PARAGON ISSUES IN PHILOSOPHY

PARAGON ISSUES IN PHILOSOPHY

THE PARAGON ISSUES
IN PHILOSOPHY SERIES

At colleges and universities, interest in the traditional areas of philosophy remains strong. Many new currents flow within them, too, but some of these—the rise of cognitive science, for example, or feminist philosophy—went largely unnoticed in undergraduate philosophy courses until the end of the 1980s. The Paragon Issues in Philosophy Series responds to both perennial and newly influential concerns by bringing together a team of able philosophers to address the fundamental issues in philosophy today and to outline the state of contemporary discussion about them.

More than twenty volumes are scheduled; they are organized into three major categories. The first covers the standard topics—metaphysics, theory of knowledge, ethics, and political philosophy—stressing innovative developments in those disciplines. The second focuses on more specialized but still vital concerns in the philosophies of science, religion, history, sport, and other areas. The third category explores new work that relates philosophy and fields such as feminist criticism, medicine, economics, technology, and literature.

The level of writing is aimed at undergraduate students who have little previous experience studying philosophy. The books provide brief but accurate introductions that appraise the state of the art in their fields and show how the history of thought about their topics developed. Each volume is complete in itself but also complements others in the series.

Traumatic change characterizes these last years of the twentieth century: all of it involves philosophical issues. The editorial staff at Paragon House has worked with us to develop this series. We hope it will encourage the understanding needed in our times, which are as complicated and problematic as they are promising.

John K. Roth
Claremont McKenna College

Frederick Sontag
Pomona College

TO
CARL G. HEMPEL
AND
WESLEY C. SALMON

FOUNDATIONS OF
PHILOSOPHY
OF SCIENCE

Edited by
JAMES H. FETZER
UNIVERSITY OF MINNESOTA, DULUTH

FOUNDATIONS OF PHILOSOPHY OF SCIENCE: RECENT DEVELOPMENTS

PARAGON HOUSE • NEW YORK

FIRST EDITION, 1993

PUBLISHED IN THE UNITED STATES BY
PARAGON HOUSE PUBLISHERS
90 FIFTH AVENUE
NEW YORK, NY 10011

COPYRIGHT © 1993 BY PARAGON HOUSE

LIBRARY OF CONGRESS CATALOGING-IN-PUBLICATION DATA

FOUNDATIONS OF PHILOSOPHY OF SCIENCE : RECENT DEVELOPMENTS / EDITED BY
    JAMES H. FETZER.—1ST ED.
        P.   CM.—(PARAGON ISSUES IN PHILOSOPHY)
    INCLUDES BIBLIOGRAPHICAL REFERENCES (P.   ) AND INDEXES.
    ISBN 1-55778-480-9
    1. SCIENCE—PHILOSOPHY.   2. SCIENCE—METHODOLOGY.   I. FETZER,
JAMES H., 1940–   .   II. SERIES.
    Q175.F715   1993
    501—DC20   91-48021
                                                         CIP

MANUFACTURED IN THE UNITED STATES OF AMERICA

CONTENTS

PREFACE

F *oundations of Philosophy of Science: Current Developments* affords an introduction to the philosophy of science by way of twenty-five studies in this field. The articles have been divided into eight subject areas of three articles apiece, each of which begins with an introduction—and study questions—to highlight the crucial issues, plus a postscript. The editor has also authored a companion volume, *Philosophy of Science,* which provides a general introduction to the field by means of a text that has been deliberately structured to correlate with the readings found in this book. The books can therefore be used together as complementary volumes or independently as separate works, depending upon the desires of the reader or the instructor.

While this is the most important feature that distinguishes these books for the purposes they are intended to serve, other features distinguish this collection as an anthology within this field. One is its emphasis on matters of methodology. If extensional languages are inherently inadequate to capture the character of natural laws, for example, then perhaps they ought to be abandoned and replaced by intensional techniques better suited to this task. Another is its consideration of conceptions of probability. The most important development involving issues of this kind is the propensity conception of probability. The consequences of the adoption of this approach, which are profound, are given the attention they deserve in this collection.

I would like to believe that this work serves the function of bringing its readers from the crucial roots of recent work in the philosophy of science to an appreciation of some of its most promising current developments. If I have been successful in attaining this objective, however, it is largely due to the opportunities I have had to study with some of the leading figures in the field during some of their most productive periods. My undergraduate thesis for Carl G. Hempel, for example, was accepted in 1962, the year that "Deductive-Nomological vs. Statistical Explanation" appeared, while my dissertation for Wesley C. Salmon was accepted in 1970, the year that "Statistical Explanations" appeared. I have benefitted from a very rich heritage.

No work of this kind could be produced without the cooperation of many authors, editors, and publishers, whose assistance I gratefully acknowledge. My original plan was to include the paper by David Lewis, "A Subjectivist's Guide to Objective Chance," in Part V, but he convinced me that this was a bad idea, and I have replaced it with "Probability and Objectivity." Each of the contributions reprinted here—not to mention Ellery Eell's valuable new paper—stands on its merits as appropriate for inclusion. It is my belief that students approaching these problems for the first time will find the sources they need to understand the field today. From this point of view, this work provides essential readings in the foundations of the philosophy of science.

J.H.F.

ACKNOWLEDGMENTS

"Principles of Definition" by Carl G. Hempel originally appeared in Carl G. Hempel, *Fundamentals of Concept Formation in Empirical Science* (Chicago: University of Chicago Press, 1952), pp. 1–14. © The University of Chicago Press. Reprinted by permission of the University of Chicago Press.

"Logical Analysis of Language" by Rudolf Carnap originally appeared in Rudolf Carnap, *Foundations of Logic and Mathematics* (Chicago: University of Chicago Press, 1939), pp. 3–11. © The University of Chicago Press. Reprinted by permission of the University of Chicago Press.

"Two Dogmas of Empiricism" by W. V. O. Quine originally appeared in W. V. O. Quine, *From a Logical Point of View* (Cambridge: Harvard University Press, 1953), pp. 20–46. © 1953, 1961 by the President and Fellows of Harvard College. Reprinted by permission of the publishers.

"The Problem of Counterfactual Conditionals" by Nelson Goodman previously appeared in Nelson Goodman, *Fact, Fiction and Forecast*, 4th ed. (Cambridge: Harvard University Press, 1983), pp. 3–27. © Nelson Goodman. Reprinted by permission of the author and *The Journal of Philosophy*.

"The Goodman Paradox and the New Riddle of Induction" by Brian Skyrms previously appeared in Brian Skyrms, *Choice and Chance*, 2d ed. (Belmont, CA: Dickinson Publishing Company, 1975), pp. 57–75. © Dickinson Publishing Company. Reprinted by permission of Wadsworth, Inc.

"Dispositions, Universals, and Natural or Physical Necessity" by Karl R. Popper originally appeared in Karl R. Popper, *The Logic of Scientific Discovery* (New York: Harper and Row, 1965), pp. 420–41. © Karl R. Popper. Reprinted by permission of the author.

"Theories and Nonobservables" by Rudolf Carnap originally appeared in Rudolf Carnap, *The Philosophy of Science* (New York: Basic Books, 1966), pp. 225–46. © Basic Books. Reprinted by permission of Basic Books.

"What's Wrong with the Received View on the Structure of Scientific Theories?" by Frederick Suppe originally appeared in *Philosophy of Science* 39 (1972), pp. 1–19. © The Philosophy of Science Association. Reprinted by permission of the author and the Philosophy of Science Association.

"Provisoes: A Problem Concerning the Inferential Function of Scientific Theories" by Carl G. Hempel originally appeared in *Erkenntnis* 28 (1988), pp. 147–64. © Carl G. Hempel. Reprinted by permission of the author.

"Explanation in Science and in History" by Carl G. Hempel originally appeared in R. G. Colodny, ed., *Frontiers of Science and Philosophy* (Pittsburgh: University of Pittsburgh Press, 1962), pp. 8–33. © University of Pittsburgh Press. Reprinted by permission of University of Pittsburgh Press.

"Statistical Explanation" by Wesley C. Salmon previously appeared in Wesley C. Salmon, *Statistical Explanation and Statistical Relevance* (Pittsburgh: University of Pittsburgh Press, 1971), pp. 29–47 and 76–87 only. © University of Pittsburgh Press. Reprinted by permission of University of Pittsburgh Press.

"A Single Case Propensity Theory of Explanation" by James H. Fetzer originally appeared in *Synthese* 28 (1974), pp.

171–98. © D. Reidel Publishing Company. Reprinted (with revised endnotes) by permission of D. Reidel Publishing Company.

"Probability and Objectivity in Deterministic and Indeterministic Situations" by James H. Fetzer originally appeared in *Synthese* 57 (1983), pp. 367–86. © D. Reidel Publishing Company. Reprinted by permission of D. Reidel Publishing Company.

"Dynamic Rationality: Propensity, Probability, and Credence" by Wesley C. Salmon originally appeared in J. H. Fetzer, ed., *Probability and Causality* (Dordrecht: D. Reidel, 1988), pp. 3–40. © D. Reidel Publishing Company. Reprinted by Permission of D. Reidel Publishing Company.

"Probability, Inference, and Decision" by Ellery Eells is an original paper that appears here for the first time. © Ellery Eells. The editor is grateful to the author for his contribution to this volume.

"An Encounter with David Hume" by Wesley C. Salmon previously appeared in J. Feinberg, ed., *Reason and Responsibility*, 3d ed. (Encino, CA: Dickenson Publishing Company, 1975), pp. 190–208. © Wesley C. Salmon. Reprinted by permission of the author.

"Recent Problems of Induction" by Carl G. Hempel originally appeared in R. G. Colodny, ed., *Mind and Cosmos* (Pittsburgh: University of Pittsburgh Press, 1966), pp. 112–34. © Pittsburgh Center for Philosophy of Science. Reprinted by permission of the author and the Pittsburgh Center for the Philosophy of Science.

"The Justification of Induction" by James H. Fetzer originally appeared in James H. Fetzer, *Scientific Knowledge* (Dordrecht: D. Reidel, 1981), pp. 175–201. © D. Reidel Publishing Company. Reprinted (abridged) by permission of D. Reidel Publishing Company.

"Science: Conjectures and Refutations" by Karl R. Popper previously appeared in Karl R. Popper, *Conjectures and Refutations* (New York: Harper and Row, 1968), pp. 33–59 only. © Karl R. Popper. Reprinted by permission of the author.

"Logic of Discovery or Psychology of Research?" by Thomas S. Kuhn originally appeared in I. Lakatos and A. Musgrave, eds., *Criticism and the Growth of Knowledge* (Cambridge, UK: Cambridge University Press, 1970), pp. 1–23. © Cambridge University Press. Reprinted by permission of the author and Cambridge University Press.

"History of Science and Its Rational Reconstruction" by Imre Lakatos originally appeared in R. Buck and R. Cohen, eds., *Boston Studies in the Philosophy of Science,* vol. 8 (Dordecht: D. Reidel, 1971), pp. 91–136. © D. Reidel Publishing Company. Reprinted by permission of D. Reidel Publishing Company.

"Three Views Concerning Human Knowledge" by Karl R. Popper previously appeared in Karl R. Popper, *Conjectures and Refutations* (New York: Harper and Row, 1968), pp. 97–119. © Karl R. Popper. Reprinted by permission of the author.

"The Nature of Natural Knowledge" by W. V. O. Quine originally appeared in S. Guttenplan, ed., *Mind and Language: Wolfson College Lectures 1974* (Oxford, UK: Oxford University Press, 1975), pp. 67–81. © Oxford University Press. Reprinted by permission of Oxford University Press.

"On Naturalizing Epistemology" by Robert Almeder originally appeared in *American Philosophical Quarterly* 27 (1990), pp. 263–279. © *American Philosophical Quarterly*. Reprinted here (revised by the author especially for this volume) by permission of Nicholas Rescher, Editor and Publisher.

"The Scientific Attitude and Fallibilism" by Charles S. Peirce previously appeared in J. Buchler, ed., *Philosophical Writings of Peirce* (London: Routledge and Kegan Paul, 1955), pp. 42–59, 36–38, and 18–19. © Routledge. Reprinted by permission of Routledge.

GENERAL INTRODUCTION

The philosophy of science today might appropriately be described as a quagmire of controversy. Almost everyone would agree that the approach represented by *logical empiricism,* which until relatively recently tended to dominate this field, no longer remains defensible, but there is considerable disagreement over what has gone wrong. This approach, represented here especially by the work of Rudolf Carnap and Carl G. Hempel, maintains that empirical science has the objective of discovering general principles which are suitable for the explanation and prediction of the occurrence of singular events, where these general principles have the character of laws of nature. Physicists search for the laws of physics, chemists the laws of chemistry, etc.

This conception, of course, is quite general. Indeed, since something like this view can be found in almost every available history of science, it is rather difficult to believe that the very idea of science as aiming at the discovery of natural laws could be entirely misguided. Such an outlook generates a specific program of philosophical research, however, which tends to focus on the nature of laws, the character of theories, and the structure of explanations and predictions. The logical empiricists went further than this by imposing certain *conditions of adequacy* upon what could properly qualify as acceptable solutions to philosophical problems. To count as adequate, such analyses had to be formalizable by means of extensional logic.

The result of their efforts was an imposing intellectual edifice founded upon three essential elements, namely: the analytic/synthetic distinction, an observational/theoretical distinction, and a methodological commitment to extensional languages as the "appropriate framework" for philosophical investigations. Although other ingredients have sometimes been identified as fundamental to this position—such as A. J. Ayer's verifiability criterion of meaningfulness, Hempel's satisfaction criterion of confirmation, or Carnap's logical interpretation of probability—these features appear to be more peripheral and less central to the epistemic motives that drove the movement.

The logical empiricists tended to view themselves as modern-day successors of David Hume, who had championed empiricism without the benefit of modern logic. Hume denied the existence of necessary connections in nature relating causes to effects or properties to proper-ties, even while he allowed the existence of habitual connections in the mind relating words to words or concepts to concepts. A consequence of this approach was that laws of nature, objectively considered, could consist of no more than constant conjunctions or relative fre-quencies, where our inevitable tendency to expect the occurrence of one event to attend the occurrence of another is nothing more than a habit of the mind, irresistible perhaps but lacking in objective foundation.

By redefining these distinctions relative to language rather than to mind, logical empiricism effectively recast Hume's approach in a methodologically sophisticated form. When W.V.O. Quine questioned the analytic/synthetic distinction, when Karl R. Popper challenged the observational/theoretical distinction, and when Nelson Goodman displayed the limitations of extensional logic, they thereby contributed to undermining the plausibility of the logical empiricist program. Yet even if most students agree that logical empiricism can no longer be defended in its classic guise, none of the views offered as alternatives has been very successful in taking its place.

One approach has been to deny the observational/theoretical distinction while (more or less) retaining the analytic/synthetic distinction and adopting an alternative conception of scientific theories, which is known as *the semantic conception*. This solution is represented here by the work of Frederick Suppe. Another approach has been to deny the analytic/synthetic distinction while (more or less) preserving the observational/theoretical distinction and adopting the conception of philosophy as continuous with rather than different from science, a view that is known as *naturalized epistemology*. This solution is represented here by the work of Quine.

More historical approaches, however, explore the dynamics of the process of discovery rather than focus on the logical structure of its products. Popper, for example, emphasizes the conception of scientific discovery as a process of conjectures and (attempted) refutations, an approach accenting the importance of *rational criticism*. Thomas S. Kuhn goes so far as to suggest that the growth of scientific knowledge involves a process of exchange of "paradigms" by mutual agreement within a scientific community, which—if there is nothing more to truth in science than consensus among scientists—may appear to lend support to various forms of *historical relativism*.

Imre Lakatos attempts to reassert the rationality of science by means of his alternative conception of the methodology of research programmes. Taking as his point of departure the dictum that, "Philosophy of science without history of science is empty; history of science without philosophy of science is blind," Lakatos contends that histories of science can only be written on the basis of normative commitments, but that alternative conceptions of science nevertheless can be subjected to empirical test on the basis of (normatively interpreted) histories of science. This paper, which is the longest in this volume, examines many of the most basic problems.

Less familiar but no less promising are attempts to improve upon the logical empiricist position by abandoning the commitment to extensional language as a necessary condition for an adequate explication. From this perspective, Wesley C. Salmon's attempts to come to grips with the issues posed by statistical explanations and by probabilistic laws while remaining faithful to the spirit of Hume provide a striking contrast to my own efforts to resolve these problems by going far beyond what Hume would allow. Indeed, no problems provide a more severe test of the scope and limits of extensional methodology than those encountered in this domain.

The pieces by Ellery Eells and by Robert Almeder are very recent contributions to understanding the subjective approach toward understanding probability and the limitations of a naturalistic approach toward epistemology. The first relates interpretations of probability to problems of inference and decision-making, while exploring the consequences of the personalist account for understanding decisions. The second examines several versions of naturalized epistemology and of evolutionary epistemology, suggesting that neither holds great promise for displacing traditional conceptions of the philosophy of science as a normative discipline.

The final paper (the "Postscript") by Charles S. Peirce elaborates the conception of scientific inquiry as a process of convergence on the truth over the long run. But this conception, which exerts immense appeal, is difficult to defend if there are any irreducibly probabilistic natural laws, which suggests there may be definite boundaries to scientific knowledge. The views Peirce advances afford some fascinating anticipations of those that Popper would propose, striking evidence of his originality and depth. The perspective Peirce supplies provides an overview to some of the most important issues that have been explored in other papers presented here.

For students approaching these problems for the very first time, perhaps three aspects of the issues that will be encountered in the pages of this book deserve to be emphasized. The first is the difference between thinking about the *products of science* and thinking about the *process of science*. A product-oriented approach that focuses on the logical structure of theories, laws, and explanations is not necessarily incompatible with a process-oriented approach that examines the individual, group, and community activities that scientists pursue in the course of their discovery. Science can involve both distinctive processes and distinctive products.

The second is the difference between *descriptive* and *normative* conceptions of the philosophy of science. A purely descriptive approach to science might attempt to answer every question about science by examining the history of science and the activities of scientists. That appears to preempt the philosophical temptation to utilize normative approaches that instead attempt to identify how science should properly be pursued. The difficulty with a purely descriptive approach, however, is that it presumes that we already know which events properly belong to the history of science as well as which persons properly qualify as scientists and why.

If the normative dimension of these investigations cannot be circumvented, then it may be beneficial to consider precisely which conditions of adequacy are appropriate for proper solutions to these problems. The choice between *extensional languages* and *intensional languages* reflects a great divide between philosophers of science today. Surely, if certain methods are inherently incapable of coping with specific problems while other methods are promising for their solution, it would be a mistake of enormous magnitude to continue to insist on those inadequate methods. Some philosophical problems exist only because of mistakes of method.

When all is said and done, the conception of science that appears to survive is not so different from that embraced by logical empiricism. Science still seems to pursue the discovery of natural laws as its objective, where those laws can be used for the explanation and prediction of singular events. What may now be better understood, however, is the relationship between the history of science and the philosophy of science, on the one hand, and the relationship between commitments to specific methodologies and the capacity to solve problems, on the other. These issues may be subtle, but they are essential to understanding science.

PART ONE

THE LANGUAGE FRAMEWORK

INTRODUCTION

By recasting Humean empiricism in a more sophisticated form, the logical empiricists refined a distinction Hume had drawn between "relations between ideas" and "matters of fact" in relation to a language L, where sentences instead of ideas became the focus of attention. A sentence may now be said to be *analytic* when its truth follows from the grammar and definitions of that language alone, and *synthetic* when its truth does not follow from L alone. In relation to a language L, the truth of an analytic sentence can be known *a priori* (independent of experience), while the truth of a synthetic sentence could only be discovered *a posteriori* (on the basis of experience).

Since synthetic knowledge requires observation, measurement, or experimentation for its evidential warrant, the issue arises of how analytic knowledge could be justified. This prospect, after all, hinges on the possibility of acquiring knowledge of the grammar and the vocabulary of a language L. One reason for the importance of the two studies with which this collection begins, therefore, is that they shed light on how it might be possible to acquire knowledge about a language L in relation to which the analytic/synthetic distinction might be sustained. Another reason is that they afford insight into how analytic philosophy itself should be justified.

Hempel's "Principles of Definition," for example, clarifies various kinds of conditions that need to be satisfied for a proper definition that relates a word, phrase, or expression to be defined (the *definiendum*) to another word, phrase, or expression by means of which it is defined (its *definiens*). Thus understood, a *definition* is a linguistic entity that relates a linguistic entity of one kind to a linguistic entity of another. Hempel assumes that the undefined (or "primitive") elements of the language are unproblematical within the context of this discussion, a practice we shall follow. This issue, however, is pursued in my book, *Philosophy and Cognitive Science*.

Hempel distinguishes four principal species of definition, the first of which is *nominal definition*. A nominal definition occurs when some new word, phrase, or expression is introduced as having the same meaning as some old word, phrase or expression. He introduces the word "tiglon" as meaning the offspring of a male tiger and a female lion, where the accept-ability of this definition is just a matter of agreement between the members of a language-using community. The definiendum and the definiens have the same meaning (become synonymous) as a matter of stipulation.

The second species of definition discussed by Hempel is *meaning analysis*. A meaning analysis represents a report upon the established usage of a word, phrase or expression within a language-using community. Thus, insofar as linguistic practices differ from one community to another and from time to time, they are relative to those communities and times. The word "fuzz," for example, was slang for policemen or officers of the law to street gangs in New York during the 1960s. Although Hempel suggests they can be validated by reflection upon their meaning, a sentence that formulates a meaning analysis will be true or false insofar as it provides an accurate or inaccurate report of the linguistic practices of the community and time.

The third species of definition that Hempel discusses is *empirical analysis*. An empirical analysis can occur when some samples or examples of the kind of thing under consideration are available for investigation, which might yield an enhanced understanding of things of that kind. Stuff of the kind *gold*, for example, was familiar to ancient peoples, who knew it was a yellowish, malleable metal. But they did not know that atoms of gold have atomic number 79 as a function of the number of protons in the nucleus of an atom of that kind. This discovery, which did not occur until the nineteenth century, thus provided a foundation for thereby redefining the meaning of the word.

The fourth species of definition that Hempel discusses is *explication*. The purpose of an explication is to take a somewhat vague and ambiguous word, phrase or expression and subject it to critical scrutiny, where the result is a recommendation or proposal as to how it might best be understood in order to achieve certain theoretical or philosophical objectives. Words such as "science," "theory," and "law," for example, might be subject to explication in an effort to develop a framework for better understanding the nature of science. Since explications have the character of suggestions, they can be qualified as more or less adequate but cannot be suitably qualified as either true or false.

One of the virtues of Hempel's conception of explication, moreover, is that it supplies a resolution of the "paradox of analysis," according to which analytic philosophy is miscon-ceived as an attempt to match definienda with corresponding definiens. For if we know what we are talking about, we already know which definiens corresponds to the definiendum under consideration, in which case it is unnecessary. But if we don't know what we are talking about, then we are in no position to match definiendum with definiens, in which case it is impossible. What we have discovered is that we can partially or vaguely understand what we are talking about and proceed from there.

Carnap's "Logical Analysis of Language" exhibits his characteristic clarity and precision. The distinction between syntax, semantics, and pragmatics is enormously important, espe-cially because it supplies a foundation for understanding the construction of a *language framework* (or of an artificial language) that corresponds to, but does not duplicate, a specific language. Thus, the construction of a model M of a language L is a process that begins with pragmatic observations of linguistic usage within a specific community as its raw data and proceeds to reconstruct its semantical and its syntactical rules by a process of abstraction, where certain decisions (such as whether or not to preserve ambiguities) may have to be made in constructing the model M.

Carnap provides a lucid conception of a model of this kind as consisting of a grammar G and a vocabulary V, where $M = < G, V >$. The vocabulary V in turn consists of logical signs LS and nonlogical signs NLS, including the names and predicates of the language, while the grammar G in its turn consists of the formation rules FR and the transformation rules TR of the model. The transformation rules, of course, govern what follows from what and are deductive rules of inference, whereas the formation rules determine which strings of signs of the vocabulary qualify as the well-formed formulae (or the sentences) of the language. The formation rules that Carnap employs, moreover, are all completely *extensional* (or truth-functional) in character.

This means that the truth-values of any sentences that are constructed out of other sentences are completely determined by the truth-values of their component sentences. Atomic sentences of the form, " . . . n is—p," where " . . . n" is replaced by a name and "—p" is replaced by a predicate, are true if the thing named by the name has the property designated by the predicate, but otherwise are false. Thus, molecular sentences of the form "not-—s" are true if sentence "—s" is not true but otherwise false; of the form "if . . . s, then—s" are true when either " . . . s" is not true or "—s" is true but otherwise false; and so forth, as Carnap explains here.

These studies, however, are preliminary to Quine's "Two Dogmas of Empiricism," which is one of the most influential papers by any contemporary philosopher. Quine challenges the analytic/synthetic distinction as "a metaphysical article of faith" on the ground that the alleged distinction has never been successfully defined. He cites four notions that have been employed in its defense—definition, analyticity, interchangeability, and semantic rule—contending that none of them can do without appeal to prior notions of analyticity and synonymy. His critique of the second alleged dogma of reductionism is also interesting to consider, but here I shall only raise some questions concerning his attack on the first dogma.

Notice how much Quine concedes along the way. He admits that there are some sentences whose truth or falsity is a function of their grammatical form alone, the logical truths. He acknowledges that there are some forms of definition, such as nominal definition, that are unobjectionable for the purpose of abbreviation. Relative to Hempel's framework, therefore, Quine's attack appears directed against meaning analyses, empirical analyses, and explications. But explications are not suitable objects of his criticism, since, as recommendations, they do not pretend to reflect previously existing relations of synonymy between definiens and definiendum.

Since Quine concedes analyticity for logical truths and for nominal definitions, he endorses the distinction for syntactical truths and for at least one kind of semantical truths. If he is contending that meaning analyses and empirical analyses are results of empirical inquiry and can never be known with certainty, his position is right but is hardly surprising. Since Carnap has elaborated how to construct a model M for a language L, the analytic/synthetic distinction can still be drawn in relation to M if not in relation to L, where M is understood as an explication of L. But if this is the case, then what Quine is rejecting is really the method of explication.

STUDY QUESTIONS

As you read the articles that appear in this section, you may want to think about their implications for understanding the nature of science and of philosophy. The following questions are intended to stimulate your thinking by focusing attention on some of the less obvious aspects of different positions.

(1) Truth conditions specify the conditions under which something (a sentence or a theory, for example) must be true. Definitions pose an interesting case. What are the truth conditions, if any, for "definitions" of each of the following kinds: nominal definitions, meaning analyses, empirical analyses, and explications? Why are there differences between them?

(2) Some kinds of definitions presuppose the prior existence of phrases or expressions that possess the same meaning as do their definienda. Which of the four kinds of definitions that Hempel discusses satisfy this condition? If some do but others do not, does that make definitions of each kind any more or less difficult to establish? Are differences of these kinds justified?

(3) Hempel suggests that explications must satisfy conditions of syntactical determinacy, of explicative relevance, and of theoretical significance. How could you decide whether or not a proposed explication did or did not satisfy these conditions? If one of them is more difficult to assess than are the others, does that make it merely a matter of subjective opinion?

(4) Carnap draws a distinction between syntax, semantics, and pragmatics, suggesting that the construction of a model of a language begins with pragmatic phenomena—the use of language by the members of a language-using community—and ends with a syntactical structure. What makes a transition of this kind possible? What kinds of decisions must be made along the way?

(5) The use of a metalanguage to specify the truth conditions for sentences in an object-language has sometimes been supposed to provide a solution to the problem of meaning, since specifying truth conditions is one manner in which the meaning of a sentence might be specified. Can you think of any difficulty that might be encountered in attempting to pursue this? Explain.

(6) Sentences whose truth conditions can be completely specified in terms of the truth conditions for other sentences are said to be "truth-functional." Can you think of any sentences where considerations that are other than or else go beyond those of the truth-values of component sentences might be relevant to the truth of those sentences as non-truth-functional sentences?

(7) Quine considers four methods for establishing the synonymy of terms: definition, analyticity, interchangeability, and semantical rule. He emphasizes that each of them appears to presuppose the prior existence of relations of synonymy. Do you think that this is a well-founded objection in view of the distinctions Hempel has drawn between kinds of definition?

(8) Quine suggests that, even though explications are intended to clarify and improve upon the meaning of terms they nevertheless rest upon preexisting synonymies between those terms and "some contexts which, as wholes, are clear and precise enough to be useful." Is this an adequate defense of his position? Do you imagine that such contexts always exist?

(9) The dogma of reductionism might be viewed as a counterpart to the dogma of analyticity by denying that the meaning of synthetic sentences is their method of confirmation or disconfirmation. Could two synthetic sentences be confirmed or disconfirmed under the same conditions, yet differ in their meaning? Could this be true for two scientific theories?

(10) Quine has suggested that the myths of the ancient Greeks and our current scientific theories "differ only in degree and not in kind," where the latter have proven "more efficacious" as instruments for anticipating the course of experience. Even if that were true, could there possibly be other features that also serve to distinguish theories from myths?

CARL G. HEMPEL

PRINCIPLES OF DEFINITION

INTRODUCTION

E mpirical science has two major objectives: to describe particular phenomena in the world of our experience and to establish general principles by means of which they can be explained and predicted. The explanatory and predictive principles of a scientific discipline are stated in its hypothetical generalizations and its theories; they characterize general patterns or regularities to which the individual phenomena conform and by virtue of which their occurrence can be systematically anticipated.

In the initial stages of scientific inquiry, descriptions as well as generalizations are stated in the vocabulary of everyday language. The growth of a scientific discipline, however, always brings with it the development of a system of specialized, more or less abstract, concepts and of a corresponding technical terminology. For what reasons and by what methods are these special concepts introduced and how do they function in scientific theory? These are the central questions which will be examined in this monograph.

It might seem plausible to assume that scientific concepts are always introduced by definition in terms of other concepts, which are already understood. As will be seen, this is by no means generally the case. Nevertheless, definition is an important method of concept formation, and we will therefore begin by surveying, in chapter I, the fundamental principles of the general theory of definition. Chapter II will analyze the methods, both definitional and nondefinitional, by means of which scientific concepts are introduced. This analysis will lead to a closer examination of the function of concepts in scientific theories and will show that concept formation and theory formation in science are so closely interrelated as to constitute virtually two different aspects of the same procedure. Chapter III, finally, will be concerned with a study of qualitative and quantitative concepts and methods in empirical science. [Editor's note: This selection reprints part of Chapter I only.]

We shall use, in this study, some of the concepts and techniques of modern logic and occasionally also a modicum of symbolic notation; these will, however, be explained, so that the main text of this monograph can be understood without any previous knowledge of symbolic logic. Some remarks of a somewhat more technical nature as well as points of detail and bibliographic references have been included in the notes at the end.[1]

PRINCIPLES OF DEFINITION

On Nominal Definition

The word "definition" has come to be used in several different senses. For a brief survey of the major meanings of the term, we choose as our point of departure the familiar distinction made in traditional logic between "nominal" and "real" definition. A real definition is conceived of as a statement of the "essential characteristics" of some entity, as when man is defined as a rational animal or a chair as a separate movable seat for one person. A nominal definition, on the other hand, is a convention which merely introduces an alternative—and usually abbreviatory—notation for a given linguistic expression, in the manner of the stipulation.

(2.1) Let the word 'tiglon' be short for (i.e., synonymous with) the phrase 'offspring of a male tiger and a female lion'

In the present section we will discuss nominal definition; in the following one, real definition and its significance for scientific inquiry.

A *nominal definition* may be characterized as a stipulation to the effect that a specified expression, the *definiendum*, is to be synonymous with a certain other expression, the *definiens*, whose meaning is already determined. A nominal definition may therefore be put into the form

(2.2) Let the expression E_2 be synonymous with the expression E_1

This form is exemplified by the definition of the popular neologism 'tiglon' in (2.1) and by the following definitions of scientific terms:

(2.3) Let the term 'Americium' be synonymous with the phrase 'the element having 95 nuclear protons'

(2.4) Let the term 'antibiotic' be synonymous with (and thus short for) the expression 'bacteriostatic or bactericidal chemical agent produced by living organisms

If a nominal definition is written in the form (2.2), it clearly speaks about certain linguistic expressions, which constitute its definiendum and its definiens; hence, it has to contain names for them. One simple and widely used method of forming a name for an expression is to put the expression between single quotation marks. This device is illustrated in the preceding examples and will frequently be used throughout this monograph.

There exists, however, an alternative way of formulating definitions, which dispenses with quotation marks, and which we will occasionally use. In its alternative form, the definition (2.3) would appear as follows:

(2.5) Americium $=_{Df}$ the element with 95 nuclear protons

The notation '$=_{Df}$' may be read 'is, by definition, to equal in meaning', or briefly, 'equals by definition'; it may be viewed as stipulating the synonymy of the expressions flanking it. Here are two additional illustrations of this manner of stating nominal definitions:

(2.6) the cephalic index of person $x =_{Df} 100 \dfrac{\text{maximum skull breadth of person } x}{\text{maximum skull length of person } x}$

(2.7) x is dolichocephalic $=_{Df} x$ is a person with a cephalic index not exceeding 75

All these definitions are of the form

(2.8) $$\underline{\qquad\qquad} =_{Df} \cdots\cdots$$

with the definiendum expression appearing to the left, and the definiens expression appearing to the right of the symbol of definitional equality.

According to the account given so far, a nominal definition introduces, or defines, a new *expression*. But it is sometimes expeditious and indeed quite customary to describe the function of nominal definition in an alternative manner: We may say that a nominal definition singles out a certain *concept*, i.e., a nonlinguistic entity such as a property, a class, a relation, a function, or the like, and, for convenient reference, lays down a special name for it. Thus conceived, the definition (2.5) singles out a certain property, namely, that of being the chemical element whose atoms have 95 nuclear protons, and gives it a brief name. This second characterization is quite compatible with the first, and it elucidates the sense in which—as is often said—a nominal definition defines a *concept* (as distinguished from the expression naming it). Henceforth, we will permit ourselves to speak of definition, and later more generally of introduction, both in regard to expressions and in regard to concepts; the definition (2.6), for example, will be alternatively said to define the expression 'cephalic index of person x' or the concept of cephalic index of a person.

The expression defined by a nominal definition need not consist of just one single word or symbol, as it does in (2.5); it may instead be a compound phrase, as in (2.6) and (2.7). In particular, if the expression to be introduced is to be used only in certain specific linguistic contexts, then it is sufficient to provide synonyms for those contexts rather than for the new term in isolation. A definition which introduces a symbol s by providing synonyms for certain expressions containing s, but not for s itself, is called a *contextual definition*. Thus, e.g., when the term 'dolichocephalic' is to be used only in contexts of the form 'so-and-so is dolich-ocephalic', then it suffices to provide means for eliminating the term from those contexts; such means are provided by (2.7), which is a contextual definition.

The idea that the definiendum expression of an adequate nominal definition must consist only of the "new" term to be introduced is a misconception which is perhaps related to the doctrine of classical logic that every definition must be stated in terms of *genus proximum* and *differentia specifica*, as in the definition

(2.9) minor $=_{Df}$ person less than 21 years of age

This definition characterizes, in effect, the class of minors as that subclass of the genus, persons, whose members have the specific characteristic of being less than 21 years old; in other words, the class of minors is defined as the logical product (the intersection) of the class of persons and the class of beings less than 21 years of age.

The doctrine that every definition must have this form is still widely accepted in elementary textbooks of logic, and it sometimes seriously hampers the adequate formulation of definitions—both nominal and "real"—in scientific writing and in dictionaries.[2] Actually, that doctrine is unjustifiable for several reasons. First, a definition by genus and differentia characterizes a class or a property as the logical product of two other classes or properties;

hence this type of definition is inapplicable when the definiendum is not a class or a property but, say, a relation or a function. Consider, for example, the following contextual definition of the relation, harder than, for minerals:

(2.10) x is harder than $y =_{Df} x$ scratches y, but y does not scratch x

or consider the contextual definition of the average density of a body—which is an example of what, in logic, is called a function:

$$(2.11) \qquad \text{average density of } x =_{Df} \frac{\text{mass of } x \text{ in grams}}{\text{volume of } x \text{ in cc.}}$$

In cases of this sort the traditional requirement is obviously inapplicable. And it is worth noting here that the majority of terms used in contemporary science are relation or function terms rather than class or property terms; in particular, all the terms representing metrical magnitudes are function terms and thus have a form which altogether precludes a definition by genus and differentia. Historically speaking, the genus-and-differentia rule reflects the fact that traditional logic has been concerned almost exclusively with class or property concepts—a limitation which renders it incapable of providing a logical analysis of modern science.

But even for class or property concepts the traditional form of definition is not always required. Thus, e.g., a property might be defined as the logical sum of certain other properties rather than as a product. This is illustrated by the following definition, which is perfectly legitimate yet states neither genus nor differentia for the definiendum:

(2.12) Scandinavian $=_{Df}$ Dane or Norwegian or Swede or Icelander

The genus-and-differentia form is therefore neither necessary nor sufficient for an adequate definition. Actually, the nominal definition of a term has to satisfy only one basic requirement: it must enable us to eliminate that term, from any context in which it can grammatically occur, in favor of other expressions, whose meaning is already understood. In principle, therefore, signs introduced by nominal definition can be dispensed with altogether: "To define a sign is to show how to avoid it."[3]

On "Real" Definition

A "real" definition, according to traditional logic, is not a stipulation determining the meaning of some expression but a statement of the "essential nature" or the "essential attributes" of some entity. The notion of essential nature, however, is so vague as to render this characterization useless for the purposes of rigorous inquiry. Yet it is often possible to reinterpret the quest for real definition in a manner which requires no reference to "essential natures" or "essential attributes," namely, as a search either for an empirical explanation of some phenomenon or for a meaning analysis. Thus, e.g., the familiar pronouncement that biology cannot as yet give us a definition of life clearly is not meant to deny the possibility of laying down some nominal definition for the term 'life'. Rather, it assumes that the term 'life' (or, alternatively, 'living organism') has a reasonably definite meaning, which we understand at least intuitively; and it asserts, in effect, that at present it is not possible to state, in a nontrivial manner, explicit and general criteria of life, i.e., conditions which are satisfied by just those phenomena which are instances of life according to the customary meaning of the term. A real definition of life would then consist in an equivalence sentence of the form

(3.1a) x is a living organism if and only if x satisfies condition C

or, in abbreviatory symbolization:

(3.1b) $$Lx \equiv Cx$$

Here, 'C' is short for an expression indicating a more or less complex set of conditions which together are necessary and sufficient for life. One set of conditions of this kind is suggested by Hutchinson in the following passage:

It is first essential to understand what is meant by a living organism. The necessary and sufficient condition for an object to be recognizable as a living organism, and so to be the subject of biological investigation, is that it be a discrete mass of matter, with a definite boundary, undergoing continual interchange of material with its surroundings without manifest alteration of properties over short periods of time, and, as ascertained either by direct observation or by analogy with other objects of the same class, originating by some process of division or fractionation from one or two pre-existing objects of the same kind. The criterion of continual interchange of material may be termed the *metabolic criterion*, that of origin from a pre-existing object of the same class, the *reproductive criterion*.[4]

If we represent the characteristic of being a discrete mass with a definite boundary by 'D' and the metabolic and reproductive criteria by 'M' and 'R', respectively, then Hutchinson's characterization of life may be written thus:

(3.2) $$Lx \equiv Dx \cdot Mx \cdot Rx$$

i.e., a thing x is a living organism if and only if x has the characteristic of being a discrete mass, etc., and x satisfies the metabolic criterion, and x satisfies the reproductive criterion.

As the quoted passage shows, this equivalence is not offered as a convention concerning the use of the term 'living' but rather as an assertion which claims to be true. How can an assertion of this kind be validated? Two possibilities present themselves:

The expression on the right-hand side of (3.2) might be claimed to be synonymous with the phrase 'x is a living organism'. In this case, the "real" definition (3.2) purports to characterize the meaning of the term 'living organism'; it constitutes what we shall call a *meaning analysis*, or an *analytic definition*, of that term (or, in an alternative locution, of the concept of living organism). Its validation thus requires solely a reflection upon the meanings of its constituent expressions and no empirical investigation of the characteristics of living organisms.

On the other hand, the "real" definition (3.2) might be intended to assert, not that the phrase 'x is a living organism' has the same meaning as the expression on the right, but rather that, as a matter of empirical fact, the three conditions D, M, and R are satisfied simultaneously by those and only those objects which are also living things. The sentence (3.2) would then have the character of an empirical law, and its validation would require reference to empirical evidence concerning the characteristics of living beings. In this case, (3.2) represents what we shall call an *empirical analysis* of the property of being a living organism.

It is not quite clear in which of these senses the quoted passage was actually intended; the first sentence suggests that a meaning analysis was aimed at.

Empirical analysis and meaning analysis differ from each other and from nominal definition. Empirical analysis is concerned not with linguistic expressions and their meanings but with empirical phenomena: it states characteristics which are, as a matter of empirical fact, both necessary and sufficient for the realization of the phenomenon under analysis. Usually, a sentence expressing an empirical analysis will have the character of a general law, as when air is characterized as a mixture, in specified proportions, of oxygen, nitrogen, and inert gases. Empirical analysis in terms of general laws is a special case of scientific *explanation*, which is aimed at the subsumption of empirical phenomena under general laws or theories.

Nominal definition and meaning analysis, on the other hand, deal with the meanings of linguistic expressions. But whereas a nominal definition introduces a "new" expression and gives it meaning by stipulation, an analytic definition is concerned with an expression which is already in use—let us call it the *analysandum expression* or, briefly, the *analysandum*—and makes its meaning explicit by providing a synonymous expression, the *analysans*, which, of course, has to be previously understood.

Dictionaries for a natural language are intended to provide analytic definitions for the words of that language; frequently, however, they supplement their meaning analyses by factual information about the subject matter at hand, as when, under the heading 'chlorine', a chemical characterization of the substance is supplemented by mentioning its use in various industrial processes.

According to the conception here outlined, an analytic definition is a statement which is true or false according as its analysans is, or is not, synonymous with its analysandum. Evidently, this conception of analytic definition presupposes a language whose expressions have precisely determined meanings—so that any two of its expressions can be said either to be, or not to be, synonymous. This condition is met, however, at best by certain artificial languages and surely is not generally satisfied by natural languages. Indeed, to determine the meaning of an expression in a given natural language as used by a specified linguistic community, one would have to ascertain the conditions under which the members of the community use—or, better, are disposed to use—the expression in question. Thus, e.g., to ascertain the meaning of the word 'hat' in contemporary English as spoken in the United States, we would have to determine to what kinds of objects—no matter whether they actually occur or not—the word 'hat' would be applied according to contemporary American usage. In this sense the conception of an analysis of "the" meaning of a given expression presupposes that the conditions of its application are (1) well determined for every user of the language and are (2) the same for all users during the period of time under consideration. We shall refer to these two presuppositions as the conditions of *determinacy* and of (personal and interpersonal) *uniformity of usage*. Clearly, neither of them is fully satisfied by any natural language. For even if we disregard ambiguity, as exhibited by such words as 'field' and 'group', each of which has several distinct meanings, there remain the phenomena of vagueness (lack of determinacy) and of inconsistency of usage.[5] Thus, e.g., the term 'hat' is vague; i.e., various kinds of objects can be described or actually produced in regard to which one would be undecided whether to apply the term or not. In addition, the usage of the term exhibits certain inconsistencies both among different users and even for the same user of contemporary American English; i.e., instances can be described or actually produced of such a kind that different users, or even the same user at different times, will pass different judgments as to whether the term applies to those instances.

These considerations apply to the analysandum as well as to the analysans of an analytic definition in a natural language. Hence, the idea of a true analytic definition, i.e., one in which the meaning of the analysans is the same as that of the analysandum, rests on an untenable assumption. However, in many cases, there exists, for an expression in a natural language, a class of contexts in which its usage is practically uniform (for the word 'hat' this class would consist of all those contexts in which practically everybody would apply the term and of those in which practically none would); analytic definitions within a natural language might, therefore, be qualified as at least more or less adequate according to the extent to which uniform usage of the analysandum coincides with that of the analysans. When subsequently we speak of, or state, analytic definitions for expressions in a natural language, we will accordingly mean characterizations of approximately uniform patterns of usage.

Meaning analysis, or analytic definition, in the purely descriptive sense considered so far has to be distinguished from another procedure, which is likewise adumbrated in the vague traditional notion of real definition. This procedure is often called logical analysis or rational reconstruction, but we will refer to it, following Carnap's proposal, as *explication*.[6] Explication is concerned with expressions whose meaning in conversational language or even in scientific discourse is more or less vague (such as 'truth', 'probability', 'number', 'cause', 'law', 'explanation'—to mention some typical objects of explicatory study) and aims at giving those expressions a new and precisely determined meaning, so as to render them more suitable for clear and rigorous discourse on the subject matter at hand. The Frege-Russell theory of arithmetic and Tarski's semantical definition of truth are outstanding examples of explication.[7] The definitions proposed in these theories are not arrived at simply by an analysis of customary meanings. To be sure, the considerations leading to the precise definitions are guided initially by reference to customary scientific or conversational usage; but eventually the issues which call for clarification become so subtle that a study of prevailing usage can no longer shed any light upon them. Hence, the assignment of precise meanings to the terms under explication becomes a matter of judicious synthesis, of rational reconstruction, rather than of merely descriptive analysis: An explication sentence does not simply exhibit the commonly accepted meaning of the expression under study but rather proposes a specified new and precise meaning for it.

Explications, having the nature of proposals, cannot be qualified as being either true or false. Yet they are by no means a matter of arbitrary convention, for they have to satisfy two major requirements: First, the explicative reinterpretation of a term, or—as is often the case—of a set of related terms, must permit us to reformulate, in sentences of a syntactically precise form, at least a large part of what is customarily expressed by means of the terms under consideration. Second, it should be possible to develop, in terms of the reconstructed concepts, a comprehensive, rigorous, and sound theoretical system. Thus, e.g., the Frege-Russell reconstruction of arithmetic gives a clear and uniform meaning to the arithmetical terms both in purely mathematical contexts, such as '7 + 5 = 12', and in their application to counting, as in the sentence 'The Sun has 9 major planets' (a purely axiomatic development of arithmetic would not accomplish this); and the proposed reconstruction provides a basis for the deductive development of pure arithmetic in such a way that all the familiar arithmetical principles can be proved.

Explication is not restricted to logical and mathematical concepts, however. Thus, e.g., the notions of purposiveness and of adaptive behavior, whose vagueness has fostered much obscure or inconclusive argumentation about the specific characteristics of biological phenomena, have become the objects of systematic explicatory efforts.[8] Again, the basic objective of the search for a "definition" of life is a precise and theoretically fruitful explication, or reconstruction, of the concept. Similarly, the controversy over whether a satisfactory definition of personality is attainable in purely psychological terms or requires reference to a cultural setting[9] centers around the question whether a sound explicatory or predictive theory of personality is possible without the use of sociocultural parameters; thus, the problem is one of explication.

An explication of a given set of terms, then, combines essential aspects of meaning analysis and of empirical analysis. Taking its departure from the customary meanings of the terms, explication aims at reducing the limitations, ambiguities, and inconsistencies of their ordinary usage by propounding a reinterpretation intended to enhance the clarity and precision of their meanings as well as their ability to function in hypotheses and theories with explanatory and predictive force. Thus understood, an explication cannot be qualified simply as true or false; but it may be adjudged more or less adequate according to the extent to which it attains its objectives.

In conclusion, let us note an important but frequently neglected requirement, which applies to analytic definitions and explications as well as to nominal definitions; we will call it the *requirement of syntactical determinacy:* A definition has to indicate the syntactical status, or, briefly, the syntax, of the expression it explicates or defines; i.e., it has to make clear the logical form of the contexts in which the term is to be used. Thus, e.g., the word 'husband' can occur in contexts of two different forms, namely, 'x is a husband of y' and 'x is a husband'. In the first type of context, which is illustrated by the sentence 'Prince Albert was the husband of Queen Victoria', the word 'husband' is used as a *relation term:* It has to be supplemented by two expressions referring to individuals if it is to form a sentence. In contexts of the second kind, such as 'John Smith is a husband', the word is used as a *property term*, requiring supplementation by only one individual name to form a sentence. Some standard English dictionaries, however, define the term 'husband' only by such phrases as 'man married to woman', which provide no explicit indication of its syntax but suggest the use of the word exclusively as a property term applying to married men; this disregards the relational use of the term, which is actually by far the more frequent. Similarly, the dictionary explication of 'twin' as 'being one of two children born at a birth' clearly suggests use of the word as a property term, i.e., in contexts of the form 'x is a twin', which is actually quite rare, and disregards its prevalent relational use in contexts of the form 'x and y are twins'. This shortcoming of many explications reflects the influence of classical logic with its insistence on construing all sentences as being of the subject-predicate type, which requires the interpretation of all predicates as property terms. Attempts to remedy this situation are likely to be impeded by the clumsiness of adequate formulations in English, which could, however, be considerably reduced by the use of variables. Thus, in a somewhat schematized form, an entry in the dictionary might read:

husband. (1) x is a h. of y: x is a male person, and x is married to y; (2) x is a h.: x is a male person who is married to some y.[10]

Nominal definitions have to satisfy the same requirement: Certainly, a term has not been defined if not even its syntax has been specified. In the definitions given in the preceding section, this condition is met by formulating the definiens in a way which unambiguously reflects its syntactical status; in some of them variables are used for greater clarity. Similarly the definition of a term such as 'force' in physics has to show that the term may occur in sentences of the form 'The force acting upon point P at time t equals vector f'. By way of contrast, consider now the concept of vital force or entelechy as adduced by neovitalists in an effort to explain certain biological phenomena which they consider as inaccessible in principle to any explanation by physicochemical theories. The term 'vital force' is used so loosely that not even its syntax is shown; no clear indication is given of whether it is to represent a property or a scalar or a vectorial magnitude, etc.; nor whether it is to be assigned to organisms, to biological processes, or to yet something else. The term is therefore unsuited for the formulation of even a moderately precise hypothesis or theory; consequently, it cannot possess the explanatory power ascribed to it.

A good illustration of the importance of syntactical determinacy is provided by the concept of probability. The definitions given in older textbooks, which speak of "the probability of an event" and thus present probabilities as numerical characteristics of individual events, overlook or conceal the fact that probabilities are relative to, and change with, some reference class (in the case of the statistical concept of probability) or some specific information (in the case of the logical concept of probability) and thus are numerical functions not of one but of two arguments. Disregard of this point is the source of various "paradoxes" of probability, in which "the same event" is shown to possess different probabilities, which actually result from a tacit shift in the reference system.

NOTES

Preliminary remark. Abbreviated titles inclosed in brackets refer to the References section which follows. Several of the previously published monographs of the *International Encyclopedia of Unified Science* contain material relevant to the problems of concept formation. For convenience, those monographs will be referred to by abbreviations; "EI3," for example, indicates volume I. no. 3.

1. I am gratefully indebted to the John Simon Guggenheim Memorial Foundation, which granted me, for the academic year 1947–48, a fellowship for work on the logic and methodology of scientific concept formation. The present monograph is part of the outcome of that work. I sincerely thank all those who have helped me with critical comments or constructive suggestions; among them, I want to mention especially Professors Rudolf Carnap, Herbert Feigl, Nelson Goodman, and Ernest Nagel, Dr. John C. Cooley, and Mr. Herbert Bohnert.
2. Thus, e.g., the genus-and-differentia rule is explicitly advocated in Hart [Report], which presents the views of a special committee on conceptual integration in the social sciences.
3. Quine [Math. Logic], p. 47.
4. Hutchinson [Biology]. (Quoted, with permission of the editor, from the 1948 copyright of Encyclopaedia Britannica.)
5. The concepts of determinacy and uniformity of usage as well as those of vagueness and inconsistency of usage are relative to some class of individuals using the language in question; they are therefore pragmatic rather than syntactic or semantic in character. On the nature of pragmatics, semantics, and syntax see Carnap [EI3], section 1, 2, and 3, and Morris [EI2].
6. See [Log. Found. Prob.], chapter I.
7. For details cf. Russell [Math. Philos.] and Tarski [Truth].
8. Cf., for example, Sommerhoff [Analyt. Biol.], which combines a lucid presentation of the general idea of explication with some useful object lessons in the explication of certain fundamental concepts of biology.
9. A spirited discussion of this issue by a group of psychologists and social scientists may be found in Sargent and Smith [Cult. and Pers.], esp. pp. 31–55. This debate illustrates the importance, for theorizing in psychology and the social sciences, of a clear distinction between the various meanings of "(real) definition."
10. Explicit (though not the fullest possible) use of this mode of formulation is made by Hogben in the presentation of his auxiliary international language, Interglossa. His English translations of Interglossa phrases include such items as these:

habe credito ex Y = owe Y; date credito Y de Z = lend Y (some) Z; X acte A Y = X performs the action A on Y ([Interglossal], pp. 45 and 49).

Similarly, Lasswell and Kaplan, in [Power and Soc.], use variables to indicate the syntax of some of their technical terms. Thus, e.g., power is defined as a triadic relation: "*Power* is participation in the making of decisions: G has power over H with respect to the values K if G participates in the making of decisions affecting the K-policies of H" (ibid., p. 75). Note that this definition is expressed contextually rather than by simulating the genus-and-differentia form, which is strictly inapplicable here.

REFERENCES

Carnap, Rudolf. [EI3]. *Foundations of Logic and Mathematics*. In EI3. Chicago, 1939.

———. [Log. Found. Prob.]. *Logical Foundations of Probability*. Chicago, 1950.

Hart, Hornell. [Report]. "Some Methods for Improving Sociological Definitions: Abridged Report of the Subcommittee on Definition of Definition of the Committee on Conceptual Integration." *American Sociological Review*. 8 (1943), pp. 333–42.

Hutchinson, G. Evelyn. [Biology]. "Biology." *Encyclopedia Brittanica* (1948).

Lasswell, Harold D., and Abraham Kaplan. [Power and Soc.]. *Power and Society*. New Haven, 1950.

Morris, Charles. [EI2]. *Foundations of the Theory of Signs*. In EI2. Chicago, 1938.

Quine, W. V. O. [Math. Logic]. *Mathematical Logic*. New York, 1940.

Russell, Bertrand. [Math. Philos.]. *Introduction to Mathematical Philosophy*. 2d ed. London, 1920.

Sargent, S. Stansfeld, and Marian W. Smith, eds. [Cult. and Pers.]. *Culture and Personality: Proceedings of an Inter-disciplinary Conference Held Under Auspices of the Viking Fund*. November 7 and 8, 1947. New York, 1949.

Sommerhoff, G. [Analyt. Biol.]. *Analytical Biology*. London, 1950.

Tarski, Alfred. [Truth]. "The Semantic Conception of Truth." *Philosophy and Phenomenological Research*, 4 (1943–44), pp. 341–75.

RUDOLF CARNAP

LOGICAL ANALYSIS OF LANGUAGE

ANALYSIS OF LANGUAGE

A language, as, e.g., English, is a system of activities or, rather, of habits, i.e., dispositions to certain activities, serving mainly for the purposes of communication and of coordination of activities among the members of a group. The elements of the language are signs, e.g., sounds or written marks, produced by members of the group in order to be perceived by other members and to influence their behavior. Since our final interest in this essay concerns the language of science, we shall restrict ourselves to the theoretical side of language, i.e., to the use of language for making assertions. Thus, among the different kinds of sentences, e.g., commands, questions, exclamations, declarations, etc., we shall deal with declarative sentences only. For the sake of brevity we shall call them here simply *sentences*.

This restriction to declarative sentences does not involve, in the investigation of processes accompanying the use of language, a restriction to theoretical thinking. Declarative sentences, e.g., 'This apple is sour', are connected not only with the theoretical side of behavior but also with emotional, volitional, and other factors. If we wish to investigate a language as a human activity, we must take into consideration all these factors connected with speaking activities. But the sentences, and the signs (e.g., words) occurring in them, are sometimes involved in still another relation. A sign or expression may concern or designate or describe something, or, rather, he who uses the expression may intend to refer to something by it, e.g., to an object or a property or a state of affairs; this we call the *designatum* of the expression. (For the moment, no exact definition for 'designatum' is intended; this word is merely to serve as a convenient, common term for different cases—objects, properties, etc.—whose fundamental differences in other respects are not hereby denied.) Thus, three components have to be distinguished in a situation where language is used. We see these in the following example: (1) the action, state, and environment of a man who speaks or hears, say, the German word 'blau'; (2) the word 'blau' as an element of the German language (meant here as a specified acoustic [or visual] design which is the common property of the many sounds produced at different times, which may be called the tokens of that design); (3) a certain property of things, viz., the color blue, to which this man—and German-speaking people in general—intends to refer (one usually says, "The man means the color by the word," or "The word means the color for these people," or " . . . within this language").

The complete theory of language has to study all these three components. We shall call *pragmatics* the field of all those investigations which take into consideration the first component, whether it be alone or in combination with the other components. Other inquiries are made in abstraction from the speaker and deal only with the expressions of the language and their relation to their designata. The field of these studies is called *semantics*. Finally, one may abstract even from the designata and restrict the investigation to formal properties—in a sense soon to be explained—of the expressions and relations among them. This field is called *logical syntax*. The distinction between the three fields will become more clear in our subsequent discussions.[1]

PRAGMATICS OF LANGUAGE *B*

In order to make clear the nature of the three fields and the differences between them, we shall analyze an example of a language. We choose a fictitious language *B*, very poor and very simple in its structure, in order to get simple systems of semantical and syntactical rules.

Whenever an investigation is made about a language, we call this language the *object-language* of the investigation, and the language in which the results of the investigation are formulated the *metalanguage*. Sometimes object-language and metalanguage are the same, e.g., when we speak in English about English. The theory concerning the object-language which is formulated in the metalanguage is sometimes called metatheory. Its three branches are the pragmatics, the semantics, and the syntax of the language in question. In what follows, *B* is our object-language, English our metalanguage.

Suppose we find a group of people speaking a language *B* which we do not understand; nor do they understand ours. After some observation, we discover which words the people use, in which forms of sentences they use them, what these words and sentences are about, on what occasions they are used, what activities are connected with them, etc. Thus we may have obtained the following results, numbered here for later reference.

Pragm. 1.—Whenever the people utter a sentence of the form '. . . ist kalt', where '. . .' is the name of a thing, they intend to assert that the thing in question is cold.

Pragm. 2a.—A certain lake in that country, which has no name in English, is usually called 'titisee'. When using this name, the people often think of plenty of fish and good meals.

Pragm. 2b.—On certain holidays the lake is called 'rumber'; when using this name, the people often think—even during good weather—of the dangers of storm on the lake.

Pragm. 3.—The word 'nicht' is used in sentences of the form 'nicht . . .', where '. . .' is a sentence. If the sentence '. . .' serves to express the assertion that such and such is the case, the whole sentence 'nicht . . .' is acknowledged as a correct assertion if such and such is not the case.

In this way we slowly learn the designata and mode of use of all the words and expressions, especially the sentences; we find out both the cause and the effect of their utterance. We may study the preferences of different social groups, age groups, or geographical groups in the choice of expressions. We investigate the role of the language in various social relations, etc.

The pragmatics of language B consists of all these and similar investigations. Pragmatical observations are the basis of all linguistic research. We see that pragmatics is an empirical discipline dealing with a special kind of human behavior and making use of the results of different branches of science (principally social science, but also physics, biology, and psychology).

SEMANTICAL SYSTEMS

We now proceed to restrict our attention to a special aspect of the facts concerning the language B which we have found by observations of the speaking activities within the group who speak that language. We study the relations between the expressions of B and their designata. On the basis of those facts we are going to lay down a system of rules establishing those relations. We call them *semantical rules*. These rules are not unambiguously determined by the facts. Suppose we have found that the word 'mond' of B was used in 98 percent of the cases for the moon and in 2 percent for a certain lantern. Now it is a matter of our decision whether we construct the rules in such a way that both the moon and the lantern are designata of 'mond' or only the moon. If we choose the first, the use of 'mond' in those 2 percent of cases was right— with respect to our rules; if we choose the second, it was wrong. The facts do not determine whether the use of a certain expression is right or wrong but only how often it occurs and how often it leads to the effect intended, and the like. A question of right or wrong must always refer to a system of rules. Strictly speaking, the rules which we shall lay down are not rules of the factually given language B; they rather constitute a language system corresponding to B which we will call the *semantical system B-S*. The language B belongs to the world of facts; it has many properties, some of which we have found, while others are unknown to us. The language system B-S, on the other hand, is something constructed by us; it has all and only those properties which we establish by the rules. Nevertheless, we construct B-S not arbitrarily but with regard to the facts about B. Then we may make the empirical statement that the language B is to a certain degree in accordance with the system B-S. The previously mentioned pragmatical facts are the basis—in the sense explained—of some of the rules to be given later (Pragm. 1 for *SD* 2a and *SL* 1, Pragm. 2a, b for *SD* 1a, Pragm. 3 for *SL* 2).

We call the elements of a semantical system *signs*; they may be words or special symbols like '0', '+', etc. A sequence consisting of one or several signs is called an *expression*. As signs of the system B-S we take the words which we have found by our observations to be words of B or, rather, only those words which we decide to accept as "correct." We divide the signs of B-S— and, in an analogous way, those of any other semantical system—into two classes: *descriptive* and *logical* signs. As descriptive signs we take those which designate things or properties of things (in a more comprehensive system we should classify here also the relations among things, functions of things, etc.). The other signs are taken as logical signs: they serve chiefly for connecting descriptive signs in the construction of sentences but do not themselves designate things, properties of things, etc. Logical signs are, e.g., those corresponding to English words like 'is', 'are', 'not', 'and', 'or', 'if', 'any', 'some', 'every', 'all'. These unprecise explanations will suffice here. Our later discussions will show some of the differentiae of the two classes of signs.[2]

RULES OF THE SEMANTICAL SYSTEM *B-S*

In order to show how semantical rules are to be formulated and how they serve to determine truth conditions and thereby give an interpretation of the sentences, we are going to construct the semantical rules for the system *B-S*. As preliminary steps for this construction we make a classification of the signs and lay down rules of formation. Each class is defined by an enumeration of the signs belonging to it. The signs of *B-S* are divided into descriptive and logical signs. The descriptive signs of *B-S* are divided into names and predicates. Names are the words 'titisee', 'rumber', 'mond', etc. (here a complete list of the names has to be given). Predicates are the words 'kalt', 'blau', 'rot', etc. The logical signs are divided into logical constants ('ist', 'nicht', 'wenn', 'so', 'fuer', 'jedes') and variables ('x', 'y', etc.). For the general description of forms of expressions we shall use blanks like '. . .', '- - -', etc. They are not themselves signs of *B-S* but have to be replaced by expressions of *B-S*. If nothing else is said, a blank stands for any expression of *B-S*. A blank with a subscript '*n*', '*p*', '*s*', or '*v*' (e.g., '. . .$_n$') stands for a name, a predicate, a sentence, or a variable, respectively. If the same blank occurs several times within a rule or a statement, it stands at all places for the same expression.

The rules of formation determine how sentences may be constructed out of the various kinds of signs.

Rules of formation.—An expression of *B-S* is called a *sentence* (in the semantical sense) or a *proposition* of *B-S*, if and only if it has one of the following forms, F 1–4. F 1: '. . .$_n$ ist- - -$_p$' (e.g., 'mond ist blau'); F 2: 'nicht . . .$_s$' (e.g., 'nicht mond ist blau'); F 3: 'wenn . . .$_s$, so- - -$_s$' (e.g., 'wenn titisee ist rot, so mond ist kalt'); F 4: 'fuer jedes . .$_v$, - . . .-', where '- . . .-' stands for an expression which is formed out of a sentence not containing a variable by replacing one or several names by the variable '. .$_v$' (e.g., 'fuer jedes *x*, *x* ist blau'; 'fuer jedes *y*, wenn *y* ist blau, so *y* ist kalt'). The partial sentence in a sentence of the form F 2 and the two partial sentences in a sentence of the form F 3 (indicated above by blanks) are called *components* of the whole sentence. In order to indicate the components of a sentence in case they are themselves compound, commas and square brackets are used when necessary.

Rules B-SD. Designata of descriptive signs:

SD 1. The *names* designate things, and especially
   a) each of the thing-names 'titisee' and 'rumber' designates the lake at such and such a longitude and latitude.
   b) 'mond' designates the moon.
   Etc. [Here is to be given a complete list of rules for all the names of *B-S*.]
SD 2. The *predicates* designate properties of things, and especially
   a) 'kalt' designates the property of being cold.
   b) 'blau' designates the property of being blue.
   c) 'rot' designates the property of being red.
   Etc. [for all predicates].

Rules B-SL. Truth conditions for the sentences of *B-S*. These rules involve the *logical signs*. We call them the L-semantical rules of *B-S*.

SL 1. 'ist', form F 1. A sentence of the form '. . .$_n$ ist- - -$_p$' is true if and only if the thing designated by '. . .$_n$' has the property designated by '- - -$_p$'.

SL 2. 'nicht', form F 2. A sentence of the form 'nicht . . .$_s$' is true if and only if the sentence '. . .$_s$' is not true.

SL 3. 'wenn' and 'so', form F 3. A sentence of the form 'wenn . . .$_s$, so - - -$_s$' is true if and only if '. . .$_s$' is not true or '- - -$_s$' is true.

SL 4. 'fuer jedes', form F 4. A sentence of the form 'fuer jedes . . $_v$, - . . -', where '- . . .-' is an expression formed out of a sentence by replacing one or several names by the variable '. .$_v$', is true if and only if all sentences of the following kind are true: namely, those sentences constructed out of the expression '- . . .-' by replacing the variable '. .$_v$' at all places where it occurs within that expression by a name, the same for all places; here names of any things may be taken, even of those for which there is no name in the list of names in *B-S*. (Example: The sentence 'fuer jedes *x*, *x* ist blau' is true if and only if every sentence of the form '. . .$_n$ ist blau' is true; hence, according to SL 1, if and only if everything is blue.)

The rule *SL1*, in combination with *SD*, provides direct truth conditions for the sentences of the simplest form; direct, since the rule does not refer to the truth of other sentences. *SL 2-4* provide indirect truth conditions for the compound sentences by referring to other sentences and finally back to sentences of the simplest form. Hence the rules *B-SD* and *SL* together give a general definition of '*true in B-S*' though not in explicit form. (It would be possible, although in a rather complicated form, to formulate an explicit definition of 'true in *B-S*' on the basis of the rules given.) A sentence of *B-S* which is not true in *B-S* is called *false* in *B-S*.

If a sentence of *B-S* is given, one can easily construct, with the help of the given rules, a direct *truth-criterion* for it, i.e., a necessary and sufficient condition for its truth, in such a way that in the formulation of this condition no reference is made to the truth of other sentences. Since to know the truth conditions of a sentence is to know what is asserted by it, the given semantical rules determine for every sentence of *B-S* what it asserts—in usual terms, its "meaning"—or, in other words, how it is to be translated into English.[3]

Therefore, we shall say that we *understand* a language system, or a sign, or an expression, or a sentence in a language system, if we know the semantical rules of the system. We shall also say that the semantical rules give an *interpretation* of the language system.[4]

NOTES

1. That an investigation of language has to take into consideration all the three factors mentioned was in recent times made clear and emphasized especially by C. S. Peirce, by Ogden and Richards, and by Morris (see vol. I, no. 2). Morris made it the basis for the three fields into which he divides semiotic (i.e., the general theory of signs), namely, pragmatics, semantics, and syntactics. Our division is in agreement with his in its chief features. For general questions concerning language and its use compare also Bloomfield, vol. I, no. 4.
2. Semantics as an exact discipline is quite new; we owe it to the very fertile school of contemporary Polish logicians. After some of this group, especially Lesniewski and Ajdukiewicz, had discussed semantical questions, Tarski, in his treatise on truth, made the first comprehensive systematic investigation in this field, giving rise to very important results.
3. Examples: (1) The sentence 'mond ist blau' is true if and only if the moon is blue. (2) The sentence 'fuer jedes *x*, wenn *x* ist blau, so *x* ist kalt' is true if and only if every thing—not only those having a name in *B-S*—either is not blue or is cold; in other words, if all blue things are cold. Hence, this sentence asserts that all blue things are cold; it is to be translated into the English sentence 'all blue things are cold'.
4. We have formulated the semantical rules of the descriptive signs by stating their designata, for the logical signs by stating truth conditions for the sentences constructed with their help. We may mention

here two other ways of formulating them which are often used in the practice of linguistics and logic. The first consists in giving *translations* for the signs and, if necessary, for the complex expressions and sentences, as it is done in a dictionary. The second way consists in stating *designata* throughout, not only for the descriptive signs as in *SD*, but also for expressions containing the logical signs, corresponding to *SL*. Example (corresponding to *SL 1*): A sentence of the form '. . .$_n$ ist - - -$_p$' designates (the state of affairs) that the thing designated by '. . .$_n$' has the property designated by '- - -$_p$'.

REFERENCES

Bloomfield, Leonard. [EI4]. *Linguistic Aspects of Science.* EI4. Chicago, 1939.
Morris, Charles. [EI2]. *Foundations of the Theory of Signs.* EI2. Chicago, 1938.

W.V.O. QUINE

TWO DOGMAS OF EMPIRICISM

Modern empiricism has been conditioned in large part by two dogmas. One is a belief in some fundamental cleavage between truths which are *analytic*, or grounded in meanings independently of matters of fact, and truths which are *synthetic*, or grounded in fact. The other dogma is *reductionism*: the belief that each meaningful statement is equivalent to some logical construct upon terms which refer to immediate experience. Both dogmas, I shall argue, are ill-founded. One effect of abandoning them is, as we shall see, a blurring of the supposed boundary between speculative metaphysics and natural science. Another effect is a shift toward pragmatism.

I. BACKGROUND FOR ANALYTICITY

Kant's cleavage between analytic and synthetic truths was foreshadowed in Hume's distinction between relations of ideas and matters of fact, and in Leibniz's distinction between truths of reason and truths of fact. Leibniz spoke of the truths of reason as true in all possible worlds. Picturesqueness aside, this is to say that the truths of reason are those which could not possibly be false. In the same vein we hear analytic statements defined as statements whose denials are self-contradictory. But this definition has small explanatory value; for the notion of self-contradictoriness, in the quite broad sense needed for this definition of analyticity, stands in exactly the same need of clarification as does the notion of analyticity itself. The two notions are the two sides of a single dubious coin.

Kant conceived of an analytic statement as one that attributes to its subject no more than is already conceptually contained in the subject. This formulation has two shortcomings: it limits itself to statements of subject-predicate form, and it appeals to a notion of containment which is left at a metaphorical level. But Kant's intent, evident more from the use he makes of the notion of analyticity than from his definition of it, can be restated thus: a statement is analytic when it is true by virtue of meanings and independently of fact. Pursuing this line, let us examine the concept of *meaning* which is presupposed.

Meaning, let us remember, is not to be identified with naming.[1] Frege's example of 'Evening Star' and 'Morning Star', and Russell's of 'Scott' and 'the author of *Waverley*', illustrate that terms can name the same thing but differ in meaning. The distinction between meaning and naming is no less important at the level of abstract terms. The terms '9' and 'the number of the planets' name one and the same abstract entity but presumably must be regarded as unlike in meaning; for astronomical observation was needed, and not mere reflection on meanings, to determine the sameness of the entity in question.

The above examples consist of singular terms, concrete and abstract. With general terms, or predicates, the situation is somewhat different but parallel. Whereas a singular term purports to name an entity, abstract or concrete, a general term does not; but a general term is *true* of an entity, or of each of many, or of none.[2] The class of all entities of which a general term is true is called the *extension* of the term. Now paralleling the contrast between the meaning of a singular term and the entity named, we must distinguish equally between the meaning of a general term and its extension. The general terms 'creature with a heart' and 'creature with kidneys', for example, are perhaps alike in extension but unlike in meaning.

Confusion of meaning with extension, in the case of general terms, is less common than confusion of meaning with naming in the case of singular terms. It is indeed a commonplace in philosophy to oppose intension (or meaning) to extension, or, in a variant vocabulary, connotation to denotation.

The Aristotelian notion of essence was the forerunner, no doubt, of the modern notion of intension or meaning. For Aristotle it was essential in men to be rational, accidental to be two-legged. But there is an important difference between this attitude and the doctrine of meaning. From the latter point of view it may indeed be conceded (if only for the sake of argument) that rationality is involved in the meaning of the word 'man' while two-leggedness is not; but two-leggedness may at the same time be viewed as involved in the meaning of 'biped' while rationality is not. Thus from the point of view of the doctrine of meaning it makes no sense to say of the actual individual, who is at once a man and a biped, that his rationality is essential and his two-leggedness accidental or vice versa. Things had essences, for Aristotle, but only linguistic forms have meanings. Meaning is what essence becomes when it is divorced from the object of reference and wedded to the word.

For the theory of meaning a conspicuous question is the nature of its objects: what sort of things are meanings? A felt need for meant entities may derive from an earlier failure to appreciate that meaning and reference are distinct. Once the theory of meaning is sharply separated from the theory of reference, it is a short step to recognizing as the primary business of the theory of meaning simply the synonymy of linguistic forms and the analyticity of statements; meanings themselves, as obscure intermediary entities, may well be abandoned.[3]

The problem of analyticity then confronts us anew. Statements which are analytic by general philosophical acclaim are not, indeed, far to seek. They fall into two classes. Those of the first class, which may be called *logically true*, are typified by:

(1)   No unmarried man is married.

The relevant feature of this example is that it not merely is true as it stands, but remains true under any and all reinterpretations of 'man' and 'married'. If we suppose a prior inventory of *logical* particles, comprising 'no', 'un-', 'not', 'if', 'then', 'and', etc., then in general a logical truth is a statement which is true and remains true under all reinterpretations of its components other than the logical particles.

But there is also a second class of analytic statements, typified by:

(2)   No bachelor is married.

The characteristic of such a statement is that it can be turned into a logical truth by putting synonyms for synonyms; thus (2) can be turned into (1) by putting 'unmarried man' for its synonym 'bachelor'. We still lack a proper characterization of this second class of analytic statements, and therewith of analyticity generally, inasmuch as we have had in the above description to lean on a notion of "synonymy" which is no less in need of clarification than analyticity itself.

In recent years Carnap has tended to explain analyticity by appeal to what he calls state-descriptions.[4] A state-description is any exhaustive assignment of truth-values to the atomic, or noncompound, statements of the language. All other statements of the language are, Carnap assumes, built up of their component clauses by means of the familiar logical devices, in such a way that the truth-value of any complex statement is fixed for each state-description by specifiable logical laws. A statement is then explained as analytic when it comes out true under every state-description. This account is an adaptation of Leibniz's "true in all possible worlds." But note that this version of analyticity serves its purpose only if the atomic statements of the language are, unlike 'John is a bachelor' and to 'John is married', mutually independent. Otherwise there would be a state-description which assigned truth to 'John is a bachelor' and to 'John is married', and consequently 'No bachelors are married' would turn out synthetic rather than analytic under the proposed criterion. Thus the criterion of analyticity in terms of state-descriptions serves only for languages devoid of extra-logical synonym-pairs, such as 'bachelor' and 'unmarried man'—synonym-pairs of the type which give rise to the "second class" of analytic statements. The criterion in terms of state-descriptions is a reconstruction at best of logical truth, not of analyticity.

I do not mean to suggest that Carnap is under any illusions on this point. His simplified model language with its state-descriptions is aimed primarily not at the general problem of analyticity but at another purpose, the clarification of probability and induction. Our problem, however, is analyticity; and here the major difficulty lies not in the first class of analytic statements, the logical truths, but rather in the second class, which depends on the notion of synonymy.

II. DEFINITION

There are those who find it soothing to say that the analytic statements of the second class reduce to those of the first class, the logical truths, by *definition*; 'bachelor', for example, is *defined* as 'unmarried man'. But how do we find that 'bachelor' is defined as 'unmarried man'? Who defined it thus, and when? Are we to appeal to the nearest dictionary, and accept the lexicographer's formulation as law? Clearly this would be to put the cart before the horse. The lexicographer is an empirical scientist, whose business is the recording of antecedent facts; and if he glosses 'bachelor' as 'unmarried man' it is because of his belief that there is a relation of synonymy between those forms, implicit in general or preferred usage prior to his own work. The notion of synonymy presupposed here has still to be clarified, presumably in terms relating to linguistic behavior. Certainly the "definition" which is the lexicographer's report of an observed synonymy cannot be taken as the ground of the synonymy.

Definition is not, indeed, an activity exclusively of philologists. Philosophers and scientists frequently have occasion to "define" a recondite term by paraphrasing it into terms of a more familiar vocabulary. But ordinarily such a definition, like the philologist's, is pure lexicography, affirming a relation of synonymy antecedent to the exposition in hand.

Just what it means to affirm synonymy, just what the interconnections may be which are necessary and sufficient in order that two linguistic forms be properly describable as synonymous, is far from clear; but, whatever these interconnections may be, ordinarily they are grounded in usage. Definitions reporting selected instances of synonymy come then as reports upon usage.

There is also, however, a variant type of definitional activity which does not limit itself to the reporting of preexisting synonymies. I have in mind what Carnap calls *explication*—an activity to which philosophers are given, and scientists also in their more philosophical moments. In explication the purpose is not merely to paraphrase the definiendum into an outright synonym, but actually to improve upon the definiendum by refining or supplementing its meaning. But even explication, though not merely reporting a preexisting synonymy between definiendum and definiens, does rest nevertheless on *other* preexisting synonymies. The matter may be viewed as follows. Any word worth explicating has some contexts which, as wholes, are clear and precise enough to be useful; and the purpose of explication is to preserve the usage of these favored contexts while sharpening the usage of other contexts. In order that a given definition be suitable for purposes of explication, therefore, what is required is not that the definiendum in its antecedent usage be synonymous with the definiens, but just that each of these favored contexts of the definiendum, taken as a whole in its antecedent usage, be synonymous with the corresponding context of the definiens.

Two alternative definientia may be equally appropriate for the purposes of a given task of explication and yet not be synonymous with each other; for they may serve interchangeably within the favored contexts but diverge elsewhere. By cleaving to one of these definientia rather than the other, a definition of explicative kind generates, by fiat, a relation of synonymy between definiendum and definiens which did not hold before. But such a definition still owes its explicative function, as seen, to preexisting synonymies.

There does, however, remain still an extreme sort of definition which does not hark back to prior synonymies at all: namely, the explicitly conventional introduction of novel notations for purposes of sheer abbreviation. Here the definiendum becomes synonymous with the definiens simply because it has been created expressly for the purpose of being synonymous with the definiens. Here we have a really transparent case of synonymy created by definition; would that all species of synonymy were as intelligible. For the rest, definition rests on synonymy rather than explaining it.

The word 'definition' has come to have a dangerously reassuring sound, owing no doubt to its frequent occurrence in logical and mathematical writings. We shall do well to digress now into a brief appraisal of the role of definition in formal work.

In logical and mathematical systems either of two mutually antagonistic types of economy may be striven for, and each has its peculiar practical utility. On the one hand we may seek economy of practical expression—ease and brevity in the statement of multifarious relations. This sort of economy calls usually for distinctive concise notations for a wealth of concepts. Second, however, and oppositely, we may seek economy in grammar and vocabulary; we may try to find a minimum of basic concepts such that, once a distinctive notation has been appropriated to each of them, it becomes possible to express any desired further concept by mere combination and iteration of our basic notations. This second sort of economy is impractical in one way, since a poverty in basic idioms tends to a necessary lengthening of discourse. But it is practical in another way: it greatly simplifies theoretical discourse *about* the language, through minimizing the terms and the forms of construction wherein the language consists.

Both sorts of economy, though prima facie incompatible, are valuable in their separate ways. The custom has consequently arisen of combining both sorts of economy by forging in effect two languages, the one a part of the other. The inclusive language, though redundant in grammar and vocabulary, is economical in message lengths, while the part, called primitive notation, is economical in grammar and vocabulary. Whole and part are correlated by rules of translation whereby each idiom not in primitive notation is equated to some complex built up of primitive notation. These rules of translation are the so-called *definitions* which appear in formalized systems. They are best viewed not as adjuncts to one language but as correlations between two languages, the one a part of the other.

But these correlations are not arbitrary. They are supposed to show how the primitive notations can accomplish all purposes, save brevity and convenience, of the redundant language. Hence the definiendum and its definiens may be expected, in each case, to be related in one or another of the three ways lately noted. The definiens may be a faithful paraphrase of the definiendum into the narrower notation, preserving a direct synonymy[5] as of antecedent usage; or the definiens may, in the spirit of explication, improve upon the antecedent usage of the definiendum; or finally, the definiendum may be a newly created notation, newly endowed with meaning here and now.

In formal and informal work alike, thus, we find that definition—except in the extreme case of the explicitly conventional introduction of new notations—hinges on prior relations of synonymy. Recognizing then that the notion of definition does not hold the key to synonymy and analyticity, let us look further into synonymy and say no more of definition.

III. INTERCHANGEABILITY

A natural suggestion, deserving close examination, is that the synonymy of two linguistic forms consists simply in their interchangeability in all contexts without change of truth-value—interchangeability, in Leibniz's phrase, *salva veritate*.[6] Note that synonyms so conceived need not even be free from vagueness, as long as the vaguenesses match.

But it is not quite true that the synonyms 'bachelor' and 'unmarried man' are everywhere interchangeable *salva veritate*. Truths which become false under substitution of 'unmarried man' for 'bachelor' are easily constructed with the help of 'bachelor of arts' or 'bachelor's buttons'; also with the help of quotation, thus:

'Bachelor' has less than ten letters.

Such counterinstances can, however, perhaps be set aside by treating the phrases 'bachelor of arts' and 'bachelor's buttons' and the quotation ''bachelor'' each as a single indivisible word and then stipulating that the interchangeability *salva veritate* which is to be the touchstone of synonymy is not supposed to apply to fragmentary occurrences inside of a word. This account of synonymy, supposing it acceptable on other counts, has indeed the drawback of appealing to a prior conception of "word" which can be counted on to present difficulties of formulation in its turn. Nevertheless some progress might be claimed in having reduced the problem of synonymy to a problem of wordhood. Let us pursue this line a bit, taking "word" for granted.

The question remains whether interchangeability *salva veritate* (apart from occurrences within words) is a strong enough condition for synonymy, or whether, on the contrary, some heteronymous expressions might be thus interchangeable. Now let us be clear that we are not concerned here with synonymy in the sense of complete identity in psychological associations or poetic quality; indeed no two expressions are synonymous in such a sense. We are concerned only with what may be called *cognitive* synonymy. Just what this is cannot be said without successfully finishing the present study; but we know something about it from the need which arose for it in connection with analyticity in section I. The sort of synonymy needed there was merely such that any analytic statement could be turned into a logical truth by putting synonyms for synonyms. Turning the tables and assuming analyticity, indeed, we could explain cognitive synonymy of terms as follows (keeping to the familiar example): to say that 'bachelor' and 'unmarried man' are cognitively synonymous is to say no more nor less than that statement:

(3)   All and only bachelors are unmarried men

is analytic.[7]

What we need is an account of cognitive synonymy not presupposing analyticity—if we are to explain analyticity conversely with help of cognitive synonymy as undertaken in section I. And indeed such an independent account of cognitive synonymy is at present up for consideration, namely, interchangeability *salva veritate* everywhere except within words. The question before us, to resume the thread at last, is whether such interchangeability is a sufficient condition for cognitive synonymy. We can quickly assure ourselves that it is, by examples of the following sort. The statement:

(4)   Necessarily all and only bachelors are bachelors

is evidently true, even supposing 'necessarily' so narrowly construed as to be truly applicable only to analytic statements. Then, if 'bachelor' and 'unmarried man' are interchangeable *salva veritate*, the result:

(5)   Necessarily all and only bachelors are unmarried men

of putting 'unmarried man' for an occurrence of 'bachelor' in (4) must, like (4), be true. But to say that (5) is true is to say that (3) is analytic, and hence that 'bachelor' and 'unmarried man' are cognitively synonymous.

Let us see what there is about the above argument that gives it its air of hocus-pocus. The condition of interchangeability *salva veritate* varies in its force with variations in the richness of the language at hand. The above argument supposes we are working with a language rich enough to contain the adverb 'necessarily', this adverb being so construed as to yield truth when and only when applied to an analytic statement. But can we condone a language which contains such an adverb? Does the adverb really make sense? To suppose that it does is to suppose that we have already made satisfactory sense of 'analytic'. Then what are we so hard at work on right now?

Our argument is not flatly circular, but something like it. It has the form, figuratively speaking, of a closed curve in space.

Interchangeability *salva veritate* is meaningless until relativized to a language whose extent is specified in relevant respects. Suppose now we consider a language containing just the following materials. There is an indefinitely large stock of one-place predicates (for example, '*F*' where '*Fx*' means that *x* is a man) and many-place predicates (for example, '*G*' where '*Gxy*' means that *x* loves *y*), mostly having to do with extralogical subject matter. The rest of the language is logical. The atomic sentences consist each of a predicate followed by one or more variables '*x*', '*y*', etc.; and the complex sentences are built up of the atomic ones by truth-functions ('not', 'and', 'or', etc.) and quantification.[8] In effect such a language enjoys the benefits also of descriptions and indeed singular terms generally, these being contextually definable in known ways.[9] Even abstract singular terms naming classes, classes of classes, etc., are contextually definable in case the assumed stock of predicates includes the two-place predicate of class membership.[10] Such a language can be adequate to classical mathematics and indeed to scientific discourse generally, except in so far as the latter involves debatable devices such as contrary-to-fact conditionals or modal adverbs like 'necessarily'.[11] Now a language of this type is extensional, in this sense: any two predicates which agree extensionally (that is, are true of the same objects) are interchangeable *salva veritate*.[12]

In an extensional language, therefore, interchangeability *salva veritate* is no assurance of cognitive synonymy of the desired type. That 'bachelor' and 'unmarried man' are interchangeable *salva veritate* in an extensional language assures us of no more than that (3) is true. There is no assurance here that the extensional agreement of 'bachelor' and 'unmarried man' rests on meaning rather than merely on accidental matters of fact, as does the extensional agreement of 'creature with a heart' and 'creature with kidneys'.

For most purposes extensional agreement is the nearest approximation to synonymy we need care about. But the fact remains that extensional agreement falls far short of cognitive synonymy of the type required for explaining analyticity in the manner of section I. The type of cognitive synonymy required there is such as to equate the synonymy of 'bachelor' and 'unmarried man' with the analyticity of (3), not merely with the truth of (3).

So we must recognize that interchangeability *salva veritate*, if construed in relation to an extensional language, is not a sufficient condition of cognitive synonymy in the sense needed for deriving analyticity in the manner of section I. If a language contains an intensional adverb 'necessarily' in the sense lately noted, or other particles to the same effect, then interchangeability *salva veritate* in such a language does afford a sufficient condition of cognitive synonymy; but such a language is intelligible only in so far as the notion of analyticity is already understood in advance.

The effort to explain cognitive synonymy first, for the sake of deriving analyticity from it afterward as in section I, is perhaps the wrong approach. Instead we might try explaining analyticity somehow without appeal to cognitive synonymy. Afterward we could doubtless derive cognitive synonymy from analyticity satisfactorily enough if desired. We have seen that cognitive synonymy of 'bachelor' and 'unmarried man' can be explained as analyticity of (3). The same explanation works for any pair of one-place predicates, of course, and it can be extended in obvious fashion to many-place predicates. Other syntactical categories can also be accommodated in fairly parallel fashion. Singular terms may be said to be cognitively synonymous when the statement of identity formed by putting '=' between them is analytic. Statements may be said simply to be cognitively synonymous when their biconditional (the result of joining them by 'if and only if') is analytic.[13] If we care to lump all categories into a single formulation, at the expense of assuming again the notion of "word" which was appealed to early in this section, we can describe any two linguistic forms as cognitively synonymous when the two forms are interchangeable (apart from occurrences within "words") *salva* (no longer *veritate* but) *analyticitate*. Certain technical questions arise, indeed, over cases of ambiguity or homonymy; let us not pause for them, however, for we are already digressing. Let us rather turn our backs on the problem of synonymy and address ourselves anew to that of analyticity.

IV. SEMANTICAL RULES

Analyticity at first seemed most naturally definable by appeal to a realm of meanings. On refinement, the appeal to meanings gave way to an appeal to synonymy or definition. But definition turned out to be a will-o'-the-wisp, and synonymy turned out to be best understood only by dint of a prior appeal to analyticity itself. So we are back at the problem of analyticity.

I do not know whether the statement 'Everything green is extended' is analytic. Now does my indecision over this example really betray an incomplete understanding, an incomplete grasp of the "meanings," of 'green' and 'extended'? I think not. The trouble is not with 'green' or 'extended', but with 'analytic'.

It is often hinted that the difficulty in separating analytic statements from synthetic ones in ordinary language is due to the vagueness of ordinary language and that the distinction is clear when we have a precise artificial language with explicit "semantical rules." This, however, as I shall now attempt to show, is a confusion.

The notion of analyticity about which we are worrying is a purported relation between statements and languages: a statement S is said to be *analytic for* a language L, and the problem is to make sense of this relation generally, that is, for variable 'S' and 'L'. The gravity of this problem is not perceptibly less for artificial languages than for natural ones. The problem of making sense of the idiom 'S is analytic for L', with variable 'S' and 'L', retains its stubbornness even if we limit the range of the variable 'L' to artificial languages. Let me now try to make this point evident.

For artificial languages and semantical rules we look naturally to the writings of Carnap. His semantical rules take various forms, and to make my point I shall have to distinguish certain of the forms. Let us suppose, to begin with, an artificial language L_0 whose semantical rules have the form explicitly of a specification, by recursion or otherwise, of all the analytic statements of L_0. The rules tell us that such and such statements, and only those, are the analytic statements of L_0. Now here the difficulty is simply that the rules contain the word 'analytic', which we do not understand! We understand what expressions the rules attribute analyticity to, but we do not understand what the rules attribute to those expressions. In short, before we can understand a rule which begins 'A statement S is analytic for language L_0 if and only if . . .', we must understand the general relative term 'analytic for'; we must understand 'S is analytic for L' where 'S' and 'L' are variables.

Alternatively we may, indeed, view the so-called rule as a conventional definition of a new simple symbol 'analytic-for-L_0', which might better be written untendentiously as 'K' so as not to seem to throw light on the interesting word 'analytic'. Obviously any number of classes K, M, N, etc. of statements of L_0 can be specified for various purposes or for no purpose; what does it mean to say that K, as against M, N, etc., is the class of the "analytic" statements of L_0?

By saying what statements are analytic for L_0 we explain 'analytic-for-L_0' but not 'analytic', not 'analytic for'. We do not begin to explain the idiom 'S is analytic for L' with variable 'S' and 'L', even if we are content to limit the range of 'L' to the realm of artificial languages.

Actually we do know enough about the intended significance of 'analytic' to know that analytic statements are supposed to be true. Let us then turn to a second form of semantical rule, which says not that such and such statements are analytic but simply that such and such statements are included among the truths. Such a rule is not subject to the criticism of containing the un-understood word 'analytic'; and we may grant for the sake of argument that there is no difficulty over the broader term 'true'. A semantical rule of this second type, a rule of truth, is not supposed to specify all the truths of the language; it merely stipulates, recursively or otherwise, a certain multitude of statements which, along with others unspecified, are to count as true. Such a rule may be conceded to be quite clear. Derivatively, afterward, analyticity can be demarcated thus: a statement is analytic if it is (not merely true but) true according to the semantical rule.

Still there is really no progress. Instead of appealing to an unexplained word 'analytic', we are now appealing to an unexplained phrase 'semantical rule'. Not every true statement which says that the statements of some class are true can count as a semantical rule—otherwise *all* truths would be "analytic" in the sense of being true according to semantical rules. Semantical rules are distinguishable, apparently, only by the fact of appearing on a page under the heading 'Semantical Rules'; and this heading is itself then meaningless.

We can say indeed that a statement is *analytic-for-L_0* if and only if it is true according to such and such specifically appended "semantical rules," but then we find ourselves back at essentially the same case which was originally discussed: 'S is analytic-for-L_0 if and only if . . . .' Once we seek to explain 'S is analytic-for-L' generally for variable 'L' (even allowing limitation of 'L' to artificial languages), the explanation 'true according to the semantical rules of L' is unavailing; for the relative term 'semantical rule of' is as much in need of clarification, at least, as 'analytic for'.

It may be instructive to compare the notion of semantical rule with that of postulate. Relative to a given set of postulates, it is easy to say what a postulate is: it is a member of the set. Relative to a given set of semantical rules, it is equally easy to say what a semantical rule is. But given simply a notation, mathematical or otherwise, and indeed as thoroughly understood a notation as you please in point of the translations or truth-conditions of its statements, who can say which of its true statements rank as postulates? Obviously the question is meaningless—as meaningless as asking which points in Ohio are starting points. Any finite (or effectively specifiable infinite) selection of statements (preferably true ones, perhaps) is as much *a* set of postulates as any other. The word 'postulate' is significant only relative to an act of inquiry; we apply the word to a set of statements just in so far as we happen, for the year or the moment, to be thinking of those statements in relation to the statements which can be reached from them by some set of transformations to which we have seen fit to direct our attention. Now the notion of semantical rule is as sensible and meaningful as that of postulate, if conceived in a similarly relative spirit—relative, this time, to one or another particular enterprise of schooling unconversant persons in sufficient conditions for truth of statements of some natural or artificial language L. But from this point of view no one signalization of a subclass of the truths of L is intrinsically more a semantical rule than another; and, if 'analytic' means 'true by semantical rules', no one truth of L is analytic to the exclusion of another.[14]

It might conceivably be protested that an artificial language L (unlike a natural one) is a language in the ordinary sense *plus* a set of explicit semantical rules—the whole constituting; let us say, an ordered pair; and that the semantical rules of *L* then are specifiable simply as the second component of the pair *L*. But, by the same token and more simply, we might construe an artificial language *L* outright as an ordered pair whose second component is the class of its analytic statements; and then the analytic statements of *L* become specifiable simply as the statements in the second component of *L*. Or better still, we might just stop tugging at our bootstraps altogether.

Not all the explanations of analyticity known to Carnap and his readers have been covered explicitly in the above considerations, but the extension to other forms is not hard to see. Just one additional factor should be mentioned which sometimes enters: sometimes the semantical rules are in effect rules of translation into ordinary language, in which case the analytic statements of the artificial language are in effect recognized as such from the analyticity of their specified translations in ordinary language. Here certainly there can be no thought of an illumination of the problem of analyticity from the side of the artificial language.

From the point of view of the problem of analyticity the notion of an artificial language with semantical rules is a *feu follet par excellence*. Semantical rules determining the analytic statements of an artificial language are of interest only in so far as we already understand the notion of analyticity; they are of no help in gaining this understanding.

Appeal to hypothetical languages of an artificially simple kind could conceivably be useful in clarifying analyticity, if the mental or behavioral or cultural factors relevant to analyticity—whatever they may be—were somehow sketched into the simplified model. But a model which takes analyticity merely as an irreducible character is unlikely to throw light on the problem of explicating analyticity.

It is obvious that truth in general depends on both language and extralinguistic fact. The statement 'Brutus killed Caesar' would be false if the world had been different in certain ways, but it would also be false if the word 'killed' happened rather to have the sense of 'begat'. Thus one is tempted to suppose in general that the truth of a statement is somehow analyzable into a linguistic component and a factual component. Given this supposition, it next seems reasonable that in some statements the factual component should be null; and these are the analytic statements. But, for all its a priori reasonableness, a boundary between analytic and synthetic statements simply has not been drawn. That there is such a distinction to be drawn at all is an unempirical dogma of empiricists, a metaphysical article of faith.

V. THE VERIFICATION THEORY AND REDUCTIONISM

In the course of these somber reflections we have taken a dim view first of the notion of meaning, then of the notion of cognitive synonymy, and finally of the notion of analyticity. But what, it may be asked, of the verification theory of meaning? This phrase has established itself so firmly as a catchword of empiricism that we should be very unscientific indeed not to look beneath it for a possible key to the problem of meaning and the associated problems.

The verification theory of meaning, which has been conspicuous in the literature from Peirce onward, is that the meaning of a statement is the method of empirically confirming or infirming it. An analytic statement is that limiting case which is confirmed no matter what.

As urged in section I, we can as well pass over the question of meanings as entities and move straight to sameness of meaning, or synonymy. Then what the verification theory says is that statements are synonymous if and only if they are alike in point of method of empirical confirmation or infirmation.

This is an account of cognitive synonymy not of linguistic forms generally, but of statements.[15] However, from the concept of synonymy of statements we could derive the concept of synonymy for other linguistic forms, by considerations somewhat similar to those at the end of section III. Assuming the notion of "word," indeed, we could explain any two forms as synonymous when the putting of the one form for an occurrence of the other in any statement (apart from occurrences within "words") yields a synonymous statement. Finally, given the concept of synonymy thus for linguistic forms generally, we could define analyticity in terms of synonymy and logical truth as in section I. For that matter, we could define analyticity more simply in terms of just synonymy of statements together with logical truth; it is not necessary to appeal to synonymy of linguistic forms other than statements. For a statement may be described as analytic simply when it is synonymous with a logically true statement.

So, if the verification theory can be accepted as an adequate account of statement synonymy, the notion of analyticity is saved after all. However, let us reflect. Statement synonymy is said to be likeness of method of empirical confirmation or infirmation. Just what are these methods which are to be compared for likeness? What, in other words, is the nature of the relation between a statement and the experiences which contribute to or detract from its confirmation?

The most naïve view of the relation is that it is one of direct report. This is *radical reductionism*. Every meaningful statement is held to be translatable into a statement (true or false) about immediate experience. Radical reductionism, in one form or another, well antedates the verification theory of meaning explicitly so called. Thus Locke and Hume held that every idea must either originate directly in sense experience or else be compounded of ideas thus originating; and taking a hint from Tooke we might rephrase this doctrine in semantical jargon by saying that a term, to be significant at all, must be either a name of a sense datum or a compound of such names or an abbreviation of such a compound. So stated, the doctrine remains ambiguous as between sense data as sensory events and sense data as sensory qualities; and it remains vague as to the admissible ways of compounding. Moreover, the doctrine is unnecessarily and intolerably restrictive in the term-by-term critique which it imposes. More reasonably, and without yet exceeding the limits of what I have called radical reductionism, we may take full statements as our significant units—thus demanding that our statements as wholes be translatable into sense-datum language, but not that they be translatable term by term.

This emendation would unquestionably have been welcome to Locke and Hume and Tooke, but historically it had to await an important reorientation in semantics—the reorientation whereby the primary vehicle of meaning came to be seen no longer in the term but in the statement. This reorientation, explicit in Frege ([5], section 60), underlies Russell's concept of incomplete symbols defined in use;[16] also it is implicit in the verification theory of meaning, since the objects of verification are statements.

Radical reductionism, conceived now with statements as units, set itself the task of specifying a sense-datum language and showing how to translate the rest of significant discourse, statement by statement, into it. Carnap embarked on this project in the *Aufbau*.

The language which Carnap adopted as his starting point was not a sense-datum language in the narrowest conceivable sense, for it included also the notations of logic, up through higher set theory. In effect it included the whole language of pure mathematics. The ontology implicit in it (that is, the range of values of its variables) embraced not only sensory events but classes, classes of classes, and so on. Empiricists there are who would boggle at such prodigality. Carnap's starting point is very parsimonious, however, in its extralogical or sensory part. In a series of constructions in which he exploits the resources of modern logic with much ingenuity,

Carnap succeeds in defining a wide array of important additional sensory concepts which, but for his constructions, one would not have dreamed were definable on so slender a basis. He was the first empiricist who, not content with asserting the reducibility of science to terms of immediate experience, took serious steps toward carrying out the reduction.

If Carnap's starting point is satisfactory, still his constructions were, as he himself stressed, only a fragment of the full program. The construction of even the simplest statements about the physical world was left in a sketchy state. Carnap's suggestions on this subject were, despite their sketchiness, very suggestive. He explained spatio-temporal point-instants as quadruples of real numbers and envisaged assignment of sense qualities to point-instants according to certain canons. Roughly summarized, the plan was that qualities should be assigned to point-instants in such a way as to achieve the laziest world compatible with our experience. The principle of least action was to be our guide in constructing a world from experience.

Carnap did not seem to recognize, however, that his treatment of physical objects fell short of reduction not merely through sketchiness, but in principle. Statements of the form 'Quality q is at point-instant $x;y;z;t$' were, according to his canons, to be apportioned truth-values in such a way as to maximize and minimize certain overall features, and with growth of experience the truth-values were to be progressively revised in the same spirit. I think this is a good schematization (deliberately oversimplified, to be sure) of what science really does; but it provides no indication, not even the sketchiest, of how a statement of the form 'Quality q is at $x;y;z;t$' could ever be translated into Carnap's initial language of sense data and logic. The connective 'is at' remains an added undefined connective; the canons counsel us in its use but not in its elimination.

Carnap seems to have appreciated this point afterward; for in his later writings he abandoned all notion of the translatability of statements about the physical world into statements about immediate experience. Reductionism in its radical form has long since ceased to figure in Carnap's philosophy.

But the dogma of reductionism has, in a subtler and more tenuous form, continued to influence the thought of empiricists. The notion lingers that to each statement, or each synthetic statement, there is associated a unique range of possible sensory events such that the occurrence of any of them would add to the likelihood of truth of the statement, and that there is associated also another unique range of possible sensory events whose occurrence would detract from that likelihood. This notion is of course implicit in the verification theory of meaning.

The dogma of reductionism survives in the supposition that each statement, taken in isolation from its fellows, can admit of confirmation or infirmation at all. My countersuggestion, issuing essentially from Carnap's doctrine of the physical world in the *Aufbau*, is that our statements about the external world face the tribunal of sense experience not individually but only as a corporate body.[17]

The dogma of reductionism, even in its attenuated form, is intimately connected with the other dogma—that there is a cleavage between the analytic and the synthetic. We have found ourselves led, indeed, from the latter problem to the former through the verification theory of meaning. More directly, the one dogma clearly supports the other in this way: as long as it is taken to be significant in general to speak of the confirmation and infirmation of a statement, it seems significant to speak also of a limiting kind of statement which is vacuously confirmed, *ipso facto*, come what may; and such a statement is analytic.

The two dogmas are, indeed, at root identical. We lately reflected that in general the truth of statements does obviously depend both upon language and upon extralinguistic fact; and we noted that this obvious circumstance carries in its train, not logically but all too naturally, a feeling that the truth of a statement is somehow analyzable into a linguistic component and a factual component. The factual component must, if we are empiricists, boil down to a range of confirmatory experiences. In the extreme case where the linguistic component is all that matters, a true statement is analytic. But I hope we are not impressed with how stubbornly the distinction between analytic and synthetic has resisted any straightforward drawing. I am impressed also, apart from prefabricated examples of black and white balls in an urn, with how baffling the problem has always been of arriving at any explicit theory of the empirical confirmation of a synthetic statement. My present suggestion is that it is nonsense, and the root of much nonsense, to speak of a linguistic component and a factual component in the truth of any individual statement. Taken collectively, science has its double dependence upon language and experience; but this duality is not significantly traceable into the statements of science taken one by one.

The idea of defining a symbol in use was, as remarked, an advance over the impossible term-by-term empiricism of Locke and Hume. The statement, rather than the term, came with Frege to be recognized as the unit accountable to an empiricist critique. But what I am now urging is that even in taking the statement as unit we have drawn our grid too finely. The unit of empirical significance is the whole of science.

VI. EMPIRICISM WITHOUT THE DOGMAS

The totality of our so-called knowledge or beliefs, from the most casual matters of geography and history to the profoundest laws of atomic physics or even of pure mathematics and logic, is a man-made fabric which impinges on experience only along the edges. Or, to change the figure, total science is like a field of force whose boundary conditions are experience. A conflict with experience at the periphery occasions readjustments in the interior of the field. Truth-values have to be redistributed over some of our statements. Reevaluation of some statements entails reevaluation of others, because of their logical interconnections—the logical laws being in turn simply certain further statements of the system, certain further elements of the field. Having reevaluated one statement we must reevaluate some others, which may be statements logically connected with the first or may be the statements of logical connections themselves. But the total field is so underdetermined by its boundary conditions, experience, that there is much latitude of choice as to what statements to reevaluate in the light of any single contrary experience. No particular experiences are linked with any particular statements in the interior of the field, except indirectly through considerations of equilibrium affecting the field as a whole.

If this view is right, it is misleading to speak of the empirical content of an individual statement—especially if it is a statement at all remote from the experiential periphery of the field. Furthermore it becomes folly to seek a boundary between synthetic statements, which hold contingently on experience, and analytic statements, which hold come what may. Any statement can be held true come what may, if we make drastic enough adjustments elsewhere in the system. Even a statement very close to the periphery can be held true in the face of recalcitrant experience by pleading hallucination or by amending certain statements of the kind called logical laws. Conversely, by the same token, no statement is immune to revision. Revision even of the logical law of the excluded middle has been proposed as a means of simplifying quantum mechanics; and what difference is there in principle between such a shift and the shift whereby Kepler superseded Ptolemy, or Einstein Newton, or Darwin Aristotle?

For vividness I have been speaking in terms of varying distances from a sensory periphery. Let me try now to clarify this notion without metaphor. Certain statements, though *about* physical objects and not sense experience, seem peculiarly germane to sense experience—and in a selective way: some statements to some experiences, others to others. Such statements, especially germane to particular experiences, I picture as near the periphery. But in this relation of "germaneness" I envisage nothing more than a loose association reflecting the relative likelihood, in practice, of our choosing one statement rather than another for revision in the event of recalcitrant experience. For example, we can imagine recalcitrant experiences to which we would surely be inclined to accommodate our system by reevaluating just the statement that there are brick houses on Elm Street, together with related statements on the same topic. We can imagine other recalcitrant experiences to which we would be inclined to accommodate our system by reevaluating just the statement that there are no centaurs, along with kindred statements. A recalcitrant experience can, I have urged, be accommodated by any of various alternative reevaluations in various alternative quarters of the total system; but, in the cases which we are now imagining, our natural tendency to disturb the total system as little as possible would lead us to focus our revisions upon these specific statements concerning brick houses or centaurs. These statements are felt, therefore, to have a sharper empirical reference than highly theoretical statements of physics or logic or ontology. The latter statements may be thought of as relatively centrally located within the total network, meaning merely that little preferential connection with any particular sense data obtrudes itself.

As an empiricist I continue to think of the conceptual scheme of science as a tool, ultimately, for predicting future experience in the light of past experience. Physical objects are conceptually imported into the situation as convenient intermediaries—not by definition in terms of experience, but simply as irreducible posits[18] comparable, epistemologically, to the gods of Homer. For my part I do, qua lay physicist, believe in physical objects and not in Homer's gods; and I consider it a scientific error to believe otherwise. But in point of epistemological footing the physical objects and the gods differ only in degree and not in kind. Both sorts of entities enter our conception only as cultural posits. The myth of physical objects is epistemologically superior to most in that it has proved more efficacious than other myths as a device for working a manageable structure into the flux of experience.

Positing does not stop with macroscopic physical objects. Objects at the atomic level are posited to make the laws of macroscopic objects, and ultimately the laws of experience, simpler and more manageable; and we need not expect or demand full definition of atomic and subatomic entities in terms of macroscopic ones, any more than definition of macroscopic things in terms of sense data. Science is a continuation of common sense, and it continues the common-sense expedient of swelling ontology to simplify theory.

Physical objects, small and large, are not the only posits. Forces are another example; and indeed we are told nowadays that the boundary between energy and matter is obsolete. Moreover, the abstract entities which are the substance of mathematics—ultimately classes and classes of classes and so on up—are another posit in the same spirit. Epistemologically these are myths on the same footing with physical objects and gods, neither better nor worse except for differences in the degree to which they expedite our dealings with sense experiences.

The overall algebra of rational and irrational numbers is underdetermined by the algebra of rational numbers, but is smoother and more convenient; and it includes the algebra of rational numbers as a jagged or gerrymandered part.[19] Total science, mathematical and natural and human, is similarly but more extremely underdetermined by experience. The edge of the system must be kept squared with experience; the rest, with all its elaborate myths or fictions, has as its objective the simplicity of laws.

Ontological questions, under this view, are on a par with questions of natural science.[20] Consider the question whether to countenance classes as entities. This, as I have argued elsewhere,[21] is the question whether to quantify with respect to variables which take classes as values. Now Carnap [3] has maintained that this is a question not of matters of fact but of choosing a convenient language form, a convenient conceptual scheme or framework for science. With this I agree, but only on the proviso that the same be conceded regarding scientific hypotheses generally. Carnap ([3], p. 32n) has recognized that he is able to preserve a double standard for ontological questions and scientific hypotheses only by assuming an absolute distinction between the analytic and the synthetic; and I need not say again that this is a distinction which I reject.[22]

The issue over there being classes seems more a question of convenient conceptual scheme; the issue over there being centaurs, or brick houses on Elm Street, seems more a question of fact. But I have been urging that this difference is only one of degree, and that it turns upon our vaguely pragmatic inclination to adjust one strand of the fabric of science rather than another in accommodating some particular recalcitrant experience. Conservatism figures in such choices, and so does the quest for simplicity.

Carnap, Lewis, and others take a pragmatic stand on the question of choosing between language forms, scientific frameworks; but their pragmatism leaves off at the imagined boundary between the analytic and the synthetic. In repudiating such a boundary I espouse a more thorough pragmatism. Each man is given a scientific heritage plus a continuing barrage of sensory stimulation; and the considerations which guide him in warping his scientific heritage to fit his continuing sensory promptings are, where rational, pragmatic.

NOTES

1. See W.V.O. Quine, [13] p. 9.
2. See ibid., pp. 10 and 107–15.
3. See ibid., pp. 11f and 48f.
4. Carnap [1], pp. 9ff; [2], pp. 70ff.
5. According to an important variant sense of 'definition', the relation preserved may be the weaker relation of mere agreement in reference; see Quine [13], p. 132. But definition in this sense is better ignored in the present connection, being irrelevant to the question of synonymy.
6. Cf. Lewis [7], p. 373.
7. This is cognitive synonymy in a primary, broad sense. Carnap ([1], pp. 56ff) and Lewis ([8], pp. 83ff) have suggested how, once this notion is at hand, a narrower sense of cognitive synonymy which is preferable for some purposes can in turn be derived. But this special ramification of concept-building lies aside from the present purposes and must not be confused with the broad sort of cognitive synonymy here concerned.
8. Quine [13], p. 81ff, contains a description of just such a language, except that there happens there to be just one predicate, the two-place predicate 'e'.
9. See ibid., pp. 5–8 85f, 166f.
10. See ibid., p. 87.
11. On such devices see also ibid., essay 8.

12. This is the substance of Quine [12], *121.
13. The 'if and only if' itself is intended in the truth-functional sense. See Carnap [1], p. 14.
14. The foregoing paragraph was not part of the present essay as originally published. It was prompted by Martin [10], as was the end of essay 7 in Quine [13].
15. The doctrine can indeed be formulated with terms rather than statements as the units. Thus Lewis describes the meaning of a term as "*a criterion in mind*, by reference to which one is able to apply or refuse to apply the expression in question in the case of presented, or imagined, things or situations" ([8], p. 133).—For an instructive account of the vicissitudes of the verification theory of meaning, centered however on the question of meaning*fulness* rather than synonymy and analyticity, see Hempel [6].
16. See Quine [13], p. 6.
17. This doctrine was well argued by Duhem [4], pp. 303–28. Or see Lowinger [9], pp. 132–40.
18. Cf. Quine [11], pp. 17f.
19. Cf. Quine [13], p. 18.
20. "L'ontologie fait corps avec la science elle-même et ne peut en être separée." Meyerson [11], p. 439.
21. Quine [13], pp. 12f, 102ff.
22. For an effective expression of further misgivings over this distinction, see White [14].

REFERENCES

Carnap, Rudolph. [1] *Meaning and Necessity*. Chicago: University of Chicago Press, 1947.
———. [2] *Logical Foundations of Probability*. Chicago: University of Chicago Press, 1950.
———. [3] "Empiricism, Semantics, and Ontology." *Revue Internationale de Philosophie* 4 (1950), pp. 20–40.
Duhem, Pierre. [4] *La Théorie Physique: Son Objet et sa Structure*. Paris, 1906.
Frege, Gottlob. [5] *Foundations of Arithmetic*. New York: Philosophical Library, 1950.
Hempel, C. G. [6] "Problems and Changes in the Empiricist Criterion of Meaning." *Revue Internationale de Philosophie* 4 (1950), pp. 41–63.
Lewis, C. I. [7] *A Survey of Symbolic Logic*. Berkeley, 1918.
———. [8] *An Analysis of Knowledge and Valuation*. LaSalle, IL: Open Court, 1946.
Lowinger, Armand. [9] *The Methodology of Pierre Duhem*. New York: Columbia University Press, 1941.
Martin, R. M. [10] "On 'Analytic.' " *Philosophical Studies* 3 (1952), pp. 42–47.
Meyerson, Emile. [11] *Identité et Realité*. Paris, 1908. 4th ed., 1932.
Quine, W.V.O. [12] *Mathematical Logic*. New York: Norton, 1940. Cambridge: Harvard University Press, 1947. Rev. ed., 1951.
———. [13] *From a Logical Point of View*. Cambridge: Harvard University Press, 1953.
White, Morton. [14] "The Analytic and the Synthetic: An Untenable Dualism." In *John Dewey: Philosopher of Science and Freedom*. Edited by Sydney Hook. New York: Dial Press, 1950, pp. 316–30.

PART TWO

LAWS AND LAWLIKENESS

INTRODUCTION

ccording to a tradition with roots in ancient history, there are basic differences between laws of nature and laws of society, on the one hand, and between laws of nature and accidental generalizations, on the other. Laws of society can be violated and can be changed, while laws of nature can neither be violated nor be changed. Laws of nature are supposed to reflect necessary connections between events of one kind and events of another (or between certain properties and other properties), which are absent in the case of merely accidental generalizations. As a consequence, while all laws are true generalizations, not all true generalizations are laws.

One of Hume's contributions to philosophy was a critique of this conception on the basis of the epistemic principle that it is rational to accept the existence of properties and relations only when they are accessible to observation. According to Hume, necessary connections are not observable and therefore should not qualify as features of an acceptable conception of causal relations, which should instead be reduced to constant conjunctions and relative frequencies between associated events (or properties). Yet there are no differences between mere generalizations and genuine laws only if there are no differences between causation and correlation.

Goodman's "The Problem of Counterfactual Conditionals" appraises the limits of extensional (or truth-functional) language for capturing the difference that is at stake here. A linguistic symptom of this difference appears to be that natural laws support subjunctive and counterfactual conditionals, while accidental generalizations do not. A *subjunctive* is an "if _____ then . . ." conditional in the subjunctive mood, which concerns what would happen if something were the case, by contrast with a material conditional, which concerns what is the case. A *material* but not a subjunctive conditional will be true if either its antecedent ("_____") is false or its consequent (". . .") is true.

An example may illustrate the difference. Consider the two sentences:

(a) If I ignite this dynamite, then it will explode;

(b) If I ignite this dynamite, then it will not explode.

We tend to believe that one of these conditionals is true and the other false. Interpreted as material conditionals, however, both are true so long as I do not ignite this dynamite. When the same sentences are instead interpreted as subjunctive conditionals, where subjunctives assume hypothetically that their antecedents are true, it is hard to imagine they could both be true:

(c) If I were to ignite this dynamite, then it would explode;

(d) If I were to ignite this dynamite, then it would not explode.

Since *counterfactuals* are subjunctives with historically false antecedents, the underlying problem is to explain which subjunctive conditionals are true and why.

Goodman maintains that there is a strong connection between various recalcitrant problems concerning counterfactuals, dispositions, and laws of nature. Suppose, for example, that the generalization that (pure) gold is malleable is a law of nature. It then seems reasonable to make the subjunctive assertion of something *a* that, if it *were* gold, then it *would be* malleable, even when that something is a piece of chalk. Malleability itself, moreover, appears to be a dispositional property of things that are gold, since it characterizes certain ways that things would behave under certain specific conditions. These appear to be closely related problems.

Goodman reviews attempts to solve the problem by techniques that remain within the scope of extensional logic. Ultimately, however, he advocates a pragmatic and historical solution that includes these two theses:

(T1) *Lawlike generalizations are those on the basis of which we find ourselves willing to assert subjunctive and counterfactual conditionals*; and,

(T2) *Lawlike generalizations are those we are willing to accept as true and project for unknown cases without having exhausted their instances.*

Indeed, the position that Goodman defends has been so influential that it has virtually defined the nature of the problem of law for other thinkers.

Skyrms' "The Goodman Paradox and the New Riddle of Induction" represents much current thought on these subjects. The "Goodman Paradox" is not the problem of counterfactual conditionals as such but rather the problem of projectible predicates, which arises from the inference that some predicates are suitable for projection to future cases, while others are not. While "blue" and "green" appear to be projectible, for example, "grue" and "bleen" do not. The "new riddle" thus appears to be Hume's old problem of induction, but appearing now in a new (linguistic) guise.

The old problem of induction concerns the rational justification of inferences about the future on the basis of regularities that have obtained in the past, when belief in necessary connections is no longer warranted. As Skyrms vividly explains, "regularities" are subject to creation as well as to discovery, provided we are ingenious enough in constructing ways to describe the evidence, where "Whatever prediction you wish to make, a regularity can be found whose projection will license that prediction." As a consequence, the prospects for a system of scientific inductive logic of the kind that he describes would seem to be difficult if not impossible.

Popper's "Universals, Dispositions, and Natural or Physical Necessity" shares Goodman's conception of the problem but diverges strongly from Goodman's conception of its solution. Popper also views the problems of subjunctive conditionals, of dispositions, and of natural law as intimately interrelated, but he rejects an historical and pragmatic approach in favor of an ontological and semantical solution. For Popper, lawlike sentences concern relations between *universals*, where universals are dispositions. It thus turns out that subjunctive and counterfactual conditionals can be explained as manifestations of underlying natural or physical necessities.

According to Popper's explication, natural or physical necessities are described by sentence functions that are satisfied in every world which differs from this world, if at all, only with respect to its initial conditions. This formulation, however, like Goodman's thesis (T1), does not differentiate logical truths from nonlogical truths, since every sentence function that is true on grammatical or definitional grounds alone can satisfy both of their conceptions. Popper's conditions (A) and (B) differentiate logical and physical necessities from material conditionals, but his conditions (A′) and (B′) do not differentiate physical necessities from logical necessities.

This problem does not appear to be too difficult to resolve, however, since physical necessities, unlike logical necessities, should *never* be true whenever either their antecedents are logically impossible or their consequents are logically necessary. The reformulation of (A′) and (B′) can be effected by substituting "never" for "always" (with related changes). Another problem that may be more threatening, however, is the claim that only *some*, but not all, universals are projectible, even when universals are understood as dispositions. The question that is raised thus becomes whether some dispositions might turn out to be unprojectible.

"Grue" and "bleen," for example, could be said to be dispositions of a funny kind, precisely because, at a certain date, something that is grue turns from green to blue, and so on, where green and blue would seem to be perfectly normal dispositions. The question that arises here, however, may have a more general character. For when we generalize upon the specific dates that occur in funny predicates (to 1990, 1980, and so forth), it should be apparent that hypotheses of this kind have not been satisfied in the past by ordinary classes of things, precisely because the members of such classes have never all changed color on any such date.

Goodman, no doubt, would not disagree but would claim further support for an historical and pragmatic solution. If universals are viewed as pure rather than funny dispositions, however, that would appear to provide an ontological and semantical solution for part of the problem. Popper's emphasis upon the character of laws as *prohibitions* that rule out certain logical possibilities as physical impossibilities, moreover, is a feature that harmonizes well with the traditional conception of laws as regularities that cannot be violated and cannot be changed. It also hints that lawlike hypotheses might be tested by attempting to refute them.

Goodman's focus on counterfactual as opposed to subjunctive conditionals appears to make a difference here. For, while it is true that no *counterfactual* can be subjected to direct test (because its antecedent is false), subjunctives, in general, *can* be subjected to direct test (because their antecedents can be true). Moreover, an ontological and semantical solution of this kind would seem to explain not only why some generalizations but not others provide support for counterfactual and subjunctive conditionals but also why the methods appropriate for establishing accidental generalizations may not be sufficient to discover natural laws. We will return to these issues in relation to the justification of induction.

STUDY QUESTIONS

As you read the articles that appear in this section, you may want to think about their implications for understanding the nature of science and of philosophy. The following questions are intended to stimulate your thinking by focusing attention on some of the less obvious aspects of different positions.

(1) The difference between laws of society and laws of nature appears to be an important one. Where do laws of each of these kinds come from? In what ways, if any, are they similar? And in what ways are they different? Do laws of both kinds support subjunctive and counter-factual conditionals?

(2) Molecular sentences that are logically equivalent to some finite conjunction of atomic sentences have finite scope. If lawlike sentences do not have finite scope, does that explain why the sentence, "All the coins in my pocket are made of silver," cannot be a law of nature? Is anything more involved?

(3) Among Goodman's examples of laws of nature are ones that assert, "All dimes are made of silver," "All butter melts at 150°F," and "All flowers of plants descended from this seed will be yellow." Do you think all three are good examples? Do any of them support or undermine Goodman's explication?

(4) Is there a difference between the question, "What is a law of nature?" and the question, "Under what conditions do we regard a sentence as a law of nature?" Which question is Goodman addressing? Which is he answering? Does a good answer to one also qualify as a good answer to the other?

(5) Things that are grue change from green to blue with respect to ordinary predicates, but they remain things that are grue with respect to Goodman predicates. This is the sense in which "linguistic machinery" makes a difference. Is this a real problem or merely a philosophical puzzle? Why?

(6) Inferences that are based on drawing samples from populations seem to involve similar problems, since each member of a sample has been observed before some time t while the other members of the population remain unobserved. Do you detect any differences which distinguish them?

(7) Would a solution to the problem of projectibility provide a solution to the problem of counterfactual conditionality? Could there be hypotheses that are expressed exclusively by means of projectible predicates but are nevertheless incapable of providing support for subjunctive conditionals?

(8) Popper suggests that universal laws transcend experience in at least two ways. They are not reducible to any finite number of their instances and the universal terms that occur in them are dispositional. In what ways does Popper's conception agree and disagree with that of Goodman?

(9) Popper defines "natural necessities" as sentences that are deducible from sentence functions that are satisfied in every world which differs from this world, if at all, only with respect to its initial conditions. Does he thereby provide a definition of "natural necessity" that is not circular?

(10) Popper tells us about an extinct species of huge birds called "moas" who, under favorable conditions, could easily have lived to be more than sixty years of age but who encountered unfavorable conditions. Now, if no moa actually lived more than fifty years, why is that not a law of nature?

NELSON GOODMAN

THE PROBLEM OF COUNTERFACTUAL CONDITIONALS[1]

I. THE PROBLEM IN GENERAL

The analysis of counterfactual conditionals is no fussy little grammatical exercise. Indeed, if we lack the means for interpreting counterfactual conditionals, we can hardly claim to have any adequate philosophy of science. A satisfactory definition of scientific law, a satisfactory theory of confirmation or of disposition terms (and this includes not only predicates ending in "ible" and "able" but almost every objective predicate, such as "is red"), would solve a large part of the problem of counterfactuals. Conversely, a solution to the problem of counterfactuals would give us the answer to critical questions about law, confirmation, and the meaning of potentiality.

I am not at all contending that the problem of counterfactuals is logically or psychologically the first of these related problems. It makes little difference where we start if we can go ahead. If the study of counterfactuals has up to now failed this pragmatic test, the alternative approaches are little better off.

What, then, is the *problem* about counterfactual conditionals? Let us confine ourselves to those in which antecedent and consequent are inalterably false—as, for example, when I say of a piece of butter that was eaten yesterday, and that had never been heated,

If that piece of butter had been heated to 150°F, it would have melted.

Considered as truth-functional compounds, all counterfactuals are of course true, since their antecedents are false. Hence

If that piece of butter had been heated to 150°F, it would not have melted

would also hold. Obviously something different is intended, and the problem is to define the circumstances under which a given counterfactual holds while the opposing conditional with the contradictory consequent fails to hold. And this criterion of truth must be set up in the face of the fact that a counterfactual by its nature can never be subjected to any direct empirical test by realizing its antecedent.

In one sense the name "problem of counterfactuals" is misleading, because the problem is independent of the form in which a given statement happens to be expressed. The problem of counterfactuals is equally a problem of factual conditionals, for any counterfactual can be transposed into a conditional with a true antecedent and consequent; e.g.,

Since that butter did not melt, it wasn't heated to 150°F.

The possibility of such transformation is of no great importance except to clarify the nature of our problem. That "since" occurs in the contrapositive shows that what is in question is a certain kind of connection between the two component sentences; and the truth of statements of this kind—whether they have the form of counterfactual or factual conditionals or some other form—depends not upon the truth or falsity of the components but upon whether the intended connection obtains. Recognizing the possibility of transformation serves mainly to focus attention on the central problem and to discourage speculation as to the nature of counterfacts. Although I shall begin my study by considering counterfactuals as such, it must be borne in mind that a general solution would explain the kind of connection involved irrespective of any assumption as to the truth or falsity of the components.

The effect of transposition upon conditionals of another kind, which I call "semifactuals," is worth noticing briefly. Should we assert

Even if the match had been scratched, it still would not have lighted,

we would uncompromisingly reject as an equally good expression of our meaning the contra-positive,

Even if the match lighted, it still wasn't scratched.

Our original intention was to affirm not that the nonlighting could be inferred from the scratching, but simply that the lighting could not be inferred from the scratching. Ordinarily a semifactual conditional has the force of denying what is affirmed by the opposite, fully counterfactual conditional. The sentence

Even had that match been scratched, it still wouldn't have lighted

is normally meant as the direct negation of

Had the match been scratched, it would have lighted.

That is to say, in practice full counterfactuals affirm, while semifactuals deny, that a certain connection obtains between antecedent and consequent.[2] Thus it is clear why a semifactual generally has not the same meaning as its contrapositive.

There are various special kinds of counterfactuals that present special problems. An example is the case of 'counteridenticals', illustrated by the statements

If I were Julius Caesar, I wouldn't be alive in the twentieth century,

and

If Julius Caesar were I, he would be alive in the twentieth century.

Here, although the antecedent in the two cases is a statement of the same identity, we attach two different consequents which, on the very assumption of that identity, are incompatible. Another special class of counterfactuals is that of the 'countercomparatives', with antecedents such as

If I had more money, . . .

The trouble with these is that when we try to translate the counterfactual into a statement about a relation between two tenseless, nonmodal sentences, we get as an antecedent something like

If "I have more money than I have" were true, . . .

which wrongly represents the original antecedent as self-contradictory. Again there are the 'counterlegals', conditionals with antecedents that either deny general laws directly, as in

If triangles were squares, . . .

or else make a supposition of particular fact that is not merely false but impossible, as in

If this cube of sugar were also spherical, ...

Counterfactuals of all these kinds offer interesting but not insurmountable special difficulties.[3] In order to concentrate upon the major problems concerning counterfactuals in general, I shall usually choose my examples in such a way as to avoid these more special complications.

As I see it, there are two major problems, though they are not independent and may even be regarded as aspects of a single problem. A counterfactual is true if a certain connection obtains between the antecedent and the consequent. But as is obvious from examples already given, the consequent seldom follows from the antecedent by logic alone. (1) In the first place, the assertion that a connection holds is made on the presumption that certain circumstances not stated in the antecedent obtain. When we say

If that match had been scratched, it would have lighted,

we mean that conditions are such—i.e., the match is well made, is dry enough, oxygen enough is present, etc.—that "That match lights" can be inferred from "That match is scratched." Thus the connection we affirm may be regarded as joining the consequent with the conjunction of the antecedent and other statements that truly describe relevant conditions. Notice especially that our assertion of the counterfactual is *not* conditioned upon these circumstances obtaining. We do not assert that the counterfactual is true *if* the circumstances obtain; rather, in asserting the counterfactual we commit ourselves to the actual truth of the statements describing the requisite relevant conditions. The first major problem is to define relevant conditions: to specify what sentences are meant to be taken in conjunction with an antecedent as a basis for inferring the consequent. (2) But even after the particular relevant conditions are specified, the connection obtaining will not ordinarily be a logical one. The principle that permits inference of

That match lights

from

That match is scratched. That match is dry enough. Enough oxygen is present. Etc.

is not a law of logic but what we call a natural or physical or causal law. The second major problem concerns the definition of such laws.

II. THE PROBLEM OF RELEVANT CONDITIONS

It might seem natural to propose that the consequent follows by law from the antecedent and a description of the actual state-of-affairs of the world, that we need hardly define relevant conditions because it will do no harm to include irrelevant ones. But if we say that the consequent follows by law from the antecedent and *all* true statements, we encounter an immediate difficulty:—among true sentences is the negate of the antecedent, so that from the antecedent and all true sentences everything follows. Certainly this gives us no way of distinguishing true from false counterfactuals.

We are plainly no better off if we say that the consequent must follow from *some* set of true statements conjoined with the antecedent; for given any counterfactual antecedent *A*, there will always be a set *S*—namely, the set consisting of *not-A*—such that from *A·S* any consequent follows. (Hereafter I shall regularly use the following symbols: "*A*" for the antecedent; "*C*" for the consequent; "*S*" for the set of statements of the relevant conditions or, indifferently, for the conjunction of these statements.)

Perhaps then we must exclude statements logically incompatible with the antecedent. But this is insufficient; for a parallel difficulty arises with respect to true statements which are not logically but are otherwise incompatible with the antecedent. For example, take

If that radiator had frozen, it would have broken.

Among true sentences may well be (*S*)

That radiator never reached a temperature below 33°F.

Now we have as true generalizations both

All radiators that freeze but never reach below 33°F break,

and also

All radiators that freeze but never reach below 33°F fail to break;

for there are no such radiators. Thus from the antecedent of the counterfactual and the given S, we can infer any consequent.

The natural proposal to remedy this difficulty is to rule that counterfactuals cannot depend upon empty laws; that the connection can be established only by a principle of the form "All x's are y's" when there are some x's. But this is ineffectual. For if empty principles are excluded, the following nonempty principles may be used in the case given with the same result:

Everything that is either a radiator that freezes but does not reach below 33°F, or that is a soap bubble, breaks;

Everything that is either a radiator that freezes but does not reach below 33°F, or is powder, does not break.

By these principles we can infer any consequent from the A and S in question.

The only course left open to us seems to be to define relevant conditions as the set of all true statements each of which is both logically and nonlogically compatible with A where nonlogical incompatibility means violation of a nonlogical law.[4] But another difficulty immediately appears. In a counterfactual beginning

If Jones were in Carolina, . . .

the antecedent is entirely compatible with

Jones is not in South Carolina

and with

Jones is not in North Carolina

and with

North Carolina plus South Carolina is identical with Carolina;

but all these taken together with the antecedent make a set that is self-incompatible, so that again any consequent would be forthcoming.

Clearly it will not help to require only that for *some* set S of true sentences, A·S be self-compatible and lead by law to the consequent; for this would make a true counterfactual of

If Jones were in Carolina, he would be in South Carolina,

and also of

If Jones were in Carolina, he would be in North Carolina,

which cannot both be true.

It seems that we must elaborate our criterion still further, to characterize a counterfactual as true if and only if there is some set S of true statements such as A·S is self-compatible and leads by law to the consequent, while there is no such set S' such that $A \cdot S'$ is self-compatible and leads by law to the negate of the consequent.[5] Unfortunately even this is not enough. For among true sentences will be the negate of the consequent: $-C$. Is $-C$ compatible with A or not? If not, then A alone without any additional conditions must lead by law to C. But if $-C$ is compatible with A (as in most cases), then if we take $-C$ as our S, the conjunction $A \cdot S$ will give us $-C$. Thus the criterion we have set up will seldom be satisfied; for since $-C$ will normally be compatible with A, as the need for introducing the relevant conditions testifies, there will normally be an S (namely, $-C$) such that $A \cdot S$ is self-compatible and leads by law to $-C$.

Part of our trouble lies in taking too narrow a view of our problem. We have been trying to lay down conditions under which an A that is known to be false leads to a C that is known to be false; but it is equally important to make sure that our criterion does not establish a similar connection between our A and the (true) negate of C. Because our S together with A was to be so chosen as to give us C, it seemed gratuitous to specify that S must be compatible with C; and because $-C$ is true by supposition, S would necessarily be compatible with it. But we are testing whether our criterion not only admits the true counterfactual we are concerned with but also excludes the opposing conditional. Accordingly, our criterion must be modified by specifying that S be compatible with both C and $-C$.[6] In other words, S by itself must not decide between C and $-C$, but S together with A must lead to C but not to $-C$. We need not know whether C is true or false.

Our rule thus reads that a counterfactual is true if and only if there is some set S of true sentences such that S is compatible with C and with $-C$, and such that $A \cdot S$ is self-compatible and leads by law to C; while there is no set S' compatible with C and with $-C$, and such that $A \cdot S'$ is self-compatible and leads by law to $-C$.[7] As thus stated, the rule involves a certain redundancy; but simplification is not in point here, for the criterion is still inadequate.

The requirement that $A \cdot S$ be self-compatible is not strong enough; for S might comprise true sentences that although *compatible with* A, were such that *they would not be true if A were true*. For this reason, many statements that we would regard as definitely false would be true according to the stated criterion. As an example, consider the familiar case where for a given match m, we would affirm

(i) If match m had been scratched, it would have lighted,

but deny

(ii) If match m had been scratched, it would not have been dry.[8]

According to our tentative criterion, statement (ii) would be quite as true as statement (i). For in the case of (ii), we may take as an element in our S the true sentence

Match m did not light,

which is presumably compatible with A (otherwise nothing would be required along with A to reach the opposite as the consequent of the true counterfactual statement (i)). As our total $A \cdot S$ we may have

Match m is scratched. It does not light. It is well made. Oxygen enough is present . . . etc.;

and from this, by means of a legitimate general law, we can infer

It was not dry.

And there would seem to be no suitable set of sentences S' such that $A \cdot S'$ leads by law to the negate of this consequent. Hence the unwanted counterfactual is established in accord with our rule. The trouble is caused by including in our S a true statement which though compatible with A would not be true if A were. Accordingly we must exclude such statements from the set of relevant conditions; S, in addition to satisfying the other requirements already laid down, must be not merely compatible with A but 'jointly tenable' or *cotenable* with A. A is cotenable with S, and the conjunction $A \cdot S$ self-cotenable, if it is not the case that S would not be true if A were.[9]

Parenthetically it may be noted that the relative fixity of conditions is often unclear, so that the speaker or writer has to make explicit additional provisos or give subtle verbal clues as to his meaning. For example, each of the following two counterfactuals would normally be accepted:

If New York City were in Georgia, then New York City would be in the South.

If Georgia included New York City, then Georgia would not be entirely in the South.

Yet the antecedents are logically indistinguishable. What happens is that the direction of expression becomes important, because in the former case the meaning is

If New York City were in Georgia, and the boundaries of Georgia remained unchanged, then . . . ,

while in the latter case the meaning is

If Georgia included New York City, and the boundaries of New York City remained unchanged, then. . . .

Without some such cue to the meaning as is covertly given by the word-order, we should be quite uncertain which of the two consequents in question could be truly attached. The same kind of explanation accounts for the paradoxical pairs of counteridenticals mentioned earlier.

Returning now to the proposed rule, I shall neither offer further corrections of detail nor discuss whether the requirement that S be cotenable with A makes superfluous some other provisions of the criterion; for such matters become rather unimportant beside the really serious difficulty that now confronts us. In order to determine the truth of a given counterfactual it seems that we have to determine, among other things, whether there is a suitable S that is cotenable with A and meets certain further requirements. But in order to determine whether or not a given S is cotenable with A, we have to determine whether or not the counterfactual "If A were true, then S would not be true" is itself true. But this means determining whether or not there is a suitable S_1, cotenable with A, that leads to $-S$ and so on. Thus we find ourselves involved in an infinite regressus or a circle; for cotenability is defined in terms of counterfactuals, yet the meaning of counterfactuals is defined in terms of cotenability. In other words, to establish any counterfactual, it seems that we first have to determine the truth of another. If so, we can never explain a counterfactual except in terms of others, so that the problem of counterfactuals must remain unsolved.

Though unwilling to accept this conclusion, I do not at present see any way of meeting the difficulty. One naturally thinks of revising the whole treatment of counterfactuals in such a way as to admit first those that depend on no conditions other than the antecedent, and then use these counterfactuals as the criteria for the cotenability of relevant conditions with antecedents of other counterfactuals, and so on. But this idea seems initially rather unpromising in view of the formidable difficulties of accounting by such a step-by-step method for even so simple a counterfactual as

If the match had been scratched, it would have lighted.

III. THE PROBLEM OF LAW

Even more serious is the second of the problems mentioned earlier: the nature of the general statements that enable us to infer the consequent upon the basis of the antecedent and the statement of relevant conditions. The distinction between these connecting principles and relevant conditions is imprecise and arbitrary; the 'connecting principles' might be conjoined to the condition-statements, and the relation of the antecedent-conjunction ($A \cdot S$) to the consequent thus made a matter of logic. But the same problems would arise as to the kind of principle that is capable of sustaining a counterfactual; and it is convenient to consider the connecting principles separately.

In order to infer the consequent of a counterfactual from the antecedent A and a suitable statement of relevant conditions S, we make use of a general statement; namely, the generalization[10] of the conditional having $A \cdot S$ for antecedent and C for consequent. For example, in the case of

If the match had been scratched, it would have lighted

the connecting principle is

Every match that is scratched, well made, dry enough, in enough oxygen, etc., lights.

But notice that *not* every counterfactual is actually sustained by the principle thus arrived at, *even* if that principle is *true*. Suppose, for example, that all I had in my right pocket on VE day was a group of silver coins. Now we would not under normal circumstances affirm of a given penny P

If P had been in my pocket on VE day, P would have been silver,[11]

even though from

P was in my pocket on VE day

we can infer the consequent by means of the general statement

Everything in my pocket on VE day was silver.

On the contrary, we would assert that if *P* had been in my pocket, then this general statement would not be true. The general statement will *not* permit us to infer the given consequent from the counterfactual assumption that *P* was in my pocket, because the general statement will not itself withstand that counterfactual assumption. Though the supposed connecting principle is indeed general, true, and perhaps even fully confirmed by observation of all cases, it is incapable of sustaining a counterfactual because it remains a description of accidental fact, not a law. The truth of a counterfactual conditional thus seems to depend on whether the general sentence required for the inference is a law or not. If so, our problem is to distinguish accurately between causal laws and casual facts.[12]

The problem illustrated by the example of the coins is closely related to that which led us earlier to require the cotenability of the antecedent and the relevant conditions, in order to avoid resting a counterfactual on any statement that would not be true if the antecedent were true. For decision as to the cotenability of two sentences depends partly upon decisions as to whether certain general statements are laws, and we are now concerned directly with the latter problem. Is there some way of so distinguishing laws from non-laws, among true universal statements of the kind in question, that laws will be the principles that will sustain counterfactual conditionals?

Any attempt to draw the distinction by reference to a notion of causative force can be dismissed at once as unscientific. And it is clear that no purely syntactical criterion can be adequate, for even the most special descriptions of particular facts can be cast in a form having any desired degree of syntactical universality. "Book *B* is small" becomes "Everything that is *Q* is small" if "*Q*" stands for some predicate that applies uniquely to *B*. What then does distinguish a law like

All butter melts at 150°F

from a true and general non-law like

All the coins in my pocket are silver?

Primarily, I would like to suggest, the fact that the first is accepted as true while many cases of it remain to be determined, the further, unexamined cases being predicted to conform with it. The second sentence, on the contrary, is accepted as a description of contingent fact *after* the determination of all cases, no prediction of any of its instances being based upon it. This proposal raises innumerable problems, some of which I shall consider presently; but the idea behind it is just that the principle we use to decide counterfactual cases is a principle we are willing to commit ourselves to in deciding unrealized cases that are still subject to direct observation.

As a first approximation then, we might say that a law is a true sentence used for making predictions. That laws are used predictively is of course a simple truism, and I am not proposing it as a novelty. I want only to emphasize the Humean idea that rather than a sentence being used for prediction because it is a law, it is called a law because it is used for prediction; and that rather than the law being used for prediction because it describes a causal connection, the meaning of the causal connection is to be interpreted in terms of predictively used laws.

By the determination of all instances, I mean simply the examination or testing by other means of all things that satisfy the antecedent, to decide whether all satisfy the consequent also.

There are difficult questions about the meaning of "instance," many of which Professor Hempel has investigated. Most of these are avoided in our present study by the fact that we are concerned with a very narrow class of sentences: those arrived at by generalizing conditionals of a certain kind. Remaining problems about the meaning of "instance" I shall have to ignore here. As for "determination," I do not mean final discovery of truth, but only enough examination to reach a decision as to whether a given statement or its negate is to be admitted as evidence for the hypothesis in question.

Our criterion excludes vacuous principles as laws. The generalizations needed for sustaining counterfactual conditionals cannot be vacuous, for they must be supported by evidence.[13] The limited scope of our present problem makes it unimportant that our criterion, if applied generally to all statements, would classify as laws many statements—e.g., true singular predictions—that we would not normally call laws.

For convenience, I shall use the term "lawlike" for sentences that, whether they are true or not, satisfy the other requirements in the definition of law. A law is thus a sentence that is both lawlike and true, but a sentence may be true without being lawlike, as I have illustrated, or lawlike without being true, as we are always learning to our dismay.

Now if we were to leave our definition as it stands, lawlikeness would be a rather accidental and ephemeral property. Only statements that happen actually to have been used for prediction would be lawlike. And a true sentence that had been used predictively would cease to be a law when it became fully tested—i.e., when none of its instances remained undetermined. The definition, then, must be restated in some such way as this: A general statement is lawlike if and only if it is acceptable prior to the determination of all its instances. This is immediately objectionable because "acceptable" itself is plainly a dispositional term; but I propose to use it only tentatively, with the idea of eliminating it eventually by means of a non-dispositional definition. Before trying to accomplish that, however, we must face another difficulty in our tentative criterion of lawlikeness.

Suppose that the appropriate generalization fails to sustain a given counterfactual because that generalization, while true, is unlawlike, as is

Everything in my pocket is silver.

All we would need to do to get a law would be to broaden the antecedent strategically. Consider, for example, the sentence

Everything that is in my pocket or is a dime is silver.

Since we have not examined all dimes, this is a predictive statement and—since presumably true—would be a law. Now if we consider our original counterfactual and choose our S so that $A \cdot S$ is

P is in my pocket. P is in my pocket or is a dime,

then the pseudo-law just constructed can be used to infer from this sentence "P is silver." Thus the untrue counterfactual is established. If one prefers to avoid an alternation as a condition-statement, the same result can be obtained by using a new predicate such as "dimo" to mean "is in my pocket or is a dime."[14]

The change called for, I think, will make the definition of lawlikeness read as follows: A sentence is lawlike if its acceptance does not depend upon the determination of any given instance.[15] Naturally this does not mean that acceptance is to be independent of all determination of instances, but only that there is no particular instance on the determination of which acceptance depends. This criterion excludes from the class of laws a statement like

That book is black and oranges are spherical

on the ground that acceptance requires knowing whether the book is black; it excludes

Everything that is in my pocket or is a dime is silver

on the ground that acceptance demands examination of all things in my pocket. Moreover, it excludes a statement like

All the marbles in this bag except Number 19 are red, and Number 19 is black

on the ground that acceptance would depend on examination of or knowledge gained otherwise concerning marble Number 19. In fact the principle involved in the proposed criterion is a rather powerful one and seems to exclude most of the troublesome cases.

We must still, however, replace the notion of the acceptability of a sentence, or of its acceptance *depending* or *not depending* on some given knowledge, by a positive definition of such dependence. It is clear that to say that the acceptance of a given statement depends upon a certain kind and amount of evidence is to say that given such evidence, acceptance of the statement is in accord with certain general standards for the acceptance of statements that are not fully tested. So one turns naturally to theories of induction and confirmation to learn the distinguishing factors or circumstances that determine whether or not a sentence is acceptable without complete evidence. But publications on confirmation not only have failed to make clear the distinction between confirmable and non-confirmable statements, but show little recognition that such a problem exists.[16] Yet obviously in the case of some sentences like

Everything in my pocket is silver

or

No twentieth-century president of the United States will be between 6 feet 1 inch and 6 feet 1½ inches tall,

not even the testing with positive results of all but a single instance is likely to lead us to accept the sentence and predict that the one remaining instance will conform to it; while for other sentences such as

All dimes are silver

or

All butter melts at 150°F

or

All flowers of plants descended from this seed will be yellow,

positive determination of even a few instances may lead us to accept the sentence with confidence and make predictions in accordance with it.

There is some hope that cases like these can be dealt with by a sufficiently careful and intricate elaboration of current confirmation theories; but inattention to the problem of distinguishing between confirmable and non-confirmable sentences has left most confirmation theories open to more damaging counterexamples of an elementary kind.

Suppose we designate the twenty-six marbles in a bag by the letters of the alphabet, using these merely as proper names having no ordinal significance. Suppose further that we are told that all the marbles except d are red, but we are not told what color d is. By the usual kind of confirmation theory this gives strong confirmation for the statement

$Ra. Rb. Rc. Rd. \ldots Rz$

because twenty-five of the twenty-six cases are known to be favorable while none is known to be unfavorable. But unfortunately the same argument would show that the very same evidence would equally confirm

$Ra. Rb. Rc. Re. \ldots Rz.-Rd,$

for again we have twenty-five favorable and no unfavorable cases. Thus "Rd" and "$-Rd$" are equally and strongly confirmed by the same evidence. If I am required to use a single predicate instead of both "R" and "$-$R" in the second case, I will use "P" to mean:

is in the bag and either is not d and is red, or is d and is not red.

Then the evidence will be twenty-five positive cases for

All the marbles are P

from which it follows that d is P, and thus that d is not red. The problem of what statements are confirmable merely becomes the equivalent problem of what predicates are projectible from known to unknown cases.

So far, I have discovered no way of meeting these difficulties. Yet as we have seen, some solution is urgently wanted for our present purpose; for only where willingness to accept a statement involves predictions of instances that may be tested does acceptance endow that statement with the authority to govern counterfactual cases, which cannot be directly tested.

In conclusion, then, some problems about counterfactuals depend upon the definition of cotenability, which in turn seems to depend upon the prior solution of those problems. Other problems require an adequate definition of law. The tentative criterion of law here proposed is reasonably satisfactory in excluding unwanted kinds of statements, and in effect, reduces one aspect of our problem to the question how to define the circumstances under which a statement is acceptable independently of the determination of any given instance. But this question I do not know how to answer.

NOTES

1. My indebtedness in several matters to the work of C. I. Lewis has seemed too obvious to call for detailed mention.

2. The practical import of a semifactual is thus different from its literal import. Literally a semifactual and the corresponding counterfactual are not contradictories but contraries, and both may be false (cf. Note 9 below). The presence of the auxiliary terms "even" and "still," or either of them, is perhaps the idiomatic indication that a not quite literal meaning is intended.

3. Of the special kinds of counterfactuals mentioned, I shall have something to say later about counter-identicals and counterlegals. As for countercomparatives, the following procedure is appropriate:— Given "If I had arrived one minute later, I would have missed the train," first expand this to "I arrived at a given time. If I had arrived one minute later than that, I would have missed the train." The counterfactual conditional constituting the final clause of this conjunction can then be treated in the usual way. Translation into "If 'I arrive one minute later than the given time' were true, then 'I miss the train' would have been true" does not give us a self-contradictory component.

4. This of course raises very serious questions, which I shall come to presently, about the nature of nonlogical law.

5. Note that the requirement that $A \cdot S$ be self-compatible can be fulfilled only if the antecedent is self-compatible; hence the conditionals I have called "counterlegals" will all be false. This is convenient for our present purpose of investigating counterfactuals that are not counterlegals. If it later appears desirable to regard all or some counterlegals as true, special provisions may be introduced.

6. It is natural to inquire whether for similar reasons we should stipulate that S must be compatible with both A and $-A$, but this is unnecessary. For if S is incompatible with $-A$, then A follows from S; therefore if S is compatible with both C and $-C$, then $A \cdot S$ cannot lead by law to one but not the other. Hence no sentence incompatible with $-A$ can satisfy the other requirements for a suitable S.

7. Since the first edition of this book, W. T. Parry has pointed out that no counterfactual satisfies this formula; for one can always take $-(A \cdot -C)$ as S, and take $-(A \cdot C)$ as S'. Thus we must add the requirement that neither S nor S' follows by law from $-A$. Of course this does not alleviate the further difficulties explained in the following paragraphs of the text above. (See Parry's "Reexamination of the Problem of Counterfactual Conditionals," *Journal of Philosophy*, 54 (1957), pp. 85–94, and my "Parry on Counterfactuals," same journal, same volume, pp. 442–45.)

8. Of course, some sentences similar to (ii), referring to other matches under special conditions, may be true; but the objection to the proposed criterion is that it would commit us to many such statements that are patently false. I am indebted to Morton G. White for a suggestion concerning the exposition of this point.

9. The double negative cannot be eliminated here; for " . . . if S would be true if A were" actually constitutes a stronger requirement. As we noted earlier (Note 2), if two conditionals having the same counterfactual antecedent are such that the consequent of one is the negate of the consequent of the other, the conditionals are contraries and both may be false. This will be the case, for example, if every otherwise suitable set of relevant conditions that in conjunction with the antecedent leads by law either to a given consequent or its negate leads also to the other.

10. The sense of "generalization" intended here is that explained by C. G. Hempel in "A Purely Syntactical Definition of Confirmation," *Journal of Symbolic Logic*, 8 (1943), pp. 122–43. See also chapter 3, section 3 of my *Fact, Fiction and Forecast*, 4th ed. (Cambridge: Harvard University Press, 1983).

11. The antecedent in this example is intended to mean "If P, while remaining distinct from the things that were in fact in my pocket on VE day, had also been in my pocket then," and *not* the quite different, counteridentical "If P had been identical with one of the things that were in my pocket on VE day." While the antecedents of most counterfactuals (as, again, our familiar one about the match) are— literally speaking—open to both sorts of interpretation, ordinary usage normally calls for some explicit indication when the counteridentical meaning is intended.

12. The importance of distinguishing laws from non-laws is too often overlooked. If a clear distinction can be defined, it may serve not only the purposes explained in the present paper but also many of those for which the increasingly dubious distinction between analytic and synthetic statements is ordinarily supposed to be needed.

13. Had it been sufficient in the preceding section to require only that $A \cdot S$ be self-*compatible*, this requirement might now be eliminated in favor of the stipulation that the generalization of the conditional having $A \cdot S$ as antecedent and C as consequent should be non-vacuous; but this stipulation would not guarantee the self-*cotenability* of $A \cdot S$.

14. Apart from the special class of connecting principles we are concerned with, note that under the stated criterion of lawlikeness, any statement could be expanded into a lawlike one; for example: given "This book is black" we could use the predictive sentence "This book is black and all oranges are spherical" to argue that the blackness of the book is the consequence of a law.

15. So stated, the definition counts vacuous principles as laws. If we read instead "given class of instances," vacuous principles will be non-laws since their acceptance depends upon examination of the null class of instances. For my present purposes the one formulation is as good as the other.

16. The points discussed in this and the following paragraph have been dealt with a little more fully in my "A Query on Confirmation," *Journal of Philosophy*, 43 (1946), pp. 383–85.

BRIAN SKYRMS

THE GOODMAN PARADOX AND THE NEW RIDDLE OF INDUCTION

I. INTRODUCTION

In chapter 2 [of Skyrms' *Choice and Chance*—Ed.] we presented some general specifications for a system of scientific inductive logic. We said it should be a system of rules for assigning inductive probabilities to arguments, with different levels of rules corresponding to the different levels of arguments. This system must accord fairly well with common sense and scientific practice. It must on each level presuppose, in some sense, that nature is uniform and that the future will resemble the past. These general specifications were sufficient to give us a foundation for surveying the traditional problem of induction and the major attempts to solve or dissolve it.

However, to be able to apply scientific inductive logic, as a rigorous discipline, we must know precisely what its rules are. Unfortunately no one has yet produced an adequate formulation of the rules of scientific inductive logic. In fact, inductive logic is in much the same state as deductive logic was before Aristotle. This unhappy state of affairs is not due to a scarcity of brainpower in the field of inductive logic. Some of the great minds of history have attacked its problems. The distance by which they have fallen short of their goals is a measure of the difficulty of the subject. Formulating the rules of inductive logic, in fact, appears to be a more difficult enterprise than doing the same for deductive logic. Deductive logic is a "yes or no" affair; an argument is either deductively valid or it is not. But inductive strength is a matter of degree. Thus while deductive logic must *classify* arguments as valid or not, inductive logic must *measure* the inductive strength of arguments.

Setting up such rules of measurement is not an easy task. It is in fact beset with so many problems that some philosophers have been convinced it is impossible. They maintain that a system of scientific induction cannot be constructed; that prediction of the future is an art, not a science; and that we must rely on the intuitions of experts, rather than on scientific inductive logic, to predict the future. We can only hope that this gloomy doctrine is as mistaken as the view of those early Greeks who believed deductive logic could never be reduced to a precise system of rules and must forever remain the domain of professional experts on reasoning.

If constructing a system of scientific inductive logic were totally impossible, we would be left with an intellectual vacuum, which could not be filled by appeal to "experts." For, to decide whether someone is an expert predictor or a charlatan, we must assess the evidence that his predictions will be correct. And to assess this evidence, we must appeal to the second level of scientific inductive logic.

Fortunately there are grounds for hope. Those who have tried to construct a system of scientific inductive logic have made some solid advances. Although the intellectual jigsaw puzzle has not been put together, we at least know what some of the pieces look like. Later we shall examine some of these "building blocks" of inductive logic, but first we shall try to put the problem of constructing a system of scientific induction in perspective by examining one of the main obstacles to this goal.

II. REGULARITIES AND PROJECTION

At this point you may be puzzled as to why the construction of a system of scientific inductive logic is so difficult. After all, we know that scientific induction assumes that nature is uniform and that the future will be like the past, so if, for example, all observed emeralds have been green, the premise embodying this information confers high probability on the conclusion that the next emerald to be observed will be green. We say that scientific inductive logic *projects an observed regularity* into the future because it assigns high inductive probability to the argument:

> All observed emeralds have been green.
> _____
> The next emerald to be observed will be green.

In contrast, counterinduction would assume that the observed regular connection between being an emerald and being green would not hold in the future, and thus would assign high inductive probability to the argument:

> All observed emeralds have been green.
> _____
> The next emerald to be observed will not be green.

So it seems that scientific induction, in a quite straightforward manner, takes observed patterns or regularities in nature and assumes that they will hold in the future. Along these same lines, the premise that 99 percent of the observed emeralds have been green would confer a slightly lower probability on the conclusion that the next emerald to be observed would be green. Why can we not simply say, then, that arguments of the form

> All observed X's have been Y's.
> _____
> The next observed X will be a Y.

have an inductive probability of 1, and that all arguments of the form

> Ninety-nine percent of the observed *X*'s have been *Y*'s.
> The next observed *X* will be a *Y*.

have an inductive probability of 99/100?

That is, why can we not simply construct a system of scientific induction by giving the following rule on each level?

Rule S: An argument of the form

> *N* percent of the observed *X*'s have been *Y*'s.
> The next observed *X* will be a *Y*.

is to be assigned the inductive probability *N*/100.

Rule S does project observed regularities into the future. But there are several reasons why it cannot constitute a system of scientific inductive logic.

The most obvious inadequacy of Rule S is that it only applies to arguments of a specific form, and we are interested in assessing the inductive strength of arguments of different forms. Consider arguments which, in addition to a premise stating the percentage of observed *X*'s that have been *Y*'s, have another premise stating how many *X*'s have been observed. Here the rule does not apply, for the arguments are not of the required form. For example, Rule S does not tell us how to assign inductive probabilities to the following arguments:

I	II
Ten emeralds have been observed	One million emeralds have been observed.
Ninety percent of the observed emeralds have been green.	Ninety percent of the observed emeralds have been green.
The next emerald to be observed will be green.	The next emerald to be observed will be green.

Obviously scientific inductive logic should tell us how to assign inductive probabilities to these arguments, and in assigning these probabilities it should take into account that the premises of Argument II bring a much greater amount of evidence to bear than the premises of Argument I.

Another type of argument that Rule S does not tell us how to evaluate is one that includes a premise stating in what variety of circumstances the regularity has been found to hold. That is, Rule S does not tell us how to assign inductive probabilities to the following arguments:

III	IV
Every person who has taken drug *X* has exhibited no adverse side reactions.	Every person who has taken drug *X* has exhibited no adverse side reactions.
Drug *X* has only been administered to persons between 20 and 25 years of age who are in good health.	Drug *X* has been administered to persons of all ages and varying degrees of health.
The next person to take drug *X* will have no adverse side reactions.	The next person to take drug *X* will have no adverse side reactions.

Again scientific inductive logic should tell us how to assign inductive probabilities to these arguments, and in doing so it should take into account the fact that the premises of Argument

IV tell us that the regularity has been found to hold in a great variety of circumstances, whereas the premises of Argument III inform us that the regularity has been found to hold in only a limited area.

There are many other types of arguments that Rule S does not tell us how to evaluate, including most of the arguments advanced as examples in chapter 1 [of *Choice and Chance*—Ed.] We can now appreciate why an adequate system of rules for scientific inductive logic must be a fairly complex structure. But there is another shortcoming of Rule S which has to do with arguments to which it does apply, that is, arguments of the form:

> *N* percent of the observed *X*'s have been *Y*'s.
>
> The next observed *X* will be a *Y*.

The following two arguments are of that form, so we can apply Rule S to evaluate them:

V	VI
One hundred percent of the observed samples of pure water have had a freezing point of +32 degrees Fahrenheit.	One hundred percent of the recorded economic depressions have occurred at the same time as large sunspots.
The next observed sample of pure water will have a freezing point of +32 degrees Fahrenheit.	The next economic depression will occur at the same time as a large sunspot.

If we apply Rule S we find that it assigns an inductive probability of 1 to each of these arguments. But surely Argument V has a much higher degree of inductive strength than Argument VI! We feel perfectly justified in projecting into the future the observed regular connection between a certain type of chemical compound and its freezing point. But we feel that the observed regular connection between economic cycles and sunspots is a coincidence, an accidental regularity or spurious correlation, which should not be projected into the future. We shall say that the observed regularity reported in the premise of Argument V is *projectible*, while the regularity reported in the premise of Argument VI is not. We must now sophisticate our conception of scientific inductive logic still further. Scientific inductive logic does project observed regularities into the future, but only projectible regularities. It does assume that nature is uniform and that the future will resemble the past, but only in certain respects. It does assume that observed patterns in nature will be repeated, but only certain types of patterns. Thus Rule S is not adequate for scientific inductive logic because it is incapable of taking into account differences in projectibility of regularities.

Exercises:

1. Construct five inductively strong arguments to which Rule S does not apply.
2. Give two new examples of projectible regularities and two new examples of unprojectible regularities.
3. For each of the following arguments, state whether Rule S is applicable. If it is applicable, what inductive probability does it assign to the argument?

   a. One hundred percent of the crows observed have been black.

   The next crow to be observed will be black.

   b. One hundred percent of the crows observed have been black.

   All crows are black.

   c. Every time I have looked at a calendar, the date has been before January 1, 1984.

     The next time I look at a calendar the date will be before January 1, 1984.

   d. Every time fire has been observed, it has continued to burn according to the laws of nature until extinguished.

     All unobserved fires continue to burn according to the laws of nature until extinguished.

   e. Eighty-five percent of the time when I have dropped a piece of silverware, company has subsequently arrived.

     The next time I drop a piece of silverware company will subsequently arrive.

III. THE GOODMAN PARADOX

If one tries to construct various examples of projectible and unprojectible regularities, one will soon come to the conclusion that projectibility is not simply a "yes or no" affair but rather a matter of degree. Some regularities are highly projectible, some have a middling degree of projectibility, and some are quite unprojectible. Just how unprojectible a regularity can be has been demonstrated by Nelson Goodman in his famous "grue-bleen" paradox.

Goodman invites us to consider a new color word "grue." It is to have the general logical features of our old color words such as "green," "blue," and "red." That is, we can speak of things being a certain color at a certain time—for example, "John's face is red now"—and we can speak of things either remaining the same color or changing colors. The new color word "grue" is defined in terms of the familiar color words "green" and "blue" as follows:

Definition 6: A certain thing X is said to be *grue* at a certain time t if and only if:

   X is green at t *and* t is before the year 2000

   or

   X is blue at t *and* t is during or after the year 2000.

Let us see how this definition works. If you see a green grasshopper today, you can correctly maintain that you have seen a grue grasshopper today. Today is before the year 2000, and before the year 2000 something is grue just when it is green. But if you or one of your descendants sees a green grasshopper during or after the year 2000, it would then be incorrect to maintain that a grue grasshopper had been seen. During and after the year 2000, something is grue just when it is blue. Thus after the year 2000, a blue sky would also be a grue sky.

Suppose now that a chameleon were kept on a green cloth until the beginning of the year 2000 and then transferred to a blue cloth. In terms of green and blue we would say that the chameleon changed color from green to blue. But in terms of the new color word "grue" we would say that it remained the same color: "grue." The other side of the coin is that when something remains the same color in terms of the old color words, it will change color in terms of the new one. Suppose we have a piece of glass that is green now and that will remain green during and after the year 2000. Then we would have to say that it was grue before the year 2000 but was not grue during and after the year 2000. At the beginning of the year 2000 it changed color from grue to some other color. To name the color that it changed to we introduce the new color word "bleen." "Bleen" is defined in terms of "green" and "blue" as follows:

Definition 7: A certain thing X is said to be *bleen* at a certain time t if and only if:

   X is blue at t *and* t is before the year 2000

   or

   X is green at t *and* t is during or after the year 2000.

Thus before the year 2000 something is grue just when it is green and bleen just when it is blue. After the year 2000 something is grue just when it is blue and bleen just when it is green. In terms of the old color words the piece of glass remains the same color (green), but in terms of the new color words the piece of glass changes color (from grue to bleen).

Imagine a tribe of people speaking a language that had "grue" and "bleen" as basic color words rather than the more familiar ones that we use. Suppose we describe a situation in our language—for example, the piece of glass being green before the year 2000 and remaining green afterward—in which we would say that there is no change in color. But if they correctly describe the same situation in their language, then, *in their terms*, there is a change. This leads to the important and rather startling conclusion that whether a certain situation involves change or not may depend on the descriptive machinery of the language used to discuss that situation.

One might object that "grue" and "bleen" are not acceptable color words because they have reference to a specific date in their definitions. It is quite true that *in our language*, in which blue and green are the basic color words, grue and bleen must be defined not only in terms of blue and green but also in terms of the date "2000 A.D." But a speaker of the grue-bleen language could maintain that definitions of our color words in his language must also have reference to a specific date. In the grue-bleen language, "grue" and "bleen" are basic, and "blue" and "green" are defined as follows:

Definition 8: A certain thing X is said to be *green* at a certain time t if and only if:

X is grue at t *and* t is before the year 2000

or

X is bleen at t *and* t is during or after the year 2000.

Definition 9: A certain thing X is said to be *blue* at a certain time t if and only if:

X is bleen at t *and* t is before the year 2000.

or

X is grue at t *and* t is during or after the year 2000.

Defining the old color words in terms of the new requires reference to a specific date as much as defining the new words in terms of the old. So the formal structure of their definitions gives no reason to believe that "grue" and "bleen" are not legitimate, although unfamiliar, color words.

Let us see what can be learned about regularities and projectibility from these new color words. We have already shown that whether there is change in a given situation may depend on what linguistic machinery is used to describe that situation. We shall now show that what regularities we find in a given situation also may depend on our descriptive machinery. Suppose that at one minute to midnight on December 31, 1999, a gem expert is asked to predict what the color of a certain emerald will be after midnight. He knows that all observed emeralds have been green. He projects this regularity into the future and predicts that the emerald will remain green. Notice that this is in accordance with Rule S, which assigns an inductive probability of 1 to the argument:

One hundred percent of the times that emeralds have been observed they have been green.

The next time that an emerald is observed it will be green.

But if the gem expert were a speaker of the grue-bleen language, he would find a different regularity in the color of observed emeralds. He would notice that every time an emerald had been observed it had been grue. (Remember that before the year 2000 everything that is green is also grue.) Now if he followed Rule S he would project *this* regularity into the future, for Rule S also assigns an inductive probability of 1 to the argument:

One hundred percent of the times emeralds have been observed they have been "grue."
The next time an emerald is observed it will be "grue."

And if he projected the regularity that all observed emeralds have been grue into the future he would predict that the emerald will remain grue. But during the year 2000 a thing is "grue" only if it is blue. So by projecting this regularity he is in effect predicting that the emerald will change from green to blue.

Now, we will all agree that this is a ridiculous prediction to make on the basis of the evidence. And no one is really claiming that it should be made. But it cannot be denied that this prediction results from the projection into the future of an observed regularity in accordance with Rule S. The point is that the regularity of every observed emerald having been grue is a totally unprojectable regularity. And the prediction of our hypothetical grue-bleen-speaking gem expert is an extreme case of the trouble we get into when we try to project, via some rule such as Rule S, regularities that are in fact unprojectible.

The trouble we get into is indeed deep, for the prediction so arrived at will conflict with the prediction arrived at by projecting a projectible regularity. If we project the projectible regularity that every time an emerald has been observed it has been green, then we arrive at the prediction that the emerald will remain green. If we project the unprojectible regularity that every time an emerald has been observed, it has been grue, then we arrive at the prediction that the emerald will change from green to blue. These two predictions clearly are in conflict.[1]

Thus the mistake of projecting an unprojectible regularity may not only lead to a ridiculous prediction. It may, furthermore, lead to a prediction that conflicts with a legitimate prediction which results from projecting a projectible regularity discovered in *the same set of data*. An acceptable system of scientific inductive logic must provide some means to escape this conflict. It must incorporate rules that tell us which regularities are projectible. From the discussion of accidental regularities and the sunspot theory of economic cycles, we already know that scientific inductive logic must have rules for determining projectibility. But the Goodman paradox gives this point new urgency by demonstrating how unprojectible a regularity can be and how serious are the consequences of projecting a totally unprojectible regularity.

Let us summarize what is to be learned from the discussion of "grue" and "bleen":

1. Whether we find change or not in a certain situation may depend on the linguistic machinery we use to describe that situation.

2. What regularities we find in a sequence of occurrences may depend on the linguistic machinery used to describe that sequence.

3. We may find two regularities in a sequence of occurrences, one projectible and one unprojectible, such that the predictions that arise from projecting them both are in conflict.

Exercises:

1. Translate the following descriptions in terms of "blue" and "green" into equivalent descriptions in terms of "grue" and "bleen":

    a. Ten million years from now the grass will be green and the sea blue.

    b. In 50 years from now the following songs will be very popular: "Green Eyes" and "My Blue Heaven."

c. In the 1950s these songs were very popular: "She Wore Blue Velvet." "The Wearing of the Green," and "Birth of the Blues."

d. There will be a miracle at the beginning of the year 2000: the color of the sky will change from blue to green.

2. Define "grue" in terms of "blue," "green," and "bleen" without mentioning the year 2000.

IV. THE GOODMAN PARADOX, REGULARITY, AND THE PRINCIPLE OF THE UNIFORMITY OF NATURE

We saw, in the last section, that projecting observed regularities into the future is not as simple as it first appears. The regularities found in a certain sequence of events may depend on the language used to describe that sequence of events. The Goodman paradox showed that if we try to project all regularities that can be found by using any language, our predictions may conflict with one another. This is a startling result, and it dramatizes the need for rules for determining projectibility in scientific induction. (This might be accomplished through the specification of the most fruitful language for the scientific description of events.)

This need is further dramatized by the following, even more startling result: For any prediction whatsoever, we can find a regularity whose projection licenses that prediction. Of course, most of these regularities will be unprojectible. The point is that we need rules to eliminate those predictions based on unprojectible regularities. I shall illustrate this principle in three ways: (1) in an example that closely resembles Goodman's "grue-bleen" paradox, (2) with reference to the extrapolation of curves on graphs, (3) with reference to the problem, often encountered on intelligence tests, of continuing a sequence of numbers. The knowledge gained from this discussion will then be applied to a reexamination of the principle of the uniformity of nature.

Example 1

Suppose you are presented with four boxes, each labeled "Excelsior!" In the first box you discover a green insect; in the second, a yellow ball of wax; in the third, a purple feather. You are now told that the fourth box contains a mask and are asked to predict its color. You must look for a regularity in this sequence of discoveries, whose projection will license a prediction as to the color of the mask. Although on the face of it, this seems impossible, with a little ingenuity a regularity can be found. What is more, for any prediction you wish to make, there is a regularity whose projection will license that prediction. Suppose you want to predict that the mask will be red. The regularity is found in the following manner.

Let us define a new word, "snarf." A snarf is something presented to you in a box labeled "Excelsior!" and is either an insect, a ball of wax, a feather, or a mask. Now you have observed three snarfs and are about to observe a fourth. This is a step toward regularity, but there is still the problem that the three observed snarfs have been different colors. One more definition is required in order to find regularity in apparent chaos. A thing X is said to be "murkle" just when:

X is an insect *and* X is green
or
X is a ball of wax and X is yellow
or
X is a feather *and* X is purple
or
X is some other type of thing *and* X is red.

Now we have found the regularity: all observed snarfs have been murkle. If we project this regularity into the future, assuming that the next snarf to be observed will be murkle, we obtain the required prediction.[2] The next snarf to be observed will be a mask, and for a mask to be murkle it must be red. Needless to say, this regularity is quite unprojectible. But it is important to see that we could discover an unprojectible regularity that, if it were projected, would lead to the prediction that the mask is red. And it is easy to see that, if we wanted to discover a regularity that would lead to a prediction that the mask will be a different color, a few alterations to the definition of "murkle" would accomplish this aim. This sort of thing can always be done and, as we shall see, in some areas we need not even resort to such exotic words as "snarf," "murkle," "grue," and "bleen."

Example 2

When basing predictions on statistical data, we often make use of graphs, which help summarize the evidence and guide us in making our predictions. To illustrate, suppose a certain small country takes a census every 10 years, and has taken three so far. The population was 11 million at the time of the first census, 12 million at the second census, and 13 million at the third. This information is represented on a graph in Figure 1. Each dot represents the information as to population size gained from one census. For example, the middle dot represents the second census, taken in the year 10, and showing a population of 12 million. Thus it is placed at the intersection of the vertical line drawn from the year 10 and the horizontal line drawn from the population of 12 million.

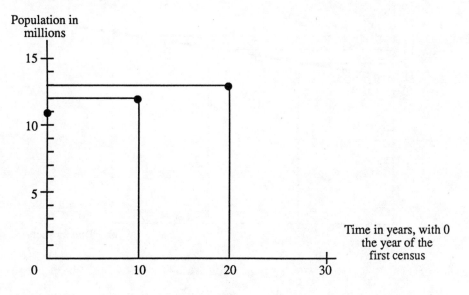

Figure 1

Suppose now you are asked to predict the population of this country at the time of the fourth census, that is, in the year 30. You would have to look for a regularity that could be projected into the future. In the absence of any further information, you would probably proceed as follows: First you would notice that the points representing the first three census all fall on the straight line labeled *A* in Figure 2, and would then project this regularity into the future. This is in accordance with Rule S, which assigns an inductive probability of 1 to the following argument:

All points representing census so far taken have fallen on line *A*.
_____
The point representing the next census to be taken will fall on line *A*.

This projection would lead you to the prediction that the population at the time of the fourth census will be 14 million, as shown by the dotted lines in Figure 2. The process by which you would arrive at your prediction is called *extrapolation*. If you had used similar reasoning to estimate the population during the year 15 at 12½ million, the process would be called *interpolation*. Interpolation is estimating the position of a point that lies *between* the points representing the data. Extrapolation is estimating the position of a point that lies *outside* the points representing the data. So your prediction would be obtained by extrapolation and your extrapolation would be a projection of the regularity that all the points plotted so far fell on line *A*.

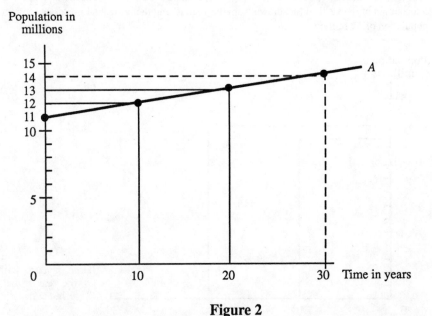

Figure 2

But it is obvious that there are quite a few other regularities to be found in the data which you did not choose to project. As shown in Figure 3 there is the regularity that all the points plotted so far fall on curve *B*, and the regularity that all the points plotted so far fall on curve *C*. The projection of one of these regularities will lead to a different prediction.

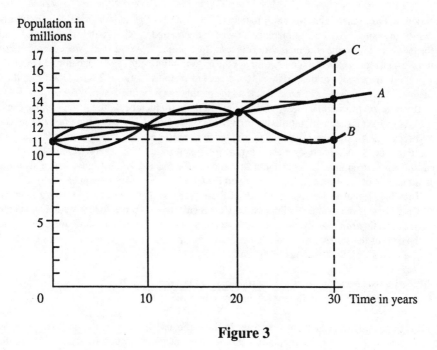

Figure 3

If you extrapolate along curve B, you can predict that the population in the year 30 will be back to 11 million. If you extrapolate along curve C, you can predict that the population will leap to 17 million. There are indeed an infinite number of curves that pass through all the points and thus an infinite number of regularities in the data. Whatever prediction you wish to make, a regularity can be found whose projection will license that prediction.

Example 3
Often intelligence and aptitude tests contain problems where one is given a sequence of numbers and asked to continue the sequence; for example:

  i. 1, 2, 3, 4, 5, . . . ;
 ii. 2, 4, 6, 8, 10, . . . ;
iii. 1, 3, 5, 7, 9, . . .

The natural way in which to continue sequence (i) is to add 6 to the end, for sequence (ii) to add 12, and for sequence (iii) to add 11. These problems are really problems of inductive logic on the intuitive level; one is asked to discover a regularity in the segment of the series given and to project that regularity in order to find the next number of the series.

Let us make this reasoning explicit for the three series given. In example (i) the first member of the series is 1, the second member is 2, the third member is 3, and, in general, for all the members given, the kth member is k. If we project this regularity to find the next member of the series, we will reason that the sixth member is 6, which is the answer intuitively arrived at before. In example (ii) the first member is twice 1, the second is twice 2, and, in general, for all the members given, the $k$the member is twice k. If we project this regularity, we will reason that the sixth member is twice 6, or 12, which is the answer intuitively arrived at before. In example (iii) the first member is twice 1 less 1, the second member is twice 2 less 1, and the third member is twice 3 less 1. In general, for all the members given, the kth member is twice k less 1. If we project this regularity, we will reason that the sixth member of the series is twice 6 less 1, or 11, which is the result intuitively arrived at. We say that k is a *generating function* for the first series, $2k$ a generating function for the second series, and $2k-1$ a generating function for the third series. Although "generating function" may sound like a very technical term, its meaning is quite simple. It is a formula with k in it, such that if 1 is substituted for k it gives the first member of the series, if 2 is substituted for k it gives the second member, etc.

Thus the regularity we found in each of these series is that a certain generating function yielded all the given members of the series. This regularity was projected by assuming that the same generating function would yield the next member of the series, and so we were able to fill in the ends of the series. For example, the prediction that the sixth member of series (iii) is 11 implicitly rests on the following argument:

For every given member of series (iii) the kth member of that series was $2k-1$.
For the next member of series (iii) the kth member will be $2k-1$.

But, as you may expect, there is a fly in the ointment. If we look more closely at these examples, we can find *other* regularities in the given members of the various series. And the projection of these other regularities conflicts with the projection of the regularities we have already noted. The generating function $(k-1)(k-2)(k-3)(k-4)(k-5)+k$ also yields the five given members of series (i). (This can be checked by substituting 1 for k, which gives 1; 2 for k, which gives 2; and so on, up through 5.) But if we project this regularity, the result is that the sixth member of the series is 126!

Indeed whatever number we wish to predict for the sixth member of the series, there is a generating function that will fit the given members of the series and that will yield the prediction we want. It is a mathematical fact that in general this is true. For any finite string of numbers which begins a series, there are generating functions that fit that string of given numbers and yield whatever next member is desired. Whatever prediction we wish to make, we can find a regularity whose projection will license that prediction.

Thus if the intelligence tests were simply looking for the projection of a regularity, any number at the end of the series would be correct. What they are looking for is not simply the projection of a regularity but the projection of an intuitively projectible regularity.

If we have perhaps belabored the point in Examples (1), (2), and (3) we have done so because the principle they illustrate is so hard to accept. Any prediction whatsoever can be obtained by projecting regularities: as Goodman puts it. "To say that valid predictions are those based on past regularities, without being able to say *which* regularities, is thus quite pointless. Regularities are where you find them, and you can find them anywhere."[3] An acceptable scientific inductive logic must have rules for determining the projectibility of regularities.

It remains to be shown how this discussion of regularities and projectibility bears on the principle of the uniformity of nature. Just as we saw that the naïve characterization of scientific inductive logic as a system that projects observed regularities into the future was pointless unless we can say which regularities it projects, so we shall see that the statement that scientific inductive logic presupposes the uniformity of nature is equally pointless unless we are able to say *in what respects* nature is presupposed to be uniform. For it is self-contradictory to say that nature is uniform in all respects, and trivial to say it is uniform in some respects.

In the original statement of the Goodman paradox, the gem expert, who spoke our ordinary language, assumed nature to be uniform with respect to the blueness or greenness of emeralds. Since observed emeralds had always been green, and since he was assuming that nature is uniform and that the future would resemble the past in this respect, he predicted that the emerald would remain green. But the hypothetical gem expert who spoke the grue-bleen language assumed nature to be uniform *with respect to the grueness or bleenness of emeralds.* Since observed emeralds had always been grue and since he was assuming that nature is uniform and that the future would resemble the past in this respect, he predicted that the emerald would remain grue. But we saw that these two predictions were in conflict. The future cannot resemble the past in both these ways. As we have seen, such conflicts can be multiplied *ad infinitum.* The future cannot resemble the past in all respects. It is self-contradictory to say that nature is uniform in all respects.

We might try to retreat to the claim that scientific induction presupposes that nature is uniform in some respects. But this claim is so weak as to be no claim at all. To say that nature is uniform in some respects is to say that it exhibits some patterns, that there are some regularities in nature taken as a whole (in both the observed and unobserved parts of nature). But as we have seen in this section, in any sequence of observations, no matter how chaotic the data may seem, there are always regularities. This holds not only for sequences of observations but also for nature as a whole. No matter how chaotic nature might be, it would always exhibit some patterns; it would always be uniform in some respects. These uniformities might seem highly artificial, such as a uniformity in terms of grue and bleen or snarf and murkle. They might be fiendishly complex. But no matter how nature might behave, there would always be some uniformity, "natural" or "artificial," simple or complex. It is therefore trivial to say that nature is uniform in some respects. Thus if the statement that scientific induction presupposes that nature is uniform is to convey any information at all, it must specify in what respects scientific induction presupposes that nature is uniform.

The points about regularities and projectibility and the uniformity of nature are really two sides of the same coin. There are so many regularities in any sequence of observations and so many ways for nature to be uniform that the statements "Scientific induction projects observed regularities into the future" and "Scientific induction presupposes the uniformity of nature" lose all meaning. They can, however, be reinvested with meaning if we can formulate *rules of projectibility* for scientific inductive logic. Then we could say that scientific inductive logic projects regularities that meet these standards. And that would be saying something informative. We could reformulate the principle of the uniformity of nature to mean: Nature is such that projecting regularities that meet these standards will lead to correct predictions most of the time. Thus the whole concept of scientific inductive logic rests on the idea of projectibility. The problem of formulating precise rules for determining projectibility is the new riddle of induction.

Exercise:

In the example of the four boxes labeled "Excelsior!" find a regularity in the observations whose projection would lead to the prediction that the mask will be blue.

V. SUMMARY

This chapter described the scope of the problem of constructing a system of scientific inductive logic. We began with the supposition that scientific inductive logic could be simply characterized as the projection of observed regularities into the future in accordance with some rule such as Rule S. We saw that this characterization of scientific inductive logic is inadequate for several reasons, the most important being that too many regularities are to be found in any given set of data. In one set of data we can find regularities whose projection leads to conflicting predictions. In fact, for any prediction we choose, there will be a regularity whose projection licenses that prediction.

Scientific inductive logic must select from the multitude of regularities present in any sequence of observations, for indiscriminate projection leads to paradox. Thus in order to characterize scientific inductive logic we must specify the rules used to determine which regularities it considers to be projectible. The problem of formulating these rules is called the new riddle of induction.

Essentially the same problem reappears if we try to characterize scientific inductive logic as a system that presupposes that nature is uniform. To say that nature is uniform in *some* respects is trivial. To say that nature is uniform in *all* respects is not only false but self-contradictory. Thus if we are to characterize scientific inductive logic in terms of some principle of the uniformity of nature which it presupposes, we must say in what respects nature is presupposed to be uniform, which in turn determines what regularities scientific inductive logic takes to be projectible. So the problem about the uniformity of nature is just a different facet of the new riddle of induction.

The problem of constructing a system of scientific inductive logic will not be solved until the new riddle of induction and other problems have been solved. Although these solutions have not yet been found, there have been developments in the history of inductive logic which constitute progress towards a system.

NOTES

1. Actually they are inconsistent only under the assumption that the emerald will not be destroyed before 2000 A.D., but presumably we will have independent inductive evidence for this assumption.
2. This projection is in accordance with Rule S, which assigns an inductive probability of 1 to the argument:

   All observed snarfs have been murkle.
   _____
   The next snarf to be observed will be murkle.
3. Nelson Goodman, *Fact, Fiction and Forecast* (Cambridge, Mass.: Harvard University Press, 1955), p. 82.

REFERENCES

Nelson Goodman, *Fact, Fiction and Forecast* (Cambridge, Mass.: Harvard University Press, 1955), chap. 3, "The New Riddle of Induction."
Bertrand Russell, "On the Notion of Cause," in *Mysticism and Logic* (New York: Anchor Books, 1957), pp. 174–201.

KARL R. POPPER

UNIVERSALS, DISPOSITIONS, AND NATURAL OR PHYSICAL NECESSITY

(1) The fundamental doctrine which underlies all theories of induction is *the doctrine of the primacy of repetitions*. Keeping Hume's attitude in mind, we may distinguish two variants of this doctrine. The first (which Hume criticized) may be called the doctrine of the logical primacy of repetitions. According to this doctrine, repeated instances furnish a kind of *justification* for the acceptance of a universal law. (The idea of repetition is linked, as a rule, with that of probability.) The second (which Hume upheld) may be called the doctrine of the temporal (and psychological) primacy of repetitions. According to this second doctrine, repetitions, even though they should fail to furnish any kind of *justification* for a universal law and for the expectations and beliefs which it entails, nevertheless induce and *arouse* these expectations and beliefs in us, as a matter of fact—however little "justified" or "rational" this fact (or these beliefs) may be.

Both variants of this doctrine of the primacy of repetitions, the stronger doctrine of their logical primacy and the weaker doctrine of their temporal (or causal or psychological) primacy, are untenable. This may be shown with the help of two entirely different arguments.

My first argument against the primacy of repetitions is the following. All the repetitions which we experience are *approximate repetitions*; and by saying that a repetition is approximate I mean that the repetition B of an event A is not identical with A, or indistinguishable from A, but only *more or less similar* to A. But if repetition is thus based upon mere similarity, it must share one of the main characteristics of similarity; that is, its relativity. Two things which are similar are always similar *in certain respects*. The point may be illustrated by a simple diagram.

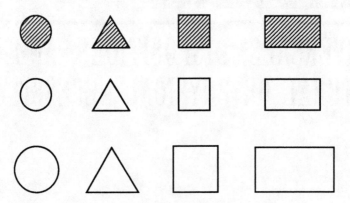

If we look at this diagram, we find that some of the figures are similar with respect to shading (hatching) or to its absence; others are similar with respect to shape; and others are similar with respect to size. The table might be extended like this.

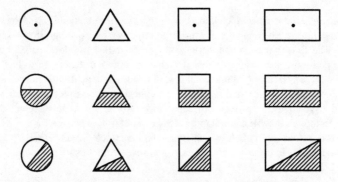

One can easily see that there is no end to the possible kinds of similarity.

These diagrams show that things may be similar in *different respects*, and that any two things which are from one point of view similar may be dissimilar from another point of view. Generally, similarity, and with it repetition, always presuppose the adoption of *a point of view*: some similarities or repetitions will strike us if we are interested in one problem, and others if we are interested in another problem. But if similarity and repetition presuppose the adoption of a point of view, or an interest, or an expectation, it is logically necessary that points of view, or interests, or expectations, are logically prior, as well as temporally (or casually or psychologically) prior, to repetition. But this result destroys both the doctrines of the logical and of the temporal primacy of repetitions.[1]

The remark may be added that for any given finite group or set of things, however variously they may be chosen, we can, with a little ingenuity, find always points of view such that all the things belonging to that set are similar (or partially equal) if considered from one of these points of view; which means that anything can be said to be a "repetition" of anything, if only we adopt the appropriate point of view. This shows how naïve it is to look upon repetition as something ultimate, or given. The point here made is closely related to the fact (mentioned in appendix *vii, footnote 9; *cf.* the property B)² that we can find, for *any* given finite sequence of noughts and ones, a mathematical rule or "law" for constructing an infinite sequence such that it commences with the given finite sequence.

I now come to my second argument against the primacy of repetitions. It is this. There are laws and theories of a character altogether different from "All swans are white," even though they may be formulated in a similar way. Take ancient atomic theory. Admittedly, it may be expressed (in one of its simplest forms) as "All material bodies are composed of corpuscles." Yet clearly, the "all"-form is comparatively unimportant in the case of this law. What I mean is this. The problem of showing that one single physical body—say, a piece of iron—is composed of atoms or "corpuscles" is at least as difficult as that of showing that *all* swans are white. Our assertions transcend, in both cases, all observational experience. It is the same with almost all scientific theories. We cannot show, directly, even of *one* physical body that, in the absence of forces, it moves along a straight line; or that it attracts, and is attracted by, one other physical body in accordance with the inverse square law. All these theories describe what we may call *structural properties of the world*; and they all transcend all possible experience. The difficulty with these structural theories is not so much to establish the universality of the law from repeated instances as to establish that it holds even for one single instance.

This difficulty has been seen by many inductivists. Most of those who saw it tried, like Berkeley, to make a sharp distinction between pure observational generalizations and more "abstract" or "occult" theories, such as the corpuscular theory, or Newton's theory; and they tried, as a rule, to resolve the problem by saying, as did Berkeley, that abstract theories are not genuine assertions about the world, but that they are *nothing but instruments*—instruments for the prediction of observable phenomena. I have called this view "*instrumentalism*," and I have criticized it in some detail elsewhere.³ Here I will only say that I reject instrumentalism, and I will give only one reason for rejecting it: that it does not solve the problem of the "abstract" or "occult" or "structural" properties. For such properties do not only occur in the "abstract" theories which Berkeley and his successors had in mind. They are mentioned all the time, by everybody, and in ordinary speech. Almost every statement we make transcends experience. There is no sharp dividing line between an "empirical language" and a "theoretical language": *we are theorizing all the time*, even when we make the most trivial singular statement. With this remark, we have arrived at the main problem which I intend to examine in this essay.

(2) Admittedly, if we say "All swans are white," then the whiteness we predicate is an observable property; and to this extent, a singular statement such as "This swan here is white" may be said to be based on observation. Yet it transcends experience—not because of the word "white," but because of the word "swan." For by calling something a "swan," we attribute to it properties which go far beyond mere observation—almost as far as when we assert that it is composed of "corpuscles."

Thus not only the more abstract explanatory theories transcend experience, but even the most ordinary singular statements. For even ordinary singular statements are always *interpretations of "the facts" in the light of theories*. (And the same holds even for "the facts" of the case. They contain *universals*; and universals always entail a *lawlike* behaviour.)

I explained briefly at the end of section 25 how it is that the use of universals such as "glass" or "water," in a statement like "here is a glass of water," necessarily transcends experience. It is due to the fact that words like "glass" or "water" are used to characterize the *lawlike behaviour* of certain things; which may be expressed by calling them "dispositional words."

Now since every law transcends experience—which is merely another way of saying that it is not verifiable—every predicate expressing lawlike behaviour transcends experience also: this is why the statement "this container contains water" is a testable but non-verifiable hypothesis, transcending experience.[4] It is for this reason impossible to "constitute" any true universal term (as Carnap tried to do) that is to say, to define it in purely experimental or observational terms—or to "reduce" it to purely experiential or observational terms: since *all universals are dispositional*, they cannot be reduced to experience. We must introduce them as undefined terms, except those which we may define in terms of other non-experiential universals (such as "water" if we choose to define it as "a compound of two atoms of hydrogen and one of oxygen").

(3) That *all* universals are dispositional is often overlooked, owing to the fact that universals can be dispositional in varying degrees. Thus "soluble" or "breakable" are clearly dispositional in a higher degree than "dissolved" or "broken." But it is sometimes not realized that even "dissolved" and "broken" are dispositional. A chemist would not say that sugar or salt had "*dissolved*" in water if he did not expect that he could get the sugar or the salt back, by evaporating the water. Thus "dissolved" denotes a dispositional state. And as to "broken," we need only consider how we proceed *if we are in doubt* whether or not a thing is broken—something we have dropped, perhaps, or say, a bone in our body: we test the behaviour of the thing in question, trying to find out whether it does not show a certain undue mobility. Thus "broken," like "dissolved," describes dispositions to behave in a certain regular or lawlike manner. Similarly, we say of a surface that it is red, or white, if it has the disposition to reflect red, or white, light, and consequently the disposition to look in daylight red, or white. In general, the dispositional character of any universal property will become clear if we consider what tests we should undertake if we are in doubt whether or not the property is present in some particular case.

Thus the attempt to distinguish between dispositional and nondispositional predicates is mistaken, just as is the attempt to distinguish between theoretical terms (or languages) and nontheoretical or empirical or observational or factual or ordinary terms (or languages). It is, perhaps, somewhat like this. What people have learnt before reaching a certain critical age, they are inclined to regard as factual, or "ordinary," and what they hear later, as theoretical or perhaps as "merely instrumental." (The critical age seems to depend on the psychological type.)

(4) Universal laws transcend experience, if only because they are universal and thus transcend any finite number of their observable instances; and singular statements transcend experience because the universal terms which normally occur in them entail dispositions to behave in a lawlike manner, so that they entail universal laws (of some lower order of universality, as a rule). Accordingly, universal laws transcend experience in at least two ways: because of their universality, and because of the occurrence of universal or dispositional terms in them. And they transcend experience in a higher degree if the dispositional terms which occur in them are dispositional in a higher degree or more abstract. There are layers of higher and higher degrees of universality, and thus of transcendence. (In section *15 of the *Postscript*, an attempt is made to explain the sense in which these are also layers of what may be called "depth.")

It is of course because of this transcendence that scientific laws or theories are non-verifiable, and that *testability* or *refutability* is the only thing that distinguishes them, in general, from metaphysical theories.

If it is asked why we use these transcendent universal laws instead of keeping more closely to "experience," two kinds of answers may be given.

(a) Because we need them: because there is no such thing as "pure experience," but only experience interpreted in the light of expectations or theories which are "transcendent."

(b) Because a theorist is a man who *wishes to explain* experiences, and because explanation involves the use of explanatory hypotheses which (in order to be independently testable; see section *15 of the *Postscript*) must transcend what we hope to explain.

The reason given under (a) is a pragmatic or instrumentalist one, and although I believe that it is true, I do not think that it is comparable in importance with the reason given under (b); for even if a programme of eliminating explanatory theories for practical purposes (say, for prediction) were to succeed, the aim of the theorist would be unaffected.[5]

(5) That theories transcend experience in the sense here indicated was asserted in many places in the book. At the same time, theories were described as strictly universal statements.

A most penetrating criticism of the view that theories, or laws of nature, can be adequately expressed by a universal statement, such as "All planets move in ellipses," has been advanced by William Kneale. I have found Kneale's criticism difficult to understand. Even now I am not entirely sure whether I understand him properly; but I hope I do.[6]

I believe that Kneale's point can be put as follows. Although universal statements are *entailed* by statements of natural law, the latter are logically stronger than the former. They do not only assert "All planets move in ellipses," but rather something like "All planets move *necessarily* in ellipses." Kneale calls a statement of this kind a "principle of necessitation." I do not think that he succeeds in making quite clear what the difference is between a universal statement and a "principle of necessitation." He speaks of "the need for a more precise formulation of the notions of contingency and necessity."[7] But a little later, one reads to one's surprise: "In fact, the word 'necessity' is the least troublesome of those with which we have to deal in this part of philosophy."[8] Admittedly, between these two passages, Kneale tries to persuade us that "the sense of this distinction"—the distinction between contingency and necessity—"can be easily understood from examples."[9] But I found his examples perplexing. Always assuming that I have succeeded in my endeavours to understand Kneale, I must say that his positive theory of natural laws seems to me utterly unacceptable. Yet his criticism seems to me most valuable.

(6) I am now going to explain, with the help of an example, what I believe to be essentially Kneale's criticism of the view that a characterization of laws of nature as universal statements is *logically sufficient* and also *intuitively adequate*.

Consider some extinct animal, say the moa, a huge bird whose bones abound in some New Zealand swamps. (I have there dug for them myself.) We decide to use the name "moa" as a universal name (rather than as a proper name; cf. section 14) of a certain biological structure; but we ought to admit that it is of course quite possible—and even quite credible—that no moas have ever existed in the universe, or will ever exist, apart from those which once lived in New Zealand; and we will assume that this credible view is correct.

Now let us assume that the biological structure of the moa organism is of such a kind that under very favourable conditions, a moa might easily live sixty years or longer. Let us further assume that the conditions met by the moa in New Zealand were far from ideal (owing, perhaps, to the presence of some virus), and that no moa ever reached the age of fifty. In this case, the strictly universal statement "All moas die before reaching the age of fifty" will be true; for according to our assumption, there never is, was, or will be a moa in the universe more than fifty years of age. At the same time, this universal statement will not be a law of nature; for according to our assumptions, it would be *possible* for a moa to live longer, and it is only due to *accidental or contingent* conditions—such as the co-presence of a certain virus—that in fact no moa did live longer.

The example shows that there may be *true, strictly universal statements* which have an accidental character rather than the character of true universal laws of nature. Accordingly, the characterization of laws of nature as strictly universal statements is logically insufficient and intuitively inadequate.

(7) The example may also indicate in what sense natural laws may be described as "principles of necessity" or "principles of impossibility," as Kneale suggests. For according to our assumptions—assumptions which are perfectly reasonable—it would be *possible*, under favourable conditions, for a moa to reach a greater age than any moa has actually reached. But were there a natural law limiting the age of any moa-like organism to fifty years, *then it would not be possible* for any moa to live longer than this. Thus natural laws set certain limits to what is possible.

I think that all this is intuitively acceptable; in fact, when I said, in several places in my book, that natural laws *forbid* certain events to happen, or that they have the character of *prohibitions*, I gave expression to the same intuitive idea. And I think that it is quite possible and perhaps even useful to speak of "natural necessity" or of "physical necessity," in order to describe this character of natural laws, and of their logical consequences.

(8) But I think it is a mistake to underrate the differences between this natural or physical necessity, and other kinds of necessity, for example, logical necessity. We may, roughly, describe as logically necessary what would hold in any conceivable world. But although Newton's inverse square law may conceivably be a true law of nature in some world, and to that extent naturally necessary in that world, a world in which it is not valid is perfectly *conceivable*.

Kneale has criticized this kind of argument by pointing out that Goldbach's conjecture (according to which any even number greater than two is the sum of two primes) may *conceivably* be true, or conceivably be false, even though it may well be demonstrable (or refutable), and in this sense mathematically or logically necessary (or impossible); and he argues that "the conceivability of the contradictory is not to be taken as a disproof of necessity in mathematics."[10] But if so, why, he asks, "should it be supposed to furnish . . . a disproof in natural science?"[11] Now I think that this argument lays too much stress on the *word* "conceivable"; moreover, it operates with a sense of "conceivable" different from the one intended: once we have a proof of Goldbach's theorem, we may say that this proof establishes precisely that an even number (greater than two) which is not the sum of two primes is inconceivable—in the sense that it leads to inconsistent results: to the assertion, among others, that o = 1, which is "inconceivable." In another sense, o = 1 may be quite conceivable: it may even be used, like any other mathematically false statement, as an assumption in an indirect proof. Indeed, an indirect proof may well be put thus: "*Conceive* that a is true. Then we should have to admit that b is true. But we know that b is absurd. Thus it is *inconceivable* that a is true." It is clear that although this use of "conceivable" and "inconceivable" is a little vague and ambiguous, it would be misleading to say that this way of arguing must be invalid since the truth of a cannot be inconceivable, considering that we did start by conceiving, precisely, the truth of a.

Thus "inconceivable" in logic and mathematics is simply another word for "leading to an obvious contradiction." *Logically* possible or "conceivable" is everything that does not lead to an obvious contradiction, and logically impossible or "inconceivable" is everything that does. When Kneale says that the contradictory of a theorem may be "conceivable," he uses the word in another sense—and in a very good sense too.

(9) Thus an assumption is logically possible if it is not self-contradictory; it is physically possible if it does not contradict the laws of nature. The two meanings of "possible" have enough in common to explain why we use the same word; but to gloss over their difference can only lead to confusion.

Compared with logical tautologies, laws of nature have a contingent, an accidental character. This is clearly recognized by Leibniz who teaches (cf. *Philos. Schriften*, Gerhardt, 7, p. 390) that the world is the work of God, in a sense somewhat similar to that in which a sonnet, or a rondeau, or a sonata, or a fugue, is the work of an artist. The artist may freely choose a certain *form*, voluntarily restricting his freedom by this choice: he imposes certain principles of impossibility upon his creation, for example upon his rhythm, and, to a lesser extent, his words which, as compared to the rhythm, may appear contingent, accidental. But this does not mean that his choice of form, or of rhythm, was not contingent also. For another form or rhythm could have been chosen.

Similarly with natural laws. They restrict the (logically) possible choice of singular facts. They are thus principles of impossibility with respect to these singular facts; and the singular facts seem highly contingent as compared with the natural laws. But the natural laws, though necessary as compared with singular facts, are contingent as compared with logical tautologies. For there may be *structurally different worlds*—worlds with different natural laws.

Thus natural necessity or impossibility is like musical necessity or impossibility. It is like the impossibility of a four-beat rhythm in a classical minuet, or the impossibility of ending it on a diminished seventh or some other dissonance. It imposes *structural* principles upon the world. But it still leaves a great deal of freedom to the more contingent singular facts—the initial conditions.

If we compare the situation in music with that of our example of the moa, we can say: there is no musical law prohibiting the writing of a minuet in G flat minor, but it is nevertheless quite possible that no minuet has ever been, or will ever be, written in this unusual key. Thus we can say that musically necessary laws may be distinguished from true universal statements about the historical facts of musical composition.

(10) The opposite view—the view that natural laws are in no sense contingent—seems to be the one which Kneale is advancing, if I understand him well. To me it seems quite as mistaken as the view which he justly criticizes—the view that laws of nature are nothing but true universal statements.

Kneale's view that laws of nature are necessary in the same sense in which logical tautologies are necessary may perhaps be expressed in religious terms thus: God may have faced the choice between creating a physical world and not creating a physical world, but once this choice was made, He was no longer free to choose the form, or the structure of the world; for since this structure—the regularities of nature, described by the laws of nature—is necessarily what it is, all He could freely choose were the initial conditions.

It seems to me that Descartes held a view very similar to this. According to him, all the laws of nature follow with necessity from the one analytic principle (the essential definition of "body") according to which "to be a body" means the same as "to be extended"; which is taken to imply that two *different* bodies cannot take up the same extension, or space. (Indeed, this principle is similar to Kneale's standard example—"that nothing which is red is also green."[12]) But it is by going beyond these "truisms" (as Kneale calls them, stressing their similarity to logical tautologies[13]) that, beginning with Newton, physical theory has reached a depth of insight utterly beyond the Cartesian approach.

It seems to me that the doctrine that the laws of nature are *in no sense contingent* is a particularly severe form of a view which I have described and criticized elsewhere as "essentialism."[14] For it entails the doctrine of the existence of *ultimate explanations*; that is to say, of the existence of explanatory theories which in their turn are neither in need of any further explanation nor capable of being further explained. For should we succeed in the task of reducing all the laws of nature to the true "principles of necessitation"—to truisms, such as that two essentially extended things cannot take up the same extension, or that nothing which is red is also green—further explanation would become both unnecessary and impossible.

I see no reason to believe that the doctrine of the existence of ultimate explanations is true, and many reasons to believe that it is false. The more we learn about theories, or laws of nature, the less do they remind us of Cartesian self-explanatory truisms or of essentialist definitions. It is not truisms which science unveils. Rather, it is part of the greatness and the beauty of science that we can learn, through our own critical investigations, that the world is utterly different from what we ever imagined—until our imagination was fired by the refutation of our earlier theories. There does not seem any reason to think that this process will come to an end.[15]

All this receives the strongest support from our considerations about content and (absolute) logical probability. If laws of nature are not merely strictly universal statements, they must be *logically stronger* than the corresponding universal statements, since the latter must be deducible from them. But the *logical necessity* of a, as we have seen (at the end of appendix *v) can be defined by the definiens

$$p(a) = p(a, \bar{a}) = 1.$$

For universal statements a, on the other hand, we obtain (cf. the same appendix and appendices *vii and *viii):

$$p(a) = p(a, \bar{a}) = 0;$$

and the same must hold for any logically stronger statement. Accordingly, a law of nature is, by its great content, as far removed from a logically necessary statement as a consistent statement can be; and it is much nearer, in its logical import, to a "merely accidentally" universal statement than to a logical truism.

(11) The upshot of this discussion is that I am prepared to accept Kneale's criticism in so far as I am prepared to accept the view that there exists a category of statements, the laws of nature, which are logically stronger than the corresponding universal statements. This doctrine is, in my opinion, incompatible with any theory of induction. To my own methodology it makes little or no difference, however. On the contrary, it is quite clear that a proposed or conjectured principle which declares the impossibility of certain events would have to be tested by trying to show that these events are possible; that is to say, by trying to bring them about. But this is precisely the method of testing which I advocate.

Thus from the point of view here adopted, no change whatever is needed, as far as methodology is concerned. The change is entirely on an ontological, a metaphysical level. It may be described by saying that if we conjecture that a is a natural law, we conjecture that a expresses a *structural property of our world*; a property which prevents the occurrence of certain logically possible singular events, or states of affairs of a certain kind—very much as explained in sections 21 to 23 of the book, and also in sections 79, 83, and 85.

(12) As Tarski has shown, it is possible to explain *logical necessity* in terms of universality: a statement may be said to be logically necessary if and only if it is deducible (for example, by particularization) from a "*universally valid*" statement function; that is to say, from a statement function which is *satisfied by every model*.[16] (This means, true in all possible worlds.)

I think that we may explain by the same method what we mean by *natural necessity*; for we may adopt the following definition:

A statement may be said to be naturally or physically necessary if, and only if, it is deducible from a statement function which is satisfied in all worlds that differ from our world, if at all, only with respect to initial conditions.

We can never *know*, of course, whether a supposed law is a genuine law or whether it only looks like a law but depends, in fact, upon certain special initial conditions prevailing in our region of the universe. (Cf. section 79.) We cannot, therefore ever find out of any given nonlogical statement that it is in fact naturally necessary: the conjecture that it is remains a conjecture for ever (not merely because we cannot search our whole world in order to ensure that no counterinstance exists, but for the even stronger reason that we cannot search all worlds that differ from ours with respect to initial conditions.) But although our proposed definition excludes the possibility of obtaining *a positive criterion* of natural necessity, we can in practice apply our definition of natural necessity in a *negative* way: by finding initial conditions under which the supposed law turns out to be invalid, we can show that it was not necessary; that is to say, not a law of nature. Thus the proposed definition fits our methodology very well indeed.

The proposed definition would, of course, make all laws of nature, together with all their logical consequences, *naturally or physically necessary.*[17]

It will be seen at once that the proposed definition is in perfect agreement with the results reached in our discussion of the moa example (cf. points 6 and 7 above): it was precisely because we thought that moas would live longer under different conditions—under more favorable ones—that we felt that a true universal statement about their actual maximal age was of an accidental character.

(13) We now introduce the symbol "N" as a name of the class of statements which are necessarily true, in the sense of natural or physical necessity; that is to say, true whatever the initial conditions may be.

With the help of "N," we can define "$a \xrightarrow{N} b$" (or in words, "If a then necessarily b") by the following somewhat obvious definition:

(D) $a \xrightarrow{N} b$ is true if, and only if, $(a \rightarrow b) \in N$.

In words, perhaps: "If a then necessarily b" holds if, and only if, "If a then b" is necessarily true. Here "$a \rightarrow b$" is, of course, the name of an ordinary conditional with the antecedent a and the consequent b. If it were our intention to define logical entailment or "strict implication," then we could also use (D), but we should have to interpret "N" as "logically necessary" (rather than as "naturally or physically necessary").

Owing to the definition (D), we can say of "$a \xrightarrow{N} b$" that it is the name of a statement with the following properties.

(A) $a \xrightarrow{N} b$ is not always true if a is false, in contradistinction to $a \rightarrow b$.

(B) $a \xrightarrow{N} b$ is not always true if b is true, in contradistinction to $a \rightarrow b$.

(A') $a \xrightarrow{N} b$ is always true if a is impossible or necessarily false, or if its negation, $\bar{a}$, is necessarily true (whether by logical or by physical necessity).

(B') $a \xrightarrow{N} b$ is always true if b is necessarily true (whether by logical or by physical necessity).

Here a and b may be either statements or statement functions.

$a \underset{N}{\rightarrow} b$ may be called a "necessary conditional" or a "nomic conditional." It expresses, I believe, what some authors have called "subjunctive conditionals," or "counterfactual conditionals." (It seems, however, that other authors—for example Kneale—meant something else by a "counterfactual conditional": they took this name to imply that a is, in fact, false.[18] I do not think that this usage is to be recommended.)

A little reflection will show that the class N of naturally necessary statements comprises not only the class of all those statements which, like true universal laws of nature, can be intuitively described as being unaffected by changes of initial conditions, but also all those statements which follow from true universal laws of nature, or from the true structural theories about the world. There will be statements among these that describe a definite set of initial conditions; for example, statements of the form "if in this phial under ordinary room temperature and a pressure of 1000 g per cm², hydrogen and oxygen are mixed . . . then. . . ." If conditional statements of this kind are deducible from true laws of nature, then their truth will be also invariant with respect to all changes of initial conditions: either the initial conditions described in the antecedent will be satisfied, in which case the consequent will be true (and therefore the whole conditional); or the initial conditions described in the antecedent will not be satisfied and therefore factually untrue ("counter-factual"). In this case the conditional will be true as vacuously satisfied. Thus the much discussed vacuous satisfaction plays its proper part to ensure that the statements deducible from naturally necessary laws are also "naturally necessary" in the sense of our definition.

Indeed, we could have defined N simply as the class of natural laws and their logical consequences. But there is perhaps a slight advantage in defining N with the help of the idea of initial conditions (of a simultaneity class of singular statements). If we define N as, for example, the class of statements which are true in all worlds that differ from our world (if at all) only with respect to initial conditions, then we avoid the use of subjunctive (or counter-factual) wording, such as "which would remain true even if different initial conditions held (in our world) than those which actually do hold."

Nevertheless, the phrase "all worlds which differ (if at all) from our world only with respect to the initial conditions" undoubtedly contains implicitly the idea of laws of nature. What we mean is "all worlds which have the same structure—or the same natural laws—as our own world." In so far as our *definiens* contains implicitly the idea of laws of nature, (D) may be said to be circular. But all definitions must be circular *in this sense*—precisely as all derivations (as opposed to proofs[19]), for example, all syllogisms, are circular: the conclusion must be contained in the premises. Our definition is not, however, circular in a more technical sense. Its *definiens* operates with a perfectly clear intuitive idea—that of varying the initial conditions of our world; for example, the distances of the planets, their masses, and the mass of the sun. It interprets the result of such changes as the construction of a kind of "model" of our world (a model or "copy" which does not need to be faithful with respect to the initial conditions); and it then imitates the well-known device of calling those statements "necessary" which are true in (the universe of) *all* these models (i.e. for all *logically possible* initial conditions).

(14) My present treatment of this problem differs, intuitively, from a version previously published.[20] I think that it is a considerable improvement, and I gladly acknowledge that I owe this improvement, in a considerable measure, to Kneale's criticism. Nevertheless, from a more technical (rather than an intuitive) point of view the changes are slight. For in that paper, I operate (a) with the idea of natural laws and (b) with the idea of conditionals which *follow*

from natural laws; but (a) and (b) together have the same extension as N, as we have seen. (c) I suggest that "subjunctive conditionals" are those that follow from (a), i.e. are just those of the class (b). And (d) I suggest (in the last paragraph) that we may have to introduce the supposition that all logically possible initial conditions (and therefore all events and processes which are compatible with the laws) are somewhere, at some time, realized in the world; which is a somewhat clumsy way of saying more or less what I am saying now with the help of the idea of all worlds that differ (if at all) from our world only with respect to the initial conditions.[21]

My position of 1949 might indeed be formulated with the help of the following statement. Although our world may not comprise all logically possible worlds, since worlds of another structure—with different laws—may be logically possible, it comprises all physically possible worlds, in the sense that all physically possible initial conditions are realized in it— somewhere, at some time. My present view is that it is only too obvious that this metaphysical assumption may possibly be true—in both senses of "possible"—but that we are much better off without it.

Yet once this metaphysical assumption is adopted, my older and my present views become (except for purely terminological differences) equivalent, as far as *the status of laws* is concerned. Thus my older view is, if anything, more "metaphysical" (or less "positivistic") than my present view, even though it does not make use of the *word* "necessary" in describing the status of laws.

(15) To a student of method who opposes the doctrine of induction and adheres to the theory of falsification, there is not much difference between the view that universal laws are nothing but strictly universal statements and the view that they are "necessary": in both cases, we can only test our conjecture by attempted refutations.

To the inductivist, there is a crucial difference here: he ought to reject the idea of "necessary" laws, since these, being logically stronger, must be even less accessible to induction than mere universal statements.

Yet inductivists do not in fact always reason in this way. On the contrary, some seem to think that a statement asserting that laws of nature are necessary may somehow be used to justify induction—perhaps somewhat on the lines of a "principle of the uniformity of nature."

But it is obvious that no principle of this kind could ever justify induction. None could make inductive conclusions valid or even probable.

It is quite true, of course, that a statement like "there exist laws of nature" might be appealed to if we wished to justify our search for laws of nature.[22] But in the context of this remark of mine, "justify" has a sense very different from the one it has in the context of the question whether we can justify induction. In the latter case, we wish to establish certain statements— the induced generalizations. In the former case, we merely wish to justify an activity, the search for laws. Moreover, even though this activity may, in some sense, be justified by the knowledge that true laws exist—that there are structural regularities in the world—it could be so justified even without that knowledge: the hope that there may be some food somewhere certainly "justifies" the search for it—especially if we are starving—even if this hope is far removed from knowledge. Thus we can say that, although the knowledge that true laws exist would add something to the justification of our search for laws, this search is justified, even if we lack knowledge, by our curiosity, and by the mere hope that we may succeed.

Moreover, the distinction between "necessary" laws and strictly universal statements does not seem to be relevant to this problem: whether necessary or not, the knowledge that laws exist would add something to the "justification" of our search, without being needed for this kind of "justification."

(16) I believe, however, that the idea that there are necessary laws of nature, in the sense of natural or physical necessity explained under point (12), is metaphysically or ontologically important, and of great intuitive significance in connection with our attempts to understand the world. And although it is impossible to establish this metaphysical idea either on empirical grounds (because it is not falsifiable) or on other grounds, I believe that it is true, as I indicated in sections 79, and 83 to 85. Yet I am now trying to go beyond what I said in these sections by emphasizing the peculiar ontological status of universal laws (for example, by speaking of their "necessity," or their "structural character"), and also by emphasizing the fact that the metaphysical character or the irrefutability of the assertion that laws of nature exist need not prevent us from discussing this assertion rationally—that is to say, critically. (See my *Postscript*, especially sections *6, *7, *15, and *120.)

Nevertheless, I regard, unlike Kneale, "necessary" as a mere word—as a label useful for distinguishing *the universality of laws* from "accidental" universality. Of course, any other label would do just as well, for there is not much connection here with logical necessity. I largely agree with the spirit of Wittgenstein's paraphrase of Hume: "A necessity for one thing to happen because another has happened does not exist. There is only logical necessity."[23] Only in one way is $a \overrightarrow{N} b$ connected with logical necessity: the necessary link between a and b is neither to be found in a nor in b, but in the fact that the corresponding ordinary conditional (or "material implication," $a \rightarrow b$ without "N") follows *with logical necessity* from a law of nature—that it is necessary, relative to a law of nature.[24] And it may be said that a law of nature is necessary in its turn because it is logically derivable from, or explicable by, a law of a still higher degree of universality, or of greater "depth." (See my *Postscript*, section *15.) One might suppose that it is this logically necessary dependence upon true statements of higher universality, conjectured to exist, which suggested in the first instance the idea of "necessary connection" between cause and effect.[25]

(17) So far as I can understand the modern discussions of "subjunctive conditionals" or "contrary-to-fact conditionals" or "counterfactual conditionals," they seem to have arisen mainly out of the problem situation created by the inherent difficulties of inductivism or positivism or operationalism or phenomenalism.

The phenomenalist, for instance, wishes to translate statements about physical objects into statements about observations. For example, "There is a flower-pot on the window sill" should be translatable into something like "If anybody in an appropriate place looks in the appropriate direction, he will see what he has learned to call a flower-pot." The simplest objection (but by no means the most important one) to regarding the second statement as a translation of the first is to point out that while the second will be (vacuously) true when nobody is looking at the window sill, it would be absurd to say that whenever nobody is looking at some window sill, there must be a flower-pot on it. The phenomenalist is tempted to reply to this that the argument depends on the truth-table definition of the conditional (or of "material implication"), and that we have to realize the need for a different interpretation of the conditional—a *modal* interpretation which makes allowance for the fact that what we mean is something like "If anybody looks, or if anybody were looking, then he will see, or would see, a flower-pot."[26]

One might think that our $a \overrightarrow{N} b$ could provide the desired modal conditional, and in a way it does do this. Indeed, it does it as well as one can possibly expect. Nevertheless, our original objection stands, because we know that if $\bar{a}$ is necessary—that is, if $\bar{a} \in N$—then $a \overrightarrow{N} b$ holds for every *b*. This means that, if for some reason or other the place where a flower-pot is (or is not) situated is such that it is physically *impossible* for anybody to look at it, then "If anybody looks, or if anybody were looking, at that place, then he will, or would, see a flower-pot" will be true, merely because nobody *can* look at it. But this means that the phenomenalist modal translation of "At the place *x* is a flower-pot" will be true for all those places *x* which, for some physical reason or other, nobody *can* look at. (Thus there is a flower-pot—or whatever else you like—in the center of the sun.) But this is absurd.

For this reason, and for many other reasons, I do not think that there is any chance of rescuing phenomenalism by this method.

As to the doctrine of operationalism—which demands that scientific terms, such as length, or solubility, should be defined in terms of the appropriate experimental procedure—it can be shown quite easily that all so-called operational definitions will be circular. I may show this briefly in the case of "soluble."[27]

The experiments by which we test whether a substance such as sugar is *soluble in water* involve such tests as the recovery of dissolved sugar from the solution (say, by evaporation of the water; cf. point 3 above). Clearly, it is necessary to identify the recovered substance, that is to say, to find out whether it has the same properties as sugar. Among these properties, *solubility in water* is one. Thus in order to define "*x* is soluble in water" by the standard operational test, we should at least have to say something like this:

"*x* is *soluble in water* if and only if (a) when *x* is put into water then it (necessarily) disappears, and (b) when after the water evaporates, a substance is (necessarily) recovered which, again, is *soluble in water*."

The fundamental reason for the circularity of this kind of definition is very simple: experiments are never conclusive; and they must, in their turn, be testable by further experiments.

Operationalists seem to have believed that once the problem of subjunctive conditionals was solved (so that the vacuous satisfaction of the defining conditional could be avoided) there would be no further obstacle in the way of operational definitions of dispositional terms. It seems that the great interest shown in the so-called problem of subjunctive (or counterfactual) conditionals was mainly due to this belief. But I think I have shown that even if we have solved the problem of logically analysing subjunctive (or "nomic") conditionals, we cannot hope to define dispositional terms, or universal terms, operationally. For universals, or dispositional terms, transcend experience, as explained here under points 1 and 2, and in section 25 of the book.

NOTES

1. Some illustrations of this argument, so far as it is directed against the doctrine of temporal primacy of repetitions (that is, against Hume) may be found in sections iv and v of my paper "Philosophy of Science: A Personal Report," in *British Philosophy in the Mid-Century*, ed. C. A. Mace, 1957.
2. *Editor's note*—All of the author's in-text references are to his book *The Logic of Scientific Discovery* (New York: Harper and Row, 1965). The present essay originally appeared as Appendix *10 to this work.
3. Cf. my papers "A Note on Berkeley as a Precursor of Mach," *B.J.P.S.* 4 (1953), and "Three Views Concerning Human Knowledge" in *Contemporary British Philosophy*, vol. 3, ed. H. D. Lewis, 1956. See also sections *11 to *15 of my *Postscript*. *Editor's note*—By "*Postscript*," Popper refers to his

(now) three volume *Postscript to the Logic of Scientific Discovery*, edited by W. W. Bartley, III, and published by Rowman and Littlefield beginning with Volume I, *Realism and the Aim of Science*, in 1983.

4. Since it is a singular statement, it is less incorrect to speak here of a symmetry between non-verifiability and non-falsifiability than in a case of universal statements; for in order to falsify it, we have to accept another singular statement, similarly non-verifiable, as true. But even here, a certain asymmetry remains. For quite generally in assuming the truth, or the falsity, of some test-statement, we can only establish the *falsity* of the statement under test, but not its truth. The reason is that the latter entails an infinite number of test statements. See also section 29 of the book, and section *22 of my *Postscript*.

5. That it is possible to do without theories is asserted by Carnap, *Logical Foundations of Probability*, p. 574 f. Yet there is no reason whatever for the belief that Carnap's analysis, even if it were otherwise defensible, could be legitimately transferred from his model language to "the language of science"; see my preface, 1958. In two very interesting articles W. Craig has discussed certain reduction programmes. (See *Journal of Symb. Logic* 18, (1953), pp. 30 f., and *Philosophical Review* 65, (1956), pp. 38 ff.) To his own excellent critical comments on his method of eliminating "auxiliary" (or "transcendent") ideas, the following might be added. (i) He achieves the elimination of explanatory theories, essentially, by promoting infinitely many theorems to the rank of axioms (or by replacing the definition of "theorem" by a new definition of "axiom" which is co-extensive with it as far as the "purified" sub-language goes). (ii) In the actual construction of the purified system, he is of course *guided by our knowledge of the theories* to be eliminated. (iii) The purified system is no longer an explanatory system, and no longer testable in the sense in which explanatory systems may be testable whose testability is, essentially, related to their informative *content* and *depth*. (One might well say that the axioms of the purified system have zero depth in the sense of section *15 of my *Postscript*.)

6. Cf. William Kneale, *Probability and Induction*, 1949. One of my minor difficulties in understanding Kneale's criticism was connected with the fact that he gives in some places very good outlines of some of my views, while in others he seems to miss my point completely. (See for example note 18 below.)

7. Ibid., p. 32.

8. Ibid., p. 80.

9. Ibid., p. 32. One of the difficulties is that Kneale at times seems to accept Leibniz's view ("A truth is necessary when its negation implies a contradiction; and when it is not necessary, it is called contingent." *Die philosophischen Schriften*, vol. 3, ed. Gerhardt, p. 400; see also vol. 7, p. 390 ff.), while at other times he seems to use "necessary" in a wider sense.

10. Ibid., p. 80.

11. Ibid.

12. Cf. Kneale, ibid., p. 32; see also, for example, p. 80.

13. Ibid., p. 33.

14. Cf. my *Poverty of Historicism*, section 10; *The Open Society*, chapter 3, section VI; chapter 11 "Three Views Concerning Human Knowledge" (*Contemporary British Philosophy* 3) and my *Postscript*, for example sections *15 and *31.

15. Cf. my *Postscript*, especially section *15.

16. Cf. my "Note on Tarski's Definition of Truth," *Mind* 64 (1955), especially p. 391.

17. Incidentally, logically necessary statements would (simply because they follow from any statement) become physically necessary also; but this does not matter, of course.

18. In my "Note on Natural Laws and So-Called Contrary-to-Fact Conditionals" (*Mind* 58, N.S., (1949), pp. 62–66) I used the term "subjunctive conditional" for what I here call "necessary" or "nomic conditional"; and I explained repeatedly that these subjunctive conditionals must be deducible from natural laws. It is therefore difficult to understand how Kneale (*Analysis* 10 (1950), p. 122) could attribute to me even tentatively the view that a subjunctive conditional or a "contrary to fact conditional" was of the form "$-\phi(a).(\phi(a)\rightarrow\psi(a))$." I wonder whether Kneale realized that this

expression of his was only a complicated way of saying "$-\phi\ (a)$"; for who would ever think of asserting that "$-\phi\ (a)$" was deducible from the law "$(\chi)(\phi(\chi)\rightarrow\psi\ (\chi))$"?

19. The distinction between derivation and proof is dealt with in my paper "New Foundations for Logic," *Mind* 56 (1947), pp. 193 f.

20. Cf. "A Note on Natural Laws and So-Called Contrary-to-Fact Conditionals," *Mind* 58, N.S. (1949), pp. 62–66. See also my *Poverty of Historicism*, 1957 (first published 1945), the footnote on p. 123.

21. I call my older formulation "clumsy" because it amounts to introducing the assumption that some-where moas have once lived, or will one day live, under ideal conditions; which seems to me a bit far-fetched. I prefer now to replace this supposition by another—that among the "models" of our world—which are not supposed to be real, but logical constructions as it were—there will be at least one in which moas live under ideal conditions. And this, indeed, seems to me not only admissible, but obvious. Apart from terminological changes, this seems to be the only change in my position, as compared with my note in *Mind* of 1949. But I think that it is an important change.

22. Cf. Wittgenstein's *Tractatus*, 6.36: "If there were a law of causality, it might run: 'There are natural laws.' But that can clearly not be said; it shows itself." In my opinion, what shows itself, if anything, is that this clearly *can* be said: it *has* been said by Wittgenstein, for example. What can clearly not be done is to *verify* the statement that there are natural laws (or even to falsify it). But the fact that a statement is not verifiable (or even that it is not falsifiable) does not mean that it is meaningless, or that it cannot be understood, or that it "can clearly not be said," as Wittgenstein believed.

23. Cf. *Tractatus*, 6.3637.

24. I pointed this out in *Aristotelian Society Supplementary Volume* 22 (1948), pp. 141–154, section 3; see especially p. 148. In this paper I briefly sketched a program which I have largely carried out since.

25. Cf. my paper quoted in the foregoing footnote.

26. It was R. B. Braithwaite who replied along similar lines as these to my objection of vacuous satisfaction after a paper he read on phenomenalism in Professor Susan Stebbing's seminar, in the spring of 1936. It was the first time that I heard, in a context like this, of what is nowadays called a "subjunctive conditional." For a criticism of phenomenalist "reduction programmes," see note 5 and text, above.

27. The argument is contained in a paper which I contributed in January 1955 to the still unpublished Carnap volume of the *Library of Living Philosophers*, ed. by P. A. Schilpp. As to the circularity of the operational definition of length, this may be seen from the following facts: (a) the "operational" definition of *length* involves *temperature* corrections, and (b) the (usual) operational definition of *temperature* involves measurements of *length*.

PART THREE

THE STRUCTURE OF THEORIES

INTRODUCTION

I f there is an alternative to the conception of the aim of science as that of discovering laws of nature, it must be that science aims at the discovery of scientific theories. Indeed, the most prevalent view would be that laws can be invoked to explain and predict the occurrence of particular events during the course of the world's history, while theories in turn may be invoked to explain those laws themselves. Alternatively, a distinction might be drawn between laws of different kinds, where theories consist of theoretical laws, but other laws may be merely empirical. On either approach, however, theories and laws are closely related, if not the very same thing.

Carnap's "Theories and Nonobservables" supplies a conception that combines features of both alternatives. Drawing a distinction between the observational and the nonobservational elements of the vocabulary of a theory, he suggests that *theoretical laws* are generalizations whose nonlogical terms are exclusively theoretical and that *empirical laws* are generalizations whose nonlogical terms are exclusively observational. A *scientific theory* consists of theoretical laws and correspondence rules, which relate theoretical laws to observable phenomena by employing a mixed nonlogical vocabulary. An empirical law might be explained by its derivation from a theory.

Carnap maintains that the distinction between the observational and the nonobservational elements of the vocabulary of a theory can be drawn two different ways. Philosophers tend to adopt a narrower sense, according to which a predicate is *observational* only if the presence or the absence of a designated property can be ascertained on the basis of direct observation. Scientists, however, tend to adopt a broader sense, according to which predicates are *observational* when the presence or the absence of such properties can be ascertained on the basis of direct observation or relatively simple measurement. No decisive reasons favor one over the other approach.

Empirical laws (such as "All swans are white") pose no special epistemic problems, since they can be discovered by means of simple inductive procedures. If m/n observed swans have been white, for example, then when an appropriate number have been observed over an appropriate range of conditions, one can infer (inductively) that m/n swans are white (or, when $m = n$, that all swans are white). This is known as *the straight rule of induction*. It thus differs from Skyrm's "Rule S," which does not lead to generalizations. According to Rule S, if m/n observed swans have been white, then the degree of support for the inference that the next swan observed will be white $= m/n$.

Theoretical laws (such as those of genetics), however, cannot be established by simple inductive procedures. The approach most appropriate to their discovery is *the hypothetico-deductive method*, according to which a theoretical hypothesis can be subjected to empirical test by deriving consequences couched in observational language. If certain hypotheses concerning the laws of genetics imply that, within suitable populations, the distribution of a specific trait (such as epilepsy, blue eyes, and so on) should assume the average relative frequency of m/n, those theoretical hypotheses can be tested indirectly within those populations when those traits are observable.

Although Carnap supports the conception of scientific theories as sets of theoretical laws and correspondence rules, he also endorses a more formal explication according to which *a scientific theory consists of an abstract calculus coupled with an empirical interpretation*. An abstract calculus, say,

(AC–I) 1. $(x)(t)(Wxt \rightarrow Xxt)$ Axiom
2. $(x)(t)[Xxt \rightarrow (Yxt \rightarrow Zxt)]$ Axiom
3. $(x)(t)[Wxt \rightarrow (Yxt \rightarrow Zzt)]$ Theorem

where "W," "X," "Y," and "Z" are predicate variables and "___ $\rightarrow$ ..." is the material conditional sign, provides a theory schema that can be converted into a theory by supplying an empirical interpretation. "W" and "X," for example, might be replaced by theoretical predicates and "Y" and "Z" by observational.

As an illustration, Carnap discusses the distinction between uninterpreted and interpreted axiom systems within geometry. Although it is possible to study formal systems as sets of axioms and deduce theorems that follow from them, it is also possible to provide them with an empirical interpretation whereby those axioms become theoretical hypotheses and those theorems empirically testable. By interpreting lines as paths of light rays and points as their intersections, Euclidean geometry can be converted from a domain of pure mathematics into one of applied mathematics, where previously purely formal claims assume the character of empirical hypotheses.

Suppe's "What's Wrong with the Received View on the Structure of Scientific Theories?" attacks the distinction between theoretical and observational language. Distinguishing between predicates and properties, Suppe suggests that sometimes *observational predicates* do not designate observable properties and that sometimes *theoretical predicates* do designate observable properties. When a blue object is shattered into minute pieces, it may no longer be possible to observe their blueness; and when I insert my thumb into a socket, I may observe an electric current. If this is the case, however, then the alleged distinction between them seems rather obscure.

Suppe also suggests the possibility of improving upon the standard conception by adopting an alternative analysis, known as *the semantic conception*. On this approach (in a simple version), *a scientific theory consists of a theoretical definition coupled with an empirical hypothesis*. A *classical particle system*, for example, might be defined as a system that obeys Newton's three laws of motion and law of universal gravitation, and the empirical hypothesis might be asserted that the sun and planets of our solar system are a classical particle system. On this view, the definition itself has the status of an analytic sentence, while the empirical hypothesis is viewed as synthetic.

Suppe wants to maintain that the semantic conception improves upon the standard conception because it sheds more light on certain important epistemic features of scientific theories. But there are at least two reasons to question such claims. The first concerns his attack upon the theoretical/observational language distinction itself. Another interpretation of Suppe's problematical cases would be to maintain that properties such as *blue* and *electrical current* exhibit diverse manifestations under different conditions precisely because they are properly viewed as dispositions. Thus, perhaps Suppe has misunderstood the ontological significance of his own examples.

The second concerns the semantic conception itself. While some definitions might stipulate that certain laws must be satisfied by systems of the kind that they define, these laws may or may not have the characteristics of natural laws. A *normal driving system* could be defined as a system of drivers, automobiles and highways that satisfies the valid-license law, the 65 mph speed-limit law, and the unexpired-auto-tag law. The empirical claim might then be made that Minnesota is a normal driving system. But even if this were true, it would completely fail to distinguish between laws of nature and laws of society or between genuine laws and merely accidental generalizations, a difficulty also confronted by the standard conception.

Hempel's "Provisoes: A Problem Concerning the Inferential Function of Scientific Theories" raises another difficulty for both of these conceptions. Suppose we assume that theories are properly understood as idealizations of the behavior that would be displayed by physical systems under certain (typically counterfactual) conditions. Then any inferences concerning past or future occurrences would depend upon logically contingent assumptions about the presence or absence of those conditions. Newton's theory of universal gravitation and three laws of motion, for example, presume that the bodies to which they are applied are unaffected by nongravitational forces.

Thus, "provisoes" should be envisioned as clauses that pertain to specific applications of a theory which asserts that, in those instances, no conditions other than those specified by the theory are present. The consequences of the role of provisoes include (i) that the falsification of a scientific theory is more complex than is commonly assumed, (ii) that programs for the elimination of theoretical terms from scientific theories are illusory, (iii) that the instrumentalist conception of scientific theories as calculating devices appears implausible, and (iv) that the notion of the empirical content of a scientific theory is far more problematic than has usually been supposed.

In view of Hempel's findings, at least two responses are available. One is to infer that scientific theories are only able to provide "explanations" or "predictions" of the behavior of actual things when they happen to display that behavior under ideal conditions. For any other conditions, those theories are, at best, mere approximations. The other is to infer that, in order to provide genuine explanations and predictions of the behavior of actual things, scientific theories must go beyond idealized conditions by taking into account every factor whose presence or absence makes a difference within that domain. As an ideal of science, mere approximation is not enough.

STUDY QUESTIONS

As you read the articles that appear in this section, you may want to think about their implications for understanding the nature of science and of philosophy. The following questions are intended to stimulate your thinking by focusing attention on some of the less obvious aspects of different positions.

(1) The standard conception of scientific theories as abstract calculi plus an *empirical* interpretation might also be employed to characterize theories in mathematics as abstract calculi plus an *abstract* interpretation. Would that make the standard conception more or less plausible? Would a distinction then have to be drawn between "pure" and "applied" mathematics as well?

(2) For a property to be observable appears to depend upon a causal interaction between observers and that property. If some persons are hard of hearing, some are color blind, and the like, how could an intersubjectively applicable standard for classifying properties be established? If none were possible, would that make observability merely a subjective phenomenon?

(3) Since the standard conception characterizes the abstract calculi which constitute the structure of scientific theories by means of extensional logic, how can it cope with the problem of distinguishing generalizations that are true and lawlike from those that are true but merely accidental? Would it be beneficial to appeal to Goodman's criteria to help resolve this problem?

(4) Suppe suggests that sometimes observation predicates designate properties that are not observable, and sometimes theoretical predicates designate properties that are observable. What do you think about the cases he uses to illustrate this difficulty? Can you think of any way in which a proponent of the standard conception could respond to examples like these?

(5) The simplest version of the semantic theory characterizes "theories" as definitions of kinds of systems, which are related to the world by means of "empirical hypotheses." The example of a normal driving system suggests that this version does not appear to be successful. Can you think of other cases that provide evidence against this version of the semantic account?

(6) If theories are counterfactual idealizations as Suppe suggests, how are they related to the world? How could we know when phenomena happen to satisfy the conditions they impose and when they do not? Are counterfactual idealizations suitable for the explanation and prediction of events?

(7) Hempel suggests that, if theories are counterfactual idealizations, then they can be applied for the purposes of explanation and prediction only in those cases in which the phenomena actually satisfy the conditions which they specify. In those cases, they will no longer be merely counterfactual idealizations. Does this consideration solve the problem or make it worse?

(8) The function of provisoes within Hempel's scheme is to affirm when the conditions specified by a theory are satisfied by physical systems in the world. Sometimes the conditions that are covered by provisoes might include the presence of nonobservable properties. Does that further undermine the old distinction between theoretical and observation language?

(9) When the empirical content of theories is supposed to be measured by the observable consequences that could be deduced from that theory, how does the problem of provisoes

render that notion more problematical than has previously been recognized? Why does Hempel think that testing theories empirically may be more complex than has commonly been assumed?

(10) An alternative conception might take the nature of *laws* to be more basic than the nature of *theories*, where a theory could be viewed as a set of laws and definitional sentences (which may be partial or complete) that apply to a common domain. Would this account improve upon the standard conception? Could it overcome problems with the semantic approach? What about the problem of provisoes?

RUDOLF CARNAP

THEORIES AND NONOBSERVABLES

I

One of the most important distinctions between two types of laws in science is the distinction between what may be called (there is no generally accepted terminology for them) empirical laws and theoretical laws. Empirical laws are laws that can be confirmed directly by empirical observations. The term "observable" is often used for any phenomenon that can be directly observed, so it can be said that empirical laws are laws about observables.

Here, a warning must be issued. Philosophers and scientists have quite different ways of using the terms "observable" and "nonobservable." To a philosopher, "observable" has a very narrow meaning. It applies to such properties as "blue," "hard," "hot." These are properties directly perceived by the senses. To the physicist, the word has a much broader meaning. It includes any quantitative magnitude that can be measured in a relatively simple, direct way. A philosopher would not consider a temperature of, perhaps, 80 degrees centigrade, or a weight of $93^{1}/_{2}$ pounds, an observable because there is no direct sensory perception of such magnitudes. To a physicist, both are observables because they can be measured in an extremely simple way. The object to be weighed is placed on a balance scale. The temperature is measured with a thermometer. The physicist would not say that the mass of a molecule, let alone the mass of an electron, is something observable, because here the procedures of measurement are much more complicated and indirect. But magnitudes that can be established by relatively simple procedures—length with a ruler, time with a clock, or frequency of light waves with a spectrometer—are called observables.

A philosopher might object that the intensity of an electric current is not really observed. Only a pointer position was observed. An ammeter was attached to the circuit and it was noted that the pointer pointed to a mark labeled 5.3. Certainly the current's intensity was not observed. It was *inferred* from what was observed.

The physicist would reply that this was true enough, but the inference was not very complicated. The procedure of measurement is so simple, so well established, that it could not be doubted that the ammeter would give an accurate measurement of current intensity. Therefore, it is included among what are called observables.

There is no question here of who is using the term "observable" in a right or proper way. There is a continuum which starts with direct sensory observations and proceeds to enormously complex, indirect methods of observation. Obviously no sharp line can be drawn across this continuum; it is a matter of degree. A philosopher is sure that the sound of his wife's voice, coming from across the room, is an observable. But suppose he listens to her on the telephone. Is her voice an observable or isn't it? A physicist would certainly say that when he looks at something through an ordinary microscope, he is observing it directly. Is this also the case when he looks into an electron microscope? Does he observe the path of a particle when he sees the track it makes in a bubble chamber? In general, the physicist speaks of observables in a very wide sense compared with the narrow sense of the philosopher, but, in both cases, the line separating observable from nonobservable is highly arbitrary. It is well to keep this in mind whenever these terms are encountered in a book by a philosopher or scientist. Individual authors will draw the line where it is most convenient, depending on their points of view, and there is no reason why they should not have this privilege.

Empirical laws, in my terminology, are laws containing terms either directly observable by the senses or measurable by relatively simple techniques. Sometimes such laws are called empirical generalizations, as a reminder that they have been obtained by generalizing results found by observations and measurements. They include not only simple qualitative laws (such as, "all ravens are black") but also quantitative laws that arise from simple measurements. The laws relating pressure, volume, and temperature of gases are of this type. Ohm's law, connecting the electric potential difference, resistance, and intensity of current, is another familiar example. The scientist makes repeated measurements, finds certain regularities, and expresses them in a law. These are the empirical laws. As indicated in earlier chapters,[1] they are used for explaining observed facts and for predicting future observable events.

There is no commonly accepted term for the second kind of laws, which I call *theoretical laws*. Sometimes they are called abstract or hypothetical laws. "Hypothetical" is perhaps not suitable because it suggests that the distinction between the two types of laws is based on the degree to which the laws are confirmed. But an empirical law, if it is a tentative hypothesis, confirmed only to a low degree, would still be an empirical law although it might be said that it was rather hypothetical. A theoretical law is not to be distinguished from an empirical law by the fact that it is not well established, but by the fact that it contains terms of a different kind. The terms of a theoretical law do not refer to observables even when the physicist's wide meaning for what can be observed is adopted. They are laws about such entities as molecules, atoms, electrons, protons, electromagnetic fields, and others that cannot be measured in simple, direct ways.

If there is a static field of large dimensions, which does not vary from point to point, physicists call it an observable field because it can be measured with a simple apparatus. But if the field changes from point to point in very small distances, or varies very quickly in time, perhaps changing billions of times each second, then it cannot be directly measured by simple techniques. Physicists would not call such a field an observable. Sometimes a physicist will distinguish between observables and nonobservables in just this way. If the magnitude remains the same within large enough spatial distances, or large enough time intervals, so that an apparatus can be applied for a direct measurement of the magnitude, it is called a *macroevent*. If the magnitude changes within such extremely small intervals of space and time that it cannot be directly measured by simple apparatus, it is a *microevent*. (Earlier authors used the terms "microscopic" and "macroscopic," but today many authors have shortened these terms to "micro" and "macro.")

A microprocess is simply a process involving extremely small intervals of space and time. For example, the oscillation of an electromagnetic wave of visible light is a microprocess. No instrument can directly measure how its intensity varies. The distinction between macro- and microconcepts is sometimes taken to be parallel to observable and nonobservable. It is not exactly the same, but it is roughly so. Theoretical laws concern nonobservables, and very often these are microprocesses. If so, the laws are sometimes called microlaws. I use the term "theoretical laws" in a wider sense than this, to include all those laws that contain nonobservables, regardless of whether they are microconcepts or macroconcepts.

It is true, as shown earlier, that the concepts "observable" and "nonobservable" cannot be sharply defined because they lie on a continuum. In actual practice, however, the difference is usually great enough so there is not likely to be debate. All physicists would agree that the laws relating pressure, volume, and temperature of a gas, for example, are empirical laws. Here the amount of gas is large enough so that the magnitudes to be measured remain constant over a sufficiently large volume of space and period of time to permit direct, simple measurements which can then be generalized into laws. All physicists would agree that laws about the behavior of single molecules are theoretical. Such laws concern a microprocess about which generalizations cannot be based on simple, direct measurements.

Theoretical laws are, of course, more general than empirical laws. It is important to understand, however, that theoretical laws cannot be arrived at simply by taking the empirical laws, then generalizing a few steps further. How does a physicist arrive at an empirical law? He observes certain events in nature. He notices a certain regularity. He describes this regularity by making an inductive generalization. It might be supposed that he could now put together a group of empirical laws, observe some sort of pattern, make a wider inductive generalization, and arrive at a theoretical law. Such is not the case.

To make this clear, suppose it has been observed that a certain iron bar expands when heated. After the experiment has been repeated many times, always with the same result, the regularity is generalized by saying that this bar expands when heated. An empirical law has been stated, even though it has a narrow range and applies only to one particular iron bar. Now further tests are made of other iron objects with the ensuing discovery that every time an iron object is heated it expands. This permits a more general law to be formulated, namely that all bodies of iron expand when heated. In similar fashion, the still more general laws "All metals . . . ," then "All solid bodies . . . ," are developed. These are all simple generalizations, each a bit more general than the previous one, but they are all empirical laws. Why? Because in each case, the objects dealt with are observable (iron, copper, metal, solid bodies); in each case the increases in temperature and length are measurable by simple, direct techniques.

In contrast, a theoretical law relating to this process would refer to the behavior of molecules in the iron bar. In what way is the behavior of the molecules connected with the expansion of the bar when heated? You see at once that we are now speaking of nonobservables. We must introduce a theory—the atomic theory of matter—and we are quickly plunged into atomic laws involving concepts radically different from those we had before. It is true that these theoretical concepts differ from concepts of length and temperature only in the degree to which they are directly or indirectly observable, but the difference is so great that there is no debate about the radically different nature of the laws that must be formulated.

Theoretical laws are related to empirical laws in a way somewhat analogous to the way empirical laws are related to single facts. An empirical law helps to explain a fact that has been observed and to predict a fact not yet observed. In similar fashion, the theoretical law helps to explain empirical laws already formulated, and to permit the derivation of new empirical laws. Just as the single, separate facts fall into place in an orderly pattern when they are generalized in an empirical law, the single and separate empirical laws fit into the orderly pattern of a theoretical law. This raises one of the main problems in the methodology of science. How can the kind of knowledge that will justify the assertion of a theoretical law be obtained? An empirical law may be justified by making observations of single facts. But to justify a theoretical law, comparable observations cannot be made because the entities referred to in theoretical laws are nonobservables.

Before taking up this problem, some remarks made in an earlier chapter, about the use of the word "fact," should be repeated. It is important in the present context to be extremely careful in the use of this word because some authors, especially scientists, use "fact" or "empirical fact" for some propositions which I would call empirical laws. For example, many physicists will refer to the "fact" that the specific heat of copper is .090. I would call this a law because in its full formulation it is seen to be a universal conditional statement: "For any x, and any time t, if x is a solid body of copper, then the specific heat of x at t is .090." Some physicists may even speak of the law of thermal expansion, Ohm's law, and others, as facts. Of course, they can then say that theoretical laws help explain such facts. This sounds like my statement that empirical laws explain facts, but the word "fact" is being used here in two different ways. I restrict the word to particular, concrete facts that can be spatio-temporally specified, not thermal expansion in general, but *the* expansion of this iron bar observed this morning at ten o'clock when it was heated. It is important to bear in mind the restricted way in which I speak of facts. If the word "fact" is used in an ambiguous manner, the important difference between the ways in which empirical and theoretical laws serve for explanation will be entirely blurred.

How can theoretical laws be discovered? We cannot say: "Let's just collect more and more data, then generalize beyond the empirical laws until we reach theoretical ones." No theoretical law was ever found that way. We observe stones and trees and flowers, noting various regularities and describing them by empirical laws. But no matter how long or how carefully we observe such things, we never reach a point at which we observe a molecule. The term "molecule" never arises as a result of observations. For this reason, no amount of generalization will ever produce a theory of molecular processes. Such a theory must arise in another way. It is stated not as a generalization of facts but as a hypothesis. The hypothesis is then tested in a manner analogous in certain ways to the testing of an empirical law. From the hypothesis, certain empirical laws are derived, and these empirical laws are tested in turn by observation of facts. Perhaps the empirical laws derived from the theory are already known and well confirmed. (Such laws may even have motivated the formulation of the theoretical law.) Regardless of whether the derived empirical laws are known and confirmed, or whether they are new laws confirmed by new observations, the confirmation of such derived laws provides indirect confirmation of the theoretical law.

The point to be made clear is this. A scientist does not start with one empirical law, perhaps Boyle's law for gases, and then seek a theory about molecules from which this law can be derived. The scientist tries to formulate a much more general theory from which a variety of empirical laws can be derived. The more such laws, the greater their variety and apparent lack of connection with one another, the stronger will be the theory that explains them. Some of these derived laws may have been known before, but the theory may also make it possible to derive new empirical laws which can be confirmed by new tests. If this is the case, it can be said that the theory made it possible to predict new empirical laws. The prediction is understood in a hypothetical way. If the theory holds, certain empirical laws will also hold. The predicted empirical law speaks about relations between observables, so it is now possible to make experiments to see if the empirical law holds. If the empirical law is confirmed, it provides indirect confirmation of the theory. Every confirmation of a law, empirical or theoretical, is, of course, only partial, never complete and absolute. But in the case of empirical laws, it is a more direct confirmation. The confirmation of a theoretical law is indirect, because it takes place only through the confirmation of empirical laws derived from the theory.

The supreme value of a new theory is its power to predict new empirical laws. It is true that it also has value in explaining known empirical laws, but this is a minor value. If a scientist proposes a new theoretical system, from which no new laws can be derived, then it is logically equivalent to the set of all known empirical laws. The theory may have a certain elegance, and it may simplify to some degree the set of all known laws, although it is not likely that there would be an essential simplification. On the other hand, every new theory in physics that has led to a great leap forward has been a theory from which new empirical laws could be derived. If Einstein had done no more than propose his theory of relativity as an elegant new theory that would embrace certain known laws—perhaps also simplify them to a certain degree—then his theory would not have had such a revolutionary effect.

Of course it was quite otherwise. The theory of relativity led to new empirical laws which explained for the first time such phenomena as the movement of the perihelion of Mercury, and the bending of light rays in the neighborhood of the sun. These predictions showed that relativity theory was more than just a new way of expressing the old laws. Indeed, it was a theory of great predictive power. The consequences that can be derived from Einstein's theory are far from being exhausted. These are consequences that could not have been derived from earlier theories. Usually a theory of such power does have an elegance, and a unifying effect on known laws. It is simpler than the total collection of known laws. But the great value of the theory lies in its power to suggest new laws that can be confirmed by empirical means.

II

An important qualification must now be added to the discussion of theoretical laws and terms given in the preceding section. The statement that empirical laws are derived from theoretical laws is an oversimplification. It is not possible to derive them directly because a theoretical law contains theoretical terms, whereas an empirical law contains only observable terms. This prevents any direct deduction of an empirical law from a theoretical one.

To understand this, imagine that we are back in the nineteenth century, preparing to state for the first time some theoretical laws about molecules in a gas. These laws are to describe the number of molecules per unit volume of the gas, the molecular velocities, and so forth. To simplify matters, we assume that all the molecules have the same velocity. (This was indeed the original assumption; later it was abandoned in favor of a certain probability distribution of velocities.) Further assumptions must be made about what happens when molecules collide. We do not know the exact shape of molecules, so let us suppose that they are tiny spheres. How do spheres collide? There are laws about colliding spheres, but they concern large bodies. Since we cannot directly observe molecules, we assume their collisions are analogous to those of large bodies; perhaps they behave like perfect billiard balls on a frictionless table. These are, of course, only assumptions; guesses suggested by analogies with known macrolaws.

But now we come up against a difficult problem. Our theoretical laws deal exclusively with the behavior of molecules, which cannot be seen. How, therefore, can we deduce from such laws a law about observable properties such as the pressure or temperature of a gas or properties of sound waves that pass through the gas? The theoretical laws contain only theoretical terms. What we seek are empirical laws containing observable terms. Obviously, such laws cannot be derived without having something else given in addition to the theoretical laws.

The something else that must be given is this: a set of rules connecting the theoretical terms with the observable terms. Scientists and philosophers of science have long recognized the need for such a set of rules, and their nature has been often discussed. An example of such a rule is: "If there is an electromagnetic oscillation of a specified frequency, then there is a visible greenish-blue color of a certain hue." Here something observable is connected with a nonobservable microprocess.

Another example is: "The temperature (measured by a thermometer and, therefore, an observable in the wider sense explained earlier) of a gas is proportional to the mean kinetic energy of its molecules." This rule connects a nonobservable in molecular theory, the kinetic energy of molecules, with an observable, the temperature of the gas. If statements of this kind did not exist, there would be no way of deriving empirical laws about observables from theoretical laws about nonobservables.

Different writers have different names for these rules. I call them "correspondence rules." P. W. Bridgman calls them "operational rules." Norman R. Campbell speaks of them as the "Dictionary."[2] Since the rules connect a term in one terminology with a term in another terminology, the use of the rules is analogous to the use of a French-English dictionary. What does the French word "cheval" mean? You look it up in the dictionary and find that it means "horse." It is not really that simple when a set of rules is used for connecting nonobservables with observables; nevertheless, there is an analogy here that makes Campbell's "Dictionary" a suggestive name for the set of rules.

There is a temptation at times to think that the set of rules provides a means for defining theoretical terms, whereas just the opposite is really true. A theoretical term can never be explicitly defined on the basis of observable terms, although sometimes an observable can be defined in theoretical terms. For example, "iron" can be defined as a substance consisting of small crystalline parts, each having a certain arrangement of atoms and each atom being a configuration of particles of a certain type. In theoretical terms then, it is possible to express what is meant by the observable term "iron," but the reverse is not true.

There is no answer to the question: "Exactly what is an electron?" Later we shall come back to this question, because it is the kind that philosophers are always asking scientists. They want the physicist to tell them just what he means by "electricity," "magnetism," "gravity," "a molecule." If the physicist explains them in theoretical terms, the philosopher may be disappointed. "That is not what I meant at all," he will say. "I want you to tell me, in ordinary language, what those terms mean." Sometimes the philosopher writes a book in which he talks about the great mysteries of nature. "No one," he writes, "has been able so far, and perhaps no one ever will be able, to give us a straightforward answer to the question: 'What is electricity?' And so electricity remains forever one of the great, unfathomable mysteries of the universe."

There is no special mystery here. There is only an improperly phrased question. Definitions that cannot, in the nature of the case, be given, should not be demanded. If a child does not know what an elephant is, we can tell him it is a huge animal with big ears and a long trunk. We can show him a picture of an elephant. It serves admirably to define an elephant in observable terms that a child can understand. By analogy, there is a temptation to believe that, when a scientist introduces theoretical terms, he should also be able to define them in familiar terms. But this is not possible. There is no way a physicist can show us a picture of electricity in the way he can show his child a picture of an elephant. Even the cell of an organism, although it cannot be seen with the unaided eye, can be represented by a picture because the cell can be seen when it is viewed through a microscope. But we do not possess a picture of the electron. We cannot say how it looks or how it feels, because it cannot be seen or touched. The best we can do is to say that it is an extremely small body that behaves in a certain manner. This may seem to be analogous to our description of an elephant. We can describe an elephant as a large animal that behaves in a certain manner. Why not do the same with an electron?

The answer is that a physicist can describe the behavior of an electron only by stating theoretical laws, and these laws contain only theoretical terms. They describe the field produced by an electron, the reaction of an electron to a field, and so on. If an electron is in an electrostatic field, its velocity will accelerate in a certain way. Unfortunately, the electron's acceleration is an unobservable. It is not like the acceleration of a billiard ball, which can be studied by direct observation. There is no way that a theoretical concept can be defined in terms of observables. We must, therefore, resign ourselves to the fact that definitions of the kind that can be supplied for observable terms cannot be formulated for theoretical terms.

It is true that some authors, including Bridgman, have spoken of the rules as "operational definitions." Bridgman had a certain justification, because he used his rules in a somewhat different way, I believe, than most physicists use them. He was a great physicist and was certainly aware of his departure from the usual use of rules, but he was willing to accept certain forms of speech that are not customary, and this explains his departure. It was pointed out in a previous chapter that Bridgman preferred to say that there is not just one concept of intensity of electric current, but a dozen concepts. Each procedure by which a magnitude can be measured provides an operational definition for that magnitude. Since there are different procedures for measuring current, there are different concepts. For the sake of convenience, the physicist speaks of just one concept of current. Strictly speaking, Bridgman believed, he should recognize many different concepts, each defined by a different operational procedure of measurement.

We are faced here with a choice between two different physical languages. If the customary procedure among physicists is followed, the various concepts of current will be replaced by one concept. This means, however, that you place the concept in your theoretical laws, because the operational rules are just correspondence rules, as I call them, which connect the theoretical terms with the empirical ones. Any claim to possessing a definition—that is, an operational definition—of the theoretical concept must be given up. Bridgman could speak of having operational definitions for his theoretical terms only because he was not speaking of a general concept. He was speaking of partial concepts, each defined by a different empirical procedure.

Even in Bridgman's terminology, the question of whether his partial concepts can be adequately defined by operational rules is problematic. Reichenbach speaks often of what he calls "correlative definitions." (In his German publications, he calls them *Zuordnungsdefinitionen*, from *zuordnen*, which means to correlate.) Perhaps correlation is a better term than definition for what Bridgman's rules actually do. In geometry, for instance, Reichenbach points out that the axiom system of geometry, as developed by David Hilbert, for example, is an uninterpreted axiom system. The basic concepts of point, line, and plane could just as well be called "class alpha," "class beta," and "class gamma." We must not be seduced by the sound of familiar words, such as "point" and "line," into thinking they must be taken in their ordinary meaning. In the axiom system, they are uninterpreted terms. But when geometry is applied to physics, these terms must be connected with something in the physical world. We can say, for example, that the lines of the geometry are exemplified by rays of light in a vacuum or by stretched cords. In order to connect the uninterpreted terms with observable physical phenomena, we must have rules for establishing the connection.

What we call these rules is, of course, only a terminological question; we should be cautious and not speak of them as definitions. They are not definitions in any strict sense. We cannot give a really adequate definition of the geometrical concept of "line" by referring to anything in nature. Light rays, stretched strings, and so on are only approximately straight; moreover, they are not lines, but only segments of lines. In geometry, a line is infinite in length and absolutely straight. Neither property is exhibited by any phenomenon in nature. For that reason, it is not possible to give an operational definition, in the strict sense of the word, of concepts in theoretical geometry. The same is true of all the other theoretical concepts of physics. Strictly speaking, there are no "definitions" of such concepts. I prefer not to speak of "operational definitions" or even to use Reichenbach's term "correlative definitions." In my publications (only in recent years have I written about this question), I have called them "rules of correspondence" or, more simply, "correspondence rules."

Campbell and other authors often speak of the entities in theoretical physics as mathematical entities. They mean by this that the entities are related to each other in ways that can be expressed by mathematical functions. But they are not mathematical entities of the sort that can be defined in pure mathematics. In pure mathematics, it is possible to define various kinds of numbers, the function of logarithm, the exponential function, and so forth. It is not possible, however, to define such terms as "electron" and "temperature" by pure mathematics. Physical terms can be introduced only with the help of nonlogical constants, based on observations of the actual world. Here we have an essential difference between an axiomatic system in mathematics and an axiomatic system in physics.

If we wish to give an interpretation to a term in a mathematical axiom system, we can do it by giving a definition in logic. Consider, for example, the term "number" as it is used in Peano's axiom system. We can define it in logical terms, by the Frege-Russell method, for example. In this way the concept of "number" acquires a complete, explicit definition on the basis of pure logic. There is no need to establish a connection between the number 5 and such observables as "blue" and "hot." The terms have only a logical interpretation; no connection with the actual world is needed. Sometimes an axiom system in mathematics is called a theory. Mathematicians speak of set theory, group theory, matrix theory, probability theory. Here the word "theory" is used in a purely analytic way. It denotes a deductive system that makes no reference to the actual world. We must always bear in mind that such a use of the word "theory" is entirely different from its use in reference to empirical theories such as relativity theory, quantum theory, psychoanalytical theory, and Keynesian economic theory.

A postulate system in physics cannot have, as mathematical theories have, a splendid isolation from the world. Its axiomatic terms—"electron," "field," and so on—must be interpreted by correspondence rules that connect the terms with observable phenomena. This interpretation is necessarily incomplete. Because it is always incomplete, the system is left open to make it possible to add new rules of correspondence. Indeed, this is what continually happens in the history of physics. I am not thinking now of a revolution in physics, in which an entirely new theory is developed, but of less radical changes that modify existing theories.

Nineteenth-century physics provides a good example, because classical mechanics and electromagnetics had been established, and, for many decades, there was relatively little change in fundamental laws. The basic theories of physics remained unchanged. There was, however, a steady addition of new correspondence rules, because new procedures were continually being developed for measuring this or that magnitude.

Of course, physicists always face the danger that they may develop correspondence rules that will be incompatible with each other or with the theoretical laws. As long as such incompatibility does not occur, however, they are free to add new correspondence rules. The procedure is never-ending. There is always the possibility of adding new rules, thereby increasing the amount of interpretation specified for the theoretical terms; but no matter how much this is increased, the interpretation is never final. In a mathematical system, it is otherwise. There a logical interpretation of an axiomatic term *is* complete. Here we find another reason for reluctance in speaking of theoretical terms as "defined" by correspondence rules. It tends to blur the important distinction between the nature of an axiom system in pure mathematics and one in theoretical physics.

Is it not possible to interpret a theoretical term by correspondence rules so completely that no further interpretation would be possible? Perhaps the actual world is limited in its structure and laws. Eventually a point may be reached beyond which there will be no room for strengthening the interpretation of a term by new correspondence rules. Would not the rules then provide a final, explicit definition for the term? Yes, but then the term would no longer be theoretical. It would become part of the observation language. The history of physics has not yet indicated that physics will become complete; there has been only a steady addition of new correspondence rules and a continual modification in the interpretations of theoretical terms. There is no way of knowing whether this is an infinite process or whether it will eventually come to some sort of end.

It may be looked at this way. There is no prohibition in physics against making the correspondence rules for a term so strong that the term becomes explicitly defined and therefore ceases to be theoretical. Neither is there any basis for assuming that it will always be possible to add new correspondence rules. Because the history of physics has shown such a steady, unceasing modification of theoretical concepts, most physicists would advise against correspondence rules so strong that a theoretical term becomes explicitly defined. Moreover, it is a wholly unnecessary procedure. Nothing is gained by it. It may even have the adverse effect of blocking progress.

Of course, here again we must recognize that the distinction between observables and nonobservables is a matter of degree. We might give an explicit definition, by empirical procedures, to a concept such as length, because it is so easily and directly measured, and is unlikely to be modified by new observations. But it would be rash to seek such strong correspondence rules that "electron" would be explicitly defined. The concept "electron" is so far removed from simple, direct observations that it is best to keep it theoretical, open to modifications by new observations.

III

In the previous section, the discussion concerned the ways in which correspondence rules are used for linking the nonobservable terms of a theory with the observable terms of empirical laws. This can be made clearer by a few examples of the manner in which empirical laws have actually been derived from the laws of a theory.

The first example concerns the kinetic theory of gases. Its model, or schematic picture, is one of small particles called molecules, all in constant agitation. In its original form, the theory regarded these particles as little balls, all having the same mass and, when the temperature of the gas is constant, the same constant velocity. Later it was discovered that the gas would not be in a stable state if each particle had the same velocity; it was necessary to find a certain probability distribution of velocities that would remain stable. This was called the Boltzmann-Maxwell distribution. According to this distribution, there was a certain probability that any molecule would be within a certain range on the velocity scale.

When the kinetic theory was first developed, many of the magnitudes occurring in the laws of the theory were not known. No one knew the mass of a molecule, or how many molecules a cubic centimeter of gas at a certain temperature and pressure would contain. These magnitudes were expressed by certain parameters written into the laws. After the equations were formulated, a dictionary of correspondence rules was prepared. These correspondence rules connected the theoretical terms with observable phenomena in a way that made it possible to determine indirectly the values of the parameters in the equations. This, in turn, made it possible to derive empirical laws. One correspondence rule states that the temperature of the gas corresponds to the mean kinetic energy of the molecules. Another correspondence rule connects the pressure of the gas with the impact of molecules on the confining wall of a vessel. Although this is a discontinuous process involving discrete molecules, the total effect can be regarded as a constant force pressing on the wall. Thus, by means of correspondence rules, the pressure that is measured macroscopically by a manometer (pressure gauge) can be expressed in terms of the statistical mechanics of molecules.

What is the density of the gas? Density is mass per unit volume, but how do we measure the mass of a molecule? Again our dictionary—a very simple dictionary—supplies the correspondence rule. The total mass M of the gas is the sum of the masses m of the molecules. M is observable (we simply weigh the gas), but m is theoretical. The dictionary of correspondence rules gives the connection between the two concepts. With the aid of this dictionary, empirical tests of various laws derived from our theory are possible. On the basis of the theory, it is possible to calculate what will happen to the pressure of the gas when its volume remains constant and its temperature is increased. We can calculate what will happen to a sound wave produced by striking the side of the vessel, and what will happen if only part of the gas is heated. These theoretical laws are worked out in terms of various parameters that occur within the equations of the theory. The dictionary of correspondence rules enables us to express these equations as empirical laws, in which concepts are measurable, so that empirical procedures can supply values for the parameters. If the empirical laws can be confirmed, this provides indirect confirmation of the theory. Many of the empirical laws for gases were known, of course, before the kinetic theory was developed. For these laws, the theory provided an explanation. In addition, the theory led to previously unknown empirical laws.

The power of a theory to predict new empirical laws is strikingly exemplified by the theory of electromagnetism, which was developed about 1860 by two great English physicists, Michael Faraday and James Clerk Maxwell. (Faraday did most of the experimental work, and Maxwell did most of the mathematical work.) The theory dealt with electric charges and how they behaved in electrical and magnetic fields. The concept of the electron—a tiny particle with an elementary electric charge—was not formulated until the very end of the century. Maxwell's famous set of differential equations, for describing electromagnetic fields, presupposed only small discrete bodies of unknown nature, capable of carrying an electric charge or a magnetic pole. What happens when a current moves along a copper wire? The theory's dictionary made this observable phenomenon correspond to the actual movement along the wire of little charged bodies. From Maxwell's theoretical model, it became possible (with the help of correspondence rules, of course) to derive many of the known laws of electricity and magnetism.

The model did much more than this. There was a certain parameter c in Maxwell's equations. According to his model, a disturbance in an electromagnetic field would be propagated by waves having the velocity c. Electrical experiments showed the value of c to be approximately 3×10^{10} centimeters per second. This was the same as the known value for the speed of light, and it seemed unlikely that it was an accident. Is it possible, physicists asked themselves, that light is simply a special case of the propagation of an electromagnetic oscillation? It was not long before Maxwell's equations were providing explanations for all sorts of optical laws, including refraction, the velocity of light in different media, and many others.

Physicists would have been pleased enough to find that Maxwell's model explained known electrical and magnetic laws; but they received a double bounty. The theory also explained optical laws! Finally, the great strength of the new model was revealed in its power to predict, to formulate empirical laws that had not been previously known.

The first instance was provided by Heinrich Hertz, the German physicist. About 1890, he began his famous experiments to see whether electromagnetic waves of low frequency could be produced and detected in the laboratory. Light is an electromagnetic oscillation and propagation of waves at very high frequency. But Maxwell's laws made it possible for such waves to have *any* frequency. Hertz's experiments resulted in his discovery of what at first were called Hertz waves. They are now called radio waves. At first, Hertz was able to transmit these waves from one oscillator to another over only a small distance—first a few centimeters, then a meter or more. Today a radio broadcasting station sends its waves many thousands of miles.

The discovery of radio waves was only the beginning of the derivation of new laws from Maxwell's theoretical model. X-rays were discovered and were thought at first to be particles of enormous velocity and penetrative power. Then it occurred to physicists that, like light and radio waves, these might be electromagnetic waves, but of extremely high frequency, much higher than the frequency of visible light. This also was later confirmed, and laws dealing with X-rays were derived from Maxwell's fundamental field equations. X-rays proved to be waves of a certain frequency range within the much broader frequency band of gamma rays. The X-rays used today in medicine are simply gamma rays of certain frequency. All this was largely predictable on the basis of Maxwell's model. His theoretical laws, together with the correspondence rules, led to an enormous variety of new empirical laws.

The great variety of fields in which experimental confirmation was found contributed especially to the strong overall confirmation of Maxwell's theory. The various branches of physics had originally developed for practical reasons; in most cases, the divisions were based on our different sense organs. Because the eyes perceive light and color, we call such phenomena optics; because our ears hear sounds, we call a branch of physics acoustics; and because our bodies feel heat, we have a theory of heat. We find it useful to construct simple machines based on the movements of bodies, and we call it mechanics. Other phenomena, such as electricity and magnetism, cannot be directly perceived, but their consequences can be observed.

In the history of physics, it is always a big step forward when one branch of physics can be explained by another. Acoustics, for instance, was found to be only a part of mechanics, because sound waves are simply elasticity waves in solids, liquids, and gases. We have already spoken of how the laws of gases were explained by the mechanics of moving molecules. Maxwell's theory was another great leap forward toward the unification of physics. Optics was found to be a part of electromagnetic theory. Slowly the notion grew that the whole of physics might some day be unified by one great theory. At present there is an enormous gap between electromagnetism on the one side and gravitation on the other. Einstein made several attempts to develop a unified field theory that might close this gap; more recently, Heisenberg and others have made similar attempts. So far, however, no theory has been devised that is entirely satisfactory or that provides new empirical laws capable of being confirmed.

Physics originally began as a descriptive macrophysics, containing an enormous number of empirical laws with no apparent connections. In the beginning of a science, scientists may be very proud to have discovered hundreds of laws. But, as the laws proliferate, they become unhappy with this state of affairs; they begin to search for underlying, unifying principles. In the nineteenth century, there was considerable controversy over the question of underlying principles. Some felt that science must find such principles, because otherwise it would be no more than a description of nature, not a real explanation. Others thought that that was the wrong approach, that underlying principles belong only to metaphysics. They felt that the scientist's task is merely to describe, to find out *how* natural phenomena occur, not *why*.

Today we smile a bit about the great controversy over description versus explanation. We can see that there was something to be said for both sides, but that their way of debating the question was futile. There is no real opposition between explanation and description. Of course, if description is taken in the narrowest sense, as merely describing what a certain scientist did on a certain day with certain materials, then the opponents of mere description were quite right in asking for more, for a real explanation. But today we see that description in the broader sense, that of placing phenomena in the context of more general laws, provides the only type of explanation that can be given for phenomena. Similarly, if the proponents of explanation mean a metaphysical explanation, not grounded in empirical procedures, then their opponents were correct in insisting that science should be concerned only with description. Each side had a valid point. Both description and explanation, rightly understood, are essential aspects of science.

The first efforts at explanation, those of the Ionian natural philosophers, were certainly partly metaphysical; the world is all fire, or all water, or all change. Those early efforts at scientific explanation can be viewed in two different ways. We can say: "This is not science, but pure metaphysics. There is no possibility of confirmation, no correspondence rules for connecting the theory with observable phenomena." On the other hand, we can say: "These Ionian theories are certainly not scientific, but at least they are pictorial visions of theories. They are the first primitive beginnings of science."

It must not be forgotten that, both in the history of science and in the psychological history of a creative scientist, a theory has often first appeared as a kind of visualization, a vision that comes as an inspiration to a scientist long before he has discovered correspondence rules that may help in confirming his theory. When Democritus said that everything consists of atoms, he certainly had not the slightest confirmation for this theory. Nevertheless, it was a stroke of genius, a profound insight, because two thousand years later his vision was confirmed. We should not, therefore, reject too rashly any anticipatory vision of a theory, provided it is one that may be tested at some future time. We are on solid ground, however, if we issue the warning that no hypothesis can claim to be scientific unless there is the *possibility* that it can be tested. It does not have to be confirmed to be a hypothesis, but there must be correspondence rules that will permit, in principle, a means of confirming or disconfirming the theory. It may be enormously difficult to think of experiments that can test the theory; this is the case today with various unified field theories that have been proposed. But if such tests are possible in principle, the theory can be called a scientific one. When a theory is first proposed, we should not demand more than this.

The development of science from early philosophy was a gradual, step-by-step process. The Ionian philosophers had only the most primitive theories. In contrast, the thinking of Aristotle was much clearer and on more solid scientific ground. He made experiments, and he knew the importance of experiments, although in other respects he was an apriorist. This was the beginning of science. But it was not until the time of Galileo Galilei, about 1600, that a really great emphasis was placed on the experimental method in preference to aprioristic reasoning about nature. Even though many of Galileo's concepts had previously been stated as theoretical concepts, he was the first to place theoretical physics on a solid empirical foundation. Certainly Newton's physics (about 1670) exhibits the first comprehensive, systematic theory, containing unobservables as theoretical concepts: the universal force of gravitation, a general concept of mass, theoretical properties of light rays, and so on. His theory of gravity was one of great generality. Between any two particles, small or large, there is a force proportional to the square of the distance between them. Before Newton advanced this theory, science provided no explanation that applied to both the fall of a stone and the movements of planets around the sun.

It is very easy for us today to remark how strange it was that it never occurred to anyone before Newton that the same force might cause the apple to drop and the moon to go around the earth. In fact, this was not a thought likely to occur to anyone. It is not that the *answer* was so difficult to give; it is that nobody had asked the *question*. This is a vital point. No one had asked: "What is the relation between the forces that heavenly bodies exert upon each other and terrestrial forces that cause objects to fall to the ground?" Even to speak in such terms as "terrestrial" and "heavenly" is to make a bipartition, to cut nature into two fundamentally different regions. It was Newton's great insight to break away from this division, to assert that there is no such fundamental cleavage. There is one nature, one world. Newton's universal law of gravitation was the theoretical law that explained for the first time both the fall of an apple and Kepler's laws for the movements of planets. In Newton's day, it was a psychologically difficult, extremely daring adventure to think in such general terms.

Later, of course, by means of correspondence rules, scientists discovered how to determine the masses of astronomical bodies. Newton's theory also said that two apples, side by side on a table, attract each other. They do not move toward each other because the attracting force is extremely small and the friction on the table very large. Physicists eventually succeeded in actually measuring the gravitational forces between two bodies in the laboratory. They used a torsion balance consisting of a bar with a metal ball on each end, suspended at its center by a long wire attached to a high ceiling. (The longer and thinner the wire, the more easily the bar would turn.) Actually, the bar never came to an absolute rest but always oscillated a bit. But the main point of the bar's oscillation could be established. After the exact position of the mean point was determined, a large pile of lead bricks was constructed near the bar. (Lead was used because of its great specific gravity. Gold has an even higher specific gravity, but gold bricks are expensive.) It was found that the mean of the oscillating bar had shifted a tiny amount to bring one of the balls on the end of the bar nearer to the lead pile. The shift was only a fraction of a millimeter, but it was enough to provide the first observation of a gravitational effect between two bodies in a laboratory—an effect that had been predicted by Newton's theory of gravitation.

It had been known before Newton that apples fall to the ground and that the moon moves around the earth. Nobody before Newton could have predicted the outcome of the experiment with the torsion balance. It is a classic instance of the power of a theory to predict a new phenomenon not previously observed.

NOTES

1. Editor's note—Here and elsewhere throughout his discussion, Carnap is referring to earlier chapters of his book *The Philosophy of Science* (New York: Basic Books, 1966). The present essay constitutes chapters 23–25 of that book.
2. See Percy W. Bridgman, *The Logic of Modern Physics* (New York: Macmillan, 1927), and Norman R. Campbell, *Physics: The Elements* (Cambridge: Cambridge University Press, 1920). Rules of correspondence are discussed by Ernest Nagel, *The Structure of Science* (New York: Harcourt, Brace & World, 1961), pp. 97–105.

FREDERICK SUPPE

WHAT'S WRONG WITH THE RECEIVED VIEW ON THE STRUCTURE OF SCIENTIFIC THEORIES?

For some time the *Received View* on scientific theories has been that theories are to be construed as axiomatic calculi in which theoretical terms are given a partial observational interpretation by means of correspondence rules; underlying this analysis is a strict bifurcation of the nonlogical terms of the theory into an observational vocabulary and a theoretical vocabulary. Recently Putnam, Achinstein, and others have urged the rejection of the received view analysis of scientific theories because (i) the notion of partial interpretation employed cannot be given a precise formulation adequate for the purposes of the received view, and (ii) the observational–theoretical distinction cannot be drawn satisfactorily.[1] It is the contention of this paper that the received view is unsatisfactory and ought to be rejected, but that reasons (i) and (ii) are the wrong reasons for rejecting it. Section I of this paper claims that reason (i) is false and that it is virtually impossible to establish reason (ii). Part II attempts to show that the received view, nonetheless, is unsatisfactory and ought to be rejected because its reliance on the observational–theoretical distinction causes it to obscure a number of epistemologically important and revealing features of the structure of scientific theories. In the process of arguing for this latter claim, a more adequate account of the epistemological structure of scientific theories is presented.

I

Achinstein's and Putnam's arguments in support of reason (i) for rejecting the received view proceed by observing that the notion of partial interpretation has not been made clear by advocates of the received view, considering a number of possible explications of the notion, and then showing that they are inadequate for the purposes of the received view. ([1], pp. 85–91; [19], pp. 244–48.) In [24] I have given a precise account of partial interpretation which is adequate for the purposes of the received view. Rather than duplicate that discussion here, I will merely claim on the basis of [24] that reason (i) is false, and confine my attention to reason (ii).

The arguments which Achinstein and Putnam advance in support of reason (ii) ([1], chapters 5, 6; [19], pp. 240–44) attempt to show that

(a) The observational-theoretical distinction cannot be drawn on the basis of the ordinary usage of scientific terms.

Of course (ii) follows from (a) only if the further assumption is made that

(b) To be tenable for the purposes of the received view, the observational–theoretical distinction must be drawn on the basis of the ordinary usage of scientific terms.

This latter assumption neither is made explicit nor argued for in [1] or [9]. As such, Achinstein and Putnam have not made their case. But I wish to establish something stronger—namely that (a) is true whereas it is virtually impossible to establish (b). However, I do not want to base my claim that (a) is true on their arguments; for I do not find them wholly satisfactory: Achinstein's arguments only show that the observational–theoretical distinction cannot be drawn on the basis of ordinary usage in the ways Carnap and others have suggested, and so establish a conclusion that is weaker than (a); and Putnam's arguments contain numerous lacunae. Rather, I will refine the sorts of considerations they raise into a much tighter and stronger argument for (a); then I will use features of that argument to argue that (b) is virtually impossible to establish.

In order to argue for my conclusions about (a) and (b), a fuller characterization of the received view is needed. Versions of the received view have been advanced by a number of authors, including Braithwaite ([2], pp. 22 ff.), Campbell ([4], chapter 6), Carnap (e.g., [5], p. 43), Duhem ([7], p. 19), Hempel ([9], [10]), Hesse ([11], [12]), Kaplan ([13], pp. 298–99), Margenau ([15]), Nagel ([16], p. 90), Northrop ([17]), Ramsay ([21], pp. 212–36), and Reichenbach ([22], chapter 8). Although there are a number of differences (some of them significant) in these various versions of the received view,[2] there is a substantial core of agreement among them. In particular, most proponents of the received view would agree on the following: The received view is not advanced as a descriptive account of how theories are formulated in actual scientific practice; rather it presents a canonical linguistic formulation for theories and claims that any scientific theory can be given an essentially equivalent reformulation in this canonical way. As such it is advanced as an explication of the notion of a scientific theory.[3] Moreover, it is claimed that this canonical linguistic formulation for theories will display the essential epistemic features of scientific theories. Such a canonical linguistic formulation will have the following epistemologically revealing features: (1) The theory consists of theoretical laws and correspondence rules formulated in a language L[4]; (2) the nonlogical vocabulary of L can be exhaustively bifurcated into a *observational vocabulary*, V_o, consisting of terms which refer to directly observable attributes or entities, and a *theoretical vocabulary*, V_T, consisting of terms which refer to attributes or entities which are not directly observable; (3) the *laws* of the theory are formulated as sentences of L whose only nonlogical terms are from V_T; (4) the *correspondence rules* are formulated as sentences of L which contain terms from V_o and also from V_T, and are intended to embody various experimental procedures, etc., for applying the laws of the theory to directly observable phenomena[5]; (5) the meanings of the V_o terms are completely specified in terms of their corresponding directly observable attributes or entities; (6) no direct observational interpretation or meaning is given to the V_T terms, they being given an indirect partial empirical interpretation by the correspondence rules and the laws of the theory.

Requirement (2) of the received view stipulates that the nonlogical terms of L be bifurcated into two disjoint classes—the observation terms and the theoretical terms. Since this distinction lies at the heart of the received view analysis, one would expect that, in advancing the received view, its proponents would have extensively discussed the nature of this bifurcation and the basis upon which it is drawn. In point of fact, however, all one usually finds in the literature is a very few examples of what would count as observation terms and what would count as theoretical terms. The most extensive discussion I have found of the observational–theoretical distinction by a proponent of the received view is in Carnap's *Philosophical Foundations of Physics*. Carnap begins by stating that "the term 'observable' is often used for any phenomenon that can be *directly observed*" ([6], p. 225, emphasis added). He then observes that this use of 'observable' is not that of the scientist, and that he intends to use the term in a very narrow sense "to apply to such properties as 'blue', 'hard', 'hot',", etc., which are "properties directly perceived by the senses" (ibid.). In defending his somewhat special sense of "observable" he says:

There is no question of who [the philosopher or the scientist] is using the term "observable" in a right or proper way. There is a continuum which starts with direct sensory observations and proceeds to enormously complex, indirect methods of observation. Obviously no sharp line can be drawn across this continuum; it is a matter of degree. . . . In general the physicist speaks of observables in a very wide sense compared with the narrow sense of the philosopher, but, in both cases, the line separating observables from nonobservables is highly arbitrary. (Ibid., p. 226.)

Thus far Carnap is discussing the use of the term "observable," and its application to attributes, things, events, objects, etc., the claim being that he is using the term to apply to such attributes and entities, etc., which can be directly perceived by the senses; from this it follows that attributes, entities, events, objects, etc., are to be divided into two classes—the observable and the nonobservable. In terms of this distinction Carnap bifurcates the nonlogical constants of L:

The terms of V_o are predicates designating observable properties of events or things (e.g., "blue," "hot," "large," etc.) or observable relationships between them (e.g., "x is warmer than y," "x is contiguous to y," etc.). ([5], p. 40.)

On the other hand, V_T contains the theoretical terms, which are often called "theoretical constructs" or "hypothetical constructs," and are intended to refer to such entities as electrons, etc., and their attributes. The vocabularies V_o and V_T constitute an exhaustive bifurcation of the nonlogical constants of L into the class of those which refer to observable attributes or entities, and the class of those which refer to nonobservable or theoretical entities or attributes.

Carnap apparently believes that the bifurcation into V_o and V_T can be drawn on the basis of the standard usages of nonlogical terms, in, e.g. scientific English. For example, Carnap writes:

For many years it has been found useful to divide *the terms of a scientific language* into three main groups.

1. Logical terms, including all of mathematics.
2. Observational terms, or O-terms.
3. Theoretical terms, or T-terms (sometimes called "constructs").

It is true, of course, as has been emphasized in earlier chapters, that no sharp boundary separates the O-terms from the T-terms. The choice of an exact line is somewhat arbitrary. From a practical point of view, however, the distinction is usually evident. Everyone would agree that words for properties, such as "blue," "hard," "cold," and words for relations, such as "warmer," "heavier," "brighter," are O-terms, whereas "electric charge," "proton," "electromagnetic field" are T-terms referring to entities that cannot be observed in a relatively simple, direct way. ([6], p. 259, emphasis added.)

Thus V_o will contain all those terms of a natural scientific language such as scientific English which in their normal usage refer to observables, and V_T will contain all the nonlogical terms of that language which refer to nonobservables in their normal usage; moreover V_o and V_T are jointly exhaustive of the nonlogical terms of the language L (cf. requirement (2) above).[6] The received view thus seems to presuppose that a bifurcation of the nonlogical terms of a natural scientific language (such as scientific English) into theoretical and observational terms can be drawn on the basis of ordinary usage. Of course, it remains to be seen whether it is necessary for the received view to make that presupposition.

Although Carnap usually does not make it clear, it is obvious from this discussion that the observational–theoretical bifurcation is a dual dichotomy. First, there is a bifurcation of entities, properties, etc., into those which are capable of direct observation and those which are not. Second, the terms in natural languages of science such as scientific English are bifurcated into two disjoint classes—the observational terms and the theoretical terms. These two bifurcations must parallel each other in the sense that a term may be included among the observational terms just in case it is used only in reference to directly observable attributes or entities. Or, differently put, the bifurcation of terms is drawn on the basis of the bifurcation of attributes and entities into the directly-observable and the nondirectly-observable. (In case an artificial language L is used, in setting up L we divide the nonlogical constants of L into those terms which are allowed to stand for, abbreviate, or correspond to observational terms of, say, scientific English and those which are not.)

Is the observational–theoretical dichotomy a viable one? The answer to this question turns on what answers can be given to the following three subsidiary questions: (1) Is it possible to dichotomize entities and attributes on the basis of whether they are directly observable or not, and if so what will be the nature of the dichotomy? (2) Is it the case that terms of, e.g. scientific English under normal scientific usage can be bifurcated into the observational and the theoretical? (3) If the answers to the first two questions are affirmative, then are the two bifurcations coextensive?

(1) In one of the quotations above Carnap suggests that the property of being blue would be a paradigmatic observable property, by which he means that it is a property the presence of which is directly ascertainable without recourse to complicated apparatus. But this is too imprecise. Is he claiming that a property is observable if its presence *sometimes* is ascertainable by direct observation? Or must it *always* be so ascertainable? If he intends the latter, then the property of being blue is not directly observable: although there are cases where I can directly ascertain whether things are blue, when objects are sufficiently small it will be impossible to do so. Similarly, consider another of Carnap's paradigm examples: being warmer than. While there are circumstances where I can directly ascertain that something is warmer than some-thing else (e.g. the water in the shower before and after adjusting it), there are numerous circumstances where it is in principle impossible to directly observe that something is warmer than another thing because my sensory apparatus will not function at the temperatures

involved. For example, although an object at $-250°C$ *is* warmer than an object at $-273°C$, I cannot directly observe that this is the case even if recourse to simple apparatus is allowed. Similarly, I cannot directly observe that one portion of the sun is warmer than another. Since direct observation precludes recourse to elaborate instrumentation, reliance on spectrographic evidence, and so on, in order to directly observe that one part of the sun is warmer than another I would have to be at those places on the sun and compare their warmth. But this is humanly impossible. Minimally, I would have to wear protective clothing which would allow only a safe amount of heat to reach me; but then I would be directly observing that the air inside my space suit was warmer when I was in one location than it was when I was in another, and not that one part of the sun is warmer than another. The latter could be determined only indirectly—e.g., by using known heat transfer properties of my protective dress. To conclude: even though it may be possible to determine by direct observation whether a particular attribute obtains under certain circumstances, the same attribute often will obtain in circumstances where it is impossible in principle to determine whether it does or does not obtain.

Since Carnap takes attributes such as being blue and being warmer than as paradigmatic examples of directly observable attributes, it follows that it is not necessary that one should be able in principle to ascertain by direct observation whether a directly observable attribute obtains in *every* circumstance in which it could obtain; rather, it is required that there be *some* circumstances in which it is possible in principle to ascertain by direct observation whether the attribute obtains. *Since there is a strict bifurcation of attributes into the directly-observable and the nondirectly-observable* (which for convenience we call *nonobservables*), *it follows that an attribute is nonobservable if, for every circumstance in which it could obtain, it is in principle impossible to ascertain by direct observation whether it obtains.* Thus, for example, the property of being a gas must be directly observable since it is possible to directly observe the presence of certain gases under certain circumstances (e.g., I can smell sulfur gas). And being electrically charged is directly observable since by sticking my finger into a socket I can directly observe the presence of the electrical charge; and similarly static electricity, forces, accelerations, gravitational attractions, etc., would qualify as directly-observables since we sometimes can directly observe their presence.[7] But this is clearly unsatisfactory since we now are forced to count as directly observable various attributes which clearly should count as nonobservables.

To summarize: if we require that an attribute's presence *always* must be ascertainable in principle by direct observation in order for it to be directly observable, then the paradigmatic directly observables (e.g., the property of being blue) fail to qualify as being so; and if we require only that their presence *sometimes* be so ascertainable, then paradigmatic nondirectly-observables (e.g., the property of being a gas) become directly observables.

The problems we are encountering in attempting to draw a line between observable and nonobservable properties, etc., stem from the fact that many attributes of scientific relevance have both directly observable and nondirectly-observable occurrences, which makes any natural division into the observable and the nonobservable impossible. If an observational–nonobservational distinction is to be drawn, this observation suggests it ought to be drawn on the basis of occurrences of attributes rather than on the basis of attributes simpliciter. Then, perhaps on the basis of the limits in discrimination of human sensory apparatus, we would say that this attribute-occurrence is observable whereas that is not. Thus we might say that an occurrence of the property blue is observable if it is characteristic of an area larger than area A; or that for objects between such and such dimension the attribute of one being longer than the

FREDERICK SUPPE • 115

other is a directly-observable attribute-occurrence, but if the objects are of larger or smaller size, then that one is longer than the other is not a directly-observable attribute-occurrence. Assuming this can be done in a sufficiently precise and general manner (which is by no means obvious), it would then be possible to distinguish observable occurrences and nonobservable occurrences of attributes and entities. What we are doing here, in effect, is defining two new attributes (e.g., *observable-red* and *nonobservable-red*) in terms of the old attribute (e.g., *red*), and replacing the old one by the two new ones. Thus we would say that the barn has the property of being O-red (observable-red) whereas the microscopic blood speck is N-red (nonobservable red). This, of course, has rather unusual consequences. If I take an O-red object of minimal area and smash it to pieces, the pieces will not be O-red, but rather N-red. And if I combine together a number of N-red blood specks I will obtain an O-red blood patch. More complicated situations are encountered in the case of relations. If I heat an object at t' to a certain degree it will be O-warmer than it was at time t, but if I heat the object still more at t'' it may be that the object is too hot for "O-warmer than" to apply: in such a case the object presumably will be N-warmer at t'' than it was at t. Some provision will have to be made to allow comparisons between nonobservable and observable occurrences of properties, and also for comparative relations whose applications straddle the observable—nonobservable boundaries. It is not clear whether this proposal is workable; but it is clear that it will be rather complicated if it is. It is equally clear from considerations raised above that some such division of attribute-occurrences into the observable and the nonobservable is required if we are to obtain an observational–nonobservational dichotomy for attributes which is anything like the one Carnap needs.

(2) Since the observational–theoretical bifurcation of terms can be drawn along Carnap's lines only if a bifurcation of properties, etc., into the observable and nonobservable can be drawn satisfactorily, let us assume that the dichotomy has been drawn along the rough lines suggested above. Is it then the case that a natural bifurcation of terms can be drawn on its basis? The linguistic analogues to the problems raised above now confront us. For we can use such paradigmatic observation terms as "blue," "is warmer than," etc., to refer to both observable and nonobservable occurrences of properties (in the discussion of (1) we used such terms in precisely this way), and so we are faced with two choices: We may employ the terms in their natural uses—in which case observational terms sometimes have nonobservable referents and theoretical terms sometimes have observable referents—or we may adopt special uses—say "red$_o$," and "red$_t$," together with the rule of usage that the former may be used to refer only to observable occurrences of red and the latter only to nonobservable occurrences. The latter option will require introducing rather complicated semantic rules into the language, including rules which enable us to use, e.g., "red$_o$" and "red$_t$," comparatively. Whether any sufficiently precise and general rules can be specified is not clear.

(3) Turning to the question whether the bifurcations discussed under (1) and (2) are coextensive, the above discussions lead immediately to the following conclusion: On the basis of ordinary linguistic usage there is no natural bifurcation of terms into the observational and the theoretical which is coextensive with any reasonable distinction between either observable and nonobservable attributes and entities, or observable and nonobservable occurrences of attributes and entities. Only in an artificial or reconstructed language L could the distinction be drawn naturally. Hence the truth of claim (a) follows.

It is notorious that Carnap and most other proponents of the received view have little respect for ordinary usage as instruments of precision in philosophical analysis, and so it would seem that the truth of claim (a) should not bother them so long as a viable observational–theoretical distinction can be drawn in some other way. For if this is possible, their mistake in supposing that it could be drawn on the basis of ordinary usage does not in itself seriously jeopardize the tenability of the received view. Can the observational–theoretical distinction be drawn in some other way? That is, what is the status of claim (b)?

The underlying motivation for the observational–theoretical distinction is the idea that statements which describe what can be directly observed are relatively nonproblematic as to truth, whereas those which describe what cannot be directly observed are more problematic as to truth; moreover, the verification of scientific theories must ultimately rest on the non-problematic evidence supplied by the senses. Accordingly, any observational–theoretical distinction which reflects the division of nonlogical statements into those which can be directly verified on the basis of the senses and those which cannot should be acceptable to proponents of the received view. In particular, a dichotomy of terms which parallels what we intuitively would accept as a bifurcation of occurrences of attributes and entities into the observable and the nonobservable should be satisfactory for the purposes of the received view. Our discussion above makes it clear that such a distinction will have to proceed roughly along the lines sketched in (1) and (2) above. Thus, demonstrating the falsity of claim (b) amounts to showing that no such distinction can be drawn on the basis of occurrences of attributes and entities. And this in turn would amount to showing that the sort of division of occurrences of attributes and entities that was proposed in (1) is impossible.

How would one show that such a division is impossible? To show that any such division will be an "artificial" convention won't do, since Carnap and others admit that it will be. To discuss problems about borderline cases won't do, since someone like Carnap can admit these and make conventional conservative decisions about how to handle these cases. And to consider various proposed divisions and attack them cannot demonstrate the impossibility of drawing such a distinction. In fact, it seems that the only way one could show such a division impossible would be to show either that no finite characterization of the division is possible or else that any possible division which clearly makes observable occurrences directly observable will result in such an impoverished stock of observable occurrences that most of science could not be confirmed. The chances of successfully demonstrating either of these contentions seems quite remote. Accordingly, it appears virtually impossible to establish claim (b). And since claim (a) leads to reason (ii) only if claim (b) can be established, it follows that reason (ii) for rejecting the received view has not been established. This together with the fact that reason (i) is false, is sufficient warrant to conclude that Achinstein and Putnam are urging the rejection of the received view for the wrong reasons.

II

Our consideration of the observational–theoretical distinction makes it clear that if the distinction can be drawn in a manner satisfactory for the purposes of the received view, things will be exceedingly complex. The fact that science manages to go about its business without involving itself in such complexities suggests that the distinction is not really required or presupposed by science, and so is extraneous to an adequate analysis of scientific theories. The question, then, is whether the observational–theoretical distinction is required for an adequate analysis of the epistemological structure of theories. More specifically, is it possible to give an analysis of the structure of theories which does not employ the observational–theoretical distinction and yet is epistemologically more revealing than the received view? If such an analysis can be shown possible, then I think we have sufficient reason for rejecting the received view.

Those who claim that the observational–theoretical distinction is an essential ingredient of an adequate analysis of scientific theories apparently justify this contention with the following line of argument.[8]:

Scientific theories are developed to explain or predict events which can be observed; however, for reasons of simplicity, scope, and economy, such theories typically must employ theoretical entities or constructs in providing these explanations or predictions; these theoretical constructs are not directly observable. Accordingly, in any theoretical explanation or prediction one finds two sorts of sentences: (a) various premises the truth of which is nonproblematic in virtue of their being confirmed by direct observation; (b) various laws the truth of which is problematic since they cannot be confirmed by direct observation. And the observational–theoretical distinction is needed to keep distinct the different statuses of these two kinds of sentences.

This picture is partially correct. Evidently it is the case that in theoretical explanation and prediction (the latter especially so when the predictions are made in order to test the theory) the truth of the laws used often is problematic, whereas the truth of the evidential premises used in conjunction with the laws is assumed to be nonproblematic. Thus far the dichotomist's argument is satisfactory. But to infer from this that the premises are nonproblematic in virtue of being observational statements and the laws problematic in virtue of being nonobservational ones is unwarranted; for it amounts to assuming as an additional premise in the argument that to be nonproblematic is to be an observational statement. Not only does this premise beg the question, but it also seems false. For the purposes of explanation and prediction all that is required is that the data premises used with the theory be considered nonproblematic relative to the theory or law which provides the prediction or explanation. That is, in application of a theory (or law) to phenomena what we do is collect data about phenomena; the process of collecting the data often involves recourse or rather sophisticated bodies of theory. If accepted standards of experimental design, control, instrumentation—and possibly involved reliability checks—are carried out, a body of "hard" data is obtained from experimentation and is taken to be relatively nonproblematic; sometimes generally accepted laws or theories are also employed in obtaining these "hard" data.[9] And it is to this body of "hard" data that the theory is applied. If the purpose of the application is explanation, then the theory explains the event under the description provided by this "hard" data by relating it to other "hard" data which function as descriptions of other features which were the cause of the event so described.[10] If the point of the application of the theory is prediction, then the initial "hard" data are used as premises from which to obtain predictions as to the "hard" data one subsequently would obtain. And these "hard" data may be quite theory-laden, hence nondirectly observable. In addition, what counts as "hard" or nonproblematic data is relative—for should the theory's predictions fail we may come to treat the data as problematic again.[11] Thus the relevant distinction is between "hard" data and the more problematic theories, and not between the directly observable and the nondirectly-observable. Accordingly, the correspondence rules for a theory should not correlate direct-observation statements with theoretical statements, but rather should correlate "hard" data with theoretical statements. Thus, it seems that the observational–theoretical distinction is not essential to an adequate analysis of the structure of scientific theories.

Suggestive as it may be, this line of argument does not establish the inadequacy of the received view. For an advocate of it could accept this line of argument and still deny the conclusion, arguing as follows: "It is true that in actual scientific practice theories are pitted against 'hard' data. But what makes these data 'hard' is that they ultimately rest on directly observable evidence; and in the received-view reconstruction of theories that dependence of 'hard' data on the direct evidence of the senses is reflected in the correspondence rules. Why, even the relativity of 'hard' data can be accommodated in terms of changes in the correspondence rules." There is little doubt that this can be built into the correspondence rules; but the relevant question is whether it can be done without obscuring important epistemological features of scientific theorizing. When one reflects that the reliance of the theory on the results and procedures of related branches of science, the design of experiments, the interpretation of theories, calibration procedures, etc., are all being lumped into the correspondence rules, there seems to be reason to suspect that, by doing so, a number of epistemologically important and revealing aspects of scientific theorizing are being obscured.

And I want to maintain that this is so: because of its reliance on the observational–theoretical distinction, the received view's account of correspondence rules must combine together a number of widely disparate aspects of the scientific enterprise in such a manner as to obscure a number of epistemologically important and revealing aspects of scientific theorizing. To support this contention it will be necessary to sketch a more adequate alternative account of scientific theories which reveals what the received view's treatment of correspondence rules obscures. The notion of a *physical system* provides us with a convenient starting point for sketching and motivating this alternative account. A science does not deal with phenomena in all of their complexity, but rather is concerned with certain kinds of phenomena only insofar as their behavior is determined by or characteristic of a small number of parameters abstracted from those phenomena. Thus, in characterizing falling bodies classical particle mechanics is concerned with only those aspects of falling-body behavior which depend upon mass, velocity, distance traveled over time, etc. The color of the object, etc., are aspects of the phenomena which are ignored. But the process of abstraction from the phenomena goes one step further— we are not concerned with actual velocities, etc., but rather with velocity under idealized conditions (e.g., in a frictionless environment, with the mass the object would have if it were concentrated at an extensionless point, etc.). Thus, for example, classical particle mechanics is concerned with the behavior of isolated systems of extensionless point-masses which interact in a vacuum, where the behavior of these point-masses depends only on their positions and momenta at a given time. A physical system for classical particle mechanics consists of such a system of point-masses undergoing a particular behavior over time. Physical systems, then, are highly abstract and idealized replicas of phenomena, being characterizations of how the phenomena *would have* behaved *had* the idealized conditions been met. And so, e.g., classical particle mechanics characterizes the phenomena within its scope in terms of the physical systems corresponding to the phenomena.

In arguing that scientific theories are concerned to characterize the behavior of physical systems, and not phenomena, I may seem to be making the case too easy for myself by using the example of classical particle mechanics—which is what Quine has called a "limit myth," and so is particularly susceptible of my treatment.[12] A brief consideration of a few examples will indicate that this is not so and display the generality of my treatment. First, classical thermodynamics, statistical mechanics, and quantum mechanics embody essentially the same "limit myth," and easily can be shown susceptible to my treatment (cf. [23], chapter 3, for details). Second, the gas laws (e.g., Boyle's law and Charles' law) describe the behavior of ideal gases, not real gases; yet they are used to work with actual gases. Here, the ideal gases described by the laws are the physical systems, and subject to appropriate experimental design, etc., they correspond to actual gases as idealized replicas. Third, the valence theory of chemical reactions describes the way theoretically pure chemical substances react together. But such pure substances are fictional ideals to which the substances in actual chemical reactions always are only approximations. The theory describes physical systems which are chemical reactions theoretically pure substances undergo, and with appropriate experimental and quality controls we can approximate the fiction that our actual substances are pure substances, and thereby treat the actual chemical reactions (phenomena) as if they were idealized reactions between pure substances (physical systems). Fourth, the genetical theory of natural selection characterizes evolutionary phenomena in terms of changes in the distributions of genotypes in populations as a function of reproductive rates, reproductive barriers, cross-over frequencies, etc. As such, the theory treats populations of individuals (phenomena) as if they were idealized populations of genotypes (physical systems) whose changes in genotypic distributions are functions of only a few selected factors. (In [26], section IX, the applicability of the analysis of theories being presented here to the genetical theory of natural selection is worked out in detail.) Fifth, stimulus-response behavioral theories attempt to characterize various kinds of behavior as functions of selected stimulus and response parameters. Such theories describe the behavior of populations of idealized individuals whose behavior is only a function of the specified stimulus and response patterns, reinforcement schedules, etc. (physical systems). The behavior of individuals in actual populations of, e.g., rats or humans (phenomena), is not simply a function of these selected parameters, etc., and only under the most strictly controlled laboratory conditions can the fiction be approximated that the behavior of individuals in actual populations is a function only of the selected parameters. The theories thus describe the behavior of physical systems, not phenomena. Similarly, consideration of grammatical theories of linguistic competence, kinship system theories, theories in animal physiology, etc., will show that they describe the behavior of idealized systems or mechanisms of which actual systems or mechanisms are only idealized approximations to varying degrees. Although brief and sketchy, these examples suffice to illustrate the variety of theories susceptible of my treatment; further, the variety of these examples strongly suggests that scientific theories in general describe the behavior of physical systems which are idealized replicas of actual phenomena.

In general a scientific theory has the task of describing, predicting, and (possibly) explaining a class of phenomena. It does so by selecting and abstracting certain idealized parameters from the phenomena, and then characterizing a class of abstract replicas of the phenomena which are characterized in terms of the selected idealized parameters; these abstract replicas are physical systems. The theory thus provides a comprehensive characterization of the behavior of phenomena under the idealized conditions characteristic of the physical systems corresponding to the phenomena; typically this characterization enables one to predict the behavior of physical systems over time.[13] When coupled with an appropriate experimental methodology, the theory can also predict, explain, etc., phenomena which do not meet these idealized conditions by displaying how these phenomena *would have* behaved *had* the idealized conditions been met. How this is accomplished is discussed below.

A central task of a theory, then, is to present descriptive, predictive, and possibly explanatory accounts of the behavior of physical systems which correspond to phenomena. The theory is not concerned merely with providing such an account for just the phenomena we do in fact observe, but rather with providing such an account for any phenomenon of the sort we *might* encounter in *any* causally possible universe.[14] That is, the theory must provide a predictive, and possibly explanatory, characterization of all those physical systems which correspond (as abstract replicas) to any phenomenon of the sort which one might encounter in any causally possible universe. Let us call this class of physical systems the class of *causally possible physical systems*. A central task of any scientific theory is to provide a precise characterization of the set of causally possible physical systems for the theory.

How does the theory provide such a characterization? Once the relevant parameters for the theory have been abstracted and selected from the phenomena, the physical systems for the theory can be specified in terms of these parameters, a physical system being a possible behavior pattern specifiable in terms of these parameters. For example, in classical particle mechanics we would specify a state of a physical system in terms of the values of the position and momentum parameters at a given time, and then characterize a physical system as a possible sequence of states over time. Of the physical systems which it is logically possible to specify in terms of the chosen parameters, only some will be empirically possible. For example, some of them will be incompatible with existing bodies of theory, etc. Of those which are compatible with accepted bodies of theory only some of them will be causally possible—in the sense that only some of them will correspond (as abstract idealized replicas) to phenomena which could be observed in some causally possible universe. The theory must specify which of the logically possible physical systems are causally possible; typically it does so by providing general laws which it is claimed characterize the behavior patterns characteristic of just the causally possible physical systems—in such a way that these laws can yield predictions of subsequent states when employed in conjunction with specifications of initial states and boundary conditions. For example, in classical particle mechanics the equations of motion provide a general description of the class of causally possible physical systems wherein the characterization of a particular causally possible physical system can be obtained by solving the equations of motion relative to specified boundary conditions and an initial state; the solution of the equations of motion together with the initial state of the physical system can then be manipulated to yield predictions of subsequent states of the system.[15]

The account of theories just sketched seems to cohere closely with the actual formulations of many theories in the physical sciences. If it is substantially correct, then an observational–theoretical distinction is not required in an adequate analysis of the structure of scientific theories; this is so because theories are not concerned primarily with applying laws directly to phenomena, but rather with using laws to predict and explain the behavior of physical systems abstracted from phenomena in such a manner that the behavior of these physical systems can be correlated with phenomena. These conclusions obviously will have important implications concerning the received view's notion of a correspondence rule—which implications we now explore. We begin by seeing how the "hard" data relate to physical systems and their corresponding phenomena. The observation reports or "hard" data to which the theory is applied are partial descriptions of the behavior of some physical system, the physical system being an abstract replica of the phenomena from which the data were collected. The collection of these data not only involves performing measurements upon the phenomena which determine the "actual" values of the chosen parameters at different times, but also involves employing various correction procedures (such as using friction coefficients, etc.) to alter the observed data into data representing the measurement results which *would have been* obtained *had* the defining features of the idealized parameters of the physical system been met by the phenomena. Thus, in classical particle mechanics our data do not represent, e.g., the velocity with which the milk bottle actually fell, but rather the velocity with which it *would have* fallen *had* it fallen in a vacuum, *had* it been a point mass, etc. That is, in a typical predictive or explanatory application of a theory, the "hard" data employed are data about the behavior of a physical system at certain times rather than about the actual behavior of the corresponding phenomena. And as such, the "hard" data will be expressed in terms of the basic parameters common to the physical systems and the theory—which is to say, in terms of what might be called the "theoretical" vocabulary. Once these "hard" data are obtained, perhaps together with "hard" data about boundary conditions, etc., they are used in conjunction with the laws of the theory to deduce various predictions, explanations, etc., about the physical systems. These deductions typically are "calculational" in nature. For example, in classical particle mechanics these calculations might consist in solving the basic equations of motion for special-case solutions, and then "plugging in" values of the parameters to calculate subsequent states of the physical system. Typically the predicted data about these subsequent states of the physical system are then converted into data about the corresponding phenomena by reversing the procedures used originally to convert the data about the phenomena to data about their corresponding physical systems.

What we have here, then, is a two-stage move from raw phenomena to statements of the theory—first a move from phenomena to "hard" data about the physical system in question, and then a second move from the physical system to the postulates, etc., of the theory.[16] The two sorts of moves are qualitatively quite different, the former being essentially empirical or experimental—being in effect a "translation" from the phenomena to an idealized description of it in the vocabulary of the theory's formalism, and the latter being essentially mathematical or computational in nature.

This perspective, together with the observation that theories have "hard" data reports as their primary subject matter rather than direct-observation reports, invites reassessment of the received view's account of the correspondence rules. For the rules of correspondence amalgamate together the two sorts of moves just discussed so as to eliminate the physical system. We might be tempted to reject the received view treatment of correspondence rules on the ground that most paradigmatic exact theories in physics and chemistry do work in terms of physical systems in the manner we've indicated, and hence the received view is inadequate since it fails to take them into account. While this is a somewhat appealing line, given the explicative character of the received view analysis it is not clear how far the criticism cuts. However, if there are important epistemological features of scientific theorizing which are obscured by failure to countenance physical systems, then we will be justified in insisting that the received view is defective and epistemologically misleading by failing to include them.

The second stage moves from data about the physical system to the theory (e.g., the various predictions, etc., about subsequent behavior of the physical system calculated on the basis of these data and the laws or postulates of the theory) are essentially computational in nature; if the theory is a quantitative one they will be essentially mathematical involving the solution of equations of motion, various auxiliary definitions and hypotheses, etc.[17]; and at no time are counterfactual inferences involved. On the other hand, the transition from phenomena to a physical system (or vice versa) involves processes of measurement equipment design, experimental techniques, interpretation and correction of raw data, the employment of theory from other branches of science, etc. And the transition from phenomena to physical system, is, as we have remarked above, fundamentally counterfactual—being a characterization of what the phenomena *would have been* under idealized circumstances. From these characteristics it follows that the ways a transition from a physical system to theory can go wrong will be quite different from the ways that the transition from phenomena to a physical system can go wrong. And in the case of a disconfirming experiment, if the source of the difficulty can be isolated as occurring in the transition from phenomenon to physical system (i.e., the data weren't as "hard" as we'd thought), the resolution of the disconfirmation does not require alteration of the theory—the theory was not at fault, but rather poor experimental procedure was followed (e.g., the instrumentation was miscalibrated, the wrong corrective factors were applied to the raw data, etc.). Only if it is the case that the disconfirmation cannot be attributed to the transition from the phenomenon to a physical system (i.e., the data are as "hard" as we had supposed) will resolution of the defects require alteration or modification of the theory itself.[18] It seems amply clear from these observations that there is considerable epistemic difference between the two transitions, and that attention to these differences exposes some rather characteristic features of the relations holding between theory and phenomena. The correspondence rules of the received view obscure these differences since they lump together all these various aspects of the relations holding between theory and phenomena into the one correspondence-rule transition. This in particular means that experimental errors, etc., which result in disconfirming instances of a theory will require modification of the correspondence rules and hence of the theory itself; for the correspondence rules are part of the theory and embody a complete specification of all allowable experimental procedures, etc. Another problem with the received view's treatment of correspondence rules is that there is little reason to suppose that an exhaustive explicit specification of allowable experimental procedures, etc., of the sort required can be given for most theories.[19]

It seems quite obvious, then, that the received view's characterization of the correspondence rules gives a quite misleading account of the ways in which theories correlate with phenomena, and that in doing so a number of characteristic and important epistemic features of scientific theorizing are obscured. If physical systems are employed as outlined above, and if the transition between phenomena and theory is characterized in the two- (or more) stage manner sketched above, not only do we obtain an epistemologically more revealing picture of scientific theorizing, but also the need for an observational–theoretical dichotomy disappears. For at no point in that picture is such a dichotomy needed. In place of that dichotomy we have a distinction between nonproblematic "hard" data about physical systems and boundary conditions, etc., and the more problematic theoretically obtained assertions about these systems.[20] And in place of the correspondence rules to provide a bridge between theory and phenomena, we have two-stage transitions: (a) the transitions from phenomena to physical systems, the characterization of which reduces to problems of measurement, experimental design, counterfactuals, etc.; and (b) the connections between the theory and physical systems which are deductively determined by the (often mathematical) apparatus of the theory and require no additional correspondence rules or postulates other than boundary conditions and data about the initial state of the physical system. The former transitions are not part of the theoretical apparatus of the theory, but rather belong to the experimental procedures used in applying the theory to phenomena; and the latter transitions are essentially computational in nature.

Our suggested alternative account of the structure of scientific theories enables us to see another way in which the received view is unsatisfactory. If we are correct that the subject matter of a theory is the behavior of physical systems and that the "hard" data include experimental data about the behavior of physical systems, then the central distinction between the nonproblematic "hard" data and the more problematic theoretical assertions about physical systems cannot be drawn on the basis of language; for the defining parameters of the physical systems (e.g., position and momentum coordinates in classical particle mechanics) are the basic parameters of the theory, and so the same "theoretical" terms will be used to provide linguistic characterizations of both the theory and the "hard" data. That is, the relevant distinction here is not a linguistic one, but rather an epistemological one. The fact that the key distinction here is not a linguistic one indicates that a number of epistemologically revealing features of the structure of scientific theories are not reflected in their linguistic formulations, and so they cannot be characterized adequately by an analysis of the language of theories. Herein lies the ultimate inadequacy of the received view.

III

To summarize, I have tried to show that the sort of criticisms raised against the received view by Achinstein and Putnam do not succeed in showing its inadequacy. Nonetheless the received view is unsatisfactory since its reliance on the observational–theoretical distinction obscures much that is epistemologically important and revealing about how theories relate to or connect with phenomena. To show this is so, I have sketched an alternative analysis of the structure of theories and used it to show how the received view obscures the role of physical systems, the way in which extratheoretical postulates provide nonexhaustive characterizations of the admissible transitions between phenomena and physical systems, and wherein lies the role of counterfactuals in connecting theories with phenomena. These epistemic revelations do not exhaust the potential of the alternative account. To indicate just some of its potential, further development of the analysis (e.g., along the lines of [28]) will reveal much more about the experimental relations holding between phenomena and physical systems; the isolation of the counterfactual component of scientific theorizing in the transition between phenomena and physical systems provides a perspective which, conceivably, could advance us towards a breakthrough on the problem of laws and counterfactuals; and for the exact sciences, there is ample evidence that this sort of account can be expanded and developed so as to give a particularly revealing account of exact theories (e.g., the sorts of revelations about phase spaces, the connections between deterministic and indeterministic theories, etc., to be found in [30] and [23], chapter 2).

What's wrong with the received view? It obscures much of epistemic importance which other analyses can reveal; and it should be rejected in favor of such an alternative analysis. In arguing for this conclusion, I have tried to sketch what that alternative analysis should be.

NOTES

1. Cf. [19] and [1], pp. 85–91, 157–58, 197–202; [1] incorporates with minor changes Achinstein's earlier writings on the subject. In [19] Putnam also urges that the observational–theoretical distinction is untenable because it is misleading both to label the class of nonobservational terms "theoretical terms" and to characterize sentences formulated solely in terms of the observational vocabulary and sentences formulated solely in terms of the theoretical vocabulary as observational sentences and theoretical sentences respectively. While this is true, it hardly necessitates rejection of the received view. In [1], pp. 199–201, Achinstein suggests that it will be epistemologically more revealing if we

avoid reliance on an observational–theoretical distinction in our analysis of theories, though he advances this as a corollary to his arguments in support of (ii). In both cases, the strength of their contention that the received view should be rejected lies in the establishment of (i) and (ii), and we shall confine our attention to those arguments.

I would like to thank Mr. Nicholas Georgalis and my colleagues, Professors Thomas Nickles and Robert Stalnaker for helpful comments on earlier drafts of this paper. I would also like to thank the referees of the journal *Philosophy of Science* for suggesting various improvements.

2. The primary disagreements are on the form of the correspondence rules. Campbell, Nagel, Hesse, and Kaplan maintain that in addition to satisfying conditions (1)–(6), the theory also must possess realizable or concrete models. Kaplan deviates from the other authors in that he claims that the analysis only works for one type of theory. Hempel no longer adheres to the received view, and now holds a similar position in which the observational–theoretical distinction is replaced by a different bifurcation of terms not drawn on the basis of direct observations; cf. [8] for details.

3. For an assessment of this claim, cf. my [23], pp. 38–46.

4. In many versions of the received view, the language L is supposed to be a symbolic language such as a first-order predicate calculus augmented by modal operators (e.g. in Carnap [5]); other authors allow L to be a natural language such as scientific English. Apparently the motivation for employing symbolic languages is the increased precision and more precise deductive mechanism of symbolic logics. We will see below that the plausibility of an observational–theoretical bifurcation of terms depends to an extent on whether L is natural or artificial.

5. Correspondence rules are referred to by various authors as *coordinating definitions, dictionaries, interpretative systems, operational definitions, epistemic correlations*, and *rules of interpretation*. Most authors impose further restrictions on the forms these correspondence rules have.

6. In case the L used in the received view canonical formulation is a symbolic language of the sort used by Carnap in [5], then V_o would contain predicates which correspond to, e.g. English observational terms, and V_T would contain predicates which correspond to, e.g. English theoretical terms. Regardless of whether the L used in the received view is a natural or an artificial language, then, the V_o–V_T distinction apparently would be drawn on the basis of standard usages in some natural language.

7. I can imagine that some proponents of the received view will protest here that I do not directly observe, e.g., that something is a gas, but rather that I observe certain manifestations of the presence of the gas; accordingly, the property of being a gas never can be directly observed. But this argument fails; for if this is legitimate, then it seems equally legitimate to argue that I do not directly observe that something is hard, but rather I observe certain manifestations of the thing being hard; and so one can never directly observe the property of being hard, and so it is not a directly observable property—contrary to the fact that Carnap advances it as a paradigmatic example of a directly observable property.

It should also be noted that the received view does not limit direct observation to visual perception; direct observation can be by any sense, as Carnap's own examples in the quotations above make clear.

Although the argument here proceeds in terms of attributes, it is clear that analogous arguments could be given, and similar conclusions drawn, for entities; for simplicity of exposition we present the arguments just for attributes.

8. At one time proponents of the received view also might have justified introducing the dichotomy by appeal to considerations of cognitive significance and a thesis about language acquisition. The apparent failure of the positivistic account of cognitive significance and the falsity of the thesis about language acquisition make it both unlikely and undesirable that the received view advocate should argue it on these grounds.

9. This discussion has benefited from conversations with Professor Don E. Dulany. Cf. [18] for Putnam's treatment of the use of such auxiliary hypotheses; cf. also [30] for related discussion.

10. This rough characterization of the role of data in explanation turns on an observation—insufficiently considered in the literature on explanation—that explanations do not explain events simpliciter, but rather explain *events under a particular description*. While it is beyond the scope of this article to

argue it here, this observation apparently can be exploited to show that the alleged symmetry between explanation and prediction collapses.

11. Cf. Quine's introduction to [20] for a discussion of this point.

12. I wish to thank the referees of *Philosophy of Science* for pointing out the need of considering this sort of objection.

13. For brevity, I confine my attention here just to theories which describe the behavior of physical systems in terms of changes in state over time. In addition to such theories with laws of succession, the analysis also will work for theories with laws of coexistence or laws of interaction. Also, it makes no difference whether the laws are deterministic or statistical. Cf. [25], section V–C, and also related discussion in [30], for details.

14. The problems of characterizing causally possible universes are many; but they can be viewed roughly as the class of universes in which all the laws assumed nonproblematic relative to the theory in question hold. For a detailed characterization of the notion of a causally possible universe, see [3], chapter 5. Our purpose in introducing the notion is to employ it in introducing the notion of a causally possible physical system. As the rough characterization just given captures those aspects of the notion of a causally possible universe which are relevant to our limited purposes here, we need not concern ourselves here with the difficult problem of providing an adequate characterization of causally possible universes.

15. On this account a theory may be construed as defining a class of theoretically possible physical systems; the theory will be empirically true just in case this class is identical with the class of causally possible physical systems. The account of empirical truth just specified is essentially a generalization of that introduced in my [24]. In both cases the idea is that you have a class of systems determined theoretically and a class determined empirically, the theory being empirically true just in case the classes are coextensive. Thus, intuitively, the class of causally possible physical systems is the class of physical systems which are empirically possible. Further consideration of this key notion of a causally possible physical system can be found in my [23], chapters 1, 2; for a detailed working-out of such an analysis of theories for the exact sciences, cf. chapter 2 of my [23]; this detailed account is similar in many respects to work on theories done by E. W. Beth and extended by B. van Fraassen in [30]. A generalization of the analyses in [23] and [30] is found in section V–C of my [25], together with further arguments in its support.

16. Actually this is still an oversimplification, the former move involving many more steps; cf. chapter 3 of my [23], Section IV–C of my [25], and also Suppes' discussion in [28] and [29].

17. For an illuminating discussion of what's involved in this sort of move, cf. [18].

18. For a detailed discussion of this point, cf. chapter 3 of my [23].

19. For a more detailed discussion of this last point, cf. [14] where Kuhn discusses the role of exemplars in the application of theories to phenomena; cf. also my commentary on [14] in [27].

20. Hempel now rejects the received view and in [8] advances an analysis based on a distinction similar to this. He distinguishes between a *theoretical vocabulary* and *an antecedently available vocabulary*, where the latter may include theoretical terms from generally accepted theories. His proposal differs from ours in that he thinks the relevant distinction can be drawn on linguistic grounds, whereas we explicitly deny that it can. His analysis differs in other respects as well—especially on the nature of the transition between the hard data and the theory of this so-called *bridge principles*.

REFERENCES

[1] Achinstein, P. *Concepts of Science*. Baltimore: Johns Hopkins Press, 1968.
[2] Braithwaite, R. B. *Scientific Explanation*. New York: Harper Torchbooks, 1953.
[3] Burks, A. *Cause, Chance, and Reason*. Ann Arbor: University of Michigan Press.
[4] Campbell, N. *Foundations of Science*. New York: Dover, 1957.

[5] Carnap, R. "Methodological Character of Theoretical Concepts." *Minnesota Studies in the Philosophy of Science*, vol. 1. Ed. H. Feigl, et al. Minneapolis: University of Minnesota Press, 1956, pp. 38–76.

[6] ———. *Philosophical Foundations of Physics*. New York: Basic Books, 1966.

[7] Duhem, P. *Aim and Structure of Physical Theory*. New York: Atheneum, 1954.

[8] Hempel, C. "Formulation and Formalization of Scientific Theories." *The Structure of Scientific Theories*. Ed. F. Suppe. Urbana: University of Illinois Press, 1972.

[9] ———. *Fundamentals of Concept Formation in Physical Science*. Chicago: University of Chicago Press, 1952.

[10] ———. "The Theoretician's Dilemma." *Minnesota Studies in the Philosophy of Science*, vol. 2. Ed. H. Feigl, et al. Minneapolis: University of Minnesota Press, 1958, pp. 37–98.

[11] Hesse, M. *Forces and Fields*. New York: Philosophical Library, 1962.

[12] ———. *Models and Analogies in Science*. London: Sheed and Ward, 1963.

[13] Kaplan, A. *The Conduct of Inquiry*. San Francisco: Chandler Publishing Co., 1964.

[14] Kuhn, T. "Second Thoughts on Paradigms." *The Structure of Scientific Theories*. Edited by F. Suppe. Urbana: University of Illinois Press, 1972.

[15] Margenau, H. *Nature of Physical Reality*. New York: McGraw-Hill, 1950.

[16] Nagel, E. *Structure of Science*. New York: Harcourt, Brace, and World, 1961.

[17] Northrop, F. S. C. *Logic of Science and Humanities*. New York: MacMillan, 1949.

[18] "Summary-Abstract: 'Scientific Explanation,' by Hilary Putnam." Forthcoming in *The Structure of Scientific Theories*. Edited by F. Suppe. Urbana: University of Illinois Press, 1972.

[19] Putnam, H. "What Theories Are Not." *Logic, Methodology, and the Philosophy of Science*. Edited by E. Nagel, P. Suppes, and A. Tarski. Stanford: Stanford University Press, 1962, pp. 240–51.

[20] Quine, W. *Methods of Logic*. Rev. ed. New York: Holt, Rinehart, and Winston, 1959.

[21] Ramsey, F. *Foundations of Mathematics*. New York: Humanities Press, 1931.

[22] Reichenbach, H. *Rise of Scientific Philosophy*. Berkeley: University of California Press, 1962.

[23] Suppe, F. *The Meaning and Use of Models in Mathematics and the Exact Sciences*. Ph.D. dissertation. Ann Arbor: University of Michigan, 1967.

[24] ———. "On Partial Interpretation." *Journal of Philosophy* 68 (1971), pp. 57–76.

[25] ———. "The Search for Philosophic Understanding of Scientific Theories." Forthcoming in *The Structure of Scientific Theories*. Ed. F. Suppe. Urbana: University of Illinois Press, 1972.

[26] ———. "Some Philosophical Problems in Biological Speciation and Taxonomy." In the proceedings of the *First Ottawa Conference on the Conceptual Basis of Classification* held at the University of Ottawa, Ottawa, Ontario, Canada, October 1–5, 1971.

[27] ———, ed. *The Structure of Scientific Theories*. Urbana: University of Illinois Press, 1972.

[28] Suppes, P. "Models of Data." *Logic, Methodology, and Philosophy of Science*. Edited by E. Nagel, et al. Stanford: Stanford University Press, 1962, pp. 252–61.

[29] ———. "What is in Scientific Theory?" *Philosophy of Science Today*. Ed. S. Morgenbesser. New York: Basic Books, 1967, pp. 55–67.

[30] van Fraassen, B. "On the Extension of Beth's Semantics of Physical Theories." *Philosophy of Science* 37 (1970): 325–39.

CARL G. HEMPEL

PROVISOES: A PROBLEM CONCERNING THE INFERENTIAL FUNCTION OF SCIENTIFIC THEORIES[1]

INTRODUCTION

The principal goal and the proudest achievement of scientific inquiry is the construction of comprehensive theories which give us an understanding of large classes of empirical phenomena and enable us to predict, to retrodict, and to explain them.

These various functions of theories are usually regarded as having the character of inferences which lead, by way of theoretical principles, from sentences expressing initial and boundary conditions to statements describing the occurrences to be predicted, retrodicted, or explained.

In this paper, I propose to examine a basic difficulty which faces this inferential construal of scientific theorizing and which has implications for some central issues in the philosophy of science. I will first present the problem by reference to a purely deductivist conception of theoretical reasoning and will then broaden its scope.

THE STANDARD DEDUCTIVIST MODEL

The best-known precise elaboration of a deductivist conception is provided by the so-called standard empiricist construal of theories and their application. It views a theory T as characterizable by an ordered pair consisting of a set C containing the basic principles of the theory and a set I of interpretative statements:

(1) $T = \langle C; I \rangle$

The sentences, or formulas, of C serve to characterize the specific entities and processes posited by the theory (e.g., elementary particles and their interactions) and to state the basic laws to which they are assumed to conform. These sentences are formulated with the help of a theoretical vocabulary, V_C, whose terms refer to the kinds and characteristics of the theoretical entities and processes in question.

The sentences of the interpretative set I serve to link the theoretical scenario represented by C to the empirical phenomena to which the theory is to be applied. These phenomena are taken to be formulated in a vocabulary V_A which is antecedently understood, i.e., which is available and understood independently of the theory. Thus, the sentences of I are said to provide partial interpretations, though not necessarily full definitions, of the theoretical terms in V_C by means of the antecedently understood terms of V_A. So-called operational definitions and reduction sentences in Carnap's sense may be viewed as special kinds of interpretative sentences.

By way of a simple example, assume that T is an elementary theory of magnetism whose theoretical vocabulary V_C contains such terms as 'magnet', 'north pole', 'south pole', and whose theoretical principles include the laws of magnetic attraction and repulsion and the law that the parts of a magnet are magnets again, while the class I includes some operational criteria for the terms of V_C.

Consider now the following application of the theory. From the sentence "b is a metal bar to which iron filings are clinging" (S_A^1), by means of a suitable operational criterion contained in the set I, infer "b is a magnet" (S_C^1); then, by way of theoretical principles in C, infer "If b is broken into two bars, b_1 and b_2, then both are magnets and their poles will attract or repel each other" (S_C^2); finally, using further operational criteria from I, derive the sentence "If b is broken into two shorter bars and these are suspended by long thin threads close to each other at the same distance from the ground, they will orient themselves so as to fall into a straight line" (S_A^2). (Note that V_A is here taken to contain not only predicates like 'metal bar', but also individual constants such as 'b'.)

The basic structure thus attributed to a theoretical inference is suggested by the following schema, in which the notation $P \overset{Q}{\rightarrow} R$ is to indicate that R can be inferred from P by using sentences from Q as additional premises.

(2)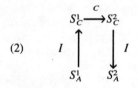

Thus, if the inferential steps in question are indeed all deductive, then the theory provides a deductive inference bridge leading from one V_A-sentence, through the theoretical realm of C, to another V_A-sentence. More precisely: S_A^1 in combination with the theory T deductively implies S_A^2; this, in turn, is tantamount to saying that T deductively implies a corresponding V_A-sentence, namely, the conditional $S_A^1 \rightarrow S_A^2$.

Carnap and other logical empiricists assumed that the vocabulary V_A, which serves to describe the phenomena to be explained by the theory, consists of terms that are "observational" at least in a broad sense, i.e., that they refer to features of the world whose presence or absence can be established by means of more or less direct observation. In recognition of the difficulties that face the notion of observability, I want to avoid any such assumption here. Indeed, I want to provide specifically for cases in which, as often happens, the vocabulary V_A was originally introduced in the context of an earlier theory. All that the standard construal needs to assume is that the phenomena for which the theory is to account are described by means of a vocabulary V_A that is "antecedently available" in the sense that it is well understood and is used with high intersubjective agreement by the scientists in the field. The interpretative sentences in I may then be viewed as interpreting the new terms introduced by the theory, i.e., those in V_C, by means of the antecedently understood terms in V_A.

This deductivist construal[2] faces two basic difficulties. I will call them the problem of theoretical ascent and the problem of provisoes. Let me spell them out in turn.

THEORETICAL OR INDUCTIVE ASCENT

The first inferential step in the schematic argument about the bar magnet presupposes that with the help of interpretative sentences belonging to part I of the theory of magnetism, S_C^1 is deducible from S_A^1. Actually, however, the theory of magnetism surely contains no general principle to the effect that when iron filings cling to a metal bar, then the bar is a magnet. The theory does not preclude the possibility, for example, that the bar is made of lead and is covered with an adhesive to which the filings stick, or that the filings are held in place by a magnet hidden under a wooden board supporting the lead bar. Thus, the theory does not warrant a deductive transition from S_A^1 to S_C^1. It is more plausible to assume that the theory contains an interpretative principle which is the converse of the one just considered, namely that if a bar is a magnet, then iron filings will cling to it. But even this is not strictly correct, as will be argued shortly.

Hence, the transition from S_A^1 to S_C^1 is not deductive even if the entire theory of magnetism is used as an additional premise. Rather, the transition involves what I will call *inductive or theoretical ascent*, i.e., a transition from a data sentence expressed in V_A to a theoretical hypothesis S_C^1 which, by way of the theory of magnetism, would explain what the data sentences describes.

This illustrates one of the two problems mentioned before that face a strictly deductivist construal of the systematic connections which a theory establishes between V_A-sentences, i.e., between sentences describing empirical phenomena in terms of V_A. This problem has been widely discussed and various efforts have been made to resolve it by constructing theories of inductive reasoning that would govern such theoretical ascent. I will not consider those efforts here, but will rather turn to the problem of provisoes, which has not, it seems to me, been investigated in the same detail.

PROVISOES

Consider the third step in our example, the transition from S_C^2 to S_A^2. Again, the theory of magnetism does not provide interpretative hypotheses which would turn this into a strictly deductive inference. The theory clearly allows for the possibility that two bar magnets, suspended by fine threads close to each other at the same level, will not arrange themselves in a straight line; for example, if a strong magnetic field of suitable direction should be present in addition, then the bars would orient themselves so as to be parallel to each other; similarly, a strong air current would foil the prediction, and so forth.

The theory of magnetism does not guarantee the absence of such disturbing factors. Hence, the inference from S_C^2 to S_A^2 presupposes the additional assumption that the suspended pieces are subject to no disturbing influence or, to put it positively, that their rotational motions are subject only to the magnetic forces they exert upon each other.

Incidentally, the explanatory inference mentioned a moment ago, from S_C^1 to S_A^1, presupposes an analogous tacit premise and thus is not deductive.

I will use the term *'provisoes'* to refer to *assumptions* of the kind just illustrated, *which are essential, but generally unstated, presuppositions of theoretical inferences.*

Provisoes are presupposed also in ostensibly deductive inferences that lead from one V_C-sentence to another. This holds, for example, in the inference from S_C^1 to S_C^2 in the case of the magnet: for if the breaking of the magnet takes place at a high temperature, the pieces may become demagnetized.

Or consider the application of the Newtonian theory of gravitation and of motion to a system of physical bodies like our solar system. In predicting, from a specification of the state of the system at a time t_o, subsequent changes of state, the basic idea is that the force acting on any one of the bodies is the vector sum of the gravitational forces exerted on it by the other bodies in accordance with the law of gravitation. That force then determines, via the second law of motion ($f = ma$), the resulting change of velocity and of position for the given body. But the quantity f in the second law is understood to be the *total* force acting on the given body; and the envisaged application of the theory therefore presupposes a proviso to the effect that the constituent bodies of the system are subject to no forces other than their mutual gravitational attraction. This proviso precludes not only gravitational forces that might be exerted by bodies outside the system, but also any electric, magnetic, frictional, or other forces to which the bodies in the system might be subject.

The absence of such forces is not, of course, vouchsafed by the principles of Newton's theory, and it is for this reason that the proviso is needed.

ESCAPE BY INTERPRETATIVE SENTENCES OF PROBABILISTIC FORM?

The foregoing considerations show in particular that when a theory contains interpretative sentences in the form of explicit definitions or of Carnapian reduction chains based on the antecedent vocabulary, the applicability of these sentences is usually subject to the fulfillment of provisoes; they cannot be regarded as unequivocal complete or partial criteria of applicability for theoretical expressions.

This thought might suggest a construal of the interpretative sentences of a theory as expressing only probabilistic rather than strictly general connections between theoretically described states or events and certain associated manifestations, or indicator phenomena, described in antecedently available terms. Such a construal might seem to come closer to scientific usage and at the same time to obviate the need for provisoes: for with probabilistic interpretation sentences, a theory would establish at best probabilistic connections between V_A-sentences. And what would otherwise appear as occasional violations of provisoes would be automatically anticipated by the merely probabilistic character of the theoretical inferences.

Interpretative sentences of probabilistic form have in fact been envisaged by several writers. Carnap did so already in his (1956) essay "The Methodological Character of Theoretical Concepts," which is, I think, his earliest full presentation of the standard empiricist construal of theories. He argues there that many terms functioning in scientific theories cannot be regarded as linked to antecedent terms ("observational terms") by interpretative sentences ("rules of correspondence") of strictly universal form. For such sentences would specify strictly necessary or sufficient observational conditions of applicability for the theoretical terms, whereas scientists, Carnap argues, will treat such conditions not as strictly binding, but as qualified by an "escape clause" to the effect that the observational criteria hold "unless there are disturbing factors," or "provided the environment is in a normal state."[3] Such escape clauses clearly have the character of provisoes in the sense adumbrated earlier. Carnap views them as probabilistic qualifiers functioning in interpretative sentences for theoretical terms. These sentences would state probabilistic rather than strictly necessary or sufficient connections between theoretical expressions and V_A-sentences. Indeed, while Carnap countenances dispositional terms, linked to V_A by strict reduction chains, he suggests that the terms characteristic of scientific theories have only probabilistic links to the observational basis.[4]

But while Carnap thus explicitly eschews a purely deductivist construal of the inferential function of theories, he does not specify the form of the probabilistic interpretation sentences he envisages. Indeed, in response to a proposal by Pap[5] concerning probabilistic reduction sentences, Carnap remarks: "it seems to me that for the time being the problem of the best form for [interpretative sentences] has not yet been sufficiently clarified."[6]

However that may be, a probabilistic construal of provisoes faces the difficulty that scientific theories do not, in general, provide probabilistic laws that would obviate the need for provisoes.

Consider, for example, the interpretative sentences that would be required for the term 'magnet'. They would have to take the form "In cases where iron filings stick to a metal bar, the probability of the bar being a magnet is p_1"; or, for inferences in the opposite direction: "Given that a metal bar is magnetic, the probability that iron filings will cling to it is p_2." But surely, the theory of magnetism contains no sentences of this kind; it is a matter quite beyond its scope to state how frequently air currents, disturbing further magnetic fields, or other factors will interfere with the effect in question. It seems to me that no scientific theory provides probabilistic interpretation statements of this sort, whose application is not itself subject to provisoes.

The same basic consideration applies also, I think, where no well-developed and sharply formulated theories are available; for example, probabilification cannot avoid the need for provisoes in the application of theoretical sentences linking psychological states or events to their behavioral manifestations.

SOME CONSEQUENCES OF THE NEED FOR PROVISOES

The conclusion that a scientific theory even of nonprobabilistic form does not, in general, establish deductive bridges between V_A-sentences has significant consequences for other issues in the philosophy of science.

I will briefly indicate four of these: (a) the idea of falsifiability, (b) the significance of so-called elimination programs for theoretical terms, (c) the instrumentalist construal of scientific theories, and (d) the idea of "the empirical content" of a theory.

(a) Falsifiability
One obvious consequence of the need for provisoes is that normally a theory is not falsifiable by V_A-sentences; otherwise, it would deductively imply the negations of the falsifying V_A-sentences, which again are V_A-sentences.

This consideration differs from the Duhem-Quine argument that individual hypotheses cannot be falsified by experiential findings because the deduction from the hypothesis of falsifying V_A-sentences requires an extensive system of background hypotheses as additional premises, so that typically only a comprehensive set of hypotheses will entail or contradict V_A-sentences. The argument from provisoes leads rather to the stronger conclusion that even a comprehensive system of hypotheses or theoretical principles will not entail any V_A-sentences because the requisite deduction is subject to provisoes.

Note that a proviso as here understood is not a clause that can be attached to a theory as a whole and vouchsafe its deductive potency by asserting that in all particular situations to which the theory is applied, disturbing factors are absent. Rather, a proviso has to be conceived as a clause which pertains to some particular application of a given theory and which asserts that in the case at hand, no effective factors are present other than those explicitly taken into account.

(b) Elimination Programs for Theoretical Terms

The need for provisoes also has a bearing on the so-called elimination programs for theoretical terms. These programs are of particular significance for philosophical qualms about the use, in scientific theories, of terms that are not explicitly defined by means of an antecedently understood vocabulary.

The ingenious and logically impeccable methods designed by Ramsey and by Craig[7] circumvent these qualms by showing that the use of theoretical expressions can always be avoided in the following sense: If a theory T consisting of two sentence classes C and I as characterized earlier does yield deductive connections between certain V_A-sentences, then it is possible to formulate a corresponding theory (class of sentences) T_A such that

(i) T_A is expressed in terms of V_A alone
(ii) T_A is logically implied by T
(iii) T_A entails '$S_A^1 \rightarrow S_A^2$' (and in this sense establishes a deductive bridge from S_A^1 to S_A^2) if and only if T entails '$S_A^1 \rightarrow S_A^2$'.[8]

If the function of a theory is taken to consist in establishing deductive bridges among V_A-sentences, then the theory T_A, which avoids the use of theoretical terms, might be called functionally equivalent to the theory T. This result might suggest the reassuring conclusion that, in principle, the use of theoretical expressions can always be avoided without any change in the "empirical content" of a theory as it is expressed by the class of V_A-sentences deducible from it, and that talk in terms of theoretical expressions is just a convenient *façon de parler* about matters that are fully expressible in the antecedently understood vocabulary V_A. Analogously, it may seem that all the problems about theoretical ascent and provisoes simply disappear if T is replaced by its functional equivalent T_A.

This impression is illusory, however. For a theory T_A constructed from T in the manner of Ramsey or of Craig yields deductive connections between V_A-sentences if and only if T yields such connections: and scientific theories do not, in general, satisfy this condition. The need for provisoes precludes the general avoidability of theoretical expressions by those elimination methods.

The verdict does not hold, however, if the provisoes qualifying the inferential applications of a theory are themselves expressible in the antecedent vocabulary. For if P_A is such a proviso governing the transition, by means of T, from S_A^1 to S_A^2, then T entails the sentence $(P_A \cdot S_A^1) \rightarrow S_A^2$ and thus establishes a deductive bridge between two V_A-sentences.

But it seems that, in general, the requisite provisoes cannot be expressed in terms of V_A alone. In the case of the theory of magnetism referred to earlier, the provisoes may assert, for example, the absence of other magnetic fields, or of disturbing forces, etc., and will then require at least the use of terms from V_C in their formulation.

(c) Provisoes and the Instrumentalist Perspective

The preceding considerations analogously cast some doubt on the instrumentalist conception of theories as purely inferential devices which, from an input in the form of V_A-sentences, generate an output of other V_A-sentences. For the need for provisoes shows that theories do not render this service. In each particular case, the applicability of the theoretical instrument would be subject to the condition that the pertinent provisoes are fulfilled; and the assertion that they are fulfilled could not just be added to the input into the theoretical calculating machine, for that assertion would not generally be expressible in V_A.

Thus, if a theory is to be thought of as a calculating instrument that generates new V_A-sentences from given ones, then it must be conceived as supplemented by an instruction manual specifying that the instrument should be used only in cases in which certain provisoes are satisfied. But the formulation of those provisoes will make use of V_C and perhaps even of terms not contained in V_C. Thus, one has to check whether certain empirical conditions not expressible in V_A are satisfied: and that surely provides a tug away from instrumentalism and in the direction of realism concerning theoretical entities.

(d) Provisoes and "the Empirical Content" of a Theory

Similar questions arise in regard to the notion of the experiential "cash value" or "empirical content" of a theory as represented by the set of all V_A-sentences entailed by the theory.

Note first, and incidentally, that thus construed the empirical content of a theory is relative to the vocabulary V_A that counts as antecedently available, so that one would properly have to speak, not of "the" empirical content of T, but of the V_A-content of T.

But the point here to be made is rather that usually a theory does not entail V_A-sentences and the proposed construal of empirical content misfires.

To be sure, there are some deductive theoretical inferences that presuppose no provisoes; for example, the inference, mediated by the law of gravitation, from a sentence S^1 specifying the masses and the distance of two bodies to a sentence S^2 specifying the gravitational attraction that the bodies exert upon each other.

But the further theoretical inference from S^2 to a sentence S^3 specifying the accelerations the bodies will undergo requires a proviso to the effect that no other forces act upon the bodies. If S^2 and S^3 are represented as theoretical sentences, then we have here an example of the need for provisoes not only in establishing theoretical inference bridges between V_A-sentences and V_C-sentences, but also in building such bridges between sentences expressed solely in terms of V_C. We will shortly return to this point.

FURTHER THOUGHTS ON THE CHARACTER OF PROVISOES

How might the notion of proviso be further illuminated? To say that provisoes are just *ceteris paribus* clauses is unhelpful, for the idea of a *ceteris paribus* clause is itself vague and elusive. "Other things being equal, such-and-so is the case." What other things, and equal to what? How is the clause to function in theoretical reasoning?

Provisoes might rather be viewed as *assumptions of completeness*. The proviso required for a theoretical inference from one sentence, S^1, to another, S^2, asserts, broadly speaking, that in a given case (e.g., in that of the metal bar considered earlier) no factors other than those specified in S^1 are present which could affect the event described by S^2.

For example, in the application of Newtonian theory to a double star it is presupposed that the components of the system are subject to no forces other than their mutual gravitational attraction and hence, that the specification given in S^1 of the initial and boundary conditions which determine that gravitational attraction is a complete or exhaustive specification of all the forces affecting the components of the system.

Such completeness is of a special kind. It differs sharply, for example, from that invoked in the requirement of complete or total evidence. This is an epistemological condition to the effect that in a probabilistic inference concerning, say, a future occurrence, the total body of evidence available at the time must be chosen as the evidential basis for the inference.[9]

A proviso, on the other hand, calls not for epistemic, but for ontic completeness: the specifics expressed by S^1 must include, not all the information available at the time (information which may well include false items), but rather all the factors present in the given case which in fact affect the outcome to be predicted by the theoretical inference; the factors in question might be said to be those which are "nomically relevant" to the outcome, i.e., those on which the outcome depends in virtue of nomic connections.

Consider once again the use of Newtonian theory to deduce, from a specification S^1 of the state of a binary star system at time t_1, a specification S^2 of its state at t_2. Let us suppose, for simplicity, that S^1 and S^2 are couched in the language of the theory; this enables us to leave on one side the problem of the inductive ascent from astronomical observation data to a theoretical redescription in terms of masses, positions, and velocities of the two objects.

The theoretical inference might then be schematized thus:

(3) $(P \cdot S^1 \cdot T) \rightarrow S^2$

Where P is a proviso to the effect that apart from the circumstances specified in S^1 the two bodies are, between t_1 and t_2, subject to no influences from within or from outside the system that would affect their motions. The proviso must thus imply the absence, in the case at hand, of electric, magnetic, and frictional forces, of radiation pressure and of any telekinetic, angelic, or diabolic influences.

One may well wonder whether this proviso can at all be expressed in the language of celestial mechanics, or even in the combined languages of mechanics and other physical theories. At any rate, neither singly nor jointly do those theories assert that forces of the kinds they deal with are the only kinds by which the motion of a physical body can be affected. A scientific theory propounds an account of certain kinds of empirical phenomena, but it does not pronounce on what other kinds there are. The theory of gravitation neither asserts nor denies the existence of non-gravitational forces, and it offers no means of characterizing or distinguishing them.

It might seem, therefore, that the formulation of the proviso transcends the conceptual resources of the theory whose deductive applicability it is to secure. That, however, is not the case in the example at hand. For in Newton's second law, $f = ma$, 'f' stands for the *total* force impressed on the body; and our proviso can therefore be expressed by asserting that the total force acting on each of the two bodies equals the gravitational force exerted upon it by the other body; and the latter force is determined by the law of gravitation.[10]

But the application of the theory to particular cases is clearly subject again to provisoes to the effect that in computing the total force, all relevant influences affecting the bodies concerned have been taken into account.

When the application of a theory to empirical subject matter is schematically represented in the form (3) with the provisoes P as one of the premises, it must be borne in mind that the language and the specific form in which P is expressed are left quite vague. The notation is not meant to be a sharp explication, but rather a convenient way of referring to the subject at issue in the context of an attempt to shed some further light on it.

Note that the proviso P does not include clauses to the effect that the establishment of S^1 has not been affected by errors of observation or measurement, by deceit or the like: that is already implied by the premise S^1 itself, which trivially asserts that S^1 is true. The proviso is to the effect, not that S^1 is true, but that it states the *whole* truth about the relevant circumstances present.

Note further that the perplexities of the reliance on provisoes cannot be avoided by adopting a structuralist, or non-statement, conception of theories broadly in the manner of Sneed and Stegmüller.[11] That conception construes theories not as classes of statements, but as deductively organized systems of statement functions, which make no assertions and have no truth-values. But such systems are presented as having empirical models; for example, the solar system might be claimed to be a model of a structuralist formalization of Newtonian celestial mechanics. But a formulation of this claim, and its inferential application to particular astronomical occurrences, again clearly assumes the fulfillment of pertinent provisoes.

METHODOLOGICAL ASPECTS OF PROVISOES

The elusive character of proviso clauses raises the question of how a theoretical inference of type (3) can be applied to particular occurrences, and more specifically, on what grounds proviso P may be taken to be satisfied or violated in specific cases.

There are circumstances that provide such grounds. If the theory T has strong previous support, but its application to a new case yields incorrect predictions S^2, then doubts may arise about S^1; but in the absence of specific grounds for such doubts, a violation of P—i.e., the presence of disturbing factors—may suggest itself. If this conjecture can be expressed in the language of the theory T and replacing S^1 by a correspondingly modified sentence $S^{1\prime}$ yields successful predictions, then this success will constitute grounds for attributing the predictive failure of the original theoretical inference to a violation of its proviso clause.

Thus, the failure of Newton's otherwise highly successful theory to predict certain perturbations in the orbit of Uranus in terms of the gravitational attraction exerted on it by the sun and by the planets known before 1846 led to the conjecture of a proviso-violation, namely the assumption that Uranus was subject to the additional attraction of a hitherto unknown planet— a conjecture borne out by the subsequent discovery of Neptune.

Sometimes predictive failure of a theory is attributed to proviso violations even though the presumably disturbing factors cannot be adequately specified.

Consider, for example, the controversy between Robert A. Millikan and Felix Ehrenhaft over the results of the famous experiments in which Millikan measured the rates at which small electrically charged oil drops rose and sank in the electric field between two horizontal electrically charged metal plates. From those rates he computed, by means of accepted theoretical principles, the size of the charges of those oil drops and found that all of them were integral multiples of a certain minimum charge e, whose numerical value he specified. Millikan presented his findings as evidence for the claim that electricity had an atomistic structure and that the atoms of electricity all had the specified charge e.

Ehrenhaft objected that in similar experiments, he had found individual charges which were not integral multiples of Millikan's value e and which, in fact, were often considerably smaller than e, suggesting the existence of "sub-electrons."[12] Ehrenhaft accordingly rejected Millikan's theoretical claims T on grounds of predictive failure.

Millikan replied in careful detail. Referring to difficulties he had encountered in his own work, he argued that Ehrenhaft's deviant results could be due to disturbing factors of various kinds. Among them, he mentions the possibility that tiny dust particles might have settled on the falling oil droplets, thus changing the total force acting on them; the possibility that evaporation might have reduced the mass of an observed drop; the possibility that the strength of the electric field might have decreased as a result of battery fatigue, and so forth.

Ehrenhaft repeated his experiments, taking great pains to screen out such disturbing factors, but he continued to obtain deviant findings. The sources of these deviations have never been fully determined; in fact, Ehrenhaft's results turned out not to be generally reproducible. Millikan's ideas, on the other hand, were sustained in various quite different applications. Thus, eventually Ehrenhaft's claims were gradually disregarded by investigators in the field, and Millikan won the day and the Nobel prize.

Interestingly, as has been pointed out by Holton,[13] Millikan himself had recorded in his laboratory diaries several sets of quite deviant measurements, but he had not published them, attributing them to disturbing factors of various kinds and sometimes not even offering a guess as to the source of the deviation.

But evidently, it cannot be made a *general* policy of scientific research to attribute predictive failures of theoretical inferences to the violation of some unspecified proviso; for this "conventionalist strategem," as Popper has called it, would deprive a theory of any predictive or explanatory force.[14]

I think that at least in periods of what Kuhn calls normal science a search for disturbing influences will consider only factors of such kinds as are countenanced by one or another of the currently accepted scientific theories as being nomically relevant to the phenomena under consideration.

Thus, if a prediction based on Newtonian mechanics fails, one might look for disturbing gravitational, electric, magnetic, and frictional forces and for still some other kinds, but not for telekinetic or diabolic ones. Indeed, since there are no currently accepted theories for such forces, we would be unable to tell under what conditions and in what manner they act; consequently, there is no way of checking on their presence or absence in any particular case.

The mode of procedure just mentioned is clearly followed also in experiments that require screening-out of disturbing outside influences—for example, in experimental studies of the frequency with which a certain kind of subatomic event occurs under specified conditions. What outside influences—such as cosmic rays—would affect the frequency in question, and what shielding devices can serve to block them and thus to ensure satisfaction of the relevant proviso, is usually determined in the light of available scientific knowledge, which again would indicate no way of screening out, say, telekinetic influences.

If a theory fails to yield correct predictions for a repeatable phenomenon by reference to factors it qualifies as relevant, then certain changes within that theory may be tried, introducing a new kind of nomically relevant factor. Roentgen's discovery of a photographic plate that had been blackened while lying in a closed desk drawer is, I think, a case in point; it led to the acknowledgment of a new kind of radiation.

Finally, persistent serious failures of a theory may lead to a revolution in Kuhn's sense, which places the phenomena into a novel theoretical framework rather than modifying the old one by piecemeal changes. In this case, the failures of the earlier theory are not attributed to proviso violations; indeed it is quite unclear what such an attribution would amount to.

Consider a theoretical inference that might have been offered some 250 years ago on the basis of the caloric fluid theory of heat or the phlogiston theory of combustion. The relevant provisoes would then have to assert, for example, that apart from the factors explicitly taken into account in the inference, no other factors are present that affect, say, the flow of caloric fluid between bodies or the degree of dephlogistication of a body. But from our present vantage point, we have to say that there are no such substances as caloric fluid or phlogiston, and that therefore there could be no proper proviso claim of the requisite sort at all.

And yet, it appears that the claims and the inferential applications of any theory have to be understood as subject to those elusive provisoes.

There is a distinct affinity, I think, between the perplexing questions concerning the appraisal of provisoes in the application of scientific theories and the recently much discussed problems of theory choice in science.

As Kuhn in particular has argued in detail, the choice between competing theories is influenced by considerations concerning the strength and the relative importance of various desirable features exhibited by the rival theories; but these considerations resist adequate expression in the form of precise explicit criteria. The choice between theories in the light of those considerations, which are broadly shared within the scientific community, is not subject to, nor learned by means of, unambiguous rules. Scientists acquire the ability to make such choices in the course of their professional training and careers, somewhat in the manner in which we acquire the use of our language largely without benefit of explicit rules, by interaction with competent speakers.

Just as, in the context of theory choice, the relevant idea of superiority of one theory to another has no precise explication and yet its use is strongly affected by considerations shared by scientific investigators, so in the inferential application of theories to empirical contexts, the idea of the relevant provisoes has no precise explication, yet it is by no means arbitrary and its use appears to be significantly affected by considerations akin to those affecting theory choice.

NOTES

* This article has grown out of a paper read in November 1980 at a workshop held under the auspices of the Center for Philosophy of Science at the University of Pittsburgh. The present, much revised, version was written for inclusion in a volume, to be published by the University of California Press, which is to contain the proceedings of that workshop.

Pending the completion of that project, which has been considerably delayed, the article appears here with the consent of the editors of the proceedings.

1. This paper is based upon work supported by National Science Foundation Grant No. SES 80–25399.
2. I have limited myself here to a schematic account of those features of the empiricist model which are of relevance to the problems subsequently to be discussed. For fuller expositions and critical discussions, and for references to the extensive literature, see, for example, Carnap (1956, 1966, chapters 23–26); Feigl (1970); Hempel (1958, 1969, 1970); Putnam (1962); and Suppe (1974), a comprehensive study which includes a large bibliography.
3. Carnap (1956), p. 69.
4. Cf. Carnap (1956), pp. 49, 72.
5. Pap (1963), section II.
6. Carnap (1963), p. 950.
7. For details, see Ramsey (1931, "Theories," section IXA); Carnap (1966, "The Ramsey Sentence," chapter 26); Craig (1956); Putnam (1965); Hempel (1965, pp. 210–17).

8. The theory T_A obtainable by Ramsey's method is quite different, in other respects, from that generated by Craig's procedure. But the differences are irrelevant to the point here under discussion.
9. Cf. Carnap (1950), pp. 211–13, 494.
10. I am indebted to Michael Friedman for having pointed this out to me.
11. Cf. Sneed (1979), Stegmüller (1976), especially chapter 7.
12. Millikan gives a detailed account of his investigations in Millikan (1917); Ehrenhaft's claims are discussed in chapter 8. The controversy is examined in a broader scientific and historical perspective in Holton (1978).
13. Holton (1978), esp. pp. 58–83.
14. See, for example, Popper (1962, pp. 33–39); Stegmüller (1976, chapter 14).

REFERENCES

Carnap, R. (1950). *Logical Foundations of Probability*. Chicago: University of Chicago Press.

———. (1956). "The Methodological Character of Theoretical Concepts." In *Minnesota Studies in the Philosophy of Science*, vol. 1. Edited by H. Feigl and M. Scriven. Minneapolis: University of Minnesota Press, pp. 38–76.

———. (1963). "Arthur Pap on Dispositions." In *The Philosophy of Rudolf Carnap*. Ed. P. A. Schilpp. Lasalle Illinois: Open Court pp. 947–52.

———. (1966). *Philosophical Foundations of Physics*. New York: Basic Books.

Craig, W. (1956). "Replacement of Auxiliary Expressions." *Philosophical Review* 65, pp. 38–55.

Feigl, H. (1970). "The 'Orthodox' View of Theories: Remarks in Defense as Well as Critique." In *Minnesota Studies in the Philosophy of Science*, vol. 4. Edited by M. Radner and S. Winokur. Minneapolis: University of Minnesota Press, pp. 3–16.

Hempel, C. G. (1958). "The Theoretician's Dilemma." In *Minnesota Studies in the Philosophy of Science*, vol. 2. Edited by H. Feigl, M. Scriven, and G. Maxwell. Minneapolis: University of Minnesota Press, pp. 37–98. Reprinted in C. G. Hempel (1965). *Aspects of Scientific Explanation*. New York: The Free Press, pp. 173–226.

———. (1969). "On the Structure of Scientific Theories." In *Isenberg Memorial Lecture Series*, 1965–66. East Lansing: Michigan State University Press, pp. 11–38.

———. (1970). "On the 'Standard Conception' of Scientific Theories." In *Minnesota Studies in the Philosophy of Science*, vol. 4. Edited by M. Radner and S. Winokur. Minneapolis: University of Minnesota Press, pp. 142–63.

Holton, Gerald. (1978). "Subelectrons, Presuppositions, and the Millikan-Ehrenhaft Dispute." In G. Holton, *The Scientific Imagination*. Cambridge: Cambridge University Press, pp. 25–83.

Millikan, Robert A. (1917). *The Electron*. Chicago: University of Chicago Press, facsimile edition, 1963.

Pap, A. (1963). "Reduction Sentences and Disposition Concepts." In *The Philosophy of Rudolf Carnap*. Edited by P.A. Schilpp. LaSalle, Illinois: Open Court, pp. 559–97.

Popper, K. (1962). *Conjectures and Refutations*, New York: Basic Books.

Putnam, H. (1962). "What Theories are Not." In *Logic, Methodology and Philosophy of Science*. Edited by E. Nagel, P. Suppes, and A. Tarski. Palo Alto: Stanford University Press, pp. 240–51.

———. (1965). "Craig's Theorem." In *The Journal of Philosophy* 62, pp. 251–60.

Ramsey, F. P. (1931). *The Foundations of Mathematics and Other Logical Essays*. Ed. R. B. Braithwaite. London: Routledge and Kegan Paul. Paperback reprint (1960). Patterson, New Jersey: Littlefield, Adams.

Sneed, J. D. (1979). *The Logical Structure of Mathematical Physics*. 2d ed. Dordrecht: D. Reidel.

Stegmüller, W. (1976). *The Structure and Dynamics of Theories*. New York: Springer Verlag.

Suppe, F. (1974). "The Search for Philosophic Understanding of Scientific Theories." In *The Structure of Scientific Theories*. Edited by F. Suppe. Chicago: University of Illinois Press, pp. 3–232. (Second edition, with an added "Afterword," 1977).

PART FOUR

EXPLANATION AND PREDICTION

INTRODUCTION

T he theory of scientific explanation has been dominated by the conception that explanations for singular events are secured by subsuming them as specific instances of natural
laws. During the 1940s, the 1950s, and the 1960s, this approach was systematically elaborated
and defended in detail by Carl G. Hempel, who developed what has come to be known as *the
covering law model* of explanation. An essential feature of Hempel's account has been the
notion that explanations can always be expressed in the form of arguments, where the premises
(called "the explanans") provide grounds, reasons, or evidence supporting the conclusion
(called "the explanandum").

Hempel's "Explanation in Science and in History" provides a general introduction to the
covering law theory. Because it has infinitely many relations to other events, no singular event
can be explained as a "concrete particular" but only as an event of a certain kind or *under a
certain description*. Thus, a distinction must be drawn between an explanandum-phenomenon
as a feature of the world's history and an explanandum-sentence as a feature of an explanatory
argument. An explanation exhibits the nomic expectability of an explanandum-phenomenon by
deriving an explanandum-sentence that describes it from an argument that includes at least one
law.

In an early paper co-authored with Paul Oppenheim, Hempel set forth a set of four conditions
that were taken to be necessary and sufficient for an explanandum-phenomenon to be given an
adequate scientific explanation:

(CA-1) the explanandum must be a deductive consequence of its explanans;

(CA-2) the explanans must include at least one lawlike sentence that is actually required for the derivation
of the explanandum from its explanans;

(CA-3) the explanans must possess empirical content; and,

(CA-4) the explanans must be true.

Strictly speaking, (CA-3) is a redundant condition, which cannot fail to be satisfied if (CA-1), (CA-2) and (CA-4) are satisfied.

As Hempel always realized, these conditions were only appropriate for explanations that appeal to natural laws of universal form, since otherwise the explanandum would not follow from the explanans and the truth of the explanans would not guarantee the truth of the explanandum. This account was therefore referred to as the *deductive-nomological* (or D-N) model of explanation. When Hempel later articulated the structure of explanations that appeal to natural laws of statistical form, he referred to their conditions as the *inductive-statistical* (or I-S) model of explanation, where explanations of this kind assume the form of inductive rather than of deductive arguments.

In spite of Hempel's best efforts, however, he was unable to provide an adequate solution for the associated problem of inductive ambiguity, which he discusses in his paper in Part VI. This obstacle, which arose because of the seeming impossibility of obtaining a completely objective conception of reference class homogeneity, forced him to introduce what he called *the requirement of maximal specificity* (or "RMS"), which makes I-S explanations relative to a knowledge context K. This difficulty, which is not elaborated here, implies a profound difference between D-N explanations, which can be true, and I-S explanations, which cannot be true, on Hempel's analysis.

Salmon's "Statistical Explanations" shares Hempel's underlying commitment to the *frequency interpretation* of probability hypotheses, according to which the probability with which an event of kind A occurs within a reference class R equals the limiting frequency with which attribute A occurs within an infinite sequence of kind R. But he does not share Hempel's pessimism over the prospect of developing a completely objective conception of reference class homogeneity. Such a conception would require that any subsequence S of the original sequence R which is "appropriately selected" yield limiting frequencies for A that equal those of the original sequence.

The principal motivation for introducing the *statistical relevance* (S-R) model of explanation is Salmon's conviction that Hempel's theory is founded upon a mistaken conception of explanatory relevance. For Hempel, a property F is explanatorily relevant to the occurrence of an attribute A if there is a lawful relationship that relates F to A. If table salt dissolves in water, then so does Morton's table salt, hexed Morton's table salt, etc., any of which can thus occur in explanations. This violates what Salmon takes to be a fundamental requirement of adequate explanations, which is that statistically irrelevant properties cannot qualify as explanatorily relevant.

In order to establish which properties should qualify as explanatorily relevant, Salmon introduces the *statistical-relevance criterion* of explanatory relevance, according to which a property F is explanatorily relevant to the occurrence of an attribute A within a reference class R just in case.

(SRC) $P(A/R\&F) = m$ and $P(A/R\&-F) = n$, where $m \neq n$;

that is, just in case the limiting frequency for A in R-and-F differs from the limiting frequency for A in R-and-not-F. Any property F for which corresponding probabilities interpreted as limiting frequencies vary is therefore supposed to be explanatorily relevant to the occurrence of A, relative to R.

This criterion enables Salmon's S-R model to deal with the hexed-salt and the birth-control pill cases, for example, a problem that Hempel's I-S model cannot solve. Salmon also rejects the requirement of a high probability relation between the explanans and the explanandum of a statistical explanation on the grounds (i) that it renders the explanation of events that only occur with low probability logically impossible, in principle, and (ii) that Carnap's conception of logical probability, which Hempel employs, is hopelessly unsuited for its intended role within the I-S model. Indeed, Hempel himself would eventually accept both of these objections as valid.

Having rejected Hempel's condition of high probability between explanans and explanandum, however, Salmon went further and even abandoned the covering law conception of explanations as arguments. Adequate scientific explanations now consist of the partition of the reference class R into various subclasses $R\&F1$ to $R\&Fn$, where each subclass is objectively homogeneous, and the singular event to be explained, such as the occurrence of Axt (attribute A of an object x at time t), is explained by assigning it to the appropriate completely objective homogeneous reference class that includes exactly those statistically relevant properties that were present in this case.

Fetzer's "A Single Case Propensity Theory of Explanation" supplies an alternative that builds upon the twin realizations that statistical relevance is neither necessary nor sufficient for causal relevance and that limiting frequency conceptions of probability cannot solve the problem of the single case. This obstacle invites the adoption of (the single-case version of) the *propensity conception* of probability, according to which probabilities are dispositional properties of physical arrangements (or of "chance set-ups") to produce one or another among various outcomes on each singular trial, where corresponding limiting frequencies are expected, but not required, were those trials endlessly repeated.

From such a point of view, probabilistic laws as well as universal laws are essentially of universal form. For a probabilistic law under the propensity interpretation no longer simply affirms that a certain percentage of a reference class also belongs to the attribute class. What it asserts is that every member of the reference class possesses a certain (logically contingent) disposition, which in the case of probabilistic laws is of probabilistic strength. Their difference is not a matter of how many members possess the property in question but of the strength of the property possessed by every member.

The single-case propensity approach supports a *causal-relevance* (C-R) model of explanation, which is based upon the *causal-relevance criterion* of explanatory relevance, according to which a property F is causally relevant to the occurrence of A in relation to reference property R just in case:

(CRC) $(Rxt\&Fxt) = m \Rightarrow Axt^*$ and $(Rxt\&-Fxt) = n \Rightarrow Axt^*$, where $m \neq n$;

that is, just in case the strength of the tendency for conditions Rxt-and-Fxt to bring about attribute A on a single trial differs from the strength of the tendency for conditions Rxt-and-not-Fxt to bring about that same attribute. Causal relevance and not statistical relevance is the fundamental notion.

This means that frequencies display but do not define probabilities as propensities and that statistical-relevance relations can serve as evidence in relation to causal-relevance hypotheses. Under this conception, lawlike sentences are true only when they are "maximally specific" by specifying within their antecedents the presence or absence of every property that makes a difference to the occurrence of attribute A. Unlike Hempel's conception, however, this *requirement of maximal specificity* is a completely objective condition whose satisfaction is independent of a knowledge context K. The analysis appeals to Reichenbach's notion of logical probability in place of Carnap's and provides conditions of adequacy that are remarkably similar to Hempel's original conception, where the key to their differences is an intensional rather than extensional conception of natural laws.

STUDY QUESTIONS

As you read the articles that appear in this section, you may want to think about their implications for understanding the nature of science and of philosophy. The following questions are intended to stimulate your thinking by focusing attention on some of the less obvious aspects of different positions.

(1) On Hempel's account, explanations are arguments involving inferences from laws. Since there appear to be several different kinds of laws, there appear to be several different kinds of explanations. Inventory how many different kinds of explanations there appear to be on a Hempelian account.

(2) A distinctive feature of the covering law theory of explanation has been the symmetry thesis, which maintains that every adequate explanation could have served as a prediction, had its explanans been taken account of in time, and conversely. Can you think of reasons why this connection might be too strong to be true?

(3) Some arguments involving inferences from law do not appear to qualify as explanations. Suppose, for example, that anyone who has ever been run over by a steamroller is dead. If you are not dead, then we can infer that you have not been run over by a steamroller. But does that explain why?

(4) Hempel has maintained that the fundamental desideratum that explanations must fulfill is that they should exhibit the nomic expectability of the explanandum phenomenon. Does exhibiting the nomic expectability of the explanandum phenomenon mean that the event could have been predicted?

(5) Salmon believes that Hempel's conception of explanation was based on a mistaken conception of relevance. That a sample of Morton's finest table salt dissolves in water could be explained by citing a law asserting that Morton's finest table salt always dissolves in water. What is wrong with that?

(6) Suppose that men whose middle names contain double vowels should turn out to have more dental problems than those who do not. Would that make this property statistically relevant to that outcome? And if it were statistically relevant, would it also qualify as explanatorily relevant as well?

(7) Salmon abandons the conception of explanations as arguments. What are his reasons for making this move? Do they appear to be good reasons? If the formulation of explanations as arguments were permissible but not required, do you think Salmon could accept that view? Why or why not?

(8) Interpretations of probability that define "probability" in terms of the long run appear to have unsolvable problems about the single case. Why do interpretations that define "probability" in terms of the single case appear to have no corresponding unsolvable problems about the long run?

(9) A crucial problem about probabilistic explanations concerns the interpretation of "degree of nomic expectability." Salmon objected to Hempel's model because it appealed to

Carnap's conception of logical probability to fulfill this role. Could he raise the same objection about Fetzer's model?

(10) Syntactical determinacy, definitional relevance, and theoretical significance are desiderata of adequacy for explications. How well do these three models fare in terms of these criteria? Which appears to clarify and illuminate the nature of explanation most adequately? How do you rate them?

CARL G. HEMPEL

EXPLANATION IN SCIENCE AND IN HISTORY

INTRODUCTION

Among the diverse factors that have encouraged and sustained scientific inquiry through its long history are two pervasive human concerns which provide, I think, the basic motivation for all scientific research. One of these is man's persistent desire to improve his strategic position in the world by means of dependable methods for predicting and, whenever possible, controlling the events that occur in it. The extent to which science has been able to satisfy this urge is reflected impressively in the vast and steadily widening range of its technological applications. But besides this practical concern, there is a second basic motivation for the scientific quest, namely, man's insatiable intellectual curiosity, his deep concern to *know* the world he lives in, and to *explain*, and thus to *understand*, the unending flow of phenomena it presents to him.

In times past questions as to the *what* and the *why* of the empirical world were often answered by myths; and to some extent, this is so even in our time. But gradually, the myths are displaced by the concepts, hypotheses, and theories developed in the various branches of empirical science, including the natural sciences, psychology, and sociological as well as historical inquiry. What is the general character of the understanding attainable by these means, and what is its potential scope? In this paper I will try to shed some light on these questions by examining what seem to me the two basic types of explanation offered by the natural sciences, and then comparing them with some modes of explanation and understanding that are found in historical studies.

First, then, a look at explanation in the natural sciences.

TWO BASIC TYPES OF SCIENTIFIC EXPLANATION.

Deductive-Nomological Explanation

In his book, *How We Think*,[1] John Dewey describes an observation he made one day when, washing dishes, he took some glass tumblers out of the hot soap suds and put them upside down on a plate: he noticed that soap bubbles emerged from under the tumblers' rims, grew for a while, came to a standstill, and finally receded inside the tumblers. Why did this happen? The explanation Dewey outlines comes to this: In transferring a tumbler to the plate, cool air is caught in it; this air is gradually warmed by the glass, which initially has the temperature of the hot suds. The warming of the air is accompanied by an increase in its pressure, which in turn produces an expansion of the soap film between the plate and the rim. Gradually, the glass cools off, and so does the air inside, with the result that the soap bubbles recede.

This explanatory account may be regarded as an argument to the effect that the event to be explained (let me call it the explanandum-event) was to be expected by reason of certain explanatory facts. These may be divided into two groups: (i) particular facts and (ii) uniformities expressed by general laws. The first group includes facts such as these: the tumblers had been immersed, for some time, in soap suds of a temperature considerably higher than that of the surrounding air; they were put, upside down, on a plate on which a puddle of soapy water had formed, providing a connecting soap film, etc. The second group of items presupposed in the argument includes the gas laws and various other laws that have not been explicitly suggested concerning the exchange of heat between bodies of different temperature, the elastic behavior of soap bubbles, etc. If we imagine these various presuppositions explicitly spelled out, the idea suggests itself of construing the explanation as a deductive argument of this form:

(D)
$$C_1, C_2, \ldots, C_k$$
$$\frac{L_1, L_2, \ldots, L_r}{E}$$

Here, $C_1, C_2, \ldots, C_k$ are statements describing the particular facts invoked; $L_1, L_2, \ldots, L_r$ are general laws: jointly, these statements will be said to form the explanans. The conclusion E is a statement describing the explanandum-event; let me call it the explanandum-statement, and let me use the word "explanandum" to refer either to E or to the event described by it.

The kind of explanation thus characterized I will call *deductive-nomological explanation*; for it amounts to a deductive subsumption of the explanandum under principles which have the character of general laws: it answers the question "*Why* did the explanandum event occur?" by showing that the event resulted from the particular circumstances specified in $C_1, C_2, \ldots, C_k$ in accordance with the laws $L_1, L_2, \ldots, L_r$. This conception of explanation, as exhibited in schema (D), has therefore been referred to as the covering law model, or as the deductive model, of explanation.[2]

A good many scientific explanations can be regarded as deductive-nomological in character. Consider, for example, the explanation of mirror-images, of rainbows, or of the appearance that a spoon handle is bent at the point where it emerges from a glass of water: in all these cases, the explanandum is deductively subsumed under the laws of reflection and refraction. Similarly, certain aspects of free fall and of planetary motion can be accounted for by deductive subsumption under Galileo's or Kepler's laws.

In the illustrations given so far the explanatory laws had, by and large, the character of empirical generalizations connecting different observable aspects of the phenomena under scrutiny: angle of incidence with angle of reflection or refraction, distance covered with falling time, etc. But science raises the question "Why?" also with respect to the uniformities expressed by such laws, and often answers it in basically the same manner, namely, by subsuming the uniformities under more inclusive laws, and eventually under comprehensive theories. For example, the question, "Why do Galileo's and Kepler's laws hold?" is answered by showing that these laws are but special consequences of the Newtonian laws of motion and of gravitation; and these, in turn, may be explained by subsumption under the more comprehensive general theory of relativity. Such subsumption under broader laws or theories usually increases both the breadth and the depth of our scientific understanding. There is an increase in breadth, or scope, because the new explanatory principles cover a broader range of phenomena; for example, Newton's principles govern free fall on the earth and on other celestial bodies, as well as the motions of planets, comets, and artificial satellites, the movements of pendulums, tidal changes, and various other phenomena. And the increase thus effected in the depth of our understanding is strikingly reflected in the fact that, in the light of more advanced explanatory principles, the original empirical laws are usually seen to hold only approximately, or within certain limits. For example, Newton's theory implies that the factor g in Galileo's law, $s = \frac{1}{2} gt^2$, is not strictly a constant for free fall near the surface of the earth; and that, since every planet undergoes gravitational attraction not only from the sun, but also from the other planets, the planetary orbits are not strictly ellipses, as stated in Kepler's laws.

One further point deserves brief mention here. An explanation of a particular event is often conceived as specifying its *cause*, or causes. Thus, the account outlined in our first illustration might be held to explain the growth and the recession of the soap bubbles by showing that the phenomenon was *caused* by a rise and a subsequent drop of the temperature of the air trapped in the tumblers. Clearly, however, these temperature changes provide the requisite explanation only in conjunction with certain other conditions, such as the presence of a soap film, practically constant pressure of the air surrounding the glasses, etc. Accordingly, in the context of explanation, a cause must be allowed to consist in a more or less complex set of particular circumstances; these might be described by a set of sentences: $C_1, C_2, \ldots, C_k$. And, as suggested by the principle "Same cause, same effect," the assertion that those circumstances jointly caused a given event—described, let us say, by a sentence E—implies that whenever and wherever circumstances of the kind in question occur, an event of the kind to be explained comes about. Hence, the given causal explanation implicitly claims that there are general laws—such as $L_1, L_2, \ldots, L_r$ in schema (D)—by virtue of which the occurrence of the causal antecedents mentioned in $C_1, C_2, \ldots, C_k$ is a sufficient condition for the occurrence of the event to be explained. Thus, the relation between causal factors and effect is reflected in schema (D): causal explanation is deductive-nomological in character. (However, the customary formulations of causal and other explanations often do not explicitly specify all the relevant laws and particular facts: to this point, we will return later.)

The converse does not hold: there are deductive-nomological explanations which would not normally be counted as causal. For one thing, the subsumption of laws, such as Galileo's or Kepler's laws, under more comprehensive principles is clearly not causal in character: we speak of causes only in reference to *particular* facts or events, and not in reference to *universal facts* as expressed by general laws. But not even all deductive-nomological explanations of particular facts or events will qualify as causal; for in a causal explanation some of the explanatory circumstances will temporally precede the effect to be explained: and there are explanations of type (D) which lack this characteristic. For example, the pressure which a gas of specified mass possesses at a given time might be explained by reference to its temperature and its volume at the same time, in conjunction with the gas law which connects simultaneous values of the three parameters.[3]

In conclusion, let me stress once more the important role of laws in deductive-nomological explanation: the laws connect the explanandum event with the particular conditions cited in the explanans, and this is what confers upon the latter the status of explanatory (and, in some cases, causal) factors in regard to the phenomenon to be explained.

Probabilistic Explanation

In deductive-nomological explanation as schematized in (D), the laws and theoretical principles involved are of *strictly universal form*: they assert that in *all* cases in which certain specified conditions are realized an occurrence of such and such a kind will result; the law that any metal, when heated under constant pressure, will increase in volume, is a typical example; Galileo's, Kepler's, Newton's, Boyle's, and Snell's laws, and many others, are of the same character.

Now let me turn next to a second basic type of scientific explanation. This kind of explanation, too, is nomological, i.e., it accounts for a given phenomenon by reference to general laws or theoretical principles; but some or all of these are of *probabilistic-statistical form*, i.e., they are, generally speaking, assertions to the effect that if certain specified conditions are realized, then an occurrence of such and such a kind will come about with such and such a statistical probability.

For example, the subsiding of a violent attack of hay fever in a given case might well be attributed to, and thus explained by reference to, the administration of 8 milligrams of chlor-trimeton. But if we wish to connect this antecedent event with the explanandum, and thus to establish its explanatory significance for the latter, we cannot invoke a universal law to the effect that the administration of 8 milligrams of that antihistamine will invariably terminate a hay fever attack: this simply is not so. What can be asserted is only a generalization to the effect that administration of the drug will be followed by relief with high statistical probability, i.e., roughly speaking, with a high relative frequency in the long run. The resulting explanans will thus be of the following type:

John Doe had a hay fever attack and took 8 milligrams of chlor-trimeton.
The probability for subsidence of a hay fever attack upon administration of 8 milligrams of chlor-trimeton is high.

Clearly, this explanans does not deductively imply the explanandum, "John Doe's hay fever attack subsided"; the truth of the explanans makes the truth of the explanandum not certain (as it does in a deductive-nomological explanation) but only more or less likely or, perhaps', "practically" certain.

Reduced to its simplest essentials, a probabilistic explanation thus takes the following form:

$$(P) \quad \frac{Fi}{p(O,F) \text{ is very high}} \quad \text{makes very likely}$$
$$Oi$$

The explanandum, expressed by the statement "Oi," consists in the fact that in the particular instance under consideration, here called i (e.g., John Doe's allergic attack), an outcome of kind O (subsidence) occurred. This is explained by means of two explanans-statements. The first of these, "Fi," corresponds to $C_1, C_2, \ldots, C_k$ in (D); it states that in case i, the factors F (which may be more or less complex) were realized. The second expresses a law of probabilistic form, to the effect that the statistical probability for outcome O to occur in cases where F is realized is very high (close to 1). The double line separating explanandum from explanans is to indicate that, in contrast to the case of deductive-nomological explanation, the explanans does not logically imply the explanandum, but only confers a high likelihood upon it. The concept of likelihood here referred to must be clearly distinguished from that of statistical probability, symbolized by "p" in our schema. A statistical probability is, roughly speaking, the long run relative frequency with which an occurrence of a given kind (say, F) is accompanied by an "outcome" of a specified kind (say, O). Our likelihood, on the other hand, is a relation (capable of gradations) not between kinds of occurrences, but between statements. The likelihood referred to in (P) may be characterized as the strength of the inductive support, or the degree of rational credibility, which the explanans confers upon the explanandum; or, in Carnap's terminology, as the *logical*, or *inductive*, (in contrast to statistical) *probability* which the explanandum possesses relative to the explanans.

Thus, probabilistic explanation, just like explanation in the manner of schema (D), is nomological in that it presupposes general laws; but because these laws are of statistical rather than of strictly universal form, the resulting explanatory arguments are inductive rather than deductive in character. An inductive argument of this kind *explains* a given phenomenon by showing that, in view of certain particular events and certain statistical laws, its occurrence was to be expected with high logical, or inductive, probability.

By reason of its inductive character, probabilistic explanation differs from its deductive-nomological counterpart in several other important respects; for example, its explanans may confer upon the explanandum a more or less high degree of inductive support; in this sense, probabilistic explanation admits of degrees, whereas deductive-nomological explanation appears as an either-or affair: a given set of universal laws and particular statements either does or does not imply a given explanandum statement. A fuller examination of these differences, however, would lead us far afield and is not required for the purposes of this paper.[4]

One final point: the distinction here suggested between deductive-nomological and probabilistic explanation might be questioned on the ground that, after all, the universal laws invoked in a deductive explanation can have been established only on the basis of a finite body of evidence, which surely affords no exhaustive verification, but only more or less strong probability for it; and that, therefore, all scientific laws have to be regarded as probabilistic. This argument, however, confounds a logical issue with an epistemological one: it fails to distinguish properly between the *claim* made by a given law-statement and the *degree of confirmation*, or *probability*, which it possesses on the available evidence. It is quite true that statements expressing laws of either kind can be only incompletely confirmed by any given finite set—however large—of data about particular facts; but law-statements of the two different types make claims of different kind, which are reflected in their logical forms: roughly, a universal law-statement of the simplest kind asserts that *all* elements of an indefinitely large reference class (e.g., copper objects) have a certain characteristic (e.g., that of being good conductors of electricity); while statistical law-statements assert that in the long run, a specified proportion of the members of the reference class have some specified property. And our distinction of two types of law and, concomitantly, of two types of scientific explanation, is based on this difference in claim as reflected in the difference of form.

The great scientific importance of probabilistic explanation is eloquently attested to by the extensive and highly successful explanatory use that has been made of fundamental laws of statistical form in genetics, statistical mechanics, and quantum theory.

ELLIPTIC AND PARTIAL EXPLANATIONS: EXPLANATION SKETCHES

As I mentioned earlier, the conception of deductive-nomological explanation reflected in our schema (D) is often referred to as the covering law model, or the deductive model, of explanation: similarly, the conception underlying schema (P) might be called the probabilistic or the inductive-statistical, model of explanation. The term "model" can serve as a useful reminder that the two types of explanation as characterized above constitute ideal types or theoretical idealizations and are not intended to reflect the manner in which working scientists actually formulate their explanatory accounts. Rather, they are meant to provide explications, or rational reconstructions, or theoretical models, of certain modes of scientific explanation.

In this respect our models might be compared to the concept of mathematical proof (within a given theory) as construed in meta-mathematics. This concept, too, may be regarded as a theoretical model: it is not intended to provide a descriptive account of how proofs are formulated in the writings of mathematicians: most of these actual formulations fall short of rigorous and, as it were, ideal, meta-mathematical standards. But the theoretical model has certain other functions: it exhibits the rationale of mathematical proofs by revealing the logical connections underlying the successive steps; it provides standards for a critical appraisal of any proposed proof constructed within the mathematical system to which the model refers; and it affords a basis for a precise and far-reaching theory of proof, provability, decidability, and related concepts. I think the two models of explanation can fulfill the same functions, if only on a much more modest scale. For example, the arguments presented in constructing the models give an indication of the sense in which the models exhibit the rationale and the logical structure of the explanations they are intended to represent.

I now want to add a few words concerning the second of the functions just mentioned; but I will have to forgo a discussion of the third.

When a mathematician proves a theorem, he will often omit mention of certain propositions which he presupposes in his argument and which he is in fact entitled to presuppose because, for example, they follow readily from the postulates of his system or from previously established theorems or perhaps from the hypothesis of his theorem, if the latter is in hypothetical form; he then simply assumes that his readers or listeners will be able to supply the missing items if they so desire. If judged by ideal standards, the given formulation of the proof is elliptic or incomplete; but the departure from the ideal is harmless: the gaps can readily be filled in. Similarly, explanations put forward in everyday discourse and also in scientific contexts are often *elliptically formulated*. When we explain, for example, that a lump of butter melted because it was put into a hot frying pan, or that a small rainbow appeared in the spray of the lawn sprinkler because the sunlight was reflected and refracted by the water droplets, we may be said to offer elliptic formulations of deductive-nomological explanations; an account of this kind omits mention of certain laws or particular facts which it tacitly takes for granted, and whose explicit citation would yield a complete deductive-nomological argument.

In addition to elliptic formulation, there is another, quite important, respect in which many explanatory arguments deviate from the theoretical model. It often happens that the statement actually included in the explanans, together with those which may reasonably be assumed to have been taken for granted in the context at hand, explain the given explanandum only *partially*, in a sense which I will try to indicate by an example. In his *Psychopathology of Everyday Life*, Freud offers the following explanation of a slip of the pen that occurred to him.

On a sheet of paper containing principally short daily notes of business interest, I found, to my surprise, the incorrect date, "Thursday, October 20th," bracketed under the correct date of the month of September. It was not difficult to explain this anticipation as the expression of a wish. A few days before I had returned fresh from my vacation and felt ready for any amount of professional work, but as yet there were few patients. On my arrival I had found a letter from a patient announcing her arrival on the 20th of October. As I wrote the same date in September I may certainly have thought "X. ought to be here already; what a pity about that whole month!" and with this thought I pushed the current date a month ahead."[5]

Clearly, the formulation of the intended explanation is *at least incomplete* in the sense considered a moment ago. In particular, it fails to mention any laws or theoretical principles in virtue of which the subconscious wish, and the other antecedent circumstances referred to, could be held to explain Freud's slip of the pen. However, the general theoretical considerations Freud presents here and elsewhere in his writings suggest strongly that his explanatory account relies on a hypothesis to the effect that when a person has a strong, though perhaps unconscious, desire, then if he commits a slip of pen, tongue, memory, or the like, the slip will take a form in which it expresses, and perhaps symbolically fulfills, the given desire.

Even this rather vague hypothesis is probably more definite than what Freud would have been willing to assert. But for the sake of the argument let us accept it and include it in the explanans, together with the particular statements that Freud did have the subconscious wish he mentions, and that he was going to commit a slip of the pen. Even then, the resulting explanans permits us to deduce only that the slip made by Freud would, *in some way or other*, express and perhaps symbolically fulfill Freud's subconscious wish. But clearly, such expression and fulfillment might have been achieved by many other kinds of slip of the pen than the one actually committed.

In other words, the explanans does not imply, and thus fully explain, that the particular slip, say s, which Freud committed on this occasion, would fall within the narrow class, say W, of acts which consist in writing the words "Thursday, October 20th"; rather, the explanans implies only that s would fall into a wider class, say F, which includes W as a proper subclass, and which consists of all acts which would express and symbolically fulfill Freud's subconscious wish *in some way or other*.

The argument under consideration might be called a *partial explanation*: it provides complete, or conclusive, grounds for expecting s to be a member of F, and since W is a subclass of F, it thus shows that the explanandum, i.e., s falling within W, accords with, or bears out, what is to be expected in consideration of the explanans. By contrast, a deductive-nomological explanation of the form (D) might then be called *complete* since the explanans here does imply the explanandum.

Clearly, the question whether a given explanatory argument is complete or partial can be significantly raised only if the explanandum sentence is fully specified; only then can we ask whether the explanandum does or does not follow from the explanans. Completeness of explanation, in this sense, is relative to our explanandum sentence. Now, it might seem much more important and interesting to consider instead the notion of a complete explanation of some *concrete event*, such as the destruction of Pompeii, or the death of Adolf Hitler, or the launching of the first artificial satellite: we might want to regard a particular event as completely explained only if an explanatory account of deductive or of inductive form had been provided for all of its aspects. This notion, however, is self-defeating; for any particular event may be regarded as having infinitely many different aspects or characteristics, which cannot all be accounted for by a finite set, however large, of explanatory statements.

In some cases, what is intended as an explanatory account will depart even further from the standards reflected in the model schemata (D) and (P) above. An explanatory account, for example, which is not explicit and specific enough to be reasonably qualified as an elliptically formulated explanation or as a partial one, can often be viewed as an *explanation sketch*: it may suggest, perhaps quite vividly and persuasively, the general outlines of what, it is hoped, can eventually be supplemented so as to yield a more closely reasoned argument based on explanatory hypotheses which are indicated more fully, and which more readily permit of critical appraisal by reference to empirical evidence.

The decision whether a proposed explanatory account is to be qualified as an elliptically formulated deductive or probabilistic explanation, as a partial explanation, as an explanation sketch, or perhaps as none of these is a matter of judicious interpretation; it calls for an appraisal of the intent of the given argument and of the background assumptions that may be assumed to have been tacitly taken for granted, or at least to be available, in the given context. Unequivocal decision rules cannot be set down for this purpose any more than for determining whether a given informally stated inference which is not deductively valid by reasonably strict standards is to count nevertheless as valid but enthymematically formulated, or as fallacious, or as an instance of sound inductive reasoning, or perhaps, for lack of clarity, as none of these.

NOMOLOGICAL EXPLANATION IN HISTORY

So far, we have examined nomological explanation, both deductive and inductive, as found in the natural sciences; and we have considered certain characteristic ways in which actual explanatory accounts often depart from the ideal standards of our two basic models. Now it is time to ask what light the preceding inquiries can shed on the explanatory procedures used in historical research.

In examining this question, we will consider a number of specific explanatory arguments offered by a variety of writers. It should be understood from the beginning that we are here concerned, not to appraise the factual adequacy of these explanations, but only to attempt an explication of the claims they make and of the assumptions they presuppose.

Let us note first, then, that some historical explanations are surely nomological in character: they aim to show that the explanandum phenomenon resulted from certain antecedent, and perhaps, concomitant, conditions; and in arguing these, they rely more or less explicitly on relevant generalizations. These may concern, for example, psychological or sociological tendencies and may best be conceived as broadly probabilistic in character. This point is illustrated by the following argument, which might be called an attempt to explain Parkinson's Law by subsumption under broader psychological principles:

As the activities of the government are enlarged, more people develop a vested interest in the continuation and expansion of governmental functions. People who have jobs do not like to lose them; those who are habituated to certain skills do not welcome change; those who have become accustomed to the exercise of a certain kind of power do not like to relinquish their control—if anything, they want to develop greater power and correspondingly greater prestige. . . . Thus, government offices and bureaus, once created, in turn institute drives, not only to fortify themselves against assault, but to enlarge the scope of their operations.[6]

The psychological generalizations here explicitly adduced will reasonably have to be understood as expressing, not strict uniformities, but strong *tendencies*, which might be formulated by means of rough probability statements; so that the explanation here suggested is probabilistic in character.

As a rule, however, the generalizations underlying a proposed historical explanation are largely left unspecified; and most concrete explanatory accounts have to be qualified as partial explanations or as explanation sketches. Consider, for example, F. J. Turner's essay "The Significance of the Frontier in American History,"[7] which amplifies and defends the view that "Up to our own day American history has been in a large degree the history of the colonization of the Great West. The existence of an area of free land, its continuous recession, and the advance of American settlement westward explain American development. . . . The peculiarity of American institutions is the fact that they have been compelled to adapt themselves . . . to the changes involved in crossing a continent, in winning a wilderness, and in developing at each area of this progress, out of the primitive economic and political conditions of the frontier, the complexity of city life."[8] One of the phenomena Turner considers in developing his thesis is the rapid westward advance of what he calls the Indian trader's frontier. "Why was it," Turner asks, "that the Indian trader passed so rapidly across the continent?"; and he answers, "The explanation of the rapidity of this advance is bound up with the effects of the trader on the Indian. The trading post left the unarmed tribes at the mercy of those that had purchased firearms—a truth which the Iroquois Indians wrote in blood, and so the remote and unvisited tribes gave eager welcome to the trader. . . . This accounts for the trader's power and the rapidity of his advance."[9] There is no explicit mention here of any laws, but it is clear that this sketch of an explanation presupposes, first of all, various particular facts, such as that the remote and unvisited tribes had heard of the efficacy and availability of firearms, and that there were no culture patterns or institutions precluding their use by those tribes; but in addition, the account clearly rests also on certain assumptions as to how human beings will tend to behave in situations presenting the kinds of danger and of opportunity that Turner refers to.

Similar comments apply to Turner's account of the westward advance of what he calls the farmer's frontier.

Omitting those of the pioneer farmers who move from the love of adventure, the advance of the more steady farmer is easy to understand. Obviously the immigrant was attracted by the cheap lands of the frontier, and even the native farmer felt their influence strongly. Year by year the farmers who lived on soil, whose returns were diminished by unrotated crops, were offered the virgin soil of the frontier at nominal prices. Their growing families demanded more lands, and these were dear. The competition of the unexhausted, cheap, and easily tilled prairie lands compelled the farmer either to go West . . . or to adopt intensive culture.[10]

This passage is clearly intended to do more than describe a sequence of particular events: it is meant to afford an understanding of the farmers' westward advance by pointing to their interests and needs and by calling attention to the facts and the opportunities facing them. Again, this explanation takes it for granted that under such conditions normal human beings will tend to seize new opportunities in the manner in which the pioneer farmers did.

Examining the various consequences of this moving-frontier history, Turner states that "the most important effect of the frontier has been in the promotion of democracy here and in Europe,"[11] and he begins his elaboration of this theme with the remark that "the frontier is productive of individualism. . . . The tendency is anti-social. It produces antipathy to control, and particularly to any direct control"[12]: and this is, of course, a sociological generalization in a nutshell.

Similarly, any explanation that accounts for a historical phenomenon by reference to economic factors or by means of general principles of social or cultural change is nomological in import, even if not in explicit formulation.

But if this be granted there still remains another question, to which we must now turn, namely, whether, in addition to explanations of a broadly nomological character, the historian also employs certain other distinctly historical ways of explaining and understanding whose import cannot be adequately characterized by means of our two models. The question has often been answered in the affirmative, and several kinds of historical explanation have been adduced in support of this affirmation. I will now consider what seem to me two especially interesting candidates for the role of specifically historical explanation; namely first, genetic explanation, and secondly, explanation of an action in terms of its underlying rationale.

GENETIC EXPLANATION IN HISTORY

In order to make the occurrence of a historical phenomenon intelligible, a historian will frequently offer a "genetic explanation" aimed at exhibiting the principal stages in a sequence of events which led up to the given phenomenon.

Consider, for example, the practice of selling indulgences as it existed in Luther's time. H. Boehmer, in his work, *Luther and the Reformation*, points out that until about the end of the nineteenth century, "the indulgence was in fact still a great unknown quantity, at sight of which the scholar would ask himself with a sigh: 'Where did it come from?' "[13] An answer was provided by Adolf Gottlob,[14] who tackled the problem by asking himself what led the Popes and Bishops to offer indulgences. As a result, ". . . origin and development of the unknown quantity appeared clearly in the light, and doubts as to its original meaning came to an end. It revealed itself as a true descendant of the time of the great struggle between Christianity and Islam, and at the same time a highly characteristic product of Germanic Christianity."[15]

In brief outline,[16] the origins of the indulgence appear to go back to the ninth century, when the popes were strongly concerned with the fight against Islam. The Mohammedan fighter was assured by the teachings of his religion that if he were to be killed in battle his soul would immediately go to heaven; but the defender of the Christian faith had to fear that he might still be lost if he had not done the regular penance for his sins. To allay these doubts, John VII, in 877, promised absolution for their sins to crusaders who should be killed in battle. "Once the crusade was so highly thought of, it was an easy transition to regard participation in a crusade as equivalent to the performance of atonement . . . and to promise remission of these penances in return for expeditions against the Church's enemies."[17] Thus, there was introduced the indulgence of the Cross, which granted complete remission of the penitential punishment to all those who participated in a religious war. "If it is remembered what inconveniences, what ecclesiastical and civil disadvantages the ecclesiastical penances entailed, it is easy to understand that the penitents flocked to obtain this indulgence."[18] A further strong incentive came from the belief that whoever obtained an indulgence secured liberation not only from the ecclesiastical penances, but also from the corresponding suffering in purgatory after death. The benefits of these indulgences were next extended to those who, being physically unfit to participate in a religious war, contributed the funds required to send a soldier on a crusade: in 1199, Pope Innocent III recognized the payment of money as adequate qualification for the benefits of a crusading indulgence.

When the crusades were on the decline, new ways were explored of raising funds through indulgences. Thus, there was instituted a "jubilee indulgence," to be celebrated every hundred years, for the benefit of pilgrims coming to Rome on that occasion. The first of these indulgences, in 1300, brought in huge sums of money; and the time interval between successive jubilee indulgences was therefore reduced to 50, 33 and even 25 years. And from 1393 on the jubilee indulgence was made available, not only in Rome, for the benefit of pilgrims, but everywhere in Europe, through special agents who were empowered to absolve the penitent of their sins upon payment of an appropriate amount. The development went even further: in 1477, a dogmatic declaration by Sixtus IV attributed to the indulgence the power of delivering even the dead from purgatory.

Undeniably, a genetic account of this kind can enhance our understanding of a historical phenomenon. But its explanatory role, far from being *sui generis*, seems to me basically nomological in character. For the successive stages singled out for consideration surely must be qualified for their function by more than the fact that they form a temporal sequence and that they all precede the final stage, which is to be explained: the mere enumeration in a yearbook of "the year's important events" in the order of their occurrence clearly is not a genetic explanation of the final event or of anything else. In a genetic explanation each stage must be shown to "lead to" the next, and thus to be linked to its successor by virtue of some general principle which makes the occurrence of the latter at least reasonably probable, given the former. But in this sense, even successive stages in a physical phenomenon such as the free fall of a stone may be regarded as forming a genetic sequence whose different stages—characterized, let us say, by the position and the velocity of the stone at different times—are interconnected by strictly universal laws; and the successive stages in the movement of a steel ball bouncing its zigzaggy way down a Galton pegboard may be regarded as forming a genetic sequence with probabilistic connections.

The genetic accounts given by historians are not, of course, of the purely nomological kind suggested by these examples from physics. Rather, they combine a certain measure of nomological interconnecting with more or less large amounts of straight description. For consider an intermediate stage mentioned in a genetic account: some aspects of it will be presented as having evolved from the preceding stages (in virtue of connecting laws, which often will be no more than hinted at); while other aspects, which are not accounted for by information about the preceding development, will be descriptively added because they are relevant to an understanding of subsequent stages in the genetic sequence. Thus, schematically speaking, a genetic explanation will begin with a pure description of an initial stage; thence, it will proceed to an account of a second stage, part of which is nomologically linked to, and explained by, the characteristic features of the initial stage; while the balance is simply described as relevant for a nomological account of some aspects of the third stage; and so forth.[19]

In our illustration the connecting laws are hinted at in the mention made of motivating factors: the explanatory claims made for the interest of the popes in securing a fighting force and in amassing ever larger funds clearly presuppose suitable psychological generalizations as to the manner in which an intelligent individual will act, in the light of his factual beliefs, when he seeks to attain a certain objective. Similarly, general assumptions underly the reference to the fear of purgatory in explaining the eagerness with which indulgences were bought. And when, referring to the huge financial returns of the first jubilee indulgence, Schwiebert says "This success only whetted the insatiable appetite of the popes. The intervening period of time was variously reduced from 100 to 50, to 33, to 25 years . . . ,"[20] the explanatory force here implied might be said to rest on some principle of reinforcement by rewards. As need hardly be added, even if such a principle were explicitly introduced, the resulting account would provide at most a partial explanation; it could not be expected to show, for example, why the intervening intervals should have the particular lengths here mentioned.

In the genetic account of the indulgences, those factors which are simply described (or tacitly presupposed) rather than explained include, for example, the doctrines, the organization, and the power of the Church; the occurrence of the crusades and their eventual decline; and innumerable other factors which are not even explicitly mentioned, but which have to be understood as background conditions if the genetic survey is to serve its explanatory purpose.

The general conception here outlined of the logic of genetic explanation could also be illustrated by reference to Turner's studies of the American frontier; this will be clear even from the brief remarks made earlier on Turner's ideas.

Some analysts of historical development put special emphasis on the importance of the laws underlying a historical explanation; thus, e.g., A. Gerschenkron maintains, "Historical research consists essentially in application to empirical material of various sets of empirically derived hypothetical generalizations and in testing the closeness of the resulting fit, in the hope that in this way certain uniformities, certain typical situations, and certain typical relationships among individual factors in these situations can be ascertained,"[21] and his subsequent substantive observations include a brief genetic survey of patterns of industrial development in nineteenth-century Europe, in which some of the presumably relevant uniformities are made reasonably explicit.

EXPLANATION BY MOTIVATING REASONS

Let us now turn to another kind of historical explanation that is often considered as *sui generis*, namely, the explanation of an action in terms of the underlying *rationale*, which will include, in particular, the ends the agent sought to attain, and the alternative courses of action he believed to be open to him. The following passage explaining the transition from the indulgence of the Cross to the institution of the jubilee indulgence illustrates this procedure: ". . . in the course of the thirteenth century the idea of a crusade more and more lost its power over men's spirits. If the Popes would keep open the important source of income which the indulgence represented, they must invent new motives to attract people to the purchase of indulgences. It is the merit of Boniface VIII to have recognized this clearly. By creating the jubilee indulgence in 1300 he assured the species a further long development most welcome to the Papal finances."[22] This passage clearly seeks to explain the establishment of the first jubilee indulgence by suggesting the reasons would include not only Boniface's objective of ensuring a continuation of the income so far derived from the indulgence of the Cross, but also his estimate of the relevant empirical circumstances, including the different courses of action open to him, and their probable efficacy as well as potential difficulties in pursuing them and adverse consequences to which they might lead.

The kind of explanation achieved by specifying the rationale underlying a given action is widely held to be fundamentally different from nomological explanation as found in the natural sciences. Various reasons have been adduced in support of this view; but I will limit my discussion largely to the stimulating ideas on the subjects that have been set forth by Dray.[23] According to Dray, there is an important type of historical explanation whose features "make the covering law model peculiarly inept"; he calls it "rational explanation," i.e., "explanation which displays the *rationale* of what was done," or, more fully, "a reconstruction of the agent's *calculation* of means to be adopted toward his chosen end in the light of the circumstances in which he found himself." The object of rational explanation is not to subsume the explanandum under general laws, but "to show that what was done was the thing to have done for the reasons given, rather than merely the thing that is done on such occasions, perhaps in accordance with certain laws." Hence, a rational explanation has "an element of *appraisal* in it: it "must exhibit what was done as appropriate or justified." Accordingly, Dray conceives a rational explanation as being based on a standard of appropriateness or of rationality of a special kind which he calls a "*principle of action*," i.e., "a judgment of the form 'When in a situation of type $C_1, C_2, \ldots, C_n$ the thing to do is X.'"

Dray does not give a full account of the kind of "situation" here referred to; but to do justice to his intentions, these situations must evidently be taken to include, at least, items of the following three types: (i) the end the agent was seeking to attain; (ii) the empirical circumstances, as seen by the agent, in which he had to act; (iii) the moral standards or principles of conduct to which the agent was committed. For while this brief list requires considerable further scrutiny and elaboration, it seems clear that only if at least these items are specified does it make sense to raise the question of the appropriateness of what the agent did in the given "situation."

It seems fair to say, then, that according to Dray's conception a rational explanation answers a question of the form "Why did agent A do X?" by offering an explanans of the following type (our formulation replaces the notation "$C_1, C_2 \ldots C_n$" by the simpler "C," without, of course, precluding that the kind of situation thus referred to may be extremely complex):

(R) A was in a situation of type C
In a situation of type C, the appropriate thing to do is X

But can an explanans of this type possibly serve to explain A's having in fact done X? It seems to me beyond dispute that in any adequate explanation of an empirical phenomenon the explanans must provide good grounds for believing or asserting that the explanandum phenomenon did in fact occur. Yet this requirement, which is necessary though not sufficient[24] for an adequate explanation, is not met by a rational explanation as conceived by Dray. For the two statements included in the contemplated explanans (R) provide good reasons for believing that the appropriate thing for A to do was X, but not for believing that A did in fact do X. Thus, a rational explanation in the sense in which Dray appears to understand it does not explain what it is meant to explain. Indeed, the expression "the thing to do" in the standard formulation of a principle of action, "functions as a value term," as Dray himself points out: but then, it is unclear, on purely logical grounds, how the valuational principle expressed by the second sentence in (R), in conjunction with the plainly empirical, non-valuational first sentence, should permit any inferences concerning empirical matters such as A's action, which could not be drawn from the first sentence alone.

To explain, in the general vein here under discussion, why A did in fact do X, we have to refer to the underlying rationale not by means of a normative principle of action, but by descriptive statements to the effect that, at the time in question A was a rational agent, or had the disposition to act rationally; and that a rational agent, when in circumstances of kind C, will always (or: with high probability) do X. Thus construed, the explanans takes on the following form:

(R')

    (a) A was in a situation of type C
    (b) A was disposed to act rationally
    (c) Any person who is disposed to act rationally will, when in a situation of type C, invariably (with high probability) do X

But by this explanans A's having done X is accounted for in the manner of a deductive or of a probabilistic nomological explanation. Thus, insofar as reference to the rationale of an agent does explain his action, the explanation conforms to one of our nomological models.

An analagous diagnosis applies, incidentally, also to explanations which attribute an agent's behavior in a given situation not to rationality and more or less explicit deliberation on his part, but to other dispositional features, such as his character and emotional make-up. The following comment on Luther illustrates this point: "Even stranger to him than the sense of anxiety was the allied sense of fear. In 1527 and 1535, when the plague broke out in Wittenberg, he was the only professor besides Bugenhagen who remained calmly at his post to comfort and care for the sick and dying. . . . He had, indeed, so little sense as to take victims of the plague into his house and touch them with his own hand. Death, martyrdom, dishonor, contempt . . . he feared just as little as infectious disease."[25] It may well be said that these observations give more than a description: that they shed some explanatory light on the particular occurrences mentioned. But in so far as they explain, they do so by presenting Luther's actions as manifestations of certain personality traits, such as fearlessness; thus, the particular acts are again subsumed under generalizations as to how a fearless person is likely to behave under certain circumstances.

It might seem that both in this case and in rational explanation as construed in (R'), the statements which we took to express general laws—namely, (c) in (R'), and the statement about the probable behavior of a fearless person in our last illustration—do not have the character of empirical laws at all, but rather that of analytic statements which simply express part of what is *meant* by a rational agent, a fearless person, or the like. Thus, in contrast to nomological explanations, these accounts in terms of certain dispositional characteristics of the agent appear to presuppose no general laws at all. Now, the idea of analyticity gives rise to considerable philosophical difficulties; but let us disregard these here and take the division of statements into analytic and synthetic to be reasonably clear. Even then, the objection just outlined cannot be upheld. For dispositional concepts of the kind invoked in our explanations have to be regarded as governed by entire clusters of general statements—we might call them symptom statements—which connect the given disposition with various specific manifestations, or symptoms, of its presence (each symptom will be a particular mode of "responding," or acting, under specified "stimulus" conditions); and the whole cluster of these symptom statements for a given disposition will have implications which are plainly not analytic (in the intuitive sense here assumed). Under these circumstances it would be arbitrary to attribute to some of the symptom statements the analytic character of partial definitions.

The logic of this situation has a precise representation in Carnap's theory of reduction sentences.[26] Here, the connections between a given disposition and its various manifest symptoms are assumed to be expressed by a set of so-called reduction sentences (these are characterized by their logical form). Some of these state, in terms of manifest characteristics, sufficient conditions for the presence of the given disposition; others similarly state necessary conditions. The reduction sentences for a given dispositional concept cannot, as a rule, all be qualified as analytic; for jointly they imply certain non-analytic consequences which have the status of general laws connecting exclusively the manifest characteristics; the strongest of the laws so implied is the so-called representative sentence, which "represents, so to speak, the factual content of the set" of all the reduction sentences for the given disposition concept. This representative sentence asserts, in effect, that whenever at least one of the sufficient conditions specified by the given reduction sentences is satisfied, then so are all the necessary conditions laid down by the reduction sentences. And when A is one of the manifest criteria sufficient for the presence of a given disposition, and B is a necessary one, then the statement that whenever A is present so is B will normally turn out to be synthetic.

So far then, I have argued that Dray's construal of explanation by motivating reasons is untenable; that the normative principles of action envisaged by him have to be replaced by statements of a dispositional kind; and that, when this is done, explanations in terms of a motivating rationale, as well as those referring to other psychological factors, are seen to be basically nomological.

Let me add a few further remarks on the idea of rational explanation. First: in many cases of so-called purposive action, there is no conscious deliberation, no rational calculation that leads the agent to his decision. Dray is quite aware of this; but he holds that a rational explanation in his sense is still possible; for "in so far as we say an action is purposive at all, no matter at what level of conscious deliberation, there is a calculation which could be constructed for it: the one the agent would have gone through if he had had time, if he had not seen what to do in a flash, if he had been called upon to account for what he did after the event, etc. And it is by eliciting some such calculation that we explain the action."[27] But the explanatory significance of reasons or "calculations" which are "reconstructed" in this manner is certainly puzzling. If, to take Dray's example, an agent arrives at his decision "in a flash" rather than by deliberation, then it would seem to be simply false to say that the decision can be accounted for by some argument which the agent might have gone through under more propitious circumstances, or which he might produce later if called upon to account for his action; for, by hypothesis, no such argument was in fact gone through by the agent at the crucial time; considerations of appropriateness or rationality played no part in shaping his decision; the rationale that Dray assumes to be adduced and appraised in the corresponding rational explanation is simply fictitious.

But, in fairness to Dray, these remarks call for a qualifying observation: in at least some of the cases Dray has in mind it might not be fictitious to ascribe the action under study to a disposition which the agent acquired through a learning process whose initial stages did involve conscious ratiocination. Consider, for example, the various complex maneuvers of accelerating, braking, signalling, dodging jaywalkers and animals, swerving into and out of traffic lanes, estimating the changes of traffic lights, etc., which are involved in driving a car through city traffic. A beginning driver will often perform these only upon some sort of conscious deliberation or even calculation; but gradually, he learns to do the appropriate thing automatically, "in a flash," without giving them any conscious thought. The habit pattern he has thus acquired may be viewed as consisting in a set of dispositions to react in certain appropriate ways in various situations; and a particular performance of such an appropriate action would then be explained, not by a "constructed" calculation which actually the agent did not perform, but by reference to the disposition just mentioned and thus, again, in a nomological fashion.

The method of explaining a given action by "constructing," in Dray's sense, the agent's calculation of means faces yet another, though less fundamental, difficulty: it will frequently yield a rationalization rather than an explanation, especially when the reconstruction relies on the reasons the agent might produce when called upon to account for his action. As G. Watson remarks, "Motivation, as presented in the perspective of history, is often too simple and straightforward, reflecting the psychology of the Age of Reason. . . . Psychology has come . . . to recognize the enormous weight of irrational and intimately personal impulses in conduct. In history, biography, and in autobiography, especially of public characters, the tendency is strong to present 'good' reasons instead of 'real' reasons."[28] Accordingly, as Watson goes on to point out, it is important, in examining the motivation of historical figures, to take into account the significance of such psychological mechanisms as reaction formation, "the dialectic dynamic by which stinginess cloaks itself in generosity, or rabid pacifism arises from the attempt to repress strong aggressive impulses."[29]

These remarks have a bearing also on an idea set forth by P. Gardiner in his illuminating book on historical explanation.[30] Commenting on the notion of the "real reason" for a man's action, Gardiner says: "In general, it appears safe to say that by a man's 'real reasons' we mean those reasons he would be prepared to give under circumstances where his confession would not entail adverse consequences to himself." And he adds "An exception to this is the psycho-analyst's usage of the expression where different criteria are adopted."[31] This observation might be taken to imply that the explanation of human actions in terms of underlying motives is properly aimed at exhibiting the agent's "real reasons" in the ordinary sense of the phrase, as just described; and that, by implication, reasons in the psychoanalyst's sense require less or no consideration. But such a construal of explanation would give undue importance to considerations of ordinary language. Gardiner is entirely right when he reminds us that the "language in which history is written is for the most part the language of ordinary speech"[32]; but the historian in search of reasons that will correctly explain human actions will obviously have to give up his reliance on the everyday conception of "real reasons" if psychological or other investigations show that real reasons, thus understood, do not yield as adequate an account of human actions as an analysis in terms of less familiar conceptions such as, perhaps, the idea of motivating factors which are kept out of the agent's normal awareness by processes of repression and reaction formation.

I would say, then, first of all, that historical explanation cannot be bound by conceptions that might be implicit in the way in which ordinary language deals with motivating reasons. But secondly, I would doubt that Gardiner's expressly tentative characterization does justice even to what we ordinarily mean when we speak of a man's "real reasons." For considerations of the kind that support the idea of subconscious motives are quite familiar in our time, and we are therefore prepared to say in ordinary, non-technical discourse that the reasons given by an agent may not be the "real reasons" behind his action, even if his statement was subjectively honest, and he had no grounds to expect that it would lead to any adverse consequences for him. For no matter whether an explanation of human actions is attempted in the language of ordinary speech or in the technical terms of some theory, the overriding criterion for what, if anything, should count as a "real," and thus explanatory, reason for a given action is surely not to be found by examining the way in which the term "real reason" has thus far been used, but by investigating what conception of real reason would yield the most satisfactory explanation of human conduct; and ordinary usage gradually changes accordingly.

CONCLUDING REMARKS

We have surveyed some of the most prominent candidates for the role of characteristically historical mode of explanation; and we have found that they conform essentially to one or the other of our two basic types of scientific explanation.

This result and the arguments that led to it do not in any way imply a mechanistic view of man, of society, and of historical processes; nor, of course, do they deny the importance of ideas and ideals for human decision and action. What the preceding considerations do suggest is, rather, that the nature of understanding, in the sense in which explanation is meant to give us an understanding of empirical phenomena, is basically the same in all areas of scientific inquiry; and that the deductive and the probabilistic model of nomological explanation accommodate vastly more than just the explanatory arguments of, say, classical mechanics: in particular, they accord well also with the character of explanations that deal with the influence of rational deliberation, of conscious and subconscious motives, and of ideas and ideals on the shaping of historical events. In so doing, our schemata exhibit, I think, one important aspect of the methodological unity of all empirical science.

NOTES

1. See John Dewey, *How We Think* (Boston, New York, Chicago, 1910), chapter 6.
2. For a fuller presentation of the model and for further references, see, for example, C. G. Hempel and P. Oppenheim, "Studies in the Logic of Explanation," *Philosophy of Science* 15 (1948), pp. 135–75 (Sections 1–7 of this article, which contain all the fundamentals of the presentation, are reprinted in H. Feigl and M. Brodbeck, eds., *Readings in the Philosophy of Science* (New York, 1953)—The suggestive term "covering-law model" is W. Dray's; cf. his *Laws and Explanation in History* (Oxford, 1957), chapter 1. Dray characterizes this type of explanation as "subsuming what is to be explained under a general law" (p. 1), and then rightly urges, in the name of methodological realism, that "the requirement of a *single* law be dropped" (p. 24; italics, the author's): it should be noted, however, that, like the schema (D) above, several earlier publications on the subject (among them the article mentioned at the beginning of this note) make explicit provision for the inclusion of more laws than one in the explanans.
3. The relevance of the covering-law model to causal explanation is examined more fully in section 4 of C. G. Hempel, "Deductive-Nomological *vs.* Statistical Explanation," in H. Feigl, et al., eds., *Minnesota Studies in the Philosophy of Science*, vol 3 (Minneapolis: University of Minnesota Press, 1962).
4. The concept of probabilistic explanation, and some of the peculiar logical and methodological problems engendered by it, are examined in some detail in Part II of the essay cited in note 3.
5. Sigmund Freud, *Psychopathology of Everyday Life*, trans. A. A. Brill (New York: Mentor Books, 1951), p. 64.
6. D. W. McConnell, et al., *Economic Behavior* (New York, 1939), pp. 894–95.
7. First published in 1893, and reprinted in several publications, among them: Everett E. Edwards, ed., *The Early Writings of Frederick Jackson Turner* (Madison, Wisconsin, 1938). Page references given in the present article pertain to this book.
8. Ibid., pp. 185–86.
9. Ibid., pp. 200–201.
10. Ibid., p. 210.
11. Ibid., p. 219.
12. Ibid., p. 220.
13. H. Boehmer, *Luther and the Reformation*, trans. E. S. G. Potter (London, 1930), p. 91.
14. Gottlob's study, *Kreuzablass und Almosenablass*, was published in 1906; cf. the references to the work of Gottlob and other investigators in E. G. Schwiebert, *Luther and His Times* (St. Louis, Missouri, 1950), notes to Chapter 10.
15. Boehmer, *Luther and the Reformation*, p. 91.
16. This outline follows the accounts given by Boehmer, ibid., chapter 3 and by Schwiebert, *Luther and His Times*, chapter 10.

17. Boehmer, ibid., p. 92.
18. Ibid., p. 93.
19. The logic of genetic explanations in history is examined in some detail in E. Nagel's book, *The Structure of Science*, (New York, 1961), pp. 564–68. The conception outlined in the present paper, though arrived at without any knowledge of Nagel's work on this subject, accords well with the latter's results.
20. Schwiebert, *Luther and His Times*, p. 304.
21. Gerschenkron, "Economic Backwardness in Historical Perspective," in B. F. Hoselitz, ed., *The Progress of Underdeveloped Areas* (Chicago, 1952), pp. 3–29.
22. Boehmer, *Luther and the Reformation*, pp. 93–94.
23. W. Dray, *Laws and Explanation in History* (Oxford, 1957), chapter 5. All quotations are from this chapter; italics in the quoted passages are Dray's.
24. Empirical evidence supporting a given hypothesis may afford strong grounds for believing the latter without providing an explanation for it.
25. Boehmer, *Luther and the Reformation*, p. 234.
26. See especially Carnap's classical essay, "Testability and Meaning," *Philosophy of Science* 3 (1936), pp. 419–71 and 4 (1937), pp. 1–40; reprinted, with some omissions, in Feigl and Brodbeck, *Readings in the Philosophy of Science*. On the point here under discussion, see section 9 and particularly section 10 of the original essay or section 7 of the reprinted version.
27. Dray, *Laws and Explanation*, p. 123.
28. G. Watson, "Clio and Psyche: Some Interrelations of Psychology and History," in C. F. Ware, ed., *The Cultural Approach to History* (New York, 1940), pp. 34–47; quotation from p. 36.
29. Ibid.
30. P. Gardiner, *The Nature of Historical Explanation* (Oxford, 1952).
31. Ibid., p. 136.
32. Ibid., p. 63.

WESLEY C. SALMON

STATISTICAL EXPLANATION*

Ever since his classic paper with Paul Oppenheim, "Studies in the Logic of Explanation," first published in 1948,[1] Carl G. Hempel has maintained that an "explanatory account [of a particular event] may be regarded as an argument to the effect that the event to be explained . . . *was to be expected* by reason of certain explanatory facts" (my italics).[2] It seems fair to say that this basic principle has guided Hempel's work on *inductive* as well as *deductive* explanation ever since.[3] In spite of its enormous intuitive appeal, I believe that this precept is incorrect and that it has led to an unsound account of scientific explanation. In this paper I shall attempt to develop a different account of explanation and argue for its superiority over the Hempelian one. In the case of inductive explanation, the difference between the two treatments hinges fundamentally upon the question of whether the relation between the explanans and the explanandum is to be understood as a relation of *high probability* or as one of *statistical relevance*. Hempel obviously chooses the former alternative; I shall elaborate an account based upon the latter one. These two alternatives correspond closely to the "concepts of firmness" and the "concepts of increase of firmness," respectively, distinguished by Rudolf Carnap in the context of confirmation theory.[4] Carnap has argued, convincingly in my opinion, that confusion of these two types of concepts has led to serious trouble in inductive logic; I shall maintain that the same thing has happened in the theory of explanation. Attention will be focused chiefly upon inductive explanation, but I shall try to show that a similar difficulty infects deductive explanation and that, in fact, deductive explanation can advantageously be considered as a special limiting case of inductive explanation. It is my hope that, in the end, the present *relevance* account of scientific explanation will be justified, partly by means of abstract "logical" considerations and partly in terms of its ability to deal with problems that have proved quite intractable within the Hempelian schema.

THE HEMPELIAN ACCOUNT

Any serious contemporary treatment of scientific explanation must, it seems to me, take Hempel's highly developed view as a point of departure. In the famous 1948 paper, Hempel and

Oppenheim offered a systematic account of deductive explanation, but they explicitly denied that all scientific explanations fit that pattern; in particular, they called attention to the fact that some explanations are of the inductive variety. In spite of fairly general recognition of the need for inductive explanations, even on the part of proponents of Hempel's deductive model, surprisingly little attention has been given to the problem of providing a systematic treatment of explanations of this type. Before 1965, when he published "Aspects of Scientific Explanation,"[5] Hempel's "Deductive-Nomological vs. Statistical Explanation"[6] was the only well-known extensive discussion. One could easily form the impression that most theorists regarded deductive and inductive explanation as quite similar in principle, so that an adequate account of inductive explanation would emerge almost routinely by replacing the universal laws of deductive explanation with statistical generalizations, and by replacing the deductive relationship between explanans and explanandum with some sort of inductive relation. Such an attitude was, of course, dangerous in the extreme, for even our present limited knowledge of inductive logic points to deep and fundamental differences between deductive and inductive logical relations. This fact should have made us quite wary of drawing casual analogies between deductive and inductive patterns of explanation.[7] Yet even Hempel's detailed examination of statistical explanation[8] may have contributed to the false feeling of security, for one of the most significant results of that study was that both deductive and inductive explanations must fulfill a *requirement of total evidence*. In the case of deductive explanations the requirement is automatically satisfied; in the case of inductive explanations that requirement is nontrivial.

Accordingly, the situation in May 1965, at the time of the Pittsburgh Workshop Conference, permitted a rather simple and straightforward characterization which would cover both deductive and inductive explanations of particular events.[9] Either type of explanation, according to Hempel, is an argument; as such, it is a linguistic entity consisting of premises and conclusion.[10] The premises constitute the explanans, and the conclusion is the explanandum. The term "explanadum event" may be used to refer to the fact to be explained; the explanandum is the statement asserting that this fact obtains. The term "explanatory facts" may be used to refer to the facts adduced to explain the explanandum event; the explanans is the set of statements asserting that these explanatory facts obtain.[11] In order to explain a particular explanandum event, the explanatory facts must include both particular facts and general uniformities. As Hempel has often said, general uniformities as well as particular facts can be explained, but for now I shall confine my attention to the explanation of particular events.

The parallel between the two types of explanation can easily be seen by comparing examples; here are two especially simple ones Hempel has offered:[12]

(1) *Deductive*
   This crystal of rock salt, when put into a Bunsen flame, turns the flame yellow, for it is a sodium salt, and all sodium salts impart a yellow color to a Bunsen flame.
(2) *Inductive*
   John Jones was almost certain to recover quickly from his streptococcus infection, for he was given penicillin, and almost all cases of streptococcus infection clear up quickly upon administration of penicillin.

These examples exhibit the following basic forms:

(3) *Deductive*
All F are G
$$\frac{x \text{ is } F}{x \text{ is } G}$$

(4) *Inductive*
Almost all F are G
$$\frac{x \text{ is } F}{x \text{ is } G}$$

There are two obvious differences between the deductive and inductive examples. First, the major premise in the deductive case is a universal generalization, whereas the major premise in the inductive case is a statistical generalization. The latter generalization asserts that a high, though unspecified, proportion of F are G. Other statistical generalizations may specify the exact numerical value. Second, the deductive schema represents a valid deductive argument, whereas the inductive schema represents a correct inductive argument. The double line in (4) indicates that the conclusion "follows inductively," that is, with high inductive probability. Hempel has shown forcefully that (4) is *not* to be construed as a deduction with the conclusion that "x is almost certain to be G."[13]

By the time Hempel had provided his detailed comparison of the two types of explanation, certain well-known conditions of adequacy had been spelled out; they would presumably apply both to deductive and to inductive explanations:[14]

(i) The explanatory argument must have correct (deductive or inductive) logical form. In a correct deductive argument the premises entail the conclusion; in a correct inductive argument the premises render the conclusion highly probable.

(ii) The premises of the argument must be true.[15]

(iii) Among the premises there must occur essentially at least one lawlike (universal or statistical) generalization.[16]

(iv) The requirement of total evidence (which is automatically satisfied by deductive explanations that satisfy the condition of validity) must be fulfilled.[17]

Explanations that conform to the foregoing conditions certainly satisfy Hempel's general principle. If the explanation is deductive, the explanandum event was to be expected because the explanandum is deducible from the explanans; the explanans necessitates the explanandum. If the explanation is inductive, it "*explains* a given phenomenon by showing that, in view of certain particular facts and certain statistical laws, its occurrence was to be expected with high logical, or inductive, probability."[18] In this case the explanandum event was to be expected because the explanans confers high probability upon the explanandum; the explanatory facts make the explanandum event highly probable.

SOME COUNTEREXAMPLES

It is not at all difficult to find cases that satisfy all of the foregoing requirements, but that certainly cannot be regarded as genuine explanations. In a previously mentioned paper[19] I offered the following inductive examples:

(5) John Jones was almost certain to recover from his cold within a week, because he took vitamin C, and almost all colds clear up within a week after administration of vitamin C.

(6) John Jones experienced significant remission of his neurotic symptoms, for he underwent extensive psychoanalytical treatment, and a substantial percentage of those who undergo psychoanalytic treatment experience significant remission of neurotic symptoms.

Both of these examples correspond exactly with Hempel's inductive example (2) above, and both conform to his schema (4). The difficulty with (5) is that colds tend to clear up within a week regardless of the medication administered, and, I understand, controlled tests indicate that the percentage of recoveries is unaffected by the use of vitamin C.[20] The problem with (6) is the substantial spontaneous remission rate for neurotic symptoms of individuals who undergo no psychotherapy of any kind. Before we accept (6) as having any explanatory value whatever, we must know whether the remission rate for psychoanalytic patients is any greater than the spontaneous remission rate. I do not have the answer to this factual question.

I once thought that cases of the foregoing sort were peculiar to inductive explanation, but Henry Kyburg has shown me to be mistaken by providing the following example:

(7) This sample of table salt dissolves in water, for it has had a dissolving spell cast upon it, and all samples of table salt that have had dissolving spells cast upon them dissolve in water.[21]

It is easy to construct additional instances:

(8) John Jones avoided becoming pregnant during the past year, for he has taken his wife's birth control pills regularly, and every man who regularly takes birth control pills avoids pregnancy.

Both of these examples correspond exactly with Hempel's deductive example (1), and both conform to his schema (3) above. The difficulty with (7) and (8) is just like that of the inductive examples (5) and (6). Salt dissolves, spell or no spell, so we do not need to explain the dissolving of this sample in terms of a hex. Men do not become pregnant, pills or no pills, so the consumption of oral contraceptives is not required to explain the phenomenon in John Jones's case (though it may have considerable explanatory force with regard to his wife's pregnancy).

Each of the examples (5) through (8) constitutes an argument to show that the explanandum event was to be expected. Each one has correct (deductive or inductive) logical form—at least it has a form provided by one of Hempel's schemata.[22] Each one has true premises (or so we may assume for the present discussion). Each one has a (universal or statistical) generalization among its premises, and there is no more reason to doubt the lawlikeness of any of these generalizations than there is to doubt the lawlikeness of the generalizations in Hempel's examples. In each case the general premise is essential to the argument, for it would cease to have correct logical form if the general premise were simply deleted. We may assume that the requirement of total evidence is fulfilled in all cases. In the deductive examples it is automatically satisfied, of course, and in the inductive examples we may safely suppose that there is no further available evidence which would alter the probability of John Jones's recovery from either his cold or his neurotic symptoms. There is nothing about any of these examples, so far as I can see, which would disqualify them in terms of the foregoing criteria without also disqualifying Hempel's examples as well.

Folklore, ancient and modern, supplies further instances that would qualify as explanatory under these conditions:

(9) The moon reappeared after a lunar eclipse, for the people made a great deal of noise, banging on pots and pans and setting off fireworks, and the moon always reappears after an eclipse when much noise occurs.[23] (Ancient Chinese folklore)
(10) An acid-freak was standing at the corner of Broadway and Forty-second Street, uttering agonizing moans, when a passerby asked him what was the matter. "Why, man, I'm keeping the wild tigers away," he answered. "But there are no wild tigers around here," replied the inquirer. "Yeah, see what a good job I'm doing!" (Modern American folklore)

A question might be raised about the significance of examples of the foregoing kind on the ground that conditions of adequacy are normally understood to be necessary conditions, not sufficient conditions. Thus, the fact that there are cases which satisfy all of the conditions of adequacy but which are not explanations is no objection whatever to the necessity of such conditions; this fact could be construed as an objection only if the conditions of adequacy are held to be jointly sufficient. In answer to this point, it must be noted that, although the Hempel-Oppenheim paper of 1948 did begin by setting out conditions of adequacy, it also offered a definition of deductive-nomological explanation, that is, explicit necessary and sufficient conditions.[24] The deductive examples offered above satisfy that definition. And if that definition is marred by purely technical difficulties, it seems clear that the examples conform to the spirit of the original definition.

One might, however, simply acknowledge the inadequacy of the early definition and maintain only that the conditions of adequacy should stand as necessary conditions for satisfactory explanations. In that case the existence of a large class of examples of the foregoing sort would seem to point only to the need for additional conditions of adequacy to rule them out. Even if one never hopes to have a set of necessary conditions that are jointly sufficient, a large and important set of examples which manifest a distinctive characteristic disqualifying them as genuine explanations demands an additional condition of adequacy. Thus, it might be said, the way to deal with the counterexamples is by adding a further condition of adequacy, much as Hempel has done in "Aspects of Scientific Explanation," where he enunciates the *requirement of maximal specificity*.[25] I shall argue, however, that this requirement does not exclude the examples I have offered, although a minor emendation will enable it to do so. Much more significantly, I shall maintain that the requirement of maximal specificity is the wrong type of requirement to take care of the difficulties that arise and that a much more fundamental revision of Hempel's conception is demanded. However, before beginning the detailed discussion of the requirement of maximal specificity, I shall make some general remarks about the counterexamples and their import—especially the inductive ones—in order to set the stage for a more enlightening discussion of Hempel's recent addition to the set of conditions of adequacy.

PRELIMINARY ANALYSIS

The obvious trouble with our horrible examples is that the "explanatory" argument is not needed to make us see that the explanandum event was to be expected. There are other, more satisfactory, grounds for this expectation. The "explanatory facts" adduced are irrelevant to the explanandum event despite the fact that the explanandum follows (deductively or inductively) from the explanans. Table salt dissolves in water regardless of hexing, almost all colds clear up within a week regardless of treatment, males do not get pregnant regardless of pills, the moon reappears regardless of the amount of Chinese din, and there are no wild tigers in Times Square regardless of our friend's moans. Each of these explanandum events has a high prior probability independent of the explanatory facts, and the probability of the explanandum event relative to the explanatory facts is the same as this prior probability. In this sense the explanatory facts are irrelevant to the explanandum event. The explanatory facts do nothing to enhance the probability of the explanandum event or to make us more certain of its occurrence than we would otherwise have been. This is not because we know that the fact to be explained has occurred; it is because we had other grounds for expecting it to occur, *even if we had not already witnessed it.*

Our examples thus show that it is not correct, even in a preliminary and inexact way, to characterize explanatory accounts as arguments showing that the explanandum event was to be expected. It is more accurate to say that an explanatory argument shows that the probability of the explanandum event relative to the explanatory facts is substantially greater than its prior probability.[26] An explanatory account, on this view, increases the degree to which the explanandum event was to be expected. As will emerge later in this paper, I do not regard such a statement as fully accurate; in fact, the increase in probability is merely a pleasant by-product which often accompanies a much more fundamental characteristic. Nevertheless, it makes a useful starting point for further analysis.

We cannot, of course, hope to understand even the foregoing rough characterization without becoming much clearer on the central concepts it employs. In particular, we must consider explicitly what is meant by "probability" and "prior probability." There are several standard views on the nature of probability, and I propose to consider briefly how the foregoing characterization of explanation, especially inductive explanation, would look in terms of each.

a. According to the *logical interpretation*, probability or degree of confirmation is a logical relation between evidence and hypothesis.[27] Degree of confirmation statements are analytic. There is no analogue of the rule of detachment (*modus ponens*), so inductive logic does not provide any basis for asserting inductive conclusions. There are certain methodological rules for the application of inductive logic, but these are not part of inductive logic itself. One such rule is the requirement of total evidence. For any given explanandum, taken as hypothesis, there are many true degrees of confirmation statements corresponding to different possible evidence statements. The probability value to be chosen for practical applications is that given by the degree of confirmation statement embodying the total available (relevant) evidence. This is the value to be taken as a fair betting quotient, as an estimate of the relative frequency, or as the value to be employed in calculating the estimated utility.

I have long been seriously puzzled as to how Carnap's conception of logical probability could be consistently combined with Hempel's views on the nature of explanation.[28] In the first place, for purposes of either deductive or inductive explanation, it is not clear how the universal or statistical generalizations demanded by Hempel's schemata are to become available, for inductive logic has no means of providing such generalizations as detachable conclusions of any argument. In the second place, degree of confirmation statements embodying particular hypothesis statements and particular evidence statements are generally available, so inductive "inferences" from particulars to particulars are quite possible. In view of this fact, it is hard to see why inductive explanation should require any sort of general premise. In the third place, the relation between explanans and explanandum would seem to me to be a degree of confirmation statement, and not an argument with premises and conclusions in the usual sense. This last point seems to me to be profoundly important. Carnap's recognition that much, if not all, of inductive logic can proceed without inductive arguments—that is, without establishing conclusions on the basis of premises—is a deep insight that must be reckoned with. As a consequence, we must seriously question whether an explanation is an argument at all. This possibility arises, as I shall try to show later, even if one does not adhere to a logical interpretation of probability. Indeed, within an account of explanation in terms of the frequency interpretation, I shall argue contra Hempel that *explanations are not arguments.*[29]

For the logical interpretation of probability, it would seem, an explanation should involve an addition of new evidence to the body of total evidence resulting in a new body of total evidence relative to which the probability of the explanandum is higher than it was relative to the old body of total evidence. In the usual situation, of course, an explanation is sought only after it is known that the explanandum event has occurred. In this case, the body of total evidence already contains the explanandum, so no addition to the body of total evidence can change its probability. We must, therefore, somehow circumscribe a body of total evidence available prior to the occurrence of the explanandum event, relative to which our prior probability is to be taken. This body of evidence must contain neither the explanans nor the explanandum.[30]

The logical interpretation of probability admits degrees of confirmation on tautological evidence, and these probabilities are not only prior but also *a priori*. But *a priori* prior probabilities are not especially germane to the present discussion. We are not concerned with the *a priori* probability of a Bunsen flame turning yellow, nor with the *a priori* probability of a cold clearing up in a week, nor with the *a priori* probability of a remission of one's neurotic symptoms, nor with the *a priori* probability of finding a wild tiger in Times Square, etc. We are concerned with the probabilities of these events relative to more or less specific factual evidence. The prior probabilities are not logically *a priori*; they are prior with respect to some particular information or investigation.

b. According to the new *subjective* or *personalistic interpretation*, probability is simply orderly opinion.[31] The required orderliness is provided by the mathematical calculus of probability. One of the main concerns of the personalists is with the revision of opinion or degree of belief in the light of new evidence. The account of explanation suggested above fits very easily with the personalistic interpretation. At some time before the explanandum event occurs, the personalist would say, an individual has a certain degree of belief that it will occur—reflected, perhaps, in the kind of odds he is willing to give or take in betting on its occurrence. According to the present view of explanation, a personalist should require that the explanatory facts be such as to increase the prior confidence in the occurrence of the explanandum event. Of course, this view deliberately introduces into its treatment of scientific explanation a large degree of subjectivity, but this is not necessarily a defect in either the account of probability or the account of explanation.

c. According to the *frequency interpretation*, a probability is the limit of the relative frequency of an attribute in an infinite sequence of events.[32] A probability cannot, therefore, literally be assigned to a single event. Since there are many occasions when we must associate probabilities with single events, and not only with large (literally, infinite) aggregates of events, a way must be found for making the probability concept applicable to single events. We wager on single events—a single toss of the dice, a single horse race, a single deal of the cards. The results of our practical planning and effort depend upon the outcomes of single occurrences, not infinite sequences of them. If probability is to be a guide of life, it must be meaningful to apply probability values to single events. This problem of the single case has traditionally been one of the difficulties confronting the frequency theory, and we shall have to examine in some detail the way in which it can be handled. With regard to the single case, the frequency interpretation is on an entirely different footing from the logical and subjective interpretations. Neither of these latter interpretations faces any special problem of the single case, for statements about single events are perfectly admissible hypotheses for the logical theory, and the subjective theory deals directly with degrees of belief regarding single events.

The central topic of concern in this paper is the explanation of single events. If the frequency theory is to approach this problem at all, it must deal directly with the problem of the single case. To some, the fact that the frequency interpretation is faced with this special problem of the single case may constitute a compelling reason for concluding that the frequency interpretation is totally unsuitable for handling the explanation of single events. Such a conclusion would, I think, be premature. On the contrary, I would argue that a careful examination of the way in which the frequency interpretation handles the single case should prove extremely illuminating with respect to the general problem of inductive explanation. Although I have strong prejudices in favor of the frequency interpretation, this paper is, nevertheless, not the place to argue for them.[33] In this context I would claim instead that frequencies play such an important role in any theory of probability that an examination of the problem of the single case cannot fail to cast light on the problem of explanation regardless of one's persuasion concerning interpretations of the probability concept.

d. In recent years there has been a good deal of discussion of the *propensity interpretation* of probability.[34] This interpretation is so similar to the frequency interpretation in fundamental respects that everything I shall say about the problem of the single case for the frequency interpretation can be made directly applicable to the propensity interpretation by a simple translation: wherever I speak of "the problem of selecting the appropriate reference class" in connection with the frequency interpretation, read "the problem of specifying the nature of the chance setup" in reference to the propensity interpretation. It seems to me that precisely parallel considerations apply for these two interpretations of probability.

THE SINGLE CASE

Let A be an unending sequence of draws of balls from an urn, and let B be the class of red things. A is known as the *reference class*, and B the *attribute class*. The probability of red draws from this urn, $P(A,B)$, is the limit of the relative frequency with which members of the reference class belong to the attribute class, that is, the limit of the relative frequency with which draws from the urn result in a red ball as the number of draws increases without any bound.[35]

Frequentists like John Venn and Hans Reichenbach have dealt with the problem of the single case by assigning each single event to a reference class and by transferring the probability value from that reference class to the single event in question.[36] Thus, if the limit of the relative frequency of red among draws from our urn is one-third, then we say that the probability of getting red on *the next draw* is one-third. In this way the meaning of the probability concept has been extended so that it applies to single events as well as to large aggregates.

The fundamental difficulty arises because a given event can be referred to any of a large number of reference classes, and the probability of the attribute in question may vary considerably from one of these to another. For instance, we could place two urns on a table, the one on the left containing only red balls, the one on the right containing equal numbers of red, white, and blue balls. The reference class A might consist of blind drawings from the right-hand urn, the ball being replaced and the urn thoroughly shaken after each draw. Another reference class A' might consist of draws made alternately from the left- and the right-hand urns. Infinitely many other reference classes are easily devised to which the next draw—the draw with which we are concerned—belongs. From which reference class shall we transfer our probability value to this single case? A method must be established for choosing the appropriate reference class. Notice, however, that there is no difficulty in selecting an attribute class. The question we ask determines the attribute class. We want to know the probability of getting red, so there is no further problem about the attribute class.

Reichenbach recommends adopting as a reference class "the narrowest class for which reliable statistics can be compiled."[37] This principle is, as Reichenbach himself has observed, rather ambiguous. Since increasing the reliability of statistics generally tends to broaden the class and since narrowing the class often tends to reduce the reliability of the statistics, the principle involves two desiderata which pull in opposite directions. It seems that we are being directed to maximize two variables that cannot simultaneously be maximized. This attempt to extend the meaning of the probability concept to single cases fails to provide a method for associating a unique probability value with a given single event. Fully aware of this fact, Reichenbach insisted that the probability concept applies *literally* only to sequences; talk about the probability of a single event is "elliptical" and the extended meaning is "fictitious." The choice of a reference class, he maintained, is often dictated by practical rather than theoretical considerations.

Although Reichenbach has not said so, it seems reasonable to suppose that he was making a distinction similar to that made by Carnap between the principles belonging to inductive logic and methodological rules for the application of inductive logic.[38] The requirement of total evidence, it will be recalled, is a methodological rule for the application of inductive logic. Reichenbach could be interpreted as suggesting analogously that probability theory itself is concerned only with limit statements about relative frequencies in infinite sequences of events, whereas the principle for selection of a reference class stands as a methodological rule for the practical application of probability statements. (A much stronger analogy between the requirement of total evidence and the principle for choosing a reference class for a single case will be shown below.) In fact, for Reichenbach, it might have been wise to withhold the term "probability" from single events, reserving his term "weight" for this purpose. We could then say that practical considerations determine what probability should be chosen to serve as a weight for a particular single event. The relative practical importance of reliability and precision would then determine the extent to which narrowness gives way to reliability of statistics (or conversely) in determining the appropriate reference class.

Although Reichenbach's formulation of the principle for the selection of reference classes is not entirely satisfactory, his intention seems fairly clear. In order to transfer a probability value from a sequence to a single case, it is necessary to have some basis for ascertaining the probability in that sequence. The reference class must, therefore, be broad enough to provide the required number of instances for examination to constitute evidence for an inductive inference. At the same time, we want to avoid choosing a reference class so broad that it includes cases irrelevant to the one with which we are concerned.

Statistical relevance is the essential notion here. It is desirable to narrow the reference class in statistically relevant ways, but not in statistically irrelevant ways. When we choose a reference class to which to refer a given single case, we must ask whether there is any statistically relevant way to subdivide that class. If so, we may choose the narrower subclass that results from the subdivision; if no statistically relevant way is known, we must avoid making the reference class any narrower. Consider, for example, the probability that a particular individual, John Smith, will still be alive ten years hence. To determine this probability, we take account of his age, sex, occupation, and health; we ignore his eye color, his automobile license number, and his last initial. We expect the relative frequency of survival for ten more years to vary among the following reference classes: humans, Americans, American males, forty-two-year-old American males, forty-two-year-old American male steeplejacks suffering from advanced cases of lung cancer. We believe that the relative frequency of survival for another ten years is the same in the following classes: forty-two-year-old American male steeplejacks with advanced cases of lung cancer, forty-two-year-old blue-eyed American male steeplejacks with advanced cases of lung cancer, and forty-two-year-old blue-eyed American male steeplejacks with even automobile license plate numbers who suffer from advanced cases of lung cancer.

Suppose we are dealing with some particular object or event x, and we seek to determine the probability (weight) that it has attribute B. Let x be assigned to a reference class A, of which it is a member. $P(A,B)$ is the probability of this attribute within this reference class. A set of mutually exclusive and exhaustive subclasses of a class is a *partition* of that class. We shall often be concerned with partitions of reference classes into two subclasses; such partitions can be effected by a property C which divides the class A into two subclasses, $A.C$ and $A.\bar{C}$. A property C is said to be *statistically relevant* to B within A if and only if $P(A.C,B) \neq P(A,B)$. This notion of statistical relevance is the fundamental concept upon which I hope to build an explication of inductive explanation.

In his development of a frequency theory based essentially upon the concept of randomness, Richard von Mises introduced the notion of a *place selection*: "By a place selection we mean the selection of a partial sequence in such a way that we decide whether an element should or should not be included without making use of the attribute of the element."[39] A place selection effects a partition of a reference class into two subclasses, elements of the place selection and elements not included in the place selection. In the reference class of draws from our urn, every third draw starting with the second, every $k$the draw where k is prime, every draw following a red result, every draw made with the left hand, and every draw made while the sky is cloudy all would be place selections. "Every draw of a red ball" and "every draw of a ball whose color is at the opposite end of the spectrum from violet" do not define place selections, for membership in these classes cannot be determined without reference to the attribute in question.

A place selection may or may not be statistically relevant to a given attribute in a given reference class. If the place selection is statistically irrelevant to an attribute within a reference class, the probability of that attribute within the subclass determined by the place selection is equal to the probability of that attribute within the entire original reference class. If every place selection is irrelevant to a given attribute in a given sequence, von Mises called the sequence *random*. If every property that determines a place selection is statistically irrelevant to B in A, I shall say that A is a *homogeneous reference class* for B. A reference class is homogeneous if there is no way, even in principle, to effect a statistically relevant partition without already knowing which elements have the attribute in question and which do not. Roughly speaking, each member of a homogeneous reference class is a random member.

The aim in selecting a reference class to which to assign a single case is not to select the narrowest, but the widest, available class. However, the reference class should be homogeneous, and achieving homogeneity requires making the reference class narrower if it was not already homogeneous. I would reformulate Reichenbach's method of selection of a reference class as follows: choose the broadest homogeneous reference class to which the single event belongs. I shall call this the *reference class rule*.

Let me make it clear immediately that, although I regard the above formulation as an improvement over Reichenbach's, I do not suppose that it removes all ambiguities about the selection of reference classes either in principle or in practice. In principle it is possible for an event to belong to two equally wide homogeneous reference classes, and the probabilities of the attribute in these two classes need not be the same. For instance, suppose that the drawing from the urn is not random and that the limit of the relative frequency of red for every kth draw (k prime) is $1/4$, whereas the limit of the relative frequency of red for every even draw is $3/4$. Each of these subsequences may be perfectly random; each of the foregoing place selections may, therefore, determine a homogeneous reference class. Since the intersection of these two place selections is finite, it does not determine a reference class for a probability. The second draw, however, belongs to both place selections; in this fictitious case there is a genuine ambiguity concerning the probability to be taken as the weight of red on the second draw.

In practice we often lack full knowledge of the properties relevant to a given attribute, so we do not know whether our reference class is homogeneous or not. Sometimes we have strong reason to believe that our reference class is not homogeneous, but we do not know what property will effect a statistically relevant partition. For instance, we may believe that there are causal factors that determine which streptococcus infections will respond to penicillin and which ones will not, but we may not yet know what these causal factors are. When we know or suspect that a reference class is not homogeneous, but we do not know how to make any statistically relevant partition, we may say that the reference class is *epistemically homogeneous*. In other cases, we know that a reference class is inhomogeneous and we know what attributes would effect a statistically relevant partition, but it is too much trouble to find out which elements belong to each subclass of the partition. For instance, we believe that a sufficiently detailed knowledge of the initial conditions under which a coin is tossed would enable us to predict (perfectly or very reliably) whether the outcome will be heads or tails, but practically speaking we are in no position to determine these initial conditions or make the elaborate calculations required to predict the outcome. In such cases we may say that the reference class is *practically homogeneous*.[40]

The reference class rule remains, then, a methodological rule for the application of probability knowledge to single events. In practice we attempt to refer our single cases to classes that are practically or epistemically homogeneous. When something important is at stake, we may try to extend our knowledge in order to improve the degree of homogeneity we can achieve. Strictly speaking, we cannot meaningfully refer to degrees of homogeneity until a quantitative concept of homogeneity has been provided.

It would, of course, be a serious methodological error to assign a single case to an inhomogeneous reference class if neither epistemic nor practical considerations prevent partitioning to achieve homogeneity. This fact constitutes another basis for regarding the reference class rule as the counterpart of the requirement of total evidence. The requirement of total evidence demands that we use all available relevant evidence; the reference class rule demands that we partition whenever we have available a statistically relevant place selection by means of which to effect the partition.

Although we require homogeneity, we must also prohibit partitioning of the reference class by means of statistically irrelevant place selections. The reason is obvious. Irrelevant partitioning reduces, for no good reason, the inductive evidence available for ascertaining the limiting frequency of our attribute in a reference class that is as homogeneous as we can make it. Another important reason for prohibiting irrelevant partitions will emerge below when we discuss the importance of multiple homogeneous reference classes.

A couple of fairly obvious facts about homogeneous reference classes should be noted at this point. If all A's are B, A is a homogeneous reference class for B. (Somewhat counterintuitively, perhaps, B occurs perfectly randomly in A.) In this case, $P(A,B) = 1$ and $P(A.C,B) = 1$ for any C whatever; consequently, no place selection can yield a probability for B different from that in the reference class A. Analogously, A is homogeneous for B if no As are B. In the frequency interpretation, of course, $P(A,B)$ can equal one even though not all As are B. It follows that a probability of one does not entail that the reference class is homogeneous.

Some people maintain, often on *a priori* grounds, that A is homogeneous (not merely practically or epistemically homogeneous) for B only if all As are B or no As are B; such people are determinists. They hold that causal factors always determine which As are not B; these causal factors can, in principle, be discovered and used to construct a place selection for making a statistically relevant partition of A. I do not believe in this particular form of determinism. It seems to me that there are cases in which A is a homogeneous reference class for B even though not all As are B. In a sample of radioactive material a certain percentage of atoms disintegrate in a given length of time; no place selection can give us a partition of the atoms for which the frequency of disintegration differs from that in the whole sample. A beam of electrons is shot at a potential barrier and some pass through while others are reflected; no place selection will enable us to make a statistically relevant partition in the class of electrons in the beam. A beam of silver atoms is sent through a strongly inhomogeneous magnetic field (Stern-Gerlach experiment); some atoms are deflected upward and some are deflected downward, but there is no way of partitioning the beam in a statistically relevant manner. Some theorists maintain, of course, that further investigation will yield information that will enable us to make statistically relevant partitions in these cases, but this is, at present, no more than a declaration of faith in determinism. Whatever the final resolution of this controversy, the homogeneity of A for B does not logically entail that all As are B. The truth or falsity of determinism cannot be settled *a priori*.

The purpose of the foregoing excursus on the frequency treatment of the problem of the single case has been to set the stage for a discussion of the explanation of particular events. Let us reconsider some of our examples in the light of this theory. The relative frequency with which we encounter instances of water-soluble substances in the normal course of things is noticeably less than one; therefore, the probability of water solubility in the reference class of samples of unspecified substances is significantly less than one. If we ask why a particular sample of unspecified material has dissolved in water, the prior weight of this explanandum event is less than one as referred to the class of samples of unspecified substances. This broad reference class is obviously inhomogeneous with respect to water solubility. If we partition it into the subclass of samples of table salt and samples of substances other than table salt, it turns out that every member of the former subclass is water-soluble. The reference class of samples of table salt is homogeneous with respect to water solubility. The weight for the single case, referred to this homogeneous reference class, is much greater than its prior weight. By referring the explanandum event to a homogeneous reference class and substantially increasing its weight, we have provided an inductive explanation of its occurrence. As the discussion develops, we shall see that the homogeneity of the reference class is the key to the explanation. The increase in weight is a fortunate dividend in many cases.

If we begin with the reference class of samples of table salt, asking why this sample of table salt dissolves in water, we already have a homogeneous reference class. If, however, we subdivide that reference class into hexed and unhexed samples, we have added nothing to the explanation of dissolving, for no new probability value results and we have not made the already homogeneous reference class any more homogeneous. Indeed, we have made matters worse by introducing a statistically irrelevant partition.

The original reference class of samples of unspecified substances can be partitioned into hexed and unhexed samples. If this partition is accomplished by means of a place selection— that is, if the hexing is done without reference to previous knowledge about solubility—the probabilities of water solubility in the subclasses will be no different from the probability in the original reference class. The reference class of hexed samples of unspecified substances is no more homogeneous than the reference class of samples of unspecified substances; moreover, it is narrower. The casting of a dissolving spell is statistically irrelevant to water solubility, so it cannot contribute to the homogeneity of the reference class, and it must not be used in assigning a weight to the single case. For this reason it contributes nothing to the explanation of the fact that this substance dissolves in water.

The vitamin C example involves the same sort of consideration. In the class of colds in general, there is a rather high frequency of recovery within a week. In the narrower reference class of colds for which the victim has taken vitamin C, the frequency of recovery within a week is no different. Vitamin C is not efficacious, and that fact is reflected in the statistical irrelevance of administration of vitamin C to recovery from a cold within a week. Subdivision of the reference class in terms of administration of vitamin C does not yield a more homogeneous reference class and, consequently, does not yield a higher weight for the explanandum event. In similar fashion, we know that noisemaking and shooting off fireworks are statistically irrelevant to the reappearance of the moon after an eclipse, and we know that our friend's loud moaning is statistically irrelevant to finding a wild tiger in Times Square. In none of these horrible examples do the "explanatory facts" contribute anything toward achieving a homogeneous reference class or to an increase of posterior weight over prior weight.

· ·

THE NATURE OF STATISTICAL EXPLANATION

Let me now, at long last, offer a general characterization of explanations of particular events. As I have suggested earlier, we may think of an explanation as an answer to a question of the form, "Why does this x which is a member of A have the property B?" The answer to such a question consists of a partition of the reference class A into a number of subclasses, all of which are homogeneous with respect to B, along with the probabilities of B within each of these subclasses. In addition, we must say which of the members of the partition contains our particular x. More formally, an explanation of the fact that x, a member of A, is a member of B would go as follows:

$$P(A.C_1,B) = p_1$$
$$P(A.C_2,B) = p_2$$

$$\cdot$$
$$\cdot$$
$$\cdot$$

$$P(A.C_n,B) = p_n$$

where

$A.C_1, A.C_2, \ldots, A.C_n$ is a homogeneous partition of A with respect to B,

$p_i = p_j$ only if $i = j$, and

$x \in A.C_k$.

With Hempel, I regard an explanation as a linguistic entity, namely, a set of statements, but unlike him, I do not regard it as an argument. On my view, an explanation is a set of probability statements, qualified by certain provisoes, plus a statement specifying the compartment to which the explanandum event belongs.

The question of whether explanations should be regarded as arguments is, I believe, closely related to the question, raised by Carnap, of whether inductive logic should be thought to contain rules of acceptance (or detachment).[41] Carnap's problem can be seen most clearly in connection with the famous lottery paradox. If inductive logic contains rules of inference which enable us to draw conclusions from premises—much as in deductive logic—then there is presumably some number r which constitutes a lower bound for acceptance. Accordingly, any hypothesis h whose probability on the total available relevant evidence is greater than or equal to r can be accepted on the basis of that evidence. (Of course, h might subsequently have to be rejected on the basis of further evidence.) The problem is to select an appropriate value for r. It seems that no value is satisfactory, for no matter how large r is, provided it is less than one, we can construct a fair lottery with a sufficient number of tickets to be able to say for each ticket that will not win, because the probability of its not winning is greater than r. From this we can conclude that no ticket will win, which contradicts the stipulation that this is a fair lottery—no lottery can be considered fair if there is *no* winning ticket.

It was an exceedingly profound insight on Carnap's part to realize that inductive logic can, to a large extent anyway, dispense entirely with rules of acceptance and inductive inferences in the ordinary sense. Instead, inductive logic attaches numbers to hypotheses, and these numbers are used to make practical decisions. In some circumstances such numbers, the degrees of confirmation, may serve as fair betting quotients to determine the odds for a fair bet on a given hypothesis. There is no rule that tells one when to accept an hypothesis or when to reject it; instead, there is a rule of practical behavior that prescribes that we so act as to maximize our expectation of utility.[42] Hence, inductive logic is simply not concerned with inductive arguments (regarded as entities composed of premises and conclusions).

Now, I do not completely agree with Carnap on the issue of acceptance rules in inductive logic; I believe that inductive logic does require some inductive inferences.[43] But when it comes to probabilities (weights) of single events, I believe that he is entirely correct. In my view, we must establish by inductive inference probability statements, which I regard as statements about limiting frequencies. But, when we come to apply this probability knowledge to single events, we procure a weight which functions just as Carnap has indicated—as a fair betting quotient or as a value to be used in computing an expectation of utility.[44] Consequently, I maintain, in the context of statistical explanation of individual events, we do not need to try to establish the explanandum as the conclusion of an inductive argument; instead, we need to establish the weights that would appropriately attach to such explanandum events for purposes of betting and other practical behavior. That is precisely what the partition of the reference class into homogeneous subclasses achieves: it establishes the correct weight to assign to *any* member of A with respect to its being a B. First, one determines to which compartment C_k it belongs, and then one adopts the value p_k as the weight. Since we adopted the *multiple homogeneity rule*, we can genuinely handle any member of A, not just those which happen to fall into one subclass of the original reference class.

One might ask on what grounds we can claim to have characterized explanation. The answer is this. When an explanation (as herein explicated) has been provided, we know exactly how to regard any A with respect to the property B. We know which ones to bet on, which to bet against, and at what odds. We know precisely what degree of expectation is rational. We know how to face uncertainty about an A's being a B in the most reasonable, practical, and efficient way. We know every factor that is relevant to an A having property B. We know exactly the weight that should have been attached to the prediction that this A will be a B. We know all of the regularities (universal or statistical) that are relevant to our original question. What more could one ask of an explanation?

There are several general remarks that should be added to the foregoing theory of explanation:

a. It is evident that explanations as herein characterized are nomological. For the frequency interpretation probability statements are statistical generalizations, and every explanation must contain at least one such generalization. Since an explanation essentially consists of a set of statistical generalizations, I shall call these explanations "statistical" without qualification, meaning thereby to distinguish them from what Hempel has recently called "inductive-statistical."[45] His inductive-statistical explanations contain statistical generalizations, but they are inductive inferences as well.

b. From the standpoint of the present theory, deductive-nomological explanations are just a special case of statistical explanation. If one takes the frequency theory of probability as literally dealing with infinite classes of events, there is a difference between the universal generalization, "All A are B," and the statistical generalization, "$P(A,B) = 1$," for the former admits no As that are not Bs, whereas the latter admits of infinitely many As that are not Bs. For this reason, if the universal generalization holds, the reference class A is homogeneous with respect to B, whereas the statistical generalization may be true even if A is not homogeneous. Once this important difference is noted, it does not seem necessary to offer a special account of deductive-nomological explanations.

c. The problem of symmetry of explanation and prediction, which is one of the most hotly debated issues in discussions of explanation, is easily answered in the present theory. To explain an event is to provide the best possible grounds we could have had for making predictions concerning it. An explanation does not show that the event was to be expected; it shows what sorts of expectations would have been reasonable and under what circumstances it was to be expected. To explain an event is to show to what degree it was to be expected, and this degree may be translated into practical predictive behavior such as wagering on it. In some cases the explanation will show that the explanandum event was not to be expected, but that does not destroy the symmetry of explanation and prediction. The symmetry consists in the fact that the explanatory facts constitute the fullest possible basis for making a prediction of whether or not the event would occur. To explain an event is not to predict it ex post facto, but a complete explanation does provide complete grounds for rational prediction concerning that event. Thus, the present account of explanation does sustain a thoroughgoing symmetry thesis, and this symmetry is not refuted by explanations having low weights.

d. In characterizing statistical explanation, I have required that the partition of the reference class yield subclasses that are, in fact, homogeneous. I have not settled for practical or epistemic homogeneity. The question of whether actual homogeneity or epistemic homogeneity is demanded is, for my view, analogous to the question of whether the premises of the explanation must be true or highly confirmed for Hempel's view.[46] I have always felt that truth was the appropriate requirement, for I believe Carnap has shown that the concept of truth is harmless enough.[47] However, for those who feel too uncomfortable with the stricter requirement, it would be possible to characterize statistical explanation in terms of epistemic homogeneity instead of actual homogeneity. No fundamental problem about the nature of explanation seems to be involved.

e. This paper has been concerned with the explanation of single events, but from the standpoint of probability theory, there is no significant distinction between a single event and any finite set of events. Thus, the kind of explanation appropriate to a single result of heads on a single toss of a coin would, in principle, be just like the kind of explanation that would be appropriate to a sequence of ten heads on ten consecutive tosses of a coin or to ten heads on ten different coins tossed simultaneously.

f. With Hempel, I believe that generalizations, both universal and statistical, are capable of being explained. Explanations invoke generalizations as parts of the explanans, but these generalizations themselves may need explanation. This does not mean that the explanation of the particular event that employed the generalization is incomplete; it only means that an additional explanation is possible and may be desirable. In some cases it may be possible to explain a statistical generalization by subsuming it under a higher level generalization; a probability may become an instance for a higher level probability. For example, Reichenbach offered an explanation for equiprobability in games of chance, by constructing, in effect, a sequence of probability sequences.[48] Each of the first level sequences is a single case with respect to the second level sequence. To explain generalizations in this manner is simply to repeat, at a higher level, the pattern of explanation we have been discussing. Whether this is or is not the only method of explaining generalizations is, of course, an entirely different question.

g. In the present account of statistical explanation, Hempel's problem of the "nonconjunctiveness of statistical systematization"[49] simply vanishes. This problem arises because in general, according to the multiplication theorem for probabilities, the probability of a conjunction is smaller than that of either conjunct taken alone. Thus, if we have chosen a value r, such that explanations are acceptable only if they confer upon the explanandum an inductive probability of at least r, it is quite possible that each of the two explananda will satisfy that condition, whereas their conjunction fails to do so. Since the characterization of explanation I am offering makes no demands whatever for high probabilities (weights), it has no problem of nonconjunctiveness.

CONCLUSION

Although I am hopeful that the foregoing analysis of statistical explanation of single events solely in terms of statistical relevance relations is of some help in understanding the nature of scientific explanation, I should like to cite, quite explicitly, several respects in which it seems to be incomplete.

First, and most obviously, whatever the merits of the present account, no reason has been offered for supposing the type of explanation under consideration to be the only legitimate kind of scientific explanation. If we make the usual distinction between empirical laws and scientific theories, we could say that the kind of explanation I have discussed is explanation by means of empirical laws. For all that has been said in this paper, theoretical explanation—explanation that makes use of scientific theories in the fullest sense of the term—may have a logical structure entirely different from that of statistical explanation. Although theoretical explanation is almost certainly the most important kind of scientific explanation, it does, nevertheless, seem useful to have a clear account of explanation by means of empirical laws, if only as a point of departure for a treatment of theoretical explanation.

Second, in remarking above that statistical explanation is nomological, I was tacitly admitting that the statistical or universal generalizations invoked in explanations should be lawlike. I have made no attempt to analyze lawlikeness, but it seems likely that an adequate analysis will involve a solution to Nelson Goodman's "grue-bleen" problem.[50]

Third, my account of statistical explanation obviously depends heavily upon the concept of *statistical relevance* and upon the *screening-off relation*, which is defined in terms of statistical relevance. In the course of the discussion, I have attempted to show how these tools enable us to capture much of the involvement of explanation with causality, but I have not attempted to provide an analysis of causation in terms of these statistical concepts alone. Reichenbach has attempted such an analysis,[51] but whether his—or any other—can succeed is a difficult question. I should be inclined to harbor serious misgivings about the adequacy of my view of statistical explanation if the statistical analysis of causation cannot be carried through successfully, for the relation between causation and explanation seems extremely intimate.

Finally, although I have presented my arguments in terms of the limiting frequency conception of probability, I do not believe that the fundamental correctness of the treatment of statistical explanation hinges upon the acceptability of that interpretation of probability. Proponents of other theories of probability, especially the personalist and the propensity interpretations, should be able to adapt this treatment of explanation to their views of probability with a minimum of effort. That, too, is left as an exercise for the reader.[52]

NOTES

* This paper grew out of a discussion of statistical explanation presented at the meeting of the American Association for the Advancement of Science, held in Cleveland in 1963, as a part of the program of Section L organized by Adolf Grünbaum, then vice-president for Section L. My paper, "The Status of Prior Probabilities in Statistical Explanation," along with Henry E. Kyburg's comments and my rejoinder, were published in *Philosophy of Science* 32, no. 2 (April 1965). The original version of this paper was written in 1964 in an attempt to work out fuller solutions to some problems Kyburg raised, and it was presented at the Pittsburgh Workshop Conference in May 1965, prior to the publication of Carl G. Hempel, *Aspects of Scientific Explanation* (New York: Free Press, 1965).

I should like to express my gratitude to the National Science Foundation for support of the research contained in this paper.

1. Carl G. Hempel and Paul Oppenheim, "Studies in the Logic of Explanation," *Philosophy of Science* 15 (1948), pp. 135–75. Reprinted, with a 1964 "Postscript," in Carl G. Hempel, *Aspects of Scientific Explanation* (New York: Free Press, 1965).
2. Carl G. Hempel, "Explanation in Science and in History," in *Frontiers in Science and Philosophy*, ed. Robert G. Colodny (Pittsburgh: University of Pittsburgh Press, 1962), p. 10.
3. See also Hempel, *Aspects of Scientific Explanation*, pp. 367–68, where he offers "a general *condition of adequacy for any rationally acceptable explanation of a particular event*," namely, that "any rationally acceptable answer to the question 'why did event X occur?' must offer information which shows that X was to be expected—if not definitely, as in the case of D-N explantion, then at least with reasonable probability."

Inductive explanations have variously been known as "statistical," "probabilistic," and "inductive-statistical." Deductive explanations have often been called "deductive-nomological." For the present I shall simply use the terms "inductive" and "deductive" to emphasize the crucial fact that the former embody inductive logical relations, whereas the latter embody deductive logical relations. Both types are nomological, for both require lawlike generalizations among their premises. Later on, I shall use the term "statistical explanation" to refer to the sort of explanation I am trying to characterize, for it is statistical in a straightforward sense, and it is noninductive in an extremely important sense.

4. Rudolf Carnap, "Preface to the Second Edition," in *Logical Foundations of Probability* (Chicago: University of Chicago Press, 1962), 2d ed., pp. xv–xx.

5. Hempel, *Aspects of Scientific Explanation*.

6. "Deductive-Nomological vs. Statistical Explanation," in *Minnesota Studies in the Philosophy of Science*, vol. 3, eds. Herbert Feigl and Grover Maxwell (Minneapolis: University of Minnesota Press, 1962).

7. I called attention to this danger in "The Status of Prior Probabilities in Statistical Explanation," *Philosophy of Science* 32, no. 2 (April, 1965), p. 137. Several fundamental disanalogies could be cited. First, the relation of deductive entailment is transitive, whereas the relation of inductive support is not; see my "Consistency, Transitivity, and Inductive Support," *Ratio* 7, no. 2 (Dec. 1965), pp. 164–69. Second, on Carnap's theory of degree of confirmation, which is very close to the notion of inductive probability that Hempel uses in characterizing statistical explanation, there is no such thing as inductive inference in the sense of allowing the detachment of inductive conclusions in a manner analogous to that in which deductive logic allows the detachment of conclusions of deductive inferences. See my contribution "Who Needs Inductive Acceptance Rules?" to the discussion of Henry E. Kyburg's "The Rule of Detachment in Inductive Logic," in *The Problem of Inductive Logic*, ed. Imre Lakatos (Amsterdam: North Holland Publishing Co., 1968), pp. 139–44, for an assessment of the bearing of this disanalogy specifically upon the problem of scientific explanation. Third, if *q* follows from *p* by a deductively valid argument, then *q* follows validly from *p* & *r*, regardless of what statement *r* is. This is the reason that the *requirement of total evidence* is automatically satisfied for deductive-nomological explanations. By contrast, even if *p* provides strong inductive support for *q*, *q* may not be inductively supported at all by *p* & *r*. Informally, a valid deductive argument remains valid no matter what premises are added (as long as none is taken away), but addition of premises to a strong inductive argument can destroy all of its strength. It is for this reason that the *requirement of total evidence* is not vacuous for statistical explanations.

8. See "Deductive-Nomological vs. Statistical Explanation."

9. See, for example, Hempel, "Explanation in Science and in History."

10. In the present context nothing important hinges upon the particular characterization of the parts of arguments. I shall refer to them indifferently as statements or propositions. Propositions may be regarded as classes of statements; so long as they are not regarded as facts of the world, or nonlinguistic states of affairs, no trouble should arise.

11. When no confusion is apt to occur, we may ignore the distinction between the explanandum and the explanandum event. It is essential to realize, however, that a given explanation must not purport to explain the explanandum event in all of its richness and full particularity; rather, it explains just those aspects of the explanandum event that are mentioned in the explanandum.

12. "Deductive-Nomological vs. Statistical Explanation," p. 125.

13. Ibid. See also "Inductive Inconsistencies," *Synthèse*, 12, no. 4 (Dec. 1960).

14. Hempel and Oppenheim, "Studies in the Logic of Explanation," and Hempel, "Deductive-Nomological vs. Statistical Explanation."

15. This condition has sometimes been weakened to the requirement that the premises be highly confirmed. I prefer the stronger requirement, but nothing very important hangs on the choice. See n. 53.

16. A premise occurs essentially in an argument if that argument would cease to be (deductively or

inductively) correct upon deletion of that premise. Essential occurrence does not mean that the argument could not be made logically correct again by replacing the premise in question with another premise. "Essential occurrence" means that the premise plays a part in the argument as given; it does not just stand there contributing nothing to the logical correctness of the argument.

17. The requirement of total evidence demands that there should be no additional statements among our available stock of statements of evidence that would change the degree to which the conclusion is supported by the argument if they were added to the argument as premises. See Carnap, *Logical Foundations of Probability*, section 45B.

18. Hempel, "Explanation in Science and in History," p. 14.

19. "The Status of Prior Probabilities in Statistical Explanation," p. 145.

20. Consumer Reports, *The Medicine Show* (New York: Simon and Schuster, 1961), pp. 17–18 (*Pace* Dr. Linus Pauling).

21. Henry E. Kyburg, "Comments," *Philosophy of Science* 32, no. 2 (April 1965), pp. 147–51.

22. Since there is no widely accepted account of inductive inference, it is difficult to say what constitutes correct logical form for inductive arguments. For purposes of the present discussion I am accepting Hempel's schema (4) as one correct inductive form.

23. The fact that the general premise in this argument refers explicitly to a particular physical object, the moon, may render this premise nonlawlike, but presumably the explanation could be reconstructed with a suitably general premise about satellites.

24. In Hempel and Oppenheim's "Studies in the Logic of Explanation," (7.5) constitutes a set of necessary but not sufficient conditions for a potential explanans, while (7.6) defines *explanans* in terms of potential explanans. However, (7.8) provides a definition of *potential explanans*, which in combination with (7.6) constitutes a set of necessary and sufficient conditions for an explanans.

25. *Aspects of Scientific Explanation*, pp. 397–403. See also Carl G. Hempel, "Maximal Specificity and Lawlikeness in Probabilistic Explanation," *Philosophy of Science*, 35 (1968), pp. 116–33, which contains a revision of this requirement. The revision does not seem to affect the objections I shall raise.

26. Salmon, "The Status of Prior Probabilities."

27. This characterization of the logical interpretation of probability is patterned closely upon Carnap, *Logical Foundations of Probability*.

28. Salmon, "Who Needs Inductive Acceptance Rules?"

29. This point was brought out explicitly and forcefully by Richard Jeffrey in "Statistical Explanation vs. Statistical Inference" presented at the meeting of the American Association for the Advancement of Science, Section L, New York, 1967. This superb paper has since been published in *Essays in Honor of Carl G. Hempel*, ed. Nicholas Rescher (Dordrecht: Reidel Publishing Co., 1969), and it is reprinted herein. Hempel discussed this issue in "Deductive-Nomological vs. Statistical Explanation," pp. 156–63.

30. For an indication of some of the difficulties involved in properly circumscribing this body of total evidence, see Kyburg's comments on my paper. "The Status of Prior Probabilities in Statistical Explanation," and my rejoinder. Hempel has discussed this problem at some length in "Deductive-Nomological vs. Statistical Explanation," pp. 145–49, and "Aspects of Scientific Explanation," section 3.4.

31. An extremely clear account of this view is given by Ward Edwards, Harold Lindman, and Leonard J. Savage in "Bayesian Statistical Inference for Psychological Research," *Psychological Review*, 70, no. 3 (May 1963). An approach which is very similar in some ways, though it is certainly not a genuinely subjective interpretation in the Bayesian sense, is given by Carnap in "The Aim of Inductive Logic," in *Logic, Methodology and Philosophy of Science*, eds. Ernest Nagel, Patrick Suppes, and Alfred Tarski (Stanford: Stanford University Press, 1962), pp. 303–18.

32. This treatment of the frequency interpretation takes its departure from Hans Reichenbach, *The Theory of Probability* (Berkeley: University of California Press, 1949), but the discussion differs from Reichenbach's in several important respects, especially concerning the problem of the single case. My

view of this matter is detailed in *The Foundations of Scientific Inference* (Pittsburgh: University of Pittsburgh Press, 1967), pp. 83–96.

33. See *Foundations of Scientific Inference*, pp. 56–96, for discussions of the various interpretations of probability.

34. See, for example, Karl Popper, "The Propensity Interpretation of the Calculus of Probability, and the Quantum Theory," in *Observation and Interpretation*, ed. S. Körner (London: Butterworth Scientific Publications, 1956), pp. 65–70, and "The Propensity Interpretation of Probability," *British Journal for the Philosophy of Science*, 10 (1960), pp. 25–42.

35. See Salmon, *The Foundations of Scientific Inference*, pp. 83–96, for fuller explanations. Note that, contrary to frequent usage, the expression "$P(A,B)$" is read "the probability *from A to B*." This notation is Reichenbach's.

36. Reichenbach, *The Theory of Probability*, section 72. John Venn, *The Logic of Chance*, 4th ed. (New York: Chelsea Publishing Co., 1962), chapter 9, sections 12–32. Venn was the first systematic exponent of the frequency interpretation, and he was fully aware of the problem of the single case. He provides an illuminating account, and his discussion is an excellent supplement to Reichenbach's well-known later treatment.

37. Reichenbach, *The Theory of Probability*, p. 374.

38. Carnap, *Logical Foundations of Probability*, section 44.

39. Richard von Mises, *Probability, Statistics and Truth*, 2d rev. ed. (London: Allen and Unwin, 1957), p. 25.

40. Also, of course, there are cases in which it would be possible in principle to make a relevant partition, but we are playing a game in which the rules prevent it. Such is the case in roulette, where the croupier prohibits additional bets after a certain point in the spin of the wheel. In these cases also we shall speak of practical homogeneity.

41. Carnap, *Logical Foundations of Probability*, section 44.

42. Ibid., sections 50–51.

43. Salmon, "Who Needs Inductive Acceptance Rules?" Because of this difference with Carnap—i.e., my claim that inductive logic requires rules of acceptance for the purpose of establishing statistical generalizations—I do not have the thoroughgoing "pragmatic" or "instrumentalist" view of science Hempel attributes to Richard Jeffrey and associates with Carnap's general conception of inductive logic. Cf. Hempel, "Deductive-Nomological vs. Statistical Explanation," pp. 156–63.

44. Salmon, *Foundations of Scientific Inference*, pp. 90–95.

45. See "Aspects of Scientific Explanation," sections 3.2–3.3. In the present essay I am not at all concerned with explanations of the type Hempel calls "deductive-statistical." For greater specificity, what I am calling "statistical explanation" might be called "statistical-relevance explanation," or "S-R explanation" as a handy abbreviation to distinguish it from Hempel's D-N, D-S, and I-S types.

46. Hempel, "Deductive-Nomological vs. Statistical Explanation," section 3.

47. Rudolf Carnap, "Truth and Confirmation," in *Readings in Philosophical Analysis*, ed. Herbert Feigl and Wilfrid Sellars (New York: Appleton-Century-Crofts, 1949), pp. 119–27.

48. Reichenbach, *Theory of Probability*, section 69.

49. Hempel, "Deductive-Nomological vs. Statistical Explanation," section 13, and "Aspects of Scientific Explanation," section 3.6. Here, Hempel says, "Nonconjunctiveness presents itself as an inevitable aspect of [inductive-statistical explanation], and thus as one of the fundamental characteristics that set I-S explanation apart from its deductive counterparts."

50. See Nelson Goodman, *Fact, Fiction, and Forecast*, 2d ed. (Indianapolis: Bobbs-Merrill Co., 1965), chapter 3. I have suggested a resolution in "On Vindicating Induction," *Philosophy of Science* 30 (July 1963), pp. 252–61, reprinted in Henry E. Kyburg and Ernest Nagel, eds., *Induction: Some Current Issues* (Middletown, Conn.: Wesleyan University Press, 1963).

51. Reichenbach, *The Direction of Time*, chapter 4.

52. The hints are provided in section 3.

JAMES H. FETZER

A SINGLE CASE PROPENSITY THEORY OF EXPLANATION*

In a recent article, "Are Statistical Hypotheses Covering Laws?" Isaac Levi has presented the provocative argument that a covering law account of statistical explanation encounters a dilemma resulting from the apparent necessity of reconciling the following desiderata:

On the one hand, statistical explanation is to be viewed as explanation by law; and, on the other hand, an account of statistical explanation must be based on an acceptable interpretation of statistical probability.[1]

Levi contends that these two desiderata cannot be simultaneously satisfied and that, as a result, the function of covering laws in Hempel's explication had better be envisioned as fulfilled by material rules of inference.[2] The force of Levi's argument, of course, rests upon his contention that there is no acceptable interpretation of statistical probability which succeeds in converting statistical hypotheses into covering laws.[3]

Levi admits that he is unable to provide an impossibility theorem here but claims that "a review of the more obvious candidates ought, at a very minimum, to place the onus of proof very squarely on the shoulders of those who believe such statements can be constructed."[4] The purpose of this paper is to demonstrate that Levi's argument is not well-founded and that, contrary to his claim, the propensity interpretation succeeds in fulfilling this goal. Implications of adopting this analysis as the standard account of statistical probability are explored, including (a) the unified theory it provides of the character of lawfulness for both universal and statistical laws and (b) the criterion it supports for the adequacy of explanations invoking laws of either kind. From this point of view, the conclusion emerges that *all* explanations in empirical science are essentially theoretical in character.

I

Levi correctly attributes to Hempel the view that statistical hypotheses are dispositional statements. He cites Hempel's interpretation of the meaning of a statistical hypothesis attributing a probability of $1/4$ to the outcome of landing on side III, given a single toss with a tetrahedron:

What the probability statement attributes to the tetrahedron is, therefore, not the frequency with which the result III is obtained in actual past or future rollings, but a certain *disposition*, namely the disposition to yield the result in about one out of four cases, in the long run. This disposition might be characterized by means of a subjunctive conditional phrase: if the tetrahedron were to be tossed a large number of times, it would yield the result III in about one-fourth of the cases. Implications in the form of counterfactual and subjunctive conditionals are thus hallmarks of lawlike statements both of strictly universal and of statistical form.[5]

Insofar as Hempel explicitly endorses a propensity interpretation similar to those of Popper and Hacking, as Levi observes, he evidently adheres to what may be referred to as the *long run* propensity concept, which may be formulated as follows:

(1) $P(E,O) = p = _{df}$ an experimental arrangement of kind E possesses the dispositional tendency to generate an outcome of kind O with the characteristic relative frequency p over the long run.

From this point of view, therefore, statistical predicates are theoretical terms attributing unobservable dispositional properties to certain experimental conditions to produce particular kinds of outcomes with characteristic relative frequencies over long runs of trials.

Levi claims, however, that although Hempel cites the capacity to sustain counterfactual and subjunctive conditionals as a crucial characteristic of lawlikeness, there appear to be examples which suggest that that characteristic is not a sufficient condition for lawlikeness; thus, for example, he argues

Consider the sentence "Jones is six feet tall." It backs the subjunctive conditional "if the angle between the sun and the earth where Jones is standing would be 45°, Jones would cast a shadow six feet long." Yet, "is six feet tall" is not a disposition predicate and "Jones is six feet tall" is not a lawlike statement. Every predicate is, in the words of Nelson Goodman, "full of threats and promises" and every singular statement backs subjunctive conditionals. If, therefore, an interesting distinction is to be made between lawlike sentences which can function as covering laws in explanation and other sentences which, if they occur in explanation at all, play a different role, the fact that disposition statements and statistical hypotheses back subjunctive conditionals is insufficient grounds for assigning them lawlike status.[6]

Levi therefore concludes that if statistical hypotheses are to be held to be lawlike then it must be on the basis of considerations other than their capacity to support counterfactual and subjunctive conditionals.

He then raises the interesting possibility that dispositional statements might be held to be lawlike on independent grounds:

This possibility deserves examination. However, in "Aspects of Scientific Explanation," Hempel rejects this point of view. According to Hempel, disposition sentences like "This piece of glass is fragile" assert that antecedent conditions of covering laws like "All fragile objects break when struck by hammers" are satisfied by individual systems. If disposition statements which are non-statistical fail to be lawlike—i.e., [fail to] function as covering laws in explanation by disposition—and statistical hypotheses are dispositional in an analogous sense, statistical hypotheses cannot be "less rigorous counterparts" for laws.[7]

Levi's argument, in other words, comes to this: if dispositional statements attribute antecedent conditions to individual systems, as Hempel maintains, then statistical hypotheses interpreted as dispositional statements must likewise fulfill the role of antecedent conditions, rather than the role of covering laws, in statistical explanations; consequently, statistical hypotheses, interpreted as dispositional statements, cannot be covering laws.

The force of Levi's argument thus far crucially depends upon two rather basic assumptions:

(i) that there are predicates, such as "is six feet tall," that sustain counterfactual and subjunctive conditionals and yet are not dispositional;

(ii) that dispositional statements fulfill the function of attributing antecedent conditions to individual systems but are not themselves lawlike.

If either or both of these assumptions is not well-founded, therefore, then Levi's argument will lose its punch. The following considerations suggest that, as a matter of fact, *neither* is well-founded.

(i) Consider, first of all, the claim that "is six feet tall" is not a dispositional predicate in spite of providing support for counterfactual and subjunctive conditionals. This argument, after all, begs the question; for if the capacity to support counterfactual and subjunctive conditionals *is* the hallmark of dispositionality, then this predicate—and every other one that satisfies this criterion—is dispositional independently of whether Levi believes it or not. The issue is therefore to determine whether or not "is six feet tall" should or should not be regarded as a dispositional predicate and by what criterion; for Levi's rejection of it in and of itself surely provides no such criterion.

If Levi's argument is construed as the claim that support for such conditionals is only a necessary but not a sufficient condition for the dispositionality of a predicate, then the problem would appear to be to ascertain what *additional* conditions must be satisfied for a predicate to qualify as dispositional. The problem as I contemplate it, however, is not one of determining what requirements in addition to providing support for such conditionals must be fulfilled for a predicate to qualify as dispositional but rather one of clarifying precisely what conditions a predicate must satisfy to be regarded as providing support for such conditionals at all.

The correct approach to this issue, in my opinion, is to notice that the question of whether or not a predicate expression provides support for counterfactual and subjunctive conditionals is only solved by ascertaining the distinctive kind of property that such predicate expressions designate. Such an expression, in other words, may serve such a purpose if and only if the property it designates is of the appropriate kind. The thesis I want to maintain, therefore, is that *a predicate expression may serve the role of providing support for such conditionals if and only if the property that expression designates is dispositional*, namely:

(a) is envisioned as a tendency to display appropriate response behavior (such as characteristic relative frequencies) under relevant test conditions (such as long runs of trials); and,

(b) is supposed to be an actual physical state, i.e., a property of some object or collection of objects (such as those constituting an experimental set-up).

From this point of view, therefore, it seems evident that the reason "is six feet tall" provides support for counterfactual and subjunctive conditionals is precisely because it *is* dispositional, i.e., it denotes a property that satisfies both of these requirements.

Dispositions, in other words, are simply tendencies—normally but not always persistent and enduring ones—to display appropriate response behavior under relevant test conditions (e.g., if the angle between the sun and the earth where Jones is standing were 45°, Jones would cast a shadow six feet long) possessed by particular objects (such as Jones) or collections of objects.

Indeed, the example cited by Levi is but one among a vast number that constitute specific manifestations of this particular property under a wide variety of relevant conditions; for example, that if Jones were to walk through a tunnel that was less than six feet high, he would have to bend over or else he would bump his head, reflects another.

This point emerges especially clearly when the empirical significance of this particular predicate is cast in the form of a series of unilateral reduction sentences along the following lines (where "Tx" stands for "x is in test conditions of type T," "Rx" stands for "x manifests behavior of kind R," and "Px" stands for "x possesses the property P," employing superscripts to indicate that different test conditions and manifest behaviors are thereby described):

(2) $T^1x \rightarrow (Px \rightarrow R^1x) \cdot$
         $T^2x \rightarrow (Px \rightarrow R^2x) \cdot$
         $\cdot$ $\cdot$ $\cdot$ $\cdot$ $\cdot$

where the set of reduction sentences characterizing the appropriate kinds of manifest behavior under appropriate kinds of test conditions is limited only by the variety of ways in which that particular property is actually—indeed, theoretically—manifest under different kinds of relevant tests.

Notice that if the property involved is of such a kind that specific kinds of response behavior under specified types of test conditions are manifest *only* by those objects (or collections of objects) that happen to possess that particular property (for example, if Jones would cast such a shadow if and only if he were six feet tall, as opposed to being less than six feet tall but wearing elevator shoes, walking on stilts, and so forth) then bilateral reduction sentences may appropriately be employed:

(3) $T^1x \rightarrow (Px \equiv R^1x) \cdot$
         $T^2x \rightarrow (Px \equiv R^2x) \cdot$
         $\cdot$ $\cdot$ $\cdot$ $\cdot$ $\cdot$ $\cdot$

Indeed, it is significant to observe that such reduction chains, although intended as specifying the meaning of particular expressions, clearly have implications of an empirical character that may be formulated as general statements of the following kinds:

(4) $(x) \, [(T^1x \cdot R^1x) \rightarrow (T^2x \rightarrow R^2x)]$ and
         $(x) - [(T^1x \cdot R^1x) \cdot (T^2x \cdot -R^2x)]$

which, as it might be expressed, reflect the "inductive risk" incurred when multiple criteria are invoked to link relevant test antecedents and outcome response consequents by means of the reduction sentence technique.[8]

As Hempel especially has pointed out, the fact that reduction chains that are intended to specify the meaning of certain predicate expressions happen to have consequences of a clearly empirical character throws grave doubt upon the possibility of sustaining the analytic-synthetic distinction with regard to terms having empirical significance and is indicative of the intimate connection between concept formation and theory construction in empirical science.[9] For it is apparent that the visualization of a wide variety of different response behaviors under different test conditions as manifestations of a single underlying dispositional property requires the establishment of theoretical connections between these various tests and behavioral responses—connections that cannot be exhausted by means of experiential considerations alone.

Indeed, the importance of this last consideration is reflected by the example at hand; for although the property of being six feet tall is typically envisioned as being a persistent and enduring tendency for an individual (or object) to display certain specifiable kinds of behavior under certain specifiable types of test conditions, there are, after all, a variety of circumstances under which it would be readily conceded that, although individual x exhibited behavior R^1 under conditions T^1 at time t_1, he would not therefore—as a matter of logical necessity— exhibit behavior R^2 under conditions T^2 at time t_2 (where t_2 was subsequent to t_1); for, to cite but one unhappy possibility, he might as a matter of fact have lost both his legs in an automobile accident in the meanwhile.

It seems clear, therefore, that although this property does support counterfactual and subjunctive conditionals and, in the absence of some well-founded criterion for its exclusion, should be regarded as dispositional in character, it does not imply that that property itself is a permanent possession. After all, objects like people have properties at one time and lose them at another; but there are surely no grounds here for supposing that this property or others like it are on that account not dispositional.

(ii) The view that dispositional statements fulfill the function of attributing antecedent conditions to individual systems but are not themselves lawlike requires further scrutiny. Consider, for example, the illustration of a dispositional explanation advanced by Levi.[10]

(5)   AX: a is fragile,
      A1: a is struck by a hammer at t,
      A2: a breaks at t.

Levi asserts of this explanation that, "As it stands, the logical structure of this argument is not that of a deductive nomological explanation or even that of a deductively valid argument."[11] It therefore requires logical reconstruction to be a candidate for covering law explanation.

Hempel refers to explanations of this kind as "dispositional explanations" because they characteristically invoke dispositional properties of individuals and objects in order to account for their manifest behavior; since they do not explicitly contain general laws in their explanans, moreover, they are often held to defy a covering law analysis.[12] Consequently, as Levi accurately reports, Hempel argues that "dispositional statements" such as "a is fragile" serve the function of describing antecedent conditions relative to such covering laws as "All fragile objects break when struck by hammers." For although the empirical significance of the predicate "fragility" is not explicitly expressed (and therefore the argument as stated does not satisfy the conditions of deductive validity), semantic considerations reflect the fact that, when the reduction chains which formalize the meaning of that predicate are taken into account, the argument itself is readily amenable to logical reconstruction in such a way that its structure is indeed that of a logically valid argument and its character that of a deductive-nomological explanation; for surely included among those reduction chains is one which states, "if x is struck by a hammer, then if x is fragile then x breaks" (or, perhaps, "if x is struck by a hammer, then x is fragile if and only if x breaks"). As a result, an explanation of this kind becomes a covering law explanation when the generalizations it implicitly invokes are explicitly expressed:

(5′)   CL: All fragile objects break when struck by hammers
       C1: a is fragile
       C2: a is struck by a hammer at t

       ES: a breaks at t

for surely the explanans invoking the covering law CL and the statements of antecedent conditions C1 and C2 fulfill the requirements for a deductive-nomological explanation of its explanandum sentence ES.

Since the statement "*a* is fragile" is indeed a statement of antecedent conditions on Hempel's account, therefore, Levi's argument—i.e., if dispositional statements attribute antecedent conditions to individual systems, as Hempel maintains, then statistical hypotheses interpreted as dispositional statements must likewise fulfill the role of antecedent conditions, rather than the role of covering laws, in statistical explanations—has about it a certain aura of plausibility. But surely this argument is woefully inadequate for its intended purpose; for it clearly fails to make any distinction at all between "dispositional statements" that attribute a dispositional property to a *single* individual (let us call them "singular dispositional statements") and "dispositional statements" that specify the kinds of response behavior under various test conditions manifest by *every* individual or object possessing that dispositional property (let us call these "general dispositional statements"). If Levi's argument as it stands were sound, therefore, it would have to be the case not only that singular dispositional statements (such as "*a* is fragile") fulfill the role of antecedent conditions but also that general dispositional statements (such as "All fragile objects break when struck by hammers") *also* fulfill the role of antecedent conditions in covering law explanations—which is surely not the case and, in effect, constitutes a *reductio* of Levi's argument.

For this argument to be sound, Levi would have to demonstrate something that, at least *prima facie*, is not true, namely: that general dispositional statements do not fulfill the role of covering laws in explanations of this kind. For unless this claim is true, statistical hypotheses may perfectly well be dispositional statements in a sense analogous to that in which *general* dispositional statements are dispositional statements and from this perspective clearly appear to be "less rigorous counterparts" of those universal generalizations. If general dispositional statements have the character of universal laws, therefore, then statistical dispositional statements may, in an analogous sense, be regarded as having the character of statistical laws. In drawing a comparison between *singular* dispositional statements and statistical hypotheses, therefore, Levi relied upon a poor analogy; for, contrary to his contention, the arguments he has advanced do not demonstrate that statistical hypotheses interpreted as "less rigorous counterparts" of general dispositional statements cannot be covering laws.

It may be worthwhile to notice in passing, moreover, that theoretical considerations come into play once again in formulating the reduction sentences expressing the empirical significance of "fragility"; for surely there are more and less fragile objects that respond to similar test conditions (such as being struck by a hammer) in different ways (since less fragile objects may not break under circumstances in which more fragile objects will). Moreover, one and the same object may possess the property in question and yet not manifest the appropriate response behavior under all variations of the relevant test conditions (such as being very lightly tapped with a hammer or struck a glancing blow); and it may even turn out to be the case that although an object possesses a property (such as fragility) at one time, it no longer possesses that property (or possesses it to a lesser degree) at some subsequent time (such as after being subjected to heat treatment). All of these considerations, therefore, serve to reinforce the point Hempel has elsewhere made so clearly, namely: that in empirical science, concept formation and theory construction go hand in hand.

The upshot is, therefore, that Levi has really not made his case; for if the considerations I have advanced above are sound, both the assumptions upon which his argument rests are faulty ones. For in the absence of some well-founded criterion for their rejection, there appear to be no reasons for supposing that predicates like "is six feet tall" should not be acknowledged to be dispositional when they support counterfactual and subjunctive conditionals nor for supposing that general dispositional statements fulfill the role of antecedent conditions rather than the role of covering laws.

II

It should be observed, however, that the force of these arguments has been essentially negative; for although Levi's underlying reasons for rejecting statistical hypotheses interpreted as dispositional statements and covering laws have been disclosed to be bad ones, I have yet to advance any good reasons for either (a) accepting Hempel's interpretation of statistical probabilities as long run propensities or (b) for replacing that interpretation with some better one. The purpose of this section, therefore, is to argue that, although the long run propensity interpretation is good as far as it goes, it does not go far enough; for there appear to be sufficient grounds for displacing that interpretation by its single case counterpart.

Suppose we consider the covering law explanation that emerges from applying the long run propensity interpretation to a particular case; for example, to the occurrence of obtaining an ace as the outcome of a single toss with a fair die. If "Dx" stands for "x is a die," "Tx" stands for "x is given a toss" and "Ax" stands for "x comes up showing an ace," then that explanation would have the following logical form:

(6) $$P(Dx \cdot Tx, Ax) = \tfrac{1}{6}$$
$$\frac{Da \cdot Ta}{Aa} \ [\tfrac{1}{6}]$$

Hempel has explained the significance of the bracketed number as indicating the strength of the inductive support conferred upon the explanandum by its explanans:

The number indicated in brackets is "the probability associated with the explanation"; it is not a statistical probability, but an inductive one in Carnap's sense, namely, the probability of the explanandum relative to the explanans. This argument *explains* a's being A by showing that this is to be expected, with probability $1/6$, in view of the general statistical law and the statement of particular facts included in the explanans.[13]

The reader may be struck by the fact that this explanation only confers an inductive probability of $1/6$ upon its explanandum in explicit contravention of the Hempelian requirement that, "The argument will be considered as explanatory only if (its inductive probability) r is sufficiently close to 1; but no specific common lower bound for r can reasonably be imposed on all probabilistic explanations."[14] A brief explanation of this departure from the Hempelian theory therefore appears to be in order.

As recent investigations by Salmon have disclosed and as I have elsewhere explained, the Hempelian requirement of a high inductive probability between explanandum and explanans has the uningratiating consequence of rendering the explanation of events which occur only comparatively rarely logically impossible, in principle.[15] These same reflections necessitate revision of the underlying Hempelian desideratum, i.e., that an explanation explains the occurrence of an event by exhibiting its *strong* nomic expectability, to indicate that an explanation explains the occurrence of an event by exhibiting its nomic expectability, which in some cases may be strong but in other cases may not be. Important as these considerations and the reasoning behind them may be, however, it seems preferable not to expand upon them here, not only since they are available elsewhere but also because they do not essentially affect the covering law position, as the arguments that follow are intended to display.

Since Levi's contention that there is no acceptable interpretation of statistical probability which succeeds in converting statistical hypotheses into covering laws has not yet been refuted, it appears appropriate to consider whether or not the long run propensity construction (which Hempel has endorsed) succeeds in this regard (now that Levi's underlying rationale for its rejection has been discovered to be ill-founded). Implicit in Levi's article are at least three desiderata that an acceptable interpretation of probability as a physical magnitude must satisfy if statistical hypotheses are to fulfill their intended role: an interpretation of probability is an acceptable interpretation for the purpose of establishing statistical hypotheses as covering laws only if those hypotheses fulfill the following conditions, namely:

(a) they must not be logically limited to a finite number of instances;
(b) they must be capable of supporting counterfactual and subjunctive conditionals; and,
(c) they must be true.[16]

Notice two aspects of these conditions: first, that insofar as they include a truth condition, they are to be regarded as necessary conditions for being a statistical law rather than for statistical lawfulness (where satisfaction of (a) and (b) but not (c) appear relevant); second, that they only establish necessary but not sufficient conditions on Levi's appraisal, which was based in large measure upon considerations that we have found to be mistaken.

Nevertheless, it seems quite relevant to consider whether or not the long run propensity interpretation fulfills these conditions as one measure of its acceptability (since they are conditions cited by Hempel as well).[17] Evidently, from the point of view of this interpretation, the (purported) statistical explanation under consideration would have to be rendered as follows:

(7) Any experimental arrangement consisting of a fair die and tossing device of kind k possesses the dispositional tendency to generate the outcome of an ace with a relative frequency of $\frac{1}{6}$ over the long run. This experimental arrangement consists of a fair die and tossing device of kind k, with which a single trial a was made at time t.

$$=== [\tfrac{1}{6}]$$

The outcome of trial a at time t was an ace.

This statistical explanation, in other words, explains the outcome of an ace on a single toss with a fair die by citing the nomic expectability for outcomes of that kind under conditions of that kind as $[\tfrac{1}{6}]$ over the long run, in accordance with which the inductive probability conferred upon this explanandum by its explanans is $\frac{1}{6}$.

It seems clear that, with respect to condition (a), the statistical hypothesis itself concerns every experimental arrangement of a certain kind, namely: all those consisting of a fair die and tossing device of kind k. Consequently, although there may, as a matter of fact, only be a finite number of experimental arrangements of this kind during the history of the physical world, this statistical hypothesis is not logically limited to a finite number of such experimental arrangements. Moreover, in fulfillment of condition (b), it explicitly asserts that statistical probabilities are to be regarded as dispositional tendencies to generate certain outcomes with characteristic relative frequencies over long runs of trials; consequently, these probabilities may be measured by means of the hypothetical relative frequencies they would generate if experimental arrangements of that kind were subjected to long runs of trials. Finally, with regard to condition (c), although it may be logically impossible to empirically verify such statistical hypotheses, they are amenable to test by means of comparisons between predicted relative frequencies and observed relative frequencies when long runs of trials actually are conducted; and although they are therefore only amenable to empirical confirmation, in principle, they are not in this respect any worse off than other theoretical statements encountered in empirical science.

The net result of these considerations, therefore, appears to be that the long run propensity interpretation is *not* an unacceptable interpretation relative to Levi's necessary conditions. In the absence of some other grounds for its rejection, therefore, it seems to be the case that this interpretation of statistical probability actually succeeds in converting statistical hypotheses into covering laws, contrary to Levi's thesis of the impossibility of such an eventuality. Yet I want to argue further that, even though the long run propensity account succeeds in these respects, it falls short in one respect not already taken into consideration and that, for this reason alone, it should be displaced by the single case propensity construction.

The difficulty which the long run propensity interpretation encounters is identical to a fundamental difficulty encountered by the entrenched frequency interpretation, according to which a statistical probability indicates the limiting frequency with which a certain kind of outcome actually occurs within a certain infinite sequence. Indeed, if the frequency interpretation is given a *hypothetical* formulation, i.e., as the limiting frequencies that *would be* generated during an infinite sequence of trials of a certain kind, then it is exceedingly difficult to distinguish between these two interpretations. Nevertheless, it can be done, as I have explained in detail elsewhere.[18] The point is, therefore, that on either the long run propensity or the hypothetical frequency or even the actual frequency interpretations, the meaning of "probability" is only significant relative to the long run. As a result, on any of these interpretations, the problem remains of explaining the meaning of "probability" relative to the occurrence of singular events.

According to the *single case* propensity interpretation, by contrast, the meaning of "probability" is fundamentally significant relative to the occurrence of singular events. That interpretation may be expressed in the following way:

(8) $P(E, O) = p = _{df}$ the strength of the dispositional tendency possessed by an experimental arrangement of kind E to produce an outcome of type O on a singular trial of that arrangement is p.

From this point of view, in other words, a statistical probability is viewed as a statistical disposition possessed by each and every experimental arrangement of a certain kind (in fulfillment of condition (a)); it asserts of each of those arrangements that they are characterized by a statistical disposition of strength p to produce a certain kind of outcome on each and every trial with that arrangement (in fulfillment of condition (b)); and although these probabilities, as theoretical properties of experimental arrangements, are not directly accessible to observational test, they may be subjected to systematic confirmation by comparing the characteristic relative frequencies they would generate during long runs of trials—as determined through application of Bernoulli's theorem—with the observable relative frequencies they actually do generate during long runs of conducted trials (in fulfillment of condition (c)).[19]

It may be worthwhile to reconsider from the point of view of the single case propensity interpretation the statistical explanation to which we applied the long run propensity interpretation, namely:

(9)   Any experimental arrangement consisting of a fair die and tossing device of kind k possesses a dispositional tendency of strength $\frac{1}{6}$ to produce the outcome of an ace on a single trial of that arrangement.

This experimental arrangement consists of a fair die and tossing device of kind k, with which a single trial a was made at time t.

$$\overline{\qquad\qquad\qquad\qquad\qquad\qquad\qquad\qquad\qquad\qquad\qquad\qquad\qquad} \; [\tfrac{1}{6}]$$

The outcome of trial a at time t was an ace.

Perhaps the most significant feature to notice by way of contrast with the long run propensity or hypothetical frequency interpretations, therefore, is that the single case propensity interpretation provides a rationale for why it should be the case that the inductive probability r reflecting the strength of support conferred by an explanans upon its explanandum should have the same numerical value as the statistical probability p pertaining to its occurrence. On the single case propensity interpretation, after all, the statistical probability p reflects the strength of the dispositional tendency for set-ups of a certain kind to produce an outcome of a certain kind *on a single trial*; consequently, it represents a marked contrast to the frequency (or even long run propensity) view that such values reflect only "fair betting quotients" assigned for reasons of practicality and convenience. Indeed, in spite of Reichenbach's resourcefulness in developing the concept of weight as a fictional derivative for application to singular events, surely the explanatory claims of such a concept—whose introduction is justified on the *ad hoc* grounds that "it serves the purpose of action to deal with such statements as meaningful"[20]—must be regarded with suspicion if not outright rejection.

The rationale, in other words, is that from the single case propensity perspective the "inductive" probability r is better thought of as a "deductive" probability in the sense of being the metalanguage analogue of the statistical probability p, i.e., they both assert the same thing but express this content from different points of view, namely: as the *strength of the dispositional tendency* for set-ups of that kind to produce an outcome of that kind on a single trial, in the case of p; and as a description of the relevant antecedent conditions and nomological regularities because of which that very *degree of nomic expectability* obtains in that specific individual instance, in the case of r. From this perspective, therefore, the single case propensity rationale for equating the numerical values of p and r is decidedly different from the standard "long run" (frequency or propensity) rationale.

There is, nevertheless, an important intersection between these two approaches to understanding the significance of the numerical value of r, for the single case propensity analysis provides an explanation for why it should be the case that r may *also* be envisioned as a "fair betting quotient." This connection is clearly established by reference to the logical interpretation of Reichenbach, according to which "probability" serves as a metalanguage operator that applies to sentences as objects. On this approach, probability statements reflect not the frequency with which a particular outcome occurs within a sequence of trials but rather the frequency with which statements describing such outcomes happen to be true relative to a sequence of statements describing those trials.[21]

From the long run point of view, of course, the probability for an outcome of a certain kind under conditions of a certain kind is simply the limiting frequency with which that outcome occurs within a sequence of trials conducted under those conditions. If the probability for an ace as the outcome within a sequence of trials consisting of tosses with a fair die and tossing device happens to be $\frac{1}{6}$, however, then it will necessarily be the case that the limiting frequency, i.e., in this case, *logical* probability, with which sentences asserting, "This outcome is an ace," accompany the members of the sequence of sentences asserting, "This trial consists of a toss with a fair die and tossing device," will also equal $\frac{1}{6}$ (since those assertions will be true if and only if the events they describe occur).

From the single case point of view, however, the probability for an outcome of a certain kind under conditions of a certain kind designates the strength of the dispositional tendency for such a set-up to produce such an outcome on its *singular* trial. As we have discovered, although these probabilities do not logically guarantee the limiting frequencies of their long run results, they do provide an overwhelming probability—through the application of Bernoulli's theorem—that those outcomes will occur with limiting frequencies that are equal to their probabilities. If the probability for an ace as the outcome within a sequence of trials consisting of tosses with a die and tossing device is $\frac{1}{6}$, therefore, it is only overwhelmingly probable that the limiting frequency, i.e., logical probability, with which sentences asserting, "This outcome is an ace," accompany the members of the sequence of sentences asserting, "This trial consists of a toss with a die and tossing device," will also equal $\frac{1}{6}$.

It might therefore be supposed that the connection between p and r on the single case account is only one of overwhelming probability, while on the long run account it is one of logical necessity. But that would be a faulty inference, for the value of r is intended to characterize the strength of an explanans relative to its explanandum—where the event to be explained is *the occurrence of a particular outcome on a single trial*. There is no doubt that the long run constructions exercise a grip upon long run results that differs categorically from the hold exerted by the single case propensity construction. But relative to the explanation of singular events, the grip exercised by single case probabilities is not matched by the hold exerted by long run probabilities. For the issue is *not* one of the limiting frequency with which an explanandum statement (such as "This outcome is an ace") accompanies a statement of initial conditions (such as "This trial consists of a toss with a fair die and tossing device") but rather of the character of the connection between the whole *explanans*, i.e., the statement of initial conditions together with the relevant statistical law, and its respective *explanandum*.

Relative to an explanation such as (6), therefore, it may be said that, on the long run analysis, this argument explains a's being A by showing that this is to be expected with the limiting frequency of $\frac{1}{6}$ *over the long run*, in view of the general statistical law and statement of particular facts included in the explanans; and for this reason, the appropriate value to assign to r as the "fair betting quotient" for an outcome of this kind under conditions of this kind is also $\frac{1}{6}$. On the single case analysis, by comparison, it may be said that this argument explains a's being A by showing that this is to be expected *on a single trial* with the dispositional strength of $\frac{1}{6}$, in view of the statistical law and statement of particular facts included in the explanans; and for this reason, the appropriate value to assign to r as the "degree of nomic expectability" for an outcome of this kind under conditions of this kind is also $\frac{1}{6}$.

The single case propensity construction, therefore, establishes the "fair betting quotient" for a particular outcome under conditions of the specified kind not only over the long run but also for the single case. For the numerical value of r, viewed as a degree of nomic expectability, not only functions as an *estimation* of the limiting frequency with which sentences describing outcomes of that kind will be true over a long sequence of trials (with the force of overwhelming probability) but also as a *designation* of the degree of entailment with which such an explanandum follows from such an explanans on any singular trial (with the force of logical necessity)! Although the long run constructions may be able to provide a *long run justification* for identifying (long run) probabilities with single case wagers, therefore, only the single case construction is able to provide a *single case justification* for identifying (single case) probabilities with single case wagers.

My motivation for characterizing *r* as a "degree of nomic expectability," however, is not only to avoid the possibly misleading connotations that would attend its unqualified endorsement as a "degree of inductive probability" but also to focus attention explicitly upon the theoretical aspects of the analysis provided by the dispositional perspective. Perhaps the most important consequences attending the adoption of this point of view, in fact, are (a) the unified theory it provides of the character of lawfulness for both statistical and universal laws and (b) the criterion it supports for the adequacy of explanations invoking laws of either kind. Consideration of these issues, therefore, will afford an opportunity to elaborate upon the conception of *r* as a "degree of nomic expectability."

III

Statistical laws are typically envisioned as attributing a specific relative frequency to the occurrence of an event of a certain kind within a specified sequence, i.e., a sequence consisting of the ordered members of a particular reference class, where the ordering relation, at least in the case of physical events, is supposed to be the temporal relations that obtain between these events. The result of thus construing probabilities as relative frequencies within temporally extended physical sequences is to reinforce the view that lawful generalizations are essentially amenable to being determined by numerical count: to ascertain whether or not a particular uniformity is universal or statistical in kind, all one has to do is to determine the ratio between the number of members belonging to the reference class and the number of members belonging to the attribute class. If every member of the reference class is also a member of the attribute class, the uniformity is universal; if not, then the relative frequency indicates the statistical distribution of that attribute within that reference class.

What is needed, therefore, is to recognize that this way of looking at the world is fundamentally mistaken by virtue of failing to provide a justifiable basis for distinguishing between mere correlations and lawful regularities. From the point of view of the propensity interpretation, a conceptual shift is in order, since now statistical laws as well as universal laws are essentially of universal form; for a statistical law under the propensity construction no longer simply affirms that a certain percentage of the reference class also belongs to the attribute class. What it asserts is that *every member of the reference class possesses a certain dispositional property*, which in the case of statistical laws is to be envisioned as a *statistical* disposition and in the case of statistical laws is to be envisioned as a *universal* disposition. The difference, in other words, is not a matter of how many members of the reference class possess the relevant attribute but rather of how strong the dispositional tendency is that is possessed by every member of that reference class.

Not the least of the reasons for adopting the propensity approach, therefore, is that it establishes a unified account of lawfulness from the point of view of dispositional properties.

This account conforms to the characterization of lawlike statements endorsed by Hempel at least in the following respect:

(I) A sentence S is *lawlike* if and only if:
  (a) S is not logically limited to a finite number of instances, i.e., S is of essentially general form; and,
  (b) S is capable of providing support for counterfactual and subjunctive conditionals.

It goes beyond the Hempelian account, however, in maintaining that only dispositional sentences, i.e., sentences making essential reference to dispositional properties, are capable of satisfying condition (b). In other words, a sentence S satisfies condition (b) *if and only if S is an essentially dispositional sentence*, i.e., a predicate expression D occurs essentially in S such that the property designated by D fulfills both of the previously specified conditions, i.e., it is a tendency to manifest appropriate response behavior under relevant test conditions that is an actual physical state of some object or collection of objects. According to the propensity account, therefore, *a sentence S is lawlike if and only if S is an essentially dispositional sentence of essentially general form.*[22]

A sentence S may fail to be lawlike, therefore, in at least these two different ways:

(1) it may be essentially dispositional in kind while failing to be essentially general in form (e.g., "This piece of glass is fragile") and consequently be capable of providing support for counterfactual and subjunctive conditionals in spite of failing to be a lawlike sentence; or, alternatively,

(2) it may be essentially general in form while failing to be essentially dispositional in kind (e.g., "All moas die before reaching the age of fifty") and consequently be incapable of providing support for counterfactual and subjunctive conditionals in spite of possessing the appropriate logical form.[23]

To determine whether or not a given sentence S is lawlike, therefore, consideration must be given not only to its logical form but also to its ontological kind. Such an undertaking is partially but not exclusively semantical in character; it is also partially but not entirely empirical in foundation. There are ample grounds, therefore, for regarding this question as only amenable to a theoretical resolution.

It is a striking result that from the propensity perspective the difference between universal and statistical laws may be characterized by means of *reduction sentences*; for universal laws only differ from statistical laws insofar as the dispositional tendencies that they attribute to objects and collections of objects that possess them are of universal rather than statistical strength, i.e., they are exceptionless rather than exceptionable tendencies to produce appropriate outcomes under relevant test conditions. If the probabilistic logical operator "$=n\Rightarrow$" is introduced as a means for symbolizing "causal conditionals" whose values n range through various statistical strengths p from zero to one, i.e., "$=p\Rightarrow$," to universal strength u (which is *not* to be confused with probabilities of one), i.e., "$=u\Rightarrow$," where the appropriate numerical value is determined by the corresponding strength of the dispositional tendency involved, then the difference between universal and statistical laws may be symbolized as follows (where the variable "x" ranges over objects and collections of objects as its values):[24]

(II) universal laws: $(x) [Tx\rightarrow(Px=p\Rightarrow Ox)]$,
  statistical laws: $(x) [Tx\rightarrow(Px=u\Rightarrow Ox)]$.

A universal law, therefore, is a statement of universal form attributing a dispositional tendency of universal strength u to produce an outcome of kind O on every single trial of kind T to every object or collection of objects that possesses the property P; and a statistical law is also a statement of universal form attributing, by contrast, a dispositional tendency of statistical strength p to produce an outcome of kind O on every single trial of kind T to every object or collection of objects that possesses the property P.

Notice that experimental set-ups, i.e., objects or collections of objects, are only characterized as experimental set-ups of a particular kind insofar as they possess or fail to possess the disposition involved. Since all dispositional properties are theoretical properties, however, evidently the identification of an experimental set-up as a set-up of a particular kind requires an essentially theoretical determination as to the dispositional properties which are distinctive of set-ups of that kind. On the other hand, it is significant to acknowledge that there may well be certain dispositional properties that are possessed by all objects or collections of objects which happen to possess certain other properties whose presence or absence may be ascertained on the basis of direct observation and relatively simple measurement alone. Thus, if an experimental set-up of kind E is characterized by the possession of a certain set of dispositional properties $P^1, P^2, \ldots, P^n$, such that

$$(x)(Ex \equiv P^1x \cdot P^2x \cdot \ldots \cdot P^nx),$$

then it is entirely possible that the possession of at least some and, perhaps, even all of these properties might be determinable by means of experiential findings alone. This possibility, I take it, is quite apparent, *provided* that the dispositions involved are specifiable by means of bilateral reduction sentences in which the relevant test and appropriate response are observationally ascertainable. In any case, although (II) represents the simplest formulation of universal and of statistical laws, they will hold for any experimental set-up E where every set-up of that kind possesses the dispositional property P as one of the necessary and sufficient conditions for being a set-up of that particular kind. Consequently, lawlike statements may also be envisioned as attributing appropriate responses under relevant test conditions to every experimental set-up of a certain kind as follows:

(II')   universal laws: $(x) [Tx \rightarrow (Ex = u \Rightarrow Ox)]$,
         statistical laws: $(x) [Tx \rightarrow (Ex = p \Rightarrow Ox)]$,

where the significance of this alternative formulation is primarily, though not exclusively of an epistemological character, i.e., the explicit recognition that it may be possible to identify experimental set-ups as experimental set-ups of a particular kind by means of observational criteria alone—provided, of course, that these observational criteria are supported on theoretical grounds.

On the basis of these considerations, it is possible to advance a single criterion for the adequacy of any explanation for the occurrence of a singular event, regardless of whether that event is envisioned as a manifestation of a universal or of a statistical regularity:

(III) A set of sentences S, known as the "explanans," provides *an adequate explanation* for the occurrence of a physical event that is described by another sentence E, known as the "explanandum," if and only if:
   (a) the explanandum is either a deductive or a probabilistic consequence of the explanans;
   (b) the explanans contains at least one general law of either universal or statistical form that is actually required for the derivation of the explanandum;
   (c) the general law(s) invoked in the explanans satisfy the requirement of statistical relevance in the form of the single case rule;[25] and
   (d) the sentences constituting the explanation—both the explanans and the explanandum—are true.

From this point of view, a set of statements satisfying conditions (a), (b), and (c) may be regarded as a "potential" explanation, while those satisfying all four are "adequate."

This criterion supports the conception that, from the logical point of view, there are two basic kinds of explanation, depending upon whether the general law(s) invoked in the explanans are essentially universal or essentially statistical in kind, i.e., depending upon whether they concern a dispositional tendency of universal or statistical strength. If the law(s) invoked in the explanans are essentially universal, the logical properties of the relationship between the sentences constituting the explanans and its explanandum will be those of complete entailment; if they are essentially statistical, they will be those of only partial entailment. Consequently, these two kinds of explanation may be called "universal-deductive" and "statistical-probabilistic," respectively.

An example of a *universal-deductive* explanation for the occurrence of an explanandum event might be the following:

(CL)   All fragile objects break when struck by hammers.
(C1) a is fragile. [Fa]
(C2) a is struck by a hammer at t. [Sa]
(ES) a breaks at t. [Ba]

for clearly the explanans invoking the covering law (CL) together with the statements of initial conditions (C1) and (C2) fulfills the criteria for an adequate explanation of its explanandum sentence (ES) (provided that the requirement of statistical relevance (c) has been fulfilled). This explanation, moreover, exemplifies the characteristics of universal-deductive explanations in general and may be schematized along these lines:

(IV) $(x) [Sx \to (Fx = u \Rightarrow Bx)]$
           $Sa \cdot Fa$
           _____ [u]
           Ba

where the single line separating the explanans from its explanandum is intended to indicate that the logical properties of the relationship between this explanans and its explanandum are those of complete, as opposed to partial, entailment; and the symbol in brackets indicates that the degree of nomic expectability for an outcome of this kind on a trial of this kind is of universal, rather than statistical, strength.

An example of a *statistical-probabilistic* explanation for another explanandum event might likewise be the following:

(CL)   The probability for obtaining an ace as the result of a toss with a fair die and tossing device of kind k is $\frac{1}{6}$.
(C1) a is a fair die. [Fa]
(C2) a is given a toss in a tossing device of kind k at t. [Ta]
(ES) a comes up showing an ace at t. [Aa]

for clearly the explanans invoking the covering law (CL) together with the statements of initial conditions (C1) and (C2) fulfills the criteria for an adequate explanation of its explanandum sentence (ES) (provided, once again, that the requirement of statistical relevance (c) has been fulfilled). This explanation similarly exemplifies the characteristics of statistical-probabilistic explanations in general and may be schematized along the following lines:

(V) $(x) [Tx{\rightarrow}(Fx= {}^1/_6 \Rightarrow Ax)]$
       $Ta \cdot Fa$

       $$\overline{\overline{}} [\tfrac{1}{6}].$$
       Aa

where the double line separating the explanans from its explanandum is intended to indicate that the logical properties of the relationship between this explanans and its explanandum are those of partial, rather than complete, entailment; and the number in brackets indicates the degree of nomic expectability for an outcome of this kind on a trial of this kind which is, of course, of statistical, as opposed to universal, strength.

It might be objected that the requirement of statistical relevance is not applicable to universal-deductive explanations, since it appears to be the case that, by virtue of the relation of complete entailment obtaining between the explanans and its explanandum, all of the relevant conditions attending the occurrence of the explanandum event must have been taken into account. From this point of view, it would be plausible to suppose that only conditions (a), (b), and (d) are relevant for the adequacy of a universal-deductive explanation, while condition (c) is applicable to statistical-probabilistic explanations alone. That this would be a mistaken assumption, however, has been clearly demonstrated by Henry Kyburg and emphasized by Salmon in the form of counterexamples of the following kind:

(i) This sample of table salt dissolves in water, for it has had a dissolving spell cast upon it, and all samples of table salt that have had dissolving spells cast upon them dissolve in water; and,

(ii) John Jones avoided becoming pregnant during the past year, for he has taken his wife's birth control pills regularly, and every man who regularly takes birth control pills avoids pregnancy.[26]

It might be said, therefore, that although the deductive character of a universal-deductive explanation guarantees that its premises establish *sufficient* conditions for the occurrence of its explanandum event, they do not thereby automatically exclude *unnecessary* circumstances that, as it were, only accidentally attend the occurrence of that event. In order to exclude these causally irrelevant conditions from the explanans of an adequate explanation, therefore, the statistical relevance rule must be employed. Indeed, the inclusion of this requirement for universal as well as statistical explanations constitutes a further strengthening of the conception of an adequate explanation as encompassing *all and only* those circumstances causally relevant to the occurrence of an explanandum event. The single case rule, therefore, may suitably be envisioned as a criterion, not just of statistical relevance, but of *causal relevance* in general.

There is an interesting property of explanations which emerges from consideration of their logical structure as exemplified in (IV) and (V). For if the reduction sentences that are employed in formulating lawlike sentences happen to be bilateral rather than unilateral in kind, then in the case of universal-deductive explanations, in particular, there is an important sense in which such explanations may be regarded as *providing evidence for themselves*. Consider, for example, the characterization of (IV) by means of bilateral reduction sentences (theoretically assuming that all and only fragile objects break when struck by hammers), which would then exemplify the following form:

(IV′) $(x) [Sx{\rightarrow}(Fx \equiv u Bx)]$
        $Sa \cdot Fa$

        $$\overline{} [u]$$
        Ba

where "$\equiv u$" is employed to symbolize the dispositional property involved as of such a character that that particular kind of outcome is *always and only* a manifestation of that specific disposition. In such a situation, the logical features of the reduction chains that formalize the meaning of the dispositional predicate "F" would be of such a kind that the satisfaction of its test condition "S" and of its response behavior condition "B" by a specific individual or object (such as a) would be logically sufficient to warrant the ascription of that property to that individual or object, i.e., "Sa" and "Ba" jointly entail "Fa." Notice that in the case of unilateral reduction chains, satisfaction of a test condition and a response behavior condition is only a necessary but not a sufficient condition for ascribing such a property to an individual or object but it would, nevertheless, constitute relevant evidence regarding its ascription.

This intriguing characteristic of explanations as thus construed, therefore, might appropriately be expressed by qualifying explanations of universal-deductive form employing bilateral reduction formulations as *fully self-evidencing* (since the occurrence of the relevant test and of the appropriate response behavior is logically sufficient to establish the presence of the dispositional property involved); while, by contrast, universal-deductive explanations employing unilateral reduction sentences may be qualified as *partially self-evidencing* (since the occurrence of the relevant test and of the appropriate response behavior is logically not sufficient—although it is logically necessary—to establish the presence of the dispositional property involved). Notice that the only sense in which statistical-probabilistic explanations may be regarded as self-evidencing is in an extremely weak, partial sense; for the logical characteristics of probabilistic reduction sentences, even when they are "bilateral," are such that a single appropriate response under a single relevant trial provides only slight—although, nevertheless, relevant—evidence for the presence of that property (whose strength, after all, is theoretically measured by the relative frequencies it would typically generate during long runs of trials).

The conception of explanations as involving essential reference to dispositional properties, of course, may be subjected to philosophical appraisal on the basis of the criteria for explicative adequacy. Among the most important considerations from this point of view, therefore, is the extent to which this conception accords with scientific practice and with ordinary language; in other words, the extent to which explanations that occur in technical scientific and ordinary conversational contexts actually conform to this conception. And, indeed, it appears as though abundant support may be found in the form of such common "explanations" as the following: "The glass broke when it was dropped, because it was fragile"; "These iron filings were attracted to this metal bar, because it is magnetic"; "That sample of table salt dissolved when put in water, because it was soluble"; "This die comes up with an ace quite often when it's tossed, because it is loaded"; "That penny yields a head only about half the time, because it is fair"; "This lump of radon disintegrated by approximately half its mass in the past few days, because the half-life of radon is 3.82 days"; and so on.

It is significant to note, therefore, that if these considerations are sound and the single case propensity interpretation should be adopted as the standard conception of statistical probability, it then becomes possible to distinguish between lawful and accidental generalizations of either universal or statistical form on the basis of theoretical grounds, namely: that lawlike generalizations are those for which we possess a theoretical warrant in the sense of attributing to the conditions they describe a dispositional property that is lacking in the case of mere correlations. From this perspective, it would be possible to claim that all explanations in empirical science—whether explanations of singular events or of general regularities either of universal or of statistical form—are fundamentally theoretical in character. Not the least of the benefits we would reap from such a move would be to discover we already possess the theoretical basis for explaining why lawful generalizations but not accidental correlations provide support for counterfactual and subjunctive conditionals.

NOTES

* This essay is dedicated to Carl G. Hempel and to Wesley C. Salmon. [The author has taken this opportunity to expand or replace several notes. These new notes appear here in brackets.]

1. Isaac Levi, "Are Statistical Hypotheses Covering Laws?" *Synthese* 20 (1969), p. 299.
2. Ibid., p. 299 and pp. 304–06.
3. Ibid., p. 303.
4. Ibid.
5. Ibid., p. 297. [While Hempel endorsed this approach in "Aspects of Scientific Explanation," *Aspects of Scientific Explanation*. (New York: The Free Press, 1965), pp. 376–80, for example, he has not pursued this approach in his subsequent published work.]
6. Ibid., p. 298.
7. Ibid.
8. Carl G. Hempel, "A Logical Appraisal of Operationalism," *Aspects of Scientific Explanation* (New York: The Free Press, 1965), p. 132, fn. 17.
9. Carl G. Hempel, *Fundamentals of Concept Formation in Empirical Science* (Chicago: University of Chicago Press, 1952), part II, esp. pp. 23–9. [The introduction of intensional operators for subjunctive and for causal conditionals, however, provides the opportunity to formally reflect the difference between subjunctive and counterfactual conditionals that are warranted on logical and on ontological grounds. See James H. Fetzer, *Scientific Knowledge* (Dordrecht: D. Reidel, 1981), part I. Also see new note 24 below.]
10. Levi, "Are Statistical Hypotheses Covering Laws?" p. 299.
11. Ibid.
12. Hempel, "Aspects of Scientific Explanation," pp. 457–63.
13. Carl G. Hempel, "Maximal Specificity and Lawlikeness in Probabilistic Explanation," *Philosophy of Science* 35 (1968), p. 117. Note that the quotation has been slightly revised to suit the example. [Hempel reconsiders the adequacy of this approach in that paper.]
14. Ibid.
15. Wesley C. Salmon, *Statistical Explanation and Statistical Relevance* (Pittsburgh: University of Pittsburgh Press, 1971); and James H. Fetzer, "Statistical Explanations," *Boston Studies in the Philosophy of Science*, vol. 20, eds., K. Schaffner and R. Cohen (Dordrecht: D. Reidel 1974) pp. 337–348.
16. Levi, "Are Statistical Hypotheses Covering Laws?" p. 303.
17. Hempel, "Aspects of Scientific Explanation," pp. 339–40.
18. [These issues are pursued in Fetzer, *Scientific Knowledge*, part I.]
19. James H. Fetzer, "Dispositional Probabilities," *Boston Studies in the Philosophy of Science*, vol. 8, eds., R. Buck and R. Cohen (Dordrecht: D. Reidel, 1971).
20. Hans Reichenbach, *The Theory of Probability* (Berkeley: University of California Press, 1949), pp. 376–77. Salmon holds essentially the same position; see Salmon, *Statistical Explanation*, pp. 77–78.
21. Reichenbach, ibid., pp. 378–82.
22. Cf. Karl R. Popper, *The Logic of Scientific Discovery* (New York: Harper and Row, 1965), New Appendix. "Universals, Dispositions, and Natural or Physical Necessity," p. 425. [This formulation should be refashioned to read: *A sentence S is lawlike if and only if S attributes a permanent dispositional property A to everything that possesses a specific reference property R.* For further discussion, see Fetzer, *Scientific Knowledge*, part I.]
23. The example is Popper's; for an illuminating discussion, see Popper, ibid., pp. 427–28.

24. [In subsequent work, I reverse the order of the first two arguments, where "Px" and "Tx" occur in the opposite order. Moreover, the subjunctive conditional should appear in place of the material conditional in order to represent logically contingent permanent property relations. The syntax and semantics for the intensional operators required to formalize lawlike sentences are presented in Fetzer, *Scientific Knowledge*, Part I.]

25. [Hempel's covering law theory, Salmon's statistical relevance theory, and the present causal relevance theory depend upon different conceptions of explanatory relevance. Salmon's frequentist approach, for example, qualifies a property F as statistically relevant to the occurrence of an attribute A within a reference class R if and only if the limiting frequency with which A occurs in R and F differs from the limiting frequency with which A occurs in R and $-F$. (We may refer to this as *the long run rule*.) On the propensity approach, by contrast, a property F qualifies as causally relevant to the occurrence of an attribute A in relation to a reference property R if and only if the strength of the dispositional tendency for A on a single trial of a chance set-up of kind R and F differs from the strength of the dispositional tendency for A on a single trial of a chance set-up of kind R and $-F$. (We may refer to this as *the single case rule*.) The theory of explanation elaborated here essentially requires the single case rule. For further elaboration, see Fetzer, *Scientific Knowledge*, part II.] Editor's note—In Fetzer's *Scientific Knowledge* and elsewhere, he refers to the condition that the antecedents of lawlike sentences must (implicitly or explicitly) *include* the presence or absence of every property that makes a difference to their consequents as *the requirement of maximal specificity*, while referring to the condition that the antecedents of lawlike sentences that appear in the explanans of adequate explanations must *exclude* any property whose presence or absence makes no difference to the occurrence of the explanandum event as *the requirement of strict maximal specificity*. The maximal specificity condition is a truth condition for lawlike sentences, while the strict maximal specificity condition is an adequacy condition for scientific explanations. The single-case rule is the causal-relevance condition that underlies these requirements for lawlike sentences and scientific explanations when they happen to be causal. For a recent discussion, see James H. Fetzer, *Philosophy of Science* (New York, NY: Paragon House Publishers, 1993), Ch. 4

26. Salmon, ibid., pp. 33–34.

PART FIVE

PROBABILITY AND INFERENCE

INTRODUCTION

he condition that lawlike sentences must have antecedents which are maximally specific to be true affords a promising solution to the problem of provisoes. The laws formulated by idealized theories, of course, can be employed to explain the behavior of actual things only when those things happen to satisfy the conditions they specify. Even idealized laws as counterfactual generalizations whose antecedents have no instances can be supplemented by less-idealized laws as subjunctive generalizations whose antecedents might have instances. The existence of such simple idealized laws does not preclude the discovery of more complex laws as science advances.

Fetzer's "Probability and Objectivity in Deterministic and Indeterministic Situations" suggests that the benefits that accrue from adopting the propensity approach extend to clarifying and illuminating problematical cases from the domain of quantum physics. Deterministic situations are those in which "the same cause" brings about "the same effect" in every case without exception. Indeterministic situations are those in which "the same cause" brings about "one or another effect" within a specific set of possible effects. If a realistic interpretation of indeterministic causation can be found, then hypotheses that describe indeterministic situations might possibly be true.

Although he sketches several kinds of cases that are encountered within the quantum domain, the primary focus of his discussion is the "one-slit" experiment, in which repetitions of what are taken to be the complete set of relevant conditions nevertheless yield different outcomes with specific probabilities. In evaluating alternative interpretations of indeterministic causation, Fetzer compares the frequency, the subjective, and the propensity approaches to understanding probabilistic hypotheses. If his analysis is well-founded, only the propensity account affords a conception which is compatible with explanatory indeterminism and predictive indeterminism.

At least two aspects of this analysis ought to be emphasized. The first is that the discovery of additional conditions (in the "one-slit" experiment) whose presence or absence makes a difference to the impact of an electron on a photographic plate when the experiment is repeated would not make the necessity for an interpretation of causal indeterminism any less pressing. The situation after these additional conditions were taken into account could continue to exemplify indeterministic causation. And other cases, including the "two-slit" experiment and the laws of radioactive decay, would still pose problems of interpretation as irreducibly probabilistic phenomena.

The second is that the constraints that must be satisfied for a set of beliefs to qualify as "rational" are subject to ambiguity. Conditions that are typically imposed include logical consistency (so that, if z believes "p" at a time t, then z does not believe "not-p" at time t) and deductive closure (so that, if z believes "$p \rightarrow q$" and "p" at time t, then z also believes "q" at time t). But it is important to notice, with respect to the condition of coherence, that *beliefs about probabilities* are not necessarily the same thing as *probabilistic beliefs*. Beliefs about objective propensities for various outcomes under various conditions do not necessarily involve any subjective probabilities at all.

Salmon's "Dynamic Rationality: Propensity, Probability, and Credence" affords a general account of the manner in which probability can function as a guide in life. Salmon identifies probabilities with limiting frequencies on the ground that the causal directedness of propensities inhibits them from qualifying as a proper interpretation of the calculus of probability. He endorses the conception of propensities as probabilistic causes, elaborating the thesis that, "We can find out about many propensities by observing frequencies." Indeed, he offers a new version of the straight rule of induction, according to which observed frequencies permit inferences about causal propensities.

Much of his discussion concerns the relationship between beliefs about probabilities and probabilistic beliefs. According to the Principal Principle advanced by David Lewis, our "degree of belief" in the proposition "that A" should equal the objective probability (or "chance") for A. Lewis accents the role of subjective probabilities in determining the values of objective chances, which for him are not unique. In Salmon's view, the inferential relations involved here are better understood the other way around, where objective chances determine degrees of belief. The moral of the analysis that he provides can be summed up by the dictim, "Respect the frequencies!" as evidence in inferring propensities.

One way to view the situation as Salmon sees it is to envision the Lewis principle as implying the evidential irrelevance of any belief E other than those about objective chance X in determining one's degree of belief in A. So it qualifies as a *subjective-probability criterion* of rational irrelevance:

(SPC) $C(A/X\&E) = x = C(A/X\&-E);$

that is, one's subjective probability (or "credence") C in A, given the belief X that the objective chance of A equals x, should equal x, no matter what other beliefs E one accepts. By this standard, every other belief has to be rationally irrelevant in arriving at the appropriate subjective probability.

Salmon's position, moreover, divides the inferential situation into (at least) two steps, the first of which involves an inference to a propensity:

(Step 1)   If z has observed that m/n Rs have been As, then z should infer that the propensity for any R to be $A = m/n$.

The second step is to use the conclusion of that inference as a premise to draw an inference about the particular instance of R under consideration:

(Step 2)   If *z* believes that the propensity for any *R* to be *A* = *m*/*n* then *z*'s degree of belief that this *R* is *A* should also = *m*/*n*.

The other steps that Salmon considers involve the use of conditionalization to adjust inferences about propensity hypotheses with the accumulation of additional frequency evidence. His discussion reviews various notions of coherence, strict coherence, and openmindedness within a Bayesian framework that is, in contrast with Lewis's account, intended to provide an objective foundation for dynamic rationality. The most fascinating feature of this discussion, however, is the introduction of principles of reasoning about propensities as counterparts to the straight rule and Skyrms' "Rule S," which have usually been employed within alternative frameworks.

Eells' "Probability, Inference, and Decision" provides an introduction to Bayesian reasoning and Bayesian decision theory which accents the role of subjective probabilities and utilities. Distinguishing between "descriptive" and "normative" conceptions of these principles, he elaborates and defends the theory that subjective probabilities and utilities lie behind and explain rational decisions and preferences. Rational decisions conform to the policy of the maximization of subjective expected utility, while rational changes in subjective probabilities conform to the process of conditionalization, even if it should turn out to be the case that few if any of us happen to be rational.

The thesis that rational changes in subjective probabilities (or "degrees of belief") conform to conditionalization requires that, whenever a person *z* acquires new evidence *E* in relation to an hypothesis *X*, the relationship between *z*'s "new" and "old" probability distributions satisfies Bayes' Theorem:

(Bayes' Theorem) $Pn(X) = Po(X/E) = Po(X\&E)/Po(E),$

where "*Po*" is the old distribution ("prior" to the acquisition of new evidence *E*) and "*Pn*" is the new distribution ("posterior" to the acquisition of evidence *E*). It serves both the static function of relating degrees of belief at any one time and the dynamic function of relating degrees of belief at any two times.

Eells' defense of conditionalization as the foundation for rational changes of belief has at least two dimensions. On the one hand, he relates conditionalization to various conditions of confirmation and problems of inference advanced in the philosophical literature, and, on the other, he relates conditionalization to a dynamic version of the "Dutch Book Theorem" in the Appendix. The Bayesian approach he recommends supports the entailment condition, the converse entailment condition, and the equivalence condition, but does not satisfy the special consequence condition. It provides a means for coping with the raven paradox and with issues involving unexpected evidence.

The policy of maximizing subjective expected utility, no doubt, is widely regarded as the appropriate decision principle to employ when quantitative information (concerning those probabilities and those utilities) happens to be available. In its absence, other qualitative principles (such as the minimax loss and the maximax gain policies) may have to be employed instead. Perhaps the most important aspect of Eells' introduction, however, concerns the general rationale he suggests for a subjective approach toward Bayesian reasoning and decision-making, which is summarized by the principle that,

(Eells' Thesis)   *We have to work with what we have to work with.*

Yet there would appear to be good reason to think that decisions which are made in the world should not be based merely on subjective opinion. Even if rational decisions do have to be based on subjective probabilities, surely those probabilities in turn should be based on information about the world.

STUDY QUESTIONS

As you read the articles that appear in this section, you may want to think about their implications for understanding the nature of science and of philosophy. The following questions are intended to stimulate your thinking by focusing attention on some of the less obvious aspects of different positions.

(1) Ontic properties are properties of the world, while epistemic properties are properties of our beliefs about the world. If the world were completely deterministic, could there be any ontic indeterminism in the world? Would any indeterminism therefore have to be because of our ignorance about the deterministic properties of the world as a function of our beliefs about it?

(2) What is the difference between the deterministic hypothesis and the so-called hidden variable hypothesis about quantum phenomena, such as the single-slit experiment? If all of the hidden variables were completely specified, would that make the formerly hidden variable hypothesis identical with an ordinary deterministic hypothesis without hidden variables?

(3) Explain the meaning of a probability hypothesis under the frequency interpretation. If probabilities are identified with limiting frequencies in infinite sequences, then what happens to probability if the history of the world is merely finite? If these limiting frequencies were identified with hypothetical instead of with actual sequences, would that solve the problem?

(4) Explain the meaning of a probability hypothesis under the subjective interpretation. If probabilities are identified with a person's degree of belief in specific propositions, then can two persons at the same time—or one person at two different times—have entirely different degrees of belief in the same propositions? Is this a vice or a virtue of this interpretation?

(5) Salmon denies that propensities can properly qualify as probabilities but nevertheless endorses the conception as appropriate for probabilistic causes in the world. Why does he qualify his acceptance of propensities in this fashion? Does this mean that propensities cannot fulfill the roles that Fetzer suggests they should assume in explanations and predictions?

(6) Lewis advances the Principal Principle as the fundamental relation that links objective chances and subjective probabilities. Does it made more sense to think that our knowledge of subjective probabilities determines the values of objective chances or to think that our knowledge of objective chances determines the values of subjective probabilities? Why?

(7) Salmon maintains that a revised version of the principle of induction by enumeration can support inferences to propensities, which should be based upon information about frequencies. Since the principle has normally been employed to make inferences about frequencies, can you think of any reasons inferences about propensities might be more problematic?

(8) If propensities were conditional probabilities, then the propensity of the joint occurrence of two outcomes A and B would be equal to the probability of A, given B, times the probability of B, and also equal to the probability of B, given A, times the probability of A. Since propensities have a "causal directedness," can they possibly qualify as conditional probabilities?

(9) Subjective probabilities are often measured by means of betting odds. If someone

would accept an even money bet (the same amount is gained if you win and lost if you lose) at odds of 2:1, for example, it means that they think the non-occurrence of the outcome is twice as likely as its occurrence. Can you think of reasons why this might ever be incorrect?

(10) As Eells explains, the principle of maximizing expected utility does not require that the probabilities involved be anything other than subjective in their character. Can you think of reasons why, even if objective probabilities are not *required* in order to employ this principle, it might nevertheless be a good idea to base decisions upon them whenever possible?

JAMES H. FETZER

PROBABILITY AND OBJECTIVITY IN DETERMINISTIC AND INDETERMINISTIC SITUATIONS*

The subject I would like to address, namely, probability and objectivity in deterministic and indeterministic situations, could be formulated by means of the question, "To what extent does the propensity approach to probability contribute to plausible solutions to various anomalies which occur in quantum physics?" In order to pursue this problem, I shall, first, sketch several of these anomalous conditions, second, clarify the difference between deterministic and indeterministic situations, and, third, consider three alternative interpretations of probability as they apply to these problems, with particular reference to Einstein's criterion of physical reality. The position I shall defend is that of these three interpretations—the frequency, the subjective, and the propensity—only the third accommodates the possibility, in principle, of providing a realistic interpretation of ontic indeterminism. If these considerations are correct, therefore, they lend support to Popper's contention that the propensity interpretation tends to remove (at least some of) the mystery from quantum phenomena (Popper 1957, 1967, 1982).

I

To offer some background for the sorts of issues that seem to be involved here, the sources of anomaly that occur in quantum physics arise from at least three apparently different types of situations. The first are characterizable by means of Heisenberg's Uncertainty Principle, according to which the measure of certainty or of precision with which the position p and the momentum q of a sub-atomic particle may be specified are inversely related, such that the more precisely its momentum can be measured, the less precisely its position, where there is a limit with respect to simultaneous measurements of position and of momentum reflected by the Uncertainty Principle itself, namely:

(1) $\Delta p \Delta q \geq h$;

where the product of Δp and of Δq as measures of uncertainty of position and of momentum, respectively, can never violate the limiting value of h, understood as Planck's constant, a very small unit of action.

Now this notion of uncertainty is amenable to at least two kinds of interpretation. One interpretation is an "ontic" interpretation, which would have us understand that sub-atomic particles simply do not *have* simultaneous position and momentum, i.e., that we ought to read formula (1) as a property of the physical world, independently of our knowledge or belief or awareness thereof. The other is an "epistemic" interpretation, which instead asserts that the uncertainty relations are properly regarded as representing limitations upon how much we can *know* about the simultaneous position and momentum of sub-atomic particles. Popper has suggested that the ontic interpretation is far-fetched, especially since determinations of momentum are usually made by means of position measurements at different times, say, t_1 and t_2, rather than by means of a simultaneous determination (Popper 1967). An arrangement consisting of two photographic plates separated by a fixed distance, say, d, could be employed to measure the location of a particle at time t_1 and later at time t_2, so that by comparing the results we can compute not only where a particle was at time t_1 but also where it was going.

The determination of momentum by this means, however, is subject to certain qualifications; for the magnitude obtained by dividing the distance, d, by the time, $t_2 - t_1$, may represent a *mean* (or "average") value—unless there are grounds to assume that particles always travel with constant momentum, a doubtful contention. Moreover, if the distance, d, were made less and less, it might still remain the case that there is a limit on the precision attainable as a function of natural law, such that formula (1) reflects an irreducible *ontic* feature of the physical world, after all. Still, I am inclined to agree with Popper that the denial that particles have simultaneous position and momentum is indeed far-fetched, even if the Uncertainty Principle does reflect a limitation, in principle, upon what we can *know*, i.e., as a function of natural law. But it would be valuable to discover an adequate explanation for this perplexing situation— perhaps, for example, by arriving at a theoretical understanding of the second source of anomaly which I would like to consider, the phenomenon known as "wave-particle duality."

Wave-particle duality may be illustrated by (what are usually described as) "one-slit" experiments, in which a source of electrons, A, let us say, is directed through a single aperture toward an apparatus, such as a photographic plate, once again, which is capable of detecting their arrival. What has been discovered is that the behavior of electrons is such that, when this experiment is subject to replication, it is not the case that they always wind up at just one place or location or area; instead, we obtain something like a distribution of impact, such that, if various areas of impact were labeled "B," "C," and so on, then with a certain probability, represented by the absolute value of the appropriate psi-function squared, $|\psi_B|^2, |\psi_C|^2$, and so forth, an electron will end up in one area, say, B, rather than another, C. The principal problem that arises here is what we are supposed to understand by the term "probability" as it is employed within this context. But notice that, even if we assume that particles always have both position and momentum during every moment of their history, nevertheless, the distribution of their impact—together with the interference patterns displayed during other, "two-slit," experiments—represents wave-like behavior by particle-like entities, which appears to be very difficult to comprehend.

The third source of anomaly I want to mention concerns the point of view known as "complementarity," which was originally introduced by Bohr to designate the necessity to depend upon two (seemingly inconsistent) conceptions of physical reality, i.e., the wave picture and the particle picture, without assuming any prospects for their theoretical reconciliation. "Complementarity," of course, has come to mean many things to many people, not least of whom are those allied with the Copenhagen Interpretation of quantum physics, according to which the human mind performs an essential role in understanding the physical world, not only in the acquisition of information about the world but in bringing about the existence of properties of the world by means of causal interaction through the process of measurement. Thus, Einstein tended to differ with Bohr with respect to the possible existence of unmeasured properties, rather than following Bohr in maintaining that,

a quantity is not real just because it *can* be measured, it is also necessary that it *is* measured. Or rather, reality cannot be attributed to the quantity itself in any case, but only to the measurement of the quantity. (Brush 1979, p.93; for alternative interpretations, see Folse 1977)

While it seems quite plausible to suppose that *measurements* arise as a result of a causal interaction between a *measuring instrument*, i.e., a device capable of making measurements, and a *measureable property*, i.e., a property which is capable of being measured, it does appear anomalous to suppose that properties themselves only exist so long as they are being subjected to measurement.

This situation is further complicated, of course, by the introduction of probabilistic properties, whose measurement involves problems not encountered within other contexts. An example sometimes offered to illustrate the difficulties confronting the Copenhagen Construction is that of Schrödinger's "Cat Paradox," which envisions an arrangement consisting of a living feline placed inside an opaque chamber that is connected to an electrical device activated by a radioactive source linked to a geiger counter. If decay occurs and registers—with a probability, let us assume, equal to $1/2$—then an impulse is activated which electrocutes the cat. From the Copenhagen Perspective, it seems, until the chamber has been opened and a live kitty or a dead corpse has been observed, the cat itself is presumed to be neither dead nor alive but rather somewhere in between, which is represented by a superposition of psi-functions for both of these events prior to this measurement being made. The procedure of taking a look and discovering, say, that the cat is dead thus effectuates (what is usually referred to as) "the reduction of the wave packet," whereby, in effect, the result of being dead or of being alive is brought about. All of this is anomalous, indeed, because we are inclined to believe that the cat, after all, is either dead or alive during each moment of its history, whether we happen to notice or not. So if there is some way around problems such as these, then it would appear very desirable to pursue, where much of what follows is intended to suggest that the Copenhagen Interpretation is not only an implausible approach toward quantum physics but also an avoidable one.

II

In order to answer the question, "Can there be a realistic interpretation of ontic indeterminism?" it is indispensable to clarify the special character of ontic indeterminism, on the one hand, and of realistic interpretations, on the other. What I want to do is to consider the criterion of reality advanced by Einstein in the famous paper he co-authored with Podolsky and Rosen— where they attempt to define conditions under which the existence of an element of physical reality should be inferred—to ascertain, in part, whether different conceptions of probability can make a difference to our understanding of what ontic indeterminism itself entails. But before going that far, let us observe that three different types of situations appear to require differentiation as follows, namely:

(2)	Three situations are possible:	Ontic Determinism	Epistemic Determinism
	a. Classical Mechanics (CM):	Yes	Yes
	b. Statistical Mechanics (SM):	Yes	No
	c. Quantum Mechanics (QM):	No	No

With respect to each of these areas of inquiry, the issue arises, "Does the domain in question—classical, statistical, and quantum phenomena, respectively—represent ontic determinism/indeterminism or does it instead reflect merely epistemic determinism/indeterminism?" Indeed, these distinctions apply to theories as well as to phenomena in each of these domains. Classical mechanics, for example, seems to represent ontically deterministic phenomena where, if only the relevant parameters (or "initial conditions") are specified with sufficient precision, then it is possible, in principle, to predict the outcome that will occur in every single case without exception, assuming, of course, some such theory happens to be true. Loosely—intuitively—let us suppose that this conception affords an appropriate foundation for understanding ontic determinism, i.e., that the same outcomes are always brought about under the same initial conditions, where exact predictions, in principle, are always possible, relative to true theories for those domains.

In classical mechanics, moreover, we are also in a situation where quite often these initial conditions are ascertainable, in practice, which makes it possible to successfully predict. Thus, under these conditions, epistemic as well as ontic determinism obtains. In the case of statistical mechanics, however, the situation appears to be somewhat different, not with respect to ontic determinism but rather with respect to epistemic determinism. For, here we seem to be dealing with circumstances—as in the case of gas laws—involving enormous numbers of very small things, where, even if we take for granted that, in principle, these enormous numbers of very small things behave in the small exactly the way billiard balls, for example, behave in the large, nevertheless, they are so many and so small that, as a practical matter, it is virtually impossible for us to possess the kind of knowledge about their initial conditions that would be required for us to be successful in predicting their behavior—even though we take it to be the case that statistical mechanistic phenomena are ultimately ontically deterministic, i.e., such that, if only we *could* have sufficiently precise measurements of these initial conditions, the appropriate laws of statistical mechanics *could* be applied and would yield an exact prediction of what would occur in every single case—without exception! Nevertheless, characteristically we are not in such a position, but rather in one of epistemic indeterminism, which can be viewed in several different ways where the phenomena are complex, where we have a lack of knowledge, and where statistical predictions are relied upon as a function of our ignorance.

In the case of quantum mechanics, by contrast, we seem to be in a rather different situation. Here it at least appears to be the case that we are possessed of enough knowledge about initial conditions that it is implausible to suppose that the situation is merely one of epistemic indeterminism. In fact, no matter how hard we look, how much we try, how many guesses we explore, it is very difficult to come up with any additional factors which make a difference, for example, to an electron's probability of landing in area B, or area C, and so on, upon its emission from the source, A. This seems to be an irreducibly probabilistic or ontically indeterministic phenomenon, where different outcomes are sometimes brought about under the same initial conditions and exact predictions, in principle, are by no means always possible. To more adequately clarify the situation encountered, let us consider the following set of five alternative hypotheses which might be thought to be applicable here:

(3)   Possible alternative hypotheses:

   h_1: the deterministic hypothesis;
   h_2: the random-walk hypothesis;
   h_3: the free-will hypothesis;
   h_4: the probabilistic hypothesis;
   h_5: the hidden-variable hypothesis.

Thus, according to h_1, the deterministic hypothesis, the relation between an electron's emission from source A and its impacting in area B, for example, is one of ontic determinism, where in every single case the same outcome occurs under the same initial conditions and exact predictions are always possible. However, if all of the known factors *are* a complete set of factors, then the deterministic hypothesis is just not true, since the available relevant evidence overwhelmingly supports the conclusion that the situation is not one of ontic determinism. So let us assume not-h_1.

According to h_2, the random-walk hypothesis, the way in which a particle gets somewhere from wherever it may be is in a wholly random way, because the particle, roughly speaking, has an equal probability (or a "classical" tendency) for travelling in every direction. The types of distributions obtained for impacts within specified areas such as B, C, and so forth, after emission from a source A, however, are not the types that would lend support to a random-walk hypothesis. So let us also assume not-h_2. According to h_3, the free-will hypothesis, of course, each electron simply "makes up its own mind" with regard to its own destination, as though electrons had minds to "make up." In the case of the free-will hypothesis, we in effect abandon predictability, because free-will, in this sense, really entails that such a phenomenon is not governed by natural laws but instead either lies beyond their scope or occurs in violation thereof. The adoption of this hypothesis would thus reflect the belief that quantum phenomena lie beyond the pale of science, which seems to be a logical possibility without adequate evidential warrant. For electrons do not behave as if they were "making up their own minds" but rather conform to probabilistic expectations, where these expectations appear to vary with variations in initial conditions. While we cannot predict where each single electron is going to impact, we can make statistical predictions of patterns of impact that will tend to be displayed by the impact of many electrons as a function of those initial conditions, which undermines a free-will hypothesis. So let us further assume not-h_3.

We seem to be left with two alternatives. According to h_4, the probabilistic hypothesis, the situation confronted here really is one of irreducible ontic indeterminism, where one or another of various different outcomes will be brought about under the same initial conditions, where exact predictions, as opposed to probabilistic expectations, are, in principle, not possible. This, of course, is a very tempting hypothesis, given the available evidence. Yet it is still not our only option, since according to h_5, the hidden-variable hypothesis, there may remain other factors, say, F^1, F^2, and so on, such that if these factors are included in a specification of initial conditions along with A, for example, then it might turn out to be the case after all that the relation between an electron's emission from a source, A, and its impacting in area B really is one of ontic determinism, relative to a complete specification of initial conditions $A \cdot F^1$, $A \cdot F^2$, and so forth. Remember that the original deterministic hypothesis, h_1, was predicated on the assumption that all of the *known* factors were all of the *relevant* factors in relation to this class of outcome phenomena, an assumption which the hidden-variable hypothesis, h_5, thus denies.

We have already discovered that the relevant evidence tends to falsify the deterministic hypothesis, h_1, but the hidden-variable hypothesis, h_5, is somewhat more subtle, insofar as it is based upon the following observation: even if we have looked very long and very hard and have not found any additional relevant factors, this in itself does not establish that they do not exist; it shows, on the contrary, that *either* they do not exist *or else* we have not yet looked in the right places to find them! Thus, someone who is very strongly committed to a deterministic thesis about the world could still preserve their commitment to determinism in the face of recalcitrant quantum phenomena by holding out for the existence of hidden variables, as hypothesis h_5 proposes, the discovery of which will eventually disclose the deterministic character thereof. Until very recently, moreover, it was very difficult to see how the hidden-variable hypothesis could be disconfirmed as well as confirmed; but the derivation of (what is known as) "Bell's inequality" has dramatically altered this situation, where Bell's inequality represents a set of relations which must be satisfied if hidden-variable hypotheses are true. When subjected to experiments (which are continuing today), the evidence has tended to falsify Bell's inequality— and with it the hidden-variable hypothesis, h_5. So let us tentatively assume not-h_5 as well.

III

These considerations, if correct, suggest that ontic indeterminism may be theoretically un-avoidable, especially if the probabilistic hypothesis h_4 happens to be true; but it sheds no light on whether or not a realistic interpretation of ontic indeterminism, in principle, might be possible at all. In order to pursue this issue, therefore, let us consider the criterion of reality advanced by Einstein in the context of his paper with Podolsky and Rosen, as follows:

(4)   If, without in any way disturbing a system, we can predict with certainty (i.e., with probability equal to unity) the value of a physical quantity, then there exists an element of physical reality corresponding to that physical quantity. (Einstein, Podolsky, and Rosen 1935, p. 777)

Certain infelicities, it must be admitted, attend this formulation. One is that it does not adequately differentiate between phenomena and theories as representatives of phenomena; for surely predictions are conclusions of inferences from premises, where lawlike sentences and descriptions of initial conditions characteristically serve as evidential warrants. Thus, it seems, we should think of Einstein as regarding a theory as describing a system in the world, where ascriptions of initial conditions assign specific values v_i which permit the derivation of specific predictions of other values v_j from certain theoretical assumptions. But another difficulty is thereby made apparent, for this formulation likewise fails to separate the ontic from the epistemic: even well-entrenched theories are likely to yield accurate predictions, without therefore being guaranteed to be true. Phlogiston, Allan Franklin reminds me, did not acquire existence as an element of physical reality in spite of innumerable "accurate predictions" of gains and losses of this property based upon phlogiston theory.

As a criterion of belief, in other words, there may be much to be said in support of the thesis that, under the conditions specified, an evidential warrant supports the *belief* that there exists an element of physical reality corresponding to such physical quantities. As a criterion of truth, however, there is little to be said in support of the claim that, under the specified conditions, an evidential warrant guarantees the *truth* that there exists an element of physical reality corresponding to such physical quantities. And clearly an adequate conception of a standard of existence should not commit any realist to the existence of properties stipulated by any theory—unless that theory is true! In order for Einstein's criterion of reality to be adequate, therefore, it has to be qualified with the condition, "so long as the theory from which those predictions were derived is true." If this condition is satisfied, however, then the rest of Einstein's criterion does not require satisfaction, since corresponding elements of physical reality must then exist whether or not they are ever subject to systematic prediction. From an ontic point of view, without this condition, Einstein's criterion is false; but with this condition, it is trivial.

These apparent shortcomings notwithstanding, Einstein's criterion has exerted considerable influence upon discussions of realism in the past and in the present; for this reason, as well as others, it will serve as an appropriate background for our discussion of ontic indeterminism. Thus, the formulation endorsed by Einstein bears a striking resemblance to a certain construction advanced by Reichenbach as his account of strict causal laws, which we shall refer to as "*Assumption D*" (for "determinism"), as follows:

> *Assumption D*: The statement that nature is governed by strict causal laws means that we can predict the future with a determinate probability and that we can push this probability as close to certainty as we want by using a sufficiently elaborate analysis of the phenomena under consideration. (Reichenbach 1944, pp. 2–3)

Indeed, the resemblance is even closer than it initially appears, insofar as Reichenbach, like Einstein, interprets "certainty" as a probability equal to unity. Moreover, as Clifford Hooker has observed, Einstein almost certainly adopted another assumption as well, which we shall refer to as "*Assumption E*" (for "Einstein"), as follows:

> *Assumption E*: A complete description of a physical system S during some time interval T is one for which every attribute of S is precisely determined for each instant $t \in T$. (Hooker 1972, p. 71)

These assumptions are theoretically significant for understanding Einstein's position, since they jointly entail the following claim, namely:

> (5)   If we can predict every attribute of a system S for each instant $t \in T$ with certainty, then (a) our description of S is complete and (b) S is governed by strict causal laws;

which supports the possibility that alternative formulations may be required to capture a realistic interpretation of ontic indeterminism.

Perhaps the most obvious logical feature of Einstein's criterion (4) is also one of its most important aspects; for, as he himself remarked, it is intended as a sufficient condition, but not as a necessary condition, for the value of a predicted quantity v_j to correspond to an element of physical reality. Its "If . . . , then _____" conditional structure reflects that this criterion of reality, such as it may be, is only meant to represent one way in which the existence of an element of physical reality may be ascertained. Thus, the crucial issue before us may be expressed in the following manner:

(6)   If, without in any way disturbing a system S, we can predict, not with certainty but with some probability less than 1, the value of a physical quantity, can there then not still exist some element of physical reality corresponding to that physical quantity?;

where it is especially important, in light of *Assumption D* and *Assumption E*, that Einstein's criterion as a *sufficient condition* not be confounded with, let us say, a *sufficient definition*, in the sense of a weakest criterion of reality, which would be a necessary and sufficient condition of the broadest general kind. For a realistic interpretation of ontic indeterminism to qualify as a theoretical possibility, in principle, after all, surely it must be at least logically possible (a') that our description of a system S could be complete even though (b') the system S is not governed by strict causal laws. Otherwise, the combined force of *Assumption D* with *Assumption E* as features of Einstein's criterion of reality strongly suggests if not strictly entails that realistic interpretations of quantum phenomena are deterministic, necessarily, in which case the probabilistic hypothesis h_4 could not possibly be true.

IV

We have discovered a striking dilemma, insofar as the arguments of section 2, which are based upon experimental findings, support the conception that a realistic interpretation of ontic indeterminism is a theoretical necessity, while the arguments of section 3, which are based upon Einstein's criterion, suggest the conclusion that a realistic interpretation of ontic indeterminism is a theoretical impossibility. This dilemma, of course, is more apparent than real, once Einstein's criterion has been diagnosed as a sufficient rather than a necessary condition. Disclosing the inadequacy of a deterministic criterion, moreover, is not the same thing as uncovering an adequate indeterministic criterion, but it still might pave the way; for the identification of "certainty" with probability equal to unity raises the possibility that the identification of "uncertainty" with probability less than unity deserves to be explored. The theoretical significance of the probabilistic hypothesis, h_4, in relation to quantum phenomena, after all, cannot be ascertained without consideration for the interpretation of probability that effects its connection with this domain, where three interpretations appear to warrant special consideration within this specific context, namely: the frequency, the subjective, and the propensity conceptions, respectively.

According to the frequency conception, probabilities are limiting frequencies for specified attributes, such as impacting in area B, within designated reference classes, such as emissions of electrons from sources such as A. A probabilistic hypothesis under the frequency interpretation may be characterized as possessing the following logical form,

(7) $P(B/A) = p$;

where "p" denotes the limiting frequency for the attribute B within an infinite reference class A. If the probability with which an electron emitted from source A lands in area B is given by the absolute value of the corresponding psi-function squared, $|\psi_B|^2 = \frac{1}{4}$, say, this means that the limiting frequency with which impacts in area B should be expected to occur over an endless sequence of emissions from source A is equal to $\frac{1}{4}$. If a reference class happens to be finite, "p" may be taken as the limit that would obtain were its members repetitiously counted over and over again. Since values of limits are logically compatible with any number of exceptions n, of course, the identification of "certainties" (in Einstein's sense) with probabilities of one (or of zero) appears to be inappropriate; but this is not a difficult problem to repair, since constant conjunctions (and constant non-occurrence) are properly entertained as the strongest (and the weakest) possible connections between the members of these classes. Thus, the identification of "uncertainties" (in a similar sense) with probabilities between zero and one inclusively promises to provide an interpretation of the probabilistic hypothesis h_4 which might support a realistic interpretation of ontic indeterminism.

Because probabilities as frequencies are physical properties of physical systems, the frequency approach exerts considerable *prima facie* appeal as an appropriate conception within the quantum context. But appearances often deceive us, and this is no exception. For in order to apply to any particular quantum outcome, such as impacting in area B, it is essential to assign each quantum experiment, such as each emission of an electron from the source A, to the proper class of trials of some kind, where the kind of trial involved is determined by the complete set of relevant properties attending its occurrence, relative to the *frequency criterion of statistical relevance*. According to this criterion of relevance, any property F with respect to which frequencies differ, i.e., such that $P(B/A \cap F) \neq P(B/A \cap -F)$, is statistically relevant, necessarily. Unfortunately, there are excellent grounds for assuming that, for any two events, say, e_1 and e_2, there is at least one property, F, such that F is an aspect of e_1 but not of e_2. But this means that, even if e_1 and e_2 both happen to be emissions of electrons from the same source, A, nevertheless, the only circumstance under which they can both be classified as members of the same reference class, such as A, under the frequency criterion of statistical relevance, is when they both happen to have the same outcome, such as B. Hence, unless a quantum experiment, e_i, is assigned to a reference class in which its outcome, B, occurs with "certainty," it is not even logically possible that experiment e_i has been assigned to the proper class of trials.

In order to avoid misunderstanding, we must keep in mind that, whenever an outcome B, $C, \ldots$, occurs, a question arises as to what set of properties $A, A \cap F^1, A \cap F^1 \cap F^2, \ldots$, so to speak, "brought it about" (or, in other words, to what reference class the single event, e_i, should be assigned). For any difference in outcomes, of course, it is entirely possible that that difference was "brought about" by the occurrence of different relevant conditions. If any two events, e_i and e_j, differ with respect to at least one property F, however, then every event, strictly speaking, qualifies as an event of a distinctive *kind*, since, with respect to any other event, there must be at least one property, F^k, that is an aspect of e_i, while $-F^k$ is an aspect of e_j. Intuitively, of course, we are inclined to believe that, even if two emissions of electrons from source A occurred at different times, under different weather conditions, in different colored rooms, and so forth, nevertheless, only some—but not all—of these conditions are explanatorily and/or predictively relevant with respect to a specific outcome, such as B, as the result of the specific event e_2, say, where e_2 belongs to many different reference classes, $A, A \cap F^1$, $A \cap F^1 \cap F^2, \ldots$. With the frequency criterion of statistical relevance, however, there is no latitude for judgments that some of these properties are, but some of these properties are not, explanatorily/predictively relevant to a specific result, other than those displayed by frequencies *per se*: when "effects" differ, their "causes" differ, necessarily. Since every single event, e_i, is different in kind from every other, e_j, if a certain result, such as B, occurs on one trial, while an incompatible outcome, such as C, occurs on another, then the frequency criterion of statistical relevance, in principle, *demands* that the differences between these events have to qualify as statistically relevant. Indeed, the frequency interpretation thus understood cannot sustain probability assignments of other than zero and one. (For detailed elaboration, see Fetzer 1981, chapter 4.)

Now if the only probabilities that are properly assignable to quantum outcomes are "certainties", i.e., degenerate probabilities of zero and of one, which actually represent constant non-occurrence and constant conjunction, respectively, then if this result follows as a matter of logical necessity from essential features of the frequency interpretation, then it is not logically possible for a probabilistic hypothesis—such as one assigning the probability of ¼ to landing in area B as an outcome of an emission from source A—to be *true*, when the probabilities involved are not degenerate probabilities of zero or of one. Moreover, since this conclusion is a necessary consequence of the frequency interpretation, it applies alike to events in the future as well as to events in the past, completely independently of our knowledge or belief or awareness thereof. But if this is the case, then it is logically impossible for the frequency interpretation to provide the theoretical foundation for a realistic interpretation of ontic indeterminism which the probabilistic hypothesis, h_4, requires. So let us assume that this approach is not what we desire.

According to the subjective conception, probabilities are supposed to be degrees of belief in particular propositions, such as, say, that an electron will impact in area B, when an individual x possesses certain other beliefs, such as that an electron has been emitted from source A. The ascription of a degree of belief thus assumes the following logical form,

$$(8) \qquad [P_A(B) = r]_{xt};$$

where "r" denotes the degree of belief in the proposition that B when individual x already possesses the belief that A. The presence of subscripts, "xt," of course, reflects that these probabilities are properties of individuals x at times t, where it is perfectly permissible for two different individuals, say, x and y, to have different degrees of belief in the same proposition, B, even when they are under the same conditions of belief, A, so long as their respective distributions of degrees of belief at any time t remain formally consistent (or "coherent"). Nevertheless, each individual x is required to preserve a special relationship between his distribution of degrees of belief at time t_i (before acquiring the belief that A) and at time t_j (after acquiring the belief that A), where his prior degree of belief in B conditional upon A, when x already holds other beliefs, say, F, is supposed to equal his posterior belief in B, when he has acquired the belief A as an addition to his other beliefs, F, i.e., $P_{F \cup A}(B) = P_F(B/A)$, a process known as "conditionalization" regulating degree of belief distributions across time. (Compare, for example, Fetzer 1981, chapters 8 and 10.)

Since probabilities as degrees of belief are mental properties of particular persons-at-times, this interpretation does not appear to hold great promise as an appropriate conception within the quantum context. The probability with which an electron emitted from source A lands in area B, for example, need not be equal to $\frac{1}{4}$ for different individuals at the same time or even for the same individual at different times. The assignment of degrees of belief, of course, is determined by the complete set of relevant beliefs for an individual x at a time t, relative to a *subjective criterion of evidential relevance*, according to which any member of the set of beliefs that x accepts at t, such as A, is evidentially relevant to the degree of belief x assigns at t to some other belief, such as B, if the truth or falsity of A "makes a difference" to that degree of belief, i.e., $P_{F \cup A}(B) \neq P_{F \cup -A}(B)$. Now while this criterion of relevance permits the possibility that particular propositions, such as B, might be assigned degrees of belief which are not equal to degenerate probabilities of zero (as "incredulity") or of one (as "indubitability"), it does *not* permit the possibility that any outcome of which x becomes aware could be assigned any degree of belief other than equal to one. For x's prior degree of belief in B conditional upon B when x already holds other beliefs, F, has to be equal to one, as a function of coherence; but then x's posterior belief in B, when he has acquired the belief B as an addition to his other beliefs, F, also has to equal one, as a function of conditionalization, where $P_{F\ B}(B) = P_F(B/B)$.

Not the least of the consequences attending this conception, therefore, is that, when probabilities are understood as degrees of belief, it is only possible for a quantum outcome to be assigned a probability value between zero and one so long as that specific outcome, such as B, remains unknown; for as soon as x becomes aware that B is the case, his degree of belief in the proposition that B has to change to one! This situation is illustrated by the Schrödinger "Cat Paradox," in fact, where the discovery that the cat is dead (or is alive) brings about a "reduction of the wave packet" in the form of an abrupt shift in subjective probabilities from $1/2$, let us say, to one! This phenomenon is not at all peculiar to quantum contexts, moreover, but commonplace with respect to tosses of coins, throws of dice, and "games of chance," in general, which are usually ontically deterministic—and only epistemically indeterministic as functions of ignorance. Although the subjective interpretation thus contributes toward clarification of the anomalous character of the "reduction of the wave packet," it does not appear to provide the theoretical foundation for a realistic interpretation of ontic indeterminism which the probabilistic hypothesis, h_4, requires. So let us assume that this approach too is not what we desire.

According to the propensity conception, finally, probabilities are to be understood as dispositional properties (or "causal tendencies") for one or another possible outcome, such as impacting in area B, in area C, etc., to be brought about (with a certain strength) by the occurrence of a test, trial, or experiment with a fixed kind of apparatus or arrangement, such as the emission of an electron from a source such as A. A probabilistic hypothesis under the propensity interpretation may be characterized as possessing the following logical form,

(9) $(x)(t)(Axt = m \Rrightarrow Bxt^*);$

where "m" denotes the strength of the tendency for an outcome of kind B at time t^* to be brought about by a single trial of kind A at time t—and t^* is equal to $t + \triangle t$. If the probability with which an electron x emitted from source A lands in area B is given by the square of the absolute value of the corresponding psi-function, $|\psi B|^2 = \frac{1}{4}$, as before, this means that a single trial of kind A would bring about an outcome of kind B with strength equal to $\frac{1}{4}$, which in turn (probabilistically) implies that a very large number of trials of kind A would tend to bring about an outcome of kind B with a relative frequency equal to $\frac{1}{4}$, where the strength of this tendency becomes enormously strong as the length of such a sequence increases without bound.

Since propensities, like frequencies, are properties of the world independently of anyone's knowledge, belief, or awareness thereof, we are again confronted by an intriguing point of view. In order to apply to any particular quantum outcome, such as impacting in area B, of course, it is essential to characterize each single trial, such as each emission of an electron from its source A, as a trial of the appropriate kind, where the kind involved is determined by the complete set of relevant properties attending its occurrence, as before, but now relative to the *propensity criterion of causal relevance*. According to this criterion of relevance, any property, F, with respect to which propensities differ, i.e., such that $(x)(t)[(Axt \cdot Fxt) = m \Rrightarrow Bxt^*]$ and $(x)(t)[(Axt - Fxt) = n \Rrightarrow Bxt^*]$, where $m \neq n$, is causally relevant to an outcome of kind B on a trial of kind A, necessarily. Since causally relevant properties need not be statistically relevant properties, the complete set of *relevant* properties present on a single trial can be a subset of the complete set of *properties* present at that trial, which means that the strength of the tendency for an outcome of kind B to be the effect of a trial of kind A can have a value between zero and one inclusively, where it is not the case that the only probabilities that are properly assignable to quantum outcomes are "certainties," i.e., degenerate probabilities with the values of zero and of one. (For further discussion, see Fetzer 1981.)

Like the frequency conception, the propensity conception is such that probabilities of zero and of one are logically compatible with any number of exceptions; consequently, "certainties" should be identified, not with constant non-occurrence and constant conjunction, but rather with null and universal strength instead. Thus, causal tendencies of universal strength obtain where, if only the relevant parameters are completely specified, it is possible, in principle, to predict the outcome that will occur in every single case without exception, assuming, of course, some such theory is true, because this situation is one of ontic determinism. And causal tendencies of probabilistic strength obtain where, if only the relevant parameters are completely specified, it is possible, in principle, not to predict the outcomes that occur in every single case without exception, but rather to derive probabilistic expectations for outcome distributions instead, assuming some such theory is true, because this situation is one of ontic indeterminism. Hence, the propensity interpretation overcomes the difficulties confronting the frequency interpretation, because it is logically possible for a probabilistic hypothesis—such as one assigning the probability of $\frac{1}{4}$ to landing in area B as an outcome of an emission from source A—to be *true*, even when the probabilities involved are not degenerate probabilities of zero or of one. And the propensity conception overcomes the difficulties confronting the subjective conception, because it is logically possible for a probabilistic hypothesis—such as one assigning the probability of $\frac{1}{4}$ to landing in area B as an outcome of an emission from source A—to be *true*, even when that outcome is known to have occurred. The situation thus appears to be as follows:

(10)	Three interpretations are possible:	Explanatory Indeterminism	Predictive Indeterminism
	a. Frequency Constructions (FC):	No	No
	b. Subjective Constructions (SC):	No	Yes
	c. Propensity Constructions (PC):	Yes	Yes

Only the propensity interpretation permits probabilistic hypotheses assigning non-degenerate probabilities to known or unknown outcomes to be true. Since this is the case, moreover, it is logically possible for the propensity conception to provide the theoretical foundation for a realistic interpretation of ontic indeterminism which the probabilistic hypothesis, h_4, requires. So let us tentatively assume that this approach *is* what we desire.

V

If these considerations are correct, then of the three interpretations which we have examined here—the frequency, the subjective, and the propensity—only the third accommodates the possibility, in principle, of providing a realistic interpretation of ontic indeterminism. Insofar as the arguments of section III, which were based upon Einstein's criterion, suggested the conclusion that a realistic interpretation of ontic indeterminism might be a theoretical impossibility, such an interpretation must satisfy another criterion of reality than the one endorsed by Einstein for this reason:

(11)   If, without in any way disturbing a system S, we can predict, not with certainty but with some probability less than 1, the value of a physical quantity, then either (a^*) our description of system S is not complete (in the sense of *Assumption E*) or (b^*) system S is not governed by strict causal laws (in the sense of *Assumption D*).

That (b^*) should be the case, of course, is entirely unproblematic, insofar as indeterministic situations are not governed by strict causal laws. But that (a^*) should be the case is highly problematic, since it invites the reintroduction of the hidden-variable hypothesis h_5. Fortunately, Feynman has supplied the missing element in the form of an alternative conception, which we shall refer to as "*Assumption F*" (for "Feynman"), as follows:

Assumption F: An ideal experiment is one in which all of the initial and final conditions of the experiment are completely specified. (Feynman 1965, vol. III, pp. 1–10)

To be precise, an ideal experiment E is one for which all the *actual* initial conditions and *possible* final conditions are completely specified. I therefore suggest the following as an improvement upon Einstein's criterion:

(12)   If an ideal experiment with a system S permits the prediction of its future states with deductive certainty or with probabilistic confidence, then that system is a deterministic or an indeterministic element of physical reality, respectively (in the sense of *Assumption F*);

where this criterion applies to indeterministic as well as to deterministic situations. And I further conclude that, while the Copenhagen Interpretation represents an unwarranted intrusion of subjectivism into physics, the propensity conception tends to remove (at least some of) the mystery from quantum phenomena, precisely as Popper has claimed.

NOTE

* This paper is an expanded and revised version of a lecture presented at the University of Colorado in February and at New College in April 1983. I am grateful to Paul Humphreys and to Stephen Brush for their comments and inquiries. In particular, Professor Brush has raised the issue of the Aspect experiments—which *seem* to confirm action at a distance—in relation to the approach defended here. As Popper (1982, p. xviii) has noted, this result need not undermine realism; but it would be remarkable if quantum mechanics could be true only if relativity were false. If situations involve propensities if and only if they are indeterministic in character, as my position implies, then if experiments such as Aspect's, Einstein-Podolsky-and-Rosen's, and others are indeterministic, then propensities are involved. If they are *both* indeterministic *and* action at a distance cannot be avoided (by appealing to non-causal, but not therefore non-lawful, relations, for example), which I doubt, then indeterministic causal concepts as well as deterministic causal concepts will almost certainly require revision. In any case, while the propensity approach can contribute to the resolution of some of the anomalies arising within the quantum domain, others—some involving questions of completeness—no doubt remain.

REFERENCES

Brush, S. (1979). "Einstein and Indeterminism." *Journal of the Washington Academy of Science* 69, pp. 89–94.

Einstein, A., B. Podolsky, and N. Rosen. (1935). "Can Quantum-Mechanical Description of Reality be Considered Complete?" *Physical Review*, series 2, 47, pp. 777–80.

Fetzer, J. H. (1981). *Scientific Knowledge*. Dordrecht: D. Reidel.

Feynman, R., R. Leighton, and M. Sands. (1965). *The Feynman Lectures on Physics*, vol. 3. Reading, Mass: Addison-Wesley.

Folse, H. J. (1977). "Complementarity and the Description of Experience." *International Philosophical Quarterly* 17, pp. 377–92.

Hooker, C. A. (1972). "The Nature of Quantum Mechanical Reality." In R. G. Colodny, ed., *Paradigms and Paradoxes*. Pittsburgh: University of Pittsburgh Press, pp. 67–302.

Popper, K. R. (1957). "The Propensity Interpretation of the Calculus of Probability, and the Quantum Theory." In S. Korner, ed., *Observation and Interpretation in the Philosophy of Physics*. Dover Publications, pp. 65–70.

———. (1967). "Quantum Mechanics without 'The Observer.' " In M. Bunge, ed. *Quantum Theory and Reality*. New York: Springer-Verlag, pp. 7–44.

———. (1982). *Quantum Theory and the Schism in Physics*. New Jersey: Rowman and Littlefield.

Reichenbach, H. (1944). *Philosophic Foundations of Quantum Mechanics*. Berkeley: University of California Press.

WESLEY C. SALMON

DYNAMIC RATIONALITY: PROPENSITY, PROBABILITY, AND CREDENCE

Since the time of Bishop Butler we have known that *probability is the very guide of life*—at least it should be if we are to behave rationally. The trouble is that we have had an extraordinarily difficult time trying to figure out what kind of thing—or things—probability is. I shall argue that causality is a key piece in the puzzle, and consequently, an indispensable aspect of rationality.

I. THE PROBLEM

EXAMPLE 1. In the autumn of 1944 I went as a student to the University of Chicago. The dormitory in which I lived was not far from Stagg Field, and I often walked by the entrance to the West Stands where a sign was posted saying "Metallurgical Laboratories." Nothing ever seemed to be going on there. Later, when I got a job as a technician at the Met Labs, I learned that this was the place where, about two years previously, the first humanly-created self-sustaining nuclear chain reaction had taken place. An atomic pile had been assembled and the decision was taken to make a trial run on 2 December 1942. The control rods were gradually withdrawn and the chain reaction occurred as predicted. It was an undertaking fraught with high risk; as one commentator has put it, "They were facing either the successful birth of the atomic age—or a catastrophic nuclear disaster within a packed metropolis."[1] I was glad I had not been there at the time. No one could be absolutely certain beforehand that the chain reaction would not spread, involving other substances in the vicinity and engulfing Chicago—or, perhaps, the entire earth—in a nuclear holocaust. On second thought, it did not much matter where one was in case of such an eventuality.

I once read that before this pile was put into operation, the probability of the spreading of the chain reaction had been calculated. The result was that this probability was no more than three in a million. I do not recall the source of this bit of information, but I do remember wondering how the probability had been calculated and how it had been decided that the risk was acceptable. I was even more curious about the meaning of the probability concept in this context.[2]

EXAMPLE 2. The foregoing perplexity was brought vivid back to mind by an article in *Science* in June of 1986 about the Rogers Commission Report on the Challenger space shuttle disaster.[3] In particular, the article reports on a press conference held by Richard Feynman, the famous and colorful physicist who was a member of that commission. Although Feynman did not refuse to sign the commission's report, he did make a supplemental statement to the press in which he sharply criticized NASA's methods of assessing risks.

Feynman objects most strongly to NASA's way of calculating risks. Data collected since the early days of the program . . . show that about one in every 25 solid rocket boosters has failed. About 2900 have been launched with 121 losses. Feynman says it is reasonable to adjust the anticipated crash rate a bit lower (to 1 in 50) to take account of today's better technology. He would even permit a little more tinkering with the numbers (to 1 in 100) to take credit for exceptionally high standards of part selection and inspection. In this way, the Challenger accident, the first solid rocket failure in 25 shuttle launches (with two boosters each), fits perfectly into Feynman's adjusted rate of one crash per 50 to 100 rocket firings.[4]

But Feynman was stunned to learn that NASA rejects the historical data and claims the actual risk of crash is only 1 in 100,000. This is the official figure as published in "Space Shuttle Data for Planetary Mission RTG Safety Analysis" on 15 February 1985.[5] . . . Feynman searched for the origin of this optimism and found that it was "engineering judgment," pure and simple. Feynman concluded that NASA "for whatever purpose . . . exaggerates the reliability of its product to the point of fantasy."

The article goes on to report a conversation with NASA's chief engineer, Milton Silveira, who stated that NASA does not "use that number as a management tool."

The 1 in 100,000 figure was hatched for the Department of Energy (DOE), he says, for use in a risk analysis DOE puts together on radioactive hazards on some devices carried aboard the shuttle. . . .

DOE and General Electric, supplier of the power units, write up a detailed risk analysis before launch. They are accustomed to expressing risk in statistical terms. NASA is not, but it must help them prepare the analysis. To speak in DOE's language, NASA translates its "engineering judgment" into numbers. How does it do this? One NASA official said, "They get all the top engineers together down at Marshall Space Flight Center and ask them to give their best judgment of the reliability of all the components involved." The engineers' adjectival descriptions are then converted to numbers. For example . . . "frequent" equals 1 in 100; "reasonably probable" equals 1 in 1000; "occasional" equals 1 in 10,000; and "remote" equals 1 in 100,000.

When all the judgments were summed up and averaged, the risk of a shuttle booster explosion was found to be 1 in 100,000. That number was then handed over to DOE for further processing. . . .

Among the things DOE did with the number was to conclude that "the overall risk of a plutonium disaster was found to be terribly, almost inexpressibly low. This is, 1 in 10,000,000, give or take a syllable."

"The process," says one consultant who clashed with NASA, "is positively medieval." He thinks Feynman hit the nail exactly on the head. . . . Unless the risk estimates are based on some actual performance data, he says, "it's all tomfoolery."

Feynman is quoted as saying, "When playing Russian roulette, the fact that the first shot got off safely is little comfort for the next."

EXAMPLE 3. Then there is the old joke about precipitation probabilities. We have seen them in weather forecasts in newspapers and on TV; sometimes they serve as some sort of guide of life. They are always given in multiples of 10—e.g., a 30 percent chance of showers. How are they ascertained and what do they mean? Well, there are 10 meteorologists, and they take a vote. If 3 of the 10 vote for showers, that makes a 30 percent chance.

II. GRADES OF RATIONALITY

When one speaks of rationality, it may refer to rational action or to rational belief. Rational action must somehow take account of probabilities of various outcomes. I am inclined to think that the policy of maximizing expected utilities—though perhaps not precisely correct—is satisfactory in most practical situations.[6] Expected utilities are defined in terms of probabilities. I want to discuss the nature of these probabilities. There is a long tradition that identifies them with degrees of belief. I am not going to deny that answer, but I want to look at it with some care. First, however, a matter of terminology.

In a recent article, Patrick Maher has argued—quite cogently, in my opinion—that belief has nothing to do with rational *behavior*.[7] He takes belief to be an all or nothing affair; one either believes a given proposition or does not believe it. Beliefs have the purely cognitive function of constituting our picture of the world. When it comes to rational behavior, he argues, we should use what he calls *degrees of confidence* to evaluate expectations of utility. Within Bayesian decision theory we can identify coherent degrees of confidence with personal probabilities. He prefers to avoid using such terminology as "degree of belief" or "degree of partial belief" in order to minimize confusion of the practical function of degrees of confidence (which can be evaluated numerically) with the cognitive function of beliefs (which are only qualitative). I have a slight preference for the term *degree of conviction* over *degree of confidence* (because "confidence" has a technical meaning in statistics that I do not want to attach to degrees of conviction), but both terms are acceptable. In addition, I shall sometimes use the more neutral term *degree of credence*, which should serve well enough for those who accept Maher's view and those who do not.[8]

There are two immediate objections to taking mere subjective degrees of conviction as probabilities. The first is that, in general, we cannot expect them to constitute an admissible interpretation of the probability calculus. The second is that we are not prepared to take raw subjective feelings as a basis for *rational* action. So, one standard suggestion is to require that the probabilities constitute *rational* degrees of conviction.

There are, I think, various grades of rationality. At the lowest level, philosophers have, for the most part, taken logical consistency as a basic rationality requirement. If one believes that no mammals hatch their young from eggs, that the spiny anteater (echidna) is a mammal, and that it hatches its young from eggs, standard deductive logic tells us that something is wrong— that some modification should be made—that at least one of these beliefs should be rejected. But logic, by itself, does not tell us what change should be made. Logical consistency can be regained—with regard to this set of beliefs—by rejecting any one of the three. Logical consistency provides one minimal sort of rationality.[9] In traditional logic, the price of adopting an inconsistent set of beliefs is that everything follows from them. Let us say that anyone whose total set of beliefs is logically consistent qualifies for *basic deductive rationality*.

A minimal kind of probabilistic rationality is represented by the subjective Bayesians who require only *coherence*. Coherence is a sort of probabilistic consistency requirement. A set of degrees of conviction that violate the relationships embodied in the standard axioms of probability is incoherent. If, for example, I hold a probability of $^2/_3$ that this coin will land heads up on the next toss, and a probability of $^2/_3$ that it will land tails up on the next toss, and that these two outcomes are mutually exclusive, then I am being incoherent. This shows that there is something fundamentally wrong with the foregoing set of degrees of conviction. As is well known, the price of incoherence is that a so-called *Dutch book* can be made against anyone who holds incoherent degrees of conviction and is prepared to use them as fair betting quotients. A set of bets constitutes a Dutch book if, no matter what the outcome, the bettor loses. It is obvious how this happens in the case in which $^2/_3$ is assigned as the probability of heads and also of tails. Adopting the terminology of L. J. Savage, we usually refer to subjective proba- bilities that are coherent as *personal probabilities*. It follows immediately from their definition that personal probabilities constitute an admissible interpretation of the probability calculus, and thus overcome the first objection to subjective probabilities.

Violation of the coherence requirement shows that something is wrong with a set of degrees of conviction. Probability theory, however, does not tell us what modification to make in order to repair the difficulty, any more than pure deductive logic tells us which statement or statements of the foregoing inconsistent triad should be rejected. In the probabilistic example, we could achieve coherence by deciding that there is a $^1/_3$ probability of heads, a $^1/_3$ probability of tails, and a $^1/_3$ probability that the coin will come to rest standing on edge, where these three alternatives are mutually exclusive and exhaustive. L. J. Savage held an official view that probabilistic coherence is the only requirement of rationality, but unofficially, so to speak, he adopted others.

Abner Shimony defined a notion of *strict coherence*, and he proved a kind of Dutch book result. Strict coherence demands, in addition to coherence, that no logically contingent molecu- lar statement (statement not involving quantifiers) should have a probability of zero or one.[10] He has shown that anyone who violates strict coherence can be put in a position of making a set of bets such that, no matter what happens, the bettor cannot win, though he or she will break even on some outcomes. Carnap has always considered strict coherence a basic rationality require- ment.

A fundamental distinction between the requirements of coherence and strict coherence should be noted. Almost without exception, coherence requirements impose restrictions on relationships among probability values, as found, for instance, in the addition rule, the multiplication rule, and Bayes's theorem. They do not generally yield individual probability values. The two exceptions are that logical truths have probability one and logical contradic- tions have probability zero. Moreover, the requirement of coherence does not constrain individ- ual probability values beyond the universal constraint that they must lie within the closed unit interval from zero to one. Strict coherence imposes a hefty restriction on a large class of probabilities, where the statements to which they apply (contingent molecular statements) are *not* logical truths or falsehoods. We shall look at the rationale for the strict coherence requirement below.

Strict coherence is a sort of *openmindedness* requirement; various authors have demanded other sorts of *openmindedness* requirements. In characterizing a view he called *tempered personalism*, Shimony[11] argues that, in evaluating and comparing scientific hypotheses, we should allow hypotheses seriously proposed by serious scientists to have nonnegligible prior probabilities. We should also accord a substantial prior probability to the *catchall hypothesis*— the "none of the above" supposition—the notion that we have not yet thought of the correct hypothesis. It is important to note that Shimony offers empirical justifications for these openmindedness conditions. He observes historically that science has progressed remarkably by taking seriously the hypotheses proposed by qualified scientists. He also points out that in many historical situations the set of hypotheses under consideration did not include some hypothesis, proposed only later, that turned out to be successful.

The principles I have mentioned thus far pertain to what might be called the *statics* of degrees of conviction. You look at your total body of knowledge at a given moment, so to speak, and try to discover whether it contains any logical inconsistencies or probabilistic incoherencies (or violations of strict coherence). If such defects are discovered some changes in degrees of conviction are required, but we have not provided any basis for determining what alterations should be made. For the inconsistent triad a modest amount of research reveals that there are several species of egg-laying mammals, and that the echidna is one of them. Hence, we should reject the first statement while retaining the other two. Additional empirical evidence has provided the solution. In the case of the coin, a modification was offered, but it was not a very satisfactory one. The reasoning might have been this. There are three possibilities: the coin could land heads up, or tails up, or on edge. Applying some crude sort of principle of indifference, we assigned equal probabilities to all of them. But silly as this may be, we did eliminate the incoherence.

Clearly we have not said nearly enough about the *kinematics* of degrees of conviction—the ways our personal probabilities should change over time. There are, I believe, three sorts of occasion for modification of personal probabilities. First, there is the kind of situation in which an incoherency is discovered, and some change is made simply to restore coherence. As we have seen, this can be accomplished without getting further information. When an alteration of this type occurs, where modifications are made willy-nilly to restore coherence (or strict coherence), there is change of degrees of conviction, but no kinematics thereof. We can speak properly of a kinematics of degrees of conviction only when we have kinematic principles that somehow direct the changes.

Second, personal probabilities are sometimes modified as a result of a new idea. Suppose we have been considering two rival hypotheses, H_1 and H_2, and the catchall H_c. We have a probability distribution over this set. Someone thinks of a new hypothesis H_3 that has never before been considered. We now have the set H_1, H_2, H_3, and a new catchall $H_{c'}$, where H_c is equivalent to $H_3 \lor H_{c'}$. It is possible, of course, to assign new probabilities in a way that does not involve changing any of the old probabilities, but that is not to be expected in all cases. Indeed, a new idea or a new hypothesis may change the whole picture as far as our plausibility considerations are concerned.[12] From what has been said so far, however, we do not have any principles to guide the way such modifications take place. At this point it looks like no more nor less than a psychological reaction to a new factor. We still have not located any kinematical principle.

Third, personal probabilities must often be modified in the light of new evidence. In many such cases the natural approach is to use Bayes's theorem. This method is known as *Bayesian conditionalization*. It is important to realize that coherence requirements alone do not mandate Bayesian conditionalization. Consider a trivial example. Suppose someone is tossing a coin in the next room. There are only two possibilities, namely, that the coin is two-headed or it is standard. I cannot examine the coin, but I do get the results of the tosses. My prior probability for the hypothesis that a two-headed coin is being tossed is $1/10$; that is, I have a fairly strong conviction that it is not two-headed. Now I learn that the coin has been tossed four times, and that each toss resulted in a head. If the coin is two-headed that result is inevitable; if the coin is standard the probability of four heads in a row is $1/16$. Using Bayes's theorem you calculate the posterior probability of the two-headed hypothesis and find that is 0.64. You tell me that I must change my mind and consider it more likely than not that the coin is two-headed. I refuse. You show me the calculation and tell me that I am being incoherent. I see that you are right, so I must somehow modify my degrees of conviction. I tell you that I was wrong about the prior probability, and I change it from $1/10$ to $1/100$. Now I calculate the posterior probability of the two-headed hypothesis using *that* value of the prior, and come out with the result that it is just about 0.14. My system of personal probabilities is now coherent and I still consider it more likely than not that the coin is a standard one. I satisfied the coherence requirement but failed to conform to Bayesian conditionalization.

To many Bayesians, Bayesian conditionalization is a cardinal kinematical principle of rationality. It says something like this. Suppose you are considering hypothesis H. Before you collect the next bit of evidence, announce your prior probabilities and your likelihoods. When the next bit of evidence comes in, calculate the posterior probability of H using those priors and likelihoods. Change your degree of conviction in H from the prior probability to the posterior probability.

Bayesian conditionalization works effectively only if the prior probabilities do not assume the extreme values of zero or one. A cursory inspection of Bayes's theorem reveals the fact that no evidence can change the probability of a hypothesis whose prior probability has one of those extreme values. As L. J. Savage once said about hypotheses being evaluated, one should have toward them a mind that is, if not open, at least slightly ajar. In addition to the requirement of coherence (or strict coherence), many Bayesians accept both Bayesian conditionalization and some sort of openmindedness condition. We shall construe the openmindedness condition as a principle of statics, since it applies to the degrees of conviction that exist at any one time. Nevertheless, we should keep in mind that the main motivation is kinematical—to enable Bayesian conditionalization to work effectively. Bayesian conditionalization is a method for modifying degrees of conviction as a result of considering new evidence.

We are now in a position to distinguish three different grades of rationality in terms of considerations already adduced. Each succeeding grade is to be understood as incorporating the principles involved in the preceding grades:

> Basic Deductive Rationality
>   Logical Consistency
> Static Probabilistic Rationality
>   Coherence
>   Strict Coherence
>   Openmindedness
> Kinematic Probabilistic Rationality
>   Bayesian Conditionalization

Later in this paper I shall add a fourth grade, to be known as *dynamic rationality*.

The division between the kinematic and static grades of rationality marks a difference between rationality principles that do, and those that do not, involve any relation to the real world. The fact that the static principles do not relate to the real world is not a fault, however, for one sort of rationality consideration is quite independent of objective fact. The basic idea is that one aspect, at least, of rationality involves simply the management of one's body of opinion in terms of its inner structure. It has no concern with the objective correctness of opinions; it deals with the avoidance of blunders of various sorts within the body of opinion—for example, the kind of mistake that occurs when logical inconsistency or probabilistic incoherence is present.

The requirement of strict coherence nicely illustrates the point. Why should we adopt a prohibition against assigning probability zero or one to all molecular statements? Do we really believe that there is a probability greater than zero, for example, of finding a piece of pure copper that is not an electrical conductor? I am inclined to believe that we could search the universe thoroughly from the big bang to the present without finding a nonconducting piece of copper, and that a search from now until the end of time (if such there is) would yield the same result. However, the requirement of strict coherence is not concerned with considerations of this sort. It is designed to prevent a person from having a set of degrees of conviction that would lead to such disadvantageous bets as wagering at odds of a million dollars to zero against someone finding a piece of nonconducting copper. It does not matter what the facts of nature are; such a bet would be at best pointless and at worst disasterous. Good housekeeping of one's stock of degrees of conviction recommends against allowing probabilities that, if they are to be used as fair betting quotients, could place one in that kind of situation.[13]

I have no desire to denigrate this type of consideration; it constitutes an important aspect of rationality. But it also seems to fall short of giving us a full-blooded concept of rationality. Surely *rational behavior* demands attention to the objective facts that are relevant to the action one contemplates or undertakes. Examples 1–3 in the first section of this paper were intended to illustrate this point dramatically.

Bayesian conditionalization does, to some extent, provide a connection between opinion and objective fact. It specifies what degrees of conviction should be held constant and which allowed to change under specified circumstances. It tells us how to respond to new items of evidence.

Nevertheless, Bayesian conditionalization cannot provide a sufficient connection between our degrees of conviction and the objective facts. One obvious restriction is that it says nothing about changing our degrees of conviction in the absence of new evidence. It could be construed as prohibiting any change of opinion without new evidence, but that would be unduly restrictive. As we have already seen, there are at least two types of occasions for revising degrees of conviction even if there is no new evidence. The first is required to restore coherence to an incoherent set of degrees of conviction. It might be said, in response, that Bayesian conditionalization presupposes a coherent set of degrees of conviction. If we have an incoherent set, any change whatever that will restore coherence (without violating any other rationality condition listed above) will do. Then Bayesian conditionalization should be used.

The second type of situation that calls for revision of degrees of conviction in the absence of new evidence is the occurrence of a new idea. Surely the Bayesian does not want to bar the sort of revision that is based on thought and reflection. However, if that sort of revision is permitted, it can be used to sever connections between degrees of conviction and objective facts. Whenever accumulating evidence—in the form of observed relative frequencies, for example— seems to mandate a certain degree of conviction, a redistribution of personal probabilities can preclude that result. It is because of this weakness of connection between degree of conviction and objective fact, given only Bayesian conditionalization, that I wish to pursue higher grades of rationality.

III. TWO ASPECTS OF PROBABILITY

In *The Emergence of Probability* Ian Hacking maintained that the concept of probability could not appear upon the scene until two notions could be brought together, namely, objective chance and degree of credence.[14] The first of these concepts is to be understood in terms of relative frequencies or propensities; the second is an epistemic notion that has to do with the degree to which one is justified in having confidence in some proposition. In our century Rudolf Carnap codified this general idea in his systems of inductive logic in which there two probability concepts—probability$_1$, inductive probability or degree of confirmation; and probability$_2$, relative frequency. The major part of Carnap's intellectual effort for many years was devoted to his various attempts to characterize degree of confirmation. Because his systems of inductive logic require *a priori* probability measures, which strike me as unavoidably arbitrary, I have never been able to accept his approach.

It is interesting to note, however, that in "The Aim of Inductive Logic," he approaches the problem by beginning with raw subjective degrees of credence and imposing rationality requirements upon them.[15] He adopts coherence, strict coherence, and Bayesian conditional-ization. He goes beyond these by imposing additional symmetry conditions. In his "Replies and Systematic Expositions" in the Schlipp volume,[16] he offers a set of fifteen axioms, all of which are to be seen as rationality conditions that narrow down the concept of degree of confirmation. These axioms, in other words, are intended to beef up the rather thin notion of rationality characterized wholly by coherence, strict coherence, and Bayesian conditionalization. It is a motley assortment of axioms that require a strange collection of considerations for their justification. The problem of arbitrary apriorism remains in all of his subsequent work.[17] Carnap has stated that the ultimate justification of the axioms is inductive intuition. I do not consider this answer an adequate basis for a concept of rationality. Indeed, I think that *every* attempt, including those by Jaakko Hintikka and his students, to ground the concept of rational degree of belief in logical probability suffers from the same unacceptable apriorism.

If the conclusion of the previous paragraph is correct, we are left with subjective proba-bilities and physical probabilities. By imposing coherence requirements on subjective proba-bilities we transform them into personal probabilities, and (trivially) these satisfy the standard probability calculus. Moreover, I am convinced—by arguments advanced by F. P. Ramsey, L. J. Savage, and others—that there *are* psychological entities that constitute degrees of conviction. We can find out about them in various ways including the observation of betting behavior. What is required if they are to qualify as *rational* degrees of conviction is the question we are pursuing.

Turning to the objective side, we find propensities and relative frequencies. Although the so-called *propensity interpretation of probability* has enjoyed considerable popularity among philosophers for the last couple of decades, it suffers from a basic defect. As Paul Humphreys pointed out, the probability calculus contains *inverse probabilities*, as in Bayes's theorem, but there are no corresponding inverse propensities. Consider a simple quality control situation. A certain factory manufactures floppy disks. There are several different machines in this factory, and these machines produce disks at different rates. Moreover, each of these machines produces a certain proportion of defective disks; suppose, if you like, that the proportions are different for different machines. If these various frequencies are given it is easy to figure the probability that a randomly selected disk will be defective. It is perfectly sensible to speak of the propensity of a given machine to produce a defective disk, and of the propensity of the factory to produce defective disks. Moreover, if we pick out a disk at random and find that it is defective, it is easy, by applying Bayes's theorem, to calculate the probability that it was produced by a particular machine. It is not sensible, however, to speak of the propensity of this disk to have been produced by a given machine. Consequently, propensities do not even provide an admissible interpretation of the probability calculus. The problem is that the term "propensity" has a causal aspect that is not part of the meaning of "probability."[18]

I have no objection to the concept of propensity as such. I believe there are probabilistic causes in the world, and they are appropriately called "propensities." There is a propensity of an atom to decay, a propensity of a tossed die to come to rest with side 6 uppermost, a propensity of a child to misbehave, a propensity of a plant sprayed with an herbicide to die, etc. Such propensities produce relative frequencies. We can find out about many propensities by observing frequencies.

Indeed, it seems to me that the propensity concept may play quite a useful role in quantum theory. In that context wave equations are often employed, and references to amplitudes are customary. To calculate a probability one squares the absolute value of the amplitude. We can, of course, speak formally about wave equations as mathematical entities, but when they are applied to the description of the physical world it is reasonable to ask what the waves are undulations of. There seems to be no answer that is generally recognized as adequate. In other realms of physics we study sound waves, vibrating strings, light waves, water waves, etc. People sometimes refer to quantum mechanical waves as waves of probability, but that is not satisfactory, for what the wave gives has to be squared to get a probability. In dealing with other kinds of waves we can say what the wave amplitude is an amplitude of: displacement of water molecules, changes in electromagnetic field strength, fluctuations of air density, etc. My suggestion is that the quantum mechanical wave is a wave of propensity—propensity to interact in certain ways given appropriate conditions. The results of such interactions are frequencies, and observed frequencies give evidence as to the correctness of the propensity we have attributed in any given case. If we adopt this terminology we can say that *propensities* exhibit interference behavior; it is no more peculiar to talk about the interference of waves of propensity than it is to speak of the interference of electromagnetic waves. In this way we can avoid the awkward necessity of saying that *probabilities* interfere with one another.

It is my view that—in quantum mechanics and everywhere else—physical probabilities are somehow to be identified with frequencies. One reason for this is that relative frequencies constitute an admissible interpretation of the probability calculus if the axioms require only finite additivity. Hans Reichenbach demonstrated that the axioms of his probability calculus are logical consequences of the definition of probabilities as limiting frequencies.[19] Van Fraassen has pointed out that the limiting frequency interpretation is not an admissible interpretation of a calculus that embodies countable additivity, but I do not consider that an insuperable objection. Complications of this sort arise when we use such mathematical idealizations as infinite sequences and limiting frequencies to describe the finite classes of events and objects with which we deal in the real world. Similar problems arise when we use geometrical descriptions of material objects, or when we use the infinitesimal calculus to deal with finite collections of such discrete entities as atoms or electric charges.

The conclusion I would draw is that there are two kinds of probabilities, personal probabilities and relative frequencies. Perhaps we can legitimately continue thinking of physical probabilities as limits of relative frequencies in infinite sequences; perhaps it will turn out that the concept has to be finitized. This is a deep and difficult issue that I shall not pursue farther in this paper. For purposes of this discussion I shall speak vaguely about long-run relative frequencies, and I shall assume that observed relative frequencies in samples of populations provide evidence regarding the relative frequencies in the entire population. The question to which I want now to turn is the relationship between personal probabilities and frequencies.

IV. ON RESPECTING THE FREQUENCIES

Section III of F. P. Ramsey's essay "Truth and Probability" is entitled "Degrees of Belief,"[20] and in it he develops a logic of partial belief. This essay is rightly regarded as a landmark in the history of the theory of subjective probability. Ramsey mentions two possible approaches to the topic, namely, (1) as a measure of intensity of belief, which could be established introspectively, and (2) from the standpoint of causes of action. He dismisses the first as irrelevant to the topic with which he is concerned, and proceeds to pursue the second. The way he does so is noteworthy.

I suggest that we introduce as a law of psychology that [the subject's] behaviour is governed by what is called the mathematical expectation; that is to say that, if p is a proposition about which he is doubtful, any goods or bads for whose realization p is in his view a necessary and sufficient condition enter into his calculations multiplied by the same fraction, which is called the 'degree of his belief in p.' We thus define degree of belief in a way which presupposes the use of the mathematical expectation.[21]

We can put this in a different way. Suppose his degree of belief in p is m/n; then his action is such as he would choose it to be if he had to repeat it exactly n times, in m of which p was true, and in the others false. . . .

This can also be taken as a definition of degree of belief, and can easily be seen to be equivalent to the previous definition.[22]

In the time since Ramsey composed the present essay (1926), a good deal of empirical work in psychology has been devoted to the behavior of subjects in gambling situations, and it seems to yield an unequivocal verdict of *false* on Ramsey's proffered law. There is, however, good reason to regard it as a normative principle of rational behavior, and that is entirely appropriate if we regard logic—including the logic of partial belief—as a normative subject.

The situation is relatively straightforward, as Ramsey shows by example. If a given type of act is to be performed n times, and if on m of these occasions it results in a good g, while in the other $n-m$ it results in a bad b (where the sign of b is taken to be negative), then the frequency m/n provides a weighting factor that enables us to calculate the average result of undertaking that action. The total outcome for n occasions is obviously

$$m \times g + (n - m) \times b;$$

the average outcome is

$$[m \times g + (n-m) \times b]/n.$$

If an individual knows the rewards (positive and negative) of the possible outcomes of an act, and also the frequencies of these outcomes, he or she can tell exactly what the total result will be. In that case planning would be altogether unproblematic, for the net result of performing any such act a given number of times could be predicted with certainty. The problem is that we do not know beforehand what the frequency will be.

In view of our advance ignorance of the frequency, we must, as Carnap repeatedly reminded us, use an estimate of the relative frequency, and we should try to obtain the best estimate that is available on the basis of our present knowledge. For Carnap, probability₁ fulfills just this function; it is the best estimate of the relative frequency. However, inasmuch as I have rejected Carnap's inductive logic on grounds of intolerable apriorism, his approach is unavailable to me.

Ramsey's approach to this problem is quite different from Carnap's. Ramsey wants to arrive at an understanding of the nature of degree of belief, and he shows that we can make sense of it if (and only if?) we identify it with the betting quotient of the subject. Using the betting quotient in this way makes sense because of its relation to frequencies. The degree of partial belief, which is to be identified with the subject's betting quotient, can thus be regarded as the subject's best guess or estimate of the relative frequency. If one repeats the same type of act in the same sort of circumstances n times, then, in addition to the actual utilities that accrue to the subject in each type of outcome, the actual frequencies with which the various outcomes occur determine the net gain or loss in utility for the subject. Because of the crucial role played by actual frequencies in this theory, I would say that Ramsey's account of degree of belief is *frequency-driven*. The whole idea is to get a handle on actual frequencies because, given the utilities, the frequency determines what you get.

Ramsey's treatment of the nature of subjective probabilities and their relations to objective probabilities stands in sharp contrast to D. H. Mellor's theory as set forth in *The Matter of Chance*.[23] In that work he explicitly adopts the strategy of basing his "account of objective probability on a concept of partial belief" instead of going at it the other way around. We can say that Mellor offers a *credence-driven* account of objective probability.

On Mellor's view, propensities are not probabilities, and they are not to be identified with chances. A propensity is a disposition of a chance set-up to display a *chance distribution* under specifiable conditions—e.g., upon being flipped in the standard way a fair coin displays the distribution {chance of heads = ½; chance of tails = ½}. The chance set-up displays this *same distribution* on *every* trial. Obviously the chance distribution, which is always the same for the same chance set-up, is not to be identified with the outcomes, which may vary from one trial to another. In addition, the chance distribution is not to be identified with the relative frequencies of outcomes generated by the chance set-up.

It might seem odd to say that chance distributions are "displayed" when clearly it is the outcome, not the distribution, that is observable. But obviously, as Mellor is clearly aware, there is nothing in the notion of a disposition that prevents it, when activated, from manifesting something that is not directly observable. A hydrogen atom, for example, has a disposition to emit photons of particular frequencies under certain specifiable circumstances. *To find out what chance distribution a given chance set-up displays*, Mellor maintains, *we must appeal to our warranted partial beliefs*. Chances are probabilities, but they are not to be identified with relative frequencies. Relative frequencies are generated by the operation of chance set-ups having chance distributions. At the foundation we have warranted partial beliefs, which determine chance distributions, which, in turn, yield relative frequencies.

A fuller elaboration of the *credence-driven* point of view, and one that differs from Mellor's in fundamental respects, is provided by David Lewis in "A Subjectivist's Guide to Objective Chance."[24] He begins,

We subjectivists conceive of probability as the measure of reasonable partial belief. But we need not make war against other conceptions of probability, declaring that where subjective credence leaves off, there nonsense begins. Along with subjective credence we should believe also in objective chance. The practice and the analysis of science require both concepts. Neither can replace the other. Among the propositions that deserve our credence we find, for instance, the proposition that (as a matter of contingent fact in our world) any tritium atom that now exists has a certain chance of decaying within a year. Why should subjectivists be less able than other folk to make sense of that?[25]

Lewis points out that there can be "hybrid probabilities of probabilities," among them credences regarding chances.

. . . we have some very firm and definite opinions concerning reasonable credence about chance. These opinions seem to me to afford the best grip we have on the concept of chance. Indeed, I am led to wonder whether anyone *but* a subjectivist is in a position to understand objective chance![26]

There is an important sense in which Lewis's guide to objective chance is extraordinarily simple. It consists of one principle that seems to him "to capture all we know about chance." Accordingly, he calls it

> **The Principal Principle.** Let C be any reasonable initial credence function. Let t be any time. Let x be any real number in the unit interval. Let X be the proposition that the chance, at time t, of A's holding equals x. Let E be any proposition compatible with X that is admissible at time t. Then
> $$C(A/XE) = x$$

"That," as Lewis says, "will need a good deal of explaining."[27] But what it says roughly is that the degree to which you believe in A should equal the chance of A. I certainly cannot disagree with that principle. The question is, who is in the driver's seat, subjective credence or objective chance? As we have seen, Lewis has stated unequivocally his view that it is subjective credence; I take myself as agreeing with Ramsey that we should leave the driving to some objective feature of the situation. Ramsey opts for relative frequencies, and in a sense I think that is correct. In a more fundamental sense, however, I shall opt for propensities.

Lewis identifies chance with propensity; I take the notion of propensity as the more basic of the two. As I said above, I do not reject that concept, when it is identified with some sort of probabilistic causality (provided it is not taken to be an interpretation of probability). Moreover, I do not have any serious misgivings about attributing causal relations in single cases. On the basis of my theory of causal processes and causal interactions—spelled out most fully in chapters 5–7 of *Scientific Explanation and the Causal Structure of the World*—I believe that individual causal processes transmit probability distributions and individual causal interactions produce probabilistic outcomes (indeterministically, in some kinds of cases, at least).[28] Scientific theories, which have been highly confirmed by massive amounts of frequency data, tell us what the values of these propensities are. Propensities are, as James H. Fetzer has often maintained, entities that are not directly observable, but about which we can and do have strong indirect evidence. Their status is fully objective.[29]

As Lewis formulates his principle, he begins by saying "Let C be *any* reasonable initial credence function."[30] This means, in part, that "C is a nonnegative, normalized, finitely additive measure defined on all propositions."[31] In addition, it is *regular*. Regularity is closely akin to strict coherence, but regularity demands that no proposition receive the value zero unless it is logically false. In addition, Lewis requires Bayesian conditionalization as *one* (but not necessarily the *only*) way of learning from experience:

In general, C is to be reasonable in the sense that if you started out with it as your initial credence function, and if you always learned from experience by conditionalizing on your total evidence, then no matter what course of experience you might undergo your beliefs would be reasonable for one who had undergone that course of experience. I do not say what distinguishes a reasonable from an unreasonable credence function to arrive at after a given course of experience. We do make the distinction, even if we cannot analyze it; and therefore I may appeal to it in saying what it means to require that C be a reasonable initial credence function.[32]

The fact that Lewis does not fully characterize reasonable functions poses problems for the interpretation of his view, but the point that is generally acknowledged by subjectivists or personalists is that reasonable credence functions are not unique. One person may have one personal probability distribution, while another in the same situation may have a radically different one. So it appears that, on Lewis's account, there is no such thing as *unique* objective chance. As I understand the Principal Principle, it goes something like this. Suppose that I have a credence function C that, in the presence of my total evidence E, assigns the *degree of credence x* to the occurrence (truth) of A. Suppose further that E says nothing to contradict X, the assertion that the *objective chance* of A is x. Then, I can try adding X to my total evidence E to see whether this would change my degree of conviction regarding A. The supposition is that in most circumstances, if my degree of credence in A is x, asserting that it is also the objective chance of A is not going to change my degree of credence to something other than x (provided, of course, that there is nothing in the evidence E that contradicts that statement about the objective chance of A). Under those circumstances I have established the objective chance of A on the basis of my degree of credence in A.

One of the main things that bothers me about this account is that it seems possible that another subject, with a different credence function C' and a different degree of conviction x' in A, will assign a different objective chance to the truth of A. There is, of course, no doubt that different subjects will have different estimates of the chance of A, or different opinions concerning the chance of A. That does not help Lewis's account, inasmuch as he is attempting to characterize *objective chance*, not *estimate of objective chance* or *guess at objective chance*. The personalist may appeal to the well-known swamping of the priors—the fact that two investigators with very different prior probabilities will experience convergence of the posterior probabilities as additional evidence accumulates if they share the same evidence and conditionalize upon it. There are two objections to this response. First, and most obviously, the convergence in question secures intersubjective agreement, without any assurance that it corresponds to objective fact. Second, the convergence cannot be guaranteed if the parties do not agree on the likelihoods, and the likelihoods are just as subjective as the prior probabilities are.

Accordingly, I would want to read the principal principle in the opposite direction, so to speak. To begin, we should use whatever empirical evidence is available—either through direct observation of relative frequencies or through derivation from a well-established theory—to arrive at a statement X that the chance (in Lewis's sense) of A is x. Taking that value of the chance, we combine X with the total evidence E, and calculate the subjective degree of conviction on the basis of the credence function C. If $C(A/XE)$ is not equal to x, then C is not a *rational* credence function. In other words, we should use our knowledge of objective chance to determine what constitutes a reasonable degree of conviction. Our knowledge of objective chance, or propensity, must ultimately be based upon observations of relative frequencies.

Epistemically speaking, this amounts to a *frequency-driven* account of rational credence. In the following section, however, I shall suggest that, ontically speaking, we should prefer a *propensity-driven* account—in my sense of the term "propensity."

V. DYNAMIC RATIONALITY

In the second section of this paper we looked at various grades of rationality, static and kinematic, that can appropriately be applied to our systems of degrees of conviction. We noted emphatically that static rationality comprises only internal "housekeeping" criteria—ones that do not appeal to external objective facts in any way. In that connection, I made mention of my view that, from the standpoint of *rational action*, it is necessary to refer to objective fact.

Kinematic rationality, which invokes Bayesian conditionalization, makes a step in that direction—it does make *some* contact with the real world. I tried to show, however, that the connection it effects is too tenuous to provide a full-blooded concept of rationality. In an attempt to see how this connection could be strengthened we considered several theories concerning the relationships between subjective and objective probabilities. We found in Ramsey a robust account of the connection between partial beliefs and relative frequencies, which led me to characterize his theory as a *frequency-driven* account of subjective probability. In both Mellor and Lewis we also saw strong connections between subjective probabilities and objective chance. Inasmuch as both of these authors base their accounts of objective chance on subjective probabilities, I characterized them as offering a *credence-driven* account of objective probability. Lewis provides a particularly strong connection in terms of his *Principal Principle*. I am prepared to endorse something like this principle, except that I think it should run in the direction opposite to that claimed by Lewis. He says, in effect, that we can plug in subjective probabilities and get out objective chance (which he identifies with propensity). I think it should be just the other way around.

I should like to confer the title *dynamic rationality* upon a form of rationality that incorporates some sort of requirement to the effect that the objective chances—whether they be interpreted as frequencies or as propensities—must be respected, as well as other such rationality principles as logical consistency, probabilistic coherence, strict coherence, open-mindedness, and Bayesian conditionalization. I believe Ramsey was offering a theory of dynamic rationality because frequencies are its driving force. My version of dynamic rationality will establish one connection between propensities and frequencies as well as another connection between propensities and personal probabilities. Since I regard propensities as probabilistic causes, the term "dynamic rationality" is especially appropriate.

In order to see how this works, let us look at an example. In the Pennsylvania State Lottery, the "daily number" consists of three digits, each of which is drawn from the chamber of a separate machine containing ten ping-pong balls numbered from 0 through 9. It is assumed that all of the balls in any of the machines have equal chances of being drawn and that the draws from the several machines are mutually independent. The winning number must have the digits in the order in which they are drawn. Since there are 1000 numbers between 000 and 999, each lottery ticket has a probability of $^1/_{1000}$ of winning. The tickets cost $1 each, and the payoff for getting the right number is $500. Thus, the expectation value of each ticket is $0.50.[33] As Ramsey emphasized, if a person played for 1000 days at the rate of one ticket per day, and if the actual frequency of wins matched exactly the probability of winning, the individual would win once for a total gain of $500 and an average loss of $0.50 per play.

Unfortunately, the lottery has not always been honest. In 1980 it was discovered that the April 24 drawing (and perhaps others) had been "fixed." On that occasion, white latex paint had been injected into all of the balls except those numbered 4 and 6, thereby making them heavier than the others. Since the balls are mixed by a jet of air through the bottom of the chamber, and are drawn by releasing one ball through the top, the heavier ones were virtually certain not to be drawn. The probabilities of drawing the untampered balls were thereby greatly increased. Those who knew about the crooked arrangement could obviously take advantage of it. If the only balls that could be drawn were 4 and 6, then each of the eight possible combinations of these two digits had a probability of $1/8$. In that case, the expectation value would work out to about $62.50, which is not bad for a ticket that can be purchased for $1.[34] The actual result was 666.

One reason for going into this example in some detail is to bring out the familiar fact that, when one is going to use knowledge of frequencies in taking some sort of action on a single outcome, it is important to use the appropriate reference class. The class must be epistemically homogeneous—that is, the agent must not know of any way to partition it in a manner that makes a difference to the probabilities of the outcomes. Someone who had no knowledge of the way the lottery had been fixed would have to assign the value $1/1000$ to the probability of any given number being the winning number. Someone who knew of the fix could assign a probability of practically zero to some of the numbers and a probability of 0.125 to the remaining ones. As we have seen, the difference between the two probabilities is sufficient to make a huge difference in the expectations.

Three steps in the decision procedure (the decision whether to purchase a lottery ticket or not) have been taken. First, the event on whose outcome the gamble depends (a particular night's drawing) is referred to a reference class (all of the nightly drawings). Second, the probability that one particular number will win is assessed relative to that reference class. Third, the epistemic homogeneity of that reference class is ascertained. If it turns out to be inhomogeneous, a relevant partition is made, and the process is repeated until an epistemically homogeneous reference class is found. This is the probability with respect to the broadest epistemically homogeneous references class (what Reichenbach and I have called "weight") that is taken as the probability value in calculating the expectation.

In any given situation, the epistemically homogeneous reference class may or may not be objectively homogeneous.[35] In cases such as the present—where we have a causal or stochastic process generating the outcomes—if the class is objectively homogeneous, I would consider the weight assigned to the outcome as the *propensity* or *objective chance* of that mechanism (chance set-up) to produce that outcome. A mechanism with this propensity generates relative frequencies, some of which are identified as probabilities if we adopt a frequency interpretation.

If the reference class is merely epistemically homogeneous, I would regard the weight as our *best available estimate* of the propensity or objective chance. That weight can easily be identified as our subjective degree of credence—or, if it is not actual, as the degree of credence we should have.

I have no wish to create the impression that any sort of crude counting of frequencies is the only way to determine the propensities of various chance set-ups. In the case of the lottery, we have enough general knowledge about the type of machine employed to conclude that the propensities for all of the different numbers from 000 to 999 are equal if all of the balls are of the same size and weight. We also have enough general background knowledge to realize that injecting some but not all of the balls with latex paint will produce a chance set-up that has different propensities for different numbers. In theoretical calculations in quantum mechanics one routinely computes propensities in order to get values of probabilities. I do think that, at the most fundamental epistemic level, it is the counting of frequencies that yields knowledge of values of propensities.

On my view, as I have said above, propensities are not probabilities; rather, they are probabilistic causes. They generate some basic probabilities directly, as, for example, when the lottery machines produce sequences of digits. From the probabilities generated directly by propensities we can compute other probabilities, such as the (inverse) probability that a given number was produced by a crooked machine.

In cases like the lottery machines, where there are actually many repetitions of the same type of event to provide a large reference class, it may seem that the foregoing account makes good sense. In many similar situations, where we do not have a large number of trials but are familiar with the sort of mechanism involved, we may justifiably feel confident that we know what kinds of frequencies would result if many trials were made. Again, the foregoing account makes sense. But how, if at all, can we extend the account to deal with nonrepetitive cases?

Let us begin by considering situations like the lottery where long sequences of trials exist, but where the subject is going to bet on only one trial in that sequence. Using the mathematical expectation, he or she can ascertain what the average return per trial would be, but what point is there in having that number if we can only apply it in a single instance? The answer is that the *same policy* can be used over and over again in connection with *different sequences*.

Imagine a gambling casino in which there are many (say 100) different games of chance, each of which generates a long sequence of outcomes. In these various games there are many different associated probabilities.[36] Let us assume that our subject knows these probabilities and decides to play each game just once. After deciding the size of the bet in each case, he or she can figure the mathematical expectation for each wager. The situation we have constructed now consists of 100 long sequences of trials, each with an associated expectation value. The subject makes a random selection of one item from each of the sequences; these constitute a new sequence of trials, each with an associated expectation value. The main differences between this new sequence and the original 100 are that each item is produced by a different chance set-up, and both the probabilities and the expectation values differ from item to item. In playing through this new sequence of trials the subject will win some and lose some, and in general the tendency will be to win more of the cases with higher probabilities and to lose more of those with low probabilities. The average gain (positive or negative) per play will tend to be close to the average of the 100 expectation values associated with the 100 different basic sequences.

We realize, of course, that our subject might be extremely unlucky one evening and lose every bet placed, but such an overall outcome will be very rare. If he or she repeats this type of performance night after night, the mathematical expectation of the evening's play will be the average outcome per evening in a sequence of evenings, and the frequency of significant departures from that amount will be small. Reichenbach proved what amounts to the same result to justify his policy for dealing with single cases.[37]

Whether we think of physical probability as propensity or as (finite or infinite) long run relative frequency, there is always the problem of the short run, as characterized elegantly by Charles Sanders Peirce:

According to what has been said, the idea of probability belongs to a kind of inference which is repeated indefinitely. An individual inference must be either true or false and can show no effect of probability; and therefore, in reference to a single case considered in itself, probability can have no meaning. Yet if a man had to choose between drawing a card from a pack containing twenty-five red cards and a black one, or from a pack containing twenty-five black cards and a red one, and that of a red one were destined to transport him to eternal felicity, and that of a black one to consign him to everlasting woe, it would be folly to deny that he ought to prefer the pack containing the larger proportion of red cards, although from the nature of the risk, it cannot be repeated.[38]

There is no question about ascertaining the probabilities in Peirce's example; they are assumed to be well known. The problem has to do with the application of this knowledge in a concrete situation. It does not much matter whether the application involves one case or a dozen or a hundred, as long as the number of cases is much smaller than the number of members of the entire population.

In a paper published many years ago, I addressed this problem and suggested a pragmatic vindication of a short run rule to the effect that one should assume that the short run frequency will match, as closely as possible, the long run probability.[39] That vindication did not hold up. Now I would be inclined to give a different argument. Assume that I am right in identifying the probability with the long run frequency, and that the long run frequency of draws resulting in red cards from the predominately red deck is 25/26. Assume that this value has been established on the basis of extensive observation of frequencies. It is not crucial to Peirce's problem that only one draw ever be made from the deck; what is essential is that a person's entire fate hinges on the outcome of one draw.

I shall now say that the drawing of a card from the deck is a chance set-up whose propensity to yield a red card is 25/26. The statement about the propensity is established on the basis of observed frequencies as well as such theoretical considerations as the symmetries of the chance set-up. As I have said above, I think of propensities as probabilistic causes. If it is extremely important to achieve a particular outcome, such as a red card, one looks for a sufficient cause to bring it about. If no sufficient cause is available, one seeks the most potent probable cause. In Peirce's example, a draw from the predominately red deck is obviously a more potent cause than is a draw from the predominately black deck. The fact that the outcome cannot be guaranteed is bad luck, but that is the kind of situation we are in all the time. One might call it *the human predicament*. That is why "*for us*, probability is the very guide of life." Taking the strongest measure possible to bring about the desired result is clearly the sensible thing to do. For the moment, at least, I am inclined to regard this as an adequate answer to the problem of the short run.

Having discussed the easy sort of case in which the frequencies, propensities, mathematical expectations, and reasonable degrees of belief are clear, we must now turn to the hard type of case in which the event whose probability we want to assess is genuinely unique in some of its most important aspects. Here the subjective probabilities may be reasonably tractable—especially in New York City, where it seems that most people will bet on anything—but the objective probabilities are much more elusive. I believe, nevertheless, that the notions of propensity and probabilistic cause can be of significant help in dealing with such cases.

Before turning to them, however, we should briefly consider an intermediate kind of case, which appears at first blush to involve a high degree of uniqueness, but where, upon reflection, we see that pertinent frequencies can be brought to bear. The Challenger disaster provides a useful instance. The life of Christa McAuliffe, the school teacher who joined the crew on that flight, was insured for a million dollars (with her family as beneficiary) by a philanthropic individual. I have no idea what premium was charged.

McAuliffe was the first female who was not a professional astronaut to go on a space shuttle flight. Since she had undergone rigorous screening and training, there was reason to believe that she was not at special risk *vis à vis* the rest of the crew, and that she did not contribute a special risk to that particular mission. As Feynman pointed out, however, there was a crucial piece of frequency information available—namely, the frequency of failure of solid rocket boosters. Taking that information into account, and even making the sort of adjustments Feynman suggested, the minimum premium (omitting profit for the insurance company) should have been $10,000.

Feynman's adjustments are worthy of comment. One adjustment was made on the basis of improved technology; whether that is reasonable or not would depend in large measure on whether the relative frequency of failures had actually decreased as time went by. The second had to do with higher standards of quality control. Perhaps there were frequency data to show that such a factor was relevant, but even in their absence one could take it as a probabilistic cause that would affect the frequency of space shuttle disasters.

Another good example comes from the continuing controversy regarding the so-called *Strategic Defense Initiative*, popularly known as *Star Wars*. Amid all the debate two facts seem incontrovertible. First, enormous technological advances will be required if the project is to be feasible at all.[40] Second, extraordinarily complicated software will be necessary to control the sensors, guidance systems, weapons, etc. This software can never be fully tested before it is used to implement a (counter?) attack. If the computers function successfully, the system will attack only in case an enemy launches an attack against the United States. The computers will have to make the decision to launch a (counter?) attack, for there will not be time for human decision-makers to intervene. What degree of confidence should we have regarding the ability of writers to produce software that is almost unimaginably complex and that will function correctly *the first time*?—Without any errors that might launch an attack against a nation that had not initiated hostilities against the United States?—Without any errors that would completely foul up the operation of the system in case of actual war, or render it completely non-operational? We all have enough experience with computers—often in use by government agencies—to make a pretty reasonable guess at *that* probability!

The moral of the consideration of these "intermediate" cases is simple. It is the point of Feynman's criticism of NASA's risk assessment. Do not ignore the available relevant information about frequencies. *Respect the frequencies.*

Let us now turn to the kind of case in which the presumption of the availability of relevant frequency information is much less plausible. Examples from history are often cited to illustrate this situation. Because of the complexity of actual historical cases, I cannot present a detailed analysis, but I hope to be able to offer some suggestive remarks.

One of the most significant occurrences of the present century was the dropping of the atomic bomb on Hiroshima. The background events leading up to the development of the atomic bomb are familiar: the discovery of nuclear fission and the possibility of a self-sustaining chain reaction, the realization that the Nazis were working on a similar project, the fear that they would succeed and—with its aid—conquer the world, and the urging by important scientists of the development of such a weapon. Before the bomb was completed, however, Germany had surrendered, and many scientists felt that the project should halt, or, if a bomb was created, it should not be put to military use. Given this situation in the spring of

1945, what were the probabilistic causes that led to the dropping of the bomb on a major Japanese city? What probabilistic causes led to rejection of the proposal by many scientists to demonstrate its power to the Japanese, and perhaps other nations, instead of using it on a civilian population?

This is obviously an extremely complicated matter, but a few factors can be mentioned. One event of great significance was the death of Franklin D. Roosevelt, and the elevation of Harry S. Truman to the presidency; this seems clearly to have raised the probability of military use. Another contributing factor was the deep racism in America during World War II, making the lives of oriental civilians seem less valuable than those of caucasians. Still another contributing factor was the failure of scientists to anticipate the devastating effects of radiation, and hence, to view the atomic bomb as just another, more powerful, conventional weapon. An additional complicating feature of the situation was the great failure of communication between scientists and politicians, and between scientists and military people.

Some scientists had suggested inviting Japanese observers to Trinity, the test explosion in Nevada, but others feared the consequences if the first bomb turned out to be a dud. Some had suggested erecting some buildings, or even constructing a model city, to demonstrate the power of the bomb, but various objections were raised. After Trinity, some scientists suggested exploding an atomic bomb over the top of Mount Fujiyama, but some of the military argued that only destruction of a city would provide an adequate demonstration.[41] The personalities of key individuals had crucial import.

As one considers a complex historical situation, such as this, it is natural, I believe, to look at the multitude of relevant items as factors that tend to produce or inhibit the outcome in question. These tendencies are propensities—contributing or counteracting probabilistic causes—and we attempt to assess their strengths. In so doing we are relying on a great deal of experience with scientific, political, economic, social, and scientific endeavors. We bring to bear an enormous amount of experience pertaining to the human interactions and the effects of various traits of personality. My claim is that, in assigning the personal probabilities that would have been appropriate in a given historical situation, we are estimating or guessing at the strengths of and interactions among probabilistic causes.

In writing about scientific explanation during a period of nearly twenty-five years, Hempel has repeatedly addressed the special problems of historical explanation.[42] He has dealt with a number of concrete examples, in an effort to show how such explanations can be understood as scientific explanations conforming to his well-known models of explanation. I would suggest that they can easily be read in terms of attributions of probabilistic causes to complex historical occurrences.

I certainly do not pretend to have numerical values to assign to the propensities involved in the dropping of the bomb on Hiroshima, given one set of conditions or another—or to any other significant historical event—and I do not think anyone else does either. But it does seem reasonable to regard each of the factors we have cited—and others, perhaps—as probabilistic causes that worked together to bring about a certain result. I would suggest that experts who are familiar with the complexities of the situation can make reasonable qualitative assessments of the strengths of the various factors, classifying them as strong, moderate, weak, or negligible. In addition, they can make assessments of the ways in which the various probabilistic causes interact, reinforcing one another or tending to cancel one another out. It is considerations such as these that can be brought to bear in arriving at personal probabilities with respect to the unique events of human history.

VI. CAUSALITY, FREQUENCY, AND DEGREE OF CONVICTION

If one were to think of causality solely in terms of constant conjunction, then it would be natural to identify probabilistic causality with relative frequency in some fashion or other. As I tried to show in *Scientific Explanation and the Causal Structure of the World*, a far more robust account of causality can be provided in terms of *causal processes* and *causal interactions*.[43] This account is intended to apply to probabilistic causal relations as well as to causal relations that can be analyzed in terms of necessary causes, sufficient causes, or any combination of them. It is also intended to give meaning to the notions of *production* and *propagation*.

My aim in the present paper is to bring these causal considerations to bear on the problem of the relationship between objective and subjective probabilities, and to relate them to rationality. As we noted above, Ramsey stressed the crucial role of mathematical expectations of utility in rational decision-making. For purposes of this discussion, let us make the grossly false assumption that we know the utilities that attach to the various possible outcomes of the actions we contemplate.[44] What we would *really* like to have, given that knowledge, is the ability to predict accurately the outcome of every choice we make, but we realize that this is impossible. Given that fact, what we would *really* like to have is knowledge of the actual frequencies with which the outcomes will occur. That would also be nice, but it, too, is impossible. Given that fact, the next best thing, I suggest, would be to know the strengths of the probabilistic causes that produce the various possible outcomes. They are the agencies that produce the actual frequencies. I think of them as actual physical tendencies, and have called them *propensities*. It is the operations of physical devices having these propensities—chance set-ups, including our own actions—that produce the actual short run frequencies, on which our fortunes depend, as well as the long run frequencies which I am calling *probabilities*.[45]

The best estimate of the actual short run frequency is, I would argue, the possible value closest to the propensity. Recall Peirce's example. If the agent draws from the deck with the preponderance of red cards, that act has a propensity of degree 25/26 to yield a red card. The actual frequency of red in a class containing only one member must be either one or zero; one is obviously closer to the propensity than is zero. In the other deck, the propensity for red is 1/26, and this value is closer to zero than it is to one. Since the agent wants a red card, he or she chooses to draw from the deck whose propensity for red is closer to the desired short run frequency.

The best way to look at an important subset of subjective or personal probabilities is, I think, to consider them as estimates of the strengths of probabilistic causes. In many cases, several probabilistic causes may be present, and the propensity of the event to occur is compounded out of them. Smoking, exercise, diet, body weight, and stress are, for example, contributing or counteracting causes of heart disease. In such cases we must estimate, not only the strengths of the several causes, but also the interactions among them. Obviously, two causes may operate synergistically to enhance the potency of one another, they may tend to cancel each other out, or they may operate independently. Our assessments of the strengths of the probabilistic causes must take into account their interactions as well as the strengths of the component causes.

The obvious problem that must now be faced is how we can justifiably estimate, guess, infer, or posit the strengths of the propensities. When we attempt to assign a propensity to a given chance set-up, we are dealing with a causal hypothesis, for a propensity is a probabilistic cause. Since Bayes's theorem is, in my view, the appropriate schema for the evaluation of scientific (including causal) hypotheses, I should like to offer a brief sketch of a Bayesian account that appeals to propensities.

There is a widely held maxim, which I regard as correct, to the effect that the meaningful collection of scientific data can occur only in the presence of one or more hypotheses upon which the data are supposed to have an evidential bearing. It is therefore important, I believe, to take a brief excursion into the context of invention (discovery) in order to consider the generation of hypotheses about propensities—i.e., about probabilistic causes.[46] It is a rather complex matter. In the first place, we have to identify the chance set-up and decide that it is an entity, or set of entities, worthy of our interest. This is analogous to selecting a reference class as a basis for an objective probability—i.e., a long run relative frequency. We must also identify the outcome (or set of outcomes) with which we are to be concerned. This is analogous to the selection of an attribute class (or sample space) for an objective probability relationship. Without these, we would have no hypothetical probabilistic causal relation to which a value of a propensity could be assigned.

But, as I emphasized above, not all objective probabilities are propensities. Inverse probabilities are not propensities.[47] Many correlations do not stand for propensities. It would be a joke to say that a barometer is a chance set-up that exhibits a high propensity for storms whenever its reading drops sharply. It would not necessarily be a joke to say that the atmosphere in a particular locale is a chance set-up with a strong propensity for storms when it experiences a sharp drop in pressure. Thus, whenever we hypothesize that a propensity exists, we are involved in a rather strong causal commitment.

When we have identified the chance set-up and the outcomes of interest, and we hypothesize a probabilistic causal relation between them, we need to make hypotheses about the strength of the propensity. The idea I want to suggest is, roughly, that an observed frequency fulfills one essential function relating to the formulation of a hypothesis about the propensity. Actually, we need more than just a single hypothesized value of the propensity; we need a prior probability distribution over the full range of possible values of the propensity, i.e., the closed unit interval. My proposal is that, in the absence of additional theoretical knowledge about the chance set-up, the observed frequency determines the value of the propensity for which the prior probability is maximal, namely, the value of the observed frequency itself.[48]

There is an additional assumption that is often made by propensity theorists. A chance set-up is defined as a mechanism that can operate repeatedly, such that, on each trial, it has the same propensity to produce the given outcome. This means that the separate instances of its operation are independent of one another; for example, the outcome in any given case does not depend probabilistically upon the outcome of the preceeding trials. This constitutes a strong factual assumption. Another, closely related, assumption has to do with the randomness of the sequence of outcomes. There is a strong temptation to make these assumptions. If we do, we can use the Bernoulli theorem to calculate the probabilities of various frequency distribution, given various values for the associated propensity.

Imagine that we have a black box with a button and two lights—one red, the other green—on the outside. We notice that, when the button is pressed, either the red or the green comes on; we have never seen both of them light up simultaneously, nor have we seen a case in which neither comes on when the button has been pushed. However, we have no *a priori* reason to believe that either of the latter two cases is impossible. This is a generic chance set-up. Suppose that we have observed 10 cases, in 6 of which the green light has been illuminated. We now have a prior distribution for green, peaking at 0.6; a prior distribution for red, peaking at 0.4; and prior distributions for both lights and for neither light, each peaking at 0. So far, I would suggest, it is all context of invention (discovery). At the same time, and in the same context, we may make hypotheses—of the sort mentioned above—about such matters as the independence of the outcomes or the randomness of the sequence. All such hypotheses can be tested by additional observational evidence. We can check such questions as whether the red light goes on every time the number of the trial is a prime number,[49] whether green goes on whenever (but not only whenever) there have been two reds in a row, or whether red occurs on every seventh trial. Answers to all of these questions depend upon the frequencies we observe.

Not all philosophers agree that there is a viable distinction between the context of invention (discovery) and the context of appraisal (justification). But those of us who do have emphasized the psychological aspects of the former context. Such psychological factors would, I believe, have considerable influence in shaping the distribution of prior probabilities—e.g., how flat it is or how sharply peaked at the value of the observed frequency. Prior probabilities represent plausibility judgments; the prior distribution exhibits the plausibilities we assign to the various possible values of the propensity.

The fact that some aspects of the context of invention (discovery) are psychological does not prevent objective features of the situation from entering as well. In particular, I am suggesting, observed frequencies—the paradigm of objective fact—play a decisive role. In this connection, I have long maintained a view regarding the confirmation of scientific hypotheses that might suitably be called *objective Bayesianism*.[50] One key feature of this approach to confirmation is that the prior probabilities of hypotheses are to be construed as frequencies. A plausibility judgment should identify a hypothesis as one of a given type, and it should estimate the frequency with which hypotheses of that type have succeeded. I shall not rehearse the arguments here, but we should recall, as noted above, that Shimony supports his treatment of prior probabilities in his *tempered personalism* by an explicit appeal to frequency considerations. This is another way in which, I believe, the frequencies should be respected as an aspect of a fully objective Bayesian account.

VII. CONCLUSION

Ramsey's conception of rationality accords a central role to mathematical expectations of utility. The probabilities occurring in the expression for the expectation are, in Ramsey's terms, degrees of partial belief. His rationale for this approach brings into sharp focus the actual short run frequencies that determine the net outcomes of our choices. It seems clear that Ramsey regarded his subjective probabilities as estimates of (short- or long- run) frequencies. For this reason I regard his view as a *frequency-driven* conception of rationality.

Dynamic rationality, as I would define it, consists in the attempt to use propensities—i.e., probabilistic causes—as the weighting factors that occur in the formula for expected utility. Since we cannot be sure that our choices and decisions will be fully efficacious in bringing about desired results, it is reasonable to rely on the strengths of probabilistic causes. This line of thought treats our voluntary choices, decisions, and actions as probabilistic causes of what happens as a result of our deliberations. Dynamic rationality involves a *propensity-driven* view of objective probabilities and short-run frequencies.

Because the values of propensities are not known with certainty, we have to make do with the best estimates we can obtain. I have been urging that some personal probabilities are, precisely, best estimates of this sort. There are, however, physical probabilities that cannot be identified with propensities; consequency, I believe, there are personal probabilities that cannot straightforwardly be construed as estimates of propensities. These personal probabilities may be taken as estimates of frequencies. Where we do not have access to the pertinent propensities, we do best by using estimates of frequencies. Since, however, I take it that frequencies are generated by propensities, my approach involves a *propensity-driven* account of degree of conviction.

In dealing with universal laws in the sciences we are used to the idea that some laws—e.g., the ideal gas law—provide empirical regularities without furnishing any causal underpinning. We look to a deeper theory—the kinetic-molecular theory—for a causal explanation of that regularity. In the domain of statistical regularities a similar distinction can be made. There are statistical laws that express statistical regularities without providing any kind of causal explanation. Such statistical regularities are physical probabilities (long run frequencies). In some cases a deeper statistical theory exists that embodies the propensities that constitute the causal underpinning. In both the universal and the statistical cases, however, the unexplained empirical regularities can serve as a basis for prediction and decision-making.

A major thesis of this paper is that observed frequencies often provide the best evidence we have concerning long run frequencies and the strengths of probabilistic causes. Sometimes our evidence is of a less direct and more theoretical variety. At the most primitive level, I believe, observed frequencies constitute the evidential base.

Induction by enumeration has traditionally been regarded as a rule of primitive induction for *justifying* inferences to values of physical probabilities (long run frequencies). Whether it may be a suitable rule for this aim is an issue I shall not go into here.[51] Since my main concern in this paper has been with propensities and probabilistic causes, it has *not* been at the level of primitive induction. Causal attributions are more complicated than mere statistical generalization. For purposes of the present discussion, I have suggested that we consider induction by enumeration instead as a method—in the context of invention (discovery)—that makes a crucial contribution to the generation of hypotheses. Used in this way, it provides, I believe, a concrete method for *respecting the frequencies*. It thereby serves as a counterpart to David Lewis's *Principal Principle*—providing the link between objective and subjective probabilities, but going *from* the objective (observed frequency) *to* the subjective (personal probabilities).

Observed frequencies furnish knowledge of physical probabilities, and propensities. They also constitute the basis for personal probabilities—both those that correspond to propensities and those that do not. These personal probabilities, in turn, provide the weights that should figure in our calculations of mathematical expectations. The mathematical expectations that result from this process then constitute our *very guide of life*.

NOTES

1. Peter Wyden, *Day One* (New York: Simon and Schuster, 1984), p. 50.
2. Ibid., pp. 50–51. Wyden mentions this incident, but without throwing any light on the questions I am raising.
3. Eliot Marshall, "Feynman Issues His Own Shuttle Report, Attacking NASA's Risk Estimates," *Science*, 232 (27 June 1986), p. 1596. All of the following quotations from this article appear on the same page.
4. [If the probability of failure of a given rocket is 0.01, the probability of at least one failure in 50 firings is 0.395; the probability of at least one failure in 100 firings is 0.634. W.C.S.]
5. [Marshall offers the following interpretation of that figure: "It means NASA thinks it could launch the shuttle, as is, every day for the next 280 years and expect not one equipment-based disaster." One could hope that NASA statisticians would not follow Marshall in making such an inference. I presume that the number 280 was chosen because that many years contain a little over 100,000 days—102,268

to be precise (allowing for leap years). However, it must be recalled, as was pointed out in the article, that each launch involves 2 rockets, so the number of rocket firings in that period of time would be 204,536. If the probability of failure on any given rocket is 1 in 100,000, the probability of at least one failure in that many firings is about 0.870. In one century of daily launches, with that probability of failure, there is about a 50–50 chance of at least one failure. This latter estimate is, of course, absurd, but to show the absurdity of the NASA estimate we should try to get the arithmetic right.]

6. A recent discussion of this issue can be found in Mark J. Machina, "Decision-Making in the Presence of Risk," *Science* 236 (1 May 1987), pp. 537–43.

7. Patrick Maher, "The Irrelevance of Belief to Practical Action," *Erkenntnis* 24 (1986), pp. 263–84.

8. Rudolf Carnap and David Lewis, among others, use the *credence* terminology.

9. I realize that a great deal of important work has been done on the handling of inconsistent systems, so that, for example, the presence of an inconsistency in a large body of data does not necessarily bring a scientific investigation to a grinding halt. See, for example, Nicholas Rescher and Robert Brandom, *The Logic of Inconsistency* (Oxford: Basil Blackwell, 1980). However, inasmuch as our main concern is with probabilistic coherence, it will not be necessary to go into that issue in detail.

10. A molecular statement is one that involves no quantifiers. The negation of a molecular statement is obviously also molecular. As the term "molecular" is being used here, basic statements (statements without quantifiers or binary connectives) are considered molecular.

11. Abner Shimony, "Scientific Inference," in Robert G. Colodny, ed., *The Nature and Function of Scientific Theories* (Pittsburgh: University of Pittsburgh Press, 1970), pp. 79–172.

12. When the modification is drastic enough, Thomas Kuhn calls it a scientific revolution.

13. Another way of handling these betting considerations—one that I would prefer—is to remember that two factors bear upon our bets. The first is the degree of probability of the event that we are betting on; the second is our degree of assurance that that probability is objectively correct. In his theory of probability$_1$ Carnap, in effect, eliminated this second consideration by making all such probability statements either logically true or logically false. This meant that the caution factor had to be built into the value of the probability; strict coherence does the job.

14. Ian Hacking, *The Emergence of Probability* (Cambridge: Cambridge University Press, 1975). Hacking argues that this could not have occurred before the seventeenth century. I am not at all sure that his historical thesis about the time at which the concept of probability emerged is correct, but his conceptual analysis strikes me as sound.

15. Rudolf Carnap, "The Aim of Inductive Logic," in Ernest Nagel, Patrick Suppes, and Alfred Tarski, *Logic, Methodology, and Philosophy of Science* (Stanford: Stanford University Press. 1962).

16. Rudolf Carnap, "Replies and Systematic Expositions," in Paul Arthur Schilpp, ed., *The Philosophy of Rudolf Carnap* (La Salle, Ill.: Open Court Publishing Co., 1963), pp. 859–1018.

17. Carnap continued work on the project of constructing an adequate inductive logic until his death in 1970. His later work on the subject is published in *Studies in Inductive Logic and Probability*, vols. 1–2 (Berkeley, Los Angeles, London: University of California Press, 1971, 1980). The first volume is edited by Rudolf Carnap and Richard C. Jeffrey. Jeffrey is the sole editor of volume 2.

18. See Wesley C. Salmon, "Propensities: A Discussion-Review", *Erkenntnis* 14 (1979), pp. 183–216, for a fuller discussion of this topic.

19. Hans Reichenbach, *The Theory of Probability* (Berkeley: University of California Press, 1949), section 18.

20. Frank Plumpton Ramsey, *The Foundations of Mathematics*, ed. R. B. Braithwaite (New York: Humanities Press, 1950), pp. 166–84. In order to discuss quotations from Ramsey's article I shall revert to his terminology and refer to *partial beliefs* and *degrees of belief*.

21. [Ramsey clearly means that the subject behaves so as to maximize his or her expected utility. W.C.S.]

22. Ibid., p. 174.

23. D. H. Mellor, *The Matter of Chance* (Cambridge: Cambridge University Press, 1971). In discussing Mellor's views I shall continue to use the traditional "partial belief" and "degree of belief" terminology.

I have treated Mellor's book in considerable detail in Wesley C. Salmon, "Propensities: A Discussion-Review." This article also contains a general discussion of propensity theory with special emphasis on the work of Karl Popper, its originator.

24. David Lewis, "A Subjectivist's Guide to Objective Chance," in Richard C. Jeffrey, ed., *Studies in Inductive Logic and Probability*, vol. 2 (Berkeley: University of California Press, 1980), pp. 263–93. In discussing Lewis's views, I shall use his terminology of "partial belief" and "credence."

25. Ibid., p. 263.

26. Ibid., p. 264, Lewis's italics.

27. Ibid., p. 266. In explaining this principle Lewis makes excursions into nonstandard analysis and possible worlds semantics. I do not think either of these tools is required for our discussion.

28. Wesley C. Salmon, *Scientific Explanation and the Causal Structure of the World* (Princeton: Princeton University Press, 1984).

29. James H. Fetzer, "Dispositional Probabilities," in R. Buck and R. Cohen, eds., *PSA 1970* (Dordrecht: D. Reidel, 1981); and *Scientific Knowledge* (Dordrecht: D. Reidel Publishing Company, 1981).

30. Lewis, "Subjectivist's Guide," p. 266, my italics.

31. Ibid., p. 267.

32. Ibid., p. 268.

33. Someone who buys a ticket each day for a year pays $365 for a set of tickets whose expectation value is $182.50. This is poor investment indeed—especially for people at or near the poverty level—but regrettably it is not an uncommon occurrence.

34. Fortunately, this particular incident was discovered, and the perpetrators were brought to trial and punished. Presumably this sort of thing is not going on any more.

35. I have attempted to characterize this rather complicated concept in *Scientific Explanation and the Causal Structure of the World* (Princeton: Princeton University Press, 1984), chapter 3.

36. We can think of different roulette wheels as different games. The same goes for slot machines, black jack tables, etc. It is not necessary that every game have a probability distribution different from all others.

37. Hans Reichenbach, *The Theory of Probability* (Berkeley: University of California Press, 1949), sections 56, 72.

38. Charles Sanders Peirce, *Collected Papers*, vol. 2, eds. Charles Hartshorne and Paul Weiss (Cambridge: Harvard University Press, 1931), section 2.652.

39. Wesley C. Salmon, "The Short Run," *Philosophy of Science* 22 (July 1955), pp. 214–21.

40. This assertion is based upon a report sponsored by the American Physical Society, reported in *Science News* 131 (May 2, 1987), p. 276. The report refers to the need for "improvements of several orders of magnitude."

41. My primary source for these remarks is Wyden, *Day One*.

42. I refer primarily to "The Function of General Laws in History," *Journal of Philosophy* 39 (1942), pp. 35–48, reprinted in Hempel, *Aspects of Scientific Explanation*; "Explanation in Science and in History," in Robert G. Colodny, ed., *Frontiers of Science and Philosophy* (Pittsburgh: University of Pittsburgh Press, 1962), pp. 7–34; "Aspects of Scientific Explanation," sections 7–10, in *Aspects of Scientific Explanation*, pp. 447–87.

43. See chapters 5–6.

44. The unrealistic nature of this assumption is nicely conveyed by the old saying. "When the gods want to punish us they grant us our prayers."

45. It may be that some probabilities are not generated by propensities as I am construing them. Ian Hacking discusses this issue in his paper, "Grounding Probabilities from Below," in P. Asquith and R. Giere, eds., *PSA 1980* (East Lansing, Mich.: Philosophy of Science Assn., 1982), pp. 110–16, and offers an interesting actual example in which this appears to be the case.

46. I am adopting the felicitous terminology, "context of invention" and "context of appraisal," proposed by Robert McLaughlin in "Invention and Appraisal," in Robert McLaughlin, ed., *What? Where?*

When? Why? (Dordrecht: D. Reidel, 1982), pp. 69–100, as a substitute for the traditional "context of discovery" and "context of justification."

47. See section III, above (text to note 18).

48. This approach bears some strong resemblances to a suggestion offered by Ian Hacking in section 9 of "One Problem About Induction," in Imre Lakatos, ed., *The Problem of Inductive Logic* (Amsterdam: North-Holland Publishing Co., 1968), pp. 52–54. It has taken me almost twenty years to appreciate the value of this suggestion.

49. Supposing that red was illuminated on the second, third, fifth, and seventh trials.

50. See, for example, Wesley C. Salmon, *The Foundations of Scientific Inference* (Pittsburgh: University of Pittsburgh Press, 1967), chapter 7.

51. The considerations advanced by Hacking—see note 45—make me suspect that it is not.

ELLERY EELLS

PROBABILITY, INFERENCE, AND DECISION*

■ *t does not depend on man to have this or that opinion in the present state, but it depends on him to prepare himself to have it eventually, . . . thus opinions are voluntary only in an indirect manner.*

—Leibniz (1765, p. 528)

I. INTRODUCTION

According to at least one conception of rationality (which I take to be a "Bayesian" one), the rationality of, say, a given person's inference or a given person's decision, on a particular occasion, should be assessed on the basis of what the person "has to work with" on that occasion: perhaps just the person's beliefs and evidence at hand, in the case of an inference, and the person's beliefs and desires, in the case of a decision. By analogy, if we want to judge a person's skill as a carpenter in terms of how nice a product, say a desk, is turned out on a particular occasion, then the quality of the desk should be assessed relative to what can be done with the kinds of tools and materials at hand to the person, and not relative to what can be done with more, or less, sophisticated, or just different, kinds of tools or materials.

On a given occasion, one happens to have certain beliefs and one happens to have certain desires, and perhaps he or she has just acquired some new evidence. (The way in which beliefs, desires, and evidence will be understood here will be clarified below.) In the spirit of the passage quoted from Leibniz above, the fact that, on a given occasion, a person has the beliefs, desires, and evidence he or she in fact has "does not depend on" the person: this fact is outside the person's control for the particular occasion in question, and the beliefs, desires, and evidence at hand are what the person "has to work with." Thus, according to the conception of rationality described above, an assessment of the rationality of an inference or decision should take this into account: one should be judged, on a particular occasion, according to what one has to work with, and not in light of what is true or in light of what desires or evidence may be optimal (in whatever sense desires or evidence may be optimal).

Of course, given a certain context, different people may have different beliefs, may have different desires, and may have different pieces of new evidence. Thus, at least the beliefs and desires relative to which an inference or decision may or may not be rational are *subjective*: different inferences and decisions may be rational for different people, depending on the specific beliefs and desires harbored by the individual. The rationality of these beliefs and desires is not in question on the particular occasion in question, since "it does not depend on" the individual to have this or that belief or desire in the particular time or occasion in question, nor does it depend on the individual at the particular time or occasion in question to have this or that piece of evidence at hand.

This conception of rationality, which may be termed "static rationality," is somewhat in contrast with, but not inconsistent with, the approach, called "dynamic rationality," urged by Wesley Salmon in the previous essay in this volume. According to Salmon's approach, a person's beliefs (or subjective probabilities) have a history and ought to be guided by one's observance of actual frequencies of one kind of event when another is present; these observed actual frequencies are evidence for the generating propensities (or probabilistic causes) and objective probabilities. I do not disagree with the idea that if one is rational then one will base his or her subjective probabilities (also called "degrees of belief") on observed actual frequencies. In fact, of course, all relevant observations should be taken into account when an appropriate way of doing so is available, an idea with which Salmon does not disagree: there may be other kinds of evidence for propensities, probabilistic causes, and objective probabilities than observed actual frequencies.

My point here is simply that the rationality of an inference or a decision can be judged independently of the history of the relevant person's subjective probability function. Although the evolution of a person's subjective probability function, as evidence has unfolded, may be criticized, there is nevertheless the separate question of how well one does in a particular situation with what he or she has to work with. Thus, in characterizing the rationality of a given inference or decision, we may restrict ourselves to strictly subjective probabilities, regardless of how they were arrived at.

Salmon concludes his essay with the idea that personal (i.e., subjective) probabilities (based on observed frequencies) are key ingredients to mathematical expectations that "constitute our *very guide of life*." Here, I shall understand rational life as including (at least) both inference and decision (which, of course, are not unrelated aspects of rational life). The purpose of this essay is to elaborate the mechanics of just how the idea of subjective probability provides a framework for understanding rational inference and rational decision making. In this essay, I will assume, and also try to make plausible, the idea that a rational person, concerned with inference or decision-making, has to work with a set of beliefs codified in a subjective probability assignment and a set of desires codified in a desirability, or utility, assignment. And I will try to show how the Bayesian approach illuminates both the nature of rational inference and the nature of rational decision in terms of these two kinds of "tools" that the rational person has to work with.

In the two sections that follow, I attempt to convey, both descriptively and critically, some of the main elements of so-called "Bayesian confirmation theory" (the subjective probabilistic theory of inference) and "Bayesian decision theory" (the subjective probabilistic theory of individual decision making).[1]

II. BAYESIAN CONFIRMATION THEORY

Bayesianism is usually characterized as the philosophical view that, for many philosophically important purposes, probability can usefully be interpreted subjectively, as an individual's "rational degree of belief," and that the rational way to assimilate new information into one's structure of beliefs is by a process called "conditionalization." The subjective interpretation of probability is connected, however, in important ways with a mathematically precise and intuitively plausible theory of rational decision called the *subjective expected utility maximization theory*. Because of this connection, and the nature of it, Bayesianism can alternatively be characterized as the view that (i) rational decision and rational preference go by subjective expected utility; (ii) subjective probabilities (and numerical subjective utilities) are more or less theoretical entities that "lie behind," explain, and are give partial empirical interpretation by, an individual's choices and preferences; and (iii) learning goes by conditionalization.

The next section will discuss the first and second aspects of Bayesianism. In this section, I will describe the third aspect: the rule of conditionalization. This will include a clarification of the rule, a brief discussion of some proposed justifications of the rule, and, not unrelatedly, how the rule itself justifies some standard canons of rational inference and also exposes others as misguided. As noted above, Bayesianism has both a static part and a dynamic part. The static part asserts that rational degrees of belief can be represented by a probability assignment over propositions (or events, event-types, sentences, etc.). One kind of justification of this idea, the so-called "Dutch book" approach, is discussed by Salmon in the previous essay, and briefly described in the appendix to this essay.[2] It is the dynamic part that asserts that learning, or inference, goes, or should go, by conditionalization. The dynamic part itself may be construed as having two parts: *descriptive* ("learning *in fact* goes by conditionalization") and *normative* ("learning *should* go by conditionalization," or "*rational* learning in fact goes by conditionalization"). Here, I will be concerned just with the normative aspect of the rule of conditionalization.[3]

As mentioned above, Bayesian learning (or confirmation or inference) theory tells you what new degree of belief assignment it is rational to adopt, when new evidence comes in, *relative to* what your prior degrees of belief are, just as Bayesian decision theory tells you what course of action it is rational to pursue *relative to* what your beliefs and desires are—all irrespective of how factually or morally or otherwise justified the beliefs, or desires, may be. Rational inference, or learning, involves both (i) having already adopted a prior degree of belief assignment and (ii) changing it to accommodate new evidence. The adoption of a particular posterior assignment accommodating new evidence may be said to be a *rational* move to the degree to which (ii) is successfully (i.e., favorably, validly, correctly) carried out, and the move may be said to be *well-grounded* to the extent to which both (i) and (ii) are successfully (favorably, validly, correctly) carried out, and thus to the extent to which the posterior assignment accommodates not only the recently acquired evidence, but also previous experiences of the agent. Bayesian learning theory is concerned with part (ii) of the process of belief change. It is a theory about how the new assignment must be related to the old one— and not how it must be related to the objective world—for it to rationally be so related, in virtue of acquisition of new evidence. Thus, the learning theory is as applicable to the learning undergone by the ignorant and inexperienced as it is to that undergone by the knowledge-able expert.

As mentioned above, the dynamic part of Bayesian theory asserts that *rational change of belief goes by conditionalization*: if one learns that some proposition E is true, then one's new degree of belief in any proposition X should equal his or her old degree of belief in X conditional on E:

$$P_n(X) = P_o(X/E) = P_o(X\&E)/P_o(E),$$

where P_o is the old (prior) subjective probability assignment and P_n is the new (posterior) assignment, the one the rational person adopts after having learning that E is true. This is the *rule of conditionalization* (or *ROC*, for short).

It is sometimes convenient to express this rule in a different form. Suppose the agent (perhaps a scientist) is considering m mutually exclusive and collectively exhaustive hypotheses H_i,[4] and has just acquired evidence E. Note that:

$$P_o(H_i/E) = \frac{P_o(H_i\&E)}{P_o(E)} = \frac{P_o(E/H_i)P_o(H_i)}{\text{SUM}_{j=1}^m P_o(E/H_j)P_o(H_j)}$$

This is known as Bayes' theorem, and the philosophical theory called "Bayesianism" is so-called because of its application, in a number of contexts, of the theorem. The rule, which is equivalent to *ROC*, that asserts that $P_n(H_i)$ is equal to the term on the right above is known as *Bayes' Rule*. $P(E/H_i)$ is called the *likelihood* of H_i on E (which, of course, is different from the *probability* of H_i given E, i.e., $P(H_i/E)$). Thus, Bayes' Rule tells you how to get the posterior probability of a hypothesis from the prior probabilities of each of the competing hypotheses and their likelihoods on the evidence. Note that if the degree of confirmation of a hypothesis H_i is construed as the difference between $P_n(H_i)$ and $P_o(H_i)$, then Bayes' Rule shows that likely hypotheses are confirmed more (or disconfirmed less) than unlikely ones: taking the ratio of Bayes' Rule with respect to two hypotheses H_i and H_j yields:

$$\frac{P_n(H_i)}{P_n(H_j)} = \frac{P_o(E/H_i)P_o(H_i)}{P_o(E/H_j)P_o(H_j)}$$

So we may think of the likelihoods as measures of the *impacts* of the evidence on the hypotheses.

Why should learning go by conditionalization? Several arguments have been advanced in the justification of *ROC*. In the appendix to this paper, I briefly describe the best known of them, the formal details of which were devised by David Lewis and reported in Teller (1976).[5] This is a "dynamic" version of the Dutch book argument that has been used to justify the idea that one's degrees of belief, at a given time ("statically"), should conform to the standard probability axioms. Just as the "static" Dutch book argument is intended to show that a person is irrational (in terms of the bets one is willing to accept) if one's degrees of belief do not conform to the probability axioms, the "dynamic" version is intended to show that one is irrational (in terms of the bets one is willing to accept) if one's degrees of belief are not revised in conformation with *ROC* when new information is absorbed into one's system of beliefs. The key novel idea in the transition from the static Dutch book argument to the dynamic Dutch book argument is that of the *conditional bet*—a bet that is called off if a certain specified condition fails to obtain. Both the static and the dynamic Dutch book arguments are described in some detail in the appendix to this paper.

I would like to emphasize that, as noted above, the Dutch book kind of justification of *ROC* has occasioned some controversy, and other kinds of approaches have been developed. In any case, adequate foundations for the theory of subjective probability, and *ROC* in particular, are very significant philosophically, especially for the theory of confirmation (that is, induction, or inference), as elaborated below.

The core of the Bayesian analysis of confirmation is in two parts. First, as alluded to above, a piece of evidence e (for example a proposition reporting an observation) *confirms, is irrelevant to*, or *disconfirms* a hypothesis h according to whether $P(h/e)$ is greater than, equal to, or less than $P(h)$ (alternatively, according to whether $P(h/e)/P(h)$ is greater than, equal to, or less than 1). And second, the *degree to which e confirms h* is equal to $P(h/e)-P(h)$ (sometimes $P(h/e)/P(h)$ is used instead). This analysis is a natural application of the Bayesian thesis that learning a proposition should alter the rest of one's belief by way of conditionalization.

Two desirable features of this approach to confirmation can immediately be noted. First, it provides a precise explication not only of the qualitative notions of confirmation, disconfirmation and evidential irrelevance, but also of the quantitative notion of *degree* of confirmation. Second, and perhaps more importantly, confirmation and degree of confirmation will, on this analysis, depend on what background beliefs (prior subjective probability distribution) we happen to possess. To take a simple example, the observation of a large number of black ravens makes us more confident that *all* ravens are black, but the observation of a large number of wooden chairs does not increase our confidence in the hypothesis that all chairs are wooden; for we already have the background information that there are non-wooden chairs. In this example it is perhaps crystal clear just what the relevant background beliefs are, and how to formulate them. However, this is not always true. As Patrick Suppes puts it,

it is impossible to express in explicit form all the evidence relevant to even our simplest beliefs. There is no canonical set of elementary propositions to be approached as an ideal for expressing exactly what evidence supports a given belief, whether it be a belief about ravens, gods, electrons or patches of red. (1966, pp. 202–203)

Bayesian confirmation theory deals with this problem in a plausible way. As Charles Chihara has put it,

To take account of heterogenous information and evidence obtained from a variety of sources, all of differing degrees of reliability and relevance, as well as of intuitive hunches and even vague memories, the Bayesian theory provides us with a subjective "prior probability distribution," which functions as a sort of systematic summary of such items. (1981, p. 433)

We will see below how significant these two features of the Bayesian theory are when we look at some of the difficulties that confront other approaches to confirmation, and at how the Bayesian approach deals with them.

To support the Bayesian theory of confirmation, we can take a kind of "metatheoretical" philosophical perspective, applying philosophical ideas, mainly developed in the philosophy of science, about confirmation of *scientific theories* to the confirmation of *theories in general*, and to *the (philosophical) Bayesian theory of confirmation itself in particular*. To the extent that a theory implies and explains what is already known or believed about its subject matter, the theory is confirmed. And this should apply not only to scientific theories but also to philosophical theories about, for example, confirmation. Thus, the Bayesian theory will be confirmed if it is shown that it is able to explain and justify accepted forms of inductive inference. Also, a theory is confirmed if it has unexpected or unaccepted consequences that are borne out in the end. Thus, the Bayesian theory of confirmation should itself be judged confirmed if, on the basis of considerations inspired by the theory, some other accepted forms of inductive inference could be exposed as incorrect, rejected, and replaced by new, more acceptable ones that are implications of the Bayesian theory. Finally, it would be important and supportive of the theory if it could be shown that it can deal with some traditionally troublesome puzzles involving confirmation in a plausible way.

I think the Bayesian theory is supported in each of these three ways. Let us first see how the theory can justify some accepted forms of inductive inference. (See also Hesse 1974, especially pp. 133–62; and for criticisms of the approach see Glymour 1980, especially pp. 75–93; and for a traditional, non-Bayesian formulation and discussion of most of the conditions discussed below, see Hempel 1945.)

Entailment condition. This is one of the conditions stated by Hempel in his "Studies in the Logic of Confirmation" (1945): If e logically implies h, then e confirms h. Of course, the condition is completely plausible. Note that when e logically implies h, the probability of h conditional on e is 1, assuming that the unconditional probability of h is not 0. So, assuming also that $P(h) < 1$ (so that h is not already, initially, known for certain), we have:

$$P(h/e) = 1 > P(h),$$

so that e confirms h in the Bayesian sense.

Converse entailment condition. It is widely accepted, especially on the hypothetico-deductive model of scientific confirmation, that a theory or hypothesis is confirmed when deductive consequences of the theory or hypothesis are verified: If h logically implies e, then e confirms h. The Bayesian approach yields this condition, assuming just that $P(h) \neq 0$ (so that also $P(e) \neq 0$) and that $P(e) \neq 1$. We have:

$$P(h/e) > P(h)$$
if and only if
$$P(e/h)P(h)/P(e) > P(h) \quad \text{(by Bayes' theorem)}$$
if and only if
$$1/P(e) > 1 \quad \text{(since } P(e/h) = 1 \text{ and dividing by } P(h))$$
if and only if
$$P(e) < 1.$$

The assumption that $P(e) \neq (<) 1$ means, intuitively, that e is not *already* known, so that it is possible to learn it and for it actually to have an evidential impact on h. However, the biconditional displayed above has recently given rise to an influential objection to the Bayesian theory of confirmation: Clark Glymour's "Problem of Old Evidence," which will be briefly discussed below.

Initially unexpected evidence. It has often been suggested that given two deductive consequences e_1 and e_2 of a hypothesis or theory h, if e_1 is initially (before h is considered) more surprising (unexpected) than e_2 is, then the discovery of e_1 should confirm h more than would the discovery of e_2. Assume that $P(e_1) < P(e_2)$, and (as above) that $P(h) \neq 0$ and that neither of $P(e_1)$ and $P(e_2)$ is equal to 1. Then the condition in question follows from the Bayesian criterion for degree of confirmation:

$$P(h/e_1) - P(h) > P(h/e_2) - P(h)$$
if and only if
$$P(h/e_1) > P(h/e_2)$$
if and only if
$$P(e_1/h)P(h)/P(e_1) > P(e_2/h)P(h)/P(e_2) \quad \text{(by Bayes' theorem)}$$
if and only if
$$1/P(e_1) > 1/P(e_2) \quad \text{(since } P(e_1/h) = P(e_2/h) = 1, \text{ and by dividing by } P(h))$$
if and only if
$$P(e_2) > P(e_1).$$

A generalized version of another of Hempel's conditions, the *equivalence condition*, can also (as the reader may verify) easily be derived from the Bayesian criterion: If *e* confirms *h* and *h* is logically equivalent to *h'*, then *e* confirms *h* to exactly the same degree as *e* confirms *h'*. However, a stronger condition, also endorsed by Hempel (and which Hempel points out implies the equivalence condition), is not satisfied by the Bayesian criterion. It is the *special consequence condition*: If *e* confirms *h* and *h* logically implies *h'*, then *e* confirms *h'* as well. Initially, it may seem highly plausible that if *e* confirms *h* then *e* must also confirm anything else that *must* be true if *h* is true. But in fact, the special consequence condition is false—at least it cannot be true if converse entailment is true—which makes it a virtue of the Bayesian criterion that it fails to satisfy special consequence. To see that special consequence conflicts with converse entailment, consider a hypothesis *f&g* and evidence *f*. Then, by converse entailment, *f* confirms *f&g*. Since *f&g* logically implies *g*, *f* would confirm *g* if the special consequence condition were true. But *f* and *g* could be any propositions whatsoever. As Hesse describes this situation,

A relation of confirmation which allows any proposition to confirm any proposition is obviously trivial and unacceptable, for it contradicts the tacit condition that confirmation must be a selective relation among propositions. A paradox has arisen by taking together a set of adequacy conditions, all of which seem to be demanded by intuition; hence, it is appropriate to call it the *transitivity paradox*. (1974, p. 143)

My view is that the situation is not a paradox, for I do not think that the special consequence condition is "demanded by intuition." I would describe the situation as showing the unacceptability of the special consequence condition. To see more intuitively why special consequence should not be expected to hold in general, consider this schema of a situation where the Bayesian criterion violates the condition. Let *e*, *h*, and *h'* be such that:

(1)   *h* logically implies *h'*
(2) $P(h') = 0.8$
(3) $P(h) = 0.2$
(4) $P(e\&h) = 0.05$
(5) $P(e\&h') = 0.05$
(6) $P(e) = 0.1$

(To visualize the situation's probabilistic structure, the reader may want to draw a Venn diagram, with the region corresponding to *h* entirely within the region corresponding to *h'*, and with half of the region corresponding to *e* within that corresponding to *h* and the other half of *e*'s region outside the region corresponding to *h'*; see Eells 1982.) Here we have,

$$P(h/e) = 0.5 > P(h) = 0.2$$

and

$$P(h'/e) = 0.5 < P(h') = 0.8$$

So it is possible for evidence *e* to raise the probability of a hypothesis *h* while at the same time lowering the probability of a deductive consequence *h'* of *h*.

To make the example more concrete, consider a subscriber to a morning newspaper, and suppose the carrier is so unreliable that on only 0.8 of all days is the paper delivered, and that on only 0.25 of *these* days does the paper arrive before 6:00 A.M. Thus, let *h* be the hypothesis that the paper will arrive before 6:00 A.M. today, and let *h'* be the hypothesis that it will arrive today at all. Suppose that the carrier every day takes a different route through the area for which he is responsible, that the subscriber knows this, and that the subscriber somehow, very early in the morning, comes into possession of the following evidence e: There is a paper shortage for today's morning edition, so that only about half the required number of newspapers could be printed. It might reasonably be inferred from e that the carrier will have a lighter load, with fewer papers to deliver, so that he will surely deliver all the papers he has—about half the usual number—by 6:00 A.M. Given e, then, it may be reasonable for the subscriber to infer that she will get her paper before 6:00 A.M. if she gets it at all. Thus, if the subscriber's subjective probabilities conform to the frequencies and reasonable inferences described above, we have: $P(h'/e) = P(h/e) =$ about 0.5. Plausibly, for the subscriber, e confirms h and e disconfirms h'.

Before leaving the topic of the special consequence condition, it is worthwhile pointing out that the Bayesian criterion focusses, as it should, on the comparison of the probability of a hypothesis after evidence with the probability of the hypothesis before the evidence; it does not invoke, as it should not, any comparison of the posterior probability with any other number. As Hesse (1974, p. 147) points out, if we use instead what she calls a "k-criterion," according to which e confirms h if and only if $P(h/e) > k > 0.5$ for some "appropriately" chosen k, then the special consequence condition would be satisfied. But, on a k-criterion, an e can confirm an h even if the result of learning e is that the probability of h is thereby decreased. And this seems contrary to an intuitive conception of confirmation which seems closely connected with the idea of rational change (in direction) of confidence. (Also, note that the converse consequence condition is not satisfied by k-criteria.)

As to diagnosing the "paradox of transitivity," it perhaps suffices to say that, when a hypothesis h logically implies a hypothesis h', then the probability of h' is at least as high as that of h, so that it is possible that a piece of evidence e can bring these two probabilities closer together, make them equal, or even reverse the inequality: e can make it "harder" for h' to be true while at the same time making it "easier" for h to be true. This, of course, speaks against only the special consequence condition, and not converse consequence, or the Bayesian criterion of confirmation.

Positive instance criterion. It is plausible, at least in a wide variety of cases, that a hypothesis that is of the logical form of a universalized conditional is confirmed by positive instances of the conditional. That is, a hypothesis of the form *All F's are G's* is confirmed by *Fa&Ga*, *Fb&Gb*, and so on. For example, the hypothesis that all emeralds are green is confirmed by the observations (or sentences reporting the observations) of objects that are emeralds and green. However, there are cases—Hempel's (1945) famous "paradoxes of confirmation," as well as other kinds of cases—where this principle seems to give the wrong answer. The Bayesian criterion of confirmation can help us see just where, and why, the principle seems to (or does) give the wrong answer; and in terms of the Bayesian criterion, we can formulate and motivate a different, more plausible version of the positive instance criterion.

Let h be the hypothesis that *All F's are G's*, and let e be a report of a positive instance of h, so that e is of the form *Fa&Ga*. Then, according to the Bayesian criterion, e confirms h if and only if:

$$P(h/Fa\&Ga) > P(h)$$

that is, if and only if:

$$P(Fa\&Ga/h)P(h)/P(Fa\&Ga) > P(h) \quad \text{(applying Bayes' theorem),}$$

that is, if and only if:

$$P(Fa/h)P(Ga/Fa\&h)/P(Fa\&Ga) > 1 \quad \text{(dividing by } P(h) \text{ and applying the multiplication rule for probability),}$$

that is, if and only if:

$$P(Fa/h)/P(Fa\&Ga) > 1 \quad \text{(since } Fa\&h \text{ logically implies } Ga).$$

Now, let's assume that Fa and h are probabilistically independent (so that $P(Fa/h) = P(Fa)$). Then, we have that e confirms h if and only if:

$$P(Fa)/P(Fa)P(Ga/Fa) > 1 \quad \text{(applying our assumption, and the multiplication rule for probability to the denominator),}$$

that is, if and only if:

$$P(Ga/Fa) < 1,$$

that is, if and only if one was not already certain that, given that something is an F, it is a G.

Thus, the Bayesian criterion of confirmation yields a restricted version of the positive instance criterion, namely: Provided that (1) Fa is probabilistically independent of h (*All F's are G's*) and that (2) $P(Ga/Fa) < 1$, then $Fa\&Ga$ confirms h. For later reference, note that the degree to which $Fa\&Ga$ confirms h equals

$$P(h)[(1/P(Ga/Fa)) - 1]$$

so that the higher $P(Ga/Fa)$ is, the lower the degree of confirmation.

Is the original, "unrestricted," positive instance criterion true? Or is only a restricted version such as the one just described true? I. J. Good (1967) has made a convincing case that the answer to the first question is "No." Significantly, the examples on which his case is based are ones in which restriction (1) of the Bayesian version of the positive instance criterion is violated. Consider this probabilistically explicit example, based on one given by Chihara (1981), which in turn was inspired by an example of Good's. There are two urns, each containing 100 marbles. Urn I contains 50 glass black marbles and 50 glass white marbles; urn II contains 5 glass black marbles and 95 plastic white marbles. Suppose you know this and suppose that one of the two urns is before you, which one it is you don't know. Now consider the hypothesis, "All the glass marbles in the urn before you are black." You are allowed to reach in and (randomly) pick one marble. It turns out to be glass and black. Your evidence, e, then, is $Ga\&Ba$. This evidence, e, is (or describes) a positive instance of the hypothesis, h, that *All the glass marbles in this urn are black marbles*. Intuitively, given the background information that you have, though, e should actually disconfirm h. Supposing that your initial subjective probability for "*Urn I is before me*" = your initial subjective probability for "*Urn II is before me*" = 0.5 (=P(h)), then $P(h/e) = 1/11 < 1/2 = P(h)$, and $P(h/e) - P(h) = -9/22$. Also note that h is not probabilistically independent of Ga, violating restriction (1) of the Bayesian version of the positive instance criterion.

We have seen that the simple Bayesian criterion of confirmation implies and constitutes a justification of the entailment condition, the converse entailment condition, the maxim of initially unexpected evidence, and the equivalence condition. On considerations inspired by the Bayesian criterion, we saw that the special consequence condition is not valid generally. And we have seen that altering the positive instance criterion in a way that makes it a consequence of the Bayesian criterion makes it immune to one kind of counterexample. All this supports the Bayesian approach to the theory of confirmation.

The approach becomes even more creditable when it is seen that it can resolve some well-known paradoxes and puzzles of confirmation. I think the Bayesian criterion offers natural and promising approaches both to the famous "raven paradox" of Hempel's (1945) as well as to Nelson Goodman's (1955) famous "grue puzzle." Below, I describe a Bayesian approach to the raven paradox; Bayesian approaches to the grue puzzle are similar in character, and for this I refer the reader to Chihara (1981) and Eells (1982).

The raven paradox is based on the positive instance criterion (either the traditional or the weaker Bayesian version) and the equivalence condition. Consider the following two logically equivalent hypotheses:

h_1: All ravens (R) are black (B)
h_2: All non-black ($-B$) things are non-ravens ($-R$),

and the following piece of evidence:

e: $-Ba\&-Ra$.

(Here, "$-$" stands for "negation," or "not," or "non-.") Plausibly, h_2 is probabilistically independent of $-Ba$, so, since e is a positive instance of h_2, e confirms h_2. Since h_1 is logically equivalent to h_2, it follows, by the equivalence condition, that e also confirms h_1. But it has been thought to be paradoxical that non-black non-ravens, such as white shoes, can confirm the hypothesis that all ravens are black.

As mentioned above, the idea of *degrees* of confirmation is a significant feature of the Bayesian theory of confirmation, and, in fact, it is central to the Bayesian resolution of the raven paradox. We will see that, plausibly, e indeed confirms h_1, but to a degree that is *negligible compared to the degree to which a piece of evidence of the form*

e': $Rb\&Bb$

confirms h_1 (and thus also h_2). Using the formula used just above, we see that the degree to which e confirms h_1 is

$$P(h_1)[(1/P(-Ra/-Ba)) - 1],$$

and the degree to which e' confirms h' is

$$P(h_1)[(1/P(Ba/Ra)) - 1].$$

Given our background information, which is supposed to be systematically summarized in the probability distribution P, the value $P(-Ra/-Ba)$ should be very close to 1—it's intuitively very unlikely that a randomly chosen non-black thing should be a raven. Thus, the degree to which e confirms h_1 should be practically 0. However, the probability that a randomly chosen raven would be black may be quite a bit smaller than 1—especially if one is initially uncertain about the truth of the hypothesis h_1 (equivalently, of course, h_2). Thus, assuming, reasonably enough it seems, that $P(-Ra/-Ba)$ is very close to 1 and that $P(Ba/Ra)$ is not, the degree to which e' confirms the hypothesis is quite high compared to the degree to which e does.

It should be noted that the above is just the gist of a Bayesian approach to the raven paradox, and that this approach to the paradox is controversial. For criticisms of this kind of approach, see, for example, Hempel (1945, pp. 20–21), Scheffler (1963, pp. 284–85), and Black (1966, 195–97); and for other formulations of the approach, see, for example, Hosiasson-Lindenbaum (1940), Pears (1950), Alexander (1958), Mackie (1963), Suppes (1966), Swinburne (1973, pp. 156–71), Hesse (1974, pp. 155–62), and Chihara (1981).

I have emphasized the advantages and versatility of the probabilistic, Bayesian approach to the theory of confirmation. It is only fair at least to mention what is probably the most important and influential recent objection to the approach, the "problem of old evidence." Clark Glymour

(1980) has pointed out that if $P(e) = 1$, then e cannot, in the Bayesian sense, confirm any hypothesis or theory, for if $P(e) = 1$, then for any h, $P(h/e) = P(h)$. However, Glymour argues, plausibly (in fact from historical examples), that facts long known to be true can be evidence for new hypotheses and theories. This can happen, for example, when a new hypothesis or theory explains in a plausible way a previously known but puzzling fact. Other philosophers have argued that when this happens, it is not the previously known fact itself that presently confirms the new hypothesis or theory, but it is rather a newly discovered logical or explanatory relation between the "old evidence" and the new hypothesis or theory that provides the confirmation. I find this latter approach quite plausible (and it is, in fact, a defense of the Bayesian confirmation theory), but it is beyond the scope of the present essay to explore the issues in any detail.[6]

As already mentioned, many of the issues remain controversial, but I have tried to convey in a general way how the idea of subjective probability provides a model showing how, in the form of Bayesian confirmation theory, probability can be the "very guide for life" at least in the area of rational *inference*. In the next section, we will look briefly at some of the outlines of Bayesian *decision* theory, including the relation between decision in general and inference (sometimes, in some contexts, called "theory choice") in particular, as well as at some of the controversies attending the theory and versions of it.

III. BAYESIAN DECISION THEORY

According to formal models of decision theory, rational deliberation is the process of envisaging the possible consequences of possible courses of action in a decision problem and *then* evaluating the merits of the possible courses of action in terms of the envisaged possible consequences of the possible actions. *First*, one must frame a decision problem in terms of what the possible *courses of action* are and what the possible *consequences* (or *outcomes*) of the actions are, where this may also include a consideration of the possible *states of nature* that either determine or probabilistically influence how the possible actions may give rise to the various possible outcomes.

Typically, *outcomes* are thought of as situations whose descriptions include everything the agent considers relevant to his or her well-being, or whatever else the agent cares about, *acts* (or the possible courses of action available) are usually characterized as the various ways things might be that are within the influence of the agent to control (or decide), and *states* (or "states of nature") are, as mentioned above, those factors that filter (determine or influence) the effect of the acts on which outcome is received. The formulation of the decision problem in terms of acts, outcomes, and states is just the *first* step of the process of deliberation.

Second, there is the problem of how to evaluate the various possible actions, in terms of the possible outcomes and the possible states that determine the effect of the acts on the outcomes. On Bayesian models of rational decision, this second part of the problem is understood as the problem of describing the correct kind of *expected utility* model for evaluating the available acts. It is assumed that the agent (decision-maker) has a subjective probability assignment P (our "very guide for life," in this case decision-making in general) and a desirability (or utility) assignment D. The subjective probability assignment attaches probabilities to states, outcomes, outcomes conditional on the various states, outcomes conditional on the various combinations of states and acts, and so on. The desirability assignment attaches numerical values to the possible outcomes of a decision problem. Then the expected utility of an act is calculated in terms of these assignments P and D.

It should be noted that, in the realm of "professional academic theory of decision," it is a not a trivial assumption (though a proposition that Bayesians argue is plausible) that an agent actually does have, to work with, a subjective probability assignment and the right kind ("interval" *versus* merely "ordinal") of desirability assignment (to put it roughly, *ordinal* desirability, or utility, assignments only represent *qualitative preferences*, while *interval* desirability, or utility, assignments represent *that as well as "intensity" of preference*.) I have tried to make this Bayesian proposition, at least for probabilities, plausible above. Other kinds of principles of decision-making have been proposed for situations in which this proposition may fail in one way or another.[7]

Before considering in detail several expected utility models, it is worth emphasizing that, on the general Bayesian model, P and D are the agent's *subjective assessments* of probabilities and desirabilities, where the actual (true or objective) probabilities and goodnesses of the relevant items (states and outcomes) are deemed irrelevant to rationality of action eventually taken: how true, reasonable, or otherwise objectively or morally sound these assessments are is regarded as a separate question. This has already been emphasized above in connection with subjective probability, especially in the context of rational inference. In the context of rational decision, we may put the point as follows: rationality is a *relation* between an agent's beliefs (subjective probabilities), desires (desirability assignment), and the preferences or choices among acts that result from the given beliefs and desires. The rationality of an act cannot be judged independently of the beliefs and desires that the agent happens to "have to work with."

Now, let $A_1, A_2, \ldots, A_n$ stand for the possible courses of action in a decision problem. For example, n may be 2, and A_1 and A_2 may be, respectively, the acts of bringing or not bringing an umbrella to work this morning. Let $S_1, S_2, \ldots, S_m$ stand for the various possible states of nature the agent deems relevant to the decision problem. For example, m may be 2, and S_1 and S_2 may be, respectively, the states of its turning out to rain today and its not turning out to rain today. And let $O_1, O_2, \ldots, O_r$ stand for the possible outcomes that the agent considers. To continue with the example, it may be that r is 4 and the possible outcomes envisioned by the agent are, corresponding to $O_1, O_2, O_3,$ and O_4 respectively: it rains but at least the agent has an umbrella, it doesn't rain and the agent is stuck carrying an umbrella, it rains and the agent is stuck without the protection of an umbrella, and it fails to rain and the agent is free from having to carry around an umbrella. As an example of a probability assignment, we may have (to specify it just partially): $P(S_1) = 0.2$ and $P(S_2) = 0.8$. And as an example of a desirability assignment, we may have: $D(O_1) = 2$, $D(O_2) = 3$, $D(O_3) = 1$, and $D(O_4) = 4$, where, of course, the higher the desirability value, the higher the desirability of the outcome.

Now that we have convenient symbols for all the five basic components of the formulation and evaluation of a decision problem (that is, acts, states, outcomes, a subjective probability assignment, and a subjective desirability assignment), we can formulate some expected utility conceptions. Maybe the simplest of such conceptions makes the assumption that outcomes are determined uniquely by an act and a state: given a particular act and a particular state, there is just one possible outcome (see, for example, Savage 1954, where acts are functions from states to outcomes). In this case, the notation for outcomes need not enter into the formula for expected utility, for each outcome corresponds uniquely the conjunction of an act and a state, and the desirabilities of outcomes can be succinctly summarized using a what is called a *utility* (or *desirability*) *matrix*, with rows corresponding to acts and columns to states. Then one conception of expected utility sets

(1) $EU(A_i) = SUM_j \, P(S_j)D(A_i \& S_j).$

The assumption that outcomes can be thought of as conjunctions of acts and states is plausible in the example described above, and we may calculate:

$$EU(A_1) = (0.2)(2) + (0.8)(3) = 2.8,$$

and

$$EU(A_2) = (0.2)(1) + (0.8)(4) = 3.4,$$

in which case the expected utility maximization rule prescribes leaving the umbrella at home.

In general, however, it is plausible that an act together with a state may give rise to different possible outcomes, with different probabilities. In this case, we should perhaps adopt an expected utility formula such as:

(2) $EU(A_i) = SUM_{j,k} \, P(S_j)P(O_k/A_i \& S_j)D(O_k).$

On the other hand, it's been suggested that the states be thought of as the form "if A_i, then O_k," in which case an act and a state do determine a unique outcome (see, for example, Jeffrey 1977, and Eells 1982, pp. 75–77, for further references).

Another twist that can arise involves the possibility that an agent's acts can influence which state of nature comes about. Although this is not plausible in the example described above, this possibility can arise in other examples. Suppose, for example, that one is trying to decide whether or not to study for an exam; the possible states may be "prepared for the exam" and "not prepared for the exam," and the possible outcomes may involve such possible eventualities as passing or not passing the exam, passing or not passing the course, graduating or not graduating, and so on. In such cases, it seems that it would be more appropriate to use an expectation rule such as one of the following:

(3) $EU(A_i) = SUM_j \, P(S_j/A_i)D(A_i \& S_j),$

or

(4) $EU(A_i) = SUM_{j,k} \, P(S_j/A_i)P(O_k/A_i \& S_j)D(O_k).$

These kinds of expected utility are often called *conditional* expected utilities, since the probabilities of the states enter into the formulas *conditional* on the act under evaluation. This idea was formulated and developed in detail by Richard Jeffrey (1965, 1983b).

There is yet a final twist that should be briefly mentioned in this brief description of Bayesian decision theory. Although the conditional expected utility idea accommodates in a plausible way the fact that acts can influence states, it has been argued that the expected utility maximization principle that is based on it (namely, choose the act that has maximum conditional expected utility) will give the wrong answer in cases in which *states can influence the acts but not vice versa*. If acts *provide evidence for* states *without being causally relevant to* the states (which can be true if the states are causal factors influencing acts but not *vice versa*), then the way in which conditional probabilities enter into the above two formulas can give a wrong evaluation. (Of course, what is relevant here is the agent's causal *beliefs* and the evidential relations embodied in the agent's conditional probabilities.) The point has been formulated as follows: a rational decision-maker should choose the act that he or she thinks would tend to *cause*, and not just provide *evidence* for, the good possible outcomes. This kind of possibility was first urged in Robert Nozick's influential paper (1969), in the form of a decision situation known as Newcomb's paradox.

One way of revising the expected utility formula to take account of this kind of possibility was urged by Brian Skyrms (1980); his formula (called "K-expectation") is:

(5) $EU(A_i) = SUM_{j,k}\, P(K_j)P(C_k/A_i\&K_j)D(C_j\&S_k\&A_i),$

where the K_j's are the states that are outside the influence of the agent's act and the C_k's are states that the agent's act can influence. The idea of maximizing conditional expected utility is sometimes called *evidential decision theory*, while Skyrms' and other proposals designed to handle the kind of case raised by Nozick are called *causal decision theories*, since they in one way or another introduce causal ideas into decision theory. The issues are subtle and cannot be described in detail here; for more on these issues, see, for example, as well as the references cited above, Gibbard and Harper (1978) and Eells (1982), as well as the references cited there.

Although it is controversial which, if any, of the proposed expected utility maximization theories is true, either descriptively or prescriptively, it is generally agreed that the basic idea is at least approximately correct, in at least a wide range of cases. If so, we can view an agent's observed preferences and choices as empirical evidence for what the individual's subjective probabilities and desirabilities are; and, thus, it has been suggested that these observed preferences and choices can give concrete meaning to the attribution of more or less particular subjective probabilities and desirabilities to the individual, thus, in particular, providing some kind of "foundations" to the theory of subjective probability. (See Eells 1982 for some details, further discussion, and references.)

In conclusion, it is worth describing, if only briefly, a way in which the theories of inference and decision have been intertwined. On the Bayesian theory of inference described in the previous section, rational agents need not actually *accept* a hypothesis, but rather only assign subjective probabilities to them and adjust these degrees of confidence as evidence comes in (although, of course, in the limiting case of the subjective probability of a hypothesis becoming unity, it makes sense to say that the agent has accepted the hypothesis); this kind of view has been urged by Jeffrey (1956). On the other hand, according to another conception of inductive inference, we should at least in some cases be prepared to *accept* a hypothesis, even if its subjective probability is less than 1. Hempel (1960) outlines an analysis of rational acceptance on which the acceptance of a given hypothesis is interpreted decision theoretically as one among several available courses of action, as described below.

Suppose an agent, perhaps a scientist, is presented with n mutually exclusive and collectively exhaustive hypotheses h_i, and that he must choose among the following $n+1$ courses of action:

A_1: accept h_1 and add it to the body of accepted knowledge;
A_2: accept h_2 and add it to the body of accepted knowledge;
•
•
•
A_n: accept h_n and add it to the body of accepted knowledge;
A_{n+1}: accept none of the h_i's (and leave the body of accepted knowledge the same).

The possible outcomes are:

O_1: enlarge the body of accepted knowledge by adding h_1, where h_1 is true;
O_2: enlarge the body of accepted knowledge by adding h_1, where h_1 is false;
•
•
•
O_{2n-1}: enlarge the body of accepted knowledge by adding h_n, where h_n is true;
O_{2n}: enlarge the body of accepted knowledge by adding h_n, where h_n is false.

Then Hempel considers the following rule of acceptance: Choose the act A_i that has the highest expected utility, that is, the highest value of the form

$$EU(A_i) = SUM_j\ P(O_j/A_i)D(O_j\&A_i).$$

Of course, application of this rule requires specification of the relevant conditional subjective probabilities and the relevant subjective desirabilities. Presumably, the conditional subjective probabilities $P(O_j/A_i)$ should correspond to the unconditional subjective probabilities of the relevant hypotheses $P(h_k)$ in the obviously natural way (which I will not formulate here). What has been more controversial, however, is what kinds of considerations should enter into the evaluation of the desirabilities $D(O_j\&A_i)$—in particular, of course, when O_j and A_i pertain to the same hypothesis h_i (that is, where j is equal to either $2i-1$ or to $2i$), or when the outcome and act both involve rejection of all the hypotheses. Some (for example, Churchman 1948, 1956; Braithwaite 1953; Rudner 1953) have argued that certain sorts of practical and ethical judgments should enter into the evaluations of these desirabilities, while others have argued that only "purely epistemic" considerations (such as truth, comprehensive truth, nothing but the truth, simplicity in describing the truth, and so on) should be relevant here (see, for example, Hempel 1960 and Levi 1961). Given the latter view, we may, following Hempel (1960), call the relevant desirabilities in the formula above "epistemic utilities." And, as noted above, there are those (for example, Jeffrey 1956) who reject altogether the idea of acceptance in the first place. The issues are too subtle to discuss in detail here, and the interested reader is directed to the references cited above, as well as Eells (1982) for further discussion and references.

There are various senses in which probability may be said to be "the very guide for life," having to do with rational inference, rational decision in general, and rational acceptance of hypotheses in particular, where the various theories and concepts that arise in these connections are not unrelated. I have attempted here to provide an introduction to the general Bayesian perspective on these issues, as well as to direct the reader to further relevant readings.

APPENDIX

Since Dutch book style justifications of the idea that one's degrees of belief should be probabilistic (conform to the probability axioms), and of the idea that one should revise one's degrees of belief in conformity with ROC, are so central to many Bayesian philosophers' conceptions of rational belief, and of rational inference, it may be useful to describe in some detail some parts and aspects of these arguments. First, there is the thesis that a rational person's degree of belief in a proposition should equal his or her *betting quotient* for the proposition. The person's betting quotient for a proposition X can be characterized in terms of the monetary value that the person places on a *gamble* on X. A gamble, $<0,X,d>$ on X is a commodity, the owner of which receives \$0 if X turns out to be false and \$$d$ if X turns out to be true. For simplicity of notation in most of what follows, let $<X>$ denote the gamble on X in which $d = 1$. Then the thesis is that a rational person's degree of belief in (subjective probability of) X is a if and only if the person values $<X>$ at \$$a$. That is, the person's subjective probability of X is a if and only if the person is indifferent between having \$$a$ and having $<X>$: the person would be willing to buy the commodity $<X>$ for \$$a$ and the person would be willing to sell (or "guarantee") the commodity $<X>$ for \$$a$. In case of gambles in which $d \neq 1$ are involved, where \$$a$ is the dollar amount at which the person values $<O,X,d>$, then the assessment of the rational person's subjective probability has to be "scaled": perhaps most straightforwardly (but see note below) such that the person's subjective probability for X, $P(X)$, $= a/d$.

The idea, of course, is just this: the more confident in X you are, the more likely you should think you'll get the \$1 (or \$$d$) if you own $<X>$ (or $<0,X,d>$), so the more you will be willing to pay for $<X>$ (or $<0,X,d>$); also, the more confident in X you are, the more likely you should think you'll have to pay out \$1 (or \$$d$) if you're sold $<X>$ (or $<0,X,d>$), so the more you'll demand if you're selling $<X>$ (or $<0,X,d>$). Consider, for example, the case in which you're fully confident in the *truth* of X (where the thesis says you should value $<X>$ at \$1 and $<0,X,d>$ at \$$d$), the case in which you are fully confident in the *falsity* of X (where the thesis says you should value each of $<X>$ and $<0,X,d>$ at \$0), and the case in which you think it's a "50–50 *toss-up*" between the truth and falsity of X (where the thesis says you should value $<X>$ and $<0,X,d>$ at \$0.5 and \$$(0.5)d$, respectively).[8]

Turning first to the static Dutch book argument, there is the mathematical result that, if a person values gambles on a *sufficiently wide domain of propositions*, and if the person's values for the gambles are *not probabilistic* (do not obey the probability axioms), then a sufficiently clever "betting opponent" can buy and sell gambles from the person in such a way that the person is *guaranteed a positive loss* (and the clever betting opponent guaranteed a positive win). (Of course, it is assumed that the person makes his or her betting quotients known to the clever betting opponent.) Such a series of transactions is called a "Dutch book" against the person. I'll illustrate this with the *additivity* axiom, which states that if X and Y are logically mutually exclusive propositions, then $P(X \vee Y) = P(X) + P(Y)$.[9] Let $Q(X)$ denote the person's betting quotient for X, for any proposition X. Then, the thesis described above can be formulated as follows: for all propositions X, $P(X) = Q(X)$, if the person is rational and P is the person's subjective probability assignment.

Suppose the person's betting quotients (values for gambles) violate the additivity axiom. For example, suppose that $Q(X \vee Y) > Q(X) + Q(Y)$. (In case it's $<$, rather than $>$, then, as explained below, the proof of the mathematical result is parallel.) Then I would buy from the person $<X>$ and $<Y>$ for a total of \$$Q(X)$ + \$$Q(Y)$, and I would sell to the person $<X \vee Y>$ for \$$Q(X \vee Y)$. Note that before we settle the payoffs, I'm ahead, because of the way the person's betting quotients have violated additivity. Now consider the various possibilities for the truth values of X and Y. Since they can't both be true, by the hypothesis that X and Y are mutually exclusive, the three possibilities are: (1) X true and Y false, (2) X false and Y true, and (3) both X and Y false. In case (1), I win (the person loses) \$1 due to the $<X>$ transaction, and I lose (the person wins) \$1 due to the $<X \vee Y>$ transaction: that's a wash, and since I was ahead (the person was behind) after the three transactions, I remain ahead (and the person behind). Case (2) is completely parallel. In case (3), I come out ahead (the person behind) not only by the initial difference of \$$Q(X \vee Y)$ − \$$Q(X)$ − \$$Q(Y)$, but by an additional \$2, since I get an additional \$1 from the person for each of $<X>$ and $<Y>$, and the person collects nothing from me as a result of my having sold him or her $<X \vee Y>$.

In case the violation of additivity goes the other way (that is, \$$Q(X \vee Y) < $$Q(X) + $$Q(Y)$), then I simply reverse the transactions, selling $<X>$ and $<Y>$ and buying $<X \vee Y>$ at the person's appraised values. As Skyrms (1975, 1986) has pointed out, owning the commodity $<X \vee Y>$ is equivalent to owning both of $<X>$ and $<Y>$, so that a violation of additivity by a person's betting quotients is the same as evaluating the same thing in different ways when they are just *described differently*. Violations of the other axioms ($P(X) > 0$ for all X, and $P(X) = 1$ of X can't be false) lead to Dutch books (series of transactions in which the person is guaranteed a loss) *via* other kinds of transactions. If it's agreed, first, that a rational person's betting quotients (valuations of gambles) numerically equal the person's subjective probabilities, and, second, that it is irrational to "leave oneself open to" a Dutch book, then it follows that a rational person's degrees of belief must be probabilistic (obey the probability axioms).

Turning now to the dynamic Dutch book argument, the idea of a conditional gamble is central. The conditional gamble $<X/Y>$ is the same as the unconditional gamble $<X>$ in case Y turns out to be true; and if Y turns out to be false, then the gamble is "called off" in the sense that all transactions conducted to obtain or sell $<X/Y>$ are undone: any purchase or sales costs are returned to the purchaser or to the seller, respectively. Recall that *ROC* says that when one learns some proposition Y to be true, then one's new degrees of belief in propositions X should equal the person's old degrees of belief in X conditional on Y. Again, this can be expressed as follows: $P_n(X) = P_o(X/Y)$, where, again, P_n stands for one's new subjective probabilities (that is, *after* Y is learned) and P_o stands for one's old degrees of belief (that is, *before* Y is learned). Now let Q_o stand for one's old (or current) betting quotients (that is, before the truth value of Y has become known), and let Q_n stand for the betting quotients one at the earlier time (or currently) *plans* to adopt at the later time *if it becomes known that Y is true* (where, as always, both in the case of P and in the case of Q, the only difference between what the person knows at the earlier time and the later time is Y). Thus, it is assumed that one at the earlier time already has a *strategy* for revising betting quotients in the event that Y becomes known (where coming to know Y is the only difference in what the person knows, across the "earlier" and the "later" times).

The mathematical result for the dynamic Dutch book argument, paralleling that for the static argument is this: if, for some X and Y, $Q_n(X) \neq Q_o(X/Y)$ (where $Q_o(X/Y)$, a "conditional betting quotient," $= Q_o(X\&Y)/Q_o(Y)$, thus defined analogously to conditional probability), then a clever betting opponent can make a series of transactions with the person, involving conditional gambles at the earlier time and possibly unconditional gambles at the later time, such that the person is guaranteed a positive loss (and the betting opponent a positive win). (Of course, it is assumed that the person's conditional and unconditional betting quotients are known to the clever betting opponent.) Such a series of transactions can be called a *dynamic* Dutch book. Analogous to the static Dutch book argument, if we assume (1) both (1a) that rational subjective probabilities are numerically equal to one's betting quotients (that is, $P = Q$) and (1b) that one's belief change strategy is numerically the same as one's betting quotient change strategy (that is, $P_n = Q_n$), and (2) that it is irrational to leave oneself open to a dynamic Dutch book, then it follows that the only rational belief change strategy is *ROC*.

Suppose that a person's betting quotients (and planned ones) violate the betting quotient analogue of *ROC* (that is, *ROC* with "Q" substituted for "P"). Suppose, for example, that $Q_o(X/Y) < Q_n(X)$, where, of course, Y is the conditioning proposition the contemplation of whose truth determines the strategy to revise Q_o to Q_n in case Y comes to be known to be true. (If it is $>$ rather than $<$, then, as explained below, the proof of the mathematical result is parallel.) In this case, I would, *at the earlier time* ("o"), buy from the person the conditional gamble $<X/Y>$ for $Q_o(X/Y)$, and I would, *at the later time* ("n"), sell to him or her the *then* *un*conditional (assuming the "condition" Y turns out to be true) gamble $<X>$ for $Q_n(X)$ (to all of which, by hypothesis, the person is agreeable). At this point I should emphasize two things: *first*, my sale, at the later time, of what I called the "*then* unconditional gamble $<X>$ for $Q_n(X)$" would only be made if in fact the condition (Y) were met (in fact, if Y turned out to be false, the person may not at the later time even value $<X>$ at $Q_n(X)$, the value we have stipulated he would attach to $<X>$ if just Y were learned); and *second*, I should note that what I have said I would do at the earlier time is not *all* I would do at the earlier time (there is a small twist that will easily be handled below).

Let us *first* assume that Y turns out to be *true*. Note that, in this case, at the later time, after Y becomes known true but before the truth value of X is determined, I am ahead, by $\$Q_n(X) - Q_o(X/Y)$. If X turns out to be true, I *win* $\$1$ from the person from having bought from him or her, at the earlier time, the conditional gamble $<X/Y>$, and I *lose* to the person the same amount, $\$1$, from having sold to him or her, at the later time, the unconditional gamble $<X>$. Thus, the final result is that I win (and the person loses) $\$Q_n(X) - \$Q_o(X/Y) + \$1 - \$1, > 0$. On the other hand, if, after the "later" time when Y turns out to be true, X then turns out to be false, then I neither win nor lose anything (further) on having bought $<X/Y>$ at the earlier time or on having sold $<X>$ at the later time (no payoffs have to be made, or "guarantees" satisfied): again, the final result is that I win (and the person loses) the same positive amount, $\$Q_n(X) - \$Q_o(X/Y)$. Thus, as long as Y turns out to be true, the way the person has violated the betting quotient version of *ROC* means that the specified series of transactions guarantees me a positive gain (and the other a positive loss). I note that if the inequality between $Q_n(X)$ and $Q_o(X/Y)$ were reversed, then I would simply reverse the transactions, my selling $<X/Y>$ for $\$Q_o(X/Y)$ at the earlier time and buying $<X>$ for $\$Q_n(X)$ at the later time.

Let us *now* assume that Y turns out to be *false*. In this case, the first of the two transactions described above (my buying $<X/Y>$ for $\$Q_o(X/Y)$) is undone, and all money transferred on this transaction is refunded (by the above definition of conditional gambles). So all that we may seem to have left is the outcome of my sale of the unconditional gamble $<X>$ for $\$Q_n(X)$ *at the later time*—however, as mentioned above, this transaction in this case will not be conducted. The condition, Y, has not been met in this case, so I will not in this case sell, at the later time, $<X>$ for $\$Q_n(X)$ (to which dollar amount the person may not have "revised" his or her betting quotient for X anyway, since Y has turned out not to be true). Thus, *given just the transactions described above*, if Y turns out to be false, no one wins and no one loses. Now is the time to describe the "small twist" mentioned above.

We have seen that if Y is *true*, then my winnings are $\$Q_n(X) - \$Q_o(X/Y)$ (>0). Let $e = Q_n(X) - Q_o(X/Y)$. Then, to guarantee a win for me against the person, whether or not Y turns out to be true, I simply make a "small side bet" *against* Y: as an example, I may, in addition to the above transactions, also, at the "earlier" time, sell to the person the gamble $<0,Y,e>$ for his or her then "fair price" of $\$Q_o(Y)e$. Now, if Y turns out to be true, then my winnings, and the person's losses are $\$e - \$e + \$Q_o(Y)e = \$Q_o(Y)e > 0$. (The first "$\$e$" in the expression just above comes from my winnings on the gambles described earlier, since Y has turned out to be true in this case; the second, subtracted, "$\$e$" comes from my loss in "guaranteeing" the $<0,Y,e>$ that I sold, and the final term, "$\$Q_o(Y)e$," represents what I get from selling $<0,Y,e>$ to the person for the indicated amount.) And if Y turns out to be false, then my winnings, and the person's losses, are $\$0 + \$0 + \$Q_o(Y)e = \$Q_o(Y)e > 0$. (The first "$\$0$" represents all the gambles described earlier being "called off," in this case of the falsity of Y, as explained above; the second "$\$0$" represents my not having to pay off on my "guarantee" after selling $<0,Y,e>$, since Y has turned out to be false; and the final term, "$\$Q_o(Y)e$," represents what I get from selling $<0,Y,e>$ to the person for the indicated amount.) Of course, other positive amounts of gain for myself (or a "clever betting opponent"), and loss to "the person" who violates the betting quotient version of *ROC*, can be guaranteed by setting different "stakes" d for the conditional, possible unconditional, and small side, bets (or gambles).

NOTES

* This essay is intended to be an introduction to subjective probabilistic, Bayesian perspectives on the theories of probability, inference, and decision. For more details on the ideas discussed here, see the references cited. I thank James H. Fetzer for helpful comments on an earlier draft.

1. The sections that follow are based on, and contain excerpts from, chapters 1 and 2 of my (1982).
2. For discussion of other attempted justifications, see Eells (1982) and references cited therein.
3. For discussion of the psychological literature on the rule of conditionalization (that is, on its descriptive adequacy), see my (1982) and references cited therein.
4. That is, a collection of hypotheses such that, by logic, exactly one of them could be true.
5. For more details and other approaches, and for discussion of controversies surrounding the Dutch book approach, see Eells (1982) and the references cited there.
6. In this connection, I refer the reader to Glymour (1980), Garber (1983), Jeffrey (1983a), Skyrms (1983), and Eells (1985) and (1990).
7. See James H. Fetzer's companion volume to this volume for a couple of samples of such principles of decisions for such "impoverished" decision-makers. See also Resnik (1987), and the references therein, for other such principles and for an introduction to decision theory in general.
8. It should be noted that this thesis has occasioned some controversy. First, it has been noted that the choice of $d = 1$ (or any other particular value, and then scaling the relationship between a and degree of belief) is arbitrary, in a way that makes a difference since there is typically a decreasing marginal utility of dollars, where the rate of decrease may be different for different individuals. Also, it's been argued that there are factors other than one's degrees of belief that can (rationally) enter into one's valuation of gambles, such as, for example, excitement or satisfaction that one can get from betting on a favorite team even when the odds are against it. See Eells (1982) for further discussion and references.
9. I assume that the reader is familiar with the standard probability calculus.

REFERENCES

Alexander, H. G. (1958). "The Paradoxes of Confirmation." *The British Journal for the Philosophy of Science* 9, pp. 227–33.

Black, M. (1966). "Notes on the 'Paradoxes of Confirmation.' " In *Aspects of Inductive Logic*. Edited by J. Hintikka and P. Suppes. Amsterdam: North Holland Publishing Company, pp. 175–97.

Braithwaite, R. B. (1953). *Scientific Explanation*. New York: Harper and Brothers, 1960.

Chihara, C. (1981). "Quine and the Confirmational Paradoxes." *Midwest Studies in Philosophy*. Vol. 6: "Foundations of Analytic Philosophy." Edited by P. French, H. Wettstein, and T. Uehling. Minneapolis: University of Minnesota Press, pp. 425–52.

Churchman, C. W. (1948). *Theory of Experimental Inference*. New York: Macmillan.

———. (1956). "Science and Decision Making." *Philosophy of Science* 23, pp. 247–49.

Eells, E. (1982). *Rational Decision and Causality*. New York: Cambridge University Press.

———. (1985). "Problems of Old Evidence." *Pacific Philosophical Quarterly* 66, pp. 283–302.

———. (1990). "Bayesian Problems of Old Evidence." *Minnesota Studies in the Philosophy of Science*. Vol. 14: "Scientific Theories." Edited by C. W. Savage. Minneapolis: University of Minnesota Press, pp. 205–23.

Garber, D. (1983). "Old Evidence and Logical Omniscience in Bayesian Confirmation Theory." *Minnesota Studies in the Philosophy of Science*. Vol. 10: "Testing Scientific Theories." Edited by J. Earman. Minneapolis: University of Minnesota Press, pp. 99–131.

Gibbard, A., and W. Harper. (1978). "Counterfactual and Two Kinds of Expected Utility." In *Foundations and Applications of Decision Theory*. Vol. 1. Edited by C. A. Hooker, J. J. Leach, and E. F. McClennen. Dordrecht: D. Reidel: pp. 125–62. Reprinted in *Ifs*. Edited by W. L. Harper, R. Stalnaker, and G. Pearce. Dordrecht: D. Reidel, pp. 153–90.

Glymour, C. (1980). *Theory and Evidence*. Princeton: Princeton University Press.

Good, I. J. (1967). "The White Shoe is a Red Herring." *The British Journal for the Philosophy of Science* 17, p. 322.

Goodman, N. (1955). *Fact, Fiction and Forecast*. 3d edition. Indianapolis: Bobbs-Merrill, 1973.

Hempel, C. (1945). "Studies in the Logic of Confirmation." In Hempel, *Aspects of Scientific Explanation and other Essays in the Philosophy of Science*. New York: The Free Press, 1965, pp. 3–46.

———. (1960). "Inductive Inconsistencies." In Hempel, *Aspects of Scientific Explanation and other Essays in the Philosophy of Science*, pp. 53–79.

Hesse, M. (1974). *The Structure of Scientific Inference*. Berkeley: University of California Press.

Hosiasson-Lindenbaum, J. (1940). "On Confirmation." *Journal of Symbolic Logic* 5, pp. 133–48.

Jeffrey, R. (1956). "Valuation and Acceptance of Scientific Hypotheses." *Philosophy of Science* 23, pp. 237–46.

———. (1965). *The Logic of Decision*. New York: McGraw-Hill.

———. (1977). "Savage's Omelet." In *PSA 1976*. Vol. 2. Edited by F. Suppe and P. D. Asquith. East Lansing: Philosophy of Science Association, pp. 361–71.

———. (1983a). "Bayesianism with a Human Face." *Minnesota Studies in the Philosophy of Science*. Vol. 10: "Testing Scientific Theories," pp. 133–56.

———. (1983b), *The Logic of Decision*. 2d edition. Chicago: University of Chicago Press.

Leibniz, G. W. (1765). *New Essays Concerning Human Understanding*. 3d ed. Trans. by A. G. Langely. La Salle, Ill: Open Court, 1949.

Levi, I. (1961). "Decision Theory and Confirmation." *The Journal of Philosophy* 58, pp. 614–25.

Mackie, J. L. (1963). "The Paradox of Confirmation." *The British Journal for the Philosophy of Science* 13, pp. 265–77.

Nozick, R. (1969). "Newcomb's Problem and Two Principles of Choice." In *Essays in Honor of Carl G. Hempel*. Edited by N. Rescher, et al. Dordrecht: D. Reidel Publishing Company, pp. 114–46.

Pears, D. (1950). "Hypotheticals." *Analysis* 10, pp. 49–63.

Resnik, M. (1987). *Choices: An Introduction to Decision Theory*. Minneapolis: University of Minnesota Press.

Rudner, R. (1953). "The Scientists *qua* Scientist Makes Value Judgments." *Philosophy of Science* 20, pp. 1–6.

Savage, L. J. (1954). *The Foundations of Statistics*. 2d ed. New York: Dover Publications, 1972.

Scheffer, I. (1963). *The Anatomy of Inquiry*. Indianapolis: Bobbs-Merrill.

Skyrms, B. (1975). *Choice and Chance*. 2d ed. Encino, CA: Dickenson.

———. (1980). *Causal Necessity: A Pragmatic Investigation of the Necessity of Laws*. New Haven: Yale University Press.

———. (1983). "Three Ways to Give a Probability Assignment a Memory." *Minnesota Studies in the Philosophy of Science*. Vol. 10: Testing Scientific Theories," pp. 157–61.

———. (1986). *Choice and Chance*. 3d ed. Belmont, California: Wadsworth.

Suppes, P. (1961). "The Philosophical Relevance of Decision Theory." *The Journal of Philosophy* 58, pp. 605–14.

———. (1966). "A Bayesian Approach to the Paradoxes of Confirmation." In *Aspects of Inductive Logic*. Edited by J. Hintikka and P. Suppes.

Swinburne, R. (1973). *An Introduction to Confirmation Theory*. London: Methuen.

Teller, P. (1976). "Conditionalization, Observation and Change of Belief." In *Foundations of Probability Theory, Statistical Inference, and Statistical Theories of Science*. Vol. 1. Edited by W. L. Harper and C. A. Hooker. Dordrecht: D. Reidel, pp. 205–59.

PART SIX

THE PROBLEM
OF INDUCTION

INTRODUCTION

cceptable solutions to problems tend to be bound by presuppositions about what kinds of proposals qualify as acceptable. In the case of the problem of induction, for example, the problem concerns the rational justification of inferences about the future on the basis of regularities that have obtained in the past. Some take for granted that any belief in necessary connections cannot be rationally warranted and therefore must not figure in an acceptable solution. Others maintain that belief in necessary connections is not only rationally warranted but also essential to an acceptable solution. And still others contend (with considerable justification) that the very idea of a regularity requires further clarification before this problem can be solved.

Salmon's "An Encounter with David Hume" provides an engaging introduction to the problem from one who tends to side with Hume in rejecting belief in necessary connections as rationally unwarranted. As "Professor Philo" observes, what scientists mean by a "proof" of a law of nature is an exemplification of the law rather than a demonstration of its truth. Since laws are unrestrictedly general, their content cannot be exhausted by any finite number of tests. Discovering that specific observations and experiments satisfy a law, therefore, can only provide partial and inconclusive inductive evidence rather than complete and conclusive deductive proofs.

Moreover, that a specific regularity has obtained in the past provides no logical guarantee that it will continue to obtain in the future. Even if the conservation of momentum, for example, has been satisfied by every object in the past, that affords no guarantee that it will continue to hold in the future. Indeed, if there are no necessary connections between various events (or properties) in nature—that is, no logically contingent natural necessities—then it is entirely possible that *every prediction on the basis of any law might turn out to be false*. The consequences of denying the existence of natural necessities thus appear to be especially profound.

The solution that Salmon embraces assumes the form of what is known as a *pragmatic vindication*, according to which scientific method provides an appropriate means for attaining the goal of discovering uniformities in nature, provided that those uniformities exist to be discovered. If no such uniformities exist, of course, then they cannot be discovered by this or by any other means. Salmon admits that there are difficulties in developing an adequate conception of a natural law, but the general features of his approach are evident. If we want to pursue the discovery of natural laws, we have everything to gain and nothing to lose by using scientific method.

Hempel's "Recent Problems of Induction" suggests that the problem of induction cannot be solved without further clarification of the notion of a natural law, on the one hand, and of the concept of inductive inference, on the other. He explains the difference between what is often referred to as the *context of discovery* and the *context of justification*, where the former involves the invention of hypotheses, while the latter concerns their acceptance. While no special requirements must be satisfied in coming up with an idea (which might occur in a dream, a daydream, etc.), whether or not the idea is worthy of acceptance depends upon meeting suitable standards.

Unfortunately, while the standards that must be met for deductive arguments to be acceptable are generally well understood, those that have to be satisfied for inductive arguments to be acceptable are not. He discusses the so-called *paradoxes of confirmation*, which arise because the conditions that seem intuitively most appropriate to capture the notion of a confirming instance of an hypothesis *h* have the paradoxical result that the hypothesis, "All ravens are black," turns out to be confirmed by a white shoe, precisely because (when this is interpreted as a truth-functional generalization) it is logically equivalent to the hypothesis, "All nonblack things are nonravens."

Hempel reviews Goodman's riddle, with which you are already familiar, and discusses the *problem of inductive ambiguity*, according to which the available evidence might provide the premises of rival arguments that are inductively acceptable, yet which have contradictory conclusions. Such an outcome cannot arise with deductive reasoning, since any conclusion which follows from specific premises continues to follow from any larger set that contains those premises. The solution to this difficulty is found in Carnap's *requirement of total evidence*, according to which the acceptability of any hypothesis must be measured relative to all the evidence that is available.

Fetzer's "The Justification of Induction" pursues a Popperian solution to the problem of induction. He agrees with Popper in holding (i) that lawlike sentences are unrestrictedly general, (ii) that universals are dispositional, and (iii) that natural necessities are not extensional (or truth-functional). This position elaborates the conception of lawlike sentences as intensional generalizations that entail corresponding extensional generalizations. The basic form of a lawlike sentence is thus taken to be that of a subjunctive generalization that ascribes a disposition to everything that has a reference property, where that sentence is not true on logical grounds alone.

The underlying conception is that an attribute is *a permanent property of a reference property* when there is no process or procedure by means of which that attribute could be taken away from something that has that reference property without taking away that reference property as well, even though the description of the reference property does not entail the presence or the absence of that attribute. When (pure) gold is defined by means of its atomic number, things that are (pure) gold have specific melting points and boiling points among their permanent properties, while their shapes and retail prices are merely transient.

Sentence functions that ascribe permanent properties are satisfied in all worlds that differ from the actual world, if at all, only with respect to their initial conditions, as Popper proposed. This view supports drawing a distinction between those subjunctives which are warranted on logical grounds ("If Smith were a bachelor, he would be unmarried") and those which are warranted on ontological grounds ("If this were made of pure gold, then it would melt at 1063°C"). It provides further evidence that Goodman's thesis (T1) cannot be sustained, since some subjunctives and counterfactuals are warranted on logical rather than ontological grounds.

You may recall that Salmon acknowledged that there appears to be a difference between the absence of material objects traveling faster than the speed of light and the absence of material objects that are enormous spheres of gold during the world's history. "The problem is," as Professor Philo remarks, "what basis do we have for claiming possibility in the one case and impossibility in the other." If the speed of light imposes an upper bound on material objects (where it is impossible to travel faster and remain a thing of that kind), while things that are gold can be of any size and shape (while remaining things of that kind), then the difference may be that things of these kinds have different permanent properties.

Hume's position, from this point of view, hinges upon the adoption of an epistemic principle that appears to be far too stringent to permit the rational belief in necessary connections, even if they exist. Their existence is not merely a matter of subjective expectation, moreover, since their presence or absence can be tested by attempting to violate them. The positive significance of unsuccessful attempts at refutation thus falls within the domain of inductive methodology, just as the negative significance of successful attempts at refutation falls within the domain of deductive methodology. The key to scientific methodology is attempts to falsify.

If this approach is right-headed, then the difference between lawlike sentences and accidental generalizations is not as simple as Goodman implies. Accidental generalizations are expressible in extensional language and are capable of confirmation by their instances, sometimes by means of simple inductive methods, such as the straight rule of induction. Lawlike sentences are only expressible in intensional language and are tested by attempts to refute them. Thus, Goodman's thesis (T2) likewise cannot be sustained. The reason why this problem has been so difficult to solve, therefore, may turn out to be a consequence of mistakes in methodology.

Indeed, an intensional construction of lawlike sentences even affords a partial vindication of the standard conception of scientific theories. The problem with (AC-I) now appears to be its choice of extensional language, which can be improved upon as follows:

(AC-II)		
	1. $(x)(t)(Wxt \gg Xxt)$	Axiom
	2. $(x)(t)[Xxt \gg (Yxt = n \gg Zxt)]$	Axiom
	3. $(x)(t)[Wxt \gg (Yxt = n \gg Zzt)]$	Theorem

where "W," "X," "Y," and "Z" are predicate variables, "____ $\gg$ ..." is the subjunctive conditional sign and "____ $= n \gg$ ..." is the (probabilistic) causal conditional sign, and (AC-II) exhibits the form of a simple scientific theory. The nature of causal conditionals, of course, is discussed in Parts IV and V.

STUDY QUESTIONS

As you read the articles that appear in this section, you may want to think about their implications for understanding the nature of science and of philosophy. The following questions are intended to stimulate your thinking by focusing attention on some of the less obvious aspects of different positions.

(1) If laws of nature are identified with limiting frequencies and the rule of induction by enumeration is identified with scientific method, then the goal of science can be attained by using the scientific method when those limits exist. How long would it take? Could we know if we had been successful?

(2) If it is *logically* possible for every prediction of any law to be false in the absence of natural necessities, is the situation any different if there are natural necessities? If there are natural necessities, would it be *physically* possible for every prediction of any law to be false? What is the difference?

(3) Why did Hume take such a strong stand against the existence of natural necessities (necessary connections) in nature? Is it possible that the problem of induction may have resisted solution for so long because Hume imposed a condition of adequacy that is too strong for its intended purpose?

(4) Hempel distinguishes between the invention of hypotheses and their acceptance as true, however tentative that may be. Why does he suggest that the invention of hypotheses does not require the satisfaction of any specific conditions of adequacy, while the acceptance of hypotheses does?

(5) The paradox of the ravens arises because an hypothesis, such as *all ravens are black*, when interpreted as a truth-functional generalization, is confirmed by *a white shoe, a brown cow*, and so on. Does this provide any grounds at all for reconsidering the use of extensional language here?

(6) What is the problem of inductive ambiguity that Hempel describes? What is the solution to the problem? Do you think that Hempel's work on induction may have influenced his work on explanation? Does the solution he proposes for induction also work in the case of explanation?

(7) On the basis of Hempel's discussion, is it plausible to suppose that scientific inquiries could ever possibly be completely value-free? Are there different senses in which or extents to which scientific inquiries are value-laden? Should scientific inquiries strive to be value-free?

(8) Is it important to distinguish between the negative significance of successful attempts at falsification and the positive significance of unsuccessful attempts at falsification? Why does one fall within the domain of deductive methodology and the other inductive methodology?

(9) There appear to be three different senses in which induction may require justification, namely: validation, vindication, and exoneration. Explain the difference between them with respect to specific arguments, specific rules of inference, and specific objectives of scientific inquiry.

(10) If we can discover laws of nature that cannot be violated and cannot be changed, then even if it remains logically possible that they might still change tomorrow, it is not physically possible that they actually will change tomorrow. Could the problem of induction thereby be resolved?

WESLEY C. SALMON

AN ENCOUNTER WITH DAVID HUME

A DAY IN THE LIFE OF A HYPOTHETICAL STUDENT

n the Physics 1a lecture hall, Professor Salvia[1] has had a bowling ball suspended from a high ceiling by a long rope so that it can swing back and forth like a pendulum. Standing well over to one side of the room, he holds the bowling ball at the tip of his nose. He releases it (taking great care not to give it a push). It swings through a wide arc, gaining considerable speed as it passes through the low portion of its swing beneath the point of suspension from the ceiling. It continues to the other side of the room, where it reaches the end of its path, and then returns. The professor stands motionless as the bowling ball moves faster and faster back toward his nose. As it passes through the midpoint of the return arc, it is again traveling very rapidly, but it begins to slow down, and it stops just at the tip of his nose. Some of the students think he is cool. "This demonstration," he says, "illustrates the faith that the physicist has in nature's regularity." (See Figure 1.)

Imagine that you have witnessed this demonstration just after your philosophy class, where the subject of discussion was Hume's *Enquiry Concerning Human Understanding*. You raise your hand. "How did you *know* that the bowling ball would stop where it did, just short of bashing your nose into your face?" you ask.

"This is a standard demonstration," he replies; "I do it every year in this class, and it has often been used by many other physics teachers." In an attempt to inject a little humor, he adds, "If I had had any doubt about its working, I'd have had the teaching assistant do it."

"Are you saying, then, that you trusted the experiment to work this time simply because it has been tried so many times in the past, and has never failed?" You recall Hume's discussion of the collisions of billiard balls. In the first instance, according to Hume, before you have any experience with material objects colliding with one another, you would not know what to expect when you see a moving billiard ball approaching a stationary one, but after a good deal of experience you confidently expect some motion to be transferred to the stationary ball as a result of the collision. As your experience accumulates, you learn to predict the exact manner in

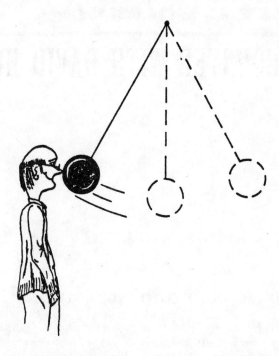

Figure 1.   Prof. Salvia's Pendulum. After swinging to the opposite side of the lecture hall, the bowling ball swings right back to the tip of the prof's nose, which remains motionless during the entire procedure.

which the second ball will move after being struck by the first. But you cannot really accept that answer, and neither, you feel sure, will your physics professor. Without waiting for an answer, you follow up your first question with another.

"I have this friend," you continue, "who drives like a maniac. It scares me to ride with him, but he always tells me not to worry—he has never had an accident, or even a traffic ticket. Should I conclude—assuming he is telling the truth (just as I assume you are telling me the truth about this demonstration)—that it is as safe for me to ride with him as it is for you to perform the bowling ball trick?"

"It's not the same thing at all," another student chimes in; "you can prove, mathematically, that the pendulum will not swing back beyond its original starting point, but you certainly can't prove mathematically that your friend won't have a wreck. In a way it's just the opposite; you can prove that he is likely to have an accident if he keeps on driving like that."

"What you say is partly right," says Professor Salvia to the second student, "but it isn't only a matter of mathematics. We have to rely upon the laws of physics as well. With the pendulum we were depending mainly upon the law of conservation of energy, one of the most fundamental laws of nature. As the pendulum goes through its swing, potential energy is transformed into kinetic energy, which is transformed back into potential energy, and so forth. As long as the total amount of energy remains unchanged, my nose is safe."

Since you have not yet studied the concept of energy, you do not worry too much about the details of the explanation. You are satisfied that you will understand why the pendulum behaves as it does when you have learned more about the concepts and laws that were mentioned. But you do remember something Hume wrote. There are two kinds of reasoning: reasoning concerning relations of ideas, and reasoning concerning matters of fact and existence. Mathematical reasoning falls into the former category (relations of ideas) and consequently, by itself, cannot provide any information about matters of fact. The pendulum and the professor's nose are, however, matters of fact, so we need something in addition to mathematics to get the information we want concerning that situation. Professor Salvia has told us what it is—we need the laws of nature as well.

Since physics is your last class in the morning, you head for the cafeteria when it is over to get a sandwich and coffee. The philosophy class is still bugging you. What was it Hume said about bread? That we do not know the "secret power" by which it nourishes us? Now we do, of course; we understand metabolism, the mechanism by which the body converts food into energy. Hume (living in the eighteenth century) did not understand about power and energy, as he said repeatedly. He did not know why bread is suitable food for humans, but not for tigers and lions. In biology class, you recall, you studied herbiverous, carnivorous, and omniverous species. Biologists must now understand why some species can metabolize vegetables and others cannot. Modern physics, chemistry, and biology can provide a complete explanation of the various forms of energy, the ways they can be converted from one form to another, and the ways in which they can be utilized by a living organism.

Taking a sip of the hot coffee, you recall some other things Hume said—for example, remarks about the "connection" between heat and flame. We now know that heat is really a form of energy; that temperature is a measure of the average kinetic energy of the molecules. Now, it seems, we know a great deal about the "secret powers," "energy," etc., that so perplexed Hume. Modern physics knows that ordinary objects are composed of molecules, which are in turn composed of atoms, which are themselves made up of sub-atomic particles. Modern science can tell us what holds atoms and molecules together, and why the things that consist of them have the properties they do. What was it that Hume said about a piece of ice and a crystal (e.g., a diamond)? That we do not know why one is caused by cold and the other by heat? I'll just bet, you think, that Salvia could answer that one without a bit of trouble. Why, you wonder, do they make us read these old philosophers who are now so out of date? Hume was, no doubt, a very profound thinker in his day, but why do we have to study him now, when we know the answers to all of those questions? If I were majoring in history that might be one thing, but that doesn't happen to be my field of interest. Oh, I suppose they'd say that getting an education means that you have to learn something about the "great minds of the past," but why doesn't the philosophy professor come right out and tell us the answers to these questions? It's silly to pretend that they are still great mysteries.

After lunch, let's imagine, you go to a class in contemporary social and political problems, a class you particularly like because of the lively discussions. A lot of time is spent talking about such topics as population growth, ecology and the environment, energy demands and uses, food production, and pollution. You discuss population trends, the extrapolation of such trends, and the prediction that by the year 2000 A.D., world population will reach 7 billion. You consider the various causes and possible effects of increasing concentrations of carbon dioxide in the atmosphere. You discuss solutions to various of these problems in terms of strict governmental controls, economic sanctions and incentives, and voluntary compliance on the part of enlightened and concerned citizens.

"If people run true to form," you interject, "if they behave as they always have, you can be sure that you won't make much progress relying on the good will and good sense of the populace at large."

"What is needed is more awareness and education," another student remarks, "for people can change if they see the need. During World War II people willingly sacrificed in order to support the war effort. They will do the same again, if they see that the emergency is really serious. That's why we need to provide more education and make stronger appeals to their humanitarian concerns."

"What humanitarian concerns?" asks still another student with evident cynicism.

"People *will* change," says another. "I have been reading that we are entering a new era, the Age of Aquarius, when man's finer, gentler, more considerate nature will be manifest."

"Well, I don't know about all of this astrology," another remarks in earnest tones, "but I do not believe that God will not let His world perish if we mend our ways and trust in Him. I have complete faith in His goodness."

You find this statement curiously reminiscent of Professor Salvia's earlier mention of his faith in the regularity of nature.

That night, after dinner, you read an English assignment. By the time you finish it, your throat feels a little scratchy, and you notice that you have a few sniffles. You decide to begin taking large doses of vitamin C; you have read that there is quite some controversy as to whether this helps to ward off colds, but that there is no harm in taking this vitamin in large quantities. Before going to the drug store to buy some vitamin C, you write home to request some additional funds; you mail your letter in the box by the pharmacy. You return with the vitamin C, take a few of the pills, and turn in for the night—confident that the sun will rise tomorrow morning, and hoping that you won't feel as miserable as you usually do when you catch a cold. David Hume is the farthest thing from your mind.

HUME REVISITED

The next morning, you wake up feeling fine. The sun is shining brightly, and you have no sign of a cold. You are not sure whether the vitamin C cured your cold, or whether it was the good night's sleep, or whether it wasn't going to develop into a real cold regardless. Perhaps, even, it was the placebo effect; in psychology you learned that people can often be cured by totally inert drugs (e.g., sugar pills) if they believe in them. You don't really know what caused your prompt recovery, but frankly, you don't really care. If it was the placebo effect that is fine with you; you just hope it will work as well the next time.

You think about what you will do today. It is Thursday, so you have a philosophy discussion section in the morning and a physics lab in the afternoon. Thursday, you say to yourself, has got to be the lousiest day of the week. The philosophy section is a bore, and the physics lab is a drag. If only it were Saturday, when you have no classes! For a brief moment you consider taking off. Then you remember the letter you wrote last night, think about your budget and your grades, and resign yourself to the prescribed activities for the day.

The leader of the discussion section starts off with the question, "What was the main problem—I mean the really *basic* problem—bothering Hume in the *Enquiry*?" You feel like saying, "Lack of adequate scientific knowledge" (or words to that effect), but restrain yourself. No use antagonizing the guy who will decide what grade to give you. Someone says that he seemed to worry quite a lot about causes and effects, to which the discussion leader (as usual) responds, "But *why*?" Again, you stifle an impulse to say, "Because he didn't know too much about them."

After much folderol, the leader finally elicits the answer, "Because he wanted to know how we can find out about things we don't actually see (or hear, smell, touch, taste, etc.)."

"In other words," the leader paraphrases, "to examine the basis for making inferences from what we observe to what we cannot (at the moment) observe. Will someone," he continues, "give me an example of something you believe in which you are not now observing?"

You think of the letter you dropped into the box last night, of your home and parents, and of the money you hope to receive. You do not see the letter now, but you are confident it is somewhere in the mails; you do not see your parents now, but you firmly believe they are back home where you left them; you do not yet see the money you hope to get, but you expect to see it before too long. The leader is pleased when you give those examples. "And what do causes and effects have to do with all of this?" he asks, trying to draw you out a little more. Still thinking of your grade, you cooperate. "I believe the letter is somewhere in the mails because I wrote it and dropped it in the box. I believe my parents are at home because they are always calling me up to tell me what to do. And I believe that the money will come as an effect of my eloquent appeal." The leader is really happy with that; you can tell you have an A for today's session.

"But," he goes on, "do you see how this leads us immediately into Hume's next question? If cause-effect relations are the whole basis for our knowledge of things and events we do not observe, how do we know whether one event causes another, or whether they just happen together as a matter of coincidence?" Your mind is really clicking now.

"I felt a cold coming on last night, and I took a massive dose of vitamin C," you report. "This morning I feel great, but I honestly don't know whether the vitamin C actually cured it."

"Well, how could we go about trying to find out," retorts the discussion leader.

"By trying it again when I have the first symptoms of a cold," you answer, "and by trying it on other people as well." At that point the bell rings, and you leave class wondering whether the vitamin C really did cure your incipient cold.

You keep busy until lunch, doing one thing and another, but sitting down and eating, you find yourself thinking again about the common cold and its cure. It seems to be a well-known fact that the cold is caused by one or more viruses, and the human organism seems to have ways of combatting virus infections. Perhaps the massive dose of vitamin C triggers the body's defenses, in some way or other, or perhaps it provides some kind of antidote to the toxic effects of the virus. You don't know much about all of this, but you can't help speculating that science has had a good deal of success in finding causes and cures of various diseases. If continued research reveals the physiological and chemical processes in the cold's infection and in the body's response, then surely it would be possible to find out whether the vitamin C really has any effect upon the common cold or not. It seems that we could ascertain whether a causal relation exists in this instance if only we could discover the relevant laws of biology and chemistry.

At this point in your musings, your notice that it is time to get over to the physics lab. You remember that yesterday morning you were convinced that predicting the outcome of an experiment is possible if you know which physical laws apply. That certainly was the outcome of the discussion in the physics class. Now, it seems, the question about the curative power of vitamin C hinges on exactly the same thing—the laws of nature. As you hurry to the lab it occurs to you that predicting the outcome of an experiment, before it is performed, is a first-class example of what you were discussing in philosophy—making inferences from the observed to the unobserved. We observe the set-up for the experiment (or demonstration) before it is performed, and we predict the outcome before we observe it. Salvia certainly was confident about the prediction he made. Also, recalling one of Hume's examples, you were at least as confident, when you went to bed last night, that the sun would rise this morning. But Hume *seemed* to be saying that the basis for this confidence was the fact that the sun has been observed to rise every morning since the dawn of history. "That's wrong," you say to yourself as you reach the physics lab. "My confidence in the rising of the sun is based upon the laws of astronomy. So here we are back at the laws again."

Inside the lab you notice a familiar gadget; it consists of a frame from which five steel balls are suspended so that they hang in a straight line, each one touching its neighbors. Your little brother got a toy like this, in a somewhat smaller size, for his birthday a couple of years ago. You casually raise one of the end balls, and let it swing back. It strikes the nearest of the four balls left hanging, and the ball at the other end swings out (the three balls in the middle keeping their place). The ball at the far end swings back again, striking its neighbor, and then the ball on the near end swings out, almost to the point from which you let it swing originally. The process goes on for a while, with the two end balls alternately swinging out and back. It has a pleasant rhythm. (See Figure 2.)

While you are enjoying the familiar toy, the lab instructor, Dr. Sagro,[2] comes over to you. "Do you know why just the ball on the far end moves—instead of, say, two on the far end, or all four of the remaining ones—when the ball on this end strikes?"

"Not exactly, but I suppose it has something to do with conservation of energy," you reply, recalling what Salvia said yesterday in answer to the question about the bowling ball.

"That's right," says Dr. Sagro, "but it also depends upon conservation of momentum." Before you have a chance to say anything she continues, "Let me ask you another question.

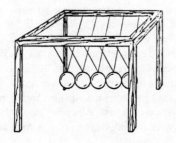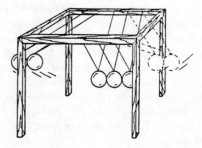

Figure 2.   The Energy-Momentum Toy. When two balls at the right collide with the remaining three, two balls swing away from the left side. What happens when three on the right collide with the remaining two?

What would happen if you raised two balls at this end, and let them swing together toward the remaining three?"

"I think two balls will swing away at the other end," you reply, remembering the way your brother's toy worked.

"Why don't you test it to find out if you are right?" says the instructor. You do, and you find that the result is as you had predicted. Without saying anything about it, you assume that this, too, can be explained by means of the laws of conservation of energy and momentum.

Dr. Sagro poses another question. "What will happen," she asks, "if you start by swinging three balls from this end?" Since there are only two remaining balls you don't know what to say, so you confess ignorance. She suggests you try it, in order to find out what will happen. When you do, you see that three balls swing to the other side, and three swing back again; the middle ball swings back and forth, acting as the third ball in each group. This was a case in which you didn't know what to expect as a result until you tried the experiment.[3] This was like some of Hume's examples; not until you have actually had the experience do you know what result to expect. But there is also something different. Hume said that you must try the experiment many times in order to know what to expect; nevertheless, after just one trial you are sure what will happen whenever the experiment is repeated. This makes it rather different from the problem of whether vitamin C cured your cold. In that case, it seemed necessary to try the experiment over and over again, preferably with a number of different people. Reflecting upon this difference, you ask the lab instructor a crucial question, "If you knew the laws of conservation of momentum and energy, but had never seen the experiment with the three balls performed, would you have been able to predict the outcome?"

"Yes," she says simply.

"Well," you murmur inaudibly, "it seems as if the whole answer to Hume's problem regarding inferences about things we do not immediately observe, including predictions of future occurrences, rests squarely upon the laws of nature."

KNOWING THE LAWS

Given that the laws are so fundamental, you decide to find out more about them. The laws of conservation of energy and momentum are close at hand, so to speak, so you decide to start there. "O.K.," you say to the lab instructor, "what are these laws of nature, which enable you to predict so confidently how experiments will turn out before they are performed? I'd like to learn something about them."

"Fine," she says, delighted with your desire to learn; "let's start with conservation of energy, and we can demonstrate it quite easily."[4] (See Figure 3.)

Your laboratory contains a standard piece of equipment—an air track—on which little cars move back and forth. The track is made of metal with many tiny holes through which air is blown. The cars thus ride on a thin cushion of air; they move back and forth almost without friction. Some of the cars are equipped with spring bumpers, so that they will bounce off of one another upon impact, while others have coupling devices which lock them together upon contact. Dr. Sagro begins by explaining what is meant by the momentum of a body—namely, its mass multiplied by its velocity.[5] "To speak somewhat quaintly," she says, "the mass is just a measure of the quantity of matter in the body.[6] Since, in all of the experiments we are going to do, it is safe to say that the mass of each body remains unchanged, we need not say more about it. You can see that each car comes with its mass labeled; this one, for instance, has a mass of

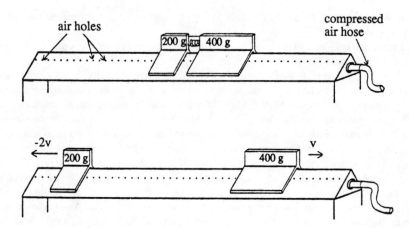

Figure 3. *Cars on the Air Track. Top: Cars tied together against spring under tension. Bottom: Cars moving apart after "explosion." 400 g × v + 200 gx (−2v) = 0. Momentum is conserved.*

200 grams, while this one has a mass of 400 grams. We have a number of different cars with quite a variety of different masses. The velocity," she continues, "is what we ordinarily mean by 'speed' along with the direction of travel. On the air track there are only two possible directions, left to right and right to left. Let us simply agree that motion from left to right has a positive velocity, while motion from right to left has a negative velocity. Mass, of course, is always a positive quantity. Thus, momentum, which is mass times velocity, may be positive, negative, or zero. When we add the momenta of various bodies together, we must always be careful of the sign (plus or minus)."

With these preliminaries, you begin to perform a variety of experiments. She has various types of fancy equipment for measuring velocities, which she shows you how to use, and she also helps you to make measurements. You find that it is fun pushing cars back and forth on the track, crashing them into one another, and measuring their velocities before and after collisions. You try it with a variety of cars of different masses and with differing velocities. You try it with the ones that bounce apart after impact and with those that stick together. You always find that the *total* momentum (the sum of the momenta for the two cars) before any collision is equal to the *total* momentum after the collision, even though the momenta of the individual cars may change markedly as a result of the collision. This, Dr. Sagro explains, is what the law of conservation of momentum demands: when two bodies (such as the cars) interact with one another (as in a collision), the total momentum of the system consisting of those two bodies is the same before and after the interaction.

You ask her whether this law applies only to collisions; she replies immediately that it applies to all kinds of interactions. "Let's see how it works for a simple type of 'explosion,' " she suggests. She helps you tie together two cars, holding a compressed spring between them. You burn the string which holds them together and they fly apart. You measure the velocities and compute the momenta of each of the cars after the "explosion." It turns out that the momentum of the one car is always equal in amount but opposite in direction to that of the other. This is true whether the cars are of equal or unequal masses and whether the tension on the spring that drives them apart is great or small. "This is just what the law of conservation of momentum tells us to expect," she explains; "the momentum of each car is zero before the 'explosion' because they are not moving (each has velocity equal to zero), and so the two momenta after the 'explosion' (one positive and one negative) must add up to zero. That is what has happened every time.

"There are many other applications of the law of conservation of momentum," she continues. "When a rifle recoils upon being fired, when a jet engine propels an airplane, when a rocket engine lifts an artificial satellite into orbit, or when you step out of an untethered rowboat and are surprised to feel it moving out from under you—these are all cases of conservation of momentum."

"Is this law ever violated?" you ask.

"No," she answers, "there are no known exceptions to it." You leave the lab with the feeling that you know at least one fundamental law, and that you have seen it proved experimentally right before your eyes. You can't wait to tell your philosophy professor about it.

When you go to your philosophy class the next morning, the topic is still Hume's *Enquiry Concerning Human Understanding* and the problem of how we can have knowledge of things we do not observe. As the lecture begins, Professor Philo[7] is saying, "As we saw during the last lecture, Hume maintains that our knowledge of what we do not observe is based entirely upon cause and effect relations, but that raises the question of how we can gain knowledge of these relations. Hume maintained that this knowledge can result only from repeated observation of one type of event (a cause) to see whether it is always followed by an event of another kind (its effect). Hume therefore analyzed the notion of causality in terms of constant conjunction of events. Consider for a moment Hume's favorite example, the colliding billiard balls. . . ."

You raise your hand. "It seems to me that Hume was wrong about this," you begin, and then you relate briefly yesterday's experiences in the physics lab. "If you know the relevant laws of nature," you conclude, "you can predict the outcomes of future experiments on the basis of a single trial, or perhaps even without benefit of any trials at all."

"But how," asks Professor Philo, "can we establish knowledge of the laws of nature?"

You had a hunch she might ask some such question, and you are ready with your reply, "We *proved* it experimentally."

"Well," says Professor Philo, "I'm not a physicist, so perhaps you had better explain in a little more detail just what the experimental proof consists of. You mentioned something about an explosion—how did that go?"

You explain carefully how the air track works, how the two cars were joined together with a spring under tension in between, and how they moved apart when the string was burned. "In every case," you conclude, "the momentum of the two cars was equal in amount and opposite in direction, just as the law of conservation of momentum says it should be."

"Now let me see if I understand your line of reasoning," says the professor in a tone that is altogether too calm to suit you. "If the law of conservation of momentum is correct, then the two cars will part in the manner you described. The cars did move apart in just that way. Therefore, the law of conservation of momentum is correct. Is that your argument?"

"I guess so," you reply a bit hesitantly, because it looks as if she is trying to trap you.

"Do you think that kind of argument is valid?" she responds.

"What do you mean?" you ask, beginning to feel a little confused.

"Well," she says, "isn't that rather like the following argument: If this defendent is guilty, he will refuse to testify at his own trial; he does refuse to testify; therefore, he is guilty. Would any judge allow that argument in a court of law?"

"Of course not," you reply, "but it isn't the same thing at all. We tested the law of conservation of momentum many times in many different ways, and in every case we got the expected result (allowing for the usual small inaccuracies in the measurements)."

"If I remember what you said," Professor Philo goes on, "in one of your experiments you had one car with a mass of 200 grams and another with a mass of 400 grams, and in that case the lighter car recoiled with twice the speed of the more massive one. How many times did you repeat this particular experiment?"

"Once or twice, as nearly as I can recall."

"Yet, you seem to believe that the result would be the same, no matter how many times the experiment was repeated—is that correct?"

"I suppose so," you reply somewhat uncomfortably.

"And with how many different masses and how many different recoil velocities did you try it? Do you believe it would work the same way if the masses were thousands or billions of kilograms instead of a few grams? And do you suppose that it would work the same way if the velocities were very great—somewhere near the speed of light?"

Since you have heard that strange things happen when speeds approach that of light, your hesitancy increases, but you reply tentatively, "Well, the lab instructor told me that there are no exceptions to the law."

"Did she say that," asks Philo, "or did she say no *known* exceptions?"

"I guess that was it," you reply lamely, feeling quite crushed.

Professor Philo endeavors to summarize the discussion. "What is considered experimental 'proof of a law of nature' is actually a process of testing *some* of its logical consequences. That is, you ask what would have to happen *if* your hypothesis is true, and then you perform an experiment to see if it turns out that way *in fact*. Since any law of nature is a generalization,[8] it has an unlimited number of consequences. We can never hope to test them all. In particular, any *useful* law of nature will have consequences that pertain to the future; they enable us to make predictions. We can never test these consequences until it is too late to use them for the purpose of prediction. To suppose that testing *some* of the consequences of a law constitutes a *conclusive proof* of the law would clearly be an outright logical fallacy." The bell rings and you leave the class, convinced that she has merely been quibbling.

During your physics class you brood about the previous discussion in the philosophy class, without paying very close attention to the lecture. Similar thoughts keep nagging at you during lunch. The objections brought up by Professor Philo seem to be well founded, you conclude, but you wonder how they can be reconciled with the apparent reliability and certainty of scientific knowledge. In desperation, you decide to talk it over with Professor Salvia during his office hour this very afternoon. When you arrive, you don't know exactly where to begin, so you decide to go back to the pendulum demonstration, which was the thing that got you started on this whole mess. "When you performed that demonstration," you ask, "were you *absolutely certain* how it would turn out? Has it never failed?"

"Well, to be perfectly honest," he says, "it has been known to fail. Once when a friend of mine was doing it in front of a large auditorium, the suspension in the ceiling broke and the ball landed right on his foot. He was in a cast for months!"

"But that's no fault of the law of conservation of energy is it?" you ask. "The breaking of the suspension didn't mean that conservation of energy is false, did it?"

"Of course not," he answers, "we still believe firmly in conservation of energy."

"But are you *certain* of the law of conservation of energy, or any other law of nature?" you ask, and before he has a chance to answer, you tell him about the discussion in the philosophy class this morning.

"So that's what's bothering you," he says, after hearing the whole story. "Professor Philo has an important point. No matter how thoroughly we have tested a scientific law—better, let's say 'hypothesis'—there is always the possibility that new evidence will show up to prove it false. For instance, around the close of the nineteenth century, many physicists seemed virtually certain that Newtonian mechanics was absolutely correct. A wide variety of its consequences had been tested under many different circumstances, and Newton's laws stood up extremely well. But early in the twentieth century it became clear that what we now call 'classical physics' would have to undergo major revisions, and a profound scientific revolution ensued. Modern physics, which includes quantum mechanics and relativity theory, was the result. We can never be sure that any hypothesis we currently accept as correct will not have to be abandoned or modified at some time in the future as a result of new evidence."

"What about the law of conservation of momentum?" you ask, recalling yesterday's experience in the lab. "The lab instructor said it has no known exceptions."

"That is correct," says Salvia, "and it is a rather interesting case. Conservation of momentum is a consequence of Newton's laws of motion; therefore, any consequence of conservation of momentum is a consequence of Newton's laws. But we now regard Newton's laws as not strictly true—they break down, for example, with objects traveling close to the speed of light—but conservation of momentum holds even in these cases. So we have a good example of a case where we believe a lot of consequences, but we do not believe in the laws (Newton's) from which the consequences follow."

It occurs to you that this is a rather important set of supposed laws; perhaps the philosophy professor was not merely quibbling when she said that it was not valid to conclude that a hypothesis is true just because we know many of its consequences to be true.

"Since you cannot be certain of any so-called law of nature," you ask, "why do you believe in them so firmly?"

"Because," answers Salvia, "we consider them very well confirmed. We accept well-confirmed hypotheses, knowing that we may later have to change our minds in the light of new evidence. Science can no longer claim infallible truth."

"Does that mean that scientific results are highly probable, but not absolutely certain?" you ask trying to be sure you have understood what he has said.

"Yes, you could put it that way," he agrees.

You leave with the feeling that you have a pretty good comprehension of the situation. As a result of your study of physics and philosophy you now understand why science cannot claim infallibility for its findings, but must be content with results that are well confirmed. With that, you take off for the weekend. (And what you do with your weekend is your own business.)

HUME'S BOMBSHELL

A little tired, but basically in a cheerful mood, you arrive at your philosophy class on Monday morning. You meet the professor a few minutes before class outside the room, and you tell her very briefly of your conversation with the physics professor. You explain that you now understand why it is that scientific laws can never be considered completely certain, but only as well-confirmed hypotheses. With her help, and with that of Professor Salvia, you now under-stand what Hume was driving at—and you see, moreover, that Hume was right. She smiles, and you both go into the classroom, where she begins her lecture.

"Last Friday, as you may recall, we had quite a lively discussion about the status of scientific laws—the law of conservation of momentum, in particular. We saw that such laws cannot be proved conclusively by any amount of experimental evidence. This is a point with which, I am happy to report, many (if not most) contemporary scientists agree. They realize that the most they can reasonably claim for their hypotheses is strong confirmation. Looking at the matter this way, one could conclude that it is wise to believe in scientific predictions, for if they are not certain to be true, they are a good bet. To believe in scientific results is to bet with the best available odds.

"However," she continues, "while this view may be correct as far as it goes, Hume was making a much more fundamental, and I should add, much more devastating point. Hume was challenging not merely our right to claim that scientific predictions will always be right, but also our right to claim that they will usually, or often, or indeed ever, be correct. Take careful note of what he says in section IV:

Let the course of things be allowed hitherto ever so regular; that alone, without some new argument or inference, proves not that, for the future, it will continue so. In vain do you pretend to have learned the nature of bodies from your past experience. Their secret nature, and consequently all their effects and influence, may change, without any change in their sensible qualities. This happens sometimes, and with regard to some objects: Why may it not happen always and with regard to all objects? What logic, what process of argument secures you against this supposition?

He is saying, as I hope you understood from your reading, that no matter how reliably a law seems to have held in the past, there is no logical reason why it must do so in the future *at all*. It is therefore possible that *every* scientific prediction, based on *any* law or laws whatever, may turn out to be false from this moment on. The stationary billiard ball that is struck by a moving one may remain motionless where it is—while the moving ball may bounce straight back in the direction from whence it came, or it may go straight up in the air, or it might vanish in a puff of smoke. Any of these possibilities can be imagined; none of them involves any logical contradic-tion. This is the force of Hume's skeptical arguments. The conclusion seems to be that we have no *reason* to believe in scientific predictions—no more reason than to believe on the basis of astrology, crystal gazing, or sheer blind guessing."

You can hardly believe your ears; what is she saying? You raise your hand, and when you are recognized, you can hardly keep your intense irritation from showing as you assert, "But certainly we can say that scientific predictions are more probable than those based, for example, upon astrology." As you speak, you are reminded of the remark in contemporary problems last Wednesday concerning the coming of the Age of Aquarius. Science has got to be better than *that!* As these thoughts cross your mind, Professor Philo is saying, ". . . but that depends upon what you mean by 'probable,' doesn't it?"

The physics lecture today is on Newton's law of gravitation, and the professor is explaining that every bit of matter in the universe is attracted to every other by a force proportional to the masses and inversely proportional to the square of the distance between them. He goes on to explain how Kepler's laws of planetary motion and Galileo's law of falling bodies are (when suitably corrected) consequences of Newton's laws. You listen carefully, but you recognize this as another law that enables scientists to make impressive predictions. Indeed, Salvia is now telling how Newton's laws were used to explain the tides on the oceans and to predict the existence of two planets, Neptune and Pluto, that had not been known before. At the same time, you are wondering whether there is anything in what Hume seemed to be saying about such laws. Is it possible that suddenly, at the very next moment, matter would cease to have gravitational attraction, so that the whole solar system would go flying apart? It's a pretty chilling thought.

At lunch you are thinking about this question, and you glance back at some of the readings that were assigned from Hume's *Enquiry*. You notice again Hume's many references to secret powers and forces. Well, gravitation is surely a force, though there has not been any great secret about it since Newton's time. It is the "power" which keeps the solar system together. You remember reading somewhere that, according to Hume, you cannot know that it is safer to leave a building by way of the halls, stairways, and doors than it would be to step out of the third-story window. Well, Newton's law makes it clear why you don't want to step out of the third-story window, but what assurance have you that the building will continue to stand, rather than crashing down around your ears before you can get out? The engineers who design and build towers and bridges have a great deal of knowledge of the "secret powers" of their materials, so they must know a great deal more than Hume did about the hidden properties of things.

At this very moment, a lucky coincidence occurs—you see Dr. Sagro, your physics lab instructor, entering the cafeteria. You wave to her, and she sits down with you, putting her coffee cup on the table. You begin to ask her some questions about structural materials, and she responds by inquiring whether you would be satisfied if she could explain how the table supports the cup of coffee. You recognize it as just the kind of question you have in mind, and urge her to proceed.

"Certain materials, such as the metal in this table," she begins, "have a rather rigid crystalline structure, and for this reason they stick together and maintain their shape unless subjected to large forces. These crystals consist of very regular (and very beautiful) arrays of atoms, and they are held together by forces, essentially electrostatic in origin, among the charged particles that make up the atoms. Have you studied Coulomb's law of electrostatic forces?"

"No," you reply, "we are just doing Newton's law of gravitation. I think Salvia said electricity and magnetism would come up next semester."

"Well," she says, "these electrostatic forces are a lot like gravitational forces (they vary inversely with the square of the distance), but there are a couple of very important differences. First, as you know, there are two types of charges, positive and negative. The proton in the nucleus of the atom carries a positive charge, and the electrons that circulate about the nuclei have a negative charge. Two particles with opposite signs (such as a proton and an electron) attract one another, while two particles with like signs (e.g., two electrons or two protons) repel each other. This is different from gravity, because all matter attracts all other matter; there is no such thing as gravitational repulsion. The second main difference is that the electrostatic force is fantastically stronger than the gravitational force—roughly a billion billion billion billion times more powerful—but we don't usually notice it because most objects we deal with in everyday life are electrically neutral, containing equal amounts of positive and negative electric charge, or very nearly so. If you could somehow strip all of the electrons away from an apple, and all of the protons away from the earth, the force of attraction between the apple and the earth would be unbelievable.

"It is these *extremely* strong attractive and repulsive forces among the electrons and protons in the metal that maintain a stable and rigid form. That's why the table doesn't collapse. And the reason the coffee cup stays on top of the table, without penetrating its surface or slipping through, is that the electrons in the surface of the cup strongly repel those in the surface of the table. Actually, there is also a quantum mechanical force that prevents the weight of the cup from noticeably compressing the table, but we needn't go into that, because the effect is mostly due to the electrostatic forces."

Pleased with this very clear explanation, you thank her, but follow it up with another question. "Is there any logical reason why it has to be that way—why opposite charges attract and like charges repel? Can you prove that it is impossible for like charges to attract and unlike charges to repel? What would happen if *that* were suddenly to become the law?"

"It would certainly result in utter catastrophe," she replies, "with all of the atomic nuclei bunching up together in one place and all of the electrons rushing away from them to congregate elsewhere. But to answer your question, no, there is no logical proof that it couldn't be that way. In our physical world we find that there are, in fact, two types of charges, and they obey the Coulomb law rather than the one you just formulated."

"Can you prove that the world will not switch from the one law to the other, say, tomorrow?" you ask.

"No, frankly, I can't," she answers, "but I, and all other physicists assume—call it an article of faith if you like—that it won't happen."

There's that word "faith" again, you muse as you leave the cafeteria.

The more you think about it, the more clearly you see that the physicists have not shown you how to get around the basic problem Hume raised; rather, they have really reinforced it. Maybe this problem is tougher than I thought, you say to yourself, and you head for Professor Philo's office to talk further about it. "I was thinking about all these 'secret powers' Hume talks about," you begin, "and so I asked my physics instructor about them. She explained, as an example, how a table supports a coffee cup, but she did it on the basis of laws of nature— Coulomb's law of electrostatics was one of them. This law is very well confirmed, I suppose, but she admitted that it is quite possible to imagine that this law would fail tomorrow, and—if you'll pardon the expression—all hell would break loose. Now, my question is, how can we find out about these secret powers that Hume keeps saying we need to know? How can we discover the real underlying causes of what happens?"

"I think you are really beginning to get the point Hume was driving at," she replies, "namely, that there is *no way*, even in principle, of finding any hidden causes or secret powers. You can, of course, find regularities in nature—such as conservation of energy, conservation of momentum, universal gravitation, and electrostatic attraction and repulsion—but these can only be known to have held up to the present. There is no further kind of hidden connection or causal relation that can be discovered by more careful observation, or examination with some kind of super-microscope. Of course, we do discover regularities, and we explain them. For instance, Kepler's laws of planetary motion are regularities that are explained by Newton's laws of motion and gravitation, but these do not reveal any secret powers. They simply provide more general regularities to cover the more restricted ones.

"In his discussion of 'the idea of necessary connection,' Hume tries to bring out precisely this point. We can observe, as you were saying in class the other day, that recoil experiments always yield a particular type of result—namely, momentum is conserved. We have observed this many times. And now we expect, on future trials, that the same thing will happen. But we do not observe, nor can we discover in any way, an *additional* factor which constitutes a necessary connection between the 'explosion' and the subsequent motion of the cars. This seems to be what Hume had in mind when he wrote:

These ultimate springs and principles are totally shut up from human curiosity and enquiry. Elasticity, gravity, cohesion of parts, communication of motion by impulse; these are probably the ultimate causes and principles which we ever discover in nature; and we may esteem ourselves sufficiently happy, if, by accurate inquiry and reasoning, we can trace up the particular phenomena to, or near to, these general principles.[9]

Hume is acknowledging that we can discover general regularities in nature, but he is denying that an additional 'connection' can be found. And Hume was dedicated to the maxim, as are modern scientists, that we have no business talking about things it is impossible in principle for us to know anything about.

"When he asks why we do, in fact, expect so confidently that the future experiments will have outcomes similar to those of the past trials, Hume finds that it is nothing other than a matter of psychological conditioning. When we see one type of cause repeatedly followed by a particular type of effect, we come to expect that the same type of effect will follow the next time we come across that kind of cause. But this is not a matter of logical reasoning. Have you heard of Pavlov's conditioning experiments with dogs?" You nod. "When the bell rings the dog starts to salivate. He is *not* reasoning that, since the sounding of the bell has, in the past, been associated with the bringing of food, therefore, on this occasion the food will (at least probably) appear soon after the bell rings. According to Hume's analysis, what is called 'scientific reasoning' is no more rational or logical than your watering at the mouth when you are hungry and hear the dinner bell. It is something you cannot help doing, Hume says, but that does not mean that it has any logical foundation."

"That brings up a question I've wanted to ask," you say. "Hume seems to think that people necessarily reason in that way—inductive reasoning, I think it is called—but I've noticed that lots of people don't seem to. For instance, many people (including a student in my current problems course) believe in things like astrology; they believe that the configuration of the planets has a bearing on human events, when experience shows that it often doesn't work that way." The professor nods in agreement. You continue, "So if there is no logical justification for believing in scientific predictions, why isn't it just as reasonable to believe in astrological predictions?"

"That" replies the prof, "is a very profound and difficult question. I doubt that any philosopher has a completely satisfactory answer to it."

MODERN ANSWERS[10]

The Wednesday philosophy lecture begins with a sort of rhetorical question, "What reason do we have (Hume is, at bottom, asking) for trusting the scientific method; what grounds do we have for believing that scientific predictions are reliable?" You have been pondering that very question quite a bit in the last couple of days, and—rhetorical or not—your hand shoots up. You have a thing or two to say on the subject.

"Philosophers may have trouble answering such questions," you assert, "but it seems to me there is an obvious reply. As my physics professor has often said, the scientist takes a very practical attitude. He puts forth a hypothesis; if it works he believes in it, and he continues to believe in it as long as it works. If it starts giving him bad predictions, he starts looking for another hypothesis, or for a way of revising his old one. Now the important thing about the scientific method, it seems to me, is that it works. Not only has it led to a vast amount of knowledge about the physical world, but it has been applied in all sorts of practical ways—and although these applications may not have been uniformly beneficial—for better or worse they were successful. Not always, of course, but by and large. Astrology, crystal gazing, and other such superstitious methods simply do not work very well. That's good enough for me."[11]

"That is, indeed, a very tempting answer," Professor Philo replies, "and in one form or another, it has been advanced by several modern philosophers. But Hume actually answered that one himself. You might put it this way. We can all agree that science has, up till now, a very impressive record of success in predicting the future. The question we are asking, however, is this: should we *predict* that science will continue to have the kind of success it has had in the past? It is quite natural to assume that its record will continue, but this is just a case of applying the scientific method to itself. In studying conservation of momentum, you inferred that future experiments would have results similar to those of your past experiments; in appraising the scientific method, you are assuming that its future success will match its past success. But using the scientific method to judge the scientific method is circular reasoning. It is as if a man goes to a bank to cash a check. When the teller refuses, on the grounds that he does not know this man, the man replies, 'That is no problem; permit me to introduce myself—I am John Smith, just as it says on the check.'

"Suppose that I were a believer in crystal gazing. You tell me that your method is better than mine because it has been more successful than mine. You say that this is a good reason for preferring your method to mine. I object. Since you are using your method to judge my method (as well as your method), I demand the right to use my method to evaluate yours. I gaze into my crystal ball and announce the result: from now on crystal gazing will be very successful in predicting the future, while the scientific method is due for a long run of bad luck."

You are about to protest, but she continues.

"The trouble with circular arguments is that they can be used to prove anything; if you assume what you are trying to prove, then there isn't much difficulty in proving it. You find the scientific justification of the scientific method convincing because you already trust the scientific method; if you had equal trust in crystal gazing, I should think you would find the crystal gazer's justification of his method equally convincing. Hume puts it this way:

When a man says, *I have found, in all past instances, such sensible qualities conjoined with such secret powers:* And when he says, *Similar sensible qualities will always be conjoined with similar secret powers,* he is not guilty of a tautology, nor are these propositions in any respect the same. You can say that the one proposition is an inference from the other. But you must confess that the inference is not intuitive; neither is it demonstrative: Of what nature is it, then? To say it is experimental is begging the question. For all inferences from experience suppose, as their foundation, that the future will resemble the past, and that similar powers will be conjoined with similar sensible qualities.[12]

If the assumption that the future is like the past is the presupposition of the scientific method, we cannot assume that principle in order to justify the scientific method. Once more, we can hardly find a clearer statement than Hume's:

We have said that all arguments concerning existence are founded on the relation of cause and effect; that our knowledge of that relation is derived entirely from experience; and that all our experimental conclusions proceed upon the supposition that the future will be conformable to the past. To endeavour, therefore, the proof of this last supposition by probable arguments, or arguments regarding existence, must evidently be going in a circle, and taking that for granted, which is the very point in question.[13]

"The principle that the future will be like the past, or that regularities which have held up to the present will persist in the future, has traditionally been called *the principle of uniformity of nature.* Some philosophers, most notably Immanuel Kant, have regarded it as an *a priori* truth.[14] It seems to me, however, that Hume had already provided a convincing refutation of that claim by arguing that irregularities, however startling to common sense, are by no means inconceivable—that is, they cannot be ruled out a priori. Recall what he said:

. . . it implies no contradiction that the course of nature may change, and that an object, seemingly like those which we have experienced, may be attended with different or contrary effects. May I not clearly and distinctly conceive that a body, falling from the clouds, and which, in all other respects, resembles snow, has yet the taste of salt or feeling of fire? . . . Now whatever is intelligible, and can be distinctly conceived, implies no contradiction, and can never be proved false by any demonstrative argument or abstract reasoning *a priori.*[15]

"Other philosophers have proposed assuming this principle (or something similar) as a postulate; Bertrand Russell, though not the only one to advocate this approach, is by far the most famous.[16] But most philosophers agree that this use of postulation is question-begging. The real question still remains: why should one adopt any such postulate? Russell himself, in another context, summed it up very well: The method of 'postulating' what we want has many advantages; they are the same as the advantages of theft over honest toil."[17]

"Nevertheless," you interject, "can't we still say that scientific predictions are more probable than, say, those of astrology or crystal gazing?"

"It seems to me you raised a similar question once before," Professor Philo replies, "and I seem to recall saying that it depends on what you mean by the term 'probable.' Maybe it would be helpful if I now explain what I meant."[18] You nod encouragement. "The concept of probability—or perhaps I should say 'concepts' of probability—are very tricky. If you were to undertake a systematic study of confirmation and induction, you would have to go into a rather technical treatment of probability, but perhaps I can give a brief hint of what is involved.[19] One thing that has traditionally been meant by this term relates directly to the frequency with which something occurs—as Aristotle put it, the probable is that which happens often. If the weather forecaster says that there is a 90 percent chance of rain, he presumably means that, given such weather conditions as are now present, rain occurs in nine out of ten cases. If these forecasts are correct, we can predict rain on such occasions and be right nine times out of ten.

"Now, if you mean that scientific predictions are probable in *this* sense, I think we must deny your claim. For Hume has argued—cogently, I think—that, for all we can know now, *every* future scientific prediction may go wrong. He was not merely saying that science is fallible, that it will sometimes err in its predictions—he was saying that nature might at any moment (for all we can know) become irregular on such a wide scale that any kind of scientific prediction of future occurrences would be utterly impossible. We have not found any reason to believe he was mistaken about this point."

"That must not be the concept of probability I had in mind," you remark; "I'm not quite sure how to express it, but it had something to do with what it would be reasonable to believe. I was thinking of the fact that, although we cannot regard scientific hypotheses as certain, we can consider them well confirmed. It is something like saying that a particular suspect is probably guilty of a crime—that the evidence, taken as a whole, seems to point to him."

"You have put your finger on another important probability concept," the professor replies. "It is sometimes known as the rational credibility concept. The most popular contemporary attempt (I believe) to deal with Hume's problem of inductive reasoning is stated in terms of this concept. The argument can be summarized in the following way. Hume has proved that we cannot *know for sure* that our scientific predictions will be correct, but that would be an unreasonable demand to place upon science. The best we can hope is for scientific conclusions that are probable. But when we ask that they be probable, in this sense, we are only asking that they be based upon the best possible evidence. Now, that is just what scientific predictions are— they are predictions based upon the best possible evidence. The scientist has fashioned his hypotheses in the light of all available information, and he has tested them experimentally on many occasions under a wide variety of circumstances. He has summoned all of the available evidence, and he has brought it to bear on the problem at hand. Such scientific predictions are obviously probable (as we are now construing this term); hence, they are rationally credible.[20] If we say that a belief is irrational, we mean that it runs counter to the evidence, or the person who holds it is ignoring the evidence. And in such contexts, when we speak of evidence, we are referring to inductive or scientific evidence.

"Now, the argument continues, to ask whether it is reasonable to believe in scientific conclusions comes right down to asking whether one ought to fashion his beliefs on the basis of the available evidence. But this is what it means to be rational. Hence, the question amounts to asking whether it is rational to be rational. If the question makes any sense at all, the obvious answer is 'Yes.' "

"That answer certainly satisfies me," you say, feeling that Dr. Philo has succeeded admirably in stating the point you were groping for. "I'm glad to know that lots of other philosophers agree with it. Do you think it is a satisfactory answer to Hume's problem of induction?" You are more than a trifle discouraged when she gives a negative response with a shake of her head. "Why not?" you demand.

"This argument seems to me to beg the question," she replies, "for it assumes that the concept of evidence is completely clear. But that is precisely the question at issue. If we could be confident that the kind of experiments you performed in the physics lab to test the law of conservation of momentum do, in fact, provide evidence for that law, then we could say that the law is well supported by evidence. But to suppose that such facts do constitute evidence amounts to saying that what has happened in the past is a sign of what will happen in the future—the fact that momentum was conserved in your 'explosion' experiments is an indication that momentum will be conserved in future experiments of a similar nature. This assumes that the future will be like the past, and that is precisely the point at issue. To say that one fact constitutes evidence for another means, in part, that the one provides some basis for inference to the occurrence of the other. The problem of induction is nothing other than the problem of determining the circumstances under which such inference is justified. Thus, we have to resolve the problem of induction—Hume's problem—before we can ascertain whether one fact constitutes evidence for another. We cannot use the concept of evidence—inductive evidence—to solve the problem of induction.

"There is another way to look at this same argument. If you ask me whether you should use the scientific method, I must find out what you hope to accomplish. If you say that you want to get a job teaching physics, I can tell you right away that you had better use the scientific method, at least in your work, because that is what is expected of a physicist. If you say that you want to enjoy the respect and prestige that accrues to scientists in certain social circles, the answer is essentially the same. If you tell me, however, that you want to have as much success as possible in predicting future events, the answer is by no means as easy. If I tell you to go ahead and make scientific predictions, because that is what is considered reasonable (that is what is meant by fashioning your beliefs on the basis of evidence), then you should ask whether being reasonable in this sense (which is obviously the commonly accepted sense) is a good way to attain your goal. The answer, 'but that's what it means to be reasonable,' is beside the point. You might say, 'I want a method that is reasonable to adopt in order to achieve my goal of successful prediction—that is what I mean by being reasonable. To tell me that the scientific method is what is usually *called* reasonable doesn't help. I want to know whether the method that is *commonly called* reasonable is *actually* a reasonable method to adopt to attain my goal of successful prediction of the future. The fact that it is usually considered reasonable cuts no ice, because an awareness of Hume's problem of induction has not filtered down into common usage.' That's what I think you should say."

"Couldn't we avoid all of these problems," suggests another student, "if we simply resisted the temptation to generalize? In social science, my area of interest, we find that it is very risky to generalize, say, from one society to another. An opinion survey on students in the far west, for example, will not be valid when applied to students attending eastern schools. Wouldn't we be better off to restrict our claims to the facts we know, instead of trying to extend them inductively to things we really don't know?"

"The opinion you have offered bears a strong resemblance (though it isn't identical) to that of an influential British philosopher.[21] He has presented his ideas persuasively, and has many followers. Hume, he says, has proved conclusively that induction is not a justifiable form of inference; it is, consequently, no part of science. The only kind of logic that has a legitimate place in science is deductive logic. Deductive inferences are demonstrative; their conclusions must be true if their premises are true. These inferences are precisely what Hume called 'reasoning concerning relations of ideas.' The crucial point is that they *do not add to our knowledge* in any way—they enable us to see the content of our premises, but they do not extend that content in the least. Thus, from premises that refer only to events in the past and present, it is impossible to *deduce* any predictions of future facts. Any kind of inference which would enable us to predict the future on the basis of facts already observed would have to be of a different sort; such inference is often called 'ampliative' or 'inductive.' If science contains only deductive inferences, but no inductive inferences, it can never provide us with any knowledge beyond the content of our immediate observations.

"Now this philosopher does not reject scientific knowledge; he simply claims that prediction of the future is no part of the business of science. Accordingly, the function of scientific investigation is to find powerful general hypotheses (he calls them *conjectures*) that adequately explain all known facts that have occurred so far. As long as such a generalization succeeds in explaining the new facts that come along it is retained; if it fails to explain new facts, it must be modified or rejected. The sole purpose of scientific experimentation is to try to find weaknesses in such hypotheses—that is to criticize them or try to refute them. He calls this the 'method of conjectures and refutations,' or sometimes simply, 'the critical approach.'

"The main difficulty with this approach—an insuperable one, in my opinion—is the fact that it completely deprives science of its predictive function. To the question of which method to use for predicting the future, it can give no answer. Astrology, crystal gazing, blind guessing, and scientific prediction are all on a par. To find out what the population of the world will be in 2000 A.D., we might as well employ a psychic seer as a scientific demographer. I find it hard to believe that this can constitute a satisfactory solution to the problem of employing our knowledge to find rational solutions to the problems that face us—problems whose solutions demand that we make predictions of the future course of events. Tempting as it is to try to evade Hume's problem in this way, I do not see how we can be satisfied to admit that there is no rational approach to our problem."

"But perhaps there is no answer to Hume's problem," says still another student; "maybe the only hope for salvation of this world is to give up our blind worship of science and return to religion. We have placed our faith in science, and look where we are as a result. I believe we should adopt a different faith."

There's that word *again*, you note to yourself, as the professor begins her answer: "Though I heartily agree that many of the results of science—*technological* results, I think we should emphasize—have been far from beneficial, I don't think we can properly condemn scientific *knowledge*. Knowledge is one thing; what we choose to do with it is quite another. But that's not the issue we are concerned with. I do not see how anyone could deny that science has had a great deal of success in making predictions; no other approach can possibly present a comparable record of success. And, as time goes on, the capability for predictive success seems only to increase. It would be an utterly astonishing piece of luck, if it were sheer coincidence, that science has been so much luckier than other approaches in making its predictions. If anyone can consistently pick a winner in every race at every track every day, we are pretty sure he has more than good luck going for him. Science isn't infallible, but it is hard to believe its predictive success is just a matter of chance. I, at least, am not prepared to say that science is just one among many equally acceptable faiths—you pays your money and you takes your choice. I feel rather sure that the scientific approach has a logical justification of some sort." With that, the bell rings, the discussion ends, and everyone leaves—none by way of the window.

It just isn't good enough, you say to yourself, after listening to your physics professor lecturing, with demonstrations, on the law of conservation of angular momentum. You don't know whether you're dizzier from the discussion of Hume's problem in the philosophy class or from watching student volunteers in this class being spun on stools mounted on turntables. In any case, you decide to look up Professor Philo after lunch, and you find her in her office.

"Look," you say a bit brusquely, "I see that Hume was right about our inability to prove that nature is uniform. But suppose that nature does play a trick on us, so to speak. Suppose that after all this time of appearing quite uniform, manifesting all sorts of regularities such as the laws of physics, she turns chaotic. Then there isn't anything we can do anyhow. Someone might make a lucky guess about some future event, but there would be no systematic method for anticipating the chaos successfully. It seems to me I've got a way of predicting the future which will work if nature is uniform—the scientific method, or if you like, the inductive method— and if nature isn't uniform, I'm out of luck whatever I do. It seems to me I've got everything to gain and nothing to lose (except a lot of hard work) if I attempt to adhere to the scientific approach. That seems good enough to me; what do you think."[22]

"Well," she says quietly, "I tend to agree with that answer, and so do a few others, but we are certainly in the minority. And many difficult problems arise when you try to work it out with precision."

"What sorts of difficulties are these?" you ask.

"There are several kinds," she begins; "for instance, what exactly do you mean by saying that nature is uniform? You cannot mean—to use Hume's quaint language—that like sensible qualities are always conjoined with like secret powers. All of us, including Hume, know this claim is false. Bread which looks and tastes completely harmless may contain a deadly poison. A gas which has exactly the appearance of normal air may suffocate living organisms and pollute the atmosphere. That kind of uniformity principle cannot be the basis of our inferences."

"That's quite true," you answer, "but perhaps we could say that nature operates according to regular laws. Ever since I began to think about Hume's problem, I have been led back to laws of nature."

"Your suggestion is a good one," she replies, "but modern philosophers have found it surprisingly difficult to say precisely what type of statement can qualify as a possible law of nature. It is a law of nature, most physicists would agree, that no material objects travel faster than light; they would refuse to admit, *as a law of nature*, that no golden spheres are more than one mile in diameter. It is not easy to state clearly the basis for this distinction. Both statements are generalizations, and both are true to the best of our knowledge."[23]

"Isn't the difference simply that you cannot, even in principle accelerate a material object to the speed of light, while it is possible in principle to fabricate an enormous sphere of gold?"

"That is precisely the question at issue," she replies. "The problem is, what basis do we have for claiming possibility in the one case and impossibility in the other. You seem to be saying that a law of nature prevents the one but not the other, which is obviously circular. And if you bring in the notion of causation—causing something to go faster than light vs. causing a large golden sphere to be created—you only compound the difficulty, for the concept of causation is itself a source of great perplexity.

"Suppose, however, that we had succeeded in overcoming that obstacle—that we could say with reasonable precision which sorts of statements are candidates for the status of laws of nature and which are not. We then face a further difficulty. It is obvious that some tests of scientific laws carry greater weight than others. The discovery of the planet Neptune, for example, confirmed Newton's laws much more dramatically than would a few additional observations of Mars. A test with particles traveling at very high velocities would be much stronger evidence for conservation of momentum than would some more experiments on the air track in the physics lab. It is not easy to see how to measure or compare the weight which different types of evidence lend to different scientific hypotheses.

"Scientific confirmation is a subtle and complex matter to which contemporary philosophers have devoted a great deal of attention; some have tried to construct systems of inductive logic that would capture this kind of scientific reasoning. Such efforts have, at best, met with limited success; inductive logic is in a primitive state compared with deductive logic. Until we have a reasonably clear idea of what such inference consists of, however, it is unlikely that we will be able to go very far in meeting the fundamental challenge Hume issued concerning the justification of scientific reasoning. Unless we can at least say what inductive inference is, and what constitutes uniformity of nature (or natural law), we can hardly argue that inductive reasoning—and only inductive reasoning—will prove successful in predicting the future if nature is uniform. And even if those concepts were clarified, the argument would still be intricate indeed."

"Do you think there is any chance that answers to such problems can be found?" you ask.

"I think it's just possible."

"Thanks," you say as you get up to leave.

"And my thanks to you," she replies. "You cannot possibly know how satisfying it is to talk with someone like you—someone intelligent—who takes such philosophical problems seriously and thinks hard about them. If you keep it up, you might be the very person to find some of the answers. I wish you well."

NOTES

1. Professor Salvia is a descendent of Salviati, the protagonist in Galileo's dialogues. The name was shortened when the family emigrated to America.
2. Dr. Sagro is married to a descent of Sagredo, another character in Galileo's dialogues.
3. If you really did know, please accept the author's apologies.
4. Please note that "demonstrate" is ambiguous. In mathematics it means "prove"; in physics it means "exemplify." Hume uses this term only in the mathematical sense.
5. Hume, using the terminology of his day, refers to it as the "moment" of the moving body.
6. This is Newton's definition; it is somewhat out of date, but adequate in the present context.
7. She is a direct descendent of Philo, the protagonist in Hume's "Dialogues Concerning Natural Religion," most of which is reprinted in *Reason and Responsibility*, 3d ed., J. Feinberg ed. (Encino, CA: Dickenson, 1975).
8. Professor Philo realizes that it would be more accurate to say that a statement or hypothesis expressing a law of nature must be a generalization, but she does not wish to introduce unnecessary terminological distinctions at this point. For further details see W. Salmon, "Determinism and Indeterminism in Modern Science," p. 351 in Feinberg, ed., *Reason and Responsibility*.
9. In section IV, part I, anticipating the results of the later discussion.
10. All of the attempts to deal with Hume's problem which are treated in this section are discussed in detail in Wesley C. Salmon, *The Foundations of Scientific Inference* (Pittsburgh: University of Pittsburgh Press, 1967); this book will be cited hereafter as *Foundations*.
11. This is an inductive justification; see *Foundations*, chapter 2, section 1.
12. David Hume, *An Enquiry Concerning Human Understanding* (hereafter, *Enquiry*), section IV, part II.
13. Ibid.
14. For discussion of justification by means of synthetic a priori principles, see *Foundations*, chapter 2, section 4.
15. *Enquiry*, section IV, part II.
16. For discussion of the postulational approach, see *Foundations*, chapter 2, section 6.
17. Bertrand Russell, *Introduction to Mathematical Philosophy* (London: Allen and Unwin, 1919), p. 71.
18. The "probabilistic approach" is discussed in *Foundations*, chapter 2, section 7.
19. An elementary survey of philosophical problems of probability is given in *Foundations*, chapters 4–7. References to additional literature on this subject can be found there.
20. We are assuming, of course, that these predictions are properly made. Scientists are only human, and they do make mistakes. One should not conclude, however, that every false prediction represents a scientific error. Impeccable scientific procedure is fallible, as we have already noted more than once.
21. This refers to the "deductivist" position of Sir Karl Popper. This approach is discussed in *Foundations*, chapter 2, section 3.
22. This approach is due mainly to Hans Reichenbach; it is known as a "pragmatic justification" and is discussed in *Foundations*, chapter 2, section 8.
23. Further elementary discussion of this issue can be found in Carl G. Hempel, *Philosophy of Natural Science* (Englewood Cliffs, N.J.: Prentice-Hall, Inc., 1966), section 5.3. A more technical and extensive treatment of related issues can be found in Nelson Goodman, *Fact, Fiction, and Forecast*, 2d ed. (Indianapolis: Bobbs-Merrill, 1965).

CARL G. HEMPEL

RECENT PROBLEMS OF INDUCTION

I. THE CLASSICAL PROBLEM OF INDUCTION

In the philosophical discussion of induction, one problem has long occupied the center of the stage—so much so, indeed, that it is usually referred to as *the* problem of induction. That is the problem of justifying the way in which, in scientific inquiry and in our everyday pursuits, we base beliefs and assertions about empirical matters on logically inconclusive evidence.

This classical problem of justification, raised by Hume and made famous by his skeptical solution, is indeed of great philosophical importance. But more recent studies, most of which were carried out during the past two or three decades, have given rise to new problems of induction, no less perplexing and important than the classical one, which are logically prior to it in the sense that the classical problem cannot even be clearly stated—let alone solved—without some prior clarification of the new puzzles.

In this paper, I propose to discuss some of these recent problems of induction.

Induction may be regarded as effecting a transition from some body of empirical information to a hypothesis which is not logically implied by it, and for this reason it is often referred to as nondemonstrative *inference*. This characterization has to be taken with a grain of salt; but it is suggestive and convenient, and in accordance with it, I will therefore sometimes refer to the sentences specifying the evidence as the *premises* and to the hypothesis based on it as the *conclusion* of an "*inductive inference.*"

Among the simplest types of inductive reasoning are those in which the evidence consists of a set of examined instances of a generalization, and the hypothesis is either the generalization itself or a statement about some unexamined instances of it. A standard example is the inference from the evidence statement that all ravens so far observed have been black to the generalization that all ravens are black or to the prediction that the birds now hatching in a given clutch of raven eggs will be black or to the retrodiction that a raven whose skeleton was found at an archeological site was black. As these examples show, induction does not always proceed from the particular to the general or from statements about the past or present to statements about the future.

The inductive procedures of science comprise many other, more complex and circumstantial, kinds of nondemonstrative reasoning, such as those used in making a medical diagnosis on the basis of observed symptoms, in basing statements about remote historical events on presently available evidence, or in establishing a theory on the basis of appropriate experimental data.

However, most of the problems to be considered here can be illustrated by inductions of the simple kind that proceed from instances of a generalization, and in general I will use these as examples.

II. THE NARROW INDUCTIVIST VIEW OF SCIENTIFIC INQUIRY

It should be stressed at the outset that what we have called inductive inference must not be thought of as an effective method of discovery, which by a mechanical procedure leads from observational data to appropriate hypotheses or theories. This misconception underlies what might be called the narrow inductivist view of scientific inquiry, a view that is well illustrated by the following pronouncement:

If we try to imagine how a mind of superhuman power and reach, but normal so far as the logical processes of its thought are concerned . . . would use the scientific method, the process would be as follows: First, all facts would be observed and recorded, *without selection* or *a priori* guess as to their relative importance. Second, the observed and recorded facts would be analyzed, compared, and classified, *without hypothesis or postulates* other than those necessarily involved in the logic of thought. Third, from this analysis of the facts, generalization would be inductively drawn as to the relations, classificatory or causal, between them. Fourth, further research would be deductive as well as inductive, employing inferences from previously established generalizations.[1]

It need hardly be argued in detail that this conception of scientific procedure, and of the role induction plays in it, is untenable; the reasons have been set forth by many writers. Let us just note that an inquiry conforming to this idea would never go beyond the first stage, for—presumably to safeguard scientific objectivity—no initial hypotheses about the mutual relevance and interconnections of facts are to be entertained in this stage, and as a result, there would be no criteria for the selection of the facts to be recorded. The initial stage would therefore degenerate into an indiscriminate and interminable gathering of data from an unlimited range of observable facts, and the inquiry would be totally without aim or direction.

Similar difficulties would beset the second stage—if it could ever be reached—for the classification or comparison of data again requires criteria. These are normally suggested by hypotheses about the empirical connections between various features of the "facts" under study. But the conception just cited would prohibit the use of such hypotheses, and the second stage of inquiry as here envisaged would again lack aim and direction.

It might seem that the quoted account of inductive scientific procedure could be rectified by simply adding the observation that any particular scientific investigation is aimed at solving a specified problem, and that the initial selection of data should therefore be limited to facts that are relevant to that problem. But this will not do, for the statement of a problem does not generally determine what kinds of data are relevant to its solution. The question as to the causes of lung cancer does not by itself determine what sorts of data would be relevant—whether, for example, differences in age, occupation, sex, or dietary habits should be recorded and studied. The notion of "relevant" facts acquires a clear meaning only when some specific answer to the problem has been suggested, however tentatively, in the form of a hypothesis: an observed fact will then be favorably or unfavorably relevant to the hypothesis according as its occurrence is by implication affirmed or denied by the hypothesis. Thus, the conjecture that smoking is a potent causative factor in lung cancer affirms by implication a higher incidence of the disease among smokers than among nonsmokers. Data showing for a suitable group of subjects that this is the case or that it is not would therefore constitute favorably relevant (confirming) or unfavorably relevant (disconfirming) evidence for the hypothesis. Generally, then, those data are relevant and need to be gathered which can support or disconfirm the contemplated hypothesis and which thus provide a basis for testing. it.

Contrary to the conception quoted above, therefore, hypotheses are put forward in science as tentative answers to the problem under investigation. And contrary to what is suggested by the description of the third stage of inquiry above, such answers in the form of hypotheses or theories cannot be inferred from empirical evidence by means of some set of mechanically applicable rules of induction. There is no generally applicable mechanical routine of "inductive inference" which leads from a given set of data to a corresponding hypothesis or theory somewhat in the way in which the familiar routine of multiplication leads from any two given integers, by a finite number of mechanically performable steps, to the corresponding product.

To be sure, mechanical induction routines can be specified for certain special kinds of cases, such as the construction of a curve, and of an analytic expression for the corresponding function, which will fit a finite set of points. Given a finite set of measurements of associated values of temperature and volume for a given body of gas under constant pressure, this kind of procedure could serve mechanically to produce a tentative general law connecting tempera-ture and volume of the gas. But for generating scientific theories, no such procedure can be devised.

Consider, for example, a theory, such as the theory of gravitation or the atomic theory of matter, which is introduced to account for certain previously established empirical facts, such as regularities of planetary motion and free fall, or certain chemmical findings such as those expressed by the laws of constant and of multiple proportions. Such a theory is formulated in terms of certain concepts (those of gravitational force, of atom, of molecule, etc.) which are novel in the sense that they had played no role in the description of the empirical facts which the theory is designed to explain. And surely, no set of induction rules could be devised which would be generally applicable to just any set of empirical data (physical, chemical, biological, etc.) and which, in a sequence of mechanically performable steps, would generate appropriate novel concepts, functioning in an explanatory theory, on the basis of a description of the data.[2]

Scientific hypotheses and theories, then, are not mechanically inferred from observed "facts": *They are invented by an exercise of creative imagination.* Einstein, among others, often emphasized this point, and more than a century ago William Whewell presented the same basic view of induction. Whewell speaks of scientific discovery as a "process of invention, trial, and acceptance or rejection" of hypotheses and refers to great scientific advances as achieved by "Happy *Guesses,*" by "felicitous and inexplicable strokes of inventive talent," and he adds: "No rules can ensure to us similar success in new cases; or can enable men who do not possess similar endowments, to make like advances in knowledge."[3] Similarly, Karl Popper has characterized scientific hypotheses and theories as conjectures, which must then be subjected to test and possible falsification.[4] Such conjectures are often arrived at by anything but explicit and systematic reasoning. The chemist Kékulé, for example, reports that his ring formula for the benzene molecule occurred to him in a reverie into which he had fallen before his fireplace. Gazing into the flames, he seemed to see snakes dancing about; and suddenly one of them moved into the foreground and formed a ring by seizing hold of its own tail. Kékulé does not tell us whether the snake was forming a *hexagonal* ring, but that was the structure he promptly ascribed to the benzene molecule.

Although no restrictions are imposed upon the *invention* of theories, scientific objectivity is safeguarded by making their *acceptance* dependent upon the outcome of careful tests. These consist in deriving, from the theory, consequences that admit of observational or experimental investigation, and then checking them by suitable observations or experiments. If careful testing bears out the consequences, the hypothesis is accordingly supported. But normally a scientific hypothesis asserts more than (i.e., cannot be inferred from) some finite set of consequences that may have been put to test, so that even strong evidential support affords no conclusive proof. It is precisely this fact, of course, that makes inductive "inference" non-demonstrative and gives rise to the classical problem of induction.

Karl Popper, in his analysis of this problem, stresses that the inferences involved in testing a scientific theory always run deductively from the theory to implications about empirical facts, never in the opposite direction; and he argues that therefore "Induction, i.e., inference based on many observations, is a myth. It is neither a psychological fact, nor a fact of ordinary life, nor one of scientific procedure";[5] and it is essentially this observation which, he holds, "solves . . . Hume's problem of induction."[6] But this is surely too strong a claim, for although the procedure of empirical science is not inductive in the narrow sense we have discussed and rejected, it still may be said to be *inductive in a wider sense*, referred to at the beginning of this paper: While scientific hypotheses and theories are not *inferred* from empirical data by means of some effective inductive procedure, they are *accepted* on the basis of observational or experimental findings which afford no deductively conclusive evidence for their truth. Thus, the classical problem of induction retains its import: What justification is there for accepting hypotheses on the basis of incomplete evidence?

The search for an answer to this question will require a clearer specification of the procedure that is to be justified; for while the hypotheses and theories of empirical science are not deductively implied by the evidence, it evidently will not count as inductively sound reasoning to accept a hypothesis on the basis of just any inconclusive evidence. Thus, there arises the logically prior problem of giving a more explicit characterization and precise criteria of what counts as sound inductive reasoning in science.

It may be instructive briefly to consider the analogue to this problem for deductive reasoning.

III. DEDUCTION AND INDUCTION; DISCOVERY AND VALIDATION

Deductive soundness, of course, is tantamount to deductive validity. This notion can be suggestively although imprecisely characterized by saying that an argument is deductively valid if its premises and its conclusion are so related that if all the premises are true, then the conclusion cannot fail to be true as well.[7]

As for *criteria* of deductive validity, the theory of deductive logic specifies a variety of forms of inference which are deductively valid, such as, for example, *modus ponens*:

$$p \rightarrow q$$
$$\underline{p}$$
$$q$$

or the inference rules of quantificational logic. Each of these represents a sufficient but not necessary condition of deductive validity. These criteria have the important characteristic of being expressible by reference to the syntactical structure of the argument, and thus without any reference to the meanings of the extralogical terms occurring in premises and conclusion. As we will see later, criteria of inductive soundness cannot be stated in purely syntactical terms.

We have already noted that whatever the rules of induction may be, they cannot be expected to specify mechanical routines leading from empirical evidence to appropriate hypotheses. Are the rules of deductive inference superior in this respect? Consider their role in logic and mathematics.

A moment's reflection shows that no interesting theorem in these fields is discovered by a mechanical application of the rules of deductive inference. Unless a putative theorem has first been put forward, such application would lack direction. Discovery in logic and mathematics, no less than in empirical science, *calls for imagination and invention*; it does not follow any mechanical rules.

Next, even when a putative theorem has been proposed, the rules of deduction do not, in general, provide a mechanical routine for proving or disproving it. This is illustrated by the famous arithmetical conjectures of Goldbach and of Fermat, which were proposed centuries ago but have remained undecided to this day. Mechanical routines for proving or disproving any given conjecture can be specified only for systems that admit of a decision procedure; and even for first-order quantificational logic and for elementary arithmetic, it is known that there can be no such procedure. In general, then, the construction of a proof or a disproof for a given logical or mathematical conjecture requires ingenuity.

But when a putative theorem has been proposed and a step-by-step argument has been offered as a presumptive proof for it, then the rules of deductive logic afford a means of establishing the validity of the argument: If each step conforms to one of those rules—a matter which can be decided by mechanical check—then the argument is a valid proof of the proposed theorem.

In sum, the formal rules of deductive inference are not rules of discovery leading mechanically to correct theorems or even to proofs for conjectured theorems which are in fact provable; rather, they provide criteria of soundness or of validity for proposed deductive proofs.

Analogously, rules of inductive inference will have to be conceived, not as canons of discovery, but as criteria of validation for proposed inductive arguments; far from generating a hypothesis from given evidence, they will *presuppose* that, in addition to a body of evidence, a hypothesis has been put forward, and they will then serve to appraise the soundness of the hypothesis on the basis of the evidence.

Broadly speaking, inductive arguments might be thought of as taking one of these forms:

$\frac{e}{h}$ (i.e., evidence e supports hypothesis h)

$\frac{e}{h}$ [r] (i.e., evidence e supports hypothesis h to degree r)

Here, the double line is to indicate that the relation of *e* to *h* is not that of full deductive implication but that of partial inductive support.

The second of these schemata incorporates the construal of inductive support as a quantitative concept. Rules of induction pertaining to it would provide criteria determining the degree of support conferred on certain kinds of hypotheses by certain kinds of evidence sentences; these criteria might even amount to a general definition assigning a definite value of *r* to any given *e* and *h*; this is one objective of Carnap's inductive logic.[8]

The first schema treats inductive support or confirmation as a qualitative concept; the corresponding inference rules would specify conditions under which a given evidence sentence supports, or confirms, a given hypothesis.[9]

The formulation of rules of these or similar kinds will be required to explicate the concept of inductive inference in terms of which the classical problem of justification is formulated. And it is in this context of explication that the newer problems of induction arise. We now turn to one of those problems; it concerns the qualitative concept of confirmation.

IV. THE PARADOXES OF QUALITATIVE CONFIRMATION

The most familiar rules of induction concern generalizations of the simple form "All *F* are *G*." According to one widely asserted rule, a hypothesis of this kind receives support from its positive instances—i.e., from cases of *F* that have been found also to be *G*. For example, the hypothesis "All ravens are black," or

$$(h) \qquad\qquad (x)(Rx \rightarrow Bx)$$

is supported, or confirmed, by any object *i* such that

$$(I) \qquad\qquad Ri \cdot Bi$$

or, as we will say, by any evidence sentence of the form "$Ri \cdot Bi$." Let us refer to such instances as *positive instances of type I for h*. Similarly, *h* is disconfirmed (invalidated) by any evidence sentence of the form $Ri \cdot -Bi$. This criterion was explicitly discussed and advocated by Jean Nicod;[10] I will therefore call it Nicod's criterion.

Now, the hypothesis *h* is logically equivalent to, and thus makes exactly the same assertion as, the statement that all nonblack things are nonravens, or

$$(h') \qquad\qquad (x)(-Bx \rightarrow -Rx)$$

According to Nicod's criterion, this generalization is confirmed by *its* instances—i.e., by any individual *j* such that

$$(II) \qquad\qquad -Bj \cdot -Rj$$

But since *h'* expresses exactly the same assertion as *h*, any such individual will also confirm *h*. Consequently, such things as a yellow rose, a green caterpillar, or a red herring confirm the generalization "All ravens are black," by virtue of being nonblack nonravens. I will call such objects *positive instances of type II for h*.

Next, the hypothesis *h* is logically equivalent also to the following statement:

$$(h'') \qquad\qquad (x)[(Rx \vee -Rx) \rightarrow (-Rx \vee Bx)]$$

in words: Anything that is a raven or not a raven—i.e., anything at all—either is not a raven or is black. Confirmatory instances for this version, which I will call *positive instances of type III for h*, consist of individuals *k* such that

(III) $-Rk \lor Bk$

This condition is met by any object *k* that is not a raven (no matter whether it is black) and by any object *k* that is black (no matter whether it is a raven). Any such object, then, affords a confirmatory instance in support of the hypothesis that all ravens are black.

On the other hand, the hypothesis *h* can be equivalently expressed by the sentence

(*h'''*) $(x)[(Rx \cdot -Bx) \to (Rx \cdot -Rx)]$

for which nothing can possibly be a confirmatory instance in the sense of Nicod's criterion, since nothing can be both a raven and not a raven.

These peculiarities, and some related ones, of the notion of confirmatory instance of a generalization have come to be referred to as the *paradoxes of confirmation.*[11] And indeed, at first glance they appear to be implausible and perhaps even logically unsound. But on further reflection one has to conclude, I think, that they are perfectly sound, that it is our intuition in the matter which leads us astray, so that the startling results are paradoxical only in a psychological, but not in a logical sense.

To see this, let us note first that the results in question follow deductively from two simple basic principles, namely: (A) A generalization of the form "All *F* are *G*" is confirmed by its positive instances—i.e., by cases of *F* that have been found also to be cases of *G*. (B) Whatever confirms a hypothesis also confirms any logically equivalent one.

Principle (A) is, in effect, part of Nicod's criterion, of which Nicod himself remarks that it "cannot claim the force of an axiom. But it offers itself so naturally and introduces such great simplicity, that reason welcomes it without feeling any imposition."[12] We will encounter some surprising exceptions to it in sections V and VI, but it does indeed seem very reasonable in cases of the kind we have considered so far—i.e., in reference to generalizations of universal conditional form containing exclusively property terms (one-place predicates).

Principle (B) may be called the equivalence condition. It simply reflects the idea that whether given evidence confirms a hypothesis must depend only on the content of the hypothesis and not on the way in which it happens to be formulated.

And once we accept these principles, we must also accept their surprising logical consequences.

Let us look at these consequences now from a different point of view, which will support the claim that they are sound. Suppose we are told that in the next room there is an object *i* which is a raven. Our hypothesis *h* then tells us about *i* that it is black, and if we find that this is indeed the case, so that we have $Ri \cdot Bi$, then this must surely count as bearing out, or confirming, the hypothesis.

Next, suppose we are told that in the adjoining room there is an object *j* that is not black. Again, our hypothesis tells us something more about it, namely, that it is not a raven. And if we find that this is indeed so—i.e., that $-Bj \cdot -Rj$, then this bears out, and thus supports, the hypothesis.

Finally, even if we are told only that in the next room there is an object *k*, the hypothesis still tells us something about it, namely, that either it is no raven or it is black—i.e., that $-Rk \lor Bk$; and if this is found to be the case, it again bears out the hypothesis.

Thus, our three types of positive instance must indeed be counted as confirmatory or supporting evidence for the generalization that all ravens are black.

Finally, the fact that the formulation h''' of our generalization admits of no confirming instances in the sense of Nicod's criterion presents no serious problem if, as here has been done, that criterion is stated as a sufficient but not necessary condition of confirmation.

But why does it seem implausible or paradoxical in the first place that positive instances of types II and III should be confirmatory for the generalization h? One important reason seems to lie in the assumption that the hypothesis "All ravens are black" is a statement about ravens and not about nonravens, let alone about all things in general. But surely, such a construal is untenable; anyone who accepts h would be bound to accept also the sentences h' and h'', which by the same token would have to be viewed as statements about nonravens and about all things, respectively. The use made of some statements of the form "All F are G" illustrates the same point. The Wassermann test, for example, is based, roughly speaking, on the generalization that any person infected with syphilis has a positive Wassermann reaction; but in view of its diagnostic implications for cases yielding a negative test result, this generalization surely cannot be said to be about syphilitically infected persons only.

To say that positive instances of types I, II, and III all confirm the hypothesis h is not to say, however, that they confirm the generalization to the same extent. Indeed, several writers have argued that the different types differ greatly in this respect and that, in particular, a positive instance of type I, i.e., a black raven, lends much stronger support to our generalization than a positive instance of type II, i.e., a nonblack object that is not a raven; and they have suggested that this is the objective basis for the first impression that instances of type I alone can count as confirmatory for our hypothesis.

This view can be made plausible by the following suggestive but imprecise consideration: Let k be the hypothesis "All marbles in this bag are red," and suppose that there are twenty marbles in the bag. Then the generalization k has twenty instances of type I, each being provided by one of the marbles. If we have checked each of the twenty objects that are marbles in the bag, we have exhaustively tested the hypothesis. And roughly speaking we might say that if we have examined one of the marbles and found it red, we have shown one twentieth of the total content of the hypothesis to be true.

Now consider the contrapositive of our generalization—i.e., the statement, "Any object that is not red is not a marble in this bag." Its instances are provided by all nonred objects. There are a large number of these in the world—perhaps infinitely many of them. Examining one of them and averring that it is not a marble in the bag is therefore to check, and corroborate, only a tiny portion of all that the hypothesis affirms. Hence, a positive finding of type II would indeed support our generalization, but only to a very small extent.

Analogously in the case of the ravens. If we may assume that there are vastly more nonblack things than there are ravens, then the observation of one nonblack thing that is not a raven would seem to lend vastly less support to the generalization that all ravens are black than would the observation of one raven that *is* black.

This argument might serve to mitigate the paradoxes of confirmation.[13] But I have stated it here only in an intuitive fashion. A precise formulation would require an explicit quantitative theory of degrees of confirmation or of inductive probability, such as Carnap's. Even within the framework of such a theory, the argument presupposes further assumptions, and the extent to which it can be sustained is not fully clear as yet.

Let us now turn to another perplexing aspect of induction. I will call it Goodman's riddle, because it was Nelson Goodman who first called attention to this problem and proposed a solution for it.[14]

V. GOODMAN'S RIDDLE: A FAILURE OF CONFIRMATION BY "POSITIVE INSTANCES"

One of the two basic principles from which we deduced the paradoxes of confirmation stated that a generalization of the form "All F are G" is confirmed, or supported, by its positive instances of type I—i.e., by objects which are F and also G. Although this principle seems entirely obvious, Goodman has shown that there are generalizations that derive no support at all from their observed instances. Take for example the hypothesis

(h)   All ravens are blite

where an object is said to be blite if it is either examined before midnight tonight and is black or is not examined before midnight and is white.

Suppose now that all the ravens examined so far have been found to be black; then, by definition, all ravens so far examined are also blite. Yet this latter information does not support the generalization h, for that generalization implies that all ravens examined after midnight will be white—and surely our evidence must be held to militate against this forecast rather than to support it.

Thus, some generalizations do derive support from their positive instances of type I; for example, "All ravens are black," "All gases expand when heated," "In all cases of free fall from rest, the distance covered is proportional to the square of the elapsed time," and so forth; but other generalizations, of which "All ravens are blite" is an example, are not supported by their instances. Goodman expresses this idea by saying that the former generalizations can, whereas the latter cannot, be *projected* from examined instances to as yet unexamined ones.

The question then arises how to distinguish between projectible and nonprojectible generalizations. Goodman notes that the two differ in the character of the terms employed in their formulation. The term "black," for example, lends itself to projection; the term "blite" does not. He traces the difference between these two kinds of term to what he calls their *entrenchment*—i.e., the extent to which they have been used in previously projected hypotheses. The word "blite," for example, has never before been used in a projection, and is thus much less entrenched than such words as "black," "raven," "gas," "temperature," "velocity," and so on, all of which have served in many previous inductive projections—successful as well as unsuccessful ones. What Goodman thus suggests is that our generalizations are chosen not only in consideration of how well they accord with the available evidence, but also in consideration of how well entrenched are their constituent extralogical terms.

By reference to the relative entrenchment of those terms, Goodman then formulates criteria for the comparison of generalizations in regard to their projectibility, and he thus constructs the beginnings of a theory of inductive projection.

I cannot enter into the details of Goodman's theory here, but I do wish to point out one of its implications which is, I think, of great importance for the conception of inductive inference.

As we noted earlier, the standard rules of deductive inference make reference only to the syntactical form of the sentences involved; the inference rules of quantification theory, for example, apply to all premises and conclusions of the requisite form, no matter whether the extralogical predicates they contain are familiar or strange, well entrenched or poorly entrenched. Thus,

All ravens are blite

and

r is a raven

deductively implies

r is blite

no less than

All ravens are black

and

r is a raven

deductively implies

r is black

But on Goodman's conception of projectibility, even elementary rules of induction cannot be similarly stated in purely syntactical terms. For example, the rule that a positive instance confirms a generalization holds only for generalizations with adequately entrenched predicates; and entrenchment is neither a syntactical nor even a semantic property of terms, but a pragmatic one; it pertains to the actual use that has been made of a term in generalizations projected in the past.

VI. A FURTHER FAILURE OF CONFIRMATION BY "POSITIVE INSTANCES"

Goodman's riddle shows that Nicod's criterion does not offer a generally adequate sufficient condition of confirmation: Positive instances do not confirm nonprojectible hypotheses.

But the criterion fails also in cases of a quite different kind, which do not hinge on the use of predicates such as "blite." Consider the hypothesis, "For any two persons x,y if it is not the case that each likes the other, then the first likes the second, but not vice versa"; in symbolic notation:

(h) $\qquad\qquad\qquad (x)(y)[-(Lxy \cdot Lyx) \rightarrow (Lxy \cdot -Lyx)]$

Let e be the information that a,b are two persons such that a likes b but not vice versa, i.e., that

(e) $\qquad\qquad\qquad Lab \cdot -Lba$

This information can equivalently be stated as follows:

(e') $\qquad\qquad\qquad -(Lab \cdot Lba) \text{ and } (Lab \cdot -Lba)$

for the first of these two sentences is a logical consequence of the second one. The sentence e' then represents a positive instance of type I for h; hence, on Nicod's criterion, e' should confirm h.[15]

But e' is equivalent to

(e'') $\qquad\qquad\qquad\qquad -(Lba \cdot Lab)$ and $(-Lba \cdot Lab)$

and this, on Nicod's criterion, disconfirms h. In intuitive terms, the preceding argument is to this effect: If a is counted as the first person and b as the second, then the information provided by e shows that, as e' makes explicit, a and b satisfy both the antecedent and the consequent of h and thus confirm the hypothesis; but if b is counted as the first person and a as the second one, then by virtue of the same information, b and a satisfy the antecedent but not the consequent of h, as is made explicit in e''. Thus, on Nicod's criterion, e constitutes both confirming and invalidating evidence for h.

Incidentally, h can be thrown into the form

(h') $\qquad\qquad\qquad\qquad (x)(y)(Lxy \cdot Lyx),$

which makes it obvious that the evidence e logically contradicts the given hypothesis; hence, the same is true of e', although Nicod's criterion qualifies e' as confirming h.[16]

Hypotheses of the form illustrated by h can be formulated in terms of well-entrenched predicate expressions, such as "x likes y" and "x is soluble in y"; the difficulty here illustrated does not, therefore, spring from the use of ill-behaved predicates of the Goodmanian variety.

The difficulty rather shows that the intuition which informs the Nicod criterion simply fails when the hypotheses under consideration include relational terms rather than only property terms. If one considers, in addition, that the Nicod criterion is limited to hypotheses of universal conditional form, then it becomes clear that it would be of great interest to develop a general characterization of qualitative confirmation which (1) affords a full definition rather than only partial criteria for the confirmation of a hypothesis h by an evidence sentence e; (2) is applicable to any hypothesis, of whatever logical form, that can be expressed within a specified language; and (3) avoids the difficulties of the Nicod criterion which have just been pointed out.

An explicit definition of this kind for the concept "h qualitatively confirms e" has in fact been constructed for the case where h and e are formulated in a formalized language that has the structure of a first-order functional calculus without identity; h may be any sentence whatsoever in such a language, and e may be any consistent sentence containing no quantifiers. The concept thus defined demonstrably avoids the difficulties encountered by the Nicod criterion in the case of hypotheses with relational predicates; and it implies the Nicod criterion in reference to those hypotheses of universal conditional form which contain only property terms. It has been argued, however, that the concept thus arrived at is not fully satisfactory as an explication of the vague idea of qualitative confirmation because it fails to capture certain characteristics which might plausibly be attributed to the relation of qualitative confirmation.[17]

VII. THE AMBIGUITY OF INDUCTION

I now turn to a further basic problem, which I will call the problem of inductive ambiguity. This facet of induction, unlike those we have considered so far, is not a recent discovery; both the problem and a possible solution of it have been recognized, if not always very explicitly, by several writers on probability, past as well as contemporary. But certain aspects of the problem are of special interest in the context of our discussion, and I will therefore consider them briefly.

Suppose that we have the following information:

(e_1)   Jones, a patient with a sound heart, has just had an appendectomy, and of all persons with sound hearts who underwent appendectomy in the past decade, 93 percent had an uneventful recovery.

This information, taken by itself, would clearly lend strong support to the hypothesis

(h_1)   Jones will have an uneventful recovery.

But suppose that we also have the information:

(e_2)   Jones is a nonagenarian with serious kidney failure; he just had an appendectomy after his appendix had ruptured; and in the past decade, of all cases of appendectomy after rupture of the appendix among nonagenarians with serious kidney failure only 8 percent had an uneventful recovery.

This information by itself lends strong support to the contradictory of h_1:

($-h_1$)   Jones will not have an uneventful recovery.

But e_1 and e_2 are logically compatible and may well both be part of the information available to us and accepted by us at the time when Jones' prognosis is being considered. In this case, our available evidence provides us with a basis for two rival arguments, both of them inductively sound, whose "conclusions" contradict each other. This is what I referred to above as the ambiguity of inductive reasoning: Inductively sound reasoning based on a consistent, and thus possibly true, set of "premises" may lead to contradictory "conclusions."

This possibility is without parallel in deductive reasoning: The consequences deducible from any premises selected from a consistent set of sentences form again a consistent set.

When two sound inductive arguments thus conflict, which conclusion, if any, is it reasonable to accept, and perhaps to act on? The answer, which has long been acknowledged, at least implicitly, is this: If the available evidence includes the premises of both arguments, it is irrational to base our expectations concerning the conclusions exclusively on the premises of one or the other of the arguments; the credence given to any contemplated hypothesis should always be determined by the support it receives from the *total* evidence available at the time. (Parts may be omitted if they are irrelevant in the sense that their omission leaves the inductive support of the contemplated hypothesis unchanged.) This is what Carnap has called the *requirement of total evidence.* According to it, an estimate of Jones' prospects of recovery should be based on all the relevant evidence at our disposal; and clearly, a physician trying to make a reasonable prognosis will try to meet this requirement as best he can.

What the requirement of total evidence demands, then, is that the credence given to a hypothesis h in a given knowledge situation should be determined by the inductive support, or confirmation, which h receives from the total evidence e available in that situation. Let us call this confirmation $c(h,e)$. Now for some brief comments on this maxim.

1. In the form just stated, the requirement presupposes a quantitative concept of the degree, $c(h,e)$, to which the evidence e confirms or supports the hypothesis h. This raises the question how such a concept might be defined and whether it can be characterized so generally that $c(h,e)$ is determined for *any* hypothesis h that might be proposed, relative to *any* body of evidence e that might be available. This issue has been much discussed in recent decades. Carnap, in his theory of inductive logic, has developed an explicit and completely general definition of the concept for the case where e and h are any two sentences expressible in one or another of certain formalized languages of relatively simple logical structure.[18] Others have

argued that the concept in question can be satisfactorily defined at best for certain special types of hypotheses and of evidential information. For example, if the total relevant evidence consists just of the sentences e_1 and e_2 listed above, certain analysts would hold that no probability or degree of confirmation can be significantly assigned to the hypothesis, "Jones will have an uneventful recovery," since the evidence provides no information about the percentage of uneventful recoveries among nonagenarians with sound hearts but seriously defective kidneys who undergo appendectomy after rupture of the appendix.

2. Next, let us note that while the requirement of total evidence is a principle concerning induction, it is not a rule of inductive inference or, more precisely, of inductive support, for it does not concern the question whether, or how strongly, a given hypothesis is supported by given evidence. The requirement is concerned rather with the rational use, or application, of inductive reasoning in the formation of empirical beliefs. This observation suggests a distinction between two kinds of rules pertaining to inductive reasoning:

(a) *Rules of inductive support, or of valid inductive inference.* These would encompass, for example, all criteria concerning the qualitative confirmation or disconfirmation of generalizations by positive or negative instances; criteria determining degrees of confirmation; and also all general principles connecting degrees of confirmation with each other, such as the law, that the degrees of confirmation of a hypothesis and of its contradictory on the same evidence add up to unity.

(b) *Rules of application.* These concern the use of rules of the former kind in the rational formation of empirical beliefs. The requirement of total evidence is one such rule of application, but not the only one, as will soon be seen.

The distinction between rules of inference and rules of application can be made also in reference to deductive reasoning. The rules of inference, as we noted earlier, provide criteria of deductive validity; but they qualify as deductively valid many particular arguments whose conclusions are false, and they do not concern the conditions under which it is reasonable to believe, or to accept, the conclusion of a deductively valid argument. To do so would be the task of rules for the rational application of deductive inference.

One such rule would stipulate, for example, that if we have accepted a set of statements as presumably true, then any logical consequence of that set (or, perhaps rather, any statement that is known to be such a consequence) should equally be accepted as presumably true.

The two kinds of rules for deduction call for quite different kinds of justification. An inference rule such as *modus ponens* might be justified by showing that when applied to true premises it will invariably yield a true conclusion—which is what is meant by the claim that an argument conforming to the rule is deductively valid.

But in order to justify a rule of application, we will have to consider what ends the acceptance or rejection of deductive conclusions is to serve. For example, if we are interested in accepting a set of statements, or of corresponding beliefs, which will afford us an emotionally reassuring or aesthetically satisfying account of the world, then it will not always be reasonable to accept, or to believe, the logical consequences of what we have previously accepted. If, on the other hand, truth is what we value in our accepted statements, and if we are accordingly concerned to give credence to all statements that are true as far as our information enables us to tell, then indeed we have to accept all the consequences of previously accepted statements; thus, justification of our rule of application requires reference to the objectives, or the values, that our acceptance procedure is meant to achieve.

VIII. INDUCTION AND VALUATION

Similarly, if we wish to devise rules for the rational application of valid inductive reasoning, or if we wish to appraise or justify such rules, we will have to take into account the objectives to be achieved by the inductive acceptance procedure, or the values or disvalues of the consequences that might result from correct or from incorrect acceptance decisions. In this sense, the construction and the justification of inductive acceptance rules for empirical statements presuppose judgments of value.

This is especially obvious when we wish to decide whether a given hypothesis is to be accepted in the strong sense of being relied on as a basis for practical action. Suppose, for example, that a new vaccine has been developed for immunization against a serious infectious disease that can afflict humans as well as chimpanzees. Let *h* be the hypothesis that the vaccine is both safe and effective in a sense specified by suitable operational criteria, and suppose that the hypothesis has been tested by examining a number of samples of the vaccine for safety and effectiveness. Let *e* be the evidence thus obtained.

Our rules of inductive support may then tell us how strongly the hypothesis is confirmed by the evidence; but in deciding whether to act on it we will have to consider, besides the strength of confirmation, also the kind of action that is contemplated, and what benefits might result from a correct decision, what harm from a mistaken one. For example, our standards of acceptance are likely to differ according as humans or chimpanzees are to be treated with the vaccine; and it may well happen that *on the same evidence* the given hypothesis is accepted as a basis of action in one case but rejected in the other.

Inductive decisions of this kind have been extensively studied in the mathematical theory of testing and decision-making. This theory deals in particular with the case where the values or disvalues attached to the possible consequences of the available decisions are expressible in numerical terms as so-called utilities. For such situations, the theory has developed a number of specific decision rules, which are rules of application in our sense. These rules—maximin, maximax, maximizing the expectable utility of the outcome, and others—make the acceptance or the rejection of the hypothesis contingent on the utilities assigned to the different possible consequences of acceptance or rejection; and when a measure for the evidential support of the hypothesis is available, that support is likewise taken into consideration.[19] In this fashion, the inductive decision rules combine empirical considerations with explicitly valuational ones.

That rules for the acceptance or rejection of empirical hypotheses thus presuppose valuational considerations has been emphasized by several writers. Some of these have made the stronger claim that the values in question are ethical values. Thus, Churchman asserts that "the simplest question of fact in science requires for even an approximation, a judgment of value," and that "the science of ethics . . . is *basic* to the meaning of any question the experimental scientist raises."[20] And in the context of a detailed study of the logic of testing statistical hypotheses, Braithwaite asserts, in a similar vein: "To say that it is 'practically certain' that the next 1000 births in Cambridge will include the birth of at least one boy includes a hedonic or ethical assessment."[21]

But while it is true that the justification of rules of acceptance for statements of fact requires reference to judgments of preference or of valuation, the claim that the values concerned are ethical values is, I think, open to question. Our argument about valuational presuppositions has so far been concerned only with the acceptance of hypotheses as a basis of specific *actions*, and in this case the underlying valuations may indeed be ethical in character. But what standards will govern the acceptance and rejection of hypotheses for which no practical application is contemplated? Braithwaite's statement about male births in Cambridge might well belong in that category, and surely so do the hypotheses examined in pure, or basic, scientific research; these might concern, for example, the rate of recession of distant galaxies or the spontaneous creation of hydrogen atoms in empty space. In such cases, it seems, we simply wish to decide, in consideration of the available evidence, whether to believe a proposed hypothesis; whether to record it, so to speak, in our book of tentative scientific knowledge, without envisaging any technological application. Here, we cannot relevantly base our decisions on any utilities or disutilities attached to practical consequences of acceptance or rejection and, in particular, ethical considerations play no part.

What will have to be taken into account in constructing or justifying inductive acceptance rules for pure scientific research are the objectives of such research or the importance attached in pure science to achieving certain kinds of results. What objectives does pure scientific research seek to achieve? Truth of the accepted statements might be held to be one of them. But surely not truth at all costs. For then, the only rational decision policy would be never to accept any hypothesis on inductive grounds since, however well supported, it might be false.

Scientific research is not even aimed at achieving very high probability of truth, or very strong inductive support, at all costs. Science is willing to take considerable chances on this score. It is willing to accept a theory that vastly outreaches its evidential basis if that theory promises to exhibit an underlying order, a system of deep and simple systematic connections among what had previously been a mass of disparate and multifarious facts.

It is an intriguing but as yet open question whether the objectives, or the values, that inform pure scientific inquiry can all be adequately characterized in terms of such theoretical desiderata as confirmation, explanatory power, and simplicity and, if so, whether these features admit of a satisfactory combination into a concept of purely theoretical or scientific utility that could be involved in the construction of acceptance rules for hypotheses and theories in pure science. Indeed, it is by no means clear whether the conception of basic scientific research as leading to the provisional acceptance or rejection of hypotheses is tenable at all. One of the problems here at issue is whether the notion of accepting a hypothesis independently of any contemplated action can be satisfactorily explicated within the framework of a purely logical and methodological analysis of scientific inquiry[22] or whether, if any illuminating construal of the idea is possible at all, it will have to be given in the context of a psychological, sociological, and historical study of scientific research.[23]

To conclude with a summary that centers about the classical problem of induction: For a clear statement of the classical problem of justification, two things are required. First, the procedure to be justified must be clearly characterized—this calls for an explication of the rules governing the inductive appraisal of hypotheses and theories; second, the intended objectives of the procedure must be indicated, for a justification of any procedure will have to be relative to the ends it is intended to serve. Concerning the first of these tasks, we noted that while there are no systematic mechanical rules of inductive discovery, two other kinds of rule have to be envisaged and distinguished, namely, rules of support and rules of application. And in our discussion of the objectives of inductive procedures we noted certain connections between rational belief on one hand and valuation on the other.

Whatever insights further inquiry may yield, the recognition and partial exploration of these basic problems has placed the classical problem of induction into a new and clearer perspective and has thereby advanced its philosophical clarification.

NOTES

1. A. B. Wolfe, "Functional Economics," in *The Trend of Economics*, ed. R. G. Tugwell (New York: Alfred A. Knopf, 1924), p. 450 (author's italics).
2. This argument does not presuppose a fixed division of the vocabulary of empirical science into observational and theoretical terms; it is quite compatible with acknowledging that as a theory becomes increasingly well established and accepted, certain statements couched in terms of its characteristic concepts may come to be qualified as descriptions of "observed facts."
3. William Whewell, *The Philosophy of the Inductive Sciences*, 2d ed. (London: John W. Parker, 1847), II, 41 (author's italics).
4. See, for example, Popper's essay, "Science: Conjectures and Refutations," in his book, *Conjectures and Refutations* (New York: Basic Books, 1962).
5. Karl Popper, "Philosophy of Science: A Personal Report," in *British Philosophy in the Mid-Century*, ed. C. A. Mace (London: Allen and Unwin, 1957), pp. 155–91, quotation from p. 181.
6. Popper, "Philosophy of Science," p. 183.
7. Precise general characterizations of deductive validity, for arguments in languages of certain specified forms, will be found, e.g., in W. V. O. Quine, *Methods of Logic*, rev. ed. (New York: Holt, Rinehart and Winston, 1959).
8. See especially the following publications by Rudolf Carnap: *Logical Foundations of Probability*, 2d ed. (Chicago: University of Chicago Press, 1962); "The Aim of Inductive Logic," in *Logic, Methodology and Philosophy of Science: Proceedings of the 1960 International Congress*, eds. E. Nagel, P. Suppes, and A. Tarski (Stanford: Stanford University Press, 1962), pp. 303–18.
9. It seems to me, therefore, that Popper begs the question when he declares: "But it is obvious that this rule or craft of 'valid induction' . . . simply does not exist. No rule can ever guarantee that a generalization inferred from true observations, however often repeated, is true" ("Philosophy of Science," p. 181). That inductive reasoning is not *deductively* valid is granted at the outset; the problem is that of constructing a concept of *inductive* validity.
10. Jean Nicod, *Foundations of Geometry and Induction* (New York: Harcourt, Brace and World, 1930), p. 219. Nicod here speaks of "truths or facts," namely, "the presence or absence of *B* in a case of *A*," as confirming or invalidating "the law *A* entails *B*" (author's italics). Such confirmatory and disconfirmatory facts can be thought of as described by corresponding evidence sentences. Nicod remarks about his criterion: "We have not seen it stated in any explicit manner. However, we do not think that anything ever written on induction is incompatible with it" (p. 220). Whether Nicod regards the specified conditions as necessary and sufficient or merely as sufficient for confirmation or invalidation is not entirely clear, although he does say: "It is conceivable that we have here the only two direct modes in which a fact can influence the probability of a law" (p. 219). We will construe his criteria simply as *sufficient* conditions of confirmation and invalidation.
11. These paradoxes were first noted in my essay "Le problème de la vérité," *Theoria* (Göteborg) 3 (1937), pp. 206–46 (see especially p. 222) and were discussed in greater detail in my articles "Studies in the Logic of Confirmation," *Mind*, 54 (1945), pp. 1–26, 97–121, and "A Purely Syntactical Definition of Confirmation," *The Journal of Symbolic Logic*, 8 (1943), pp. 122–43.
12. Nicod, *Geometry and Induction*, pp. 219–20.
13. It was first offered by Janina Hosiasson-Lindenbaum in her article "On Confirmation," *The Journal of Symbolic Logic* 5 (1940), pp. 133–48. Similar ideas were proposed by, among others, D. Pears, "Hypotheticals," *Analysis* 10 (1950), pp. 49–63; I. J. Good, "The Paradoxes of Confirmation," Parts I and II, *The British Journal for the Philosophy of Science* 11 (1960), pp. 145–48; 12 (1961), pp. 63–64. A detailed and illuminating study of qualitative confirmation and its paradoxes is offered in section 3, Part I of Israel Scheffler, *The Anatomy of Inquiry* (New York: Alfred A. Knopf, 1963).
14. Nelson Goodman, *Fact, Fiction, and Forecast* (Cambridge: Harvard University Press, 1955); 2d, rev. ed. (Indianapolis: Bobbs-Merrill, 1965).

15. Nicod does not explicitly deal with hypotheses which, like *h*, contain relational terms rather than only property terms such as "raven" and "black"; but the application here suggested certainly seems to be in full accord with his basic conception.
16. This further paradox of qualitative confirmation was briefly noted in my article "Studies in the Logic of Confirmation," p. 13.
17. The general definition is developed in "A Purely Syntactical Definition of Confirmation"; the gist of it is presented in sec. 9 of my article essay, "Studies in the Logic of Confirmation." The objections in question were raised especially by R. Carnap in *Logical Foundations of Probability*, sections 86–88. Briefly, Carnap's principal objection is to the effect that under an adequate definition of qualitative confirmation, *e* should confirm *h* only if, in the sense of inductive probability theory, *e* raises the prior probability of *h*; and my definition of confirmation is not compatible with such a construal.
18. See especially the following publications: "On Inductive Logic," *Philosophy of Science* 12 (1945), pp. 72–97; *Logical Foundations of Probability; The Continuum of Inductive Methods* (Chicago: University of Chicago Press, 1952).
19. A lucid account of these rules and of their theoretical use will be found in R. D. Luce and H. Raiffa, *Games and Decisions* (New York: Wiley, 1957).
20. C. W. Churchman, *Theory of Experimental Inference* (New York: Macmillan, 1948), pp. vii, viii (author's italics).
21. R. B. Braithwaite, *Scientific Explanation* (Cambridge: Cambridge University Press, 1953), p. 251.
22. For a fuller discussion and bibliographic references concerning these issues, see, e.g., section 12 of C. G. Hempel, "Deductive-Nomological *vs.* Statistical Explanation," in *Scientific Explanation, Space, and Time*, eds. H. Feigl and G. Maxwell, Minnesota Studies in the Philosophy of Science, vol. 3 (Minneapolis: University of Minnesota Press, 1962), pp. 98–169. Some of the basic issues are examined in R. B. Braithwaite's paper, "The Role of Values in Scientific Inference," and especially the discussion of that paper in *Induction: Some Current Issues*, eds. H. E. Kyburg, Jr., and E. Nagel (Middletown, CT: Wesleyan University Press, 1963), pp. 180–204.
23. Such an alternative conception is represented, e.g., by T. S. Kuhn's work, *The Structure of Scientific Revolutions* (Chicago: University of Chicago Press, 1962).

JAMES H. FETZER

THE JUSTIFICATION OF INDUCTION

The "problem of induction" is perhaps as clear a paradigm of a purely philosophical difficulty as one is likely to find: it has been advanced in many different forms, for which a wide variety of disparate solutions have been proposed, about the correctness of which few philosophers have tended to agree. It has been variously characterized as subject to an inductive solution, a deductive solution, a linguistic resolution, or as incapable of solution; it has been diversely appraised as an important problem, as an unimportant problem, and as no problem at all. Perhaps even more remarkably, it appears to be a problem possessing no practical significance for anyone at all, since the particular form that its solution might take seems to be a matter of no more and no less practical consequence than whether it is amenable to any resolution after all. No doubt a problem whose "successful' resolution has no different practical implications than no solution at all has the *sine qua non* of every truly philosophical problem. It thus appears to be a paradigm, indeed.

One of the most interesting attempts to come to grips with the problem of induction is also one of the most controversial, namely: Popper's solution, which emphasizes the asymmetry between *verification* and *falsification* as (general) scientific procedures (especially Popper 1965, part I; and Popper 1972, chapter 1). The purpose of this chapter is to maintain that, although Popper's position may easily be misunderstood, when appropriate attention is given to,

(i) the fundamental distinction between lawlike and accidental generalizations;

(ii) the important differences between inductive confirmation and Popperian corroboration; and,

(iii) the theoretical significance of Popper's principle of empiricism as opposed to traditional principles of induction;

it becomes apparent that, whether or not Popper's arguments are mistaken in detail, his solution, in principle, is correct. The point, therefore, is to propose a Popperian defense of Popper's own position.

Not the least of the difficulties which this investigation confronts arises from a certain ambiguity afflicting our conception of induction itself, for the term, "induction", may be employed in at least two distinct senses. In its *broad* sense, an argument or an inference may be described as "inductive" whenever its conclusion, no matter how tentatively or provisionally entertained, contains more content than do its premises; while, in its *narrow* sense, an argument or inference is described as "inductive" whenever it conforms to certain specific "inductive rules" exemplified in particular by probabilistic conceptions of confirmation as well as by traditional principles of induction. Let us note, therefore, that, although procedures which are "inductive" in the narrow sense are also "inductive" in the broad sense, necessarily, those which are "inductive" in the broad sense are not necessarily also "inductive" in the narrow sense.

This distinction becomes especially important insofar as the position Popper has promoted fits within the category of those which are "inductive" in the broad sense but not in the narrow, a circumstance that has been obscured, at least in part, due to two quite different factors: first, the negative significance of *successful* attempts at falsification falls within the domain of deductive methodology; second, the very conception of "rules of induction" tends to be identified with precisely those procedures which Popper vehemently rejects. The complexity of the situation, however, calls for more subtle discriminations, insofar as Popper has sought to provide techniques and procedures, i.e., a set of rules, for assessing the acceptability of alternative hypotheses, where the positive significance of *unsuccessful* attempts at falsification clearly falls within the domain of inductive methodology, as the considerations which follow should explain.

Popper's analysis itself involves distinguishing between different versions of the *philosophical* problem (which he refers to as the "traditional" problem and its "methodological" variant, respectively) and what may be characterized as the *pragmatical* problem, which concerns decision-making and practical life. One significant feature of Popper's approach, therefore, is to seek to define the character of the problem at hand before undertaking its solution, which, in this case especially, should be viewed as an indispensable ingredient of rational procedure. In order to present Popper's solution within an appropriate context, however, I would like to begin by considering the distinction drawn between *validation* and *vindication* as modes of justification that apply to individual arguments and to inferential principles, respectively; for it will be my contention that preoccupation with vindication and validation has tended to obscure an important aspect of the problem of induction which, I believe, should be acknowledged as the foundation of any successful solution.

THE TRADITIONAL PROBLEM OF INDUCTION

Induction and deduction are generally supposed to be mutually exclusive and jointly exhaustive modes of propositional inference, i.e., which regulate inferences from propositional premises to propositional conclusions, as chapter 1[1] has also explained. As modes of inference, of course, each may be envisioned as an accepted "set of rules" in accordance with which inferences must be drawn to qualify either as *deductively valid* or, let us say, as *inductively proper*. Analogously, proper arguments with true premises will be *correct*, just as valid arguments with true premises are *sound*. Provided we consider "arguments" as sets of propositions (or sentences) divided into two parts, i.e., "premises" and "conclusions", then whether or not a particular argument (or inference) belongs to the class of proper inductive arguments may only be determined relative to the set of accepted inductive rules; and whether or not a particular argument (or inference) is a member of the class of valid deductive arguments may only be determined relative to the set of accepted deductive rules. The establishment of a specific argument as in conformity with accepted rules of either set is thus sufficient to warrant the acceptance of that argument (or inference) as either inductively proper or deductively valid. The justification of an inference through such a procedure, of course, is known as *validation* (Feigl 1963).

Since there are infinitely many possible rules of either kind, however, the selection of some finite set of rules of each type as acceptable rules has come to be regarded as a matter of considerable philosophical interest. The process of selection necessarily involves reference to certain characteristics which acceptable rules are supposed to possess. The establishment of a specific rule as possessing those characteristics thus constitutes a sufficient condition for the inclusion of that rule as a member of the set of acceptable rules. The justification of a rule by means of this procedure, moreover, is known as *vindication* (Salmon 1967). Although validation and vindication are both familiar conceptions of justification, their application, in principle, depends upon a logically prior process of establishing those specific characteristics whose possession renders a rule acceptable. These characteristics, in other words, are ascertained in relation to the objective, purpose, or program of the enterprise itself, which, of course, in this case distinguishes a mode of inference, i.e., they are *pragmatically* determined.

The inductive and deductive modes of inference, therefore, may be analyzed into three constitutive components, namely: a class of inferences, a set of rules, and a program. The *class of inferences* which are acceptable within each mode of inference is determined by some set of accepted rules. The *set of rules* which are acceptable within each mode of inference, in turn, is determined by the accepted program. And the *program* which is acceptable for each mode of inference is determined by the purpose for which that mode of inference is intended. The residual problem, therefore, is one of ascertaining the purpose to be fulfilled by each of these modes of inference, a matter about which there appears to be considerable agreement with respect to the deductive mode. Thus, deductive inferences, in general, are supposed to be *truth-preserving*, in the sense that deductive rules of inference are acceptable if and only if, when applied to true premises, only true conclusions follow (Beth 1969). The establishment of a set of rules and a class of inferences which fulfills this purpose thus defines the deductive program.

The selection of a set of accepted rules from within the set of acceptable rules normally involves both logical and non-logical considerations. The *logical* considerations, of course, include the soundness and completeness properties of a contemplated set of rules, since any such set which permitted some inferences to be drawn which are *not* valid would fail to satisfy the deductive program, just as such a set which does not permit other inferences to be drawn which *are* valid falls short of its complete satisfaction. Apart from these purely deductive conditions, however, *nonlogical* considerations, such as balancing theoretical elegance against practical convenience, fulfill an important role; for, there are those who desire to derive a maximal set of theorems from a minimal set of axioms, even though the resulting proofs may be tedious and complex, while others wish to secure a modest set of axioms which, although not equally elegant, provides a more flexible foundation for constructing relatively simple and obvious proofs. Those who belong to the first group, of course, tend to take a dim view of those who belong to the second, while the latter, in turn, are themselves rather intimidated by the former—all of which tends to account for the enormous variety of different textbooks currently available within this field.

In the case of inductive inference, by contrast, there has been an absence of general agreement beyond the tendency to assume that induction is supposed to be *knowledge-*

extending, insofar as inductive rules of inference are envisioned as regulating inferences whose conclusions contain more content than do their premises. This conception itself, however, provides (at best) a necessary but not sufficient condition for defining the program of the inductive mode of inference, since this requirement is satisfied by innumerable invalid deductive arguments that, nevertheless, would not qualify as inductively proper. One attempt to deal with this difficulty has been to seek to combine the *ampliative* (or knowledge-extending) function of the inductive mode with the *demonstrative* (or truth-preserving) function of the deductive mode to generate a class of ampliative-demonstrative inferences. Rules of inference that satisfy one of these conditions, however, do so at the expense of the other, which dictates the result that this contradictory conception of the inductive program cannot possibly succeed.

Another attempt to deal with this difficulty has been to recommend a rather specific conception of the purpose of induction, namely: to ascertain the limiting frequencies with which different attributes occur within different reference classes during the course of the world's history (Reichenbach 1949, and Salmon 1967, for example). Assuming this conception itself is logically consistent, it remains to be determined whether or not the inductive program is thereby adequately defined. Among the most important problems confronting this conception, for example, are (a) the extent to which scientific practice actually fulfills this interpretation and (b) the extent to which its objectives and procedures are illuminated by such a construction. The first problem might be described as one of *definitional relevance*, insofar as a conception that altogether ignores actual scientific practice is surely irrelevant as a definition of the inductive program; while the second problem might be described as one of *theoretical significance*, since a conception of induction that fails to clarify scientific procedure should certainly not define its foundations (conditions which parallel Hempel's [1952] requirements of adequacy for explications).

Not the least of the reasons for objecting to this conception, therefore, is that actual scientific practice appears to pursue the discovery of scientific laws rather than ascertaining limiting frequencies, to search for principles of prediction for the past and the present as well as for the distant future, and to value explanations for "the single case" in addition to those accessible for long and short runs. The point, let me emphasize, is not that the case for one conception rather than the other is clear-cut and beyond debate, but rather that there is an issue here which requires explicit attention and careful argumentation for its tentative resolution, namely: *the problem of defining the inductive program*. And insofar as there appear to be objective standards of logical consistency, of definitional relevance, and of theoretical significance which are applicable to such a dispute, the defense of some specific conception of the inductive program is an indispensable ingredient of attempts to provide an adequate justification for induction, an aspect we may refer to as *the process of exoneration*.

The three constitutive components of modes of inference, therefore, are attended by three distinct modes of justification, insofar as a class of inferences must be validated, a set of rules must be vindicated, and a program must be exonerated, for its comprehensive justification. (Distinctions such as these, incidentally, also apply to forming beliefs, making decisions, and so forth, which we will consider in chapters to come.) Thus, the foundation for Popper's analysis of induction consists in the conception of its program as one of *providing for the acceptance, rejection, or modification of hypotheses and theories of broad scope and systematic power which may be employed for the purposes of explanation and prediction, with special concern for the provisional and tentative quality of the results of scientific inquiry*. But the crucial difference between Popper's program and similar conceptions that others have endorsed is reflected by the difference between alternative formulations of "the problem of induction" itself (Popper 1972, p. 7), namely:

(1) as the *traditional* problem, which asks, "Can the claim that an explanatory universal theory is *true* be justified on empirical grounds, i.e., by assuming the truth of certain test statements or experiential findings?"; and,

(2) as the *methodological* problem, which asks, "Can the claim that an explanatory universal theory is *true* or that it is *false* be justified on empirical grounds, i.e., by assuming the truth of certain test statements or experiential findings?"

For Popper maintains that the answer to the traditional question is, "No," but that the answer to the methodological question is, "Yes," on the basis of certain asymmetrical characteristics of *verification* and *falsification* as (general) scientific procedures (Popper 1965, p. 265), which we shall now consider.

Not the least of Popper's contributions to philosophical discussion has been his unrelenting assault upon the *desideratum of certainty* as an indispensable foundation of scientific knowledge: in opposition to those who defend the conception of "incorrigible" sense data or of "irrevocable" observation reports, he has promoted the position that observation statements represent interpretations of perceptual experience by means of presupposed theories. Popper contends that, "since there can be no theory-free observation, and no theory-free language, there can of course be no theory-free rule or principle of induction" upon which all theories could be based (Popper 1976, p. 148). For the present, let us understand his position as undermining the conception of observation sentences as establishing an infallible evidential resource for subjecting scientific hypotheses and theories to empirical test, rather than as an objection to any principles of induction *per se*. Thus, to emphasize the fallibility of all experiential data, let us also refer to these reports as *basic statements* (Popper 1965, pp. 104–105).

These considerations make it clear that the differences between verification and falsification, whatever they may be, do not consist in the alleged incorrigibility of one of these procedures in comparison with the other: our supposition, therefore, denies the defensibility of "dogmatic" versions of either methodology, but instead only supports the possibility of relative, rather than absolute, verifiability and falsifiability, i.e., in application to basic statements, these procedures yield only *fallible* results (as Hempel [1965, pp. 39–46] has also observed). The principle of verifiability, accordingly, may be formulated as follows:

An hypothesis *h* is *verifiable* within a language L if and only if *h* is not analytic but follows from some logically consistent finite set of potential basic statements expressible in L;

where the cumbersome phrase, "potential basic statements expressible in L," is required to implement the semantical analogue of the pragmatical notion of basic statements as singular sentences whose truth or falsity is decided by tentative agreement among relevant members of the language-using community, as Popper (1965, pp. 100–106) suggests. Analogously, the principle of falsifiability may be formulated as follows:

An hypothesis *h* is *falsifiable* within a language L if and only if the negation of *h* is not analytic but follows from some logically consistent finite set of potential basic statements expressible in L;

where, as before, the results of neither process are regarded as infallible.

The principal attraction of these principles, of course, is that they offer the prospect of characterizing scientific procedure entirely by means of the application of deductive principles to basic statements as empirical premises; as a consequence, however, they fulfill the ampliative function of inductive inference in a psychological, but not in a logical, sense, insofar as the results of these procedures may amount to the *transformation* of what we may consider as "existing knowledge," but not in its addition, rejection, or modification—at least to the extent to which that "knowledge" itself is consistent. The psychological benefits that accrue from reliance upon these demonstrative procedures, of course, are not therefore without value; on the contrary, the deductive transformation of tentatively agreed-upon conclusions concerning the data of more-or-less immediate experience may not only expose unexpected contradictions in the state of "existing knowledge" but also dictate further observation and experimentation to reestablish consistency, a circumstance which may become acute with the sudden acquisition of enormous quantities of unfamiliar evidence through the introduction of technological innovations such as the microscope, the telescope, x-ray diagnosis, and so on. (Thus, Ackermann [1976] refers to the sets of data available by means of fixed sets of technical instruments as "data domains".)

Of course, if all of the objectives of scientific inquiry could be attained by means of deductive procedures alone, there would be nothing more to be desired; it seems clear, however, that verification and falsification, individually or in combination, do not suffice for such a purpose, since in particular, as is indeed well-known, different classes of sentences are amenable to each of these procedures. Thus, for example,

Sentence Type	Verifiable	Falsifiable
Existential Generalizations	Yes	No
Finite Frequency Statements	Yes	Yes
Limiting Frequency Statements	No	No
Mixed Quantification Statements	No	No
Statistical Lawlike Statements	No	No
Universal Lawlike Statements	No	Yes

which reflects the incapacity of deductive methodology alone to justify the claim that some specific limiting frequency statement, statement of mixed quantification, or statistical lawlike statement either *is true* or *is false* on the basis of any logically consistent and finite set of basic statements (an issue Hempel [1965, especially pp. 102–107] has also discussed). A number of explanatory comments could be made relative to these considerations; for example, if statistical lawlike sentences were to be *identified* with limiting frequency statements, then only five, rather than six, distinct sentence types would actually be required. Other considerations, however, suggest that a *seventh* kind is called for instead.

The distinction between a criterion of cognitive significance (which distinguishes between meaningful and meaningless sentences) and a criterion of demarcation (for distinguishing between "scientific" and "nonscientific" sentences), I take it, is sufficiently familiar to us all as to warrant no detailed elaboration. Popper's employment of falsifiability as a criterion of demarcation appears to have the uningratiating consequence of rendering existential generalizations, limiting frequency statements, statements of mixed quantification, and statistical lawlike statements, not meaningless, but *nonscientific*. This, of course, creates an immediate quandary, since such sentences as, "There are black holes," "In arbitrarily large populations of natural childbirths, the limiting frequency for male children is .514," and, "Every metal has a melting point," seem to represent at least *some* of the kinds of knowledge which scientific inquiry should be able to supply. (Popper himself, of course, has discussed most of these problems; see, for example, Popper 1965, pp. 100–103; and especially Schilpp, ed., 1974, pp. 1038–39.) Rather than evaluate Popper's criterion of demarcation, however, I would like to consider the problems implicitly created for his program.

These difficulties, moreover, are less severe with respect to limiting frequency statements and statements of mixed quantification, for example, provided they do not also qualify as *lawlike* generalizations; for the principal objective of Popper's program is to provide for the acceptance, rejection, and modification of hypotheses and theories of broad scope and systematic power which are applicable for the purposes of explanation and prediction, i.e., *the members of the class of scientific laws.* Thus, if statistical lawlike statements, for example, are not amenable to empirical test on the basis of Popper's principle of falsifiability, then either (a) Popper's set of rules of induction lacks an adequate vindication, or (b) Popper's program lacks a satisfactory exoneration, or, perhaps, (c) both. If statistical lawlike statements are identifiable with limiting frequency statements, however, then a solution may present itself, insofar as limiting frequency statements in turn may be identified with nondecreasing sequences of finite sets of elements, each of which might be described as a finite frequency and therefore be not only falsifiable but also verifiable.

This problem, of course, was very much on Popper's mind while writing *The Logic of Scientific Discovery*, which was in large part devoted to this problem's resolution. According to the methodological principles developed there, important aspects of testing and evaluating hypotheses and theories are determined by conventional decisions and procedures of several different kinds, namely: (1) an hypothesis or theory under test must be delineated from (provisionally unproblematic) background knowledge and auxiliary hypotheses; (2) decision procedures must be agreed upon for the acceptance and rejection of basic statements describing experimental outcomes as well as initial conditions; (3) the decision must be made to regard particular experiments (or sets of experiments) as tests of the relevant kinds (usually, although not always, by means of experimental repetitions); and, (4) in the case of statistical (or probabilistic) hypotheses, agreements must also be reached rendering specific patterns of outcome distributions "compatible" or "incompatible" with the hypothesis under investigation. (Concerning (4), see especially Popper 1965, pp. 198–205; and Lakatos 1970, especially pp. 106–11.)

The peculiar difficulty with statistical hypotheses, of course, stems from the fact that any limiting frequency over an infinite sequence is logically compatible with any relative frequency within a finite segment; but Popper recognized that, although arbitrary deviations from limiting values within (normal) sequences were *logically possible*, they were not therefore *equally probable*. Thus, by exploiting the results of Bernoulli's theorem, among others, Popper extended the principle of falsifiability for statistical statements by adopting the *supplementary principle* that, since almost all possible finite segments of large size will very probably exhibit relative frequencies that are very close to the limiting frequencies of these infinite sequences, *highly improbable outcomes deserve systematic neglect*. (See especially Popper 1965, pp. 410–19.) Popper has thus sought to defend the position that the testing of statistical hypotheses, like that of all other scientific hypotheses, is deductive: for, the probabilities of various frequency distributions over large (but finite) samples are mathematically derived employing the principles of the calculus of probability, highly improbable results are supposed not to occur, and the hypotheses under consideration are confronted by experience. (See Gillies 1973 as well.)

Now while these considerations tend to justify Popper's program and to salvage his criterion of demarcation, there appear to be further grounds in support of the principle of falsifiability as a fundamental scientific rule, namely: the theoretical distinction between *lawlike sentences* and (merely) *accidental generalizations*. For, as we have discovered, by introducing the conception of a single case statistical predicate as a refinement of Popper's propensity interpretation of probability, it has proven possible to develop an account of statistical laws as universal generalizations attributing statistical properties, i.e., probabilistic dispositions, to every member of appropriately specified reference classes, which in turn has led to the emergence of a unified theory of the character of universal and statistical laws on the basis of a dispositional analysis. The pursuit of this objective has also brought about the elaboration of a single case dispositional predicate possible-world formal semantics in order to formalize the logical relations that obtain between logical, subjunctive, and nomological conditionals within scientific language, which was presented in chapter 3.

The account of *scientific conditionals* that has resulted from these investigations reflects the following suppositions:

(1) that subjunctive conditionals may be justified on the basis of either logical or nomological considerations, but not on other grounds;

(2) that nomological conditionals are themselves of two different kinds: "simple" nomic conditionals and "causal" nomic conditionals;

(3) that "causal" nomic conditionals are likewise of two kinds, i.e., "universal" and "statistical" (or "probabilistic") causal conditionals;

(4) that true scientific conditionals satisfy a requirement of maximal specificity, which is not generally applicable in ordinary discourse; and,

(5) that lawlike sentences are logically general nomological conditionals, i.e., that nomological conditionals are instantiated lawlike sentences.

The most important feature of this analysis for Popper's inductive program, moreover, is that it reflects three desiderata concerning the character of scientific laws which Popper has sought to emphasize, namely: (a) that lawlike sentences are unrestrictedly general; (b) that all universals are dispositional; and, (c) that lawlike sentences are not extensional (or, truth-functional) generalizations (especially Popper 1965, pp. 420–41).

Indeed, it is the characteristic of lawlike sentences as *intensional generalizations* that provides the ultimate grounds for preferring Popper's conception of the importance of falsifiability over alternative principles. Whereas the truth-values of extensional generalizations are determined by the history of the actual world—they are true if they describe that history and otherwise they are false—the crucial ingredient for an adequate solution to the problem of induction consists in the recognition that lawlike sentences as intensional generalizations entail, but are not entailed by, corresponding extensional generalizations. For, the truth conditions for generalizations that describe classes of possible worlds are strictly determined by the truth conditions for generalizations describing the history of the actual world *only when those extensional generalizations happen to be false*. Since the actual world is the only world in which generalizations may be subjected to (more or less) direct empirical test, however, it should be apparent that Popper's solution, in principle, is correct.

If the objects of scientific inquiry are intensional generalizations, then it is as important to distinguish between universal lawlike sentences and universal material conditionals as it is to differentiate statistical lawlike sentences from limiting frequency statements. For every universal lawlike sentence semantically entails a corresponding set of universal material conditionals, and every statistical lawlike sentence probabilistically implies innumerable possible frequency distributions for runs short and long; yet intensional statements of neither kind are logically equivalent to their extensional counterparts. As a result, therefore, one more class of sentences is required for a more adequate classification, namely: *universal material generalizations*, which, of course, are falsifiable but not verifiable—unless the universe itself is finite. These observations, we now know, suggest an appropriate criterion for separating lawlike sentences from accidental generalizations and display the inadequacy of any scientific program focused exclusively upon extensional distributions.

The falsifiability of universal material generalizations, moreover, strongly suggests that Popper's criterion of demarcation may be necessary but not sufficient to fulfill its intended objective, so long as (merely) accidental generalizations should not qualify as "scientific" statements. This difficulty, of course, remains whether sentences of this kind happen to be true or happen to be false, since *falsifiability* does not depend upon a sentence's truth-value; however, it does support the view that, as a criterion of demarcation, falsifiability may be too weak instead of being too strong, depending upon matters of interpretation. The most important difference distinguishing accidental generalizations and lawlike sentences, therefore, is not that sentences of one of these kinds are falsifiable and the other not, but that lawlike sentences possess nomological significance, i.e., they reflect nonlogical relations of necessary connection.

The differences involved here, although enormously important, are not infrequently obscured because the "deep structure" of a lawlike sentence is not always represented by its "surface grammar"; thus, the statement, "Fat men are jolly," might be interpreted *either* as a material conditional, say, (A) "For all x and all t, if x is a fat man at t, then x is jolly at t," which does not pretend to be lawlike; *or* as a subjunctive conditional, say, (B) "For all x and all t, if x were a fat man at t, then x would be jolly at t," which does. The truth of an accidental generalization, such as (A), however, is compatible with the existence of processes or procedures which could produce or provide a fat man who is not jolly, while the truth of a lawlike statement, such as (B), precludes that possibility. Falsification practices provide crucial opportunities for discriminating between them in principle, therefore, since statements which are not both *lawlike* and *true* are theoretically vulnerable to the eventual discovery of such refutations—where the class of quasi-accidental (or, quasi-lawlike) sentences qualifies as the intriguing case that "proves the rule": for, *if it were physically impossible to falsify* (A), *then the corresponding lawlike sentence*, (B), *would have to be true*!

Popper (1968, pp. 54–55) has portrayed the problem of induction as arising from an apparent contradiction between Hume's realization that ampliative arguments are deductively invalid, necessarily, and *the principle of empiricism*, i.e., that, in science, only observation and experiment may decide the acceptance or the rejection of hypotheses and theories. Most prior attempts to resolve this dilemma have tended to flounder upon a certain unwarranted assumption, namely: that all scientific statements must be *completely* (if fallibly) *decidable*, in principle, i.e., both verifiable and falsifiable. But once this (misleading) assumption has been abandoned, it becomes possible to resolve this apparent contradiction by interpreting scientific laws and theories as only *partially* (and fallibly) *decidable*, in principle, i.e., as statements that may be tested by systematic attempts at their refutation (as Popper [1965, especially pp. 312–13] has emphasized). Moreover, there is a telling precedent for Popper's asymmetrical conception, since whether or not a specific conclusion *follows from* specified premises, within the context of deduction, may only be established, in the absence of a valid demonstration, in general, by systematic attempts to provide one.

THE "PARADOXES" OF CONFIRMATION

One measure of the theoretical significance of the Popperian program, of course, is the extent to which it succeeds in clarifying various difficulties that have beset alternative conceptions. Given the character of the enterprise before us, it would appear appropriate to consider whether or not this approach is capable of illuminating such perplexing aspects of the underlying problems as Goodman's *riddle of induction*, Hempel's *paradox of confirmation*, and Hume's *critique of causation*. In order to undertake this arduous endeavor, however, it is necessary to review at least some of the details of the dispositional construction of lawlike sentences; thus, as an alternative definition, *S is a lawlike sentence of "simple" form in a language Lzt* if and only if (a) S is logically general, (b) S is not logically true, and (c) S is of the form, "For all x and all t, if x were K at t, then x would be X at t," where "X" is a (purely) dispositional predicate of universal or statistical strength in *Lzt* (a formulation suggested to the author by Evan K. Jobe). On this analysis, let us note, a lawlike sentence S, as before, is an unrestrictedly general subjunctive conditional attributing a (universal or statistical) dispositional property X to every member of a reference class K under an appropriate description.

Goodman's *riddle of induction* may be viewed as a special case of the general difficulty which Hempel has referred to as *inductive inconsistency*, i.e., the problem of ascertaining which members, if any, of a set of inconsistent hypotheses are inductively confirmed by a logically consistent but finite set of basic statements (Hempel 1965, pp. 53–73). The essential elements of this predicament, if such it be, are illustrated by curve-fitting problems, in which, no matter how many points appear upon a graph, so long as they are finite, an infinite number of mutually incompatible lines may be drawn to connect those points, where all these lines differ with respect to other locations. The statistical version of this difficulty, of course, arises due to the circumstance that any relative frequency within a finite segment of an infinite sequence is logically compatible with any limiting frequency, which suggests that an infinite number of mutually inconsistent hypotheses might be confirmed by that same data. Goodman presented a metalinguistic version of this difficulty, while seeking to define its ramifications and significance (Goodman 1965, especially pp. 72–92).

A simple example of Goodman's riddle is represented by a finite set of logically consistent basic statements reporting observations of green emeralds. All of these reports, of course, have been made prior to some time t, which, let us assume, might be midnight tonight. Goodman notes, however, that, although this evidence does not contradict the hypothesis H_1: "All emeralds are green," it also does not contradict the alternate hypothesis H_2: "All emeralds are grue," where something is "grue" just in case it is green before midnight tonight and blue thereafter; nor the hypothesis H_3: "All emeralds are gruple," where something is "gruple" just in case it is green before midnight tonight and purple thereafter; and so forth. But if all of these hypotheses are regarded as confirmed by this same data, then should one predict that an emerald that might be observed tomorrow will be green? Or blue? Or purple? And so on. The solution Goodman was to recommend consisted in the suggestion that the attribute predicates, "green," "grue," and so on differed significantly in their linguistic histories within the language-using community, insofar as some of these, such as "green," have frequently occurred in successful predictions in the past, while certain others, such as "grue," have not. On the basis of considerations such as these, therefore, Goodman developed his *theory of projectibility*, according to which the reliability-rating (as it were) of different predicates in the formulation of predictions is taken to be a function of their past successful employment, i.e., of their *degree of entrenchment*, which might be described as the result of a process of linguistic evolution.

The general conclusions that Goodman derives from his investigations, however, are especially noteworthy, since Goodman infers that *only a statement that is lawlike is capable of being confirmed by its instances*: the residual problem, therefore, is one of ascertaining, "what distinguishes lawlike or confirmable hypotheses from accidental or non-confirmable ones" (Goodman 1965, p. 80). From the perspective of the present program, of course, Goodman's analysis is confused and his solution is mistaken. For, in spite of its apparent plausibility, the thesis that accidental generalizations are incapable of being confirmed by their instances cannot be sustained: recall the examples of chapter 6, including, "All moas die before the age of fifty." Indeed, Goodman's contention strongly suggests that the truth of accidental generalizations is beyond the scope of human knowledge. If that were the case, then the problem of separating lawlike from accidental generalizations would have a trivial, but effective solution, namely: if the truth of a generalization is determinable on the basis of its instances, then that generalization must be lawlike. The very opposite, however, appears to be far closer to the truth.

Consider, for example, *the satisfaction criterion of confirmation* that Hempel has constructed in application to Goodman's problem. The basic idea behind this conception is that *an hypothesis h is confirmed by a logically consistent finite set of basic statements* for example if that hypothesis is satisfied by the finite class of individuals mentioned in those statements (Hempel 1965, especially pp. 35–39). Let the evidence class consist of the sentences, "John Jones is a professor and John Jones is bald," "Bill Smith is a professor and Bill Smith is bald," and, "Mary Clark is a professor and Mary Clark is bald"; and let the hypothesis under consideration be H_4: "All professors are bald." Then, according to Hempel's satisfaction criterion of confirmation, H_4 is confirmed by the specified class of evidence; yet surely no one doubts that the hypothesis, even if it were true, is not a lawlike statement, since (to cite at least one desideratum with which Goodman has been concerned) it does not support the subjunctive conditional, "For all x and all t, if x were a professor at t, then x would be bald at t." But this hypothesis *is* capable of being confirmed by its instances, nevertheless, as we have ascertained.

It might be objected, of course, that Goodman himself was attempting to overcome, if not outright rejecting, Hempel's satisfaction criterion, which should therefore not be relied upon as a source of counterexamples, even if the hypotheses under consideration contain only well-entrenched constituent predicates, such as "professor" and "bald." Indeed, the force of the objection to Goodman's conception does not depend upon the source of our examples at all and *a fortiori* does not depend upon specific accounts of confirmation. Consider, for example, any circumstance of custom, practice, or tradition in which it is plausible to suppose that a certain pattern of behavior might be conformed to for an indefinite temporal interval. Imagine that within many agrarian communities, say, it is a tradition to clip the ears of every dog at three years of age; then, when the only dogs of a species D happen to belong to those communities, it might easily turn out to be the case that the hypothesis, "All dogs of species D over three years old have clipped ears," is true. But surely the only way to ascertain whether or not this claim *is* true would be to examine its instances, for customs may change, traditions may wane, and practices may be violated. This phenomenon, moreover, may be characterized quite generally; for with respect to any arbitrarily selected reference class, R, and any arbitrarily selected attribute, A, either,

All Rs are As; or,
.99 Rs are As; or,
. . . . ; or,
.01 Rs are As; or
All Rs are non-As.

So long as the presence or the absence of the attribute, A, is not entailed by the description of the reference class, R, the truth of sentences such as these will be determinable, in general, only on the basis of their instances, even though, as extensional distributions, none of them happens to be lawlike.

The difficulties with Goodman's analysis in attempting to differentiate lawlike from accidental generalizations on the basis of their capacity to be confirmed by their instances arises from implicitly mistaking a semantic and ontological problem for an epistemic and pragmatic one. The crucial difference to be drawn is that lawlike sentences are subjunctive generalizations, which characterize classes of possible worlds by means of their ontological structure, while accidental generalizations are extensional sentences which characterize the actual world by describing (some segment of) its history. Thus, the relevant issue concerns the kind of connection claimed to obtain between the reference class property, K, and the attribute class property, X, where *there is a nomological relationship between K and X*, for example, when X is a permanent property of every member of the reference class, K, under the appropriate description within the language Lzt. Consequently, it is not the case that the hypothesis, "All professors are bald," would be a lawlike statement, provided it were true, because there *are* processes and procedures, including hair transplants, by means of which individuals could lose their baldness without also losing their professorships.

The situation is quite different, of course, with such hypotheses as, "Gold is malleable," "Sugar is soluble," "The half-life of polonium^{218} is 3.05 minutes," and so on, since there are no processes or procedures that would render gold nonmalleable without altering its atomic structure, or make sugar nonsoluble without changing its chemical composition, and so forth. Indeed, it seems quite plausible to assume that Goodman's account of the character of projectible predicates is similarly beside the point; for the explanation is not merely that predicates such as "grue" lack the history of past successful projection that typify such predicates as, say, "green," but that predicates such as "grue" are the wrong kind of predicate, namely: "green" is a *purely dispositional predicate*, whereas "grue" is not. "Grue" is a dispositional predicate to the extent to which the property it designates (i) is a (complex) tendency to display appropriate outcome responses when subjected to appropriate singular trials, and (ii) is an actual (complex) physical state of some object individually or of some arrangement of things collectively (when it happens to be satisfied at all). By virtue of its explicit definition by means of a temporal reference uniquely denoting a particular moment in the history of the actual world, however, "grue" is not a property that is predicable, in principle, of any member of the history of any possible world and therefore fails to designate a *pure* disposition: *for pure dispositions are universals*, and conversely.

. . . .

Hempel's *paradox of confirmation*, by contrast, poses different kinds of difficulties, which the Popperian program also clarifies. The paradox itself, of course, arises from an intuitively plausible "condition of adequacy" for any acceptable conception of confirmation, namely: *the equivalence condition*, according to which, if a logically consistent finite set of basic statements confirms an hypothesis h, then it also confirms every hypothesis which is logically equivalent with h (Hempel 1965, especially pp. 14–20). Although this requirement appears to be logically impeccable, it nevertheless creates a paradox to the extent to which evidence that intuitively confirms one formulation of an hypothesis h does not invariably intuitively confirm another: for example, the hypothesis H_5: "All nonblack things are nonravens," is extensionally equivalent with the hypothesis H_6: "All ravens are black"; yet certain evidence, such as the observation of red pencils, yellow cows, or white handkerchiefs, which would intuitively confirm H_5 does not intuitively confirm H_6, which instead appears to concern only ravens and their color.

Hempel's own explanation of this paradox relies upon the recognition that the specific phrasing by which an hypothesis is formulated does not dictate its logical content, since, in particular, within an extensional language framework, hypotheses H_5 and H_6 are both logically equivalent to hypothesis H_7: "All things are either nonravens or black," which surely receives intuitive confirmation from observations of red pencils or yellow cows as well as those of black ravens. Hempel (1965, pp. 14–20 and pp. 47–48) concludes, therefore, that the paradoxical cases have to be counted as confirmatory, while their counterintuitive character may be accounted for by virtue of *pragmatical circumstances*, such as background knowledge. The explanation that emanates from our preliminary deliberations, however, suggests that these paradoxes are not merely psychological, but are rooted in an inadequate conception of the logical structure of lawlike sentences, which cannot be formulated by means of extensional language alone; hence, properly understood, these paradoxes invite attention to one of the most important philosophical problems confronting the theory of science.

In order to perceive this connection, remember that the hypothesis, "All ravens are black," interpreted as a lawlike sentence, represents a *subjunctive generalization*, namely: "For all x and all t, if x were a raven at t, then x would be black at t," which will turn out to be true if and only if, although "(being) black" does not follow from the reference class description, "(being a) raven," nevertheless, *being black* is a permanent property of everything that happens to be a *raven*, which, of course, will be the case only if there is no process or procedure whereby something could lose the color *black*, while remaining throughout a *raven*. But the most important syntactical feature that distinguishes these lawlike sentences from material conditionals, on the one hand, and logical necessities, on the other, is that these intensional generalizations are not subject to principles of transposition, which would affect a trivialization of the significance of the conception of permanent properties as the ontological foundation for an adequate explication of scientific laws. For with transposition, the distinction between subjunctive conditionals which are warranted on logical grounds as opposed to those which are warranted on nomological grounds cannot be sustained, while the invocation of permanent properties becomes theoretically superfluous (for the recognition of which the author is indebted to Charles E. M. Dunlop).

. . . .

The deductive principle, *modus tollens*, of course, continues to serve as a valid rule of inference relative to arguments with "simple" lawlike premises in general. Among other authors who have also rejected transposition for subjunctive or for lawlike conditionals, moreover, are Stalnaker (1968, especially p. 110), and Pollock (1972, especially p. 307). Indeed, when considered along with certain other semantical properties distinguishing the logical from the physical modalities, the nontransposability of scientific conditionals does not seem to be especially surprising. In particular, when an "if . . . then____" statement, S, is interpreted as *nomological*, then:

(i) *S* is not always true when its antecedent is false, in contradistinction to corresponding material conditionals;

(ii) *S* is never true when its antecedent is logically impossible (or necessarily false), in contradistinction to corresponding logical truths;

(iii) *S* is not always true when its consequent is true, in contradistinction to corresponding material conditionals; and,

(iv) *S* is never true when its consequent is logically necessary (or necessarily true), in contradistinction to corresponding logical truths;

which underscores the theoretical necessity for distinguishing between them (as Popper [1965, pp. 432–41 and especially p. 434] has also emphasized).

It is extremely interesting to observe, moreover, that, even though principles of transposition for lawlike sentences would reinstate the paradoxes of *confirmation* within our intensional language, there are no corresponding paradoxes of *falsification* (intensional or otherwise). Thus, notice that the evidence which would falsify the hypothesis, "All ravens are black," and the evidence which would falsify its extensional equivalent, "All nonblack things are non-ravens," is *identical*, i.e., ravens that are nonblack or nonblack things that are non-nonravens. Consequently, considered purely as a *methodological* problem, for example, concerning the techniques of hypothesis testing, rather than as a *semantical* one, i.e., concerning the logical structure of lawlike sentences, this asymmetry itself might reasonably be regarded as the foundation for a resolution of Hempel's paradoxes in favor of falsification; indeed, this is essentially the position adopted by Popper himself (Schilpp, ed., 1974, especially pp. 990–91) and by Watkins (1964).

As a result, Hempel's paradoxes not only implicitly display the essential inadequacy of extensional language for the formalization of lawlike sentences but also serve to emphasize the fundamental role of falsification procedures; for, as Popper, especially, has maintained, all laws have *the force of prohibitions*, i.e., they forbid the occurrence of any event of a certain kind, not only during the history of the actual world but also during the history of any other possible world. An "inventory" of the history of the actual world, therefore, does not provide a basis for evaluating the truth of every lawlike statement, for the particular sequence of events which constitutes that history does not necessarily reflect all of the world's physical possibilities: the problem, therefore, is *to attempt to arrange this world's history* so that it should include sets of events evidentially relevant to testing alternative hypotheses and theories, which requires, in general, controlled experiments and systematic observations. We thus have to decide, in part, which hypotheses to test. (The view that deliberate experimentation affords an avenue for testing subjunctives which might otherwise remain counterfactual during the history of the actual world is also advanced by von Wright [1971].)

Of course, it would be wrong to conclude that no hypothesis is subjected to test during the course of the world's "natural" history, i.e., without intervention by means of deliberate experimentation. Numberless hypotheses are tacitly tested by the observation of a single red pencil, for example, which could provide sufficient evidence to *falsify* enormous numbers of lawlike hypotheses, such as, "All pencils are purple," "All pencils are elastic," "All pencils are soluble," and so on, while simultaneously affording appropriate evidence to *confirm* enormous numbers of extensional statements, such as, "All pencils are red," "All pencils are wooden," "All pencils are broken," and so forth. Although the equivalence class of extensional generalizations is closed under transposition, moreover, the equivalence class of intensional generalizations is not. The problem, therefore, is not to distinguish between *confirmable* and *accidental* generalizations, as Goodman misleadingly suggests, but to distinguish between *testing lawlike hypotheses* and *confirming extensional generalizations*; for the evidence that confirms a generalization does not necessarily support a law.

A CRITIQUE OF HUME'S CRITIQUE

Hume's *critique of causation*, finally, is important not only because permanent properties as intensional relations are a species of necessary connection but also because every lawlike sentence, in principle, may be expressed in the form of a causal conditional as well. This result is a consequence of the conception of dispositional properties as *single-case causal tendencies*, which is reflected by their mode of definition, since a dispositional predicate may be (partially) defined by a conjunction of relevant-test/outcome-response conditions by invoking the "probabilistic causal conditional" as follows: "x is malleable at t," means, by definition, "hammering x into shape S^1 at t would invariably (or, probably) bring about x's having shape S^1 at t^*; and, pressing x into shape S^2 at t would invariably (or, probably) bring about x's having shape S^2 at t^*; and, . . . ," where t^* is either simultaneous with or subsequent to t. The "causal" form of a lawlike sentence is thus obtained by substituting one of its defining conjuncts for a dispositional predicate, as follows: "For all x and all t, if x were gold at t, then hammering x into shape S^1 at t would invariably bring about x's having shape S^1 at t^*," which is a partial reflection of the causal significance of the lawlike statement, "Gold is malleable," on this intensional program. The question therefore arises of the extent to which conceptions such as these actually satisfy Hume's strictures.

Without providing a detailed reconstruction of the specifics of Hume's position, let us assume that Hume's motivation was not merely to establish the meaning of a certain term within a community of language users, but to ascertain the extent to which claims of a certain kind might be justified on the basis of experiential considerations alone, i.e., on the basis of (more or less) direct observation and relatively simple measurement. The ordinary usage of causal language thus suggests that the term "cause" is characteristically employed to assert that one event (called "the cause") bears a certain relationship to another event (called "its effect") where this relation of causation embraces the following components, namely: (a) *resemblance*, i.e., similar causes are attended by similar effects (which, we may assume, may be either their invariable or their probable outcomes); (b) *regular association*, i.e., causes are temporally simultaneous or prior to and spatially contiguous with their effects, conforming to a repeatable pattern which, for probabilistic causes, is that of a relative frequency; and, (c) *necessary connection*, i.e., effects are necessarily, rather than accidentally, related to their causes, even though this relation is not a matter of logical necessity.

The classical result of this inquiry was Hume's determination that, although the relations of resemblance and of regular association were experientially ascertainable, relations of necessary connection could not be detected on the basis of experiential considerations alone. Consequently, the attribution of relations of necessary connection between events, Hume reasoned, must be a result of human frailty, i.e., an inevitable habit of the mind, which, however, is epistemically unwarranted and therefore philosophically inexcusable. The benefit of this analysis was a clarification of the concept of causation that it should no longer embrace any notion of necessary connection between events but encompass only those aspects whose presence or absence could be experientially established: resemblance and regular association. And as a philosophical legacy, Hume (implicitly) bequeathed the following argument:

Necessary connections between events are either observable and objective or psychological and subjective; but they cannot be ascertained on the basis of experiential considerations alone; consequently, they must be merely psychological and subjective.

Indeed, this argument has been among the most pervasive and influential in the history of Western philosophy.

It is my contention, however, that Hume has presented a misleading dilemma in the form of the premise that necessary conditions must be *either* observable and objective *or* psychological and subjective. This crucial assumption precludes the possibility that necessary connections, as theoretical properties of the physical world, might be unobservable and *nevertheless* objective. If the logical foundation supporting Hume's argument should prove to be insecure, therefore, then the critique of the concept of causation based upon it should pose no insurmountable obstacle to adopting an intensional conception of lawlike statements. Moreover, once these logical foundations are clearly displayed, it becomes apparent that there are important reasons for abandoning them; indeed, my argument will be that rigid adherence to the epistemological principles implicit in the Humean approach would itself pose a virtually insurmountable obstacle to the progress of empirical science.

The logical foundation of Hume's argument, therefore, is the thesis that *properties of the physical world are objective if and only if they are observable.* Notice that, although this thesis is directly applicable to terms that designate properties of the physical world, it is indirectly applicable to statements that describe the world as well. In its direct application, in other words, it serves as a criterion for distinguishing "objective" from "subjective" *predicates*; in its indirect application, by contrast, it functions as a criterion for differentiating between "cognitively significant" and "cognitively insignificant" *sentences*. Thus, the obvious complement to Hume's position is the thesis that an hypothesis or a theory is empirically meaningful (or scientifically significant) if and only if it is *verifiable* on the basis of a logically consistent finite set of observation sentences.

The first difficulty encountered by this thesis is that it imposes an excessive restriction upon the language of empirical science; for the Humean position entails that scientific language, if it is to be "objective," must be constructed exclusively from a nonlogical vocabulary that is limited to observational predicates alone. The only permissible predicates, presumably, would be those designating (more or less) directly observable properties of (more or less) directly observable entities, perhaps, e.g., the color of the sky or the shape of a die. Those that designate (more or less) unobservable properties of observable entities, e.g., the fragility of a vase or the flexibility of a rubber band, or designating unobservable properties of unobservable entities, such as the strength of gravitational fields or the transmission of a recessive trait, would not be permissible predicates. All dispositional and theoretical predicates would accordingly be excluded from the language of empirical science. (Compare Hempel's discussion [1965, especially pp. 107–13].)

The second difficulty is that scientific laws, whether of universal or statistical form, would have to be given an entirely extensional analysis in order to guarantee their complete verifiability. But this would entail abandoning established criteria for lawlike statements, since their "objectivity" would require (i) that they be logically equivalent with a finite conjunction of singular sentences and (ii) that they be incapable of providing support for counterfactual and for subjunctive conditionals. Indeed, under such a strict conception, subjunctives and counterfactuals would have no scientific significance at all. Any true generalizations describing (segments of) the world's history accessible to observations and measurement might have to be accorded the status of a scientific law; for there would be no syntactical or semantical basis for distinguishing between genuinely lawlike and merely accidental generalizations. (Again compare Hempel's discussion [1965, especially pp. 338–43].)

The third difficulty is that empirical science would have to dispense with scientific theories, at least insofar as such theories are envisioned as encompassing "objective" properties of the physical world. But scientific theories have proven to be exceptionally beneficial to the progress of science, for they provide the opportunity to systematically incorporate broad ranges of experiential data by means of general principles in terms of which past events may be explained and future events predicted. A further advantage of scientific theories is their heuristic fertility and conceptual economy, in the sense that their pursuit has stimulated the discovery of unsuspected connections between natural occurrences in an attempt to account for the largest variety of phenomena while relying upon the smallest set of assumptions. Indeed, the development of scientific theories has been a distinguishing characteristic of the history of science itself. (Compare Hempel's discussion once again [1965, especially pp. 210–22].)

Not the least of the difficulties confronting this Humean position, I might add, is the defense of the very distinction upon which its fundamental principles depend, for the difference between observational and nonobservational language has proven notoriously difficult to successfully define; indeed, if the Popperian conception of universals as dispositional is correct, there is, in principle, no theoretical warrant for that distinction at all, since observational, dispositional, and theoretical language represent only differing degrees of epistemic accessibility, from the ontological point of view. But even if the distinction at issue were to be assumed, the underlying inadequacy of Hume's analysis should by now have been made apparent; for Hume relies upon an excessively narrow conception of objectivity. Surely a scientific assertion need not be couched exclusively in observation language in order to be cognitively significant in relation to the data of experience; for an empirical hypothesis is epistemically permissible when it can be subjected to objective tests by means of systematic observation and controlled experimentation in accordance with Popper's principle of empiricism.

The deficiencies of Hume's critique of causation, however, should not be supposed to affect the results of his critique of induction; for whether or not there are any nonlogical necessary connections, there are certainly no ampliative-demonstrative arguments. Thus, to perceive that this is the case, simply notice that no logical inconsistency arises from admitting:

(a) the kinds of tests that have verified in the past might not verify in the future;
(b) the kinds of tests that have falsified in the past might not falsify in the future;
(c) the predicates that have been projectible in the past might not be projectible in the future; and,
(d) the necessary connections that have obtained in the past might not obtain in the future.

Perhaps more importantly, however, if we acknowledge that our conception of scientific laws entails that *when they are true, they do not change*, then a conditional argument that relates the past and the future is possible, after all, with respect to the members of the class of presumptive scientific laws as follows, namely:

Even if the world *is* as we believe it to be in these specific respects, it remains *logically possible* that they might still change tomorrow; but *if* the world is as we believe it to be in these specific respects, then it is not *physically possible* that they actually will change tomorrow.

And this, perhaps, is as much as we should ask of any "inductive" procedure.

The general conception of the Popperian program that emerges from these considerations at last, therefore, suggests that empirical science endeavors to fulfill (at least) two complementary objectives: *first*, to ascertain the historical patterns displayed by the world's history, which are expressible in extensional language and are capable of confirmation by their instances; and, *second*, to discover the lawlike relations constitutive of the world's structure, which are expressible in intensional language and, in principle, are subject to procedures of falsification but not to those of verification. These historical patterns, moreover, may be described by means of frequency distributions and by material conditionals to which traditional conceptions of induction apparently apply; their principal importance, however, resides in their usefulness as *evidence* for discovering the lawlike relations which they covertly display and which in turn implicitly explain them. Although the confirmation of extensional generalizations thus fulfills a necessary condition for the conduct of scientific inquiry, therefore, the principles of fallibilistic falsification are indispensable for its ultimate success.

NOTE

1. Editor's note—All chapter references are to Fetzer's *Scientific Knowledge* (Dordrecht, Holland: D. Reidel, 1981). The present essay originally appeared as chapter 7 of that work.

REFERENCES

Ackermann, R. (1976). *The Philosophy of Karl Popper.* Amherst: University of Massachusetts Press.

Beth, E. W. (1969). "Semantic Entailment and Formal Derivability." In *The Philosophy of Mathematics.* Edited by J. Hintikka. Oxford: Oxford University Press, 1969, pp. 9–41.

Feigl, H. (1963). "De Principiis Non Disputandum . . . ?" In *Philosophical Analysis.* Edited by M. Black. Englewood Cliffs, NJ: Prentice-Hall, 1963, pp. 113–47.

Gillies, D. A. (1973). *An Objective Theory of Probability.* London: Methuen.

Goodman, N. (1965). *Fact, Fiction, and Forecast.* Indianapolis: Bobbs-Merrill.

Hempel, C. G. (1952). *Fundamentals of Concept Formation in Empirical Science.* Chicago: University of Chicago Press.

———. (1965). *Aspects of Scientific Explanation.* New York: The Free Press.

Lakatos, I. (1970). "Falsification and the Methodology of Scientific Research Programmes." In *Criticism and the Growth of Knowledge.* Edited by I. Lakatos and A. Musgrave. Cambridge: Cambridge University Press, 1970, pp. 91–195.

Pollock, J. (1972). "Subjunctive Generalizations." *Synthese* 28 (1974), pp. 199–214.

Popper, K. R. (1965). *The Logic of Scientific Discovery.* New York: Harper and Row.

———. (1968). *Conjectures and Refutations.* New York: Harper and Row.

———. (1972). *Objective Knowledge.* Oxford: Oxford University Press.

———. (1976). *Unended Quest.* La Salle, IL: Open Court.

Reichenbach, H. (1949). *The Theory of Probability.* Berkeley: University of California Press.

Salmon, W. C. (1967). *The Foundations of Scientific Inference.* Pittsburgh: University of Pittsburgh Press.

Schilpp, P., ed. (1974). *The Philosophy of Karl Popper.* La Salle, IL: Open Court.

Stalnaker, R. (1968). "A Theory of Conditionals." *American Philosophical Quarterly, Supplementary Monographs* no. 2, Oxford: Basil Blackwell, 1968, pp. 987–1112.

von Wright, G. H. (1971). *Explanation and Understanding.* Ithaca: Cornell University Press.

Watkins, J. W. N. (1964). "Confirmation, the Paradoxes, and Positivism." In *The Critical Approach to Science and Philosophy.* Edited by M. Bunge. New York: The Free Press, 1964, pp. 92–115.

PART SEVEN

THE GROWTH OF SCIENTIFIC KNOWLEDGE

INTRODUCTION

hile the authors we have studied up to now have tended to emphasize the products of science as opposed to the process of science, others have focused their attention upon the history of science as a guide to the philosophy of science. Upon initial consideration, after all, it seems enormously promising to suppose that the questions we have been considering might be settled by the study of the history of science, where the actual practice of scientists could provide a basis for arbitrating between conflicting conceptions. Thus, the normative questions that have preoccupied philosophers might be amenable to descriptive solutions by increased sensitivity to the historical record.

Popper's "Conjectures and Refutations" pursues the *problem of demarcation*, which involves separating science from nonscience, as opposed to the *problem of meaningfulness*, which attempts to distinguish sense from nonsense. In the process of elaborating the virtues of his falsificationist methodology, he discusses various theories of the past, including the dialectical materialism of Marx, the psychoanalytic theory of Freud, and the "individual psychology" of Adler. These "theories," however, do not fare well in comparison to other theories, such as the theory of relativity of Einstein, because the former, unlike the latter, appear to be compatible with virtually any possible outcome.

Popper emphasizes what he takes to be the crucial characteristics of scientific theories, which assert prohibitions about the world's behavior. The more a theory prohibits, the greater its content and the greater its testability. As a result, "A theory which is not refutable by any conceivable event is nonscientific." Every genuine test of a theory is an effort to falsify or to refute it, where apparently confirming evidence does not properly count as supporting a theory except when it results from a sincere attempt to falsify or to refute it. The findings supplied by inductive confirmations, therefore, should not be mistaken for the evidence provided by attempted refutations.

Without doubt, Popper's position in this essay is strongly deductivist, insofar as he maintains, "Only the falsity of a theory can be inferred from empirical evidence, and this inference is a purely deductive one." As we have already discovered, however, a distinction must be drawn between "induction" in its broad and in its narrow senses. Popper may be on solid ground in rejecting the straight rule of induction or probabilistic measures of confirmation, but scientific inquiries would still remain ampliative. And even if decision-making does not require the acceptance as true of any theories, the situation appears to be different with respect to scientific explanation.

Kuhn's "Logic of Discovery or Psychology of Research?" challenges Popper's position on historical grounds, contending that the history of science reflects a great deal of scientific activity that cannot be accurately described in falsificationist language. Kuhn maintains that a fundamental distinction must be drawn between "normal science" and "revolutionary science," where Popper's conceptions, at best, characterize extraordinary events during revolutionary periods rather than the typical conduct of normal practice. Most scientists spend most of their time attempting to display the power of widely accepted theories (or "paradigms") and are not trying to refute them.

Kuhn thus distinguishes between "problem solving" in a Popperian sense and "puzzle solving" in his sense, where *problem solving* involves establishing a paradigm, but *puzzle solving* involves extending an accepted paradigm. Although Popper considers critical discourse and severe testing as criteria of scientific activity, Kuhn considers the abandonment of criticism and the conduct of puzzle solving as typical of normal science. Even though Kuhn tends to agree with Popper's position as a description of revolutionary activities in science, he disagrees with Popper's position as a description of the ordinary activity of scientists. Most of scientific activity is normal, not revolutionary.

Their most striking differences emerge from the respective roles which they assign to logic and to psychology. Kuhn contends that normal science can be conducted even when confronted with "anomalies," phenomena that do not fit the accepted paradigm. Since anomalies are inconsistent with or otherwise contravene the adopted theory, they should qualify as falsifying instances that warrant its rejection, from the Popperian perspective. Kuhn contends that scientists will persist in attempting to extend their paradigm until they discover an alternative theory with the capacity to resolve a substantial proportion of accumulated anomalies without generating new ones.

The difficulty encountered at this juncture by Kuhn's conception is that it can easily give rise to the impression that changes in paradigm are more a matter of psychology than they are of logic. Indeed, if there is nothing more to truth in science than consensus among scientists, then it might be said that accepted theories are on a par with political ideologies and that paradigm changes are on a par with religious conversions. Kuhn takes for granted that the members of the scientific community have the right kind of background, education, and training. But this raises the further question of just what kind of background, education, and training is the right kind.

One mode of reconciliation between their divergent views is to consider them as complementary rather than competitive. While bold conjectures are typical of revolutionary science, cautious conjectures are characteristic of normal science. With respect to the kinds of results that make the most contribution to the advance of science, however, corroborations dominate revolutionary science, because they point the way toward new paradigms and because the falsification of bold conjectures is expected. Falsifications dominate normal science, ironically, because they are not expected and because they indicate that scientists may have adopted the wrong paradigm.

Lakatos's "History of Science and Its Rational Reconstructions" surveys inductivism, conventionalism, falsificationism, and the methodology of research programmes as alternative conceptions of the nature of science. He shares with Kuhn the conviction that scientists should persist in nurturing an infant theory by deflecting the falsifying significance of apparently incompatible findings ("anomalies") onto the background knowledge, the auxiliary hypotheses, and the initial conditions attending its obtainment. This approach thus incorporates the realization that, as a point of logic, theories are never subject to direct tests but only in combination with other claims.

The subtle hazard thereby generated, however, is that the methodology that protects the hard core of basic assumptions that constitute a theory by granting it temporary immunity from empirical falsification has to specify how long "temporary immunity" should endure. Otherwise, the transition from Popperian principles to Lakatosian programs may degenerate from a methodology emphasizing that the fate of theories must be decided on the basis of experiments and observation to a platform that endorses "the conventionalist stratagem," according to which a theory is retained in spite of its experiential refutation. When, after all, should a theory be abandoned?

For Lakatos, the critical measure of the scientific significance of alternative programs is a function of the extent to which their hard cores contribute to the discovery of novel phenomena (thereby qualifying as *progressive*, since they promote the growth of scientific knowledge, whereas those that do not are *degenerative* and therefore should be abandoned). Because future discoveries might revive an abandoned theory or undermine its successors, the progress of science is never conclusive. The shift from Popperian falsification to Kuhnian paradigms to Lakatosian programmes thus ultimately leads to a theory where successes count but failures do not.

Perhaps the most valuable aspect of Lakatos's study is the difficulties it discloses for purely descriptive approaches. Each methodology yields a distinctive *internal history* as a rational reconstruction of the history of science from its point of view. Each of these normative interpretations will have to be supplemented by empirical *external histories* to account for the nonrational factors that affect the growth of science. In this sense, he maintains, "The history of science is always richer than its rational reconstructions." But rational reconstructions (or internal histories) are always primary and empirical descriptions (or external histories) are always secondary, because the role of external histories is to explain the anomalies of internal histories.

At a deeper level, however, it should be obvious that purely descriptive approaches to science are fundamentally misconceived. Historians cannot study the history of science without having some idea of which persons are scientists and which activities are scientific and why. "Science" could be defined as what the members of the presumptive community of scientists do only by taking for granted that they are not frauds, quacks, or incompetents. The possibility of malpractice guarantees that the principles and procedures by means of which a discipline is properly defined cannot be adequately ascertained by empirical methods alone. The appropriate methodology here is not meaning analysis but rather explication. After all, "science" is not what the scientists do. On the contrary, the "scientists" are those who do science.

STUDY QUESTIONS

As you read the articles that appear in this section, you may want to think about their implications for understanding the nature of science and of philosophy. The following questions are intended to stimulate your thinking by focusing attention on some of the less obvious aspects of different positions.

(1) If there is a difference between the problem of meaningfulness and the problem of demarcation, then a proper solution to them would still permit some hypotheses, conjectures, or theories to be meaningful even when they are not scientific. Can you think of any examples that would satisfy these conditions by being meaningful in spite of being incapable of falsification?

(2) Popper stresses the differences between searching for *positive* (or confirming) instances and searching for *negative* (or disconfirming) instances. Why does he seem to think—why does he actively insist—that the absence of negative (disconfirming) instances should not be mistaken for the mere presence of positive (confirming) instances? Why is this issue important?

(3) Popper has often been accused of promoting a conception of scientific methodology according to which scientific method is completely deductive. Were this account of his views correct, then science could only eliminate hypotheses and never accept them. On this basis of what Popper has said here, do you think he believes in tentative acceptance as well as rejection?

(4) There is more than one version of principles of empiricism. One holds that there is no synthetical *a priori* knowledge. Another holds that acceptance and rejection of theories in science must be based upon observation and experimentation. Which "principle of empiricism" does Popper endorse here? Can you think of any connections between these two versions?

(5) Why does Kuhn disagree with Popper? How deep do their differences run? If Popper thinks that science proceeds by the method of conjectures and (attempted) refutations, does Kuhn think that science proceeds *without* the benefits of (attempted) refutations? What characteristics make a good scientist on Kuhn's account? And on Popper's? Are they the same?

(6) Kuhn contends that the *puzzle solving* traditions that accompany normal science are very different in kind from the *problem solving* traditions that accompany revolutionary science. What does he mean when he says that puzzle solving tests a scientist's ability, while problem solving tests a theory's ability? Is the distinction between these activities fundamental?

(7) According to Popper, the growth of scientific knowledge is promoted by testing and rejecting various theories in succession. According to Kuhn, the growth of scientific knowledge is promoted by adopting and changing different paradigms in succession. Under what circumstances should the members of the scientific community exchange one paradigm for another?

(8) According to Lakatos, a fundamental distinction should be drawn between "internal" history and "external" history, where internal histories are normative accounts of science, while external accounts of science are descriptive accounts of science. What does he have in mind? Why do we need internal histories of science if we have external histories available?

(9) Lakatos suggests that infant theories need to be protected from the falsifying significance of incompatible evidence, which should be deflected onto the background knowledge, the auxiliary hypotheses, and the initial conditions attending their obtainment. This conveys a very different attitude from Popper's. Which of them seems to be correct? Why?

(10) Lakatos investigates inductivism, conventionalism, methodological falsificationism, and the methodology of scientific research programmes. What are the reasons he advances for preferring one of these to another? Are they good reasons? Do you think that the methodology of scientific research programmes provides the most adequate account or not? Why?

KARL R. POPPER

SCIENCE: CONJECTURES AND REFUTATIONS*

 r. Turnbull had predicted evil consequences, . . . and was now doing the best in his power to bring about the verification of his own prophecies.
—Anthony Trollope

I

When I received the list of participants in this course and realized that I had been asked to speak to philosophical colleagues I thought, after some hesitation and consultation, that you would probably prefer me to speak about those problems which interest me most, and about those developments with which I am most intimately acquainted. I therefore decided to do what I have never done before: to give you a report on my own work in the philosophy of science, since the autumn of 1919 when I first began to grapple with the problem, *"When should a theory be ranked as scientific?"* or *"Is there a criterion for the scientific character or status of a theory?"*

The problem which troubled me at the time was neither, "When is a theory true?" nor, "When is a theory acceptable?" My problem was different. I *wished to distinguish between science and pseudo-science*; knowing very well that science often errs, and that pseudo-science may happen to stumble on the truth.

I knew, of course, the most widely accepted answer to my problem: that science is distinguished from pseudo-science—or from "metaphysics"—by its *empirical method*, which is essentially *inductive*, proceeding from observation or experiment. But this did not satisfy me. On the contrary, I often formulated my problem as one of distinguishing between a genuinely empirical method and a non-empirical or even a pseudo-empirical method—that is to say, a method which, although it appeals to observation and experiment, nevertheless does not come up to scientific standards. The latter method may be exemplified by astrology, with its stupendous mass of empirical evidence based on observation—on horoscopes and on biographies.

But as it was not the example of astrology which led me to my problem I should perhaps briefly describe the atmosphere in which my problem arose and the examples by which it was stimulated. After the collapse of the Austrian Empire there had been a revolution in Austria: the air was full of revolutionary slogans and ideas, and new and often wild theories. Among the theories which interested me Einstein's theory of relativity was no doubt by far the most important. Three others were Marx's theory of history, Freud's psychoanalysis, and Alfred Adler's so-called "individual psychology."

There was a lot of popular nonsense talked about these theories, and especially about relativity (as still happens even today), but I was fortunate in those who introduced me to the study of this theory. We all—the small circle of students to which I belonged—were thrilled with the result of Eddington's eclipse observations which in 1919 brought the first important confirmation of Einstein's theory of gravitation. It was a great experience for us, and one which had a lasting influence on my intellectual development.

The three other theories I have mentioned were also widely discussed among students at that time. I myself happened to come into personal contact with Alfred Adler, and even to co-operate with him in his social work among the children and young people in the working-class districts of Vienna where he had established social guidance clinics.

It was during the summer of 1919 that I began to feel more and more dissatisfied with these three theories—the Marxist theory of history, psychoanalysis, and individual psychology; and I began to feel dubious about their claims to scientific status. My problem perhaps first took the simple form, "What is wrong with Marxism, psychoanalysis, and individual psychology? Why are they so different from physical theories, from Newton's theory, and especially from the theory of relativity?"

To make this contrast clear I should explain that few of us at the time would have said that we believed in the *truth* of Einstein's theory of gravitation. This shows that it was not my doubting the *truth* of those other three theories which bothered me, but something else. Yet neither was it that I merely felt mathematical physics to be more *exact* than the sociological or psychological type of theory. Thus what worried me was neither the problem of truth, at that stage at least, nor the problem of exactness or measurability. It was rather that I felt that these other three theories, though posing as sciences, had in fact more in common with primitive myths than with science; that they resembled astrology rather than astronomy.

I found that those of my friends who were admirers of Marx, Freud, and Adler, were impressed by a number of points common to these theories, and especially by their apparent *explanatory power*. These theories appeared to be able to explain practically everything that happened within the fields to which they referred. The study of any of them seemed to have the effect of an intellectual conversion or revelation, opening your eyes to a new truth hidden from those not yet initiated. Once your eyes were thus opened you saw confirming instances everywhere: the world was full of *verifications* of the theory. Whatever happened always confirmed it. Thus its truth appeared manifest; and unbelievers were clearly people who did not want to see the manifest truth; who refused to see it, either because it was against their class interest, or because of their repressions which were still "unanalyzed" and crying aloud for treatment.

The most characteristic element in this situation seemed to me the incessant stream of confirmations, of observations which "verified" the theories in question; and this point was constantly emphasized by their adherents. A Marxist could not open a newspaper without finding on every page confirming evidence for his interpretation of history; not only in the news, but also in its presentation—which revealed the class bias of the paper—and especially of course in what the paper did *not* say. The Freudian analysts emphasized that their theories were constantly verified by their "clinical observations." As for Adler, I was much impressed by a personal experience. Once, in 1919, I reported to him a case which to me did not seem particularly Adlerian, but which he found no difficulty in analysing in terms of his theory of inferiority feelings, although he had not even seen the child. Slightly shocked, I asked him how he could be so sure. "Because of my thousandfold experience," he replied; whereupon I could not help saying: "And with this new case, I suppose, your experience has become thousand-and-one-fold."

What I had in mind was that his previous observations may not have been much sounder than this new one; that each in its turn had been interpreted in the light of "previous experience," and at the same time counted as additional confirmation. What, I asked myself, did it confirm? No more than that a case could be interpreted in the light of the theory. But this meant very little, I reflected, since every conceivable case could be interpreted in the light of Adler's theory, or equally of Freud's. I may illustrate this by two very different examples of human behaviour: that of a man who pushes a child into the water with the intention of drowning it; and that of a man who sacrifices his life in an attempt to save the child. Each of these two cases can be explained with equal ease in Freudian and in Adlerian terms. According to Freud the first man suffered from repression (say, of some component of his Oedipus complex), while the second man had achieved sublimation. According to Adler the first man suffered from feelings of inferiority (producing perhaps the need to prove to himself that he dared to commit some crime), and so did the second man (whose need was to prove to himself that he dared to rescue the child). I could not think of any human behaviour which could not be interpreted in terms of either theory. It was precisely this fact—that they always fitted, that they were always confirmed—which in the eyes of their admirers constituted the strongest argument in favour of these theories. It began to dawn on me that this apparent strength was in fact their weakness.

With Einstein's theory the situation was strikingly different. Take one typical instance—Einstein's prediction, just then confirmed by the findings of Eddington's expedition. Einstein's gravitational theory had led to the result that light must be attracted by heavy bodies (such as the sun), precisely as material bodies were attracted. As a consequence it could be calculated that light from a distant fixed star whose apparent position was close to the sun would reach the earth from such a direction that the star would seem to be slightly shifted away from the sun; or, in other words, that stars close to the sun would look as if they had moved a little away from the sun, and from one another. This is a thing which cannot normally be observed since such stars are rendered invisible in daytime by the sun's overwhelming brightness; but during an eclipse it is possible to take photographs of them. If the same constellation is photographed at night one can measure the distances on the two photographs, and check the predicted effect.

Now the impressive thing about this case is the *risk* involved in a prediction of this kind. If observation shows that the predicted effect is definitely absent, then the theory is simply refuted. The theory is *incompatible with certain possible results of observation*—in fact with results which everybody before Einstein would have expected.[1] This is quite different from the situation I have previously described, when it turned out that the theories in question were compatible with the most divergent human behaviour, so that it was practically impossible to describe any human behaviour that might not be claimed to be a verification of these theories.

These considerations led me in the winter of 1919–20 to conclusions which I may now reformulate as follows.

(1) It is easy to obtain confirmations, or verifications, for nearly every theory—if we look for confirmations.

(2) Confirmations should count only if they are the result of *risky predictions*; that is to say,

if, unenlightened by the theory in question, we should have expected an event which was incompatible with the theory—an event which would have refuted the theory.

(3) Every "good" scientific theory is a prohibition: it forbids certain things to happen. The more a theory forbids, the better it is.

(4) A theory which is not refutable by any conceivable event is nonscientific. Irrefutability is not a virtue of a theory (as people often think) but a vice.

(5) Every genuine *test* of a theory is an attempt to falsify it, or to refute it. Testability is falsifiability; but there are degrees of testability: some theories are more testable, more exposed to refutation, than others; they take, as it were, greater risks.

(6) Confirming evidence should not count *except when it is the result of a genuine test of the theory*; and this means that it can be presented as a serious but unsuccessful attempt to falsify the theory. (I now speak in such cases of "corroborating evidence.")

(7) Some genuinely testable theories, when found to be false, are still upheld by their admirers—for example by introducing *ad hoc* some auxiliary assumption, or by reinterpreting the theory *ad hoc* in such a way that it escapes refutation. Such a procedure is always possible, but it rescues the theory from refutation only at the price of destroying, or at least lowering, its scientific status. (I later described such a rescuing operation as a "*conventionalist twist*" or a "*conventionalist stratagem.*")

One can sum up all this by saying that *the criterion of the scientific status of a theory is its falsifiability, or refutability, or testability.*

II

I may perhaps exemplify this with the help of the various theories so far mentioned. Einstein's theory of gravitation clearly satisfied the criterion of falsifiability. Even if our measuring instruments at the time did not allow us to pronounce on the results of the tests with complete assurance, there was clearly a possibility of refuting the theory.

Astrology did not pass the test. Astrologers were greatly impressed, and misled, by what they believed to be confirming evidence—so much so that they were quite unimpressed by any unfavourable evidence. Moreover, by making their interpretations and prophecies sufficiently vague they were able to explain away anything that might have been a refutation of the theory had the theory and the prophecies been more precise. In order to escape falsification they destroyed the testability of their theory. It is a typical soothsayer's trick to predict things so vaguely that the predictions can hardly fail: that they become irrefutable.

The Marxist theory of history, in spite of the serious efforts of some of its founders and followers, ultimately adopted this soothsaying practice. In some of its earlier formulations (for example in Marx's analysis of the character of the "coming social revolution") their predictions were testable, and in fact falsified.[2] Yet instead of accepting the refutations the followers of Marx reinterpreted both the theory and the evidence in order to make them agree. In this way they rescued the theory from refutation; but they did so at the price of adopting a device which made it irrefutable. They thus gave a "conventionalist twist" to the theory; and by this stratagem they destroyed its much advertised claim to scientific status.

The two psychoanalytic theories were in a different class. They were simply nontestable, irrefutable. There was no conceivable human behaviour which could contradict them. This does not mean that Freud and Adler were not seeing certain things correctly: I personally do not doubt that much of what they say is of considerable importance, and may well play its part one day in a psychological science which is testable. But it does mean that those "clinical observations" which analysts naïvely believe confirm their theory cannot do this any more than the daily confirmations which astrologers find in their practice.[3] And as for Freud's epic of the ego, the super-ego, and the Id, no substantially stronger claim to scientific status can be made for it than for Homer's collected stories from Olympus. These theories describe some facts, but in the manner of myths. They contain most interesting psychological suggestions, but not in a testable form.

At the same time I realized that such myths may be developed, and become testable; that historically speaking all—or very nearly all—scientific theories originate from myths, and that a myth may contain important anticipations of scientific theories. Examples are Empedocles' theory of evolution by trial and error, or Parmenides' myth of the unchanging block universe in which nothing ever happens and which, if we add another dimension, becomes Einstein's block universe (in which, too, nothing ever happens, since everything is, four-dimensionally speaking, determined and laid down from the beginning). I thus felt that if a theory is found to be nonscientific, or "metaphysical" (as we might say), it is not thereby found to be unimportant, or insignificant, or "meaningless," or "nonsensical."[4] But it cannot claim to be backed by empirical evidence in the scientific sense—although it may easily be, in some genetic sense, the "result of observation."

(There were a great many other theories of this prescientific or pseudo-scientific character, some of them, unfortunately, as influential as the Marxist interpretation of history; for example, the racialist interpretation of history—another of those impressive and all-explanatory theories which act upon weak minds like revelations.)

Thus the problem which I tried to solve by proposing the criterion of falsifiability was neither a problem of meaningfulness or significance, nor a problem of truth or acceptability. It was the problem of drawing a line (as well as this can be done) between the statements, or systems of statements, of the empirical sciences, and all other statements—whether they are of a religious or of a metaphysical character, or simply pseudo-scientific. Years later—it must have been in 1928 or 1929—I called this first problem of mine the *"problem of demarcation."* The criterion of falsifiability is a solution to this problem of demarcation, for it says that statements or systems of statements, in order to be ranked as scientific, must be capable of conflicting with possible, or conceivable, observations.

III

Today I know, of course, that this *criterion of demarcation*—the criterion of testability, or falsifiability, or refutability—is far from obvious; for even now its significance is seldom realized. At that time, in 1920, it seemed to me almost trivial, although it solved for me an intellectual problem which had worried me deeply, and one which also had obvious practical consequences (for example, political ones). But I did not yet realize its full implications, or its philosophical significance. When I explained it to a fellow student of the Mathematics Department (now a distinguished mathematician in Great Britain), he suggested that I should publish it. At the time I thought this absurd; for I was convinced that my problem, since it was so important for me, must have agitated many scientists and philosophers who would surely have reached my rather obvious solution. That this was not the case I learnt from Wittgenstein's work, and from its reception; and so I published my results thirteen years later in the form of a criticism of Wittgenstein's *criterion of meaningfulness*.

Wittgenstein, as you all know, tried to show in the *Tractatus* (see for example his propositions 6.53, 6.54, and 5) that all so-called philosophical or metaphysical propositions were actually non-propositions or pseudo-propositions: that they were senseless or meaningless. All genuine (or meaningful) propositions were truth functions of the elementary or atomic propositions which described "atomic facts," i.e.,—facts which can in principle be ascertained by observation. In other words, meaningful propositions were fully reducible to elementary or atomic propositions which were simple statements describing possible states of affairs, and which could in principle be established or rejected by observation. If we call a statement an "observation statement" not only if it states an actual observation but also if it states anything that *may* be observed, we shall have to say (according to the *Tractatus*, 5 and 4.52) that every genuine proposition must be a truth-function of, and therefore deducible from, observation statements. All other apparent propositions will be meaningless pseudo-propositions; in fact they will be nothing but nonsensical gibberish.

This idea was used by Wittgenstein for a characterization of science, as opposed to philosophy. We read (for example in 4.11, where natural science is taken to stand in opposition to philosophy): "The totality of true propositions is the total natural science (or the totality of the natural sciences)." This means that the propositions which belong to science are those deducible from *true* observation statements; they are those propositions which can be *verified* by true observation statements. Could we know all true observation statements, we should also know all that may be asserted by natural science.

This amounts to a crude verifiability criterion of demarcation. To make it slightly less crude, it could be amended thus: "The statements which may possibly fall within the province of science are those which may possibly be verified by observation statements; and these statements, again, coincide with the class of *all* genuine or meaningful statements." For this approach, then, *verifiability, meaningfulness, and scientific character all coincide.*

I personally was never interested in the so-called problem of meaning; on the contrary, it appeared to me a verbal problem, a typical pseudo-problem. I was interested only in the problem of demarcation, i.e., in finding a criterion of the scientific character of theories. It was just this interest which made me see at once that Wittgenstein's verifiability criterion of meaning was intended to play the part of a criterion of demarcation as well; and which made me see that, as such, it was totally inadequate, even if all misgivings about the dubious concept of meaning were set aside. For Wittgenstein's criterion of demarcation—to use my own terminology in this context—is verifiability, or deducibility from observation statements. But this criterion is too narrow (*and* too wide): it excludes from science practically everything that is, in fact, characteristic of it (while failing in effect to exclude astrology). No scientific theory can ever be deduced from observation statements, or be described as a truth-function of observation statements.

All this I pointed out on various occasions to Wittgensteinians and members of the Vienna Circle. In 1931–32, I summarized my ideas in a largish book (read by several members of the Circle but never published; although part of it was incorporated in my *Logic of Scientific Discovery*); and in 1933 I published a letter to the Editor of *Erkenntnis* in which I tried to compress into two pages my ideas on the problems of demarcation and induction.[5] In this letter and elsewhere I described the problem of meaning as a pseudo-problem, in contrast to the problem of demarcation. But my contribution was classified by members of the Circle as a proposal to replace the verifiability criterion of *meaning* by a falsifiability criterion of *meaning*—which effectively made nonsense of my views.[6] My protests that I was trying to solve, not their pseudo-problem of meaning, but the problem of demarcation, were of no avail.

My attacks upon verification had some effect, however. They soon led to complete confusion in the camp of the verificationist philosophers of sense and nonsense. The original proposal of verifiability as the criterion of meaning was at least clear, simple, and forceful. The modifications and shifts which were now introduced were the very opposite.[7] This, I should say, is now seen even by the participants. But since I am usually quoted as one of them I wish to repeat that although I created this confusion I never participated in it. Neither falsifiability nor testability were proposed by me as criteria of meaning; and although I may plead guilty to having introduced both terms into the discussion, it was not I who introduced them into the theory of meaning.

Criticism of my alleged views was widespread and highly successful. I have yet to meet a criticism of my views.[8] Meanwhile, testability is being widely accepted as a criterion of demarcation.

IV

I have discussed the problem of demarcation in some detail because I believe that its solution is the key to most of the fundamental problems of the philosophy of science. I am going to give you later a list of some of these other problems, but only one of them—the *problem of induction*—can be discussed here at any length.

I had become interested in the problem of induction in 1923. Although this problem is very closely connected with the problem of demarcation, I did not fully appreciate the connection for about five years.

I approached the problem of induction through Hume. Hume, I felt, was perfectly right in pointing out that induction cannot be logically justified. He held that there can be no valid logical[9] arguments allowing us to establish *"that those instances, of which we have had no experience, resemble those, of which we have had experience."* Consequently *"even after the observation of the frequent or constant conjunction of objects, we have no reason to draw any inference concerning any object beyond those of which we have had experience."* For "shou'd it be said that we have experience"[10]—experience teaching us that objects constantly conjoined with certain other objects continue to be so conjoined—then, Hume says, "I wou'd renew my question, *why from this experience we form any conclusion beyond those past instances, of which we have had experience.*" In other words, an attempt to justify the practice of induction by an appeal to experience must lead to an *infinite regress*. As a result we can say that theories can never be inferred from observation statements, or rationally justified by them.

I found Hume's refutation of inductive inference clear and conclusive. But I felt completely dissatisfied with his psychological explanation of induction in terms of custom or habit.

It has often been noticed that this explanation of Hume's is philosophically not very satisfactory. It is, however, without doubt intended as a *psychological* rather than a philosophical theory; for it tries to give a causal explanation of a psychological fact—*the fact that we believe in laws*, in statements asserting regularities or constantly conjoined kinds of events—by asserting that this fact is due to (i.e. constantly conjoined with) custom or habit. But even this reformulation of Hume's theory is still unsatisfactory; for what I have just called a "psychological fact" may itself be described as a custom or habit—the custom or habit of believing in laws or regularities; and it is neither very surprising nor very enlightening to hear that such a custom or habit must be explained as due to, or conjoined with, a custom or habit (even though a different one). Only when we remember that the words "custom" and "habit" are used by Hume, as they are in ordinary language, not merely to *describe* regular behaviour, but rather to *theorize about its origin* (ascribed to frequent repetition), can we reformulate his psychological theory in a more satisfactory way. We can then say that, like other habits, *our habit of believing in laws is the product of frequent repetition*—of the repeated observation that things of a certain kind are constantly conjoined with things of another kind.

This genetico-psychological theory is, as indicated, incorporated in ordinary language, and it is therefore hardly as revolutionary as Hume thought. It is no doubt an extremely popular psychological theory—part of "common sense," one might say. But in spite of my love of both common sense and Hume, I felt convinced that this psychological theory was mistaken; and that it was in fact refutable on purely logical grounds.

Hume's psychology, which is the popular psychology, was mistaken, I felt, about at least three different things: (*a*) the typical result of repetition; (*b*) the genesis of habits; and especially (*c*) the character of those experiences or modes of behaviour which may be described as "believing in a law" or "expecting a lawlike succession of events."

(*a*) The typical result of repetition—say, of repeating a difficult passage on the piano—is that movements which at first needed attention are in the end executed without attention. We might say that the process becomes radically abbreviated, and ceases to be conscious: it becomes "physiological." Such a process, far from creating a conscious expectation of lawlike succession, or a belief in a law, may on the contrary begin with a conscious belief and destroy it by making it superfluous. In learning to ride a bicycle we may start with the belief that we can avoid falling if we steer in the direction in which we threaten to fall, and this belief may be useful for guiding our movements. After sufficient practice we may forget the rule; in any case, we do not need it any longer. On the other hand, even if it is true that repetition may create unconscious expectations, these become conscious only if something goes wrong (we may not have heard the clock tick, but we may hear that it has stopped).

(*b*) Habits or customs do not, as a rule, *originate* in repetition. Even the habit of walking, or of speaking, or of feeding at certain hours, *begins* before repetition can play any part whatever. We may say, if we like, that they deserve to be called "habits" or "customs" only after repetition has played its typical part; but we must not say that the practices in question originated as the result of many repetitions.

(*c*) Belief in a law is not quite the same thing as behaviour which betrays an expectation of a lawlike succession of events; but these two are sufficiently closely connected to be treated together. They may, perhaps, in exceptional cases, result from a mere repetition of sense impressions (as in the case of the stopping clock). I was prepared to concede this, but I contended that normally, and in most cases of any interest, they cannot be so explained. As Hume admits, even a single striking observation may be sufficient to create a belief or an expectation—a fact which he tries to explain as due to an inductive habit, formed as the result of a vast number of long repetitive sequences which had been experienced at an earlier period of life.[11] But this, I contended, was merely his attempt to explain away unfavourable facts which threatened his theory; an unsuccessful attempt, since these unfavourable facts could be observed in very young animals and babies—as early, indeed, as we like. "A lighted cigarette was held near the noses of the young puppies," reports F. Bäge. "They sniffed at it once, turned tail, and nothing would induce them to come back to the source of the smell and to sniff again. A few days later, they reacted to the mere sight of a cigarette or even of a rolled piece of white paper, by bounding away, and sneezing."[12] If we try to explain cases like this by postulating a vast number of long repetitive sequences at a still earlier age we are not only romancing, but forgetting that in the clever puppies' short lives there must be room not only for repetition but also for a great deal of novelty, and consequently of nonrepetition.

But it is not only that certain empirical facts do not support Hume; there are decisive arguments of a *purely logical* nature against his psychological theory.

The central idea of Hume's theory is that of *repetition, based upon similarity* (or "resemblance"). This idea is used in a very uncritical way. We are led to think of the water-drop that hollows the stone: of sequences of unquestionably like events slowly forcing themselves upon us, as does the tick of the clock. But we ought to realize that in a psychological theory such as Hume's, only repetition-for-us, based upon similarity-for-us, can be allowed to have any effect upon us. We must respond to situations as if they were equivalent; *take* them as similar; *interpret* them as repetitions. The clever puppies, we may assume, showed by their response, their way of acting or of reacting, that they recognized or interpreted the second situation as a repetition of the first: that they expected its main element, the objectionable smell, to be present. The situation was a repetition-for-them because they responded to it by *anticipating* its similarity to the previous one.

This apparently psychological criticism has a purely logical basis which may be summed up in the following simple argument. (It happens to be the one from which I originally started my criticism.) The kind of repetition envisaged by Hume can never be perfect; the cases he has in mind cannot be cases of perfect sameness; they can only be cases of similarity. Thus *they are repetitions only from a certain point of view.* (What has the effect upon me of a repetition may not have this effect upon a spider.) But this means that, for logical reasons, there must always be a point of view—such as a system of expectations, anticipations, assumptions, or interests—*before* there can be any repetition; which point of view, consequently, cannot be merely the result of repetition. (See now also appendix *x, (1), to my *L.Sc.D.*)

We must thus replace, for the purposes of a psychological theory of the origin of our beliefs, the naïve idea of events which *are* similar by the idea of events to which we react by *interpreting* them as being similar. But if this is so (and I can see no escape from it) then Hume's psychological theory of induction leads to an infinite regress, precisely analogous to that other infinite regress which was discovered by Hume himself, and used by him to explode the logical theory of induction. For what do we wish to explain? In the example of the puppies we wish to explain behaviour which may be described as *recognizing or interpreting* a situation as a repetition of another. Clearly, we cannot hope to explain this by an appeal to earlier repetitions, once we realize that the earlier repetitions must also have been repetitions-for-them, so that precisely the same problem arises again: that of *recognizing or interpreting* a situation as a repetition of another.

To put it more concisely, similarity-for-us is the product of a response involving interpretations (which may be inadequate) and anticipations or expectations (which may never be fulfilled). It is therefore impossible to explain anticipations, or expectations, as resulting from many repetitions, as suggested by Hume. For even the first repetition-for-us must be based upon similarity-for-us, and therefore upon expectations—precisely the kind of thing we wished to explain.

This shows that there is an infinite regress involved in Hume's psychological theory.

Hume, I felt, had never accepted the full force of his own logical analysis. Having refuted the logical idea of induction he was faced with the following problem: How do we actually obtain our knowledge, as a matter of psychological fact, if induction is a procedure which is logically invalid and rationally unjustifiable? There are two possible answers: (1) We obtain our knowledge by a non-inductive procedure. This answer would have allowed Hume to retain a form of rationalism. (2) We obtain our knowledge by repetition and induction, and therefore by a logically invalid and rationally unjustifiable procedure, so that all apparent knowledge is merely a kind of belief—belief based on habit. This answer would imply that even scientific knowledge is irrational, so that rationalism is absurd, and must be given up. (I shall not discuss here the age-old attempts, now again fashionable, to get out of the difficulty by asserting that though induction is of course logically invalid if we mean by "logic" the same as "deductive logic," it is not irrational by its own standards, as may be seen from the fact that every reasonable man applies it *as a matter of fact*: it was Hume's great achievement to break this uncritical identification of the question of fact—*quid facti?*—and the question of justification or validity—*quid juris?* (See below, point (13) of the appendix to the present essay [Editor's note: the appendix is not reprinted here].)

It seems that Hume never seriously considered the first alternative. Having cast out the logical theory of induction by repetition he struck a bargain with common sense, meekly allowing the reentry of induction by repetition, in the guise of a psychological theory. I proposed to turn the tables upon this theory of Hume's. Instead of explaining our propensity to expect regularities as the result of repetition, I proposed to explain repetition-for-us as the result of our propensity to expect regularities and to search for them.

Thus I was led by purely logical considerations to replace the psychological theory of induction by the following view. Without waiting, passively, for repetitions to impress or impose regularities upon us, we actively try to impose regularities upon the world. We try to discover similarities in it, and to interpret it in terms of laws invented by us. Without waiting for premises we jump to conclusions. These may have to be discarded later, should observation show that they are wrong.

This was a theory of trial and error—of *conjectures and refutations*. It made it possible to understand why our attempts to force interpretations upon the world were logically prior to the observation of similarities. Since there were logical reasons behind this procedure, I thought that it would apply in the field of science also; that scientific theories were not the digest of observations, but that they were inventions—conjectures boldly put forward for trial, to be eliminated if they clashed with observations; with observations which were rarely accidental but as a rule undertaken with the definite intention of testing a theory by obtaining, if possible, a decisive refutation.

V

The belief that science proceeds from observation to theory is still so widely and so firmly held that my denial of it is often met with incredulity. I have even been suspected of being insincere—of denying what nobody in his senses can doubt.

But in fact the belief that we can start with pure observations alone, without anything in the nature of a theory, is absurd; as may be illustrated by the story of the man who dedicated his life to natural science, wrote down everything he could observe, and bequeathed his priceless collection of observations to the Royal Society to be used as inductive evidence. This story should show us that though beetles may profitably be collected, observations may not.

Twenty-five years ago I tried to bring home the same point to a group of physics students in Vienna by beginning a lecture with the following instructions: "Take pencil and paper; carefully observe, and write down what you have observed!" They asked, of course, *what* I wanted them to observe. Clearly the instruction, "Observe!" is absurd.[13] (It is not even idiomatic, unless the object of the transitive verb can be taken as understood.) Observation is always selective. It needs a chosen object, a definite task, an interest, a point of view, a problem. And its description presupposes a descriptive language, with property words; it presupposes similarity and classification, which in its turn presupposes interests, points of view, and problems. "A hungry animal," writes Katz,[14] "divides the environment into edible and inedible things. An animal in flight sees roads to escape and hiding places. . . . Generally speaking, objects change . . . according to the needs of the animal." We may add that objects can be classified, and can become similar or dissimilar, *only* in this way—by being related to needs and interests. This rule applies not only to animals but also to scientists. For the animal a point of view is provided by its needs, the task of the moment, and its expectations; for the scientist by his theoretical interests, the special problem under investigation, his conjectures and anticipations, and the theories which he accepts as a kind of background: his frame of reference, his "horizon of expectations."

The problem "Which comes first, the hypothesis (H) or the observation (O)," is soluble; as is the problem, "Which comes first, the hen (H) or the egg (O)." The reply to the latter is, "An earlier kind of egg"; to the former, "An earlier kind of hypothesis." It is quite true that any particular hypothesis we choose will have been preceded by observations—the observations, for example, which it is designed to explain. But these observations, in their turn, presupposed the adoption of a frame of reference: a frame of expectations: a frame of theories. If they were significant, if they created a need for explanation and thus gave rise to the invention of a hypothesis, it was because they could not be explained within the old theoretical framework, the old horizon of expectations. There is no danger here of an infinite regress. Going back to more and more primitive theories and myths we shall in the end find unconscious, *inborn* expectations.

The theory of inborn *ideas* is absurd, I think; but every organism has inborn *reactions* or *responses*; and among them, responses adapted to impending events. These responses we may describe as "expectations" without implying that these "expectations" are conscious. The newborn baby "expects," in this sense, to be fed (and, one could even argue, to be protected and loved). In view of the close relation between expectation and knowledge we may even speak in quite a reasonable sense of "inborn knowledge." This "knowledge" is not, however, *valid a priori*; an inborn expectation, no matter how strong and specific, may be mistaken. (The newborn child may be abandoned, and starve.)

Thus we are born with expectations; with "knowledge" which, although not *valid a priori*, is *psychologically or genetically a priori*, i.e., prior to all observational experience. One of the most important of these expectations is the expectation of finding a regularity. It is connected with an inborn propensity to look out for regularities, or with a *need* to *find* regularities, as we may see from the pleasure of the child who satisfies this need.

This "instinctive" expectation of finding regularities, which is psychologically *a priori*, corresponds very closely to the "law of causality" which Kant believed to be part of our mental outfit and to be *a priori* valid. One might thus be inclined to say that Kant failed to distinguish between psychologically *a priori* ways of thinking or responding and *a priori* valid beliefs. But I do not think that his mistake was quite as crude as that. For the expectation of finding regularities is not only psychologically *a priori*, but also logically *a priori*: it is logically prior to all observational experience, for it is prior to any recognition of similarities, as we have seen; and all observation involves the recognition of similarities (or dissimilarities). But in spite of being logically *a priori* in this sense the expectation is not valid *a priori*. For it may fail: we can easily construct an environment (it would be a lethal one) which, compared with our ordinary environment, is so chaotic that we completely fail to find regularities. (All natural laws could remain valid: environments of this kind have been used in the animal experiments mentioned in the next section.)

Thus Kant's reply to Hume came near to being right; for the distinction between an *a priori* valid expectation and one which is both genetically *and* logically prior to observation, but not *a priori* valid, is really somewhat subtle. But Kant proved too much. In trying to show how knowledge is possible, he proposed a theory which had the unavoidable consequence that our quest for knowledge must necessarily succeed, which is clearly mistaken. When Kant said, "Our intellect does not draw its laws from nature but imposes its laws upon nature," he was right. But in thinking that these laws are necessarily true, or that we necessarily succeed in imposing them upon nature, he was wrong.[15] Nature very often resists quite successfully, forcing us to discard our laws as refuted; but if we live we may try again.

To sum up this logical criticism of Hume's psychology of induction we may consider the idea of building an induction machine. Placed in a simplified "world" (for example, one of sequences of coloured counters) such a machine may through repetition "learn," or even "formulate," laws of succession which hold in its "world." If such a machine can be constructed (and I have no doubt that it can) then, it might be argued, my theory must be wrong; for if a machine is capable of performing inductions on the basis of repetition, there can be no logical reasons preventing us from doing the same.

The argument sounds convincing, but it is mistaken. In constructing an induction machine we, the architects of the machine, must decide *a priori* what constitutes its "world"; what things are to be taken as similar or equal; and what *kind* of "laws" we wish the machine to be able to "discover" in its "world." In other words we must build into the machine a framework determining what is relevant or interesting in its world: the machine will have its "inborn" selection principles. The problems of similarity will have been solved for it by its makers who thus have interpreted the "world" for the machine.

VI

Our propensity to look out for regularities, and to impose laws upon nature, leads to the psychological phenomenon of *dogmatic thinking* or, more generally, dogmatic behaviour: we expect regularities everywhere and attempt to find them even where there are none; events which do not yield to these attempts we are inclined to treat as a kind of "background noise"; and we stick to our expectations even when they are inadequate and we ought to accept defeat. This dogmatism is to some extent necessary. It is demanded by a situation which can only be dealt with by forcing our conjectures upon the world. Moreover, this dogmatism allows us to approach a good theory in stages, by way of approximations: if we accept defeat too easily, we may prevent ourselves from finding that we were very nearly right.

It is clear that this *dogmatic attitude*, which makes us stick to our first impressions, is indicative of a strong belief; while a *critical attitude*, which is ready to modify its tenets, which admits doubt and demands tests, is indicative of a weaker belief. Now according to Hume's theory, and to the popular theory, the strength of a belief should be a product of repetition; thus it should always grow with experience, and always be greater in less primitive persons. But dogmatic thinking, an uncontrolled wish to impose regularities, a manifest pleasure in rites and in repetition as such, are characteristic of primitives and children; and increasing experience and maturity sometimes create an attitude of caution and criticism rather than of dogmatism.

I may perhaps mention here a point of agreement with psychoanalysis. Psychoanalysts assert that neurotics and others interpret the world in accordance with a personal set pattern which is not easily given up, and which can often be traced back to early childhood. A pattern or scheme which was adopted very early in life is maintained throughout, and every new experience is interpreted in terms of it; verifying it, as it were, and contributing to its rigidity. This is a description of what I have called the dogmatic attitude, as distinct from the critical attitude, which shares with the dogmatic attitude the quick adoption of a schema of expectations—a myth, perhaps, or a conjecture or hypothesis—but which is ready to modify it, to correct it, and even to give it up. I am inclined to suggest that most neuroses may be due to a partially arrested development of the critical attitude; to an arrested rather than a natural dogmatism; to resistance to demands for the modification and adjustment of certain schematic interpretations and responses. This resistance in its turn may perhaps be explained, in some cases, as due to an injury or shock, resulting in fear and in an increased need for assurance or certainty, analogous to the way in which an injury to a limb makes us afraid to move it, so that it becomes stiff. (It might even be argued that the case of the limb is not merely analogous to the dogmatic response, but an instance of it.) The explanation of any concrete case will have to take into account the weight of the difficulties involved in making the necessary adjustments—difficulties which may be considerable, especially in a complex and changing world: we know from experiments on animals that varying degrees of neurotic behaviour may be produced at will by correspondingly varying difficulties.

I found many other links between the psychology of knowledge and psychological fields which are often considered remote from it—for example the psychology of art and music; in fact, my ideas about induction originated in a conjecture about the evolution of Western polyphony. But you will be spared this story.

VII

My logical criticism of Hume's psychological theory, and the considerations connected with it (most of which I elaborated in 1926–7, in a thesis entitled "On Habit and Belief in Laws"[16]) may seem a little removed from the field of the philosophy of science. But the distinction between dogmatic and critical thinking, or the dogmatic and the critical attitude, brings us right back to our central problem. For the dogmatic attitude is clearly related to the tendency to *verify* our laws and schemata by seeking to apply them and to confirm them, even to the point of neglecting refutations, whereas the critical attitude is one of readiness to change them—to test them; to refute them; to *falsify* them, if possible. This suggests that we may identify the critical attitude with the scientific attitude, and the dogmatic attitude with the one which we have described as pseudo-scientific.

It further suggests that genetically speaking the pseudo-scientific attitude is more primitive than, and prior to, the scientific attitude: that it is a prescientific attitude. And this primitivity or priority also has its logical aspect. For the critical attitude is not so much opposed to the dogmatic attitude as superimposed upon it: criticism must be directed against existing and influential beliefs in need of critical revision—in other words, dogmatic beliefs. A critical attitude needs for its raw material, as it were, theories or beliefs which are held more or less dogmatically.

Thus science must begin with myths, and with the criticism of myths; neither with the collection of observations, nor with the invention of experiments, but with the critical discussion of myths, and of magical techniques and practices. The scientific tradition is distinguished from the prescientific tradition in having two layers. Like the latter, it passes on its theories; but it also passes on a critical attitude towards them. The theories are passed on, not as dogmas, but rather with the challenge to discuss them and improve upon them. This tradition is Hellenic: it may be traced back to Thales, founder of the first *school* (I do not mean "of the first *philosophical* school," but simply "of the first school") which was not mainly concerned with the preservation of a dogma.[17]

The critical attitude, the tradition of free discussion of theories with the aim of discovering their weak spots so that they may be improved upon, is the attitude of reasonableness, of rationality. It makes far-reaching use of both verbal argument and observation—of observation in the interest of argument, however. The Greeks' discovery of the critical method gave rise at first to the mistaken hope that it would lead to the solution of all the great old problems; that it would establish certainty; that it would help to *prove* our theories, to *justify* them. But this hope was a residue of the dogmatic way of thinking; in fact nothing can be justified or proved (outside of mathematics and logic). The demand for rational proofs in science indicates a failure to keep distinct the broad realm of rationality and the narrow realm of rational certainty: it is an untenable, an unreasonable demand.

Nevertheless, the role of logical argument, of deductive logical reasoning, remains all-important for the critical approach; not because it allows us to prove our theories, or to infer them from observation statements, but because only by purely deductive reasoning is it possible for us to discover what our theories imply, and thus to criticize them effectively. Criticism, I said, is an attempt to find the weak spots in a theory, and these, as a rule, can be found only in the more remote logical consequences which can be derived from it. It is here that purely logical reasoning plays an important part in science.

Hume was right in stressing that our theories cannot be validly inferred from what we can know to be true—neither from observations nor from anything else. He concluded from this that our belief in them was irrational. If "belief" means here our inability to doubt our natural laws, and the constancy of natural regularities, then Hume is again right: this kind of dogmatic belief has, one might say, a physiological rather than a rational basis. If, however, the term "belief" is taken to cover our critical acceptance of scientific theories—a *tentative* acceptance combined with an eagerness to revise the theory if we succeed in designing a test which it cannot pass—then Hume was wrong. In such an acceptance of theories there is nothing irrational. There is not even anything irrational in relying for practical purposes upon well-tested theories, for no more rational course of action is open to us.

Assume that we have deliberately made it our task to live in this unknown world of ours; to adjust ourselves to it as well as we can; to take advantage of the opportunities we can find in it; and to explain it, *if* possible (we need not assume that it is), and as far as possible, with the help of laws and explanatory theories. *If we have made this our task, then there is no more rational procedure than the method of trial and error—of conjecture and refutation:* of boldly proposing theories; of trying our best to show that these are erroneous; and of accepting them tentatively if our critical efforts are unsuccessful.

From the point of view here developed all laws, all theories, remain essentially tentative, or conjectural, or hypothetical, even when we feel unable to doubt them any longer. Before a theory has been refuted we can never know in what way it may have to be modified. That the sun will always rise and set within twenty-four hours is still proverbial as a law "established by induction beyond reasonable doubt." It is odd that this example is still in use, though it may have served well enough in the days of Aristotle and Pytheas of Massalia—the great traveller who for centuries was called a liar because of his tales of Thule, the land of the frozen sea and the *midnight sun*.

The method of trial and error is not, of course, simply identical with the scientific or critical approach—with the method of conjecture and refutation. The method of trial and error is applied not only by Einstein but, in a more dogmatic fashion, by the amoeba also. The difference lies not so much in the trials as in a critical and constructive attitude towards errors; errors which the scientist consciously and cautiously tries to uncover in order to refute his theories with searching arguments, including appeals to the most severe experimental tests which his theories and his ingenuity permit him to design.

The critical attitude may be described as the conscious attempt to make our theories, our conjectures, suffer in our stead in the struggle for the survival of the fittest. It gives us a chance to survive the elimination of an inadequate hypothesis—when a more dogmatic attitude would eliminate it by eliminating us. (There is a touching story of an Indian community which disappeared because of its belief in the holiness of life, including that of tigers.) We thus obtain the fittest theory within our reach by the elimination of those which are less fit. (By "fitness" I do not mean merely "usefulness" but truth; see chapters 3 and 10 of my book *Conjectures and Refutations*.) I do not think that this procedure is irrational or in need of any further rational justification.

VIII

Let us now turn from our logical criticism of the *psychology of experience* to our real problem—the problem of *the logic of science*. Although some of the things I have said may help us here, in so far as they may have eliminated certain psychological prejudices in favour of induction, my treatment of the *logical problem of induction* is completely independent of this criticism, and of all psychological considerations. Provided you do not dogmatically believe in the alleged psychological fact that we make inductions, you may now forget my whole story with the exception of two logical points: my logical remarks on testability or falsifiability as the criterion of demarcation; and Hume's logical criticism of induction.

From what I have said it is obvious that there was a close link between the two problems which interested me at that time: demarcation, and induction or scientific method. It was easy to see that the method of science is criticism, i.e. attempted falsifications. Yet it took me a few years to notice that the two problems—of demarcation and of induction—were in a sense one.

Why, I asked, do so many scientists believe in induction? I found they did so because they believed natural science to be characterized by the inductive method—by a method starting from, and relying upon, long sequences of observations and experiments. They believed that the difference between genuine science and metaphysical or pseudo-scientific speculation depended solely upon whether or not the inductive method was employed. They believed (to put it in my own terminology) that only the inductive method could provide a satisfactory *criterion of demarcation*.

I recently came across an interesting formulation of this belief in a remarkable philosophical book by a great physicist—Max Born's *Natural Philosophy of Cause and Chance*.[18] He writes: "Induction allows us to generalize a number of observations into a general rule: that night follows day and day follows night. . . . But while everyday life has no definite criterion for the validity of an induction, . . . science has worked out a code, or rule of craft, for its application." Born nowhere reveals the contents of this inductive code (which, as his wording shows, contains a "definite criterion for the validity of an induction"); but he stresses that "there is no logical argument" for its acceptance: "it is a question of faith"; and he is therefore "willing to call induction a metaphysical principle." But why does he believe that such a code of valid inductive rules must exist? This becomes clear when he speaks of the "vast communities of people ignorant of, or rejecting, the rule of science, among them the members of anti-vaccination societies and believers in astrology. It is useless to argue with them; I cannot compel them to accept the same criteria of valid induction in which I believe: the code of scientific rules." This makes it quite clear that "*valid induction*" *was here meant to serve as a criterion of demarcation between science and pseudo-science.*

But it is obvious that this rule or craft of "valid induction" is not even metaphysical: it simply does not exist. No rule can ever guarantee that a generalization inferred from true observations, however often repeated, is true. (Born himself does not believe in the truth of Newtonian physics, in spite of its success, although he believes that it is based on induction.) And the success of science is not based upon rules of induction, but depends upon luck, ingenuity, and the purely deductive rules of critical argument.

I may summarize some of my conclusions as follows:

(1) Induction, i.e. inference based on many observations, is a myth. It is neither a psychological fact, nor a fact of ordinary life, nor one of scientific procedure.

(2) The actual procedure of science is to operate with conjectures: to jump to conclusions— often after one single observation (as noticed for example by Hume and Born).

(3) Repeated observations and experiments function in science as *tests* of our conjectures or hypotheses, i.e. as attempted refutations.

(4) The mistaken belief in induction is fortified by the need for a criterion of demarcation which, it is traditionally but wrongly believed, only the inductive method can provide.

(5) The conception of such an inductive method, like the criterion of verifiability, implies a faulty demarcation.

(6) None of this is altered in the least if we say that induction makes theories only probable rather than certain. (See especially chapter 10 of *Conjectures and Refutations.*)

IX

If, as I have suggested, the problem of induction is only an instance or facet of the problem of demarcation, then the solution to the problem of demarcation must provide us with a solution to the problem of induction. This is indeed the case, I believe, although it is perhaps not immediately obvious.

For a brief formulation of the problem of induction we can turn again to Born, who writes: ". . . no observation or experiment, however extended, can give more than a finite number of repetitions"; therefore, "the statement of a law—B depends on A—always transcends experience. Yet this kind of statement is made everywhere and all the time, and sometimes from scanty material."[19]

In other words, the logical problem of induction arises from (*a*) Hume's discovery (so well expressed by Born) that it is impossible to justify a law by observation or experiment, since it "transcends experience"; (*b*) the fact that science proposes and uses laws "everywhere and all the time." (Like Hume, Born is struck by the "scanty material," i.e., the few observed instances upon which the law may be based.) To this we have to add (*c*) *the principle of empiricism* which asserts that in science, only observation and experiment may decide upon the *acceptance or rejection* of scientific statements, including laws and theories.

These three principles, (*a*), (*b*), and (*c*), appear at first sight to clash; and this apparent clash constitutes the *logical problem of induction*.

Faced with this clash, Born gives up (*c*), the principle of empiricism (as Kant and many others, including Bertrand Russell, have done before him), in favour of what he calls a "metaphysical principle"; a metaphysical principle which he does not even attempt to formulate; which he vaguely describes as a "code or rule of craft"; and of which I have never seen any formulation which even looked promising and was not clearly untenable.

But in fact the principles (*a*) to (*c*) do not clash. We can see this the moment we realize that the acceptance by science of a law or of a theory is *tentative only*; which is to say that all laws and theories are conjectures, or tentative *hypotheses* (a position which I have sometimes called "hypotheticism"); and that we may reject a law or theory on the basis of new evidence, without necessarily discarding the old evidence which originally led us to accept it.[20]

The principle of empiricism (*c*) can be fully preserved, since the fate of a theory, its acceptance or rejection, is decided by observation and experiment—by the result of tests. So long as a theory stands up to the severest tests we can design, it is accepted; if it does not, it is rejected. But it is never inferred, in any sense, from the empirical evidence. There is neither a psychological nor a logical induction. *Only the falsity of the theory can be inferred from empirical evidence, and this inference is a purely deductive one.*

Hume showed that it is not possible to infer a theory from observation statements; but this does not affect the possibility of refuting a theory by observation statements. The full appreciation of this possibility makes the relation between theories and observations perfectly clear.

This solves the problem of the alleged clash between the principles (*a*), (*b*), and (*c*), and with it Hume's problem of induction.

X

Thus the problem of induction is solved. But nothing seems less wanted than a simple solution to an age-old philosophical problem. Wittgenstein and his school hold that genuine philosophical problems do not exist;[21] from which it clearly follows that they cannot be solved. Others among my contemporaries do believe that there are philosophical problems, and respect them; but they seem to respect them too much; they seem to believe that they are insoluble, if not taboo; and they are shocked and horrified by the claim that there is a simple, neat, and lucid, solution to any of them. If there is a solution it must be deep, they feel, or at least complicated.

However this may be, I am still waiting for a simple, neat and lucid criticism of the solution which I published first in 1933 in my letter to the Editor of *Erkenntnis*,[22] and later in *The Logic of Scientific Discovery*.

Of course, one can invent new problems of induction, different from the one I have formulated and solved. (Its formulation was half its solution.) But I have yet to see any reformulation of the problem whose solution cannot be easily obtained from my old solution. I am now going to discuss some of these reformulations.

One question which may be asked is this: How do we really jump from an observation statement to a theory?

Although this question appears to be psychological rather than philosophical, one can say something positive about it without invoking psychology. One can say first that the jump is not from an observation statement, but from a problem-situation, and that the theory must allow us *to explain* the observations which created the problem (that is, *to deduce* them from the theory strengthened by other accepted theories and by other observation statements, the so-called initial conditions). This leaves, of course, an immense number of possible theories, good and bad; and it thus appears that our question has not been answered.

But this makes it fairly clear that when we asked our question we had more in mind than, "How do we jump from an observation statement to a theory?" The question we had in mind was, it now appears, "How do we jump from an observation statement to a *good* theory?" But to this the answer is: by jumping first to *any* theory and then testing it, to find whether it is good or not; i.e., by repeatedly applying the critical method, eliminating many bad theories, and inventing many new ones. Not everybody is able to do this; but there is no other way.

Other questions have sometimes been asked. The original problem of induction, it was said, is the problem of *justifying* induction, i.e. of justifying inductive inference. If you answer this problem by saying that what is called an "inductive inference" is always invalid and therefore clearly not justifiable, the following new problem must arise: how do you justify your method of trial and error? Reply: the method of trial and error is a *method of eliminating false theories* by observation statements; and the justification for this is the purely logical relationship of deducibility which allows us to assert the falsity of universal statements if we accept the truth of singular ones.

Another question sometimes asked is this: why is it reasonable to prefer non-falsified statements to falsified ones? To this question some involved answers have been produced, for example pragmatic answers. But from a pragmatic point of view the question does not arise, since false theories often serve well enough: most formulae used in engineering or navigation are known to be false, although they may be excellent approximations and easy to handle; and they are used with confidence by people who know them to be false.

The only correct answer is the straightforward one: because we search for truth (even though we can never be sure we have found it), and because the falsified theories are known or believed to be false, while the non-falsified theories may still be true. Besides, we do not prefer *every* non-falsified theory—only one which, in the light of criticism, appears to be better than its competitors: which solves our problems, which is well tested, and of which we think, or rather conjecture or hope (considering other provisionally accepted theories), that it will stand up to further tests.

It has also been said that the problem of induction is, "Why is it *reasonable* to believe that the future will be like the past?" and that a satisfactory answer to this question should make it plain that such a belief is, in fact, reasonable. My reply is that it is reasonable to believe that the future will be very different from the past in many vitally important respects. Admittedly it is perfectly reasonable to *act* on the assumption that it will, in many respects, be like the past, and that well-tested laws will continue to hold (since we can have no better assumption to act upon); but it is also reasonable to believe that such a course of action will lead us at times into severe trouble, since some of the laws upon which we now heavily rely may easily prove unreliable. (Remember the midnight sun!) One might even say that to judge from past experience, and from our general scientific knowledge, the future will *not* be like the past, in perhaps most of the ways which those have in mind who say that it will. Water will sometimes not quench thirst, and air will choke those who breathe it. An apparent way out is to say that the future will be like the past *in the sense that the laws of nature will not change*, but this is begging the question. We speak of a "law of nature" only if we think that we have before us a regularity which does not change; and if we find that it changes then we shall not continue to call it a "law of nature." Of course our search for natural laws indicates that we hope to find them, and that we believe that there are natural laws; but our belief in any particular natural law cannot have a safer basis than our unsuccessful critical attempts to refute it.

I think that those who put the problem of induction in terms of the *reasonableness* of our beliefs are perfectly right if they are dissatisfied with a Humean, or post-Humean, sceptical despair of reason. We must indeed reject the view that a belief in science is as irrational as a belief in primitive magical practices—that both are a matter of accepting a "total ideology," a convention or a tradition based on faith. But we must be cautious if we formulate our problem, with Hume, as one of the reasonableness of our *beliefs*. We should split this problem into three—our old problem of demarcation, or of how to *distinguish* between science and primitive magic; the problem of the rationality of the scientific or critical *procedure*, and of the role of observation within it; and lastly the problem of the rationality of our *acceptance* of theories for scientific and for practical purposes. To all these three problems solutions have been offered here.

One should also be careful not to confuse the problem of the reasonableness of the scientific procedure and the (tentative) acceptance of the results of this procedure—i.e., the scientific theories—with the problem of the rationality or otherwise *of the belief that this procedure will succeed*. In practice, in practical scientific research, this belief is no doubt unavoidable and reasonable, there being no better alternative. But the belief is certainly unjustifiable in a theoretical sense, as I have argued (in section v). Moreover, if we could show, on general logical grounds, that the scientific quest is likely to succeed, one could not understand why anything like success has been so rare in the long history of human endeavours to know more about our world.

Yet another way of putting the problem of induction is in terms of probability. Let t be the theory and e the evidence: we can ask for $P(t,e)$, that is to say, the probability of t, given e. The problem of induction, it is often believed, can then be put thus: construct a *calculus of probability* which allows us to work out for any theory t what its probability is, relative to any given empirical evidence e; and show that $P(t,e)$ increases with the accumulation of supporting evidence, and reaches high values—at any rate values greater than $\frac{1}{2}$.

In *The Logic of Scientific Discovery* I explained why I think that this approach to the problem is fundamentally mistaken.[23] To make this clear, I introduced there the distinction between *probability* and *degree of corroboration or confirmation*. (The term "confirmation" has lately been so much used and misused that I have decided to surrender it to the verificationists and to use for my own purposes "corroboration" only. The term "probability" is best used in some of the many senses which satisfy the well-known calculus of probability, axiomatized, for example, by Keynes, Jeffreys, and myself; but nothing of course depends on the choice of words, as long as we do not *assume*, uncritically, that degree of corroboration must also be a probability—that is to say, that it must satisfy the calculus of probability.)

I explained in my book why we are interested in theories with a *high degree of corroboration*. And I explained why it is a mistake to conclude from this that we are interested in *highly probable* theories. I pointed out that the probability of a statement (or set of statements) is always the greater the less the statement says: it is inverse to the content or the deductive power of the statement, and thus to its explanatory power. Accordingly every interesting and powerful statement must have a low probability; and *vice versa*: a statement with a high probability will be scientifically uninteresting, because it says little and has no explanatory power. Although we seek theories with a high degree of corroboration, *as scientists we do not seek highly probable theories but explanations; that is to say, powerful and improbable theories.*[24] The opposite view—that science aims at high probability—is a characteristic development of verificationism: if you find that you cannot verify a theory, or make it certain by induction, you may turn to probability as a kind of *"Ersatz"* for certainty, in the hope that induction may yield at least that much.

I have discussed the two problems of demarcation and induction at some length. Yet since I set out to give you in this lecture a kind of report on the work I have done in this field I shall have to add, in the form of an appendix, a few words about some other problems on which I have been working, between 1934 and 1953. I was led to most of these problems by trying to think out the consequences of the solutions to the two problems of demarcation and induction. But time does not allow me to continue my narrative, and to tell you how my new problems arose out of my old ones. Since I cannot even start a discussion of these further problems now, I shall have to confine myself to giving you a bare list of them, with a few explanatory words here and there. But even a bare list may be useful, I think. It may serve to give an idea of the fertility of the approach. It may help to illustrate what our problems look like; and it may show how many there are, and so convince you that there is no need whatever to worry over the question whether philosophical problems exist, or what philosophy is really about. So this list contains, by implication, an apology for my unwillingness to break with the old tradition of trying to solve problems with the help of rational argument, and thus for my unwillingness to participate wholeheartedly in the developments, trends, and drifts, of contemporary philosophy.

(Editor's note—The Appendix is not reprinted here.)

NOTES

* A lecture given at Peterhouse, Cambridge, in Summer 1953, as part of a course on developments and trends in contemporary British philosophy, organized by the British Council: originally published under the title "Philosophy of Science: a Personal Report" in *British Philosophy in Mid-Century*, ed. C. A. Mace, 1957.

1. This is a slight oversimplification, for about half of the Einstein effect may be derived from the classical theory, provided we assume a ballistic theory of light.

2. See, for example, my *Open Society and Its Enemies*, (London, Routledge, 1945) chapter 15, section III, and notes 13–14.

3. "Clinical observations," like all other observations, are *interpretations in the light of theories* (see below, sections IV ff.); and for this reason alone they are apt to seem to support those theories in the light of which they were interpreted. But real support can be obtained only from observations undertaken as tests (by "attempted refutations"); and for this purpose *criteria of refutation* have to be laid down beforehand: it must be agreed which observable situations, if actually observed, mean that the theory is refuted. But what kind of clinical responses would refute to the satisfaction of the analyst not merely a particular analytic diagnosis but psychoanalysis itself? And have such criteria ever been discussed or agreed upon by analysts? Is there not, on the contrary, a whole family of analytic concepts, such as "ambivalence" (I do not suggest that there is no such thing as ambivalence), which would make it difficult, if not impossible, to agree upon such criteria? Moreover, how much headway has been made in investigating the question of the extent to which the (conscious or unconscious) expectations and theories held by the analyst influence the "clinical responses" of the patient? (To say nothing about the conscious attempts to influence the patient by proposing interpretations to him, etc.) Years ago I introduced the term *"Oedipus effect"* to describe the influence of a theory or expectation or prediction *upon the event which it predicts* or describes: it will be remembered that the causal chain leading to Oedipus' parricide was started by the oracle's prediction of this event. This is a characteristic and recurrent theme of such myths, but one which seems to have failed to attract the interest of the

analysts, perhaps not accidentally. (The problem of confirmatory dreams suggested by the analyst is discussed by Freud, for example in *Gesammelte Schriften*, vol. 3 (1925), where he says on p. 314: "If anybody asserts that most of the dreams which can be utilized in an analysis . . . owe their origin to [the analyst's] suggestion,' then no objection can be made from the point of view of analytic theory. Yet there is nothing in this fact," he surprisingly adds, "which would detract from the reliability of our results.")

4. The case of astrology, nowadays a typical pseudo-science, may illustrate this point. It was attacked, by Aristotelians and other rationalists, down to Newton's day, for the wrong reason—for its now accepted assertion that the planets had an "influence" upon terrestrial ("sublunar") events. In fact Newton's theory of gravity, and especially the lunar theory of the tides, was historically speaking an offspring of astrological lore. Newton, it seems, was most reluctant to adopt a theory which came from the same stable as for example the theory that "influenza" epidemics are due to an astral "influence." And Galileo, no doubt for the same reason, actually rejected the lunar theory of the tides; and his misgivings about Kepler may easily be explained by his misgivings about astrology.

5. My *Logic of Scientific Discovery* (London: Hutchinson, 1985, 1959, 1960, 1961), here usually referred to as *L.Sc.D.*, is the translation of *Logik der Forschung* (Wien: Springer, 1934), with a number of additional notes and appendices, including (on pp. 312–14) the letter to the Editor of *Erkenntnis* mentioned here in the text which was first published in *Erkenntnis* 3, (1933), pp. 426 f.

Concerning my never published book mentioned here in the text, see R. Carnap's paper *"Ueber Protokollstäze"* (On Protocol-Sentences), *Erkenntnis* 3, (1932), pp. 215–28 where he gives an outline of my theory on pp. 223–8, and accepts it. He calls my theory "procedure B," and says (p. 224, top): "Starting from a point of view different from Neurath's" (who developed what Carnap calls on p. 223 "procedure A"), "Popper developed procedure B as part of his system." And after describing in detail my theory of tests, Carnap sums up his views as follows (p. 228): "After weighing the various arguments here discussed, it appears to me that the second language form with procedure B—that is in the form here described—is the most adequate among the forms of scientific language at present advocated . . . in the . . . theory of knowledge." This paper of Carnap's contained the first published report of my theory of critical testing. (See also, my critical remarks in *L.Sc.D.*, note 1 to section 29, p. 104, where the date "1933" should read "1932"; and chapter 11 of my *Conjectures and Refutations* (New York: Harper and Row, 1968), text to note 39.)

6. Wittgenstein's example of a nonsensical pseudo-proposition is: "Socrates is identical." Obviously, "Socrates is not identical" must also be nonsense. Thus the negation of any nonsense will be nonsense, and that of a meaningful statement will be meaningful. *But the negation of a testable (or falsifiable) statement need not be testable*, as was pointed out, first in my *L.Sc.D.*, (e.g., pp. 38 f.) and later by my critics. The confusion caused by taking testability as a criterion of *meaning* rather than of *demarcation* can easily be imagined.

7. The most recent example of the way in which the history of this problem is misunderstood is A. R. White's 'Note on Meaning and Verification', *Mind*, 63, 1954, pp. 66 ff. J. L. Evans's article, *Mind* 62, (1953), pp. 1 ff., which Mr. White criticizes, is excellent in my opinion, and unusually perceptive. Understandably enough, neither of the authors can quite reconstruct the story. (Some hints may be found in my *Open Society*, notes 46, 51 and 52 to chapter 11.)

8. In *L.Sc.D.* I discussed, and replied to, some likely objections which afterwards were indeed raised, without reference to my replies. One of them is the contention that the falsification of a natural law is just as impossible as its verification. The answer is that this objection mixes two entirely different levels of analysis (like the objection that mathematical demonstrations are impossible since checking, no matter how often repeated, can never make it quite certain that we have not overlooked a mistake). On the first level, there is a logical asymmetry: one singular statement—say about the perihelion of Mercury—can formally falsify Kepler's laws; but these cannot be formally verified by any number of singular statements. The attempt to minimize this asymmetry can only lead to confusion. On another level, we may hesitate to accept any statement, even the simplest observation statement; and we may

point out that every statement involves *interpretation in the light of theories*, and that it is therefore uncertain. This does not affect the fundamental asymmetry, but it is important: most dissectors of the heart before Harvey observed the wrong things—those, which they expected to see. There can never be anything like a completely safe observation, free from the dangers of misinterpretation. (This is one of the reasons why the theory of induction does not work.) The "empirical basis" consists largely of a mixture of *theories* of lower degree of universality (of "reproducible effects"). But the fact remains that, relative to whatever basis the investigator may accept (at his peril), he can test his theory only by trying to refute it.

9. Hume does not say "logical" but "demonstrative," a terminology which, I think, is a little misleading. The following two quotations are from the *Treatise of Human Nature*, Book I, Part III, sections vi and xii. (The italics are all Hume's.)

10. Ibid. This and the next quotation are from section vi. See also Hume's *Enquiry Concerning Human Understanding*, section IV, Part II, and his *Abstract*, edited 1938 by J. M. Keynes and P. Sraffa, p. 15, and quoted in *L.Sc.D.*, new appendix *VII, text to note 6.

11. *Treatise*, section xiii; section xv, rule 4.

12. F. Bäge, "Zur Entwicklung, etc.," *Zeitschrift f. Hundeforschung* (1933); cp. D. Katz, *Animals and Men*, chapter 6, footnote.

13. See section 30 of *L.Sc.D.*

14. Katz, *Animals and Men*.

15. Kant believed that Newton's dynamics was *a priori* valid. (See his *Metaphysical Foundations of Natural Science*, published between the first and the second editions of the *Critique of Pure Reason*.) But if, as he thought, we can explain the validity of Newton's theory by the fact that our intellect imposes its laws upon nature, it follows, I think, that our intellect *must succeed* in this; which makes it hard to understand why *a priori* knowledge such as Newton's should be so hard to come by. A somewhat fuller statement of this criticism can be found in chapter 2, especially section ix, and chapters 7 and 8 of *Conjectures and Refutations*.

16. A thesis submitted under the title "*Gewohnheit und Gesetzerlebnis*" to the Institute of Education of the City of Vienna in 1927. (Unpublished.)

17. Further comments on these developments may be found in chapters 4 and 5 of *Conjectures and Refutations*.

18. Max Born, *Natural Philosophy of Cause and Chance* (Oxford, 1949), p. 7.

19. Ibid., p. 6.

20. I do not doubt that Born and many others would agree that theories are accepted only tentatively. But the widespread belief in induction shows that the far-reaching implications of this view are rarely seen.

21. Wittgenstein still held this belief in 1946; see note 8 to chapter 2 of *Conjectures and Refutations*.

22. See note 5 above.

23. *L.Sc.D.* (see note 5 above), chapter 10, especially sections 80 to 83, also section 34 ff. See also my note "A Set of Independent Axioms for Probability" *Mind* N.S. 47 (1938), p. 275. (This note has since been reprinted, with corrections, in the new appendix *ii of *L.Sc.D.* See also the next note but one to the present chapter.)

24. A definition, in terms of probabilities of $C(t,e)$, i.e. of the degree of corroboration (of a theory t relative to the evidence e) satisfying the demands indicated in my *L.Sc.D.*, sections 82 to 83, is the following:

$$C(t, e) = E(t,e)(1 + P(t)P(t,e)),$$

where $E(t,e) = (P(e,t) - P(e))/(P(e,t) + P(e))$ is a (non-additive) measure of the explanatory power of t with respect to e. Note that $C(t,e)$ is not a probability: it may have values between -1 (refutation of t by e) and $C(t,t) \leq +1$. Statements t which are lawlike and thus non-verifiable cannot even reach $C(t,e) = C(t,t)$ upon empirical evidence e, $C(t,e)$ is the *degree of corroborability* of t, and is equal to the *degree of testability* of t, or to the *content* of t. Because of the demands implied in point (6) at the end of section I above, I do not think, however, that it is possible to give a complete formalization of the idea of corroboration (or, as I previously used to say, of confirmation).

(Added 1955 to the first proofs of this paper:)

See also my note "Degree of Confirmation," *British Journal for the Philosophy of Science* 5, (1954), pp. 143 ff. (See also 5, pp. 334.) I have since simplified this definition as follows (*B.J.P.S.* 5 (1955), p. 359:)

$$C(t,e) = (P(e,t) - P(e))/(P(e,t) - P(et) + P(e))$$

For a further improvement, see *B.J.P.S.* 6 (1955), p. 56.

THOMAS S. KUHN

LOGIC OF DISCOVERY OR PSYCHOLOGY OF RESEARCH?[1]

My object in these pages is to juxtapose the view of scientific development outlined in my book, *The Structure of Scientific Revolutions*, with the better known views of our chairman, Sir Karl Popper.[2] Ordinarily I should decline such an undertaking, for I am not so sanguine as Sir Karl about the utility of confrontations. Besides, I have admired his work for too long to turn critic easily at this date. Nevertheless, I am persuaded that for this occasion the attempt must be made. Even before my book was published two and a half years ago, I had begun to discover special and often puzzling characteristics of the relation between my views and his. That relation and the divergent reactions I have encountered to it suggest that a disciplined comparison of the two may produce peculiar enlightenment. Let me say why I think this could occur.

On almost all the occasions when we turn explicitly to the same problems, Sir Karl's view of science and my own are very nearly identical.[3] We are both concerned with the dynamic process by which scientific knowledge is acquired rather than with the logical structure of the products of scientific research. Given that concern, both of us emphasize, as legitimate data, the facts and also the spirit of actual scientific life, and both of us turn often to history to find them. From this pool of shared data, we draw many of the same conclusions. Both of us reject the view that science progresses by accretion; both emphasize instead the revolutionary process by which an older theory is rejected and replaced by an incompatible new one[4]; and both deeply underscore the role played in this process by the older theory's occasional failure to meet challenges posed by logic, experiment, or observation. Finally, Sir Karl and I are united in opposition to a number of classical positivism's most characteristic theses. We both emphasize, for example, the intimate and inevitable entanglement of scientific observation with scientific theory; we are correspondingly sceptical of efforts to produce any neutral observation language; and we both insist that scientists may properly aim to invent theories that *explain* observed phenomena and that do so in terms of *real* objects, whatever the latter phrase may mean.

That list, though it by no means exhausts the issues about which Sir Karl and I agree,[5] is already extensive enough to place us in the same minority among contemporary philosophers of science. Presumably that is why Sir Karl's followers have with some regularity provided my most sympathetic philosophical audience, one for which I continue to be grateful. But my gratitude is not unmixed. The same agreement that evokes the sympathy of this group too often misdirects its interest. Apparently Sir Karl's followers can often read much of my book as chapters from a late (and, for some, a drastic) revision of his classic, *The Logic of Scientific Discovery*. One of them asks whether the view of science outlined in my *Scientific Revolutions* has not long been common knowledge. A second, more charitably, isolates my originality as the demonstration that discoveries-of-fact have a life cycle very like that displayed by innovations of theory. Still others express general pleasure in the book but will discuss only the two comparatively secondary issues about which my disagreement with Sir Karl is most nearly explicit: my emphasis on the importance of deep commitment to tradition and my discontent with the implications of the term "falsification." All these men, in short, read my book through a quite special pair of spectacles, and there is another way to read it. The view through those spectacles is not wrong—my agreement with Sir Karl is real and substantial. Yet readers outside of the Popperian circle almost invariably fail even to notice that the agreement exists, and it is these readers who most often recognize (not necessarily with sympathy) what seem to me the central issues. I conclude that a gestalt switch divides readers of my book into two or more groups. What one of these sees as striking parallelism is virtually invisible to the others. The desire to understand how this can be so motivates the present comparison of my view with Sir Karl's.

The comparison must not, however, be a mere point by point juxtaposition. What demands attention is not so much the peripheral area in which our occasional secondary disagreements are to be isolated but the central region in which we appear to agree. Sir Karl and I do appeal to the same data; to an uncommon extent we are seeing the same lines on the same paper; asked about those lines and those data, we often give virtually identical responses, or at least responses that inevitably seem identical in the isolation enforced by the question-and-answer mode. Nevertheless, experiences like those mentioned above convince me that our intentions are often quite different when we say the same things. Though the lines are the same, the figures which emerge from them are not. That is why I call what separates us a gestalt switch rather than a disagreement and also why I am at once perplexed and intrigued about how best to explore the separation. How am I to persuade Sir Karl, who knows everything I know about scientific development and who has somewhere or other said it, that what he calls a duck can be seen as a rabbit? How am I to show him what it would be like to wear my spectacles when he has already learned to look at everything I can point to through his own?

In this situation a change in strategy is called for, and the following suggests itself. Reading over once more a number of Sir Karl's principal books and essays, I encounter again a series of recurrent phrases which, though I understand them and do not quite disagree, are locutions that *I* could never have used in the same places. Undoubtedly they are most often intended as metaphors applied rhetorically to situations for which Sir Karl has elsewhere provided unexceptionable descriptions. Nevertheless, for present purposes these metaphors, which strike me as patently inappropriate, may prove more useful than straightforward descriptions. They may that is, be symptomatic of contextual differences that a careful literal expression hides. If that is so, then these locutions may function not as the lines-on-paper but as the rabbit-ear, the shawl, or the ribbon-at-the-throat which one isolates when teaching a friend to transform his way of seeing a gestalt diagram. That, at least, is my hope for them. I have four such differences of locutions in mind and shall treat them *seriatim*.

I

Among the most fundamental issues on which Sir Karl and I agree is our insistence that an analysis of the development of scientific knowledge must take account of the way science has actually been practiced. That being so, a few of his recurrent generalizations startle me. One of these provides the opening sentences of the first chapter of the *Logic of Scientific Discovery:* "A scientist," writes Sir Karl, "whether theorist or experimenter, puts forward statements, or systems of statements, and tests them step by step. In the field of the empirical sciences, more particularly, he constructs hypotheses, or systems of theories, and tests them against experience by observation and experiment.[6] The statement is virtually a cliché, yet in application it presents three problems. It is ambiguous in its failure to specify which of two sorts of "statements" or "theories" are being tested. That ambiguity can, it is true, be eliminated by reference to other passages in Sir Karl's writings, but the generalization that results is historically mistaken. Furthermore, the mistake proves important, for the unambiguous form of the description misses just that characteristic of scientific practice which most nearly distinguishes the sciences from other creative pursuits.

There is one sort of "statement" or "hypothesis" that scientists do repeatedly subject to systematic test. I have in mind statements of an individual's best guesses about the proper way to connect his own research problem with the corpus of accepted scientific knowledge. He may, for example, conjecture that a given chemical unknown contains the salt of a rare earth, that the obesity of his experimental rats is due to a specified component in their diet, or that a newly discovered spectral pattern is to be understood as an effect of nuclear spin. In each case, the next steps in his research are intended to try out or test the conjecture or hypothesis. If it passes enough or stringent enough tests, the scientist has made a discovery or has at least resolved the puzzle he had been set. If not, he must either abandon the puzzle entirely or attempt to solve it with the aid of some other hypothesis. Many research problems, though by no means all, take this form. Tests of this sort are a standard component of what I have elsewhere labelled "normal science" or "normal research," an enterprise which accounts for the overwhelming majority of the work done in basic science. In no usual sense, however, are such tests directed to current theory. On the contrary, when engaged with a normal research problem, the scientist must *premise* current theory as the rules of his game. His object is to solve a puzzle, preferably one at which others have failed, and current theory is required to define that puzzle and to guarantee that, given sufficient brilliance, it can be solved.[7] Of course the practitioner of such an enterprise must often test the conjectural puzzle solution that his ingenuity suggests. But only his personal conjecture is tested. If it fails the test, only his own ability not the corpus of current science is impugned. In short, though tests occur frequently in normal science, these tests are of a peculiar sort, for in the final analysis it is the individual scientist rather than current theory which is tested.

This is not, however, the sort of test Sir Karl has in mind. He is above all concerned with the procedures through which science grows, and he is convinced that "growth" occurs not primarily by accretion but by the revolutionary overthrow of an accepted theory and its replacement by a better one.[8] (The subsumption under "growth" of "repeated overthrow" is itself a linguistic oddity whose *raison d'être* may become more visible as we proceed.) Taking this view, the tests which Sir Karl emphasizes are those which were performed to explore the limitations of accepted theory or to subject a current theory to maximum strain. Among his favourite examples, all of them startling and destructive in their outcome, are Lavoisier's experiments on calcination, the eclipse expedition of 1919, and the recent experiments on parity conservation.[9] All, of course, are classic tests, but in using them to characterize scientific activity Sir Karl misses something terribly important about them. Episodes like these are very rare in the development of science. When they occur, they are generally called forth either by a prior crisis in the relevant field (Lavoisier's experiments or Lee and Yang's[10]) or by the existence of a theory which competes with the existing canons of research (Einstein's general relativity). These are, however, aspects of or occasions for what I have elsewhere called "extraordinary research," an enterprise in which scientists do display very many of the characteristics Sir Karl emphasizes, but one which, at least in the past, has arisen only intermittently and under quite special circumstances in any scientific speciality.[11]

I suggest then that Sir Karl has characterized the entire scientific enterprise in terms that apply only to its occasional revolutionary parts. His emphasis is natural and common: the exploits of a Copernicus or Einstein make better reading than those of a Brahe or Lorentz; Sir Karl would not be the first if he mistook what I call normal science for an intrinsically uninteresting enterprise. Nevertheless, neither science nor the development of knowledge is likely to be understood if research is viewed exclusively through the revolutions it occasionally produces. For example, though testing of basic commitments occurs only in extraordinary science, it is normal science that discloses both the points to test and the manner of testing. Or again, it is for the normal, not the extraordinary practice of science that professionals are trained; if they are nevertheless eminently successful in displacing and replacing the theories on which normal practice depends, that is an oddity which must be explained. Finally, and this is for now my main point, a careful look at the scientific enterprise suggests that it is normal science, in which Sir Karl's sort of testing does not occur, rather than extraordinary science which most nearly distinguishes science from other enterprises. If a demarcation criterion exists (we must not, I think, seek a sharp or decisive one), it may lie just in that part of science which Sir Karl ignores.

In one of his most evocative essays, Sir Karl traces the origin of "the tradition of critical discussion [which] represents the only practicable way of expanding our knowledge" to the Greek philosophers between Thales and Plato, the men who, as he sees it, encouraged critical discussion both between schools and within individual schools.[12] The accompanying description of Presocratic discourse is most apt, but what is described does not at all resemble science. Rather it is the tradition of claims, counterclaims, and debates over fundamentals which, except perhaps during the Middle Ages, have characterized philosophy and much of social science ever since. Already by the Hellenistic period mathematics, astronomy, statics and the geometric parts of optics had abandoned this mode of discourse in favour of puzzle solving. Other sciences, in increasing numbers, have undergone the same transition since. In a sense, to turn Sir Karl's view on its head, it is precisely the abandonment of critical discourse that marks the transition to a science. Once a field has made that transition, critical discourse recurs only at moments of crisis when the bases of the field are again in jeopardy.[13] Only when they must choose between competing theories do scientists behave like philosophers. That, I think, is why Sir Karl's brilliant description of the reasons for the choice between metaphysical systems so closely resembles my description of the reasons for choosing between scientific theories.[14] In neither choice, as I shall shortly try to show, can testing play a quite decisive role.

There is, however, good reason why testing has seemed to do so, and in exploring it Sir Karl's duck may at last become my rabbit. No puzzle-solving enterprise can exist unless its practitioners share criteria which, for that group and for that time, determine when a particular puzzle has been solved. The same criteria necessarily determine failure to achieve a solution, and anyone who chooses may view that failure as the failure of a theory to pass a test. Normally, as I have already insisted, it is not viewed that way. Only the practitioner is blamed, not his tools. But under the special circumstances which induce a crisis in the profession (e.g., gross failure, or repeated failure by the most brilliant professionals) the group's opinion may change. A failure that had previously been personal may then come to seem the failure of a theory under test. Thereafter, because the test arose from a puzzle and thus carried settled criteria of solution, it proves both more severe and harder to evade than the tests available within a tradition whose normal mode is critical discourse rather than puzzle solving.

In a sense, therefore, severity of test-criteria is simply one side of the coin whose other face is a puzzle-solving tradition. That is why Sir Karl's line of demarcation and my own so frequently coincide. That coincidence is, however, only in their *outcome*; the *process* of applying them is very different, and it isolates distinct aspects of the activity about which the decision—science or nonscience—is to be made. Examining the vexing cases, for example, psychoanalysis or Marxist historiography, for which Sir Karl tells us his criterion was initially designed,[15] I concur that they cannot now properly be labelled "science." But I reach that conclusion by a route far surer and more direct than his. One brief example may suggest that of the two criteria, testing and puzzle solving, the latter is at once the less equivocal and the more fundamental.

To avoid irrelevant contemporary controversies, I consider astrology rather than, say, psychoanalysis. Astrology is Sir Karl's most frequently cited example of a "pseudo-science."[16] He says: "By making their interpretations and prophecies sufficiently vague they [astrologers] were able to explain away anything that might have been a refutation of the theory had the theory and the prophecies been more precise. In order to escape falsification they destroyed the testability of the theory.[17] Those generalizations catch something of the spirit of the astrological enterprise. But taken at all literally, as they must be if they are to provide a demarcation criterion, they are impossible to support. The history of astrology during the centuries when it was intellectually reputable records many predictions that categorically failed.[18] Not even astrology's most convinced and vehement exponents doubted the recurrence of such failures. Astrology cannot be barred from the sciences because of the form in which its predictions were cast.

Nor can it be barred because of the way its practitioners explained failure. Astrologers pointed out, for example, that, unlike general predictions about, say, an individual's propensities or a natural calamity, the forecast of an individual's future was an immensely complex task, demanding the utmost skill, and extremely sensitive to minor errors in relevant data. The configuration of the stars and eight planets was constantly changing; the astronomical tables used to compute the configuration at an individual's birth were notoriously imperfect; few men knew the instant of their birth with the requisite precision.[19] No wonder, then, that forecasts often failed. Only after astrology itself became implausible did these arguments come to seem question-begging.[20] Similar arguments are regularly used today when explaining, for example, failures in medicine or meteorology. In times of trouble they are also deployed in the exact sciences, fields like physics, chemistry, and astronomy.[21] There was nothing unscientific about the astrologer's explanation of failure.

Nevertheless, astrology was not a science. Instead it was a craft, one of the practical arts, with close resemblances to engineering, meteorology, and medicine as these fields were practised until little more than a century ago. The parallels to an older medicine and to contemporary psychoanalysis are, I think, particularly close. In each of these fields shared theory was adequate only to establish the plausibility of the discipline and to provide a rationale for the various craft-rules which governed practice. These rules had proved their use in the past, but no practitioner supposed they were sufficient to prevent recurrent failure. A more articulated theory and more powerful rules were desired, but it would have been absurd to abandon a plausible and badly needed discipline with a tradition of limited success simply because these desiderata were not yet at hand. In their absence, however, neither the astrologer nor the doctor could do research. Though they had rules to apply, they had no puzzles to solve and therefore no science to practice.[22]

Compare the situations of the astronomer and the astrologer. If an astronomer's prediction failed and his calculations checked, he could hope to set the situation right. Perhaps the data were at fault: old observations could be reexamined and new measurements made, tasks which posed a host of calculational and instrumental puzzles. Or perhaps theory needed adjustment, either by the manipulation of epicycles, eccentrics, equants, etc., or by more fundamental reforms of astronomical technique. For more than a millennium these were the theoretical and mathematical puzzles around which, together with their instrumental counterparts, the astronomical research tradition was constituted. The astrologer, by contrast, had no such puzzles. The occurrence of failures could be explained, but particular failures did not give rise to research puzzles, for no man, however skilled, could make use of them in a constructive attempt to revise the astrological tradition. There were too many possible sources of difficulty, most of them beyond the astrologer's knowledge, control or responsibility. Individual failures were correspondingly uninformative, and they did not reflect on the competence of the prognosticator in the eyes of his professional compeers.[23] Though astronomy and astrology were regularly practised by the same people, including Ptolemy, Kepler, and Tycho Brahe, there was never an astrological equivalent of the puzzle-solving astronomical tradition. And without puzzles, able first to challenge and then to attest the ingenuity of the individual practitioner, astrology could not have become a science even if the stars had, in fact, controlled human destiny.

In short, though astrologers made testable predictions and recognized that these predictions sometimes failed, they did not and could not engage in the sorts of activities that normally characterize all recognized sciences. Sir Karl is right to exclude astrology from the sciences, but his over-concentration on science's occasional revolutions prevents his seeing the surest reason for doing so.

That fact, in turn, may explain another oddity of Sir Karl's historiography. Though he repeatedly underlines the role of tests in the replacement of scientific theories, he is also constrained to recognize that many theories, for example the Ptolemaic, were replaced before they had in fact been tested.[24] On some occasions, at least, tests are not requisite to the revolutions through which science advances. But that is not true of puzzles. Though the theories Sir Karl cites had not been put to the test before their displacement, none of these was replaced before it had ceased adequately to support a puzzle-solving tradition. The state of astronomy was a scandal in the early sixteenth century. Most astronomers nevertheless felt that normal adjustments of a basically Ptolemaic model would set the situation right. In this sense the theory had not failed a test. But a few astronomers, Copernicus among them, felt that the difficulties must lie in the Ptolemaic approach itself rather than in the particular versions of Ptolemaic theory so far developed, and the results of that conviction are already recorded. The situation is typical.[25] With or without tests, a puzzle-solving tradition can prepare the way for its own displacement. To rely on testing as the mark of ascience is to miss what scientists mostly do and, with it, the most characteristic feature of their enterprise.

II

With the background supplied by the preceding remarks we can quickly discover the occasion and consequences of another of Sir Karl's favourite locutions. The preface to *Conjectures and Refutations* opens with the sentence: "The essays and lectures of which this book is composed, are variations upon one very simple theme—the thesis that *we can learn from our mistakes.*" The emphasis is Sir Karl's; the thesis recurs in his writing from an early date[26]; taken in isolation, it inevitably commands assent. Everyone can and does learn from his mistakes; isolating and correcting them is an essential technique in teaching children. Sir Karl's rhetoric has roots in everyday experience. Nevertheless, in the contexts for which he invokes this familiar imperative, its applications seems decisively askew. I am not sure a mistake has been made, at least not a mistake to learn from.

One need not confront the deeper philosophical problems presented by mistakes to see what is presently at issue. It is a mistake to add three plus three and get five, or to conclude from "All men are mortal" to "All mortals are men." For different reasons, it is a mistake to say, "He is my sister," or to report the presence of a strong electric field when test charges fail to indicate it. Presumably there are still other sorts of mistakes, but all the normal ones are likely to share the following characteristics. A mistake is made, or is committed, at a specifiable time and place by a particular individual. That individual has failed to obey some established rule of logic, or of language, or of the relations between one of these and experience. Or he may instead have failed to recognize the consequences of a particular choice among the alternatives which the rules allow him. The individual can learn from his mistake only because the group whose practice embodies these rules can isolate the individual's failure in applying them. In short, the sorts of mistakes to which Sir Karl's imperative most obviously applies are in individual's failure of understanding or of recognition within an activity governed by preestablished rules. In the sciences such mistakes occur most frequently and perhaps exclusively within the practice of normal puzzle-solving research.

That is not, however, where Sir Karl seeks them, for his concept of science obscures even the existence of normal research. Instead, he looks to the extraordinary or revolutionary episodes in scientific development. The mistakes to which he points are not usually acts at all but rather out-of-date scientific theories: Ptolemaic astronomy, the phlogiston theory, or Newtonian dynamics, and "learning from our mistakes" is, correspondingly, what occurs when a scientific community rejects one of these theories and replaces it with another.[27] If this does not immediately seem an odd usage, that is mainly because it appeals to the residual inductivist in us all. Believing that valid theories are the product of correct inductions from facts, the inductivist must also hold that a false theory is the result of a mistake in induction. In principle, at least, he is prepared to answer the questions: what mistake was made, what rule broken, when and by whom, in arriving at, say, the Ptolemaic system? To the man for whom those are sensible questions and to him alone, Sir Karl's locution presents no problems.

But neither Sir Karl nor I is an inductivist. We do not believe that there are rules for inducing correct theories from facts, or even that theories, correct or incorrect, are induced at all. Instead we view them as imaginative posits, invented in one piece for application to nature. And though we point out that such posits can and usually do at last encounter puzzles they cannot solve, we also recognize that those troublesome confrontations rarely occur for some time after a theory has been both invented and accepted. In our view, then, no mistake was made in arriving at the Ptolemaic system, and it is therefore difficult for me to understand what Sir Karl has in mind when he calls that system, or any other out-of-date theory, a mistake. At most one may wish to say that a theory which was not previously a mistake has become one or that a scientist has made the mistake of clinging to a theory for too long. And even these locutions, of which at least the first is extremely awkward, do not return us to the sense of mistake with which we are most familiar. Those mistakes are the normal ones which a Ptolemaic (or a Copernican) astronomer makes within his system, perhaps in observation, calculation, or the analysis of data. They are, that is, the sort of mistake which can be isolated and then at once corrected, leaving the original system intact. In Sir Karl's sense, on the other hand, a mistake infects an entire system and can be corrected only by replacing the system as a whole. No locutions and no similarities can disguise these fundamental differences, nor can they hide the fact that before infection set in the system had the full integrity of what we now call sound knowledge.

Quite possibly Sir Karl's sense of "mistake" can be salvaged, but a successful salvage operation must deprive it of certain still current implications. Like the term "testing," "mistake" has been borrowed from normal science, where its use is reasonably clear, and applied to revolutionary episodes, where its application is at best problematic. That transfer creates, or at least reinforces, the prevalent impression that whole theories can be judged by the same sort of criteria that one employs when judging a theory's individual research applications. The discovery of applicable criteria then becomes a primary desideratum for many people. That Sir Karl should be among them is strange, for the search runs counter to the most original and fruitful thrust in his philosophy of science. But I can understand his methodological writings since the *Logik der Forschung* in no other way. I shall now suggest that he has, despite explicit disclaimers, consistently sought evaluation procedures which can be applied to theories with the apodictic assurance characteristic of the techniques by which one identifies mistakes in arithmetic, logic, or measurement. I fear that he is pursuing a will-o'-the-wisp born from the same conjunction of normal and extraordinary science which made tests seem so fundamental a feature of the sciences.

III

In his *Logik der Forschung*, Sir Karl underlined the asymmetry of a generalization and its negation in their relation to empirical evidence. A scientific theory cannot be shown to apply successfully to all its possible instances, but it can be shown to be unsuccessful in particular applications. Emphasis upon that logical truism and its implications seems to me a forward step from which there must be no retreat. The same asymmetry plays a fundamental role in my *Structure of Scientific Revolutions*, where a theory's failure to provide rules that identify solvable puzzles is viewed as the source of professional crises which often result in the theory's being replaced. My point is very close to Sir Karl's, and I may well have taken it from what I had heard of his work.

But Sir Karl describes as "falsification" or "refutation" what happens when a theory fails in an attempted application, and these are the first of a series of related locutions that again strike me as extremely odd. Both "falsification" and "refutation" are antonyms of "proof." They are drawn principally from logic and from formal mathematics; the chains of argument to which they apply end with a "Q.E.D."; invoking these terms implies the ability to compel assent from any member of the relevant professional community. No member of this audience, however, still needs to be told that, where a whole theory or often even a scientific law is at stake, arguments are seldom so apodictic. All experiments can be challenged, either as to their relevance or their accuracy. All theories can be modified by a variety of *ad hoc* adjustments without ceasing to be, in their main lines, the same theories. It is important, furthermore, that this should be so, for it is often by challenging observations or adjusting theories that scientific knowledge grows. Challenges and adjustments are a standard part of normal research in empirical science, and adjustments, at least, play a dominant role in informal mathematics as well. Dr. Lakatos's brilliant analysis of the permissible rejoinders to mathematical refutations provides the most telling arguments I know against a naïve falsificationist position.[28]

Sir Karl is not, of course, a naïve falsificationist. He knows all that has just been said and has emphasized it from the beginning of his career. Very early in his *Logic of Scientific Discovery*, for example, he writes: "In point of fact, no conclusive disproof of a theory can ever be produced; for it is always possible to say that the experimental results are not reliable or that the discrepancies which are asserted to exist between the experimental results and the theory are only apparent and that they will disappear with the advance of our understanding."[29] Statements like these display one more parallel between Sir Karl's view of science and my own, but what we make of them could scarcely be more different. For my view they are fundamental, both as evidence and as source. For Sir Karl's, in contrast, they are an essential qualification which threatens the integrity of his basic position. Having barred conclusive disproof, he has provided no substitute for it, and the relation he does employ remains that of logical falsification. Though he is not a naïve falsificationist, Sir Karl may, I suggest, legitimately be treated as one.

If his concern were exclusively with demarcation, the problems posed by the unavailability of conclusive disproofs would be less severe and perhaps eliminable. Demarcation might, that is, be achieved by an exclusively syntactic criterion.[30] Sir Karl's view would then be, and perhaps is, that a theory is scientific if and only if *observation statements*—particularly the negations of singular existential statements—can be logically deduced from it, perhaps in conjunction with stated background knowledge. The difficulties (to which I shall shortly turn) in deciding whether the outcome of a particular laboratory operation justifies asserting a particular observation statement would then be irrelevant. Perhaps, though the basis for doing so is less apparent, the equally grave difficulties in deciding whether an observation statement deduced from an approximate (e.g., mathematically manageable) version of the theory should be considered consequences of the theory itself could be eliminated in the same way. Problems like these would belong not to the syntactics but to the pragmatics or semantics of the language in which the theory was cast, and they would therefore have no role in determining its status as a science. To be scientific a theory need be falsifiable only by an observation statement not by actual observation. The relation between statements, unlike that between a statement and an observation, could be the conclusive disproof familiar from logic and mathematics.

For reasons suggested above (text to footnote 22) and elaborated immediately below, I doubt that scientific theories can without decisive change be cast in a form which permits the purely syntactic judgements which this version of Sir Karl's criterion requires. But even if they could, these reconstructed theories would provide a basis only for his demarcation criterion, not for the logic of knowledge so closely associated with it. The latter has, however, been Sir Karl's most persistent concern, and his notion of it is quite precise. "The logic of knowledge . . . ," he writes; "consists solely in investigating the methods employed in those systematic tests to which every new idea must be subjected if it is to be seriously entertained."[31] From this investigation, he continues, result methodological rules or conventions like the following: "Once a hypothesis has been proposed and tested, and has proved its mettle, it may not be allowed to drop out without 'good reason.' A 'good reason' may be, for instance . . . the falsification of one of the consequences of the hypothesis."[32]

Rules like these, and with them the entire logical enterprise described above, are no longer simply syntactic in their import. They require that both the epistemological investigator and the research scientist be able to relate sentences derived from a theory not to other sentences but to actual observations and experiments. This is the context in which Sir Karl's term "falsification" must function, and Sir Karl is entirely silent about how it can do so. What is falsification if it is not conclusive disproof? Under what circumstances does the *logic* of knowledge require a scientist to abandon a previously accepted theory when confronted, not with statements about experiments, but with experiments themselves? Pending clarification of these questions, I am not clear that what Sir Karl has given us is a logic of knowledge at all. In my conclusion I shall suggest that, though equally valuable, it is something else entirely. Rather than a logic, Sir Karl has provided an ideology; rather than methodological rules, he has supplied procedural maxims.

That conclusion must, however, be postponed until after a last deeper look at the source of the difficulties with Sir Karl's notion of falsification. It presupposes, as I have already suggested, that a theory is cast, or can without distortion be recast, in a form which permits scientists to classify each conceivable event as either a confirming instance, a falsifying instance, or irrelevant to the theory. That is obviously required if a general law is to be falsifiable: to test the generalization $(x) \phi (x)$ by applying it to the constant a, we must be able to tell whether or not a lies within the range of the variable x and whether or not $\phi (a)$. The same presupposition is even more apparent in Sir Karl's recently elaborated measure of verisimilitude. It requires that we first produce the class of all logical consequences of the theory and then choose from among these, with the aid of background knowledge, the classes of all true and of all false consequences.[33] At least, we must do this if the criterion of verisimilitude is to result in a *method* of theory choice. None of these tasks can, however, be accomplished unless the theory is fully articulated logically and unless the terms through which it attaches to nature are sufficiently defined to determine their applicability in each possible case. In practice, however, no scientific theory satisfies these rigorous demands, and many people have argued that a theory would cease to be useful in research if it did so.[34] I have myself elsewhere introduced the term "paradigm" to underscore the dependence of scientific research upon concrete examples that bridge what would otherwise be gaps in the specification of the content and application of scientific theories. The relevant arguments cannot be repeated here. But a brief example, though it will temporarily alter my mode of discourse, may be even more useful.

My example takes the form of a constructed epitome of some elementary scientific knowledge. That knowledge concerns swans, and to isolate its presently relevant characteristics I shall ask three questions about it: (*a*) How much can one know about swans without introducing explicit generalizations like "All swans are white" ? (*b*) Under what circumstances and with what consequences are such generalizations worth adding to what was known without them? (*c*) Under what circumstances are generalizations rejected once they have been made? In raising these questions my object is to suggest that, though logic is a powerful and ultimately an essential tool of scientific enquiry, one can have sound knowledge in forms in which logic can scarcely be applied. Simultaneously, I shall suggest that logical articulation is not a value for its own sake, but is to be undertaken only when and to the extent that circumstances demand it.

Imagine that you have been shown and can remember ten birds which have authoritatively been identified as swans; that you have a similar acquaintance with ducks, geese, pigeons, doves, gulls, etc.; and that you are informed that each of these types constitutes a natural family. A natural family you already know as an observed cluster of like objects, sufficiently important and sufficiently discrete to command a generic name. More precisely, though here I introduce more simplification than the concept requires, a natural family is a class whose members resemble each other more closely than they resemble the members of other natural families.[35] The experience of generations has to date confirmed that all observed objects fall into one or another natural family. It has, that is, shown that the entire population of the world can always be divided (though not once and for all) into perceptually discontinuous categories. In the perceptual spaces between these categories there are believed to be no objects at all.

What you have learned about swans from exposure to paradigms is very much like what children first learn about dogs and cats, tables and chairs, mothers and fathers. Its precise scope and content are, of course, impossible to specify, but it is sound knowledge nonetheless. Derived from observation, it can be infirmed by further observation, and it meanwhile provides a basis for rational action. Seeing a bird much like the swans you already know, you may reasonably presume that it will require the same food as the others and will breed with them. Provided swans are a natural family, no bird which closely resembles them on sight should display radically different characteristics on closer acquaintance. Of course you may have been misinformed about the natural integrity of the swan family. But that can be discovered from experience, for example, by the discovery of a number of animals (note that more than one is required) whose characteristics bridge the gap between swans and, say, geese by barely perceptible intervals.[36] Until that does occur, however, you will know a great deal about swans though you will not be altogether sure what you know or what a swan is.

Suppose now that all the swans you have actually observed are white. Should you embrace the generalization, "All swans are white" ? Doing so will change what you know very little; that change will be of use only in the unlikely event that you meet a nonwhite bird which otherwise resembles a swan; by making the change you increase the risk that the swan family will prove not to be a natural family after all. Under those circumstances you are likely to refrain from generalizing unless there are special reasons for doing so. Perhaps, for example, you must describe swans to men who cannot be directly exposed to paradigms. Without superhuman caution both on your part and on that of your readers, your description will acquire the force of a generalization; this is often the problem of the taxonomist. Or perhaps you have discovered some grey birds that look otherwise like swans but eat different food and have an unfortunate disposition. You may then generalize to avoid a behavioural mistake. Or you may have a more theoretical reason for thinking the generalization worthwhile. For example, you may have observed that the members of other natural families share coloration. Specifying this fact in a form which permits the application of powerful logical techniques to what you know may enable you to learn more about the animal colour in general or about animal breeding.

Now, having made the generalization, what will you do if you encounter a black bird that looks otherwise like a swan? Almost the same things, I suggest, as if you had not previously committed yourself to the generalization at all. You will examine the bird with care, externally and perhaps internally as well, to find other characteristics that distinguish this specimen from your paradigms. That examination will be particularly long and thorough if you have theoretical reasons for believing that color characterizes natural families or if you are deeply ego involved with the generalization. Very likely the examination will disclose other differentiae, and you will announce the discovery of a new natural family. Or you may fail to find such differentiae and may then announce that a black swan has been found. Observation cannot, however, force you to that falsifying conclusion, and you would occasionally be the loser if it could do so. Theoretical considerations may suggest that colour alone is sufficient to demarcate a natural family: the bird is not a swan because it is black. Or you may simply postpone the issue pending the discovery and examination of other specimens. Only if you have previously committed yourself to a full definition of "swan," one which will specify its applicability to every conceivable object, can you be logically *forced* to rescind your generalization.[37] And why should you have offered such a definition? It could serve no cognitive function and would expose you to tremendous risks.[38] Risks, of course, are often worth taking, but to say more than one knows solely for the sake of risk is foolhardy.

I suggest that scientific knowledge, though logically more articulate and far more complex, is of this sort. The books and teachers from whom it is acquired present concrete examples together with a multitude of theoretical generalizations. Both are essential carriers of knowledge, and it is therefore Pickwickian to seek a methodological criterion that supposes the scientist can specify in advance whether each imaginable instance fits or would falsify his theory. The criteria at his disposal, explicit and implicit, are sufficient to answer that question only for the cases that clearly do fit or that are clearly irrelevant. These are the cases he expects, the ones for which his knowledge was designed. Confronted with the unexpected, he must always do more research in order further to articulate his theory in the area that has just become problematic. He may then reject it in favor of another and for good reason. But no exclusively logical criteria can entirely dictate the conclusion he must draw.

IV

Almost everything said so far rings changes on a single theme. The criteria with which scientists determine the validity of an articulation or an application of existing theory are not by themselves sufficient to determine the choice between competing theories. Sir Karl has erred by transferring selected characteristics of everyday research to the occasional revolutionary episodes in which scientific advance is most obvious and by thereafter ignoring the everyday enterprise entirely. In particular, he has sought to solve the problem of theory choice during revolutions by logical criteria that are applicable in full only when a theory can already be presupposed. That is the largest part of my thesis in this paper, and it could be the entire thesis if I were content to leave altogether open the questions that have been raised. How do the scientists make the choice between competing theories? How are we to understand the way in which science does progress?

Let me at once be clear that having opened that Pandora's box, I shall close it quickly. There is too much about these questions that I do not understand and must not pretend to. But I believe I see the directions in which answers to them must be sought, and I shall conclude with an attempt briefly to mark the trail. Near its end we shall once more encounter a set of Sir Karl's characteristic locutions.

I must first ask what it is that still requires explanation. Not that scientists discover the truth about nature, nor that they approach ever closer to the truth. Unless, as one of my critics suggests,[39] we simply define the approach to truth as the result of what scientists do, we cannot recognize progress towards that goal. Rather we must explain why science—our surest example of sound knowledge—progresses as it does, and we must first find out how, in fact, it does progress.

Surprisingly little is yet known about the answer to that descriptive question. A vast amount of thoughtful empirical investigation is still required. With the passage of time, scientific theories taken as a group are obviously more and more articulated. In the process, they are matched to nature at an increasing number of points and with increasing precision. Or again, the number of subject matters to which the puzzle-solving approach can be applied clearly grows with time. There is a continuing proliferation of scientific specialities, partly by an extension of the boundaries of science and partly by the subdivision of existing fields.

Those generalizations are, however, only a beginning. We know, for example, almost nothing about what a group of scientists will sacrifice in order to achieve the gains that a new theory invariably offers. My own impression, though it is no more than that, is that a scientific community will seldom or never embrace a new theory unless it solves all or almost all the quantitative, numerical puzzles that have been treated by its predecessor.[40] They will, on the other hand, occasionally sacrifice explanatory power, however reluctantly, sometimes leaving previously resolved questions open and sometimes declaring them altogether unscientific.[41] Turning to another area, we know little about historical changes in the unity of the sciences. Despite occasional spectacular successes, communication across the boundaries between scientific specialties becomes worse and worse. Does the number of incompatible viewpoints employed by the increasing number of communities of specialists grow with time? Unity of the sciences is clearly a value for scientists, but for what will they give it up? Or again, though the bulk of scientific knowledge clearly increases with time, what are we to say about ignorance? The problems solved during the last thirty years did not exist as open questions a century ago. In any age, the scientific knowledge already at hand virtually exhausts what there is to know, leaving visible puzzles only at the horizon of existing knowledge. Is it not possible, or perhaps even likely, that contemporary scientists know less of what there is to know about their world than the scientists of the eighteenth century knew of theirs? Scientific theories, it must be remembered, attach to nature only here and there. Are the interstices between those points of attachment perhaps now larger and more numerous than ever before?

Until we can answer more questions like these, we shall not know quite what scientific progress is and cannot therefore quite hope to explain it. On the other hand, answers to those questions will very nearly provide the explanation sought. The two come almost together. Already it should be clear that the explanation must, in the final analysis, be psychological or sociological. It must, that is, be a description of a value system, an ideology, together with an analysis of the institutions through which that system is transmitted and enforced. Knowing what scientists value, we may hope to understand what problems they will undertake and what choices they will make in particular circumstances of conflict. I doubt that there is another sort of answer to be found.

What form that answer will take is, of course, another matter. At this point, too, my sense that I control my subject matter ends. But again, some sample generalizations will illustrate the sorts of answers which must be sought. For a scientist, the solution of a difficult conceptual or instrumental puzzle is a principal goal. His success in that endeavour is rewarded through recognition by other members of his professional group and by them alone. The practical merit of his solution is at best a secondary value, and the approval of men outside the specialist group is a negative value or none at all. These values, which do much to dictate the form of normal science, are also significant at times when a choice must be made between theories. A man trained as a puzzle-solver will wish to preserve as many as possible of the prior puzzle-solutions obtained by his group, and he will also wish to maximize the number of puzzles that can be solved. But even these values frequently conflict, and there are others which make the problem of choice still more difficult. It is just in this connection that a study of what scientists will give up would be most significant. Simplicity, precision, and congruence with the theories used in other specialties are all significant value for the scientists, but they do not all dictate the same choice nor will they all be applied in the same way. That being the case, it is also important that group unanimity be a paramount value, causing the group to minimize the occasions for conflict and to reunite quickly about a single set of rules for puzzle solving even at the price of subdividing the specialty or excluding a formerly productive member.[42]

I do not suggest that these are the right answers to the problem of scientific progress, but only that they are the types of answers that must be sought. Can I hope that Sir Karl will join me in this view of the task still to be done? For some time I have assumed he would not, as a set of phrases that recurs in his work seems to bar the position to him. Again and again he has rejected "the psychology of knowledge" or the "subjective" and insisted that his concern was instead with the "objective" or "the logic of knowledge."[43] The title of his most fundamental contribution to our field is *The* Logic *of Scientific Discovery*, and it is there that he most positively asserts that his concern is with the logical spurs to knowledge rather than with the psychological drives of individuals. Until very recently I have supposed that this view of the problem must bar the sort of solution I have advocated.

But now I am less certain, for there is another aspect of Sir Karl's work, not quite compatible with what precedes. When he rejects "the psychology of knowledge," Sir Karl's explicit concern is only to deny the methodological relevance of an *individual's* source of inspiration or of an individual's sense of certainty. With that much I cannot disagree. It is, however, a long step from the rejection of the psychological idiosyncrasies of an individual to the rejection of the common elements induced by nurture and training in the psychological make-up of the licensed membership of a *scientific group.* One need not be dismissed with the other. And this, too, Sir Karl seems sometimes to recognize. Though he insists he is writing about the logic of knowledge, an essential role in his methodology is played by passages which I can only read as attempts to inculcate moral imperatives in the membership of the scientific group.

"Assume," Sir Karl writes, "that we have deliberately made it our task to live in this unknown world of ours; to adjust ourselves to it as well as we can; . . . and to explain it, *if* possible (we need not assume that it is) and as far as possible, with help of laws and explanatory theories. *If we have made this our task, then there is no more rational procedure than the method of . . . conjecture and refutation:* of boldly proposing theories; of trying our best to show that these are erroneous: and of accepting them tentatively if our critical efforts are unsuccessful."[44] We shall not, I suggest, understand the success of science without understanding the full force of rhetorically induced and professionally shared imperatives like these. Institutionalized and articulated further (and also somewhat differently) such maxims and values may explain the outcome of choices that could not have been dictated by logic and experiment alone. The fact that passages like these occupy a prominent place in Sir Karl's writing is therefore further evidence of the resemblance of our views. That he does not, I think, ever see them for the social-psychological imperatives that they are is further evidence of the gestalt switch that still divides us deeply.

NOTES

1. This paper was initially prepared at the invitation of P. A. Schilpp for, *The Philosophy of Karl R. Popper*, to be published by The Open Court Publishing Company, La Salle, Ill., in The Library of Living Philosophers. I am most grateful to both Professor Schilpp and the publishers for permission to print it as part of the proceedings of this symposium.

2. For purposes of the following discussion I have reviewed Sir Karl Popper's [1959], his [1963], and his [1957]. I have also occasionally referred to his original [1935] and his [1945]. My own [1962] provides a more extended account of many of the issues discussed below.

3. More than coincidence is presumably responsible for this extensive overlap. Though I had read none of Sir Karl's work before the appearance in 1959 of the English translation of his [1935] (by which time my book was in draft), I had repeatedly heard a number of his main ideas discussed. In particular, I had heard him discuss some of them as William James Lecturer at Harvard in the spring of 1950. These circumstances do not permit me to specify an intellectual debt to Sir Karl, but there must be one.

4. Elsewhere I use the term "paradigm" rather than "theory" to denote what is rejected and replaced during scientific revolutions. Some reasons for the change of term will emerge below.

5. Underlining one additional area of agreement about which there has been much misunderstanding may further highlight what I take to be the real differences between Sir Karl's views and mine. We both insist that adherence to a tradition has an essential role in scientific development. He has written, for example, "Quantitatively and qualitatively by far the most important source of our knowledge—apart from inborn knowledge—is tradition" (Popper 1963, p. 27). Even more to the point, as early as 1948 Sir Karl wrote, "I do not think that we could ever free ourselves entirely from the bonds of tradition. The so-called freeing is really only a change from one tradition to another" [1963], p. 122).

6. Popper (1959), p. 27.

7. For an extended discussion of normal science, the activity which practitioners are trained to carry on, see my (1962), pp. 23–42, and 135–42. It is important to notice that when I describe the scientist as a puzzle solver and Sir Karl describes him as a problem solver (e.g., in his 1963, pp. 67, 222), the similarity of our terms disguises a fundamental divergence. Sir Karl writes (the italics are his), "Admittedly, our expectations, and thus our theories, may precede, historically, even our problems. *Yet science starts only with problems.* Problems crop up especially when we are disappointed in our expectations, or when our theories involve us in difficulties, in contradictions." I use the term "puzzle" in order to emphasize that the difficulties which *ordinarily* confront even the very best scientists are, like crossword puzzles or chess puzzles, challenges only to his ingenuity. *He* is in difficulty, not current theory. My point is almost the converse of Sir Karl's.

8. Cf. Popper (1963), pp. 129, 215 and 221, for particularly forceful statements of this position.

9. For example, Popper (1963), p. 220.

10. For the work on calcination see Guerlac (1961). For the background of the parity experiments see Hafner and Presswood (1965).

11. The point is argued at length in my (1962), pp. 52–97.

12. Popper (1963), chapter 5, especially pp. 148–52.

13. Though I was not then seeking a demarcation criterion, just these points are argued at length in my (1962), pp. 10–22 and 87–90.

14. Cf. Popper (1963), pp. 192–200, with my (1962), pp. 143–58.

15. Popper (1963), p. 34.

16. The index to Popper (1963) has eight entries under the heading "astrology as a typical pseudo science."

17. Popper (1963), p. 37.

18. For examples, see Thorndike (1923–58), vol. 5, pp. 225 ff.; vol. 6, pp. 71, 101, 114.

19. For reiterated explanations of failure see, ibid., vol. I, pp. 11 and 514 f.; vol. 4, p. 368; vol. 5, p. 279.

20. A perceptive account of some reasons for astrology's loss of plausibility is included in Stahlman (1956). For an explanation of astrology's previous appeal, see Thorndike (1955).

21. Cf. my (1962), pp. 66–76.

22. This formulation suggests that Sir Karl's criterion of demarcation might be saved by a minor restatement entirely in keeping with his apparent intent. For a field to be a science its conclusions must be *logically derivable* from *shared premises*. On this view astrology is to be barred not because its forecasts were not testable but because only the most general and least testable ones could be derived from accepted theory. Since any field that did satisfy this condition *might* support a puzzle-solving tradition, the suggestion is clearly helpful. It comes close to supplying a sufficient condition for a field's being a science. But in this form, at least, it is not even quite a sufficient condition, and it is surely not a necessary one. It would, for example, admit surveying and navigation as sciences, and it would bar taxonomy, historical geology, and the theory of evolution. The conclusions of a science may be both precise and binding without being fully derivable by logic from accepted premises. Cf. my (1962), pp. 35–51, and also the discussion in section III.

23. This is not to suggest that astrologers did not criticize each other. On the contrary, like practitioners of philosophy and some social sciences, they belonged to a variety of different schools, and the inter-school strife was sometimes bitter. But these debates ordinarily revolved about the *implausibility* of the particular theory employed by one or another school. Failures of individual predictions played very little role. Compare Thorndike (1923–58), vol. 5, p. 233.

24. Cf. Popper (1963), p. 246.

25. Cf. my (1962), pp. 77–87.

26. The quotation is from Popper (1963), p. vii, in a preface dated 1962. Earlier Sir Karl had equated "learning from our mistakes" with "learning by trial and error" ([1963], p. 216), and the trial-and-error formulation dates from at least 1937 ([1963], p. 312) and is in spirit older than that. Much of what is said below about Sir Karl's notion of "mistake" applies equally to his concept of "error."

27. Popper (1963), pp. 215 and 220. In these pages Sir Karl outlines and illustrates his thesis that science grows through revolutions. He does not, in the process, ever juxtapose the term "mistake" with the name of an out-of-date scientific theory, presumably because his sound historic instinct inhibits so gross an anachronism. Yet the anachronism is fundamental to Sir Karl's rhetoric, which does repeatedly provide clues to more substantial differences between us. Unless out-of-date theories are mistakes, there is no way to reconcile, say, the opening paragraph of Sir Karl's preface ([1963], p. vii: "learn from our mistakes," "our often mistaken attempts to solve our problems"; "tests which may help us in the discovery of our mistakes") with the view ([1963], p. 215) that "the growth of scientific knowledge . . . [consists in] the repeated overthrow of scientific theories and their replacement by better or more satisfactory ones."

28. Lakatos (1963–64).

29. Popper (1959), p. 50.

30. Though my point is somewhat different, I owe my recognition of the need to confront this issue to C. G. Hempel's strictures on those who misinterpret Sir Karl by attributing to him a belief in absolute rather than relative falsification. See his (1965), p. 45. I am also indebted to Professor Hempel for a close and perceptive critique of this paper in draft.

31. Popper (1959), p. 31.

32. Popper (1959), pp. 53. f.

33. Popper (1963), pp. 233–35. Notice also, at the foot of the last of these pages, that Sir Karl's comparison of the relative verisimilitude of two theories depends upon there being "no revolutionary changes in our background knowledge," an assumption which he nowhere argues and which is hard to reconcile with his conception of scientific change by revolutions.

34. Braithwaite (1953), pp. 50–87, especially p. 76, and my (1962), pp. 97–101.

35. Note that the resemblance between members of a natural family is here a learned relationship and one which can be unlearned. Contemplate the old saw, "To an occidental, all chinamen look alike." That

example also highlights the most drastic of the simplification introduced at this point. A fuller discussion would have to allow for hierarchies of natural families with resemblance relations between families at the higher levels.

36. This experience would not necessitate the abandonment of either the category "swans" or the category "geese," but it would necessitate the introduction of an *arbitrary* boundary between them. The families "swans" and "geese" would no longer be natural families, and you could conclude nothing about the character of a new swan-like bird that was not also true of geese. Empty perceptual space is essential if family membership is to have cognitive content.

37. Further evidence for the unnaturalness of any such definition is provided by the following question. Should "whiteness" be included as a defining characteristic of swans? If so, the generalization "All swans are white" is immune to experience. But if "whiteness" is excluded from the definition, then some other characteristic must be included for which "whiteness" might have substituted. Decisions about which characteristics are to be parts of a definition and which are to be available for the statement of general laws are often arbitrary and, in practice, are seldom made. Knowledge is not usually articulated in that way.

38. This incompleteness of definitions is often called "open texture" or "vagueness of meaning," but those phrases seem decisively askew. Perhaps the definitions are incomplete, but nothing is wrong with the meanings. That is the way meanings behave!

39. Hawkins (1963).

40. Cf. Kuhn (1958).

41. Cf. Kuhn (1962), pp. 102–108.

42. Cf. my (1962), pp. 161–169.

43. Popper (1959), pp. 22 and 31 f., 46; and (1963), p. 52.

44. Popper (1963), p. 51. Italics in original.

REFERENCES

Braithwaite, R.B (1953). *Scientific Explanation.*

Guerlac, H. (1961). *Lavoisier—The Crucial Year.*

Hafner and Presswood, S. (1965). "Strong Interference and Weak Interactions." *Science* 149, pp. 503–10.

Hawkins, D. (1963). Review of Kuhn's "Structure of Scientific Revolutions." *American Journal of Physics*, 31.

Hempel, C.G. (1965). *Aspects of Scientific Explanation.*

Lakatos, I. (1963–64). "Proofs and Refutations." *The British Journal for the Philosophy of Science* 14, pp. 1–25, 120–39, 221–43, 296–342.

Kuhn, T.S. (1958). "The Role of Measurement in the Development of Physical Science." *Isis* 49, pp. 161–93.

———. (1962). *The Structure of Scientific Revolutions.*

Popper, K.R. (1935). *Logik der Forschung.*

———. (1945). *The Open Society and its Enemies*, 2 vols.

———. (1957). *The Poverty of Historicism.*

———. (1959). *Logic of Scientific Discovery.*

———. (1963). *Conjectures and Refutations.*

Stahlman, W. (1956). "Astrology in Colonial America: An Extended Query." *William and Mary Quarterly*, 13, pp. 551–63.

Thorndike, L. (1923–58). *A History of Magic and Experimental Science*, 8 vols.

———. (1955). "The True Place of Astrology in the History of Science." *Isis*, 46, pp. 273–78.

IMRE LAKATOS

HISTORY OF SCIENCE AND ITS RATIONAL RECONSTRUCTIONS*

INTRODUCTION

"**P**hilosophy of science without history of science is empty; history of science without philosophy of science is blind." Taking its cue from this paraphrase of Kant's famous dictum, this paper intends to explain *how* the historiography of science should learn from the philosophy of science and *vice versa*. It will be argued that (a) philosophy of science provides normative methodologies in terms of which the historian reconstructs "internal history" and thereby provides a rational explanation of the growth of objective knowledge; (b) two competing methodologies can be evaluated with the help of (normatively interpreted) history; (c) any rational reconstruction of history needs to be supplemented by an empirical (socio-psychological) "external history."

The vital demarcation between normative-internal and empirical-external is different for each methodology. Jointly, internal and external historiographical theories determine to a very large extent the choice of problems for the historian. But some of external history's most crucial problems can be formulated only in terms of one's methodology; thus internal history, so defined, is primary, and external history only secondary. Indeed, in view of the autonomy of internal (but not of external) history, external history is irrelevant for the understanding of science.[1]

I. RIVAL METHODOLOGIES OF SCIENCE; RATIONAL RECONSTRUCTIONS AS GUIDES TO HISTORY

There are several methodologies afloat in contemporary philosophy of science; but they are all very different from what used to be understood by "methodology" in the seventeenth or even eighteenth century. Then it was hoped that methodology would provide scientists with a mechanical book of rules for solving problems. This hope has now been given up: modern methodologies or "logics of discovery" consist merely of a set of (possibly not even tightly knit, let alone mechanical) rules for the *appraisal* of ready, articulated theories.[2] Often these rules, or systems of appraisal, also serve as "theories of scientific rationality," "demarcation criteria" or "definitions of science."[3] Outside the legislative domain of these normative rules there is, of course, an empirical psychology and sociology of discovery.

I shall now sketch four different "logics of discovery." Each will be characterised by rules governing the (scientific) *acceptance* and *rejection* of theories or research programmes.[4] These rules have a double function. First, they function as *a code of scientific honesty* whose violation is intolerable; secondly, as hard cores of (*normative*) *historiographical research programmes*. It is their second function on which I should like to concentrate.

A. Inductivism

One of the most influential methodologies of science has been inductivism. According to inductivism only those propositions can be accepted into the body of science which either describe hard facts or are infallible inductive generalizations from them.[5] When the inductivist *accepts* a scientific proposition, he accepts it as provenly true; he *rejects* it if it is not. His scientific rigor is strict: a proposition must be either proven from facts, or—deductively or inductively—derived from other propositions already proven.

Each methodology has its specific epistemological and logical problems. For example, inductivism has to establish with certainty the truth of "factual" ("basic") propositions and the validity of inductive inferences. Some philosophers get so preoccupied with their epistemological and logical problems that they never get to the point of becoming interested in actual history; if actual history does not fit their standards they may even have the temerity to propose that we start the whole business of science anew. Some others take some crude solution of these logical and epistemological problems for granted and devote themselves to a rational reconstruction of history without being aware of the logico-epistemological weakness (or, even, untenability) of their methodology.[6]

Inductivist criticism is primarily sceptical: it consists in showing that a proposition is unproven, that is, pseudo-scientific, rather than in showing that it is false.[7] When the inductivist historian writes the *prehistory* of a scientific discipline, he may draw heavily upon such criticisms. And he often explains the early dark age—when people were engrossed by "unproven ideas"—with the help of some "external" explanation, like the socio-psychological theory of the retarding influence of the Catholic church.

The inductivist historian recognizes only two sorts of *genuine scientific discoveries*: *hard factual propositions* and inductive *generalizations*. These and only these constitute the backbone of his *internal history*. When writing history, he looks out for them—finding them is quite a problem. Only when he finds them, can he start the construction of his beautiful pyramids. Revolutions consist in unmasking (irrational) errors which then are exiled from the history of science into the history of pseudo-science, into the history of mere beliefs: genuine scientific progress starts with the latest scientific revolution in any given field.

Each internal historiography has its characteristic victorious paradigms.[8] The main paradigms of inductivist historiography were Kepler's generalizations from Tycho Brahe's careful observations; Newton's discovery of his law of gravitation by, in turn, inductively generalizing Kepler's "phenomena" of planetary motion; and Ampère's discovery of his law of electrodynamics by inductively generalizing his observations of electric currents. Modern chemistry too is taken by some inductivists as having really started with Lavoisier's experiments and his "true explanations" of them.

But the inductivist historian cannot offer a *rational* "internal" explanation for *why* certain facts rather than others were selected in the first instance. For him this is a *nonrational, empirical, external* problem. Inductivism as an "internal" theory of rationality is compatible with many different supplementary empirical or external theories of problem-choice. It is, for instance, compatible with the vulgar Marxist view that problem-choice is determined by social needs;[9] indeed, some vulgar Marxists identify major phases in history of science with the major phases of economic development.[10] But choice of facts need not be determined by social factors; it may be determined by extrascientific intellectual influences. And inductivism is equally compatible with the "external" theory that the choice of problems is primarily determined by inborn, or by arbitrarily chosen (or traditional) theoretical (or "metaphysical") frameworks.

There is a radical brand of inductivism which condemns all external influences, whether intellectual, psychological or sociological, as creating impermissible bias: radical inductivists allow only a (random) selection by the empty mind. Radical inductivism is, in turn, a special kind of *radical internalism*. According to the latter, once one establishes the existence of some external influence on the acceptance of a scientific theory (or factual proposition) one must withdraw one's acceptance: proof of external influence means invalidation:[11] but since external influences always exist, radical internalism is utopian, and, as a theory of rationality, self-destructive.[12]

When the radical inductivist historian faces the problem of why some great scientists thought highly of metaphysics and, indeed, why they thought that their discoveries were great for reasons which, in the light of inductivism, look very odd, he will refer these problems of "false consciousness" to psychopathology, that is, to external history.

B. Conventionalism

Conventionalism allows for the building of any system of pigeon holes which organizes facts into some coherent whole. The conventionalist decides to keep the centre of such a pigeonhole system intact as long as possible: when difficulties arise through an invasion of anomalies, he only changes and complicates the peripheral arrangements. But the conventionalist does not regard any pigeonhole system as provenly true, but only as "true by convention" (or possibly even as neither true nor false). In *revolutionary* brands of conventionalism one does not have to adhere forever to a given pigeonhole system: one may abandon it if it becomes unbearably clumsy and if a simpler one is offered to replace it.[13] This version of conventionalism is epistemologically, and especially logically, much simpler than inductivism: it is in no need of valid inductive inferences. Genuine *progress* of science is cumulative and takes place on the ground level of "proven" facts,[14] the *changes* on the theoretical level are merely instrumental. Theoretical "progress" is only in convenience ("simplicity"), and not in truth-content.[15] One may, of course, introduce revolutionary conventionalism also at the level of "factual" propositions, in which case one would accept "factual" propositions by decision rather than by experimental "proofs." But then, if the conventionalist is to retain the idea that the growth of "factual" science has anything to do with objective, factual truth, he must devise some metaphysical principle which he then has to superimpose on his rules for the game of science.[16] If he does not, he cannot escape scepticism or, at least, some radical form of instrumentalism.

(It is important to clarify the *relation between conventionalism and instrumentalism*. Conventionalism rests on the recognition that false assumptions may have true consequences; therefore false theories may have great predictive power. Conventionalists had to face the problem of comparing rival false theories. Most of them conflated truth with its signs and found themselves holding some version of the pragmatic theory of truth. It was Popper's theory of truth-content, verisimilitude and corroboration which finally laid down the basis of a philosophically flawless version of conventionalism. On the other hand some conventionalists did not have sufficient logical education to realise that some propositions may be true whilst being unproven; and others false whilst having true consequences, and also some which are both false and approximately true. These people opted for "instrumentalism": they came to regard theories as neither true nor false but merely as "instruments" for prediction. Conventionalism, as here defined, is a philosophically sound position; instrumentalism is a degenerate version of it, based on a mere philosophical muddle caused by lack of elementary logical competence.)

Revolutionary conventionalism was born as the Bergsonians' philosophy of science: free will and creativity were the slogans. The code of scientific honor of the conventionalist is less rigorous than that of the inductivist: it puts no ban on unproven speculation, and allows a pigeonhole system to be built around *any* fancy idea. Moreover, conventionalism does not brand discarded systems as unscientific: the conventionalist sees much more of the actual history of science as rational ("internal") than does the inductivist.

For the conventionalist historian, major discoveries are primarily inventions of new and simpler pigeonhole systems. Therefore he constantly compares for simplicity: the complications of pigeonhole systems and their revolutionary replacement by simpler ones constitute the backbone of his internal history.

The paradigmatic case of a scientific revolution for the conventionalist has been the Copernican revolution.[17] Efforts have been made to show that Lavoisier's and Einstein's revolutions too were replacements of clumsy theories by simple ones.

Conventionalist historiography cannot offer a *rational* explanation of why certain facts were selected in the first instance or of why certain particular pigeonhole systems were tried rather than others at a stage when their relative merits were yet unclear. Thus conventionalism, like inductivism, is compatible with various supplementary empirical-"externalist" programmes.

Finally, the conventionalist historian, like his inductivist colleague, frequently encounters the problem of "false consciousness." According to conventionalism, for example, it is a "matter of fact" that great scientists arrive at their theories by flights of their imaginations. Why then do they often claim that they derived their theories from facts? The conventionalist's rational reconstruction often differs from the great scientists' own reconstruction—the conventionalist historian relegates these problems of false consciousness to the externalist.[18]

C. Methodological Falsificationism

Contemporary falsificationism arose as a logico-epistemological criticism of inductivism and of Duhemian conventionalism. Inductivism was criticised on the grounds that its two basic assumptions, namely, that factual propositions can be "derived" from facts and that there can be valid inductive (content-increasing) inferences, are themselves unproven and even demonstrably false. Duhem was criticised on the grounds that comparison of intuitive simplicity can only be a matter for subjective taste and that it is so ambiguous that no hard-hitting criticism can be based on it. Popper, in his *Logik der Forschung*, proposed a new "falsificationist" methodology.[19] This methodology is another brand of revolutionary conventionalism: the main difference is that it allows factual, spatio-temporally singular "basic statements," rather than spatio-temporally universal theories, to be accepted by convention. In the code of honor of the falsificationist a theory is scientific only if it can be *made* to conflict with a basic statement; and a theory must be eliminated if it conflicts with an accepted basic statement. Popper also indicated a further condition that a theory must satisfy in order to qualify as scientific: it must predict facts which are *novel*, that is, unexpected in the light of previous knowledge. Thus it is against Popper's code of scientific honor to propose unfalsifiable theories or "*ad hoc*" hypotheses (which imply no *novel* empirical predictions)—just as it is against the (classical) inductivist code of scientific honor to propose unproven ones.

The great attraction of Popperian methodology lies in its clarity and force. Popper's deductive model of scientific criticism contains empirically falsifiable spatio-temporally universal propositions, initial conditions and their consequences. The weapon of criticism is the *modus tollens*: neither inductive logic nor intuitive simplicity complicate the picture.[20]

(Falsificationism, though logically impeccable, has epistemological difficulties of its own. In its "dogmatic" proto-version it assumes the provability of propositions from facts and thus the disprovability of theories—a false assumption.[21] In its Popperian "conventionalist" version it needs some (extramethodological) "inductive principle" to lend epistemological weight to its decisions to accept "basic" statements, and in general to connect its rules of the scientific game with verisimilitude.[22])

The Popperian historian looks for great, "bold," falsifiable theories and for great negative crucial experiments. These form the skeleton of his rational reconstruction. The Popperians' favorite paradigms of great falsifiable theories are Newton's and Maxwell's theories, the radiation formulas of Rayleigh, Jeans and Wien, and the Einsteinian revolution; their favorite paradigms for crucial experiments are the Michelson-Morley experiment, Eddington's eclipse experiment, and the experiments of Lummer and Pringsheim. It was Agassi who tried to turn this naïve falsificationism into a systematic historiographical research programme.[23] In particular he predicted (or "postdicted," if you wish) that behind each great experimental discovery lies a theory which the discovery contradicted; the importance of a factual discovery is to be measured by the importance of the theory refuted by it. Agassi seems to accept at face value the value judgments of the scientific community concerning the importance of factual discoveries like Galvani's, Oersted's, Priestley's, Roentgen's and Hertz's; but he denies the "myth" that they were chance discoveries (as the first four were said to be) or confirming instances (as Hertz first thought his discovery was).[24] Thus Agassi arrives at a bold prediction: all these five experiments were successful refutations—in some cases even *planned* refutations—of theories which he proposes to unearth, and, indeed, in most cases, claims to have unearthed.[25]

Popperian internal history, in turn, is readily supplemented by external theories of history. Thus Popper himself explained that (on the positive side) (1) the main *external* stimulus of scientific theories comes from unscientific "metaphysics," and even from myths (this was later beautifully illustrated mainly by Koyré); and that (on the negative side) (2) facts do *not* constitute such external stimulus—factual discoveries belong completely to internal history, emerging as refutations of some scientific theory, so that facts are only noticed if they conflict with some previous expectation. Both theses are cornerstones of Popper's *psychology* of discovery.[26] Feyerabend developed another interesting *psychological* thesis of Popper, namely, that proliferation of rival theories may—*externally*—speed up *internal* Popperian falsification.[27]

But the external supplementary theories of falsificationism need not be restricted to purely intellectual influences. It has to be emphasized (*pace* Agassi) that falsificationism is no less compatible with a vulgar Marxist view of what makes science progress than is inductivism. The only difference is that while for the latter Marxism might be invoked to explain the discovery of *facts*, for the former it might be invoked to explain the invention of *scientific theories*; while the choice of facts (that is, for the falsificationist, the choice of "potential falsifiers") is primarily determined internally by the theories.

"False awareness"—"false" from the point of view of *his* rationality theory—creates a problem for the falsificationist historian. For instance, why do some scientists believe that crucial experiments are positive and verifying rather than negative and falsifying? It was the falsificationist Popper who, in order to solve these problems, elaborated better than anybody else before him the cleavage between objective knowledge (in his "third world") and its distorted reflections in individual minds.[28] Thus he opened up the way for my demarcation between internal and external history.

D. Methodology of Scientific Research Programmes

According to my methodology the greatest scientific achievements are research programmes which can be evaluated in terms of progressive and degenerating problem-shifts; and scientific revolutions consist of one research programme superseding (overtaking in progress) another.[29] This methodology offers a new rational reconstruction of science. It is best presented by contrasting it with falsificationism and conventionalism, from both of which it borrows essential elements.

From conventionalism, this methodology borrows the licence rationally to accept by convention not only spatio-temporally singular "factual statements" but also spatio-temporally universal theories: indeed, this becomes the most important clue to the continuity of scientific growth.[30] The basic unit of appraisal must not be an isolated theory or conjunction of theories but rather a *"research programme,"* with a conventionally accepted (and thus by provisional decision "irrefutable") *"hard core"* and with a *"positive heuristic"* which defines problems, outlines the construction of a belt of auxiliary hypotheses, foresees anomalies and turns them victoriously into examples, all according to a preconceived plan. The scientist lists anomalies, but as long as his research programme sustains its momentum, he may freely put them aside. *It is primarily the positive heuristic of his programme, not the anomalies, which dictate the choice of his problems.*[31] Only when the driving force of the positive heuristic weakens, may more attention be given to anomalies. The methodology of research programmes can explain in this way *the high degree of autonomy of theoretical science*; the naïve falsificationist's disconnected chains of conjectures and refutations cannot. What for Popper, Watkins and Agassi is *external*, influential metaphysics, here turns into the *internal* "hard core" of a programme.[32]

The methodology of research programmes presents a very different picture of the game of science from the picture of the methodological falsificationist. The best opening gambit is not a falsifiable (and therefore consistent) hypothesis, but a research programme. Mere "falsification" (in Popper's sense) must not imply rejection.[33] Mere "falsifications" (that is, anomalies) are to be recorded but need not be acted upon. Popper's great negative crucial experiments disappear; "crucial experiment" is an honorific title, which may, of course, be conferred on certain anomalies, but only *long after the event*, only when one programme has been defeated by another one. According to Popper a crucial experiment is described by an accepted basic statement which is inconsistent with a theory—according to the methodology of scientific research programmes no accepted basic statement *alone* entitles the scientist to reject a theory. Such a clash may present a problem (major or minor), but in no circumstance a "victory."

Nature may shout *no*, but human ingenuity—contrary to Weyl and Popper[34]—may always be able to shout louder. With sufficient resourcefulness and some luck, any theory can be defended "progressively" for a long time, even if it is false. The Popperian pattern of "conjectures and refutations," that is the pattern of trial-by-hypothesis followed by error-shown-by-experiment, is to be abandoned: no experiment is crucial at the time—let alone before—it is performed (except, possibly, psychologically).

It should be pointed out, however, that the methodology of scientific research programmes has more teeth than Duhem's conventionalism: instead of leaving it to Duhem's unarticulated common sense[35] to judge when a "framework" is to be abandoned, I inject some hard Popperian elements into the appraisal of whether a programme progresses or degenerates or of whether one is overtaking another. That is, I give criteria of progress and stagnation within a programme and also rules for the "elimination" of whole research programmes. A research programme is said to be *progressing* as long as its theoretical growth anticipates its empirical growth, that is, as long as it keeps predicting novel facts with some success (*"progressive problem-shift"*); it is *stagnating* if its theoretical growth lags behind its empirical growth, that is, as long as it gives only *post-hoc* explanations either of chance discoveries or of facts anticipated by, and discovered in, a rival programme (*"degenerating problem-shift"*).[36] If a research programme progressively explains more than a rival, it "supersedes" it, and the rival can be eliminated (or, if you wish, "shelved").[37]

(*Within* a research programme a theory can only be eliminated by a better theory, that is, by one which has excess empirical content over its predecessors, some of which is subsequently confirmed. And for this replacement of one theory by a better one, the first theory does not even have to be "falsified" in Popper's sense of the term. Thus progress is marked by instances verifying excess content rather than by falsifying instances,[38] empirical "falsification" and actual "rejection" become independent.[39] Before a theory has been modified we can never know in what way it had been "refuted," and some of the most interesting modifications are motivated by the "positive heuristic" of the research programme rather than by anomalies. This difference alone has important consequences and leads to a rational reconstruction of scientific change very different from that of Popper's.[40])

It is very difficult to decide, especially since one must not demand progress at each single step, when a research programme has degenerated hopelessly or when one of two rival programmes has achieved a decisive advantage over the other. In this methodology, as in Duhem's conventionalism, there can be no instant—let alone mechanical—rationality. *Neither the logician's proof of inconsistency nor the experimental scientist's verdict of anomaly can defeat a research programme in one blow.* One can be "wise" only after the event.[41]

In this code of scientific honor modesty plays a greater role than in other codes. One *must* realize that one's opponent, even if lagging badly behind, may still stage a comeback. No advantage for one side can ever be regarded as absolutely conclusive. There is never anything inevitable about the triumph of a programme. Also, there is never anything inevitable about its defeat. Thus pigheadedness, like modesty, has more "rational" scope. *The scores of the rival sides, however, must be recorded*[42] *and publicly displayed at all times.*

(We should here at least refer to the main epistemological problem of the methodology of scientific research programmes. As it stands, like Popper's methodological falsificationism, it represents a very radical version of conventionalism. One needs to posit some extramethodological inductive principle to relate—even if tenuously—the scientific gambit of pragmatic acceptances and rejections to verisimilitude.[43] Only such an "inductive principle" can turn science from a mere game into an epistemologically rational exercise; from a set of lighthearted sceptical gambits pursued for intellectual fun into a—more serious—fallibilist venture of approximating the Truth about the Universe.[44])

The methodology of scientific research programmes constitutes, like any other methodology, a historiographical research programme. The historian who accepts this methodology as a guide will look in history for rival research programmes, for progressive and degenerating problem shifts. Where the Duhemian historian sees a revolution merely in simplicity (like that of Copernicus), he will look for a large scale progressive programme overtaking a degenerating one. Where the falsificationist sees a crucial negative experiment, he will "predict" that there was none, that behind any alleged crucial experiment, behind any alleged single battle between theory and experiment, there is a hidden war of attrition between two research programmes. The outcome of the war is only later linked in the falsificationist reconstruction with some alleged single "crucial experiment."

The methodology of research programmes—like any other theory of scientific rationality— must be supplemented by empirical-external history. No rationality theory will ever solve problems like why Mendelian genetics disappeared in Soviet Russia in the 1950s, or why certain schools of research into genetic racial differences or into the economics of foreign aid came into disrepute in the Anglo-Saxon countries in the 1960s. Moreover, to explain different speeds of development of different research programmes we may need to invoke external history. Rational reconstruction of science (in the sense in which I use the term) cannot be comprehensive since human beings are not *completely* rational animals; and even when they act rationally they may have a false theory of their own rational actions.[45]

But the methodology of research programmes draws a demarcation between internal and external history which is markedly different from that drawn by other rationality theories. For instance, what for the falsificationist looks like the (regrettably frequent) phenomenon of irrational adherence to a "refuted" or to an inconsistent theory and which he therefore relegates to *external* history, may well be explained in terms of my methodology *internally* as a rational defence of a promising research programme. Or, the successful *pre*dictions of novel facts which constitute serious evidence for a research programme and therefore vital parts of internal history, are irrelevant both for the inductivist and for the falsificationist.[46] For the inductivist and the falsificationist it does not really matter whether the discovery of a fact preceded or followed a theory: only their logical relation is decisive. The "irrational" impact of the historical coincidence that a theory happened to have *anticipated* a factual discovery, has no internal significance. Such anticipations constitute "not proof but (mere) propaganda."[47] Or again, take Planck's discontent with his own 1900 radiation formula, which he regarded as "arbitrary." For the falsificationist the formula was a bold, falsifiable hypothesis and Planck's dislike of it a nonrational mood, explicable only in terms of psychology. However, in my view, Planck's discontent can be explained internally: it was a rational condemnation of an "*ad hoc*," theory.[48] To mention yet another example: for falsificationism irrefutable "metaphysics" is an external intellectual influence, in my approach it is a vital part of the rational reconstruction of science.

Most historians have hitherto tended to regard the solution of some problems as being the monopoly of externalists. One of these is the problem of the high frequency of *simultaneous discoveries*. For this problem vulgar Marxists have an easy solution: a discovery is made by many people at the same time, once a social need for it arises.[49] Now what constitutes a "discovery," and especially a major discovery, depends on one's methodology. For the inductivist, the most important discoveries are factual, and, indeed, such discoveries are frequently made simultaneously. For the falsificationist a *major* discovery consists in the discovery of a theory rather than of a fact. Once a theory is discovered (or rather invented), it becomes public property; and nothing is more obvious than that several people will test it simultaneously and make, simultaneously, (minor) factual discoveries. Also, a published theory is a challenge to devise higher-level, independently testable explanations. For example, given Kepler's ellipses and Galileo's rudimentary dynamics, simultaneous "discovery" of an inverse square law is not so very surprising: a problem-situation being public, simultaneous solutions can be explained on *purely internal* grounds.[50] The discovery of a new problem however may not be so readily explicable. If one thinks of the history of science as of one of rival research programmes, then most simultaneous discoveries, theoretical or factual, are explained by the fact that research programmes being public property, many people work on them in different corners of the world, possibly not knowing of each other. However, really *novel, major, revolutionary* developments are rarely invented simultaneously. Some alleged simultaneous discoveries of novel programmes are seen as having been simultaneous discoveries only with false hindsight: in fact they are *different* discoveries, merged only later into a single one.[51]

A favorite hunting ground of externalists has been the related problem of why so much importance is attached to—and energy spent on—*priority disputes*. This can be explained only *externally* by the inductivist, naïve falsificationist, or the conventionalist; but in the light of the methodology of research programmes some priority disputes are vital *internal* problems, since in this methodology *it becomes all-important for rational appraisal which programme was first in anticipating a novel fact and which fitted in the by now old fact only later*. Some priority disputes can be explained by rational interest and not simply by vanity and greed for fame. It then becomes important that Tychonian theory, for instance, succeeded in explaining—only *post hoc*—the observed phases of, and the distance to, Venus which were originally precisely anticipated by Copernicans;[52] or that Cartesians managed to explain everything that the Newtonians *pre*dicted—but only *post hoc*. Newtonian optical theory explained *post hoc* many phenomena which were anticipated and first observed by Huyghensians.[53]

All these examples show how the methodology of scientific research programmes turns many problems which had been *external* problems for other historiographies into internal ones. But occasionally the borderline is moved in the opposite direction. For instance there may have been an experiment which was accepted *instantly*—in the absence of a better theory—as a negative crucial experiment. For the falsificationist such acceptance is part of internal history; for me it is not rational and has to be explained in terms of external history.

Note. The methodology of research programmes was criticised both by Feyerabend and by Kuhn. According to Kuhn: "[Lakatos] must specify criteria which can be used *at the time* to distinguish a degenerative from a progressive research programme; and so on. Otherwise, *he has told us nothing at all.*"[54] Actually, I *do* specify such criteria. But Kuhn probably meant that "[my] standards have practical force only if they are combined with a *time limit* (what looks like a degenerating problem-shift may be the beginning of a much longer period of advance)."[55] Since I specify no such time limit, Feyerabend concludes that my standards are no more than "*verbal ornaments.*"[56] A related point was made by Musgrave in a letter containing some major constructive criticisms of an earlier draft, in which he demanded that I specify, for instance, at what point dogmatic adherence to a programme ought to be explained "externally" rather than "internally."

Let me try to explain why such objections are beside the point. One may rationally stick to a degenerating programme until it is overtaken by a rival *and even after*. What one must *not* do is to deny its poor public record. Both Feyerabend and Kuhn conflate *methodological* appraisal of a programme with firm *heuristic* advice about what to do.[57] It is perfectly rational to play a risky game: what is irrational is to deceive oneself about the risk.

This does not mean as much licence as might appear for those who stick to a degenerating programme. For they can do this mostly only in private. Editors of scientific journals should refuse to publish their papers which will, in general, contain either solemn reassertions of their position or absorption of counterevidence (or even of rival programmes) by *ad hoc*, linguistic adjustments. Research foundations, too, should refuse money.[58]

These observations also answer Musgrave's objection by separating rational and irrational (or honest and dishonest) adherence to a degenerating programme. They also throw further light on the demarcation between internal and external history. They show that internal history is self-sufficient for the presentation of the history of disembodied science, including degenerating problem-shifts. External history explains why some people have false beliefs about scientific progress, and how their scientific activity may be influenced by such beliefs.

E. Internal and External History

Four theories of the rationality of scientific progress—or logics of scientific discovery—have been briefly discussed. It was shown how each of them provides a theoretical framework for the rational reconstruction of the history of science.

Thus the internal history of *inductivists* consists of alleged discoveries of hard facts and of so-called inductive generalizations. The internal history of *conventionalists* consists of factual discoveries and of the erection of pigeonhole systems and their replacement by allegedly simpler ones.[59] The internal history of *falsificationists* dramatises bold conjectures, improvements which are said to be *always* content-increasing and, above all, triumphant "negative crucial experiments." The *methodology of research programmes*, finally, emphasizes long-extended theoretical and empirical rivalry of major research programmes, progressive and degenerating problem-shifts, and the slowly emerging victory of one programme over the other.

Each rational reconstruction produces some characteristic pattern of rational growth of scientific knowledge. But all of these *normative* reconstructions may have to be supplemented by *empirical* external theories to explain the residual nonrational factors. The history of science is always richer than its rational reconstruction. *But rational reconstruction or internal history is primary, external history only secondary, since the most important problems of external history are defined by internal history.* External history either provides nonrational explanation of the speed, locality, selectiveness, etc., of historic events *as interpreted* in terms of internal history; or, when history differs from its rational reconstruction, it provides an empirical explanation of why it differs. But the *rational* aspect of scientific growth is fully accounted for by one's logic of scientific discovery.

Whatever problem the historian of science wishes to solve, he has first to reconstruct the relevant section of the growth of objective scientific knowledge, that is, the relevant section of "internal history." As it has been shown, what constitutes for him internal history, depends on his philosophy, whether he is aware of this fact or not. Most theories of the growth of knowledge are theories of the growth of disembodied knowledge: whether an experiment is crucial or not, whether a hypothesis is highly probable in the light of the available evidence or not, whether a problem-shift is progressive or not, is not dependent in the slightest on the scientists' beliefs, personalities or authority. These subjective factors are of no interest for any internal history. For instance, the "internal historian" records the Proutian programme with its hard core (that atomic weights of pure chemical elements are whole numbers) and its positive heuristic (to overthrow, and replace, the contemporary false observational theories applied in measuring atomic weights). This programme was later carried through.[60] The internal historian will waste little time on Prout's *belief* that if the "experimental techniques" *of his time* were "carefully" applied, and the experimental findings properly interpreted, the anomalies would *immediately* be seen as mere illusions. The internal historian will regard this historical fact as a fact in the second world which is only a caricature of its counterpart in the third world.[61] *Why* such caricatures come about is none of his business; he might—in a footnote—pass on the externalist the problem of why certain scientists had "false beliefs" about what they were doing.[62]

Thus in constructing internal history the historian will be highly selective: he will omit everything that is irrational in the light of his rationality theory. But this normative selection still does not add up to a fully fledged rational reconstruction. For instance, Prout never articulated the "Proutian programme": the Proutian programme is not Prout's programme. *It is not only the ("internal") success or the ("internal") defeat of a programme which can only be judged with hindsight: it is frequently also its content.* Internal history is not just a *selection* of methodologically interpreted facts: it may be, on occasions, their *radically improved version*. One may illustrate this using the Bohrian programme. Bohr, in 1913, may not have even thought of the possibility of electron spin. He had more than enough on his hands without the spin. Nevertheless, the historian, describing with hindsight the Bohrian programme, should include electron spin in it, since electron spin fits naturally in the original outline of the programme. Bohr might have referred to it in 1913. Why Bohr did not do so, is an interesting problem which deserves to be indicated in a footnote.[63] (Such problems might then be solved either internally by pointing to rational reasons in the growth of objective, impersonal knowledge; or externally by pointing to psychological causes in the development of Bohr's personal beliefs.)

One way to indicate discrepancies between history and its rational reconstruction is to relate the internal history *in the text*, and indicate *in the footnotes* how actual history "misbehaved" in the light of its rational reconstruction.[64]

Many historians will abhor the idea of *any* rational reconstruction. They will quote Lord Bolingbroke: "History is philosophy teaching by example." They will say that before philosophising "we need a lot more examples."[65] But such an inductivist theory of historiography is utopian.[66] *History without some theoretical "bias" is impossible.*[67] Some historians look for the discovery of hard facts, inductive generalizations, others for bold theories and crucial negative experiments, yet others for great simplifications, or for progressive and degenerating problem-shifts; all of them have *some* theoretical "bias." This bias, of course, may be obscured by an eclectic variation of theories or by theoretical confusion: but neither eclecticism nor confusion amounts to an atheoretical outlook. What a historian regards as an external problem is often an excellent guide to his implicit methodology: some will ask why a "hard fact" or a "bold theory" was discovered exactly when and where it actually was discovered; others will ask why a "degenerating problem-shift" could have wide popular acclaim over an incredibly long period or why a "progressive problem-shift" was left "unreasonably" unacknowledged.[68] Long texts have been devoted to the problem of whether, and if so, why, the emergence of science was a purely European affair; but such an investigation is bound to remain a piece of confused rambling until one clearly defines "science" according to some normative philosophy of science. One of the most interesting problems of external history is to specify the psychological, and indeed, social conditions which are necessary (but, of course, never sufficient) to make scientific progress possible; but in the very formulation of this "external" problem *some* methodological theory, *some* definition of science is bound to enter. History of *science* is a history of events which are selected and interpreted in a normative way.[69] This being so, the hitherto neglected problem of appraising rival logics of scientific discovery and, hence, rival reconstructions of history, acquires paramount importance. I shall now turn to this problem.

II. CRITICAL COMPARISON OF METHODOLOGIES: HISTORY AS A TEST OF ITS RATIONAL RECONSTRUCTIONS

Theories of scientific rationality can be classified under two main heads.

(1) *Justificationist methodologies* set very high epistemological standards: for classical justificationists a proposition is "scientific" only if it is *proven*, for neojustificationists, if it is *probable* (in the sense of the probability calculus) or *corroborated* (in the sense of Popper's third note on corroboration) to a proven degree.[70] Some philosophers of science gave up the idea of proving or of (provably) probabilifying scientific theories but remained dogmatic empiricists: whether inductivists, probabilists, conventionalists or falsificationist, they still stick to the provability of "factual" propositions. By now, of course, all these different forms of justificationism have crumbled under the weight of *epistemological and logical criticism*.

(2) The only alternatives with which we are left are *pragmatic-conventionalist methodologies*, crowned by some global principle of induction. Conventionalist methodologies first lay down rules about "acceptance" and "rejection" of factual and theoretical propositions—without yet laying down rules about proof and disproof, truth and falsehood. We then get *different systems of rules of the scientific game*. The inductivist game would consist of collecting "acceptable" (not proven) data and drawing from them "acceptable" (not proven) inductive generalizations. The conventionalist game would consist of collecting "acceptable" data and ordering them into the simplest possible pigeonhole systems (or devising the simplest possible pigeonhole systems and filling them with acceptable data). Popper specified yet another game as "scientific."[71] Even methodologies which have been epistemologically and logically discredited, may go on functioning, in these emasculated versions, as guides for the rational reconstruction of history. But these *scientific games* are without any genuine epistemological relevance *unless* we superimpose on them some sort of metaphysical (or, if you wish, "inductive") principle which will say that the game, as specified by the methodology, gives us the best chance of approaching the Truth. Such a principle then turns the pure conventions of the game into fallible conjectures; but without such a principle the scientific game is just like any other game.[72]

It is very difficult to criticise conventionalist methodologies like Duhem's and Popper's. There is no obvious way to criticise either a game or a metaphysical principle of induction. In order to overcome these difficulties I am going to propose a new theory of how to appraise such methodologies of science (the ones, which—at least in the first stage, before the introduction of an inductive principle—are conventionalist). I shall show that methodologies may be criticised without any direct reference to any epistemological (or even logical) theory, and without using directly any logico-epistemological criticism. The basic idea of this criticism is that *all methodologies function as historiographical (or meta-historical) theories (or research programmes) and can be criticised by criticising the rational historical reconstructions to which they lead*.

I shall try to develop this historiographical method of criticism in a dialectical way. I start with a special case: I first "refute" falsificationism by "applying" falsificationism (on a normative historiographical meta-level) to itself. Then I shall apply falsificationism also to inductivism and conventionalism, and, indeed, argue that all methodologies are bound to end up "falsified" with the help of this Pyrrhonian *machine de guerre*. Finally, I shall "apply" not falsificationism but the methodology of scientific research programmes (again on a normative-historiographical meta-level) to inductivism, conventionalism, falsificationism and to itself, and show that—on this metacriterion—methodologies can be constructively criticised and compared. This normative-historiographical version of the methodology of scientific research programmes supplies a general theory of how to compare rival logics of discovery in which (in a sense carefully to be specified) *history may be seen as a "test" of its rational reconstructions.*

A. Falsificationism as a Metacriterion: History "falsifies" Falsificationism (and any other Methodology)

In their purely "methodological" versions scientific appraisals, as has already been said, are *conventions* and can always be formulated as a definition of science.[73] How can one criticise such a definition? If one interprets it nominalistically,[74] a definition is a mere abbreviation, a terminological suggestion, a tautology. How can one criticise a tautology? Popper, for one, claims that his definition of science is "fruitful" because "a great many points can be clarified and explained with its help." He quotes Menger: "Definitions are dogmas; only the conclusions drawn from them can afford us any new insight."[75] But how can a definition have explanatory power or afford new insights? Popper's answer is this: "It is only from the consequences of my definition of empirical science, and from the methodological decisions which depend upon this definition, that the scientist will be able to see how far it conforms to his intuitive idea of the goal of his endeavours."[76]

The answer complies with Popper's general position that conventions can be criticised by discussing their "suitability" relative to some purpose: "As to the suitability of any convention opinions may differ; and a reasonable discussion of these questions is only possible between parties having some purpose in common. The choice of that purpose . . . goes beyond rational argument."[77] Indeed, Popper never offered a theory of rational criticism of consistent conventions. He does not raise, let alone answer, the question: "*Under what conditions would you give up your demarcation criterion?*"[78]

But the question can be answered. I give my answer in two stages: I propose first a naïve and then a more sophisticated answer. I start by recalling how Popper, according to his own account,[78a] arrived at his criterion. He thought, like the best scientists of his time, that Newton's theory, although refuted, was a wonderful scientific achievement; that Einstein's theory was still better; and that astrology, Freudianism and twentieth-century Marxism were pseudo-scientific. His problem was to find a definition of science which yielded these "*basic judgments*" concerning particular theories; and he offered a novel solution. Now let us consider the proposal that *a rationality theory—or demarcation criterion—is to be rejected if it is inconsistent with an accepted "basic value judgment" of the scientific élite.* Indeed, this meta-methodological rule (*metafalsificationism*) would seem to correspond to Popper's methodological rule (falsificationism) that a scientific theory is to be rejected if it is inconsistent with an ("empirical") basic statement unanimously accepted by the scientific community. Popper's whole methodology rests on the contention that there exist (relatively) singular statements on whose truth-value scientists can reach unanimous agreement; without such agreement there would be a new Babel and "the soaring edifice of science would soon lie in ruins."[79] But even if

394 • THE GROWTH OF SCIENTIFIC KNOWLEDGE

there were an agreement about "basic" statements, if there were no agreement about how to appraise scientific achievement relative to this "empirical basis," would not the soaring edifice of science equally soon lie in ruins? No doubt it would. While there has been little agreement concerning a *universal* criterion of the scientific character of theories, there has been considerable agreement over the last two centuries concerning *single* achievements. While there has been no *general* agreement concerning a theory of scientific rationality, there has been considerable agreement concerning whether a particular single step in the game was scientific or crankish, or whether a particular gambit was played correctly or not. A general definition of science thus must reconstruct the acknowledgedly best gambits as "scientific": if it fails to do so, it has to be rejected.[80]

Then let us propose tentatively that *if a demarcation criterion is inconsistent with the "basic" appraisals of the scientific élite, it should be rejected.*

Now *if* we apply this quasi-empirical metacriterion (which I am going to reject later), Popper's demarcation criterion—that is, Popper's rules of the game of science—has to be rejected.[81]

Popper's basic rule is that the scientist must specify in advance under what experimental conditions he will give up even his most basic assumptions. For instance, he writes, when criticising psychoanalysis: "*Criteria of refutation* have to be laid down beforehand: it must be agreed which observable situations, if actually observed, mean that the theory is refuted. But what kind of clinical responses would refute to the satisfaction of the analyst *not merely a particular analytic diagnosis but psychoanalysis itself*? And have such criteria ever been discussed or agreed upon by analysts?"[82] In the case of psychoanalysis Popper was right: no answer has been forthcoming. Freudians have been nonplussed by Popper's basic challenge concerning scientific honesty. Indeed, they have refused to specify experimental conditions under which they would give up their basic assumptions. For Popper this was the hallmark of their intellectual dishonesty. But what if we put Popper's question to the Newtonian scientist: "What kind of observation would refute to the satisfaction of the Newtonian not merely a particular Newtonian explanation but Newtonian dynamics and gravitational theory itself? And have such criteria ever been discussed or agreed upon by Newtonians?" The Newtonian will, alas, scarcely be able to give a positive answer.[83] But then if analysts are to be condemned as dishonest by Popper's standards, Newtonians must also be condemned. Newtonian science, however, in spite of this sort of "dogmatism," is highly regarded by the greatest scientists, and, indeed, by Popper himself. Newtonian "dogmatism" then is a "falsification" of Popper's definition: it defies Popper's rational reconstruction.

Popper may certainly withdraw his celebrated challenge and demand falsifiability—and rejection on falsification—only for systems of theories, including initial conditions and all sorts of auxiliary and observational theories.[84] This is a considerable withdrawal, for it allows the imaginative scientist to save his pet theory by suitable lucky alterations in some odd, obscure corner on the periphery of his theoretical maze. But even Popper's mitigated rule will show up even the most brilliant scientists as irrational dogmatists. For in large research programmes there are always known anomalies: normally the researcher puts them aside and follows the positive heuristic of the programme.[85] In general he rivets his attention on the positive heuristic rather than on the distracting anomalies, and hopes that the "recalcitrant instances" will be turned into confirming instances as the programme progresses. On Popper's terms the greatest scientists in these situations used forbidden gambits, *ad hoc* stratagems: instead of regarding Mercury's anomalous perihelion as a falsification of the Newtonian theory of our planetary system and thus as a reason for its rejection, most physicists shelved it as a problematic instance to be solved at some later stage—or offered *ad hoc* solutions. This methodological attitude of treating as (mere) *anomalies* what Popper would regard as (dramatic) counterexamples is commonly accepted by the best scientists. Some of the research programmes now held in highest esteem by the scientific community progressed in an ocean of anomalies.[86] That in their choice of problems the greatest scientists "uncritically" ignore anomalies (and that they isolate them with the help of *ad hoc* stratagems) offers, at least on our metacriterion, a further falsification of Popper's methodology. He cannot interpret as rational some most important patterns in the growth of science.

Furthermore, for Popper, working on *an inconsistent system* must invariably be regarded as irrational "a self-contradictory system must be rejected . . . [because it] is uninformative. . . . No statement is singled out . . . since all are derivable."[87] But some of the greatest scientific research programmes progressed on inconsistent foundations.[88] Indeed in such cases the best scientists' rule is frequently: *"Allez en avant et la foi vous viendra."* This anti-Popperian methodology secured a breathing space both for the infinitesimal calculus and for naïve set theory when they were bedevilled by logical paradoxes.

Indeed, if the game of science had been played according to Popper's rule book, Bohr's 1913 paper would never have been published because it was inconsistently grafted on to Maxwell's theory, and Dirac's delta functions would have been suppressed until Schwartz. All these examples of research based on inconsistent foundations constitute further "falsifications" of falsificationist methodology.[89]

Thus several of the "basic" appraisals of the scientific *élite* "falsify" Popper's definition of science and scientific ethics. The problem then arises, to what extent, given these considerations, can falsificationism function as a guide for the historian of science. The simple answer is, to a very small extent. Popper, the leading falsificationist, never wrote any history of science; possibly because he was too sensitive to the judgment of great scientists to pervert history in a falsificationist vein. One should remember that while in his autobiographical recollections he mentions Newtonian science as the paradigm of scientificness, that is, of falsifiability, in his classical *Logik der Forschung* the falsifiability of Newton's theory is nowhere discussed. The *Logik der Forschung*, on the whole, is dryly abstract and highly ahistorical.[90] Where Popper does venture to remark casually on the falsifiability of major scientific theories, he either plunges into some logical blunder,[91] or distorts history to fit his rationality theory. If a historian's methodology provides a poor rational reconstruction, he may either misread history in such a way that it coincides with his rational reconstruction, or he will find that the history of science is highly irrational. Popper's respect for great science made him choose the first option, while the disrespectful Feyerabend chose the second.[92] Thus Popper, in his historical asides, tends to turn anomalies into "crucial experiments" and to exaggerate their immediate impact on the history of science. Through his spectacles, great scientists accept refutations readily and this is the primary source of their problems. For instance, in one place he claims that the Michelson-Morley experiment decisively overthrew classical ether theory; he also exaggerates the role of this experiment in the emergence of Einstein's relativity theory.[93] It takes a naïve falsificationist's simplifying spectacles to see, with Popper, Lavoisier's classical experiments as refuting (or as "tending to refute") the phlogiston theory; or to see the Bohr-Kramers-Slater theory as being knocked out with a single blow from Compton; or to see the parity principle "rejected" by "counterexample."[94]

Furthermore, if Popper wants to reconstruct the provisional acceptance of theories as rational on *his* terms, he is bound to ignore the historical fact that most important theories are born refuted and that some laws are further explained, rather than rejected, in spite of the known counterexamples. He tends to turn a blind eye on all anomalies known before the one which later was enthroned as "crucial counterevidence." For instance, he mistakenly thinks that "neither Galileo's nor Kepler's theories were refuted before Newton."[95] The context is significant. Popper holds that the most important pattern of scientific progress is when a crucial experiment leaves one theory *unrefuted* while it refutes a rival one. But, as a matter of fact, in most, if not in all, cases where there are two rival theories, both are known to be simultaneously infected by anomalies. In such situations Popper succumbs to the temptation to simplify the situation into one to which his methodology is applicable.[96]

Falsificationist historiography is then "falsified." But if we apply the same metafalsificationist method to inductivist and conventionalist historiographies, we shall "falsify" them too.

The best logico-epistemological demolition of inductivism is, of course, Popper's; but even if we assumed that inductivism were philosophically (that is, epistemologically and logically) sound, Duhem's historiographical criticism falsifies it. Duhem took the most celebrated *"successes" of inductivist historiography*: Newton's law of gravitation and Ampère's electromagnetic theory. These were said to be two most victorious applications of inductive method. But Duhem (and, following him, Popper and Agassi) showed that they were not. Their analyses illustrate how the inductivist, if he wants to show that the growth of actual science is rational, must falsify actual history out of all recognition.[97] Therefore, if the rationality of science is inductive, actual science is not rational; if it is rational, it is not inductive.[98]

Conventionalism—which, unlike inductivism, is no easy prey to logical or epistemological criticism[99]—can also be historiographically falsified. One can show that the clue to scientific revolutions is not the replacement of cumbersome frameworks by simpler ones.

The Copernican revolution was generally taken to be the *paradigm of conventionalist historiography*, and it is still so regarded in many quarters. For instance Polanyi tells us that Copernicus's "simpler picture" had "striking beauty" and "[justly] carried great powers of conviction."[100] But modern study of primary sources, particularly by Kuhn,[101] has dispelled this myth and presented a clear-cut historiographical refutation of the conventionalist account. It is now agreed that the Copernican system was "at least as complex as the Ptolemaic."[102] But if this is so, then, if the acceptance of Copernican theory was rational, it was not for its superlative objective simplicity.[103]

Thus inductivism, falsificationism and conventionalism can be falsified as rational reconstructions of history with the help of the sort of historiographical criticism I have adduced.[104] Historiographical falsification of inductivism, as we have seen, was initiated already by Duhem and continued by Popper and Agassi. Historiographical criticisms of (naïve) falsificationism have been offered by Polanyi, Kuhn, Feyerabend and Holton.[105] The most important historiographical criticism of conventionalism is to be found in Kuhn's—already quoted—masterpiece on the Copernican revolution.[106] The upshot of these criticisms is that all these rational reconstructions of history force history of science into the Procrustean bed of their hypocritical morality, thus creating fancy histories, which hinge on mythical "inductive bases," "valid inductive generalizations," "crucial experiments," "great revolutionary simplifications," etc. But critics of falsificationism and conventionalism drew very different conclusions from the falsification of these methodologies than Duhem, Popper and Agassi did from their own falsification of inductivism. Polanyi (and, seemingly, Holton) concluded that while proper, rational scientific appraisal can be made in *particular* cases, there can be no *general* theory of scientific rationality.[107] *All* methodologies, *all* rational reconstructions can be historiographically "falsified": science *is* rational, but its rationality cannot be subsumed under the general laws of any methodology.[108] Feyerabend, on the other hand, concluded that not only can there be no general theory of scientific rationality but also that there is no such thing as scientific rationality.[109] Thus Polanyi swung towards conservative authoritarianism, while Feyerabend swung towards sceptical anarchism. Kuhn came up with a highly original vision of irrationally changing rational authority.[110]

Although, as it transpires from this section, I have high regard for Polanyi's, Feyerabend's and Kuhn's criticisms of extant ("internalist") theories of method, I drew a conclusion completely different from theirs. I decided to look for an improved methodology which offers a better *rational* reconstruction of science.

Feyerabend and Kuhn immediately tried to "falsify" my improved methodology in turn.[111] I soon had to discover that, at least in the sense described in the present section, my methodology too—and any methodology whatsoever—*can* be "falsified," for the simple reason that no set of human judgments is completely rational and thus no rational reconstruction can ever coincide with actual history.[112]

This recognition led me to propose a new *constructive* criterion by which methodologies *qua* rational reconstructions of history might be appraised.

B. The Methodology of Historiographical Research Programmes. History—to Varying Degrees—Corroborates Its Rational Reconstructions

I should like to present my proposal in two stages. First, I shall amend slightly the falsificationist historiographical metacriterion just discussed, and then replace it altogether with a better one.

First, the slight amendment. If a universal rule clashes with a particular "normative basic judgment," one should allow the scientific community time to ponder the clash: they may give up their particular judgment and submit to the general rule. "Second-order"—historiographical—falsifications must not be rushed any more than "first-order"—scientific—ones.[113]

Secondly, since we have abandoned naïve falsificationism in *method*, why should we stick to it in *metamethod*? We can easily replace it with a methodology of scientific research programmes of second order, or if you wish, a methodology of historiographical research programmes.

While maintaining that a theory of rationality has to try to organize basic value judgments in universal, coherent frameworks, we do not have to reject such a framework immediately merely because of some anomalies or other inconsistencies. We should, of course, insist that a good rationality theory must anticipate further basic value judgments unexpected in the light of its predecessors or that it must even lead to the revision of previously held basic value judgments.[114] We then reject a rationality theory only for a better one, for one which, in this "quasi-empirical" sense, represents a *progressive shift* in the sequence of research programmes of rational reconstructions. Thus this new—more lenient—metacriterion enables us to compare rival logics of discovery and discern growth in "metascientific"—methodological—knowledge.

For instance, Popper's theory of scientific rationality need not be rejected simply because it is "falsified" by some actual "basic judgments" of leading scientists. Moreover, on our new criterion, Popper's demarcation criterion clearly represents progress over its justificationist predecessors, and in particular, over inductivism. For, contrary to these predecessors, it rehabilitated the scientific status of falsified theories like phlogiston theory, thus reversing a value judgment which had expelled the latter from the history of science proper into the history of irrational beliefs.[115] Also, it successfully rehabilitated the Bohr-Kramers-Slater theory.[116] In the light of most justificationist theories of rationality the history of science is, at its best, a history of *prescientific* preludes to some *future* history of science.[117] Popper's methodology enabled the historian to interpret more of the *actual* basic value judgments in the history of science as rational: in *this* normative-historiographical sense Popper's theory constituted progress. In the light of better rational reconstructions of science one can always reconstruct more of actual great science as rational.[118]

I hope that my modification of Popper's logic of discovery will be seen, in turn—on the criterion I specified—as yet a further step forward. For it seems to offer a coherent account of *more* old, isolated basic value judgments; moreover, it has led to new and, at least for the justificationist or naïve falsificationist, surprising basic value judgments. For instance, according to Popper's theory, it was irrational to retain and further elaborate Newton's gravitational theory after the discovery of Mercury's anomalous perihelion; or again, it was irrational to develop Bohr's old quantum theory based on inconsistent foundations. From my point of view these were perfectly rational developments: some rearguard actions in the defence of defeated programmes—even after the so-called "crucial experiments"—are perfectly rational. Thus my methodology leads to the reversal of those historiographical judgments which deleted these rearguard actions both from inductivist and from falsificationist party histories.[119]

Indeed, this methodology confidently predicts that where the falsificationist sees the instant defeat of a theory through a simple battle with some fact, the historian will detect a complicated war of attrition, starting long before, and ending after, the alleged "crucial experiment"; and where the falsificationist sees consistent and unrefuted theories, it predicts the existence of hordes of known anomalies in research programmes progressing on possibly inconsistent foundations.[120] Where the conventionalist sees the clue to the victory of a theory over its predecessor in the former's intuitive simplicity, this methodology predicts that it will be found that victory was due to empirical degeneration in the old and empirical progress in the new programme.[121] Where Kuhn and Feyerabend see irrational change, I predict that the historian will be able to show that there has been rational change. The methodology of research programmes thus predicts (or, if you wish, "postdicts") novel historical facts, unexpected in the light of extant (internal and external) historiographies and these predictions will, I hope, be corroborated by historical research. If they are, then the methodology of scientific research programmes will itself constitute a progressive problem-shift.

Thus progress in the theory of scientific rationality is marked by discoveries of novel historical facts, by the reconstruction of a growing bulk of value-impregnated history as rational.[122] In other words, the theory of scientific rationality progresses if it constitutes a "progressive" historiographical research programme. I need not say that no such historiographical research programme can or should explain *all* history of science as rational: even the greatest scientists make false steps and fail in their judgment. Because of this *rational reconstructions remain for ever submerged in an ocean of anomalies. These anomalies will eventually have to be explained either by some better rational reconstruction or by some "external" empirical theory.*

This approach does not advocate a cavalier attitude to the "basic normative judgments" of the scientist. "Anomalies" may be rightly ignored by the internalist *qua* internalist and relegated to external history only as long as the internalist historiographical research programme is *progressing*; or if a supplementary empirical externalist historiographical programme absorbs them *progressively*. But if in the light of a rational reconstruction the history of science is seen as increasingly irrational *without* a progressive externalist explanation (such as an explanation of the degeneration of science in terms of political or religious terror, or of an anti-scientific ideological climate, or of the rise of a new parasitic class of pseudo-scientists with vested interests in rapid "university expansion"), then historiographical innovation, proliferation of historiographical theories, is vital. Just as scientific progress is possible even if one never gets rid of scientific anomalies, progress in rational historiography is also possible even if one never gets rid of historiographical anomalies. The rationalist historian need not be disturbed by the fact that actual history is more than, and, on occasions, even different from, internal history, and that he may have to relegate the explanation of such anomalies to external history. But this unfalsifiability of internal history does not render it immune to constructive, but only to negative, criticism—just as the unfalsifiability of a scientific research programme does not render it immune to constructive, but only to negative, criticism.

Of course, one can criticise internal history only by making the historian's (usually latent) methodology explicit, showing how it functions as a historiographical research programme. Historiographical criticism frequently succeeds in destroying much of fashionable externalism. An "impressive," "sweeping," "far-reaching" external explanation is usually the hallmark of a weak methodological substructure; and, in turn, the hallmark of a relatively weak internal history (in terms of which most actual history is either inexplicable or anomalous) is that it leaves too much to be explained by external history. When a better rationality theory is produced, internal history may expand and reclaim ground from external history. The competition, however, is not as open in such cases as when two rival scientific research programmes compete. Externalist historiographical programmes which supplement internal histories based on naïve methodologies (whether aware or unaware of the fact) are likely either to degenerate quickly or never even to get off the ground, for the simple reason that they set out to offer psychological or sociological "explanations" of methodologically induced fantasies rather than of (more rationally interpreted) historical facts. Once an externalist account uses, whether consciously or not, a naïve methodology (which can so easily creep into its "descriptive" language), it turns into a fairy tale which, for all its apparent scholarly sophistication, will collapse under historiographical scrutiny.

Agassi already indicated how the poverty of inductivist history opened the door to the wild speculations of vulgar Marxists.[123] His falsificationist historiography, in turn, flings the door wide open to those trendy "sociologists of knowledge" who try to explain the further (possibly unsuccessful) development of a theory "falsified" by a "crucial experiment" as the manifestation of the irrational, wicked, reactionary resistance by established authority to enlightened revolutionary innovation.[124] But in the light of the methodology of scientific research programmes such rearguard skirmishes are perfectly explicable *internally*: where some externalists see power struggle, sordid personal controversy, the rationalist historian will frequently find rational discussion.[125]

An interesting example of how a poor theory of rationality may impoverish history is the treatment of degenerating problemshifts by historiographical positivists.[126] Let us imagine for instance that in spite of the objectively progressing astronomical research programmes, the astronomers are suddenly all gripped by a feeling of Kuhnian "crisis," and then they all are converted, by an irresistible *Gestalt*-switch, to astrology. I would regard this catastrophe as a horrifying *problem*, to be accounted for by some empirical externalist explanation. But not a Kuhnian. All he sees is a "crisis" followed by a mass conversion effect in the scientific community: an ordinary revolution. Nothing is left as problematic and unexplained.[127] The Kuhnian psychological epiphenomena of "crisis" and "conversion" can accompany either objectively progressive or objectively degenerating changes, either revolutions or counter-revolutions. But this fact falls outside Kuhn's framework. Such historiographical anomalies cannot be formulated, let alone be progressively absorbed, by his historiographical research programme, in which there is no way of distinguishing between, say, a "crisis" and "degenerating problem-shift." But such anomalies might even be predicted by an externalist historiographical theory based on the methodology of scientific research programmes that would specify social conditions under which degenerating research programmes may achieve socio-psychological victory.

C. Against Aprioristic and Anti-theoretical Approaches to Methodology

Finally, let us contrast the theory of rationality here discussed with the strictly aprioristic (or, more precisely, "Euclidean") and with the anti-theoretical approaches.[128]

"Euclidean" methodologies lay down *a priori general rules* for scientific appraisal. This approach is most powerfully represented today by Popper. In Popper's view there must be the constitutional authority of an *immutable statute law* (laid down in his demarcation criterion) to distinguish between good and bad science.

Some eminent philosophers, however, ridicule the idea of statute law, the possibility of any valid demarcation. According to Oakeshott and Polanyi there must be—and can be—no statute law at all: only case law. They may also argue that even if one mistakenly allowed for statute law, statute law too would need authoritative interpreters. I think that Oakeshott's and Polanyi's position has a great deal of truth in it. After all, one must admit (*pace* Popper) that until now all the "laws" proposed by the apriorist philosophers of science have turned out to be wrong in the light of the verdicts of the best scientists. Up to the present day it has been the scientific standards, as applied "instinctively" by the scientific *élite* in *particular* cases, which have constituted the main—although not the exclusive—yardstick of the philosopher's *universal* laws. But if so, methodological progress, at least as far as the most advanced sciences are concerned, still lags behind common scientific wisdom. Is it not then *hubris* to try to impose some *a priori* philosophy of science on the most advanced sciences? Is it not *hubris* to demand that if, say, Newtonian or Einsteinean science turns out to have violated Bacon's, Carnap's or Popper's *a priori* rules of the game, the business of science should be started anew?

I think it is. And, indeed, the methodology of historiographical research programmes implies a pluralistic system of authority, partly because the wisdom of the scientific jury and its case law has not been, and cannot be, fully articulated by the philosopher's statute law, and partly because the philosopher's statute law may occasionally be right when the scientists' judgment fails. I disagree, therefore, both with those philosophers of science who have taken it for granted that general scientific standards are immutable and reason can recognise them *a priori*,[129] and with those who have thought that the light of reason illuminates only particular cases. The methodology of historiographical research programmes specifies ways both for the philosopher of science to learn from the historian of science and *vice versa*.

But this two-way traffic need not always be balanced. The statute law approach should become much more important when a tradition degenerates[130] or a new bad tradition is founded.[131] In such cases statute law may thwart the authority of the corrupted case law, and slow down or even reverse the process of degeneration.[132] When a scientific school degenerates into pseudo-science, it may be worthwhile to force a methodological debate in the hope that working scientists will learn more from it than philosophers (just as when ordinary language degenerates into, say, journalese, it may be worthwhile to invoke the rules of grammar).[133]

D. Conclusion

In this paper I have proposed a "historical" method for the evaluation of rival methodologies. The arguments were primarily addressed to the philosopher of science and aimed at showing how he can—and should—learn from the history of science. But the same arguments also imply that the historian of science must, in turn, pay serious attention to the philosophy of science and decide upon which methodology he will base his internal history. I hope to have offered some strong arguments for the following theses. First, each methodology of science determines a characteristic (and sharp) demarcation between (primary) internal history and (secondary) external history and, secondly, both historians and philosophers of science must make the best of the critical interplay between internal and external factors.

Let me finally remind the reader of my favourite—and by now well-worn—joke that history of science is frequently a caricature of its rational reconstructions; that rational reconstructions are frequently caricatures of actual history; and that some histories of science are caricatures both of actual history and of its rational reconstructions.[134] This paper, I think, enables me to add: *Quod erat demonstandum.*

NOTES

* Earlier versions of this paper were read and criticized by Colin Howson, Alan Musgrave, John Watkins, Elie Zahar, and especially John Worrall.

The present paper further develops some of the theses proposed in my (1970). I have tried, at the cost of some repetition, to make it self-contained.

1. "Internal history" is usually defined as intellectual history, "external history" as social history (cf. e.g. Kuhn [1968]). My unorthodox, new demarcation between "internal" and "external" history constitutes a considerable problem-shift and may sound dogmatic. But my definitions form the hard core of a historiographical research programme; their evaluation is part and parcel of the evaluation of the fertility of the whole programme.

2. This is an all-important shift in the problem of normative philosophy of science. The term "norma-tive" no longer means rules for arriving at solutions, but merely directions for the appraisal of solutions already there. Thus *methodology* is separated from *heuristics*, rather as value judgments are from ought statements. (I owe this analogy to John Watkins.)

3. This profusion of synonyms has proved to be rather confusing.

4. The epistemological significance of scientific "acceptance" and "rejection" is, as we shall see, far from being the same in the four methodologies to be discussed.

5. "*Neo*-inductivism" demands only (provably) highly probable generalizations. In what follows I shall only discuss classical inductivism; but the watered down neo-inductivist variant can be similarly dealt with.

6. Cf. Section IE of the present essay.

7. For a detailed discussion of inductivist (and, in general, justificationist) criticism cf. my (1966).

8. I am now using the term "paradigm" in its pre-Kuhnian sense.

9. This compatibility was pointed out by Agassi on pp. 23–27 of his (1963). But did he not point out the analogous compatibility within his own falsificationist historiography; cf. Section IC of the present essay.

10. Cf. e.g. Bernal (1965), p. 377.

11. Some logical positivists belonged to this set: one recalls Hempel's horror at Popper's casual praise of certain external metaphysical influences upon science (Hempel, [1937]).

12. When German obscurantists scoff at "positivism," they frequently mean radical internalism, and in particular, radical inductivism.

13. For what I here call *revolutionary conventionalism*, see my (1970), pp. 105–106 and 187–189.

14. I mainly discuss here only one version of revolutionary conventionalism, the one which Agassi, in his (1966), called "unsophisticated": the one which assumes that factual propositions—unlike pigeonhole systems—can be "proven." (Duhem, for instance, draws no clear distinction between facts and factual propositions.)

15. It is important to note that most conventionalists are reluctant to give up inductive generalizations. They distinguish between the "*floor of facts*," the "*floor of laws*" (i.e. inductive generalizations from "facts") and the "*floor of theories*" (or of pigeonhole systems) which classify, conveniently, both facts and inductive laws. (Whewell, the conservative conventionalist and Duhem, the revolutionary conventionalist differ less than most people imagine.)

16. One may call such metaphysical principles "inductive principles." For an "inductive principle" which—roughly speaking—makes Popper's "degree of corroboration" (a conventionalist appraisal) the measure of Popper's verisimilitude (truth-content minus falsity-content) see my (1968a), pp. 390–408 and my (1971a), section 2. (Another widely spread "inductive principle" may be formulated like this: "What the group of trained—or up-to-date, or suitably purged—scientists decide to *accept* as 'true,' is true.")

17. Most historical accounts of the Copernican revolution are written from the conventionalist point of view. Few claimed that Copernicus's theory was an "inductive generalization" from some "factual discovery"; or that it was proposed as a bold theory to replace the Ptolemaic theory which had been "refuted" by some celebrated "crucial" experiment.

   For a further discussion of the historiography of the Copernican revolution, cf. my (1971b).

18. For example, for non-inductivist historians Newton's "*Hypotheses non fingo*" represents a major problem. Duhem, who unlike most historians did not over-indulge in Newton-worship, dismissed Newton's inductivist methodology as logical nonsense; but Koyré, whose many strong points did not include logic, devoted long chapters to the "hidden depths" of Newton's muddle.

19. *In this paper I use this term to stand exclusively for one version of falsificationism, namely for "naïve methodological falsificationism," as defined in my* (1970), *pp.* 93–116.

20. Since in his methodology the *concept* of intuitive simplicity has no place, Popper was able to use the term "simplicity" for "degree of falsifiability." But there is more to simplicity than this: cf. my (1970), pp. 131ff.

21. For a discussion cf. my (1970), especially pp. 99–100.

22. For further discussion cf. pp. 108–109.

23. Agassi (1963).

24. An experimental discovery is *a chance discovery in the objective sense* if it is neither a confirming nor a refuting instance of some theory in the objective body of knowledge of the time; it is *a chance discovery in the subjective sense* if it is made (or recognised) by the discoverer neither as a confirming nor as a refuting instance of some theory he personally had entertained at the time.

25. Agassi (1963), pp. 64–74.

26. Within the Popperian circle, it was Agassi and Watkins who particularly emphasized the importance of unfalsifiable or barely testable "*empirical*" theories in providing *external* stimulus to later properly *scientific* developments. (Cf. Agassi, [1964] and Watkins, [1958]). This idea, of course, is already there in Popper's (1934) and (1960). Cf. my (1970), p. 184; but the new formulation of the

difference between their approach and mine which I am going to give in this paper will, I hope, be much clearer.

27. Popper occasionally—and Feyerabend systematically—stressed the catalytic (*external*) role of alternative theories in devising so-called "crucial experiments." But alternatives are not merely catalysts, which can be later removed in the rational reconstruction, they are *necessary* parts of the falsifying process. Cf. Popper (1940) and Feyerabend (1965); but cf. also Lakatos (1970), especially p. 121, footnote 4.

28. Cf. Popper (1968a) and (1968b).

29. The terms "progressive" and "degenerating problem-shifts," "research programmes," and "superseding" will be crudely defined in what follows—for more elaborate definitions see my (1968b) and especially my (1970).

30. Popper does not permit this: "There is a vast difference between my views and conventionalism. I hold that what characterises the empirical method is just this: our conventions determine the acceptance of the *singular*, not of the *universal* statements" (Popper, [1934], section 30).

31. The falsificationist hotly denies this: "Learning from experience is learning from a refuting instance. The refuting instance then becomes a problematic instance." (Agassi [1964], p. 201). In his (1969) Agassi attributed to Popper the statement that "we learn from experience by refutations" (p. 169), and adds that according to Popper one can learn *only* from refutation but not from corroboration (p. 167). Feyerabend, even in his (1969), says that "*negative instances suffice in science.*" But these remarks indicate a very one-sided theory of learning from experience. (Cf. my [1970], p. 121, footnote 1, and p. 123.)

32. Duhem, as a staunch positivist within philosophy of science, would, no doubt, exclude most "metaphysics" as unscientific and would not allow it to have any influence on science proper.

33. Cf. my (1968a), pp. 383–386, my (1968b), pp. 162–167, and my (1970), pp. 116ff. and pp. 155ff.

34. Cf. Popper (1934), section 85.

35. Cf. Duhem (1906), part II, chapter 6, section 10.

36. In fact, I define a research programme as degenerating even if it anticipates novel facts but does so in a patched-up development rather than by a coherent, pre-planned positive heuristic. I distinguish three types of *ad hoc* auxiliary hypotheses: those which have no excess empirical content over their predecessor ("*ad hoc$_1$*"), those which do have such excess content but none of it is corroborated ("*ad hoc$_2$*") and finally those which are not *ad hoc* in these two senses but do not form an integral part of the positive heuristic ("*ad hoc$_3$*"). Examples for an *ad hoc$_1$* hypothesis are provided by the linguistic prevarications of pseudo-sciences, or by the conventionalist stratagems discussed in my (1963–64), like "monsterbarring," "exceptionbarring," "monsteradjustment," etc. A famous example of an *ad hoc$_2$* hypothesis is provided by the Lorentz-Fitzgerald contraction hypothesis; an example of an *ad hoc$_3$* hypothesis is Planck's first correction of the Lummer-Pringsheim formula (also cf. p. 103). Some of the cancerous growth in contemporary social "sciences" consists of a cobweb of such *ad hoc$_3$* hypotheses, as shown by Meehl and Lykken. (For references, cf. my [1970], p. 175, footnotes 2 and 3.)

37. The rivalry of two research programmes is, of course, a protracted process during which it is rational to work in either (*or, if one can, in both*). The latter pattern becomes important, for instance, when one of the rival programmes is vague and its opponents wish to develop it in a sharper form in order to show up its weakness. Newton elaborated Cartesian vortex theory in order to show that it is inconsistent with Kepler's laws. (Simultaneous work on rival programmes, of course, undermines Kuhn's thesis of the psychological incommensurability of rival paradigms.)

    The progress of one programme is a vital factor in the degeneration of its rival. If programme P_1 constantly produces "novel facts" these, by definition, will be anomalies for the rival programme P_2. If P_2 accounts for these novel facts only in an *ad hoc* way, it is degenerating by definition. Thus the more P_1 progresses, the more difficult it is for P_2 to progress.

38. Cf. especially my (1970), pp. 120–121.

39. Cf. especially my (1968a), p. 385 and (1970), p. 121.

40. For instance, a rival theory, which acts as an *external* catalyst for the Popperian falsification of a theory, here becomes an *internal* factor. In Popper's (and Feyerabend's) reconstruction such a theory, after the falsification of the theory under test, can be removed from the rational reconstruction; in my reconstruction it has to stay within the internal history lest the falsification be undone. (Cf. note 27.)

  Another important consequence is the difference between Popper's discussion of the Duhem-Quine argument and mine; cf. on the one hand Popper (1934), last paragraph of section 18 and section 19, footnote 1; Popper (1957b), pp. 131–133; Popper (1963a), p. 112, footnote 26, pp. 238–239 and p. 243; and on the other hand, my (1970), pp. 184–189.

41. For the falsificationist this is a repulsive idea; cf. e.g. Agassi (1963), pp. 48ff.

42. Feyerabend seems now to deny that even this is a possibility; cf. his (1970a) and especially (1970b) and (1971).

43. I use "verisimilitude" here in Popper's technical sense, as the difference between the truth content and falsity content of a theory. Cf. his (1963a), chapter 10.

44. For a more general discussion of this problem, cf. pp. 108–109.

45. Also cf. p. 94, 96, 98, 106, 120.

46. The reader should remember that in this paper I discuss only naïve falsificationism; cf. note 19.

47. This is Kuhn's comment on Galileo's successful *prediction* of the phases of Venus (Kuhn, [1957], p. 224). Like Mill and Keynes before him, Kuhn cannot understand why the historic order of theory and evidence should count, and he cannot see the importance of the fact that Copernicans *predicted* the phases of Venus, while Tychonians only explained them by *post hoc* adjustments. Indeed, since he does not see the importance of the fact, he does not even care to mention it.

48. Cf. note 36.

49. For a statement of this position and an interesting critical discussion cf. Polanyi (1951), pp. 4ff and 78ff.

50. Cf. Popper (1963b) and Musgrave (1969).

51. This was illustrated convincingly, by Elkana, for the case of the so-called simultaneous discovery of the conservation of energy; cf. his (1971).

52. Also cf. note 47.

53. For the Mertonian brand of functionalism—as Alan Musgrave pointed out to me—priority disputes constitute a *prima facie* disfunction and therefore an anomaly for which Merton has been labouring to give a general socio-psychological explanation. (Cf. e.g. Merton 1957, 1963 and 1969.) According to Merton "scientific *knowledge* is not the richer or the poorer for having credit given where credit is due: it is the social *institution* of science and individual men of science that would suffer from repeated failures to allocate credit justly" (Merton, [1957], p. 648). But Merton overdoes his point: in important cases (like in some of Galileo's priority fights) there was more at stake than institutional interests: the problem was whether the Copernican research programme was progressive or not. (Of course, not all priority disputes have scientific relevance. For instance, the priority dispute between Adams and Leverrier about who was first to discover Neptune had no such relevance: whoever discovered it, the discovery strengthened the same (Newtonian) programme. In such cases Merton's external explanation may well be true.)

54. Kuhn (1970), p. 239; my italics.

55. Feyerabend (1970), p. 215.

56. Ibid.

57. Cf. note 2.

58. I do, of course, *not* claim that such decisions are necessarily uncontroversial. In such decisions one has to use also one's *common sense*. Common sense (that is, judgment in *particular* cases which is not made according to mechanical rules but only follows general principles which leave some *Spielraum*) plays a role in all brands of non-mechanical methodologies. The Duhemian conventionalist needs common sense to decide when a theoretical framework has become sufficiently cumbersome to be replaced by a "simpler" one. The Popperian falsificationist needs common sense to decide when a

basic statement is to be "accepted," or to which premise the *modus tollens* is to be directed. (Cf. my [1970], pp. 106ff.) But neither Duhem, nor Popper gives a blank cheque to "common sense." They give very definite guidance. The Duhemian judge directs the jury of common sense to agree on comparative simplicity; the Popperian judge directs the jury to look out primarily for, and agree upon, accepted basic statements which clash with accepted theories. My judge directs the jury to agree on appraisals of progressive and degenerating research programmes. But, for example, there may be conflicting views about whether an accepted basic statement expresses a *novel* fact or not. Cf. my (1970), p. 156.

Although it is important to reach agreement on such verdicts, there must also be the possibility of appeal. In such appeals inarticulated common sense is questioned, articulated and criticised. (The criticism may even turn from a criticism of law interpretation into a criticism of the law itself.)

59. Most conventionalists have also an intermediate inductive layer of "laws" between facts and theories; cf. note 15.

60. The proposition "the Proutian programme was carried through" looks like a "factual" proposition. But there are no "factual" propositions: the phrase only came into ordinary language from dogmatic empiricism. *Scientific "factual" propositions* are theory-laden: the theories involved are "observational theories." *Historiographical "factual" propositions* are also theory-laden: the theories involved are methodological theories. In the decision about the truth-value of the "factual" proposition, "the Proutian programme was carried through," two methodological theories are involved. First, the theory that the units of scientific appraisal are research programmes; secondly, some *specific* theory of how to judge whether a programme was "in fact" carried through. For all these considerations a Popperian internal historian will not need to take any interest whatsoever in the *persons* involved, or in their beliefs about their own activities.

61. The "first world" is that of matter, the "second" the world of feelings, beliefs, consciousness, the "third" the world of objective knowledge, articulated in propositions. This is an age-old and vitally important trichotomy; its leading contemporary proponent is Popper. Cf. Popper (1968a), (1968b) and Musgrave (1969) and (1971a).

62. Of course what, in this context, constitutes "false belief" (or "false consciousness"), depends on the rationality theory of the critic: cf. pp. 94, 96 and 98. But no rationality theory can ever succeed in leading to "true consciousness."

63. If the publication of Bohr's programme had been delayed by a few years, further speculation might even have led to the spin problem without the previous observation of the anomalous Zeeman effect. Indeed, Compton raised the problem in the context of the Bohrian programme in his (1919).

64. I first applied this expositional device in my (1963–64); I used it again in giving a detailed account of the Proutian and the Bohrian programmes; cf. my (1970), pp. 138, 140, 146. This practice was criticised at the 1969 Minneapolis conference by some historians. McMullin, for instance, claimed that this presentation may illuminate a *methodology*, but certainly not real *history*: the text tells the reader what ought to have happened and the footnotes what in fact happened (cf. McMullin, [1970]). Kuhn's criticism of my exposition ran essentially on the same lines: he thought that it was a specifically *philosophical* exposition: "a *historian* would not include *in his narrative* a factual report which he knows to be false. If he had done so, he would be so sensitive to the offence that he could not conceivably compose a footnote calling attention to it." (Cf. Kuhn, [1970], p. 256.)

65. Cf. L. P. Williams (1970).

66. Perhaps I should emphasize the difference between on the one hand, *inductivist historiography of science*, according to which *science* proceeds through discovery of hard facts (in nature) and (possibly) inductive generalizations, and, on the other hand, the *inductivist theory of historiography of science* according to which *historiography of science* proceeds through discovery of hard facts (in history of science) and (possibly) inductive generalizations. "Bold conjectures," "crucial negative experiments," and even "progressive and degenerating research programmes" may be regarded as "hard historical facts" by some inductivist historiographers. One of the weaknesses of Agassi's

406 • THE GROWTH OF SCIENTIFIC KNOWLEDGE

(1963) is that he omitted to emphasize this distinction between scientific and historiographical inductivism.

67. Cf. Popper (1957b), section 31.

68. This thesis implies that the work of those 'externalists' (mostly trendy 'sociologists of science') who claim to do social history of some scientific discipline without having mastered the discipline itself, and its internal history, is worthless. Also cf. Musgrave (1971a).

69. Unfortunately there is only one single word in most languages to denote history₁ (the set of historical events) and history₂ (a set of historical propositions). Any history₂ is a theory and value-laden reconstruction of history₁.

70. That is, a hypothesis h is scientific only if there is a number q such that $p(h,e) = q$ where e is the available evidence and $p(h,e) = q$ can be *proved*: It is irrelevant whether p is a Carnapian confirmation function or a Popperian corroboration function as long as $p(h,e) = q$ is allegedly proved. (Popper's third note on corroboration, of course, is only a curious slip which is out of tune with his philosophy: cf. my (1968a), pp. 411–17.)

   Probabilism has never generated a programme of historiographical reconstruction; it has never emerged from grappling—unsuccessfully—with the very problems it created. As an epistemological programme it has been degenerating for a long time; as a historiographical programme it never even started.

71. Popper (1934), sections 11 and 85. Also cf. the comment in my (1971a), footnote 13.

   The methodology of research programmes too is, in the first instance, defined as a game; cf. especially pp. 99–100.

72. This whole problem area is the subject of my (1968a), pp. 390ff, but especially of my (1971a).

73. Cf. Popper (1934), sections 4 and 11. Popper's definition of science is, of course, his celebrated "demarcation criterion."

74. For an excellent discussion of the distinction between nominalism and realism (or, as Popper prefers to call it, "essentialism") in the theory of definitions, cf. Popper (1945), vol. 2, chapter 11, and (1963a), p. 20.

75. Popper (1934), section 11.

76. Ibid.

77. Popper (1934), section 4. But Popper, in his *Logik der Forschung* never specifies a *purpose* of the game of science that would go beyond what is contained in its rules. The thesis that the *aim* of science is *truth*, occurs only in his writings since 1957. All that he says in his *Logik der Forschung* is that the quest for truth may be a psychological *motive* of scientists. For a detailed discussion cf. my (1971a).

78. This flaw is the more serious since Popper himself has expressed qualifications about his criterion. For instance in his (1963a) he describes "dogmatism," that is, treating anomalies as a kind of "background noise," as something that is "to some extent necessary" (p. 49). But on the next page he identifies this "dogmatism" with "pseudo-science." Is then pseudo-science "to some extent necessary"? Also, cf. my (1970), p. 177, footnote 3.

78a. Cf. Popper (1963), pp. 33–37.

79. Popper (1934), section 29.

80. This approach, of course, does not imply that we *believe* that the scientists "basic judgments" are unfailingly rational; it only means that we *accept* them in order to criticise universal definitions of science. (If we were to add that no such *universal* definition has been found and no such *universal* definition will ever be found, the stage would be set for Polanyi's conception of the lawless closed autocracy of science.)

   My metacriterion may be seen as a "quasi-empirical" self-application of Popperian falsificationism. I introduced this "quasi-empiricalness" earlier in the context of mathematical philosophy. We may abstract from *what* flows in the logical channels of a deductive system, whether it is something certain or something fallible, whether it is truth and falsehood or probability and improbability, or even moral or scientific desirability and undesirability: it is the *how* of the flow which decides whether the system is negativist, "quasi-empirical," dominated by *modus tollens* or whether it is justification-ist, "quasi-Euclidean," dominated by *modus ponens*. (Cf. my [1967].) This "quasi-empirical" approach may be applied to *any* kind of normative knowledge: Watkins has already applied it to ethics in his (1963) and (1967). But now I prefer another approach: cf. note 122.

81. It may be noted that this metacriterion does not have to be construed as psychological, or "naturalis-tic" in Popper's sense. (Cf. his [1934], section 10.) The definition of the "scientific *élite*" is not simply an empirical matter.

82. Popper (1963a), p. 38, footnote 3; my italics. This, of course, is equivalent to his celebrated "demarcation criterion" between (internal, rationally reconstructed) science and nonscience (or "metaphysics"). The latter may be (externally) "influential" and has to be branded as pseudo-science only if it declares itself to be science.

83. Cf. my (1970), pp. 100–101.

84. Cf. e.g. his (1934), section 18.

85. Cf. my (1970), especially pp. 135ff.

86. Ibid., pp. 138ff.

87. Cf. Popper (1934), section 24.

88. Cf. my (1970), especially pp. 140ff.

89. In general Popper stubbornly overestimates the immediate striking force of purely negative criticism. "Once a mistake, or a contradiction, is pinpointed, there can be no verbal evasion: it can be proved, and that is that" (Popper, [1959], p. 394). He adds: "Frege did not try evasive manoeuvres when he received Russell's criticism." But of course he did. (Cf. Frege's *Postscript* to the second edition of his *Grundgesetze*.)

90. Interestingly, as Kuhn points out, "a consistent interest in historical problems and a willingness to engage in original historical research distinguishes the men [Popper] has trained from the members of any other current school in the philosophy of science" (Kuhn [1970], p. 236). For a hint at a possible explanation of the apparent discrepancy cf. note 129.

91. For instance, he claims that a perpetual motion machine would "refute" (on his terms) the first law of thermodynamics ([1934], section 15). But how can one interpret, on Popper's own terms, the statement that "*K* is a perpetual motion machine" as a "basic," that is, as a spatio-*temporally* singular statement?

92. I am referring to Feyerabend's (1970) and (1971).

93. Cf. Popper (1934), section 30 and Popper (1945), vol. 2, pp. 220–21. He stressed that Einstein's problem was how to account for experiments "refuting" classical physics and he "did not . . . set out to criticise our conceptions of space and time." But Einstein certainly did. His Machian criticism of our concepts of space and time, and, in particular his operationalist criticism of the concept of simultaneity played an important role in his thinking.

I discussed the role of the Michelson-Morley experiments at some length in my (1970).

Popper's competence in physics would never, of course, have allowed him to distort the history of relativity theory as much as Beveridge, who wanted to persuade economists to an empirical approach by setting them Einstein as an example. According to Beveridge's falsificationist reconstruction, Einstein "started [in his work on gravitation] from facts [which refuted Newton's theory, that is,] from the movements of the planet Mercury, the unexplained aberrancies of the moon" (Beveridge, [1937]). Of course, Einstein's work on gravitation grew out from a "creative shift" in the positive heuristic of his special relativity programme, and certainly not from pondering over Mercury's anomalous peri-helion or the moon's devious, unexplained aberrancies.

94. Popper (1963a), pp. 220, 239, 242–243 and (1963b), p. 965. Popper, of course, is left with the problem why "counterexamples" (that is, anomalies) are not recognized immediately as causes for rejection. For instance, he points out that in the case of the breakdown of parity "there had been many observations—that is, photographs of particle tracks—from which we might have read off the result, but the observations had been either ignored or misinterpreted" ([1963b], p. 965). Popper's—

external—explanation seems to be that scientists have not yet learned to be sufficiently critical and revolutionary. But is not it a better—and internal—explanation that the anomalies *had* to be ignored until some progressive alternative theory was offered which turned the counterexamples into examples?

95. Ibid., p. 246.
96. As I mentioned, one Popperian, Agassi, did write a book on the historiography of science (Agassi, [1963]). The book has some incisive critical sections flogging inductivist historiography, but he ends up by replacing inductivist mythology by falsificationist mythology. For Agassi *only* those facts have scientific (internal) significance which can be expressed in propositions which conflict with some extant theory: only their discovery deserves the honorific title "factual discovery"; factual propositions which *follow from* rather than *conflict with* known theories are irrelevant; so are factual propositions which are *independent of* them. If some valued factual discovery in the history of science is known as a confirming instance or chance discovery, Agassi boldly predicts that on *close* investigation they will turn out to be refuting instances, and he offers five case-studies to support his claim (pp. 60–74). Alas, on *closer* investigation it turns out that Agassi got wrong all the five examples which he adduced as confirming instances of his historiographical theory. In fact all the five examples (in our normative metafalsificationist sense) "falsify" his historiography.
97. Cf. Duhem (1906), Popper (1948) and (1957), Agassi (1963).
98. Of course, an inductivist may have the temerity to claim that genuine science has not yet started and may write a history of extant science as a history of bias, superstition and false belief.
99. Cf. Popper (1934), section 19.
100. Cf. Polanyi (1951), p. 70.
101. Kuhn (1957). Also cf. Price (1959).
102. Cohen (1960), p. 61. Bernal, in his (1954), says that "[Copernicus's] reasons for [his] revolutionary change were essentially philosophic and aesthetic [that is, in the light of conventionalism, scientific];" but in later editions he changes his mind: "[Copernicus's] reasons were mystical rather than scientific."
103. For a more detailed sketch cf. my (1971b).
104. Other types of criticism of methodologies may, of course, be easily devised. We may, for instance, apply the standards of each methodology (not only falsificationism) to itself. The result, for most methodologies, will be equally destructive: inductivism cannot be proved inductively, simplicity will be seen as hopelessly complex. (For the latter cf. end of note 106.)
105. Cf. Polanyi (1958), Kuhn (1962), Holton (1969), Feyerabend (1970) and (1971). I should also add Lakatos (1963–64), (1968b), and (1970).
106. Kuhn (1957). Such historiographical criticism can easily drive some rationalists into an irrational defence of their favourite falsified rationality theory. Kuhn's historiographical criticism of the simplicity theory of the Copernican revolution shocked the conventionalist historian Richard Hall so much that he published a polemic article in which he singled out and reasserted those aspects of Copernican theory which Kuhn himself had mentioned as possibly having a claim to higher simplicity, and ignored the rest of Kuhn's—valid—argument (Hall, [1970]). No doubt, simplicity can always be defined for *any* pair of theories T_1 and T_2 in such a way that the simplicity of T_1 is greater than that of T_2.

For further discussion of conventionalist historiography cf. my (1971b).
107. Thus Polanyi is a conservative rationalist concerning science, and an "irrationalist" concerning the philosophy of science. But, of course, this meta-"irrationalism" is a perfectly respectable brand of rationalism: to claim that the concept of "scientifically acceptable" cannot be further defined, but only transmitted by the channels of "personal knowledge," does not make one an outright irrationalist, only an outright conservative. Polanyi's position in the philosophy of natural science corresponds closely to Oakeshott's ultra-conservative philosophy of political science. (For references and an excellent criticism of the latter cf. Watkins [1952]). Also cf. section IIC of this essay.

108. Of course, none of the critics were aware of the exact logical character of meta-methodological falsificationism as explained in this section and none of them applied it completely consistently. One of them writes: "At this stage we have not yet developed a general theory of criticism even for scientific theories, let alone for theories of rationality: therefore if we want to falsify methodological falsificationism, we have to do it before having a theory of how to do it" (Lakatos [1970], p. 114).

109. I used the critical machinery developed in this paper against Feyerabend's epistemological anarchism in my (1971b).

110. Kuhn's vision was criticised from many quarters; cf. Shapere (1964 and 1967) Scheffler (1967) and especially the critical comments by Popper, Watkins, Toulmin, Feyerabend and Lakatos—and Kuhn's reply—in Lakatos and Musgrave (1970). But none of these critics applied a systematic *historiographical* criticism to his work. One should also consult Kuhn's 1970 Postscript to the second edition of his (1962) and its review by Musgrave (Musgrave [1971b]).

111. Cf. Feyerabend (1970a, 1970b and 1971); and Kuhn (1970).

112. For instance, one may refer to the actual immediate impact of at least *some* "great" negative crucial experiments, like that of the falsification of the parity principle. Or one may quote the high respect for at least *some* long, pedestrian, trial-and-error procedures which occasionally precede the announcement of a major research programme, which in the light of my methodology is, at best, "immature science." (Cf. my [1970]), p. 175; also cf. L. P. Williams's reference to the history of spectroscopy between 1870 and 1900 in his (1970). Thus the judgment of the scientific élite, on occasions, goes also against *my* universal rules too.

113. There is a certain analogy between this pattern and the occasional appeal procedure of the theoretical scientist against the verdict of the experimental jury; cf. my (1970), pp. 127–31.

114. This latter criterion is analogous to the exceptional "depth" of a theory which clashes with some basic statements available at the time and, at the end, emerges from the clash victoriously. Cf. Popper (1957a). Popper's example was the inconsistency between Kepler's laws and the Newtonian theory which set out to explain them.

115. Conventionalism, of course, had performed this historic role to a great extent before Popper's version of falsificationism.

116. Van der Waerden had thought that the Bohr-Kramers-Slater theory was bad: Popper's theory showed it to be good. Cf. Van der Waerden (1967), p. 13 and Popper (1963a), pp. 242ff; for a critical discussion cf. my (1970), p. 168, footnote 4 and p. 169, footnote 1.

117. The attitude of some modern logicians to the history of mathematics is a typical example; cf. my (1963–64), p. 3.

118. This formulation was suggested to me by my friend Michael Sukale.

119. Cf. my (1970), section 3(c).

120. Cf. my (1970), pp. 138–73.

121. Duhem himself gives only one explicit example: the victory of wave optics over Newtonian optics (1906), Chapter 6, section 10 (also see chapter 4, section 4). But where Duhem relies on intuitive "common sense," I rely on an analysis of rival problem-shifts (cf. my [1972]).

122. One may introduce the notion of "*degree of correctness*" into the metatheory of methodologies, which would be analogous to Popper's empirical content. Popper's empirical "basic statements" would have to be replaced by quasi-empirical "normative basic statements" (like the statement that "Planck's radiation formula is arbitrary").

Let me point out here that the methodology of research programmes may be applied not only to norm-impregnated historical knowledge but to any normative knowledge, including even ethics and aesthetics. This would then supersede the naive falsificationist "quasi-empirical" approach as outlined on note 80.

123. Cf. text to note 9. (The term "wild speculation" is, of course, a term inherited from inductivist methodology. It should now be reinterpreted as "degenerating programme.")

124. The fact that even degenerating externalist theories have been able to achieve some respectability was to a considerable extent due to the weakness of their previous internalist rivals. Utopian Victorian morality either creates false, hypocritical accounts of bourgeois decency, or adds fuel to the view that mankind is totally depraved; utopian scientific standards either create false, hypocritical accounts of scientific perfection, or add fuel to the view that scientific theories are no more than mere beliefs bolstered by some vested interests. This explains the "revolutionary" aura which surrounds some of the absurd ideas of contemporary sociology of knowledge: some of its practitioners claim to have unmasked the bogus rationality of science, while, at best, they exploit the weakness of outdated theories of scientific rationality.

125. For examples cf. Cantor (1971) and the Forman-Ewald debate (Forman [1969] and Ewald, [1969]).

126. I call "*historiographical positivism*" the position that history can be written as a completely *external* history. For historiographical positivists history is a purely empirical discipline. They deny the existence of objective standards as opposed to mere beliefs about standards. (Of course, they too hold beliefs about standards which determine the choice and formulation of their historical problems.) This position is typically Hegelian. It is a special case of *normative positivism*, of the theory that sets up might as the criterion of right. (For a criticism of Hegel's ethical positivism cf. Popper [1945], vol. 1, pp. 71–72, vol. 2, pp. 305–306 and Popper [1961].) Reactionary Hegelian obscurantism pushed values back completely into the world of facts; thus reversing their separation by Kantian philosophical enlightenment.

127. Kuhn seems to be in two minds about objective scientific progress. I have no doubt that, being a devoted scholar and scientist, he *personally* detests relativism. But his *theory* can either be interpreted as denying scientific progress and recognizing only scientific change; or, as recognizing scientific progress but as "progress" marked solely by the march of actual history. Indeed, on his criterion, he would have to describe the catastrophe mentioned in the text as a proper "revolution." I am afraid this might be one clue to the unintended popularity of his theory among the New Left busily preparing the 1984 "revolution."

128. The technical term "Euclidean" (or rather "quasi-Euclidean") means that one starts with universal, high level propositions ("axioms") rather than singular ones. I suggested in my (1967) and (1962) that the "quasi-Euclidean" versus "quasi-empirical" distinction is more useful than the "*a priori*" versus "*a posteriori*" distinction.

    Some of the "apriorists" are, of course, empiricists. But empiricists may well be apriorists (or, rather, "Euclideans") on the meta-level here discussed.

129. Some might claim that Popper does *not* fall into this category. After all, Popper defined "science" in such a way that it should include the refuted Newtonian theory and exclude unrefuted astrology, Marxism and Freudianism.

130. This seems to be the case in modern particle physics; or according to some philosophers and physicists even in the Copenhagen school of quantum physics.

131. This is the case with some of the main schools of modern sociology, psychology and social psychology.

132. This, of course, explains why a good methodology "distilled" from the mature sciences—may play an important role for immature and, indeed, dubious disciplines. While Polanyiite academic autonomy should be defended for departments of theoretical physics, it must not be tolerated, say, in institutes for computerised social astrology, science planning or social imagistics. (For an authoritative study of the latter, cf. Priestley [1968].)

133. Of course, a critical discussion of scientific standards, possibly leading even to their improvement, is impossible without articulating them in general terms; just as if one wants to challenge a language, one has to articulate its grammar. Neither the conservative Polanyi nor the conservative Oakeshott seem to have grasped (or to have been inclined to grasp) the *critical* function of language—Popper has. (Cf. especially Popper [1963a]), p. 135).

134. Cf. e.g. my (1962), p. 157 or my (1968a), p. 387, footnote 1.

REFERENCES

Agassi, J. (1963). *Towards an Historiography of Science.*

———. (1964). "Scientific Problems and their Roots in Metaphysics." In *The Critical Approach to Science and Philosophy.* edited by M. Bunge, pp. 189–211.

———. (1966). "Sensationalism." *Mind* 75, pp. 1–24.

———. (1969). "Popper on Learning from Experience." In *Studies in the Philosophy of Science.* edited by N. Rescher, pp. 162–171.

Bernal, J. D. (1954). *Science in History.* 1st ed.

———. (1965). *Science in History.* 3rd ed.

Beveridge, W. (1937). "The Place of the Social Sciences in Human Knowledge." *Politica* 2, pp. 459–79.

Cantor, G. (1971). "A Further Appraisal of the Young-Brougham Controversy." In *Studies in the History and Philosophy of Science.*

Cohen, I. B. (1960). *The Birth of a New Physics.*

Compton, A. H. (1919). "The Size and Shape of the Electron." *Physical Review* 14, pp. 20–43.

Duhem, P. (1905). *La Théorie Physique: Son objet et sa structure* (English trans. of 2d (1914) edition: *The Aim and Structure of Physical Theory*, 1954).

Elkana, Y. (1971). "The Conservation of Energy: a Case of Simultaneous Discovery?" *Archives Internationales d'Histoire des Sciences* 24, pp. 31–60.

Ewald, P. (1969). "The Myth of Myths." *Archive for the History of Exact Science* 6, pp. 72–81.

Feyerabend, P. K. (1964). "Realism and Instrumentalism: Comments on the Logic of Factual Support." In *The Critical Approach to Science and Philosophy.* (ed. by M. Bunge), pp. 280–308.

———. (1965). "Reply to Criticism." *Boston Studies in the Philosophy of Science* 2. Edited by R. S. Cohen and M. Wartofsky, pp. 223–61.

———. (1969). "A Note on Two 'Problems' of Induction." *British Journal for the Philosophy of Science* 19, pp. 251–53.

———. (1970a). "Consolations for the Specialist." In *Criticism and the Growth of Knowledge.* Edited by I. Lakatos and A. Musgrave, pp. 197–230.

———. (1970b). "Against Method." *Minnesota Studies for the Philosophy of Science* 4.

———. (1971). *Against Method* (expanded version of Feyerabend [1970b]).

Forman, P. (1969). "The Discovery of the Diffraction of X-Rays by Crystals: A Critique of the Critique of the Myths." *Archive for the History of Exact Sciences* 6, pp. 38–71.

Hall, R. J. (1970). "Kuhn and the Copernican Revolution." *British Journal for the Philosophy of Science* 21, pp. 196–97.

Hempel, C. G. (1937). Review of Popper (1934), *Deutsche Literaturzeitung*, pp. 309–14.

Holton, G. (1969). "Einstein, Michelson, and the 'Crucial' Experiment." *Isis* 6, pp. 133–97.

Kuhn, T. S. (1957). *The Copernican Revolution.*

———. (1962). *The Structure of Scientific Revolutions.*

———. (1968). "Science: The History of Science." In *International Encyclopedia of the Social Sciences.* Vol. 14. Edited by D. L. Sills, pp. 74–83.

———. (1970). "Reflections on my Critics." In *Criticism and the Growth of Knowledge.* Edited by I. Lakatos and A. Musgrave, pp. 237–78.

Lakatos, I. (1962). "Infinite Regress and the Foundations of Mathematics." *Aristotelian Society Supplementary Volume* 36, pp. 155–84.

———. (1963–64). "Proofs and Refutations." *The British Journal for the Philosophy of Science* 14, pp. 1–25, 120–39, 221–43, 296–342.

———. (1966). "Popkin on Skepticism." In *Logic, Physics and History.* Edited by W. Yourgrau and A. D. Breck, (1970), pp. 220–23.

———. (1967). "A Renaissance of Empiricism in the Recent Philosophy of Mathematics." In *Problems in the Philosophy of Mathematics.* Edited by I. Lakatos, pp. 199–202.

————. (1968a). "Changes in the Problem of Inductive Logic." In *The Problem of Inductive Logic*. Edited by I. Lakatos, pp. 315–417.

————. (1968b). "Criticism and the Methodology of Scientific Research Programmes." *Proceedings of the Aristotelian Society* 69, pp. 149–86.

————. (1970). "Falsification and the Methodology of Scientific Research Programmes." In *Criticism and the Growth of Knowledge*. Edited by I. Lakatos and A. Musgrave.

————. (1971a). "Popper on Demarcation and Induction." In *The Philosophy of Sir Karl Popper*. Edited by P. A. Schilpp. (Available in German in *Neue Aspekte der Wissenschaftstheorie* Edited by H. Lenk.

————. (1971b). "A Note on the Historiography of the Copernican Revolution."

————. (1972). *The Changing Logic of Scientific Discovery*.

Lakatos, I. and Musgrave, A. (1970). *Criticism and the Growth of Knowledge*.

McMullin, E. (1970). "The History and Philosophy of Science: a Taxonomy." *Minnesota Studies in the Philosophy of Science* 5, pp. 12–67.

Merton, R. (1957). "Priorities in Scientific Discovery." *American Sociological Review* 22, pp. 635–59.

————. (1963). "Resistance to the Systematic Study of Multiple Discoveries in Science." *European Journal of Sociology* 4, pp. 237–82.

————. (1969). "Behaviour Patterns of Scientists." *American Scholar* 38, pp. 197–225.

Musgrave, A. (1969). *Impersonal Knowledge: A Criticism of Subjectivism*. Ph. D. thesis, University of London.

————. (1971a). "The Objectivism of Popper's Epistemology." In *The Philosophy of Sir Karl Popper*. Edited by P. A. Schilpp.

————. (1971b). "Kuhn's Second Thoughts." *British Journal for the Philosophy of Science* 22, pp. 287–97.

Polanyi, M. (1951). *The Logic of Liberty*.

————. (1958). *Personal Knowledge, Towards a Post-Critical Philosophy*.

Popper, K. R. (1935). *Logik der Forschung*.

————. (1940). "What is Dialectic?" *Mind* 49, pp. 403–26. Reprinted in Popper (1963), pp. 312–35.

————. (1945). *The Open Society and Its Enemies*. Vols. 1–2.

————. (1948). "Naturgesetze und theoretische Systeme." In *Gesetz und Wirklichkeit*. Edited by S. Moser, pp. 65–84.

————. (1963). "Three Views Concerning Human Knowledge." In *Contemporary British Philosophy*. Edited by H. D. Lewis (1957), pp. 355–88. Reprinted in Popper (1963), pp. 97–119.

————. (1957a). "The Aim of Science." *Ratio* 1, pp. 24–35.

————. (1957b). *The Poverty of Historicism*.

————. (1959). *The Logic of Scientific Discovery*.

————. (1960). "Philosophy and Physics." *Atti del XII Congresso Internazionale di Filosofia* 2, pp. 363–74.

————. (1961). "Facts, Standards, and Truth: A Further Criticism of Relativism." Addendum to the 4th edition of Popper (1945).

————. (1963a). *Conjectures and Refutations*.

————. (1963b). "Science: Problems, Aims, Responsibilities." *Federation Proceedings* 22, pp. 961–72.

————. (1968a). "Epistemology Without a Knowing Subject." In *Proceedings of the Third International Congress for Logic, Methodology and Philosophy of Science*. Edited by B. Rootselaar and J. Staal. Amsterdam, pp. 333–73.

————. (1968b). "On the Theory of the Objective Mind." In *Proceedings of the XIV International Congress of Philosophy*. Vol. 1, pp. 25–33.

Price, D. J. (1959). "Contra Copernicus: A Critical Re-estimation of the Mathematical Planetary Theory of Ptolemy, Copernicus and Kepler." In *Critical Problems in the History of Science*. Edited by M. Clagett, pp. 197–218.

Priestley, J. B. (1968). *The Image Men*.

Scheffler, I. (1967). *Science and Subjectivity*.

Shapere, D. (1964). "The Structure of Scientific Revolutions." In *Philosophical Review*, pp. 383–84.

Shapere, S. (1967). "Meaning and Scientific Change." In *Mind and Cosmos*. Edited by R. G. Colodny, pp. 41–85.

Van der Waerden, B. (1967). *Sources of Quantum Mechanics*.

Watkins, J. W. N. (1952). "Political Tradition and Political Theory: an Examination of Professor Oakeshott's Political Philosophy." *Philosophical Quarterly* 2, pp. 323–37.

———. (1958). "Influential and Confirmable Metaphysics." *Mind* 67, pp. 344–65.

———. (1963). "Negative Utilitarianism." *Aristotelian Society Supplementary* 37, pp. 95–114.

———. (1967). "Decision and Belief." In *Decision Making*. Edited by R. Hughes, pp. 9–26.

———. (1970). "Against Normal Science." In *Criticism and the Growth of Knowledge*. Edited by I. Lakatos and A. Musgrave, pp. 25–38.

Williams, L. P. (1970). "Normal Science and its Dangers." In *Criticism and the Growth of Knowledge*. Edited by I. Lakatos and A. Musgrave, pp. 49–50.

PART EIGHT

THE NATURE OF SCIENTIFIC KNOWLEDGE

INTRODUCTION

The general conception that emerges from the perspective of what has gone before suggests that empirical science endeavors to fulfill at least two complementary objectives. The first is to ascertain the historical patterns displayed by the world's history, which are expressible in extensional language and are capable of confirmation by their instances. The second is to discover the lawful relations constituting the world's structure, which are expressible in intensional language and can be tested by attempts to refute them. The principal importance of these historical patterns is to serve as evidence in discovering the laws they display, which in turn explain them.

Popper's "Three Views Concerning Human Knowledge," however, hints that more than one attitude can be adopted concerning the nonobservable. Essentialism, for example, holds that science aims at ultimate explanations in terms of essences, where the best theories describe the essences that lie behind appearances. Popper denies that essentialism provides an appropriate foundation for understanding science, however, not because it assumes that things have essences but rather because there is no reason why scientists should assume their existence. Belief in the existence of essences also has the unhappy effect of "preventing fruitful questions from being raised."

Instrumentalism, by contrast, holds that, whether or not essences exist, they lie beyond the possibility of human discovery, which means that science can never provide ultimate explanations for things. Instrumentalism thus abandons the search for explanations altogether, substituting the aim of description and prediction, which might be attained by means of extensional language alone. Scientific theories, from this perspective, are nothing but calculating devices (or "instruments") for predicting future events and thereby contributing to decision-making. The world is as it appears to be (through observation), while our theories (about nonobservables) are not.

Realism, by comparison, holds that science aims at true descriptions of the world, which can provide explanations of the phenomena accessible to experience. These descriptions typically assume the form of theories that are expressed by means of predicates that designate nonobservable properties and laws that designate natural necessities. These theories typically explain the familiar by the unfamiliar or the known by the unknown. Although theories are conjectures whose truth cannot be established beyond all doubt, science is capable of discovering previously unsuspected objects and properties, which makes possible genuine forms of scientific progress.

It would be a mistake to view permanent properties as a species of essential properties, which are properties of individual things "by their nature" that appear in proper definitions of those things. Permanent properties are not definitional but logically contingent properties of things as instances of other kinds defined by reference properties. Essentialism also imposes boundaries on scientific knowledge, while the requirement of strict maximal specificity, in particular, insists that adequate explanations explain phenomena exclusively by means of lawfully relevant properties. There are no *a priori* guarantees that explanations we accept today could not be superseded by the discovery of alternative explanations tomorrow.

Quine's "The Nature of Natural Knowledge" represents a sophisticated form of instrumentalism, according to which, "The utility of science, from a practical point of view, lies in fulfilled expectation: true prediction." In Quine's view, we fashion our expectations on the basis of experience using subjective standards of similarity in discerning resemblance relations between various events. The inferential foundation for shaping expectations is simple induction, envisioned as the expectation that events which have been attended by other events in the past will continue to do so in the future. The similarities between the views of Quine and Hume are striking.

The advance of science depends on ongoing observation and expectation modification. Science goes beyond simple induction as "a ponderous linguistic structure, fabricated of theoretical terms linked by fabricated hypotheses, and keyed to observable events here and there." Like other instrumentalists, Quine retains the observational/theoretical distinction, while implying that theoretical language possesses no ontological import. The themes of his essay are continuous with "Two Dogmas of Empiricism," where he describes the theories of modern science as "on a par" with the myths of ancient peoples; they are simply better as devices of prediction.

Although he supports the hypothetico-deductive method as delivering knowledge "hand over fist," the measure of that knowledge is facilitating successful prediction. There is "vast freedom" in constructing theories on the basis of observations, because even access to the totality of true observation sentences would not suffice to arbitrate between the totality of possible theories, which means that theories are invariably underdetermined by observation. Indeed, he also wants to claim that there has to be more to theories than their observational consequences. If there were no meaning but empirical meaning and theories with the same empirical meaning were the same theory, there could be no underdetermination of theories.

Precisely what that meaning beyond empirical meaning may come to, however, is not a matter about which Quine is entirely clear. And he still maintains that the conception of a single true theory of the universe is an "illusion" which has been fostered by the success of science in narrowing the range of acceptable theories on the basis of accumulated observations. Even more importantly, Quine views epistemology as an enterprise which falls within the domain of science itself. The theory of knowledge thus becomes a branch of empirical science, a science of science which cannot lay claim to methods of inquiry or to forms of knowledge of a distinctive kind.

Almeder's "On Naturalizing Epistemology" affords a systematic survey of positions in support of this approach. He distinguishes between three theses: the *replacement* thesis, which holds that science can replace traditional epistemology; the *transformation* thesis, which holds that traditional epistemology requires supplementation from psychology, biology, and cognitive science; and (let us call it) an *autonomy* thesis, which holds that natural science has a privileged role in addressing questions about natural phenomena. His discussion focuses on the first of these three.

Almeder examines Quine's views in some detail. The most important arguments which he has advanced in support of this position derive from his critique of the analytic/synthetic distinction, his endorsement of Hume's critique of induction ("the Humean predicament is the human predicament"), and his own views about the nature of meaning, where "the only meaningful questions are questions answerable by science." Almeder, however, thinks there is something "radically incoherent" in offering philosophical arguments for naturalized epistemology and suggests that coherent arguments in its support may be impossible.

Indeed, the naturalization of epistemology appears to generate inherent problems. Change in accepted theories may lead to change in the contents of observation. Change in accepted methods, of course, must lead to change in the practice of science. Change in the practice of science in turn must lead to change in naturalized epistemology. Yet the very possibility of changes of these kinds should invite consideration of whether the available theories, methods or practices are the most reliable, the most efficient, or the most effective to achieve their respective aims, objectives, or goals. Inquiries of this kind, however, reaffirm the primacy of the normative in epistemology and therefore lie beyond the scope of Quinean methodology.

During the course of investigation, Almeder examines arguments concerning evolutionary epistemology as a special case of naturalized epistemology. Insofar as human intellectual endowments have emerged as a result of an evolutionary process, perhaps the way we reason is the way we ought to reason. If our mental abilities are the products of natural selection, after all, how could we imagine they could be improved upon? Other versions maintain that the growth of scientific knowledge has to be understood as a manifestation of biological evolution. These arguments, however, like others Almeder considers, appear to carry no real weight.

Evolution, after all, is a dynamic process, which has not yet run its course. For all we know, we represent a relatively primitive stage in the emergence of mental phenomena. And cultural evolution, including the growth of scientific knowledge, operates by means of Lamarckian mechanisms rather than by means of the Darwinian mechanisms that govern genetic evolution. So the principles that govern biological evolution are not the same as those that govern the growth of scientific knowledge. Evolution may be a paradigm of scientific achievement, but accounting for the nature of knowledge is more than it seems able to bear. So there may be a place for normative epistemology, after all.

STUDY QUESTIONS

As you read the articles that appear in this section, you may want to think about their implications for understanding the nature of science and of philosophy. The following questions are intended to stimulate your thinking by focusing attention on some of the less obvious aspects of different positions.

(1) Popper suggests that essentialism "prevents fruitful questions from being raised." Could the reason essentialism inhibits inquiry be because once we believe we have found them, no

further questions seem to remain to be explored? Can you think of other reasons why essentialism is a bad thing?

(2) Realism differs from instrumentalism because realism maintains that theories are attempts to provide true descriptions of the world. If theories are merely calculating devices, as instrumentalism maintains, then do theories describe nothing? Is there no more to the world than meets the eye?

(3) With reference to the problem of provisoes, what is it about provisoes that makes the instrumentalist conception of scientific theories as calculating devices appear implausible? And why do programs for the elimination of theoretical terms from scientific theories likewise appear to be illusory?

(4) Quine has sometimes argued strongly in favor of the thesis that there is no meaning but stimulus meaning. He has also argued equally strongly in favor of the thesis of the underdetermination of theories by evidence. Can both theses be true? If one of them is true, must the other be false?

(5) Quine's critique of the analytic/synthetic distinction seems to make analytic sentences a special kind of synthetic proposition, as Almeder observes. But we have discovered reasons to doubt the success of his rejection of the analytic/synthetic distinction. What difference does it make?

(6) Would it make more sense for advocates of naturalized epistemology to cease the practice of philosophy and pursue empirical science instead? If epistemology could be replaced by science, then what would be left of philosophy? Would philosophy itself disappear along with epistemology?

(7) Almeder considers several reasons for thinking that deductive arguments are trivial and uninteresting. If that were the case, would Popper's conception of science as a process of conjectures and (attempted) refutations have to be trivial and uninteresting as well? If not, then why not?

(8) In the "Postscript," Peirce endorses the conception of truth as that opinion which the community of inquirers is destined to converge upon over the long run. Apply what you have learned about interpretations of probability to this claim and assess whether or not it can be justified.

(9) Peirce discusses several different ways in which evolution might be able to shed light on the nature of inquiry. Consider what he has to say and attempt to determine whether there is any ground here in support of a version of evolutionary epistemology that warrants consideration.

(10) Peirce also describes the robust realism that tends to characterize scientists. Considering everything that you have learned about science from what you have found here, do you think that essentialism, instrumentalism, or realism yields the strongest motive for scientific inquiry?

KARL R. POPPER

THREE VIEWS CONCERNING HUMAN KNOWLEDGE

I. THE SCIENCE OF GALILEO AND ITS NEW BETRAYAL

Once upon a time there was a famous scientist whose name was Galileo Galilei. He was tried by the Inquisition, and forced to recant his teaching. This caused a great stir; and for well over two hundred and fifty years the case continued to arouse indignation and excitement—long after public opinion had won its victory, and the Church had become tolerant of science.

But this is by now a very old story, and I fear it has lost its interest. For Galilean science has no enemies left, it seems: its life hereafter is secure. The victory won long ago was final, and all is quiet on this front. So we take a detached view of the affair nowadays, having learned at last to think historically, and to understand both sides of a dispute. And nobody cares to listen to the bore who can't forget an old grievance.

What, after all, was this old case about? It was about the status of the Copernican "System of the World" which, besides other things, explained the diurnal motion of the sun as only apparent, and as due to the rotation of our own earth. [1] The Church was very ready to admit that the new system was simpler than the old one: that it was a more convenient *instrument* for astronomical calculations, and for predictions. And Pope Gregory's reform of the calendar made full practical use of it. There was no objection to Galileo's teaching the mathematical theory, so long as he made it clear that its value was *instrumental* only; that it was nothing but a "supposition," as Cardinal Bellarmino put it; [2] or a "mathematical hypothesis"—a kind of mathematical trick, "invented and assumed in order to abbreviate and ease the calculations." [3] In other words there were no objections so long as Galileo was ready to fall into line with Andreas Osiander who had said in his preface to Copernicus's *De revolutionibus*: "There is no need for these hypotheses to be true, or even to be at all like the truth; rather, one thing is sufficient for them—that they should yield calculations which agree with the observations."

Galileo himself, of course, was very ready to stress the superiority of the Copernican system as an *instrument of calculation*. But at the same time he conjectured, and even believed, that it was *a true description of the world*; and for him (as for the Church) this was by far the most important aspect of the matter. He had indeed some good reasons for believing in the truth of the theory. He had seen in his telescope that Jupiter and its moons formed a miniature model of the Copernican solar system (according to which the planets were moons of the sun). Moreover, if Copernicus was right the inner planets (and they alone) should, when observed from the earth, show phases like the moon; and Galileo had seen in his telescope the phases of Venus.

The Church was unwilling to contemplate the truth of a New System of the World which seemed to contradict a passage in the Old Testament. But this was hardly its main reason. A deeper reason was clearly stated by Bishop Berkeley, about a hundred years later, in his criticism of Newton.

In Berkeley's time the Copernican System of the World had developed into Newton's Theory of gravity, and Berkeley saw in it a serious competitor to religion. He was convinced that a decline of religious faith and religious authority would result from the new science if its interpretation by the "free-thinkers" was correct; for they saw in its success a proof of *the power of the human intellect, unaided by divine revelation, to uncover the secrets of our world*—the reality hidden behind its appearance.

This, Berkeley felt, was to misinterpret the new science. He analysed Newton's theory with complete candour and great philosophical acumen; and a critical survey of Newton's concepts convinced him that this theory could not possibly be anything but a "mathematical hypothesis," that is, a convenient *instrument* for the calculation and prediction of phenomena or appearances; that it could not possibly be taken as a true description of anything real.[4]

Berkeley's criticism was hardly noticed by the physicists; but it was taken up by philosophers, sceptical as well as religious. As a weapon it turned out to be a boomerang. In Hume's hands it became a threat to all belief—to all knowledge, whether human or revealed. In the hands of Kant, who firmly believed both in God and in the truth of Newtonian science, it developed into the doctrine that theoretical knowledge of God is impossible, and that Newtonian science must pay for the admission of its claim to truth by the renunciation of its claim to have discovered the real world behind the world of appearance: it was a true science of nature, but *nature* was precisely the world of mere phenomena, the world as it appeared to our assimilating minds. Later certain pragmatists based their whole philosophy upon the view that the idea of "pure" knowledge was a mistake; that there could be no knowledge in any other sense but in the sense of *instrumental* knowledge; that knowledge was power, and that truth was usefulness.

Physicists (with a few brilliant exceptions[5]) kept aloof from all these philosophical debates, which remained completely inconclusive. Faithful to the tradition created by Galileo, they devoted themselves to the search for truth, as he had understood it.

Or so they did until very recently. For all this is now past history. Today the view of physical science founded by Osiander, Cardinal Bellarmino, and Bishop Berkeley,[6] has won the battle without another shot being fired. Without any further debate over the philosophical issue, without producing any new argument, the *instrumentalist view* (as I shall call it) has become an accepted dogma. It may well now be called the "official view" of physical theory since it is accepted by most of our leading theorists of physics (although neither by Einstein nor by Schrödinger). And it has become part of the current teaching of physics.

II. THE ISSUE AT STAKE

All this looks like a great victory of philosophical critical thought over the naïve realism of the physicists. But I doubt whether this interpretation is right.

Few if any of the physicists who have now accepted the instrumentalist view of Cardinal Bellarmino and Bishop Berkeley realize that they have accepted a philosophical theory. Nor do they realize that they have broken with the Galilean tradition. On the contrary, most of them think that they have kept clear of philosophy; and most of them no longer care anyway. What they now care about, as physicists, is (a) *mastery of the mathematical formalism*, i.e., of the instrument, and (b) *its applications*; and they care for nothing else. And they think that by thus excluding everything else they have finally got rid of all philosophical nonsense. This very attitude of being tough and not standing any nonsense prevents them from considering seriously the philosophical arguments for and against the Galilean view of science (though they will no doubt have heard of Mach[7]). Thus the victory of the instrumentalist philosophy is hardly due to the soundness of its arguments.

How then did it come about? As far as I can see, through the coincidence of two factors, (a) difficulties in the interpretation of the formalism of the Quantum Theory, and (b) the spectacular practical success of its applications.

(a) In 1927 Niels Bohr, one of the greatest thinkers in the field of atomic physics, introduced the so-called *principle of complementarity* into atomic physics, which amounted to a "renunciation" of the attempt to interpret atomic theory as a description of anything. Bohr pointed out that we could avoid certain contradictions (which threatened to arise between the formalism and its various interpretations) only by reminding ourselves that the formalism as such was self-consistent, and that each single case of its application (or each kind of case) remained consistent with it. The contradictions only arose through the attempt to comprise within *one* interpretation the formalism together with more than one case, or kind of case, of its experimental application. But, as Bohr pointed out, any two of these conflicting applications were physically incapable of ever being combined in one experiment. Thus, the result of *every single* experiment was consistent with the theory, and unambiguously laid down by it. This, he said, was all we could get. The claim to get more, and even the hope of ever getting more, we must renounce; physics remains consistent only if we do not try to interpret, or to understand, its theories beyond (a) mastering the formalism, and (b) relating them to each of their actually realizable cases of application separately.[8]

Thus the instrumentalist philosophy was used here *ad hoc* in order to provide an escape for the theory from certain contradictions by which it was threatened. It was used in a defensive mood—to rescue the existing theory; and the principle of complementarity has (I believe for this reason) remained completely sterile within physics. In twenty-seven years it has produced nothing except some philosophical discussions, and some arguments for the confounding of critics (especially Einstein).

I do not believe that physicists would have accepted such an *ad hoc* principle had they understood that it was *ad hoc*, or that it was a philosophical principle—part of Bellarmino's and Berkeley's instrumentalist philosophy of physics. But they remembered Bohr's earlier and extremely fruitful "principle of correspondence" and hoped (in vain) for similar results.

(b) Instead of results due to the principle of complementarity other and more practical results of atomic theory were obtained, some of them with a big bang. No doubt physicists were perfectly right in interpreting these successful applications as corroborating their theories. But strangely enough they took them as confirming the instrumentalist creed.

Now this was an obvious mistake. The instrumentalist view asserts that theories are *nothing but* instruments, while the Galilean view was that they are not only instruments but also—and mainly—descriptions of the world, or of certain aspects of the world. It is clear that in this disagreement even a proof showing that theories are instruments (assuming it possible to "prove" such a thing) could not seriously be claimed to support either of the two parties to the debate, since both were agreed on this point.

If I am right, or even roughly right, in my account of the situation, then philosophers, even instrumentalist philosophers, have no reason to take pride in their victory. On the contrary, they should examine their arguments again. For at least in the eyes of those who like myself do not accept the instrumentalist view, there is much at stake in this issue.

The issue, as I see it, is this.

One of the most important ingredients of our Western civilization is what I may call the "rationalist tradition" which we have inherited from the Greeks. It is the tradition of critical discussion—not for its own sake, but in the interests of the search for truth. Greek science, like Greek philosophy, was one of the products of this tradition,[9] and of the urge to understand the world in which we live; and the tradition founded by Galileo was its renaissance.

Within this rationalist tradition science is valued, admittedly, for its practical achievements; but it is even more highly valued for its informative content, and for its ability to free our minds from old beliefs, old prejudices, and old certainties, and to offer us in their stead new conjectures and daring hypotheses. Science is valued for its liberalizing influence—as one of the greatest of the forces that make for human freedom.

According to the view of science which I am trying to defend here, this is due to the fact that scientists have dared (since Thales, Democritus, Plato's *Timaeus*, and Aristarchus) to create myths, or conjectures, or theories, which are in striking contrast to the everyday world of common experience, yet able to explain some aspects of this world of common experience. Galileo pays homage to Aristarchus and Copernicus precisely because they dared to go beyond this known world of our senses: "I cannot," he writes,[10] "express strongly enough my unbounded admiration for the greatness of mind of these men who conceived [the heliocentric system] and held it to be true . . . , in violent opposition to the evidence of their own senses. . . ." This is Galileo's testimony to the liberalizing force of science. Such theories would be important even if they were no more than exercises for our imagination. But they are more than this, as can be seen from the fact that we submit them to severe tests by trying to deduce from them some of the regularities of the known world of common experience—i.e., by trying to *explain* these regularities. And these attempts to *explain the known by the unknown* (as I have described them elsewhere[11]) have immeasurably extended the realm of the known. They have added to the facts of our everyday world the invisible air, the antipodes, the circulation of the blood, the worlds of the telescope and the microscope, of electricity, and of tracer atoms showing us in detail the movements of matter within living bodies. All these things are far from being mere instruments: they are witness to the intellectual conquest of our world by our minds.

But there is another way of looking at these matters. For some, science is still nothing but glorified plumbing, glorified gadget-making—"mechanics"; very useful, but a danger to true culture, threatening us with the domination of the near-illiterate (of Shakespeare's "mechanicals"). It should never be mentioned in the same breath as literature or the arts or philosophy. Its professed discoveries are mere mechanical inventions, its theories are instruments—gadgets again, or perhaps super-gadgets. It cannot and does not reveal to us new worlds behind our everyday world of appearance; for the physical world is just surface: it has no depth. *The world is just what it appears to be. Only the scientific theories are not what they appear to be.* A scientific theory neither explains nor describes the world; it is nothing but an instrument.

I do not present this as a complete picture of modern instrumentalism, although it is a fair sketch, I think, of part of its original philosophical background. Today a much more important part of it is, I am well aware, the rise and self-assertion of the modern "mechanic" or engineer.[12] Still, I believe that the issue should be seen to lie between a critical and adventurous rationalism—the spirit of discovery—and a narrow and defensive creed according to which we cannot and need not learn or understand more about our world than we know already. A creed, moreover, which is incompatible with the appreciation of science as one of the greatest achievements of the human spirit.

Such are the reasons why I shall try, in this paper, to uphold at least part of the Galilean view of science against the instrumentalist view. But I cannot uphold all of it. There is a part of it which I believe the instrumentalists were right to attack. I mean the view that in science we can aim at, and obtain, *an ultimate explanation by essences*. It is in its opposition to this Aristotelian view (which I have called[13] "essentialism") that the strength and the philosophical interest of instrumentalism lies. Thus I shall have to discuss and criticize two views of human knowledge—*essentialism* and *instrumentalism*. And I shall oppose to them what I shall call *the third view*—what remains of Galileo's view after the elimination of essentialism, or more precisely, after allowance has been made for what was justified in the instrumentalist attack.

III. THE FIRST VIEW: ULTIMATE EXPLANATION BY ESSENCES

Essentialism, the first of the three views of scientific theory to be discussed, is part of the Galilean philosophy of science. Within this philosophy three elements or doctrines which concern us here may be distinguished. Essentialism (our "first view") is that part of the Galilean philosophy which I do not wish to uphold. It consists of a combination of the doctrines (2) and (3). These are the three doctrines:

(1) *The scientist aims at finding a true theory or description of the world* (and especially of its regularities or "laws"), *which shall also be an explanation of the observable facts*. (This means that a description of these facts must be deducible from the theory in conjunction with certain statements, the so-called "initial conditions.")

This is a doctrine I wish to uphold. It is to form part of our "third view."

(2) *The scientist can succeed in finally establishing the truth of such theories beyond all reasonable doubt.*

This second doctrine, I think, needs correction. All the scientist can do, in my opinion, is to test his theories, and to eliminate all those that do not stand up to the most severe tests he can design. But he can never be quite sure whether new tests (or even a new theoretical discussion) may not lead him to modify, or to discard, his theory. In this sense all theories are, and remain hypotheses: they are conjecture (*doxa*) as opposed to indubitable knowledge (*epistēmē*).

(3) *The best, the truly scientific theories, describe the "essences" or the "essential natures" of things—the realities which lie behind the appearances*. Such theories are neither in need nor susceptible of further explanation: they are *ultimate explanations*, and to find them is the ultimate aim of the scientist.

This third doctrine (in connection with the second) is the one I have called "essentialism." I believe that like the second doctrine it is mistaken.

Now what the instrumentalist philosophers of science, from Berkeley to Mach, Duhem, and Poincaré, have in common is this. They all assert that explanation is not an aim of physical science, since physical science cannot discover "the hidden essences of things." The argument shows that what they have in mind is what I call *ultimate* explanation.[14] Some of them, such as Mach and Berkeley, hold this view because they do not believe that there is such a thing as an essence of anything physical: Mach, because he does not believe in essences at all; Berkeley, because he believes only in spiritual essences, and thinks that the only essential explanation of the world is God. Duhem seems to think (on lines reminiscent of Kant[15]) that there are essences but that they are undiscoverable by human science (though we may, somehow, move towards them); like Berkeley he thinks that they can be revealed by religion. But all these philosophers agree that (ultimate) scientific explanation is impossible. And from the absence of a hidden essence which scientific theories could describe they conclude that these theories (which clearly do not describe our ordinary world of common experience) describe nothing at all. Thus they are mere instruments.[16] And what may appear as the growth of theoretical knowledge is merely the improvement of instruments.

The instrumentalist philosophers therefore reject the third doctrine, i.e., the doctrine of essences. (I reject it too, but for somewhat different reasons.) At the same time they reject, and are bound to reject, the second doctrine; for if a theory is an instrument, then it cannot be true (but only convenient, simple, economical, powerful, etc.). They even frequently call the theories "hypotheses"; but they do not, of course, mean by this what I mean: that a theory is *conjectured to be true*, that it is a descriptive though possibly a false statement; although they do mean to say that theories are uncertain: "And as to the usefulness of hypotheses," Osiander writes (at the end of his preface), "nobody should expect anything certain to emerge from astronomy, for nothing of the kind can ever come out of it." Now I fully agree that there is no certainty about theories (which may always be refuted); and I even agree that they are instruments, although I do not agree that this is the reason why there can be no certainty about theories. (The correct reason, I believe, is simply that our tests can never be exhaustive.) There is thus a considerable amount of agreement between my instrumentalist opponents and myself over the second and third doctrines. But over the first doctrine there is complete disagreement.

To this disagreement I shall return later. In the present section I shall try to criticize (3), the essentialist doctrine of science, on lines somewhat different from the arguments of the instrumentalism which I cannot accept. For its argument that there can be no "hidden essences" is based upon its conviction that *there can be nothing hidden* (or that if anything is hidden it can be only known by divine revelation). From what I said in the last section it will be clear that I cannot accept an argument that leads to the rejection of the claim of science to have discovered the rotation of the earth, or atomic nuclei, or cosmic radiation, or the "radio stars."

I therefore readily concede to essentialism that much is hidden from us, and that much of what is hidden may be discovered. (I disagree profoundly with the spirit of Wittgenstein's dictum, "The riddle does not exist.") And I do not even intend to criticize those who try to understand the "essence of the world." The essentialist doctrine I am contesting is solely *the doctrine that science aims at ultimate explanation*; that is to say, an explanation which (essentially, or by its very nature) cannot be further explained; and which is in no need of any further explanation.

Thus my criticism of essentialism does not aim at establishing the nonexistence of essences; it merely aims at showing the obscurantist character of the role played by the idea of essences in the Galilean philosophy of science (down to Maxwell, who was inclined to believe in them but whose work destroyed this belief). In other words my criticism tries to show that whether essences exist or not the belief in them does not help us in any way and indeed is likely to hamper us; so that there is no reason why the scientist should *assume* their existence.[17]

This, I think, can be best shown with the help of a simple example—*the Newtonian theory of gravity*.

The essentialist interpretation of Newtonian theory is due to Roger Cotes.[18] According to him Newton discovered that every particle of matter was endowed with *gravity*, i.e., with an inherent power or force to attract other matter. It was also endowed with *inertia*—an inherent power to resist a change in its state of motion (or to retain the direction and velocity of its motion). Since both gravity and inertia inhere in each particle of matter it follows that both must be strictly proportional to the amount of matter in a body, and therefore to each other; hence the law of proportionality of inert and gravitating mass. Since gravity radiates from each particle we obtain the square law of attraction. In other words, Newton's laws of motion simply describe in mathematical language the state of affairs due to the inherent properties of matter: they describe the *essential nature of matter.*

Since Newton's theory described in this way the essential nature of matter, he could explain the behaviour of matter with its help, by mathematical deduction. But Newton's theory, in its turn, is neither capable of, nor in need of, further explanation, according to Cotes—at least not within physics. (The only possible further explanation was that God has endowed matter with these essential properties.[19])

This essentialist view of Newton's theory was on the whole the accepted view until the last decades of the nineteenth century. That it was obscurantist is clear: *it prevented fruitful questions from being raised*, such as, "What is the cause of gravity?" or more fully, "Can we perhaps explain gravity by deducing Newton's theory, or a good approximation of it, from a more general theory (which should be independently testable)?"

Now it is illuminating to see that Newton himself had not considered *gravity* as an essential property of matter (although he considered *inertia* to be essential, and also, with Descartes, *extension*). It appears that he had taken over from Descartes the view that the essence of a thing must be a true or absolute property of the thing (i.e., a property which does not depend on the existence of other things) such as extension, or the power to resist a change in its state of motion, and not a relational property, i.e., a property which, like gravity, determines the relations (interactions in space) between one body and other bodies. Accordingly, he strongly felt the incompleteness of this theory, and the need to explain gravity. "That gravity," he wrote,[20] "should be innate, inherent, and essential to matter, so that one body may act upon another at a distance . . . is to me so great an absurdity that I believe no man who has in philosophical matters a competent faculty of thinking can ever fall into it."

It is interesting to see that Newton condemned here, in anticipation, the bulk of his followers. To them, one is tempted to remark, the properties of which they had learned in school appeared to be essential (and even self-evident), although to Newton, with his Cartesian background, the same properties had appeared to be in need of explanation (and indeed to be almost paradoxical).

Yet Newton himself was an essentialist. He had tried hard to find an acceptable ultimate explanation of gravity by trying to deduce the square law from the assumption of a mechanical push—the only kind of causal action which Descartes had permitted, since only push could be explained by the essential property of all bodies, extension.[21] But he failed. Had he succeeded we can be certain that he would have thought that his problem was finally solved—that he had found the ultimate explanation of gravity.[22] But here he would have been wrong. The question, "Why can bodies push one another?" *can* be asked (as Leibniz first saw), and it is even an extremely fruitful question. (We now believe that they push one another because of certain repulsive electric forces.) But Cartesian and Newtonian essentialism, especially if Newton had been successful in his attempted explanation of gravity, might have prevented this question from ever being raised.

These examples, I think, make it clear that the belief in essences (whether true or false) is liable to create obstacles to thought—to the posing of new and fruitful problems. Moreover, it cannot be part of science (for even if we should, by a lucky chance, hit upon a theory describing essences, we could never be sure of it). But a creed which is likely to lead to obscurantism is certainly not one of those extrascientific beliefs (such as a faith in the power of critical discussion) which a scientist need accept.

This concludes my criticism of essentialism.

IV. THE SECOND VIEW: THEORIES AS INSTRUMENTS

The instrumentalist view has great attractions. It is modest, and it is very simple, especially if compared with essentialism.

According to essentialism we must distinguish between (i) the universe of essential reality, (ii) the universe of observable phenomena, and (iii) the universe of descriptive language or of symbolic representation. I will take each of these to be represented by a square.

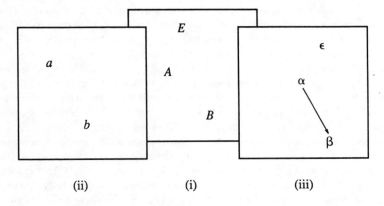

The function of a theory may here be described as follows.

a, b are phenomena; A, B are the corresponding realities behind these appearances; and α, β the descriptions or symbolic representations of these realities. E are the essential properties of A, B, and ϵ is the theory describing E. Now from ϵ and α we can deduce β; this means that we can explain, with the help of our theory, why a leads to, or is the cause of, b.

A representation of instrumentalism can be obtained from this schema simply by omitting (i), i.e., the universe of the realities behind the various appearances. α then directly describes a, and β directly describes b; and ϵ describes nothing—it is merely an instrument which helps us to deduce β from α. (This may be expressed by saying—as Schlick did, following Wittgenstein—that a universal law or a theory is not a proper statement but rather "a rule, or a set of instructions, for the derivation of singular statements from other singular statements."[23])

This is the instrumentalist view. In order to understand it better we may again take Newtonian dynamics as an example. a and b may be taken to be two positions of two spots of light (or two positions of the planet Mars); α and β are the corresponding formulae of the formalism; and ϵ is the theory strengthened by a general description of the solar system (or by a "model" of the solar system). Nothing corresponds to ϵ in the world (in the universe ii): there simply are no such things as attractive forces, for example. Newtonian forces are not entities which determine the acceleration of bodies: they are nothing but mathematical tools whose function is to allow us to deduce β from α.

No doubt we have here an attractive simplification, a radical application of Ockham's razor. But although this simplicity has converted many to instrumentalism (for example Mach) it is by no means the strongest argument in its favour.

Berkeley's strongest argument for instrumentalism was based upon his nominalistic philosophy of language. According to this philosophy the expression "force of attraction" must be a meaningless expression, since forces of attraction can never be observed. What can be observed are movements, not their hidden alleged "causes." This is sufficient, on Berkeley's view of language, to show that Newton's theory cannot have any informative or descriptive content.

Now this argument of Berkeley's may perhaps be criticized because of the intolerably narrow theory of meaning which it implies. For if consistently applied it amounts to the thesis that all dispositional words are without meaning. Not only would Newtonian "attractive forces" be without meaning, but also such ordinary dispositional words and expressions as "breakable" (as opposed to "broken"), or "capable of conducting electricity" (as opposed to "conducting electricity"). These are not names of anything observable, and they would therefore have to be treated on a par with Newtonian forces. But it would be awkward to classify all these expressions as meaningless, and *from the point of view of instrumentalism* it is quite unnecessary to do so: all that is needed is an analysis of the meaning of dispositional terms and dispositional statements. This will reveal that they have meaning. But from the point of view of instrumentalism they do not have a descriptive meaning (like nondispositional terms and statements). Their function is not to report events, or occurrences, or "incidents," in the world, or to describe facts. Rather, their meaning exhausts itself in the permission or licence which they give us to draw inferences or to argue from some matters of fact to other matters of fact. Nondispositional statements which describe observable matters of fact ("this leg is broken") have cash value, as it were; dispositional statements, to which belong the laws of science, are not like cash, but rather like legal *"instruments"* creating rights to cash.

One need only proceed one step further in the same direction, it appears, in order to arrive at an instrumentalist argument which it is extremely difficult, if not impossible, to criticize; for our whole question—whether science is descriptive or instrumental—is here exposed as a pseudo-problem.[24]

The step in question consists, simply, in not only allowing meaning—an instrumental meaning—to dispositional terms, but also a kind of *descriptive meaning*. Dispositional words such as "breakable," it may be said, certainly describe something; for to say of a thing that it is breakable is to describe it as a thing that can be broken. But to say of a thing that it is breakable, or soluble, is to describe it in a different way, and by a different method, from saying that it is broken or dissolved; otherwise we should not use the suffix "able." The difference is just this— that we describe, by using dispositional words, what may happen to a thing (in certain circumstances). Accordingly, dispositional descriptions *are* descriptions, but they have nevertheless a purely instrumental function. In their case, knowledge *is* power (the power to foresee). When Galileo said of the earth "and yet, it moves," then he uttered, no doubt, a descriptive statement. But the function or meaning of this statement turns out nevertheless to be purely instrumental: it exhausts itself in the help it renders in deducing certain nondispositional statements.

Thus the attempt to show that theories have a descriptive meaning *besides* their instrumental meaning is misconceived, according to this argument; and the whole problem—the issue between Galileo and the Church—turns out to be a pseudo-problem.

In support of the view that Galileo suffered for the sake of a pseudo-problem it has been asserted that in the light of a logically more advanced system of physics Galileo's problem has in fact dissolved into nothing. Einstein's general principle, one often hears, makes it quite clear that it is meaningless to speak of absolute motion, even in the case of rotation; for we can freely choose whatever system we wish to be (relatively) at rest. Thus Galileo's problem vanishes. Moreover, it vanishes precisely for the reasons given above. Astronomical knowledge can be nothing but knowledge of how the stars behave; thus it cannot be anything but the power to describe and predict our observations; and since these must be independent of our free choice of a coordinate system, we now see more clearly why Galileo's problem could not possible be real.

I shall not criticize instrumentalism in this section, or reply to its arguments, except the very last one—the argument from general relativity. This argument is based on a mistake. From the point of view of general relativity, there is very good sense—even an absolute sense—in saying that the earth rotates: *it rotates in precisely that sense in which a bicycle wheel rotates.* It rotates, that is to say, with respect to *any* chosen local inertia system. Indeed relativity describes the solar system in such a way that from this description we can deduce that *any* observer situated on *any* sufficiently distant freely moving physical body (such as our moon, or another planet, or a star outside the system) would see the earth rotating, and could deduce, from this observation, that for its inhabitants there would be an apparent diurnal motion of the sun. But it is clear that this is precisely the sense of the words "it moves" which was at issue; for part of the issue was whether the solar system was a system like that of Jupiter and his moons, only bigger; and whether it would look like this system, if seen from outside. On all these questions Einstein unambiguously supports Galileo.

My argument should not be interpreted as an admission that the whole question can be reduced to one of observations, or of possible observations. Admittedly both Galileo and Einstein intend, among other things, to deduce what an observer, or a possible observer, would see. But this is not their main problem. Both investigate physical systems and their movements. It is only the instrumentalist philosopher who asserts that what they discussed, or "really meant" to discuss, were not physical systems but *only* the results of possible observations; and that their so-called "physical systems," which *appeared* to be their objects of study, were *in reality* only instruments for predicting observations.

V. CRITICISM OF THE INSTRUMENTALIST VIEW

Berkeley's argument, we have seen, depends upon the adoption of a certain philosophy of language, convincing perhaps at first, but not necessarily true. Moreover, it hinges on the *problem of meaning*,[25] notorious for its vagueness and hardly offering hope of a solution. The position becomes even more hopeless if we consider some more recent development of Berkeley's arguments, as sketched in the preceding section. I shall try, therefore, to force a clear decision on our problem by a different approach—by way of an analysis of science rather than an analysis of language.

My proposed criticism of the instrumentalist view of scientific theories can be summarized as follows.

Instrumentalism can be formulated as the thesis that scientific theories—the theories of the so-called "pure" sciences—are nothing but computation rules (or inference rules); of the same character, fundamentally, as the computation rules of the so-called "applied" sciences. (One might even formulate it as the thesis that 'pure' science is a misnomer, and that all science is "applied.")

Now my reply to instrumentalism consists in showing that there are profound differences between "pure" theories and technological computation rules, and that instrumentalism can give a perfect description of these rules but is quite unable to account for the difference between them and the theories. Thus instrumentalism collapses.

The analysis of the many functional differences between computation rules (for navigation, say) and scientific theories (such as Newton's) is a very interesting task, but a short list of results must suffice here. The logical relations which may hold between theories and computation rules are not symmetrical; and they are different from those which may hold between various theories, and also from those which may hold between various computation rules. The way in which computation rules are *tried out* is different from the way in which theories are *tested*; and the skill which the application of computation rules demands is quite different from that needed for their (theoretical) discussion, and for the (theoretical) determination of the limits of their applicability. These are only a few hints, but they may be enough to indicate the direction and the force of the argument.

I am now going to explain one of these points a little more fully, because it gives rise to an argument somewhat similar to the one I have used against essentialism. What I wish to discuss is the fact that theories are tested by *attempts to refute them* (attempts from which we learn a great deal), while there is nothing strictly corresponding to this in the case of technological rules of computation or calculation.

A theory is tested not merely by applying it, or by trying it out, but by applying it to very special cases—cases for which it yields results different from those we should have expected without that theory, or in the light of other theories. In other words we try to select for our tests those crucial cases in which we should expect the theory to fail if it is not true. Such cases are "crucial" in Bacon's sense; they indicate the crossroads between *two* (or more) theories. For to say that without the theory in question we should have expected a different result implies that our expectation was the result of some other (perhaps an older) theory, however dimly we may have been aware of this fact. But while Bacon believed that a crucial experiment may establish or verify a theory, we shall have to say that it can at most refute or falsify a theory.[26] It is an attempt to refute it; and if it does not succeed in refuting the theory in question—if, rather, the theory is successful with its unexpected prediction—then we say that it is corroborated by the experiment. (It is the better corroborated[27] the less expected, or the less probable, the result of the experiment has been.)

Against the view here developed one might be tempted to object (following Duhem[28]) that in every test it is not only the theory under investigation which is involved, but also the whole system of our theories and assumptions—in fact, more or less the whole of our knowledge—so that we can never be certain which of all these assumptions is refuted. But this criticism overlooks the fact that if we take each of the two theories (between which the crucial experiment is to decide) *together* with all this background knowledge, as indeed we must, then we decide between two systems which differ *only* over the two theories which are at stake. It further overlooks the fact that we do not assert the refutation of the theory as such, but of the theory *together* with that background knowledge; parts of which, if other crucial experiments can be designed, may indeed one day be rejected as responsible for the failure. (Thus we may even characterize a *theory under investigation* as that part of a vast system for which we have, if vaguely, an alternative in mind, and for which we try to design crucial tests.)

Now nothing sufficiently similar to such tests exists in the case of instruments or rules of computation. An instrument may break down, to be sure, or it may become outmoded. But it hardly makes sense to say that we submit an instrument to the severest tests we can design in order to reject it if it does not stand up to them: every air frame, for example, can be "tested to destruction," but this severe test is undertaken not in order to reject every frame when it is destroyed but to obtain information about the frame (i.e., to test a theory about it), so that it may be used *within the limits of its applicability* (or safety).

For instrumental purposes of practical application a theory may continue to be used *even after its refutation*, within the limits of its applicability: an astronomer who believes that Newton's theory has turned out to be false will not hesitate to apply its formalism within the limits of its applicability.

We may sometimes be disappointed to find that the range of applicability of an instrument is smaller than we expected at first; but this does not make us discard the instrument *qua* instrument—whether it is a theory or anything else. On the other hand a disappointment of this kind means that we have obtained new *information* through refuting a *theory*—that theory which implied that the instrument was applicable over a wider range.

Instruments, even theories *insofar as they are instruments*, cannot be refuted, as we have seen. The instrumentalist interpretation will therefore be unable to account for real tests, which are attempted refutations, and will not get beyond the assertion that *different theories have different ranges of application*. But then it cannot possibly account for scientific progress. Instead of saying (as I should) that Newton's theory was falsified by crucial experiments which failed to falsify Einstein's, and that Einstein's theory is therefore better than Newton's, the consistent instrumentalist will have to say, with reference to his "new" point of view, like Heisenberg: "It follows that we do not say any longer: Newton's mechanics is false. . . . Rather, we now use the following formulation: Classical mechanics . . . is everywhere exactly 'right' where its concepts can be applied."[29]

Since "right" here means "applicable," this assertion merely amounts to saying, "Classical mechanics is applicable where its concepts can be applied"—which is not saying much. But be this as it may, the point is that *by neglecting falsification, and stressing application, instrumentalism proves to be as obscurantist a philosophy as essentialism*. For it is only in searching for refutations that science can hope to learn and to advance. It is only in considering how its various theories stand up to tests that it can distinguish between better and worse theories and so find a criterion of progress. (See chapter 10 of my *Conjectures and Refutations*.)

Thus a mere instrument for prediction cannot be falsified. What may appear to us at first as its falsification turns out to be no more than a rider cautioning us about its limited applicability. This is why the instrumentalist view may be used *ad hoc* for rescuing a physical theory which is threatened by contradictions, as was done by Bohr (if I am right in my interpretation, given in section II, of his principle of complementarity). If theories are mere instruments of prediction we need not discard any particular theory even though we believe that no consistent physical interpretation of its formalism exists.

Summing up we may say that instrumentalism is unable to account for the importance to pure science of testing severely even the most remote implications of its theories, since it is unable to account for the pure scientist's interest in truth and falsity. In contrast to the highly critical attitude requisite in the pure scientist, the attitude of instrumentalism (like that of applied science) is one of complacency at the success of applications. Thus it may well be responsible for the recent stagnation in quantum theory. (This was written before the refutation of parity.)

VI. THE THIRD VIEW: CONJECTURES, TRUTH, AND REALITY

Neither Bacon nor Berkeley believed that the earth rotates, but nowadays everybody believes it, including the physicists. Instrumentalism is embraced by Bohr and Heisenberg only as a way out of the special difficulties which have arisen in quantum theory.

The motive is hardly sufficient. It is always difficult to interpret the latest theories, and they sometimes perplex even their own creators, as happened with Newton. Maxwell at first inclined towards an essentialist interpretation of his theory: a theory which ultimately contributed more than any other to the decline of essentialism. And Einstein inclined at first to an instrumentalist interpretation of relativity, giving a kind of operational analysis of the concept of simultaneity which contributed more to the present vogue for instrumentalism than anything else; but he later repented.[30]

I trust that physicists will soon come to realize that the principle of complementarity is *ad hoc*, and (what is more important) that its only function is to avoid criticism and to prevent the discussion of physical interpretations; though criticism and discussion are urgently needed for reforming any theory. They will then no longer believe that instrumentalism is forced upon them by the structure of contemporary physical theory.

Anyway, instrumentalism is, as I have tried to show, no more acceptable than essentialism. Nor is there any need to accept either of them, for there is a third view.[31]

This "third view" is not very startling or even surprising, I think. It preserves the Galilean doctrine that the scientist aims at a true description of the world, or of some of its aspects, and at a true explanation of observable facts; and it combines this doctrine with the non-Galilean view that though this remains the aim of the scientist, he can never know for certain whether his findings are true, although he may sometimes establish with reasonable certainty that a theory is false.[32]

One may formulate this "third view" of scientific theories briefly by saying that they are *genuine conjectures*—highly informative guesses about the world which although not verifiable (i.e., capable of being shown to be true) can be submitted to severe critical tests. They are serious attempts to discover the truth. In this respect scientific hypotheses are exactly like Goldbach's famous conjecture in the theory of numbers. Goldbach thought that it might possibly be true; and it may well be true in fact, even though *we do not know, and may perhaps never know, whether it is true or not.*

I shall confine myself to mentioning only a few aspects of my "third view," and only such aspects as distinguish it from essentialism and instrumentalism; and I shall take essentialism first.

Essentialism looks upon our ordinary world as mere appearance behind which it discovers the real world. This view has to be discarded once we become conscious of the fact that the world of each of our theories may be explained, in its turn, by further worlds which are described by further theories—theories of a higher level of abstraction, of universality, and of testability. The doctrine of an *essential or ultimate reality* collapses together with that of ultimate explanation.

Since according to our third view the new scientific theories are, like the old ones, genuine conjectures, they are genuine attempts to describe these further worlds. Thus we are led to take all these worlds, including our ordinary world, as equally real; or better, perhaps, as equally real aspects or layers of the real world. (If looking through a microscope we change its magnification, then we may see various completely different aspects or layers of the same thing, all equally real.) It is thus mistaken to say that my piano, as I know it, is real, while its alleged molecules and atoms are mere "logical constructions" (or whatever else may be indicative of their unreality); just as it is mistaken to say that atomic theory shows that the piano of my everyday world is an appearance only—a doctrine which is clearly unsatisfactory once we see that the atoms in their turn may perhaps be explained as disturbances, or structures of disturbances, in a quantised field of forces (or perhaps of probabilities). All these conjectures are equal in their claims to describe reality, although some of them are more conjectural than others.

Thus we shall not, for example, describe only the so-called "primary qualities" of a body (such as its geometrical shape) as real, and contrast them as the essentialists once did, with its unreal and merely apparent "secondary qualities" (such as colour). For the extension and even the shape of a body have since become *objects of explanation* in terms of theories of a higher level; of theories describing a further and deeper layer of reality—forces, and field of forces—which are related to the primary qualities in the same way as these were believed by the essentialists to be related to the secondary ones; and the secondary qualities, such as colors, are just as real as the primary ones—though our color-experiences have to be distinguished from the color-properties of the physical things, exactly as our geometrical-shape-experiences have to be distinguished from the geometrical-shape-properties of the physical things. From our point of view both kinds of qualities are equally real; and so are forces, and fields of forces—in spite of their undoubted hypothetical or conjectural character.

Although in one sense of the word "real," all these various levels are equally real, there is another yet closely related sense in which we might say that the higher and more conjectural levels are the *more real* ones—in spite of the fact that they are more conjectural. They are, according to our theories, more real (more stable in intention, more permanent) in the sense in which a table, or a tree, or a star, is more real than any of its aspects.

But is not just this conjectural or hypothetical character of our theories the reason why we should not ascribe reality to the worlds described by them? Should we not (even if we find Berkeley's "to be is to be perceived" too narrow) *call only those states of affairs "real" which are described by true statements*, rather than by conjectures which may turn out to be false? With these questions we turn to the discussion of the instrumentalist doctrine, which with its assertion that theories are mere instruments intends to deny the claim that anything like a real world is described by them.

I accept the view (implicit in the classical or correspondence theory of truth[33]) that we should call a state of affairs "real" if, and only if, the statement describing it is true. But it would be a grave mistake to conclude from this that the uncertainty of a theory, i.e., its hypothetical or conjectural character, diminishes in any way its implicit *claim* to describe something real. For every statement s is equivalent to a statement claiming that s is true. And as to s being a conjecture, we must remember that, first of all, a conjecture *may* be true, and thus describe a real state of affairs. Secondly, if it is false, then it contradicts some real state of affairs (described by its true negation). Moreover, if we test our conjecture, and succeed in falsifying it, we see very clearly that there was a reality—something with which it could clash.

Our falsifications thus indicate the points where we have touched reality, as it were. And our latest and best theory is always an attempt to incorporate all the falsifications ever found in the field, by explaining them in the simplest way; and this means (as I have tried to show in *The Logic of Scientific Discovery*, sections 31 to 46) in the most testable way.

Admittedly, if we do not know how to test a theory we may be doubtful whether there is anything at all of the kind (or level) described by it; and if we positively know that it cannot be tested, then our doubts will grow; we may suspect that it is a mere myth, or a fairy tale. *But if a theory is testable, then it implies that events of a certain kind cannot happen; and so it asserts something about reality.* (This is why we demand that the more conjectural a theory is, the higher should be its degree of testability.) Testable conjectures or guesses, at any rate, are thus conjectures or guesses about reality; from their uncertain or conjectural character it only follows that our knowledge concerning the reality they describe is uncertain or conjectural. And although only that is certainly real which can be known with certainty, it is a mistake to think that only that is real which is known to be certainly real. We are not omniscient and, no doubt, much is real that is unknown to us all. It is thus indeed the old Berkeleian mistake (in the form "to be is to be known") which still underlies instrumentalism.

Theories are our own inventions, our own ideas; they are not forced upon us, but are our self-made instruments of thought: this has been clearly seen by the idealist. But some of these theories of ours can clash with reality; and when they do, we know that there is a reality; that there is something to remind us of the fact that our ideas may be mistaken. And this is why the realist is right.

Thus I agree with essentialism in its view that *science is capable of real discoveries*, and even in its view that in discovering new worlds our intellect triumphs over our sense experience. But I do not fall into the mistake of Parmenides—of denying reality to all that is colorful, varied, individual, indeterminate, and indescribable in our world.

Since I believe that science can make real discoveries I take my stand with Galileo against instrumentalism. I admit that our discoveries are conjectural. But this is even true of geographical explorations. Columbus' conjectures as to what he had discovered were in fact mistaken; and Peary could only conjecture—on the basis of theories—that he had reached the Pole. But these elements of conjecture do not make their discoveries less real, or less significant.

There is an important distinction which we can make between two kinds of scientific prediction, and which instrumentalism cannot make; a distinction which is connected with the problem of scientific discovery. I have in mind the distinction between the prediction of *events of a kind which is known*, such as eclipses or thunderstorms on the one hand and, on the other hand, the prediction of *new kinds of events* (which the physicist calls "new effects") such as the prediction which led to the discovery of wireless waves, or of zero-point energy, or to the artificial building up of new elements not previously found in nature.

It seems to me clear that instrumentalism can account only for the first kind of prediction: if theories are instruments for prediction, then we must assume that their purpose must be determined in advance, as with other instruments. Predictions of the second kind can be fully understood only as discoveries.

It is my belief that our discoveries are guided by theory in these as in most other cases, rather than that theories are the result of discoveries "due to observation"; for observation itself tends to be guided by theory. Even geographical discoveries (Columbus, Franklin, the two Nordenskjölds, Nansen, Wegener, and Heyerdahl's Kon-Tiki expedition) are often undertaken with the aim of testing a theory. Not to be content with offering predictions, but to create new situations for new kinds of tests: this is a function of theories which instrumentalism can hardly explain without surrendering its main tenets.

But perhaps the most interesting contrast between the "third view" and instrumentalism arises in connection with the latter's denial of the descriptive function of abstract words, and of disposition-words. This doctrine, by the way, exhibits an essentialist strain within instrumentalism—the belief that events or occurrences or "incidents" (which are directly observable) must be, in a sense, more real than dispositions (which are not).

The "third view" of this matter is different. I hold that most observations are more or less indirect, and that it is doubtful whether the distinction between directly observable incidents and whatever is only indirectly observable leads us anywhere. I cannot but think that it is a mistake to denounce Newtonian forces (the "causes of acceleration") as occult, and to try to discard them (as has been suggested) in favour of accelerations. For accelerations cannot be observed any more directly than forces; and they are *just as dispositional*: the statement that a body's velocity is accelerated tells us that the body's velocity in the next second from now will exceed its present velocity.

In my opinion *all universals are dispositional*. If "breakable" is dispositional, so is "broken," considering for example how a doctor decides whether a bone is broken or not. Nor should we call a glass "broken" if the pieces would fuse the moment they were put together: the criterion of being broken is behaviour *under certain conditions*. Similarly, "red" is dispositional: a thing is red if it is able to reflect a certain kind of light—if it "looks red" in certain situations. But even "looking red" is dispositional. It describes the disposition of a thing to make onlookers agree that it looks red.

No doubt there are *degrees* of dispositional character: "able to conduct electricity" is dispositional in a higher degree than "conducting electricity now" which is still very highly dispositional. These degrees correspond fairly closely to those of the conjectural or hypothetical character of theories. But there is no point in denying reality to dispositions, not even if we deny reality to all universals and to all states of affairs, including incidents, and confine ourselves to using that sense of the word "real" which, from the point of view of ordinary usage, is the narrowest and safest: to call only physical bodies "real," and only those which are neither too small nor too big nor too distant to be easily seen and handled.

For even then we should realize (as I wrote twenty years ago) that

every description uses . . . universals; every statement has the character of a theory, a hypothesis. The statement, "Here is a glass of water," cannot be (completely) verified by any sense-experience, because the universals which appear in it cannot be correlated with any particular sense-experience. (An "immediate experience" is *only once* "immediately given"; it is unique.) By the word "glass," for example, we denote physical bodies which exhibit a certain *law-like behaviour*; and the same holds of the word "water."[34]

I do not think that a language without universals could ever work; and the use of universals commits us to asserting, and thus (at least) to conjecturing, the reality of dispositions—though not of ultimate and inexplicable ones, that is, of essences. We may express all this by saying that the customary distinction between *"observational terms"* (or *"nontheoretical terms"*) and *theoretical terms* is mistaken, since all terms are theoretical to some degree, though some are more theoretical than others; just as we said that all theories are conjectural, though some are more conjectural than others.

But if we are committed, or at least prepared, to conjecture the reality of forces, and of fields of forces, then there is no reason why we should not conjecture that a die has a definite *propensity* (or disposition) to fall on one or another of its sides; that this propensity can be changed by loading it; that propensities of this kind may change continuously; and that we may operate with fields of propensities, or of entities which determine propensities. An interpretation of probability on these lines might allow us to give a new physical interpretation to quantum theory—one which differs from the purely statistical interpretation, due to Born, while agreeing with him that probability statements can be tested only statistically.[35] And this interpretation may, perhaps, be of some little help in our efforts to resolve those grave and challenging difficulties in quantum theory which today seem to imperil the Galilean tradition.

NOTES

1. I emphasize here the diurnal as opposed to the annual motion of the sun because it was the theory of the diurnal motion which clashed with Joshua 10, 12f., and because the explanation of the diurnal motion of the sun by the motion of the earth will be one of my main examples in what follows. (This explanation is, of course, much older than Copernicus—older even than Aristarchus—and it has been repeatedly re-discovered; for example by Oresme.)
2. ". . . Galileo will act prudently," wrote Cardinal Bellarmino (who had been one of the inquisitors in the case against Giordano Bruno) ". . . if he will speak hypothetically, *ex suppositione* . . .: to say that we give a better account of the appearances by supposing the earth to be moving, and the sun at rest, than we could if we used eccentrics and epicycles is to speak properly; there is no danger in that, and it is all that the mathematician requires." Cf. H. Grisar, *Galileistudien*, (1882), appendix ix. (Although this passage makes Bellarmino one of the founding fathers of the epistemology which Osiander had suggested some time before and which I am going to call "instrumentalism," Bellarmino—unlike Berkeley—was by no means a convinced instrumentalist himself, as other passages in this letter show. He merely saw in instrumentalism one of the possible ways dealing with inconvenient scientific hypotheses. The same remarks might well be true of Osiander. See also note 6, in section II below.)
3. The quotation is from Bacon's criticism of Copernicus in the *Novum Organum*, vol. 2, 36. In the next quotation (from *De revolutionibus*) I have translated the term "*verisimilis*" by "like the truth." It should certainly not be translated here by "probable"; for the whole point here is the question whether Copernicus's system is, or is not, similar in structure to the world; that is, whether it is truthlike. The questions of degree of certainty or probability does not arise. See also chapter 10 of my *Conjectures and Refutations* (New York: Harper and Row, 1968), especially sections 3, 10, and 14; and Addendum 6.
4. See also chapter 6 of *Conjectures and Refutations*.
5. The most important of them are Mach, Kirchhoff, Hertz, Duhem, Poincaré, Bridgman, and Eddington—all instrumentalists in various ways.
6. Duhem, in his famous series of papers, *Sōzein ta phainómena'* (*Ann. de philos. chrétienne*, anneé 79, tom 6, 1908, nos. 2 to 6), claimed for instrumentalism a much older and much more illustrious ancestry than is justified by the evidence. For the postulate that, with their hypotheses, scientists ought to "*account for the observed facts*," rather than "do violence to them by trying to squeeze or fit them into their theories" (Aristotle, *De Caelo*, 293a25; 296b6; 297a4, b24ff; *Met.* 1073b37, 1074al) has little to do with the instrumentalist thesis (that our theories can do *nothing but this*). Yet this postulate is essentially the same as that we ought to "*preserve the phenomena*" or "save" them ([*dia-*]*sōzein ta phainómena*). The phrase seems to be connected with the astronomical branch of the Platonic School tradition. (See especially the most interesting passage on Aristarchus in Plutarch's *De Facie in Orbe Lunae*, 923a; see also 933a for the "confirmation of the cause" by the phenomena, and Cherniss's note *a* on p. 168 of his edition of this work of Plutarch's; furthermore, Simplicius's commentaries on *De Caelo* where the phrase occurs, e.g., on pp. 497 1.21, 506 1.10, and 488 1.23 f, of Heiberg's edition, in commentaries on *De Caelo* 293a4 and 292b10.) We may well accept Simplicius's report that

Eudoxus, under Plato's influence, in order to account for the observable phenomena of planetary motion, set himself the task of evolving an abstract geometrical system of rotating spheres *to which he did not attribute any physical reality.* (There seems to be some resemblance between this program and that of the *Epinomis*, 990–91, where the study of abstract geometry—of the theory of the irrationals, 990d–991b—is described as a necessary preliminary to planetary theory; another such preliminary is the study of number—i.e., the odd and the even, 990c.) Yet even this would not mean that either Plato or Eudoxus accepted an instrumentalist epistemology: they may have consciously (and wisely) confined themselves to a preliminary problem.

7. But they seem to have forgotten that Mach was led by his instrumentalism to fight against atomic theory—a typical example of *the obscurantism of instrumentalism* which is the topic of section V below.

8. I have explained Bohr's "Principle of Complementarity" as I understand it after many years of effort. No doubt I shall be told that my formulation of it is unsatisfactory. But if so I am in good company; for Einstein refers to it as "Bohr's principle of complementarity, a sharp formulation of which . . . I have been unable to attain despite much effort which I have expended on it." Cf. *Albert Einstein: Philosopher-Scientist*, ed. by P. A. Schilpp (1949), p. 674.

9. See chapter 4 of *Conjectures and Refutations*.

10. Salviati says so several times, with hardly a verbal variation, on the Third Day of *The Two Principal Systems*.

11. See the appendix, point (10) to chapter 1 of *Conjectures and Refutations*, and the penultimate paragraph of chapter 6 to the same work.

12. The realization that natural science is not indubitable *epistēmē* (*scientia*) has led to the view that it is *technē* (technique, art, technology); but the proper view, I believe, is that it consists of *doxai* (*opinions, conjectures*), controlled by critical discussion as well as by experimental *technē*. Cf. chapter 20 of *Conjectures and Refutations*.

13. See section 10 of my *Poverty of Historicism*, and my *Open Society and its Enemies* (London: Hutchinson, 1945), vol. 1, chapter 3 section 6 and vol. 2, ch. 11, sections 1 and 2.

14. The issue has been confused at times by the fact that the instrumentalist criticism of (ultimate) explanation was expressed by some with the help of the formula: the aim of science is *description rather than explanation.* But what was here meant by "description" was the description *of the ordinary empirical world*; and what the formula expressed, indirectly, was that those theories which do not describe *in this sense* do not explain either, but are nothing but convenient instruments to help us in the description of ordinary phenomena.

15. Cf. Kant's letter to Reinhold, May 12, 1789, in which the "real essence" or "nature" of a thing (e.g. of matter) is said to be inaccessible to human knowledge.

16. See chapter 6 of *Conjectures and Refutations*.

17. This criticism of mine is thus frankly utilitarian, and it might be described as instrumentalist; but I am concerned here with a *problem of method* which is always a problem of the fitness of means to ends.

My attacks upon *essentialism*—i.e., upon the *doctrine of ultimate explanation*—have sometimes been countered by the remark that I myself operate (perhaps unconsciously) with the idea of an *essence of science* (or an *essence of human knowledge*), so that my argument, if made explicit, would run: "It is of the essence or of the nature of human science (or human knowledge) that we cannot know, or search for, such things as essences or natures." I have however answered, by implication, this particular objection at some length in *L.Sc.D.* (sections 9 and 10, "The Naturalist View of Method") and I did so before it was ever raised—in fact before I ever came to describe, and to attack, essentialism. Moreover, one might adopt the view that certain *things of our own making*—such as clocks—may well be said to have "essences," viz. their "purposes" (and what makes them serve these "purposes"). And science, as a human, purposeful activity (or a method), *might* therefore be claimed by some to have an "essence," even if they deny that natural objects have essences. (This denial is not, however, implied in my criticism of essentialism.)

18. R. Cotes' Preface to the second edition of Newton's *Principia*.
19. There is an essentialist theory of Time and Space (similar to this theory of matter) which is due to Newton himself.
20. Letter to Richard Bentley, February 25, 1692–93 (i.e., 1693); cf. also the letter of January 17.
21. This Cartesian theory of causality is of decisive importance for the whole history of physics. It led to the principle of action by contact, and later to the more abstract "principle of *action at vanishing distances*" (as I may call it), of an action propagated from each point to its immediate vicinity; i.e., to the principle of differential equations.
22. Newton was an essentialist for whom gravity was not acceptable as an ultimate explanation, but he was unsuccessful in his attempts to explain it further mathematically. Descartes, in such a situation, would have postulated the existence of some push-mechanism: he would have proposed what he called a "hypothesis." But Newton, with a critical allusion to Descartes, said that, in this situation, he was not going to invent arbitrary *ad hoc* hypotheses (*hypotheses non fingo*). Of course, he could not but operate constantly with hypotheses (e.g. with an atomistic theory of light "rays"); but this saying of his has been interpreted as an authoritative criticism of the method of hypotheses, or (by Duhem) as a declaration of his instrumentalism.
23. For an analysis and criticism of this view see my *L.Sc.D.* especially note 7 to section 4, and my *Open Society*, note 51 to chapter 11. The idea that universal statements may function in this way can be found in Mill's *Logic*, Book II, chapter III, 3: "All inference is from particulars to particulars." See also G. Ryle, *The Concept of Mind* (1949), chapter 5, pp. 121 ff., for a more careful and critical formulation of the same view.
24. I have not so far encountered in the literature this particular form of the instrumentalist argument; but if we remember the parallelism between problems concerning the *meaning* of an expression and problems concerning the *truth* of a statement (see for example the table in the Introduction to *Conjectures and Refutations*, section 12), we see that this argument closely corresponds to William James's definition of "truth" as "usefulness."
25. For this problem see my two books mentioned here in footnote 23, and chapters 1, 11, 13 and 14 of *Conjectures and Refutations*.
26. Duhem, in his famous criticism of crucial experiments (in his *Aim and Structure of Physical Theory*), succeeds in showing that crucial experiments can never *establish* a theory. He fails to show that they cannot *refute* it.
27. The degree of corroboration will therefore increase with the improbability (or the content) of the corroborating cases. See my "Degree of Confirmation," *British Journal for the Philosophy of Science*. 5, pp. 143ff., now among the new appendices of my *L.Sc.D.*, and chapter 10 of *Conjectures and Refutations*, (including the Addenda).
28. See note 26.
29. See W. Heisenberg in *Dialectica*, 2 (1948), p. 333 f. Heisenberg's own instrumentalism is far from consistent, and he has many anti-instrumentalist remarks to his credit. But this article here quoted may be described as an out-and-out attempt to prove that his quantum theory leads of necessity to an instrumentalist philosophy, and thereby to the result that physical theory can never be unified, or even made consistent.
30. *Note added to the proofs.* When this paper went to press Albert Einstein was still alive, and I intended to send him a copy as soon as it was printed. My remark referred to a conversation we had on the subject in 1950.
31. Cf. section V of chapter 6 of *Conjectures and Refutations*.
32. Cf. the discussion of this point in section V, above, and *L.Sc.D.* (*passim*); also chapter 1 of *Conjectures and Refutations*, and Xenophanes' fragments quoted towards the end of chapter 5 to the same work.
33. See A. Tarski's work on the *Concept of Truth* (*Der Wahrheitsbegriff, etc., Studia Philosophica*, (1935), text to note 1: "true = in agreement with reality"). (See the English translation in A. Tarski, *Logic, Semantics, Metamathematics* (1956), p. 153; the translation says "corresponding" where I translated

440 • THE NATURE OF SCIENTIFIC KNOWLEDGE

"in agreement.") The following remarks (and also the penultimate paragraph before the one to which this footnote is appended) have been added in an attempt to answer a friendly criticism privately communicated to me by Professor Alexander Koyré to whom I feel greatly indebted.

I do not think that, if we accept the suggestion that "in agreement with reality" and "true" are equivalent, we are seriously in danger of being led up the path to idealism. I do not propose to *define* "real" with the help of this equivalence. (And even if I did, there is no reason to believe that a definition necessarily determines the ontological status of the term defined.) What the equivalence should help us to see is that the *hypothetical character* of a statement—i.e., our *uncertainty as to its truth*—implies that we are making *guesses concerning reality.*

34. See my *L.Sc.D.*, end of section 25; see also New Appendix *x*, (1) to (4), and chapter 1 of *Conjectures and Refutations*; also chapter 11, section 5, text to notes 58–62.

35. Concerning the propensity theory of probability, see my papers in *Observation and Interpretation*, ed. S. Körner (1957), pp. 65 ff., and in the *B.J.P.S.* 10 (1959), pp. 25 ff.

W.V.O. QUINE

THE NATURE OF NATURAL KNOWLEDGE[1]

Doubt has oft been said to be the mother of philosophy. This has a true ring for those of us who look upon philosophy primarily as the theory of knowledge. For the theory of knowledge has its origin in doubt, in scepticism. Doubt is what prompts us to try to develop a theory of knowledge. Furthermore, doubt is also the first step to take in developing a theory of knowledge, if we adopt the line of Descartes.

But this is only half of a curious interplay between doubt and knowledge. Doubt prompts the theory of knowledge, yes; but knowledge, also, was what prompted the doubt. Scepticism is an offshoot of science. The basis for scepticism is the awareness of illusion, the discovery that we must not always believe our eyes. Scepticism battens on mirages, on seemingly bent sticks in water, on rainbows, after-images, double images, dreams. But in what sense are these illusions? In the sense that they seem to be material objects which they in fact are not. Illusions are illusions only relative to a prior acceptance of genuine bodies with which to contrast them. In a world of immediate sense data with no bodies posited and no questions asked, a distinction between reality and illusion would have no place. The positing of bodies is already rudimentary physical science; and it is only after that stage that the sceptic's invidious distinctions can make sense. Bodies have to be posited before there can be a motive, however tenuous, for acquiescing in a non-committal world of the immediate given.

Rudimentary physical science, that is, common sense about bodies, is thus needed as a springboard for scepticism. It contributes the needed notion of a distinction between reality and illusion, and that is not all. It also discerns regularities of bodily behaviour which are indispensable to that distinction. The sceptic's example of the seemingly bent stick owes its force to our knowledge that sticks do not bend by immersion; and his examples of mirages, after-images, dreams, and the rest are similarly parasitic upon positive science, however primitive.

I am not accusing the sceptic of begging the question. He is quite within his rights in assuming science in order to refute science; this, if carried out, would be a straightforward argument by *reductio ad absurdum*. I am only making the point that sceptical doubts are scientific doubts.

Epistemologists have coped with their sceptical doubts by trying to reconstruct our knowledge of the external world from sensations. A characteristic effort was Berkeley's theory of vision, in which he sought our clues for a third dimension, depth, in our two-dimensional visual field. The very posing of this epistemological problem depends in a striking way upon acceptations of physical science. The goal of the construction, namely the depth dimension, is of course deliberately taken from the science of the external world; but what particularly wants noticing is that also the accepted basis of the construction, the two-dimensional visual field, was itself dictated by the science of the external world as well. The light that informs us of the external world impinges on the two-dimensional surface of the eye, and it was Berkeley's awareness of this that set his problem.

Epistemology is best looked upon, then, as an enterprise within natural science. Cartesian doubt is not the way to begin. Retaining our present beliefs about nature, we can still ask how we can have arrived at them. Science tells us that our only source of information about the external world is through the impact of light rays and molecules upon our sensory surfaces. Stimulated in these ways, we somehow evolve an elaborate and useful science. How do we do this, and why does the resulting science work so well? These are genuine questions, and no feigning of doubt is needed to appreciate them. They are scientific questions about a species of primates, and they are open to investigation in natural science, the very science whose acquisition is being investigated.

The utility of science, from a practical point of view, lies in fulfilled expectation: true prediction. This is true not only of sophisticated science, but of its primitive progenitor as well; and it may be good strategy on our part to think first of the most primitive case. This case is simple induction. It is the expectation, when some past event recurs, that the sequel of that past event will recur too. People are prone to this, and so are other animals.

It may be felt that I am unduly intellectualizing the dumb animals in attributing expectation and induction to them. Still the net resultant behaviour of dumb animals is much on a par with our own, at the level of simple induction. In a dog's experience, a clatter of pans in the kitchen has been followed by something to eat. So now, hearing the clatter again, he goes to the kitchen in expectation of dinner. His going to the kitchen is our evidence of his expectation, if we care to speak of expectation. Or we can skip this intervening variable, as Skinner calls it, and speak merely of reinforced response, conditioned reflex, habit formation.

When we talk easily of repetition of events, repetition of stimuli, we cover over a certain significant factor. It is the *similarity* factor. It can be brought into the open by speaking of events rather as unique, dated, unrepeated particulars, and then speaking of similarities between them. Each of the noisy episodes of the pans is a distinct event, however similar, and so is each of the ensuing dinners. What we can say of the dog in those terms is that he hears something similar to the old clatter and proceeds to expect something similar to the old dinner. Or, if we want to eliminate the intervening variable, we can still say this: when the dog hears something similar to the old dinner, he is reinforced in his disposition to go to the kitchen after each further event similar to the old clatter.

What is significant about this similarity factor is its subjectivity. Is similarity the mere sharing of many attributes? But any two things share countless attributes—or anyway any two objects share membership in countless classes. The similarity that matters, in the clatter of the pans, is similarity for the dog. Again I seem to appeal to the dog's mental life, but again I can eliminate this intervening variable. We can analyse similarity, for the dog, in terms of his dispositions to behaviour: his patterns of habit formation. His habit of going to the kitchen after a clatter of pans is itself our basis for saying that the clatter events are similar for the dog, and that the dinner events are similar for the dog. It is by experimental reinforcement and extinction along these lines that we can assess similarities for the dog, determining whether event *a* is more similar to *b* than to *c* for him. Meanwhile his mental life is as may be.

Now our question "Why is science so successful?" makes some rudimentary sense already at this level, as applied to the dog. For the dog's habit formation, his primitive induction, involved extrapolation along similarity lines: episodes similar to the old clattering episode engendered expectation of episodes similar to the old dinner episode. And now the crux of the problem is the subjectivity of similarity. Why should nature, however lawful, match up at all with the dog's subjective similarity ratings? Here, at its most primitive, is the question "Why is science so successful?"

We are taking this as a scientific question, remember, open to investigation by natural science itself. Why should the dog's implicit similarity ratings tend to fit world trends, in such a way as to favor the dog's implicit expectations? An answer is offered by Darwin's theory of natural selection. Individuals whose similarity groupings conduce largely to true expectations have a good chance of finding food and avoiding predators, and so a good chance of living to reproduce their kind.

What I have said of the dog holds equally of us, at least in our pursuit of the rudimentary science of common sense. We predict in the light of observed uniformities, and these are uniformities by our subjective similarity standards. These standards are innate ones, overlaid and modified by experience; and natural selection has endowed us, like the dog, with a head start in the way of helpful, innate similarity standards.

I am not appealing to Darwinian biology to justify induction. This would be circular, since biological knowledge depends on induction. Rather I am granting the efficacy of induction, and then observing that Darwinian biology, if true, helps explain why induction is as efficacious as it is.

We must notice, still, a further limitation. Natural selection may be expected only to have encouraged similarity standards conducive to rough and ready anticipations of experience in a state of nature. Such standards are not necessarily conducive to deep science. Color is a case in point. Color dominates our scene; similarity in color is similarity at its most conspicuous. Yet, as J.J.C. Smart points out, color plays little role in natural science. Things can be alike in color even though one of them is reflecting green light of uniform wave length while the other is reflecting mixed waves of yellow and blue. Properties that are most germane to sophisticated science are camouflaged by color more than revealed by it. Over-sensitivity to color may have been all to the good when we were bent on quickly distinguishing predator from prey or good plants from bad. But true science cuts through all this and sorts things out differently, leaving color largely irrelevant.

Color is not the only such case. Taxonomy is rich in examples to show that visual resemblance is a poor index of kinship. Natural selection has even abetted the deception; thus some owls have grown to resemble cats, for their own good, and others resemble monkeys. Natural selection works both to improve a creature's similarity standards and to help him abuse his enemies' similarity standards.

For all their fallibility, our innate similarity standards are indispensable to science as an entering wedge. They continue to be indispensable, moreover, even as science advances. For the advance of science depends on continued observation, continued checking of predictions. And there, at the observational level, the unsophisticated similarity standards of common sense remain in force.

An individual's innate similarity standards undergo some revision, of course, even at the common-sense level, indeed even at the subhuman level, through learning. An animal may learn to tell a cat from an owl. The ability to learn is itself a product of natural selection, with evident survival value. An animal's innate similarity standards are a rudimentary instrument for prediction, and then learning is a progressive refinement of that instrument, making for more dependable prediction. In man, and most conspicuously in recent centuries, this refinement has consisted in the development of a vast and bewildering growth of conceptual or linguistic apparatus, the whole of natural science. Biologically, still, it is like the animal's learning about cats and owls; it is a learned improvement over simple induction by innate similarity standards. It makes for more and better prediction.

Science revises our similarity standards, we saw; thus we discount color, for some purposes, and we liken whales to cows rather than to fish. But this is not the sole or principal way in which science fosters prediction. Mere improvement of similarity standards would increase our success at simple induction, but this is the least of it. Science departs from simple induction. Science is a ponderous linguistic structure, fabricated of theoretical terms linked by fabricated hypotheses, and keyed to observable events here and there. Indirectly, via this labyrinthine superstructure, the scientist predicts future observations on the basis of past ones; and he may revise the superstructure when the predictions fail. It is no longer simple induction. It is the hypothetico-deductive method. But, like the animal's simple induction over innate similarities, it is still a biological device for anticipating experience. It owes its elements still to natural selection—notably, the similarity standards that continue to operate at the observational level. The biological survival value of the resulting scientific structure, however, is as may be. Traits that were developed by natural selection have been known to prove lethal, through over-development or remote effects or changing environment. In any event, and for whatever good it may do us, the hypothetico-deductive method is delivering knowledge hand over fist. It is facilitating prediction.

I said that science is a linguistic structure that is keyed to observation at some points. Some sentences are keyed directly to observation: the observation sentences. Let us examine this connection. First I must explain what I mean by an observation sentence. One distinctive trait of such a sentence is that its truth value varies with the circumstances prevailing at the time of the utterance. It is a sentence like "This is red" or "It is raining," which is true on one occasion and false on another; unlike "Sugar is sweet," whose truth value endures regardless of occasion of utterance. In a word, observation sentences are occasion sentences, not standing sentences.

But their being occasion sentences is not the only distinctive trait of observation sentences. Not only must the truth value of an observation sentence depend on the circumstances of its utterance; it must depend on intersubjectively observable circumstances. Certainly the fisherman's sentence "I just felt a nibble" is true or false depending on the circumstances of its utterance; but the relevant circumstances are privy to the speaker rather than being out in the open for all present witnesses to share. The sentence "I just felt a nibble" is an occasion sentence but not an observation sentence, in my sense of the term.

An observation sentence, then, is an occasion sentence whose occasion is intersubjectively observable. But this is still not enough. After all, the sentence "There goes John's old tutor" meets these requirements; it is an occasion sentence, and all present witnesses can see the old tutor plodding by. But the sentence fails of a third requirement: the witnesses must in general be able to appreciate that the observation which they are sharing is one that verifies the sentence. They must have been in a position, equally with the speaker, to have assented to the sentence on their own in the circumstances. They are in that position in the case of "This is red" and "It is raining" and "There goes an old man," but not in the case of "There goes John's old tutor."

Such, then, is an observation sentence: it is an occasion sentence whose occasion is not only intersubjectively observable but is generally adequate, moreover, to elicit assent to the sentence from any present witness conversant with the language. It is not a report of private sense data; typically, rather, it contains references to physical objects.

These sentences, I say, are keyed directly to observation. But how *keyed*, now—what is the nature of the connection? It is a case of conditioned response. It is not quite the simplest kind; we do not say "red" or "This is red" whenever we see something red. But we do assent if asked. Mastery of the term "red" is acquisition of the habit of assenting when the term is queried in the presence of red, and only in the presence of red.

At the primitive level, an observation sentence is apt to take the form of a single word, thus "ball," or "red." What makes it easy to learn is the intersubjective observability of the relevant circumstances at the time of utterance. The parent can verify that the child is seeing red at the time, and so can reward the child's assent to the query. Also the child can verify that the parent is seeing red when the parent assents to such a query.

In this habit formation the child is in effect determining, by induction, the range of situations in which the adult will assent to the query "red," or approve the child's utterance of "red." He is extrapolating along similarity lines; this red episode is similar to that red episode by his lights. His success depends, therefore, on substantial agreement between his similarity standards and those of the adult. Happily the agreement holds; and no wonder, since our similarity standards are a matter partly of natural selection and partly of subsequent experience in a shared environment. If substantial agreement in similarity standards were not there, this first step in language acquisition would be blocked.

We have been seeing that observation sentences are the starting-points in the learning of language. Also, they are the starting-points and the check points of scientific theory. They serve both purposes for one and the same reason: the intersubjective observability of the relevant circumstances at the time of utterance. It is this, intersubjective observability at the time, that enables the child to learn when to assent to the observation sentence. And it is this also, intersubjective observability at the time, that qualifies observation sentences as check points for scientific theory. Observation sentences state the evidence, to which all witnesses must accede.

I had characterized science as a linguistic structure that is keyed to observation at some points. Now we have seen how it is keyed to observation: some of the sentences, the observation sentences, are conditioned to observable events in combination with a routine of query and assent. There is the beginning, here, of a partnership between the theory of language learning and the theory of scientific evidence. It is clear, when you think about it, that this partnership must continue. For when a child learns his language from his elders, what has he to go on? He can learn observation sentences by consideration of their observable circumstances, as we saw. But how can he learn the rest of the language, including the theoretical sentences of science? Somehow he learns to carry his observation terms over into theoretical contexts, variously embedded. Somehow he learns to connect his observation sentences with standing sentences, sentences whose truth-values do not depend on the occasion of utterance. It is only by such moves, however ill understood, that anyone masters the nonobservational part of his mother tongue. He can learn the observational part in firm and well-understood ways, and then he must build out somehow, imitating what he hears and linking it tenuously and conjecturally to what he knows, until by dint of trial and social correction he achieves fluent dialogue with his community. This discourse depends, for whatever empirical content it has, on its devious and tenuous connections with the observation sentences; and those are the same connections, nearly enough, through which one has achieved one's fluent part in that discourse. The channels by which, having learned observation sentences, we acquire theoretical language, are the very channels by which observation lends evidence to scientific theory. It all stands to reason; for language is man-made and the locutions of scientific theory have no meaning but what they acquired by our learning to use them.

We see, then, a strategy for investigating the relation of evidential support, between observation and scientific theory. We can adopt a genetic approach, studying how theoretical language is learned. For the evidential relation is virtually enacted, it would seem, in the learning. This genetic strategy is attractive because the learning of language goes on in the world and is open to scientific study. It is a strategy for the scientific study of scientific method and evidence. We have here a good reason to regard the theory of language as vital to the theory of knowledge.

When we try to understand the relation between scientific theory and the observation sentences, we are brought up short by the break between occasion sentences and standing sentences; for observation sentences are of the one kind while theoretical sentences are of the other. The scientific system cannot digest occasion sentences; their substance must first be converted into standing sentences. The observation sentence "Rain" or "It is raining" will not do; we must put the information into a standing sentence: "Rain at Heathrow 1600 G.M.T. 23 February 1974." This report is ready for filing in the archives of science. It still reports an observation, but it is a standing report rather than an occasion sentence. How do we get from the passing observation of rain to the standing report?

This can be explained by a cluster of observations and observation sentences, having to do with other matters besides the rain. Thus take the term "Heathrow." Proper names of persons, buildings, and localities are best treated as observation terms, on a par with "red" and "rain." All such terms can be learned by ostension, repeated sufficiently to suggest the intended scope and limits of application. "Here is Heathrow," then, is an observation sentence on a par with "It is raining"; and their conjunction, "Raining at Heathrow," is an observation sentence as well. It is an occasion sentence still, of course, and not a standing report of observation. But now the two further needed ingredients, hour and date, can be added as pointer readings: "The clock reads 1600" and "The calendar reads 23 February 1974" are further observation sentences. Taking the conjunction of all four, we still have an observation sentence: "Rain at Heathrow with clock at 1600 and calendar at 23 February 1974." But it is an observation sentence with this curious trait: it gives lasting information, dependent no longer on the vicissitudes of tense or of indicator words like "here" and "now." It is suitable for filing.

True, the clock and calendar may have been wrong. As an observation sentence our report must be viewed as stating the temporal readings and not the temporal facts. The question of the temporal facts belongs to scientific theory, somewhat above the observational level. Theoretical repercussions of this and other observations could eventually even prompt a modest scientific hypothesis to the effect that the clock or the calendar had been wrong.

I think this example serves pretty well as a paradigm case, to show how we can get from the occasion sentences of observation to the standing reports of observation that are needed for scientific theory. But this connection is by no means the only connection between observation sentences and standing sentences. Thus consider the universal categorical, "A dog is an animal." This is a standing sentence, but it is not, like the example of rain at Heathrow, a standing report of observation. Let us resume our genetic strategy: how might a child have mastered such a universal categorical?

I shall venture one hypothesis, hoping that it may be improved upon. The child has learned to assent to the observation term "a dog" when it is queried in the conspicuous presence of dogs, and he has learned to assent to "an animal" likewise when it is queried in the conspicuous presence of dogs (though not only dogs). Because of his close association of the word "dog" with dogs, the mere sound of the word "dog" disposes him to respond to the subsequent query "an animal" as he would have done if a dog had been there; so he assents when he hears "a dog" followed by the query, "an animal?" Being rewarded for so doing, he ever after assents to the query "A dog is an animal?" In the same way he learns a few other examples of the universal categorical. Next he rises to a mastery of the universal categorical construction "An S is a P" in general: he learns to apply it to new cases on his own. This important step of abstraction can perhaps be explained in parallel fashion to the early learning of observation sentences, namely, by simple induction along similarity lines; but the similarity now is a language-dependent similarity.

Much the same account can be offered for the learning of the seemingly simpler construction, mere predication: "Fido is a dog," "Sugar is sweet."

The child has now made creditable progress from observation sentences towards theoretical language, by mastering predication and the universal categorical construction. Another important step will be mastery of the relative clause; and I think I can give a convincing hypothesis of how this comes about. What is conspicuous about the relative clause is its role in predication. Thus take a relative clause, "something that chases its tail," and predicate it of Dinah: "Dinah is something that chases its tail." This is equivalent to the simple sentence "Dinah chases its tail" (or "her tail"). When we predicate the relative clause, the effect is the same as substituting the subject of the predication for the pronoun of the relative clause. Now my suggestion regarding the learning of the relative clause is that the child learns this substitution transformation. He discovers that the adult is prepared to assent to a predication of a relative clause in just the circumstances where he is prepared to assent to the simpler sentence obtained by the substitution.

This explains how the child could learn relative clauses in one standard position: predicative position. He learns how to eliminate them, in that position, by the substitution transformation—and how to introduce them into that position by the converse transformation, superstitution. But then, having learned this much, he is struck by an analogy between relative clauses and ordinary simple predicates or general terms; for these also appear in predicative position. So, pursuing the analogy, he presses relative clauses into other positions where general terms have been appearing—notably into the universal categorical construction. Or, if the child does not press this analogy on his own, he is at any rate well prepared to grasp adult usage and follow it in the light of the analogy. In this way the relative clause gets into the universal categorical construction, from which it cannot be eliminated by the substitution transformation. It is there to stay.

We can easily imagine how the child might learn the truth functions—negation, conjunction, alternation. Take conjunction: the child notices, by degrees, that the adult affirms "p and q" in only those circumstances where he is disposed, if queried, to assent to "p" and also to "q."

We have now seen, in outline and crude conjecture, how one might start at the observational edge of language and work one's way into the discursive interior where scientific theory can begin to be expressed. Predication is at hand, and the universal categorical, the relative clause, and the truth-functions. Once this stage is reached, it is easy to see that the whole strength of logical quantification is available. I shall not pause over the details of this, except to remark that the pronouns of relative clauses take on the role of the bound variable of quantification. By further conjectures in the same spirit, some of them more convincing and some less, we can outline the learner's further progress, to where he is bandying abstract terms and quantifying over properties, numbers, functions, and hypothetical physical particles and forces. This progress is not a continuous derivation, which, followed backward, would enable us to reduce scientific theory to sheer observation. It is a progress rather by short leaps of analogy. One such was the pressing of relative clauses into universal categoricals, where they cease to be eliminable. There are further such psychological speculations that I could report, but time does not allow.

Such speculations would gain, certainly, from experimental investigation of the child's actual learning of language. Experimental findings already available in the literature could perhaps be used to sustain or correct these conjectures at points, and further empirical investigations could be devised. But a speculative approach of the present sort seems required to begin with, in order to isolate just the factual questions that bear on our purposes. For our objective here is still philosophical—a better understanding of the relations between evidence and scientific theory. Moreover, the way to this objective requires consideration of linguistics and logic along with psychology. This is why the speculative phase has to precede, for the most part, the formulation of relevant questions to be posed to the experimental psychologist.

In any event the present speculations, however inaccurate, are presumably true to the general nature of language acquisition. And already they help us to understand how the logical links are forged that connect theoretical sentences with the reports of observation. We learn the grammatical construction "p and q" by learning, among other things, to assent to the compound only in circumstances where we are disposed to assent to each component. Thus it is that the logical law of inference which leads from "p and q" to "p" is built into our habits by the very learning of "and." Similarly for the other laws of conjunction, and correspondingly for the laws of alternation and other truth-functions. Correspondingly, again, for laws of quantification. The law of inference that leads from "$(x)Fx$" to "Fa" should be traceable back, through the derivation of quantification that I have passed over, until it is found finally to hinge upon the substitution transformation by which we learn to use the relative clause. Thus, in general, the acquisition of our basic logical habits is to be accounted for in our acquisition of grammatical constructions.

Related remarks hold true of inferential habits that exceed pure logic. We learn when to assent to "dog," and to "animal," only by becoming disposed to assent to "animal" in all circumstances where we will assent to "dog." Connections more accidental and casual in aspect can also come about through the learning of words; thus a child may have begun to learn the term "good" in application to chocolate.

I characterized science as a linguistic structure that is keyed to observation here and there. I said also that it is an instrument for predicting observations on the basis of earlier observations. It is keyed to observations, earlier and later, forming a labyrinthine connection between them; and it is through this labyrinth that the prediction takes place. A powerful improvement, this, over simple induction from past observations to future ones; powerful and costly. I have now sketched the nature of the connection between the observations and the labyrinthine interior of scientific theory. I have sketched it in terms of the learning of language. This seemed reasonable, since the scientist himself can make no sense of the language of scientific theory beyond what goes into his learning of it. The paths of language learning, which lead from observation sentences to theoretical sentences, are the only connection there is between observation and theory. This has been a sketch, but a fuller understanding may be sought along the same line: by a more painstaking investigation of how we learn theoretical language.

One important point that already stands forth, regarding the relation of theory to observation, is the vast freedom that the form of the theory must enjoy, relative even to all possible observation. Theory is empirically underdetermined. Surely even if we had an observational oracle, capable of assigning a truth-value to every standing observational report expressible in our language, still this would not suffice to adjudicate between a host of possible physical theories, each of them completely in accord with the oracle. This seems clear in view of the tenuousness of the connections that we have noted between observation sentences and theoretical ones. At the level of observation sentences, even the general form of the eventual theoretical language remained indeterminate, to say nothing of the ontology. The observation sentences were associated, as wholes, with the stimulatory situations that warranted assent to them; but there was in this no hint of what aspects of the stimulatory situations to single out somehow as objects, if indeed any. The question of ontology simply makes no sense until we get to something recognizable as quantification, or perhaps as a relative clause, with pronouns as potential variables. At the level of observation sentences there was no foreseeing even that the superimposed theoretical language would contain anything recognizable as quantification or relative clauses. The steps by which the child was seen to progress from observational language to relative clauses and categoricals and quantification had the arbitrary character of historical accident and cultural heritage; there was no hint of inevitability.

It was a tremendous achievement, on the part of our long-term culture and our latter-day scientists, to develop a theory that leads from observation to predicted observation as successfully as ours. It is a near miracle. If our theory were in full conformity with the observational oracle that we just now imagined, which surely it is not, that would be yet a nearer miracle. But if, even granted that nearer miracle, our theory were not still just one of many equally perfect possible theories to the same observational effect, that would be too miraculous to make sense.

But it must be said that the issue of underdetermination proves slippery when we try to grasp it more firmly. If two theories conform to the same totality of possible observations, in what sense are they two? Perhaps they are both stated in English, and they are alike, word for word, except that one of them calls molecules electrons and electrons molecules. Literally the two theories are in contradiction, saying incompatible things about so-called molecules. But of course we would not want to count this case; we would call it terminological. Or again, following Poincaré, suppose the two theories are alike except that one of them assumes an infinite space while the other has a finite space in which bodies shrink in proportion to their distance from center. Even here we want to say that the difference is rather terminological than real; and our reason is that we see how to bring the theories into agreement by translation: by reconstruing the English of one of the theories.

At this point it may be protested that after all there can never be two complete theories agreeing on the total output of the observational oracle. It may be protested that since such theories would be empirically equivalent, would have the same empirical meaning, their difference is purely verbal. For surely there is no meaning but empirical meaning, and theories with the same meaning must be seen as translations one of the other. This argument simply rules out, by definition, the doctrine that physical theory is underdetermined by all possible observation.

The best reaction at this point is to back away from terminology and sort things out on their merits. Where the significant difference comes is perhaps where we no longer see how to state rules of translation that would bring the two empirically equivalent theories together. Terminology aside, what wants recognizing is that a physical theory of radically different form from ours, with nothing even recognizably similar to our quantification or objective reference, might still be empirically equivalent to ours, in the sense of predicting the same episodes of sensory bombardment on the strength of the same past episodes. Once this is recognized, the scientific achievement of our culture becomes in a way more impressive than ever. For, in the midst of all this formless freedom for variation, our science has developed in such a way as to maintain always a manageably narrow spectrum of visible alternatives among which to choose when need arises to revise a theory. It is this narrowing of sights, or tunnel vision, that has made for the continuity of science, through the vicissitudes of refutation and correction. And it is this also that has fostered the illusion of there being only one solution to the riddle of the universe.

NOTE

1. This paper is meant as a summary statement of my attitude towards our knowledge of nature. Consequently I must warn the more omnivorous of my readers (dear souls) that they are apt to experience a certain indefinable sense of *déjà vu*. The main traces of novelty come towards the end.

ROBERT ALMEDER

ON NATURALIZING EPISTEMOLOGY*

I. INTRODUCTION

There are three distinct forms of naturalized epistemology. The first form asserts that the only legitimate questions about the nature of human knowledge are those we can answer in natural science. So described, naturalized epistemology is a branch of natural science wherein the questions asked about the nature of human knowledge make sense only because they admit of resolution under the methods of such natural sciences as biology and psychology. Characterized in this way, naturalized epistemology consists in empirically describing and scientifically explaining how our various beliefs originate, endure, deteriorate or grow. Unlike traditional epistemology, this form of naturalized epistemology does not seek to determine whether the claims of natural science are more or less justified. For this reason, it is not "normative" in the way traditional epistemology is normative. Not surprisingly, this first form of naturalized epistemology regards traditional "philosophical" questions about human knowledge, questions whose formulation and solution do not emerge solely from the practice of natural science, as pointless. Accordingly, this first form of naturalized epistemology seeks to *replace* traditional epistemology with the thesis that while we certainly have scientific knowledge, and whatever norms are appropriate for the successful conduct of natural science, we have no philosophical theory of knowledge sitting in judgment over the claims of natural science to determine whether they live up to a philosophically congenial analysis of justification or knowledge. As we shall see shortly, the classical defense of this first form of naturalized epistemology appears in Quine's "Naturalized Epistemology."[1]

The second form of naturalized epistemology seeks less to *replace* traditional epistemology than it does to *transform* and supplement it by connecting it with the methods and insights of psychology, biology and cognitive science. In *Epistemology and Cognition*, for example, Alvin Goldman has argued for this second form which allows for traditionally normative elements but is "naturalized" for the reason that the practitioners of natural science, especially biology and psychology, will have the last word on whether anybody knows what they claim to know. For

Goldman, although defining human knowledge and other epistemic concepts is legitimately philosophical and traditionally normative, whether anybody knows what they claim to know, and just what cognitive processes are involved, is ultimately a matter we must consign to psychologists or cognitive scientists. Unlike the first form of naturalized epistemology, this second form allows traditional epistemology to sit in judgment on the claims of natural science but the judgment must be made by the practitioners of natural science using the methods of natural science.

The third distinct form of naturalized epistemology simply insists that the method of the natural sciences is the only method for acquiring a proper understanding of the nature of the physical universe. On this view, natural science, and all that it implies, is the most epistemically privileged activity for understanding the nature of the physical world. Adopting this last form of naturalized epistemology is, however, quite consistent with rejecting both of the above forms of naturalized epistemology. This third form is quite compatible with traditional epistemology because it does not seek to *replace* traditional epistemology in the way that the Quine thesis does; nor does it seek to *transform* traditional epistemology by turning the question of who knows what over to psychologists and cognitive scientists in the way that the Goldman thesis does.

At any rate, the most currently pervasive and challenging form of naturalized epistemology is the radically anti-traditional, anti-philosophical thesis offered originally by Quine and recently defended by others. So, in the next few pages we shall focus *solely* on the Quinean thesis and five distinct arguments recently offered in defense of it. Along the way, we will discuss various objections to such a naturalized epistemology, objections proponents of the thesis have recently confronted. Unfortunately, because space is here limited, we will not examine the second and distinct form of naturalized epistemology offered by Alvin Goldman. To do so would involve a long discussion of the merits of the reliabilist theory of justification upon which Goldman's type of naturalism squarely rests.[2]

Finally, the modest conclusion of this paper is that there is no sound argument available for the Quinean form of naturalized epistemology. The immodest conclusion is that any argument proposed for the thesis will be incoherent, and that consequently there is no rational justification for anybody taking such a naturalistic turn.

II. QUINE'S ARGUMENT

In "Epistemology Naturalized," Quine begins his defense of naturalized epistemology by asserting that traditional epistemology is concerned with the foundations of science, broadly conceived. As such, it is supposed to show how the foundations of knowledge, whether it be the foundations of mathematics or natural science, reduce to certainty. In short, showing how certainty obtains is the core of traditional epistemology, and this implies that the primary purpose of traditional epistemology is to refute the Cartesian sceptic whose philosophical doubts over whether we can attain certainty has set the program for traditional epistemology.

But, for Quine, traditional epistemology has failed to refute the sceptic, and will never succeed in refuting the sceptic. Mathematics reduces only to set theory and not to logic; and even though this reduction enhances clarity it does nothing by way of establishing certainty because the axioms of set theory have less to recommend them by way of certainty than do most of the mathematical theorems we would derive from them. As he says:

Reduction in the foundations of mathematics remains mathematically and philosophically fascinating, but it does not do what the epistemologist would like of it: it does not reveal the ground of mathematical knowledge, it does not show how mathematical certainty is possible. (p. 71)

Moreover, mathematics aside, the attempt to reduce natural knowledge to a foundation in the certainty of statements of sense experience has also failed miserably. Common sense about sensory impressions provides no certainty. And, when it comes to justifying our knowledge about truths of nature, Hume taught us that general statements and singular statements about the future do not admit of justification by way of allowing us to ascribe certainty to our beliefs associated with such statements. For Quine, the problem of induction is still with us; "The Humean predicament is the human predicament" (p. 72). As Quine sees it, Hume showed us quite clearly that any attempt to refute the sceptic by uncovering some foundation of certainty associated with sense statements, whether about sense impressions or physical objects, is doomed equally to failure (p. 72).

This last consideration is crucial because as soon as we accept Quine's rejection of the analytic/synthetic distinction in favor of only synthetic propositions, Hume's argument casts a long despairing shadow over our ever being able to answer the sceptic because such propositions could never be certain anyway. The conclusion Quine draws from all this is that traditional epistemology is dead. There is no "first philosophy." There are no strictly philosophical truths validating the methods of the natural sciences. Nor can we validate in any non-circular way the methods of the natural sciences by appeal to psychology or the methods of the natural sciences. As he says, "If the epistemologist's goal is validation of the grounds of empirical science, he defeats his purpose by using psychology or other empirical science in the validation" (pp. 75–76). We may well have justified beliefs based upon induction, but we cannot have any justified belief that we can have justified beliefs based upon induction. Accordingly, if epistemology is to have any content whatever, it will seek to explain, *via* the methods of natural science, the origin and growth of beliefs we take to be human knowledge and natural science. Construed in this way, epistemology continues as a branch of natural science wherein the only meaningful questions are questions answerable in science by scientists using the methods of natural science. This reconstrual of the nature of epistemology consigns the enterprise to a descriptive psychology whose main function is to describe the origin of our beliefs and the conditions under which we take them to be justified. On this view, all questions and all doubts are scientific and can only be answered or resolved in science by the methods of science. Philosophical discussions on the nature and limits of scientific knowledge, questions that do not lend themselves to resolution via the methods of natural science, are simply a part of traditional philosophy that cannot succeed. What can we say about all this?

III. RESPONSE TO QUINE'S ARGUMENT

In "The Significance of Naturalized Epistemology," Barry Stroud criticizes Quine's defense of naturalized epistemology.[3] After a brief description of Quine's position, Stroud argues that Quince is inconsistent for arguing *both* that there is no appeal to scientific knowledge that could non-circularly establish the legitimacy of scientific knowledge in the presence of the traditional epistemological sceptic, *and*, in *Roots of Reference*, that we should take seriously the project of validating our knowledge of the external world.[4] For Stroud, it was in *Roots of Reference* that Quine came to believe in the coherent use the resources of natural science to validate the

454 • THE NATURE OF SCIENTIFIC KNOWLEDGE

deliverances of natural science. But that would be to countenance the basic question of traditional epistemology when in fact the thrust of Quine's thesis on naturalized epistemology is that such a question forms part of "first philosophy" which is impossible. Apart from such an inconsistency, Stroud also argues that Quine's attempt to validate scientific inference fails (p. 81). Stroud's thesis here is that Quine attempts to offer a naturalized defense of science in "The Nature of Natural Knowledge,"[5] but the effort fails because, on Quine's reasoning, we can see how others acquire their beliefs but we are denied thereby any evidence of whether such beliefs are correct beliefs about the world. By implication, we have no reason for thinking our own beliefs are any better off (p. 81). In commenting on Quine's defense, Stroud says:

Therefore, if we follow Quine's instructions and try to see our own position as "just like" the position we can find another "positing" or "projecting" subject to be in, we will have to view ourselves as we view another subject when we can know nothing more than what is happening at his sensory surfaces and what he believes or is disposed to assert. (p. 81)

His point here is that when we examine how another's beliefs originate, we have no way to look beyond his positing to determine whether his beliefs are true or correct. In that position we never can understand how the subject's knowledge or even true belief is possible. Therefore, we never can understand how our own true beliefs are possible either. Stroud says:

The possibility that our own view of the world is a *mere* projection is what had to be shown not to obtain in order to explain how our knowledge is possible. Unless that challenge has been met, or rejected, we will never understand how our knowledge is possible at all. (p. 83)
    . . . if Quine's naturalized epistemology is taken as an answer to the philosophical question of our knowledge of the external world, then I think that for the reasons I have given, no satisfactory explanation is either forthcoming or possible. (p. 83)

He goes on to conclude that if naturalized epistemology is *not* taken as an answer to the philosophical question of our knowledge of the external world, and if the question is a legitimate question (and Quine has not shown that it is not) then naturalized epistemology cannot answer the question:

I conclude that even if Quine is right in saying that sceptical doubts are scientific doubts, the scientific source of these doubts has no anti-sceptical force in itself. Nor does it establish the relevance and legitimacy of a scientific epistemology as an answer to the traditional epistemological question. If Quine is confident that a naturalized epistemology can answer the traditional question about knowledge, he must have some other reason for that confidence. He believes that sceptical doubts are scientific doubts and he believes that in resolving those doubts we may make free use of all the scientific knowledge we possess. But if, as he allows, it is possible for the sceptic to argue by *reductio* that science is not known, then it cannot be that the second of those beliefs (that a naturalized epistemology is all we need) follows from the first.
    Until the traditional philosophical question has been exposed as in some way illegitimate or incoherent, there will always appear to be an intelligible question about human knowledge in general which, as I have argued, a naturalized epistemology cannot answer. And Quine himself seems committed at least to the coherence of that traditional question by his very conception of knowledge. (pp. 85–86)

Stroud's closing remark is that the traditional question has not been demonstrated as illegitimate, and Quine's attempt to resolve sceptical doubts as scientific doubts within science has failed. Moreover, for Stroud, apart from the question of whether Quine succeeded, his effort is predicated on the legitimacy of the traditional question of whether science provides us with knowledge of the external world.

Some naturalized epistemologists will probably disagree with Stroud's analysis and urge that Quine's attempt to validate scientific knowledge is misunderstood when construed as an attempt to establish first philosophy. Better by far that we read Quine as asserting that there is simply no way to validate the deliverances of science as more or less warranted. Whether this last response is adequate, we cannot now discuss.

At any rate, Quine has responded to Stroud with the following remarks:

What then does our overall scientific theory really claim regarding the world? Only that it is somehow structured as to assure the sequences of stimulation that our theory gives us to expect. . . .

In what way then do I see the Humean predicament as persisting? Only in the fallibility of prediction: the fallibility of induction and the hypothetico-deductive method in anticipating experience.

I have depicted a barren scene. The furniture of our world, the people and sticks and stones along with the electrons and molecules, have dwindled to manners of speaking. And other purported objects would serve as well, and may as well be said already to be doing so.

So it would seem. Yet people, sticks, stones, electrons and molecules are real indeed, on my view, and it is these and no dim proxies that science is all about. Now, how is such robust realism to be reconciled with what we have just been through? The answer is naturalism: the recognition that it is within science itself, and not in some prior philosophy, that reality is properly to be identified and described.[6]

In reflecting on this response to Stroud, Ernest Sosa has been quick to note the incoherence involved in accepting science as the "reality-claims court coupled with denial that it is anything but free and arbitrary creation."[7] Continuing his criticism of Quine, Sosa goes on to say:

The incoherence is not removed, moreover, if one now adds:

(Q1) What then does our overall scientific theory really claim regarding the world? Only that it is somehow so structured as to assure the sequence of stimulation that our theory gives us to expect.
(Q2) Yet people, sticks, stones, electrons and molecules are real indeed.
(Q3) [It] . . . is within science itself and not in some prior philosophy, that reality is properly to be identified and described.

If it is within science that we settle, to the extent possible for us, the contours of reality; and if science really claims regarding the world only that it is so structured as to assure certain sequences of stimulation; then how can we possibly think reality to assume the contours of people, sticks, stones and so on?

We cannot have it all three ways: (Q1), (Q2) and (Q3) form an incoherent triad. If we trust science as the measure of reality, and if we think there really are sticks and stones, then we can't have science accept only a world "somehow so structured as to assure" certain sequences of stimulations or the like. Our science must also claim that there really are sticks and stones.

What is more, if science really is the measure of reality it cannot undercut itself by saying that it really isn't, that it is only convenient "manners of speaking" to guide us reliably from stimulation to stimulation. (p. 69)

Sosa's criticism seems quite pointed. Moreover, even if the critique offered by both Stroud and Sosa should turn out to be a misconstrual of Quine's position, there are other plausible objections we might raise to Quine's argument for naturalized epistemology. For one thing, it is obvious that Quine's argument itself for naturalized epistemology is a philosophical argument, which, *ex hypothesi*, should not count by way of providing evidence for the thesis of naturalized epistemology. Further, the thesis of naturalized epistemology is arguably fundamentally incoherent. It argues against there being a "first philosophy" by appealing to two premises both of which are sound only if philosophical arguments about the limits of human knowledge are permissible and sound. The first premise consists in asserting that Hume's scepticism about factual knowledge is indeed established. Hume's thesis is certainly not empirically confirmable. The so-called "problem of induction" is a philosophical problem based upon a certain philosophical view about what is necessary for scientific knowledge. It is certainly not a problem in natural science or naturalized epistemology. The second premise is the denial of the analytic/synthetic distinction; and that is a thesis largely resting on a philosophical argument about the nature of meaning. Such premises only make sense within a commitment to the validity of some form of first philosophy and the legitimacy of traditional epistemology. Finally, there is the problematic premise that traditional epistemology has been exclusively concerned to establish the foundations of certainty in order to show that we have knowledge of the world. A close look at traditional epistemology, however, suggests that the primary concern is as much a matter of getting clear on, or (as Sosa has noted) understanding just what it *means* to know, and just what the concept of certainty relative to different senses of "knows" consists in, as it is a matter of validating knowledge claims or seeking the foundations of certainty (pp. 50–51). Indeed, there is good reason to think that the primary concern of traditional epistemology is one of *defining* concepts of knowledge, certainty, justification and truth; and only then of determining whether anybody has the sort of certainty associated with the correct definition of knowledge. The history of epistemology is as apt to criticize the program of the Cartesian sceptic (and the definition of knowledge implied therein) as it is to accept it. Certainly, if the concepts of knowledge and justification had been defined differently than Hume had defined them, Hume's predicament would never have occurred. Traditional epistemology is probably as concerned with what it means for a belief to be certain, as it is with determining whether scientific knowledge is certain. With these few considerations in mind, and realizing that much more can be said on the issue, it would appear that Quine's defense of naturalized epistemology admits of a number of solid objections. Let us turn to a more recent and quite distinct defense of the Quinean thesis.

IV. THE "PHILOSOPHY IS SCIENCE" ARGUMENT

Among recent arguments for the Quine thesis, the argument offered by William Lycan in *Judgement and Justification* is quite different from Quine's.[8] Unlike the Quinean argument, it does not rest on the alleged failure of the analytic/synthetic distinction and upon the subsequent classification of all propositions as synthetic. Nor does it feed upon Quine's Humean argument that synthetic propositions cannot be justified from the viewpoint of a first philosophy and so, if epistemology is to continue, it can only be in terms of the deliverances of a descriptive psychology. What is the argument?

Lycan begins by characterizing classical philosophy in terms of the deductivist model. He calls it "deductivism" and under this model philosophy gets characterized in a certain way:

. . . the deductivist holds that philosophy and science differ in that deductive argument from self-evident premises pervades the former but not the latter. . . . Now Quine (1960, 1963, 1970) has a rather special reason for rejecting the dichotomy between philosophy and science, or, to put the point more accurately, between philosophical method and scientific method. He rejects the analytic/synthetic distinction, and thus the proposal that there are two kinds of truths ("conceptual" or "a priori," and "empirical" or scientific), one of which is the province of philosophy and the other the province of science. . . .

I side with Smart and Quine against the deductivist, but for what I think is a more fundamental and compelling reason, one that does not depend on the rejection of the analytic/synthetic distinction. If my argument is sound, then one can countenance that distinction and still be forced to the conclusion that the Smart/Quine methodological view is correct.

Suppose we try to take a strict deductivist stance. Now, as is common knowledge, one cannot be committed (by an argument) to the conclusion of that argument unless one accepts the premises. Upon being presented with a valid argument, I always have the option of denying its conclusion, so long as I am prepared to accept the denial of at least one of the premises.

Thus, every deductive argument can be set up as an inconsistent set. (Let us, for simplicity, consider only arguments whose premises are internally consistent.) Given an argument

$$\frac{P}{Q}$$
$$/ \therefore R$$

The cognitive cash value of which is that R follows deductively from the set of P and Q, we can exhaustively convey its content simply by asserting that the set (P, Q, not-R) is inconsistent, and all the original argument has told us, in fact, is that for purely logical reasons we must deny either P, Q, or not-R. The proponent of the original argument, of course, holds that P and Q are true; therefore, she says, we are committed to the denial of not-R, that is, to R. But how does she know that P and Q are true? Perhaps she has constructed deductive arguments with P and Q as conclusions. But, if we are to avoid regress, we must admit that she relies ultimately on putative knowledge gained non-deductively; so let us suppose that she has provided non-deductive arguments for P and Q. On what grounds then does she accept them? The only answer that can be given is that she finds each of P and Q more plausible than not-R, just as Moore found the statement "I had breakfast before I had lunch" more plausible than any of the metaphysical premises on which rested the fashionable arguments against the reality of time.

But these are just the sorts of considerations to which the theoretical scientist appeals. If what I have said here is (more or less) right, then we appear to have vindicated some version of the view that (1) philosophy, except for that relatively trivial part of it that consists in making sure that controversial arguments are formally valid, is just very high level science and that consequently (2) the proper philosophical method for acquiring interesting new knowledge cannot differ from proper scientific method. (pp. 116–118)

In defending this general argument, Lycan then responds to two basic objections which he offers against his own thesis. The first objection is that even if all philosophical arguments rest on plausibility arguments, the above argument has not established what is necessary, namely, that considerations that make for plausibility in science are the same considerations that make for plausibility in philosophy. The second objection is that even if we were to establish as much, it would not thereby obviously follow that philosophy is just very high-level science. After all, philosophy and science might have the same method but differ by way of subject matter (pp. 116–118). The core of Lycan's defense of his general argument consists in responding to the first objection. So, let us see whether the response overcomes the objection.

In response to the first objection, Lycan constructs the following argument:

P1. The interesting principles of rational acceptance are not the deductive ones (even in philosophy).

P2. There are, roughly speaking, three kinds of ampliative, non-deductive principles of inference: principles of self-evidence (gnostic access, incorrigibility, apriority, clarity and distinctness, etc.), principles of what might be called "textbook induction" (enumerative induction, eliminative induction, statistical syllogism, Mill's Methods, etc.), and principles of sophisticated ampliative inference (such as PS principles and the other considerations of theoretical elegance and power mentioned earlier, which are usually construed as filling out the "best" in "inference to the best explanation").

P3. Principles of textbook induction are not the interesting principles of rational acceptance in philosophy.

P4. Principles of "self-evidence," though popular throughout the history of philosophy and hence considered interesting principles of rational acceptance, cannot be used to settle philosophical disputes.

Therefore: If there are any interesting and decisive principles of rational acceptance in philosophy, they are the elegance principles.

Lycan adds that the elegance principles are to be extracted mainly from the history of science, and that we can obtain precise and useful statements of such principles only by looking to the history of science, philosophy, and logic in order to see exactly what considerations motivate the replacement of an old theory by a new theory (pp. 119–120). So, the answer to the question "Why does it follow that the considerations that make for plausibility in philosophy are the same as those that make for plausibility in science?" is simply "there is nowhere else to turn" (p. 120). For a number of reasons, however, this response to the objection seems problematic.

To begin with, P1 is not true. It is common knowledge that one cannot be rationally justified in accepting the conclusion of a deductive argument unless the argument is valid and consistent in addition to the premises being true. So, we cannot construe P1 to assert that validity and consistency are redundant or eliminable as conditions necessary for the rational acceptability of a deductive argument. Lycan does not seek to argue that point. Rather P1 asserts that even though validity and consistency are necessary conditions for the soundness of a deductive argument, validity and consistency provide no grounds for thinking that the conclusion deduced is plausible. In short, P1 asserts that it is not even a necessary condition for the *plausibility* of a proposed argument that it be both sound and consistent. The reasons offered for P1, however, seem particularly questionable, and the reasons for thinking P1 false seem straightforwardly compelling. Let me explain.

Lycan claims that P1 is true because deductive rules are not controversial in their application (p. 119). But how exactly would that establish that such rules of inference are not interesting, meaning thereby not plausibility-conferring on the conclusion? Why not say instead that *because* such rules are noncontroversially applied they are interesting, that is, plausibility. conferring? In other words, what does the fact that such rules are noncontroversial in their application have to do with their not being plausibility-conferring on the conclusions that follow from them? Is it meant to be obvious that a deductive rule of inference is plausibility-conferring only when its application is controversial? Why should anyone accept such a definition of plausibility, especially because it seems to endorse saying such things as "Your argument is perfectly plausible even though it is both invalid and inconsistent." Why aren't deductive rules interesting (or plausibility-conferring) because they are more likely to guarantee truth from premises that are true? If "interest" is relative to purpose and, if one's purpose is to provide a system of inferential rules that is strongly truth-preserving, then such rules are truly quite interesting. This in itself is sufficient to show P1 is involved in a questionable bit of semantic legislation.

Moreover, Lycan's second reason for P1 is that deductive inference is such that any invalid argument can be made valid trivially by the addition of some inference-licensing premise. But how exactly does it follow from the fact (if it be a fact) that any deductive argument can be made trivially valid that no deductive principle (including consistency) is interesting in the sense of conferring plausibility in any degree on what follows from the deductive principle? Here again, is it meant to be obvious that deductive principles are plausibility-conferring only if they function in arguments incapable of being rendered valid and consistent in nontrivial ways? Does such a claim presuppose a definition of plausibility which, by stipulation, asserts that the plausibility of a deductive conclusion has nothing to do with the fact that the argument is valid and consistent? And is that not precisely what needs to be shown? Indeed, if any deductive argument could be rendered valid and consistent in wholly trivial ways and the conclusion still be plausible, why insist, as we do, on validity and consistency for soundness as a necessary condition for rational acceptance? Why insist on rules that are truth-preserving for soundness if one can get it in trivial ways and it has nothing to do with the plausibility of the conclusion?

Lycan's third reason for P1 is that deductive rules are not plausibility-conferring because such rules are uninteresting. They are uninteresting precisely because deductive inferences obviously do not accomplish the expansion of our total store of explicit and implicit knowledge, since they succeed only in drawing out information already implicit in the premises (p. 119). Here again, however, even if Lycan were right in this latter claim, that would only show that deductive inference is not inductive inference, and, unless one *assumes* that the only plausibility considerations that will count are those relevant to expanding our factual knowledge base, why would the fact that deductive inference is not inductive inference be a sufficient reason for thinking that deductive inference is uninteresting as a way of enhancing the plausibility of one's conclusions deductively inferred? The reason Lycan offers here (like the two offered above) strongly implies that the plausibility of a person's beliefs has nothing to do with whether it is internally consistent, or follows logically from well-confirmed beliefs, or is consistent with a large body of well-confirmed beliefs; and this just flies in the face of our epistemic practices.

Lycan's last reason for P1 is that any deductive argument can be turned upon its head. Once again, what needs proving is assumed. Even if we can turn a valid deductive argument on its head, so to speak, does that mean that there are no valid arguments? If the answer is yes, why say that valid deductive inference is uninteresting rather than impossible? But if we are not arguing that valid deductive inference is impossible, why exactly would such inference be uninteresting if it is truth-preserving, and would guarantee consistency, coherence with well-confirmed beliefs, and the explicit addition of true verifiable sentences not formerly in the corpus of our beliefs? If such considerations do not count as plausibility-conferring, it could only be because "plausibility" is stipulatively defined to rule out such consideration as plausibility-conferring. Such a definition needs defending rather than pleading.

By way of general observation with regard to P1, it seems clear that plausibility considerations rest quite squarely on questions of consistency and derivability. One of the traditional tests for theory confirmation (and hence by implication for plausibility) is derivability from above. For example, the fact that Balmer's formula for the emission spectra for gases derives logically from Bohr's theory on the hydrogen atom, counts strongly in favor of Balmer's formula above and beyond the evidence Balmer gave for his formula. What is that to say except that considerations purely deductive in nature function to render theories more or less plausible? What about the rest of Lycan's argument against the first objection to his general argument?

Well, suppose, for the sake of discussion that P2 and P3 are true. Will P4 be true? In other words, will it be true that principles of self-evidence do not count for plausibility unless they can be used to settle some philosophical disputes. Here the argument seems to be suggesting that a common-sense principle will be plausibility-conferring only if it can be used to "settle" (in the sense of everybody agreeing henceforth to the answer) some philosophical dispute. But such a requirement seems arbitrarily too strong. Obviously, a conclusion can be plausible and worthy of rational acceptance even when others will disagree to some degree. Two mutually exclusive conclusions may both be rationally plausible without the principle that renders them plausible "settling" the dispute once and for all. Moreover, are we sure that appeals to common-sense principles have failed to resolve or settle philosophical disputes? In a very strong sense of "settle," of course, nothing is settled in philosophy. But that would be to impose an arbitrarily strong sense of "settle" on philosophy, a sense we certainly would not impose on science. In a suitably weak sense, "appeals to obviousness or self-evidence" often, but not always, settles disputes. Indeed, isn't the basic reason that the question of solipsism consistently fails to capture anybody's sustained attention is that it is so implausible by way of appeal to common sense? Who these days really takes the possibility of solipsism seriously? Isn't that a philosophical problem pretty much settled by appeal to common sense or self-evidence? Of course, not all appeals to common sense are so successful, and some are more successful than others as clean "conversation stoppers."

These reasons show that Lycan's reply to the first objection fails. Further, it would have been surprising if the reply had succeeded because it seems clear that in science, but not in philosophy, a necessary condition for any explanation being even remotely plausible is that it be in principle empirically testable. As a matter of fact, if we consult practicing scientists and not philosophers, unless one's scientific explanations are ultimately testable, and we know what empirical evidence would need to occur to falsify the hypothesis, we say that the explanation is not plausible. We may even go so far as to say that it is meaningless because it is not testable. Minimally, in science a hypothesis or a theory will be plausible only if it is empirically testable, and it will be testable only if what the hypothesis virtually predicts is in principle observable under clearly specifiable conditions, and would occur as expected if we were to accept the hypothesis as worthy. On the other hand, if we are not to beg the question against philosophy as distinct from science, and look at philosophical theses, we will find that a philosophical thesis can be more or less plausible quite independently of whether the thesis is empirically confirmable or testable. As a matter of fact, consider, for example, the dispute between classical scientific realists and classical anti-realists of an instrumental sort. What empirical test might one perform to establish or refute the view that the long-term predictive success of some scientific hypotheses is a function of the truth of claims implied or assumed by the hypotheses? Surely one of these theses must be correct, and yet neither the realist nor the anti-realist position here is testable by appeal to any known experimental or non-experimental test.[9] Does that mean that while one position must be correct *neither* is plausible? Paradox aside, if we say yes, how is that anything more than assuming what needs to be proven, namely that considerations that count for plausibility in science are the same as those that count for plausibility in philosophy?

Surely, however, there are also other philosophical arguments that in fact do depend for their plausibility on the verification and falsification of certain factual claims. For example, Aristotle once argued that humans are quite different from animals because they use tools, whereas animals do not. Aristotle's argument here is implausible because it is readily falsified by careful observations of the sort Jane Goodall and others continually make. So, in philosophy plausibility may sometimes be rooted in considerations of testability just because one of the premises in the argument asserts that some factual claim about the world is true or false. But, as we just showed in the case of the dispute between the scientific realist and the scientific anti-realist, plausibility may have very little or nothing to do with the empirical testability of the hypothesis. It may simply be a matter of showing the internal inconsistency of a particular argument, or the dire consequences of adopting one position over the other, or the informal (or formal) fallacies attending the argumentation of one position over the other. In short, as practiced, philosophical reasoning often requires both deductive and inductive principles of rational acceptance for plausibility. But it certainly is not a necessary condition for philosophical plausibility that one's philosophical positions be testable or explainable in a way that accommodates empirical test-ability as a necessary condition for significance. Moreover, it should be apparent by now that to insist that plausibility in philosophy must accommodate the canons of empirical testability or the canons of explanation in the natural sciences is simply a blatant question-begging move against the objection offered against Lycan's main argument. As such, it would be a rationally unmoti-vated stipulation against philosophy as distinct from natural science.

In sum, Lycan's reply to the first objection to his general argument fails unless one wants to suppose that there is nothing at all plausible about any philosophical argument primarily because philosophical arguments are not straightforwardly verifiable or falsifiable in the way that empirical claims are. Besides, it seems that the dark shadow of Quine's "Epistemology Naturalized" is having an unrealized effect on the main argument Lycan offers. This is because if one excludes philosophical arguments from the realm of the analytic or *a priori*, (as Quine does), it would appear that if there is anything to them at all, they must fall into the realm of the synthetic; and hence it seems only too natural to suppose that synthetic claims are meaningful only if testable and confirmable in some basic way by the method of the natural sciences. But the very argument offered from this view supposes, once again, what needs defending, namely, that philosophical plausibility depends on plausibility considerations that are appropriate only to the methods of the natural sciences. When we look to the actual practice of philosophy that assumption seems quite false or the argument Lycan offers begs the question against the distinctness of philosophy. Let's turn to another recent argument for the Quine thesis.

V. THE "TRADITIONAL EPISTEMOLOGY WILL BECOME IRRELEVANT" ARGUMENT

In his recent book *Explaining Science: A Cognitive Approach*, Ron Giere argues that the justification for the naturalizing of philosophy will not come from explicitly refuting the old paradigm of traditional epistemology, by explicitly refuting on a philosophical basis the philosophical arguments favoring the traditional posture. Rather the argument for naturalizing epistemology will simply be a function of the empirical success of those practitioners in showing how to answer certain questions and, at the same time, showing the irrelevance of the questions asked under the old paradigm.[10] Comparing the naturalized epistemologist with the proponents of seventeenth-century physics, he says:

Proponents of the new physics of the seventeenth century won out not because they explicitly refuted the arguments of the scholastics but because the empirical success of their science rendered the scholastic's arguments irrelevant. (p. 9)

This same sort of argument has been offered by philosophers such as Patricia Churchland and Paul Churchland, who have claimed that traditional epistemology or "first philosophy" will disappear as a consequence of the inevitable elimination of folk psychology in favor of some future successful neuroscientific account of cognitive functioning.[11]

While there are various reasons for thinking that the eliminative materialism implied by the above argument cannot occur,[12] what seems most obvious is that the assertion made by Giere and the Churchlands is simply not an *argument* for naturalized epistemology. Rather, it is a buoyantly optimistic prediction that, purely and simply because of the expected empirical success of the new model, we will naturally come to regard traditional epistemology (normative epistemology) as having led us nowhere. In short, we will come to view the questions of traditional epistemology as sterile and no longer worth asking. In spite of the optimism of this prediction, it is difficult to see what successes to date justify such a prediction. What central traditional epistemological problems or questions have been rendered trivial or meaningless by the advances in natural science or neuroscience? Unless one proves that a basic question in traditional epistemology is "How does the Brain Work?" the noncontroversial advances made in neuroscience will be quite irrelevant to answering the questions of traditional epistemology. While some people seem to have *assumed* as much,[13] it is by no means clear that knowing how one's beliefs originate is in any way relevant to their being justified or otherwise worthy of acceptance.[14] Without being able to point to such successes, the eliminative thesis amounts to an unjustified assertion that traditional philosophy is something of a unwholesome disease for which the doing of natural science or neuroscience is the sure cure. In the absence of such demonstrated success, however, no traditional epistemologist need feel compelled by the prediction to adopt the posture of naturalized epistemology.

As a program committed to understanding the mechanisms of belief-acquisition, naturalized epistemology may very well come to show that our traditional ways of understanding human knowledge are in important respects flawed and, as a result, we may indeed need to recast dramatically our understanding of the nature of human knowledge. It would be silly to think that this could not happen. After all, Aristotle's conception of human rationality, and the way in which it was allegedly distinct from animal rationality, was shown to be quite wrong when we all saw Jane Goodall's films showing gorillas making and using tools. Thereafter, Aristotle's philosophical argument that humans think, whereas animals do not, because the former but not the latter use tools, disappeared from the philosophical landscape. So, it is quite possible that there are certain empirical assumptions about the nature of human knowledge that may well be strongly and empirically falsified in much the same way that Aristotle's position was falsified. But even that sort of progress is still quite consistent with construing epistemology in non-naturalized ways. Traditional epistemology should have no difficulty with accepting the view that some philosophical theses can be conclusively refuted by the occurrence of certain facts. That would be simply to acknowledge that philosophy, and philosophical arguments, are not purely *a priori* and hence immune from rejection by appeal to the way the world is. So, the traditional epistemologist will need to wait and see just what naturalized epistemology comes up with. Whether it lives up to the expectations of Giere and others who, like the Churchlands, offer the same basic argument is still an open question, at best. As things presently stand, there are good reasons, as we shall see, for thinking that no amount of naturalized epistemology will ever be able in principle to answer certain crucial questions about the nature of justification.

Otherwise Giere's defense of naturalized epistemology consists in responding to others who argue against naturalized epistemology. In responding to these objections, Giere seeks to show that there is certainly no compelling reason why one should not proceed on the new model. He considers the following three arguments.

A. Putnam's Objection

In his "Why Reasons Can't be Naturalized" (*Synthese* 52 [1982], pp. 3–23) Putnam says:

A cognitive theory of science would require a definition of rationality of the form: A belief is rational if and only if it is acquired by employing some specified cognitive capacities. But any such formula is either obviously mistaken or vacuous, depending on how one restricts the range of beliefs to which the definition applies. If the definition is meant to cover *all* beliefs, then it is obviously mistaken because people do sometimes acquire irrational beliefs using the same cognitive capacities as everyone else. But restricting the definition to rational beliefs renders the definition vacuous. And so the program of constructing a naturalistic philosophy of science goes nowhere. (As cited by Giere on p. 9)

In response to this particular argument, Giere says:

The obvious reply is that a naturalistic theory of science need not require any such definition. A naturalist in epistemology, however, is free to deny that such a conception can be given any coherent content. For such a naturalist, there is only hypothetical rationality which many naturalists, including me, would prefer to describe simply as "effective goal-directed action," thereby dropping the word "rationality" altogether. (p. 9)

In short, for Giere, Putnam is just begging the question by insisting that there must be a coherent concept of categorical rationality. In defense of Putnam's intuition, however, one can argue that Giere missed Putnam's point. Putnam's point is just as easily construed as asserting that if the naturalized epistemologist is not to abandon altogether the concept of rationality, (and thereby abandon any way of sorting justifiable or warranted beliefs from those that are not) the rationality of a belief will be purely and simply a function of the reliability of the mechanisms that cause the beliefs. But because a belief can be produced by reliable belief-making mechanisms and can still be rationally unjustified, such a definition will not work. Putnam's objection, when construed in this way, is compelling. Unfortunately, Giere's response seems to miss the point Putnam makes. Presumably, Putnam would respond that even if we were to stop talking about rationality, we would still need some way of determining which beliefs are more or less justified; and the naturalized epistemologist would need to define such concepts in terms of the mechanisms that produce certain beliefs. And Putnam's point is that that just will not work because unjustified beliefs can emerge just as easily from reliable mechanisms.

B. Siegel's Objection

In his "Justification, Discovery and the Naturalizing of Epistemology,"[15] Harvey Siegel challenges the naturalistic approach by arguing that rationality of means is not enough. There must be a rationality of goals as well because there is no such thing as rational action in pursuit of an irrational goal. In response to this objection, Giere notes:

This sort of argument gains its plausibility mainly from the way philosophers use the vocabulary of "rationality". If one simply drops this vocabulary, the point vanishes. Obviously, there can be effective action in pursuit of any goal whatsoever—as illustrated by the proverbial case of the efficient Nazi. . . ."

Nor does the restriction to instrumental rationality prevent the study of science from yielding normative claims about how science should be pursued. Indeed, it may be argued that the naturalistic study of science provides the only legitimate basis for sound science policy (Campbell, 1985). (p. 10)

Along with Giere, we may find it difficult to take Siegel's objection seriously for two reasons. Firstly, it is not at all obvious that naturalized epistemology is committed to rationality of means only and not also to the rationality of goals. It is not even clear what that claim amounts to. Secondly, as Giere also points out, there certainly seem to be cases in which irrational ends can be pursued by rational action. Anyway, as we shall see later, there are much more persuasive objections to naturalized epistemology.

C. The Objection from Vicious Circularity

There is another common objection to eliminating traditional epistemological questions in favor of questions about effective means to desired goals. Giere characterizes it in the following way:

To show that some methods are effective, one must be able to show that they can result in reaching the goal. And this requires being able to say what it is like to reach the goal. But the goal in science is usually taken to be "true" or "correct" theories. And the traditional epistemological problem has always been to justify the claim that one has in fact found a correct theory. Any naturalistic theory of science that appeals only to effective means to the goal of discovering correct theories must beg this question. Thus a naturalistic philosophy of science can be supported only by a circular argument that assumes some means to the goal are in fact effective. (p. 11)

Giere then proceeds to show that this sort of objection (which he does not cite anybody in fact offering) is based on some dubious items of Cartesian epistemology. A more direct response, however, is that this objection is unacceptable because it assumes rather than proves that the goal of scientific theories is to achieve truth rather than empirical adequacy. In other words, a proper response would consist in straightforwardly denying that the goal of science is to discover "true" or "correct" theories rather than ones that are instrumentally reliable as predictive devices. So, for other reasons, we need not take this objection very seriously. In the end, apart from Putnam's objection, these last two objections to naturalized epistemology do not have the necessary bite, and Giere seems quite justified in rejecting them. Later we shall see better objections. For now, however, we need only note that the above argument in favor of naturalized epistemology is not an argument, and that the author's response to the above three objections to naturalized epistemology selects only three and fails to deal effectively with Putnam's objection.

In the end, for Giere, evolutionary theory provides an alternative foundation for the study of science:

It explains why the traditional projects of epistemology, whether in their Cartesian, Humean, or Kantian form, were misguided. And it shows why we should not fear the charge of circularity. (p. 12)

But what exactly is it about traditional epistemology that made it misguided? That it sought to refute universal scepticism? Whoever said that was *the goal* of traditional epistemology? As we noted earlier when we examined Quine's argument, to define the concept of knowledge and then to determine whether, and to what extent, human knowledge exists in the various ways we define it seems equally the major goal of traditional epistemology. And why, exactly, is that a misguided activity? Such an activity seems justified by the plausible goal that if we get very clear on just what we mean by basic epistemological concepts, we might just be in a better position to determine the snake-oil artist from those whose views are worthy of adoption. This goal is based on the noncontroversial point that knowledge just isn't a matter of accepting everything a passerby might say. At the root of most arguments for naturalized epistemology, as we shall see, is this peculiar claim to the effect that traditional epistemology somehow has failed or been misguided in its search for some cosmic skyhook. Certainly we saw as much when we examined Quine's argument. But when the arguments are laid on the table, some philosophers may come to think that what gets characterized as traditional epistemology is quite different from the real thing. Socrates, after all, began his discussion in *Theaetetus* with the question "What is knowledge?" and not "Is human knowledge possible?" or "How does the mind represent reality?" or (as one philosopher recently claimed) "How does the brain work?"[16] That anybody could seriously think that Socrates was really asking for an account of how the brain works is difficult to comprehend. And to say that that is what he *should* have been asking (because nobody has or can answer whatever other question he might have asked) presupposes that one can show that the questions he did ask are misguided or bad questions, and that is yet to be shown in any way that does not beg the question against philosophy. We may now turn to the fourth argument in favor of Quine's thesis.

VI. THE ARGUMENT FROM EVOLUTIONARY THEORY

Evolutionary epistemology is a form of naturalized epistemology which insists that the only valid questions about the nature of human knowledge are those that can be answered in biological science by appeal to evolutionary theory. For the evolutionary epistemologist, the Darwinian revolution underscored the point that human beings, as products of evolutionary development, are natural beings whose capacities for knowledge and belief can be understood by appeal to the basic laws of biology under evolutionary theory. As Michael Bradie has recently noted, evolutionary epistemologists often seem to be claiming that Darwin or, more generally, biological considerations are relevant in deciding in favor of a non-justificational or purely descriptive approach to the theory of knowledge.[17] When we examine the arguments proposed by specific evolutionary epistemologists, there seem to emerge two distinct arguments. The first argument, allegedly offered by philosophers such as Karl Popper, and reconstructed by Peter Munz, is as follows:

P1. We do in fact have human knowledge.

P2. No justification is possible.

Therefore: P3. Human knowledge does not involve justification.

Therefore: P4. Every item of knowledge is a provisional proposal or hypothesis subject to revision.[18]

For this reason Popper held that the only problem in epistemology was the problem of the growth of human knowledge, or the biological question of how human knowledge originates and grows. Therefore, epistemology is not normative in the way that traditional epistemology is normative but rather purely descriptive. As Bradie has noted, Popper's argument for P2 is based on his acceptance of Hume's critique of induction and the corollary that no empirical universal statements are provable beyond doubt (p. 10). The second argument, inspired by Quine's reference to Darwin, is offered by Hilary Kornblith and reconstructed by Bradie as follows:

P1. Believing truths has survival value.

Therefore: P2. Natural selection guarantees that our innate intellectual endowment gives us a predisposition for believing truths.

Therefore: P3. Knowledge is a necessary by-product of natural selection.

In order to get the desired conclusion of a purely descriptive epistemology, Kornblith supplies the following premise:

Therefore: P4. If nature has so constricted us that our belief-generating processes are inevitably biased in favor of true beliefs, then it must be that the processes by which we arrive at beliefs just are those by which we ought to arrive at them.

This premise is said to warrant the final conclusion:

Therefore: P5. The processes by which we arrive at our beliefs are just those by which we ought to arrive at them.[19]

What can we say about these two arguments?

With regard to the first argument, the one Peter Munz ascribes to Popper, the first thing to note is that there is nothing particularly "biological" or "evolutionary" about it at all. It is simply a philosophical argument based on a philosophical acceptance of Hume's philosophical scepticism to the effect that no factual claim about the world could be justified sufficiently for knowledge. So, the argument does not provide a justification deriving from evolutionary theory for taking the naturalistic turn. Secondly, as we saw when we discussed Quine's argument above, accepting a philosophical argument for a purely descriptive epistemology is radically incoherent. A philosophical argument to the effect that there is no first philosophy because Hume was correct in his defense of the problem of induction, is radically incoherent and self-defeating in a way apparently not yet appreciated by naturalized epistemologists.

The second argument has already been well criticized by Michael Bradie who has noted (along with many others, including Stitch, Leowontin, and Wilson) that P2 is quite questionable. The fact that certain beliefs endure and have survival value by no means implies that they are the product of natural selection. There are many traits that evolve culturally which have no survival value. (Bradie, 16) Moreover, even if it were true that our cognitive capacities have evolved by natural selection, the important point is that that by itself is no reason for thinking that we are naturally disposed to believe truths rather than falsity. On the contrary, the evidence seems pretty strong that, given the history of scientific theorizing, the species is more disposed to accept empirically adequate rather than true hypotheses.

One interesting response to this last line of reasoning comes from Nicholas Rescher who, in *Methodological Pragmatism*, has argued that say what we will, the methods of the natural sciences have indeed been selected out by nature, otherwise they would not have endured as such reliable instruments for prediction and control. Rescher's basic point is that on any given occasion, an instrumentally reliable belief or thesis may well fail to be true. But that is no reason for thinking that nature has not selected out the methods of the natural sciences because in the long run the methods of the natural sciences provide truth.[20] Rescher's point is well taken, but it is certainly not an argument for the thesis that epistemology is purely descriptive. Rescher certainly is not a naturalized epistemologist in that sense. Rather it is an argument for regarding the deliverances of the methods of natural science as epistemically privileged. In offering the argument he does here, Rescher is merely showing how the usual arguments against pragmatism hold for *thesis* pragmatism and not for *methodological* pragmatism. Nor does his argument provide the evidence necessary for making sound Kornblith's reconstructed argument from evolution. This is because Kornblith's proposed argument still falters on P2. Rescher's argument by no means shows or supports the view that people by nature are innately disposed to believe only true propositions. If that were so, it would be difficult to see why we would ever need the methods of the natural sciences anyway. Nature selected out the methods of the natural sciences just *because* we are not natively disposed to believe only true propositions.

But, if the above two arguments are the best evolutionary biologists can offer in defense of the first form of naturalized epistemology, it would seem that biology itself, and especially evolutionary biology, is yet to offer a persuasive argument for naturalized epistemology. Along with Bradie, we can only conclude that there does not seem to be any persuasive argument from evolutionary theory in favor of the first form of naturalized epistemology.[21]

VII. THE "IMPOSSIBILITY OF DEFINING JUSTIFICATION" ARGUMENT

The last, and perhaps the most interesting, argument for the first form of naturalized epistemology appears in a recent paper by Richard Ketchum entitled "The Paradox of Epistemology: A Defense of Naturalism." Ketchum's argument is the following.

An adequate traditional epistemology will require, among other things, an acceptable definition, or explication of the concept of justification. But there is no non-question-begging definition, or explication of the concept of justification. After all, whatever definition one would offer for the concept of justification admits of the question "Are you justified in accepting or believing this definition of justification?" Presumably if one were to answer yes and then defend the answer, the stated defense would need to be an instance of the original definition—thereby rendering the defense question-begging, because what is at issue is whether the original definition itself is justified. Appealing to the analysans of the definition to justify the definition is patently circular and hence question-begging; and appealing to anything else would be logically contradictory because it would be a matter of ultimately asserting and denying one's stated definition of justification. No matter what one's definition might be, there would be no non-question-begging way of answering the question of whether one is justified in accepting that definition. Thus, traditional epistemology is dead.[22] What about this argument?

A. Various Unacceptable Responses

One possible response is that while one may not be justified in believing one's definition of justification, one might certainly have good reasons for accepting one's definition of justification. But the problem with this response is that it arbitrarily prevents one from defining justification in terms of having good reasons. Besides, if having good reasons for accepting a definition of justification is sufficient for accepting it, then why is that not the definition of justification? Can one have sufficient reasons for accepting something and not be justified in accepting it?

Another possible response asserts that the problem with this argument is not in the assumption that we must be justified in believing our definition of justification. Rather it is in the assumption that "justification" in believing a definition has the same meaning as "justification" when the term applies to nondefinitions. On this view, being justified in believing a definition is simply a matter of whether one has correctly generalized from the conditions of correct usage in natural or scientific discourse (or, if our definitions are stipulative, a matter of whether they lead us to conclusions that satisfy the purpose behind defining things the way we do); whereas being justified in believing a nondefinition, or a proposition about the world, is a matter of whether one can give (if necessary) good reasons for thinking that the proposition is a reasonably adequate description of one's mental content or of the nonmental world. Is there anything wrong with this proposed solution?[23]

Yes, and it is this: The original question returns in the form of the question "Are you justified in believing that the concept of justification differs for reportive definitions and nondefinitions in the way indicated?" Here again, if one answers affirmatively, one could only defend the answer by making it an instance of the concept of justification appropriate for nondefinitions, and that is what is at issue. In short, the question returns with a sting even when we try to distinguish various senses of justification.

By implication, suppose one were to say "I am justified in accepting my definition of justification because the definition conforms to the rules we require for generating acceptable definitions." Once again, the obvious response is "Are you justified in accepting the rules for generating acceptable definitions?" If the answer is yes (as presumably it would be), then the answer is defensible only if it is an instance of one's definition of justification for nondefinitions; but one's definition of justification for nondefinitions is justifiable only if it is an instance of the definition of justification for nondefinitions. But the latter is itself what is at issue, and so we come back to the original question and the impossibility of answering it in a non-question-begging way.

A third reply consists in trying to rule against the meaningfulness of the question on the grounds that if we take it seriously, then it would lead to an infinite regress and that in itself is good evidence for the inappropriateness of the question. On this view, whatever answer one gives, the respondent could still ask "But are you justified in believing that?" Differently stated, to countenance the question in the first instance is to countenance more properly the assumption that one must be justified in all one's beliefs and, as we know from Aristotle's argument in the first book of *Prior Analytics*, that requirement guarantees scepticism, because the need for an infinite amount of justification prevents there ever being any demonstrative knowledge. Is this response acceptable?

To begin with, the question does not obviously imply that one must be justified in all one's beliefs, but it does imply that one must be justified in one's definition of justification just because there are mutually exclusive proposals on the nature of epistemic justification.

Even so, this way of establishing nontraditional epistemology is initially problematic because the same question seems to cut equally strongly against the naturalized epistemologist. The naturalized epistemologist, like Quine, still says that one's beliefs about the world are more or less justified by appeal to the canons of scientific inference. Accordingly, suppose we grant that traditional epistemology is dead and that one could still be justified in one's beliefs about the world because we need only follow the canons of justification as specified and practiced in science. But if the question "Are you justified in believing that your definition of justification is appropriate or correct?" is a legitimate question to ask of the classical epistemologist, it is also seems to be a legitimate question to ask of the naturalized epistemologist, who asserts that "In natural science, being justified in one's beliefs is simply a matter of accommodating the basic rules of inductive inference as stipulated in current scientific practice." And if this is so, justification in science is as problematic as it is in traditional epistemology. The traditional epistemologist may want to know why the naturalized epistemologist, or the natural scientist (but not the traditional epistemologist), is at liberty to ignore the philosopher's question "Are you justified in accepting x as the correct definition of justification in science?" Does it not seem that the question cuts both ways, and is not any more devastating for the traditional epistemologist than it is for the practice of science in general or for the naturalized epistemologist? If the naturalized epistemologist feels justified in ignoring such questions because they are so obviously philosophical, why exactly is that an argument in favor of naturalized epistemology rather than an unargued rejection of philosophy in general? Thus, for the traditional epistemologist if the original question is persuasive, it arguably tends to show the truth of scepticism in general and not simply the failure of traditional epistemology. This is hardly a desirable result for anybody except the general sceptic. Can the naturalized epistemologist respond to this objection?

In all likelihood, the naturalized epistemologist might reply that there is an important disanalogy showing that the question does not cut both ways. She may urge that in natural science, but not in philosophy or traditional epistemology, there is solid agreement on what counts for justification in science. So the question does not have the same urgency among the practitioners of science. The confusion and disagreement in traditional epistemology requires that a proposed definition be justified as more or less persuasive relative to other proposals on the table. But the fact that practicing scientists have no real doubt about what they accept as a community in the name of justified belief, undermines philosophers' attempt to show that scientists too must answer the question "Are you justified in accepting your definition of justification?" Their reply is that they do not need to answer such a question because there is simply no problem with what counts for being justified in science; such canons are agreed upon as necessary for what scientists perceive as being minimally necessary for prediction and control. This is the typical attitude on the part of practicing scientists to Hume's agony over justifying induction. And there is much to be said for the view that the need for giving a justification is context-sensitive and that when the question "How do you know?" is not appropriate for the splendid reason that nobody but the philosopher really doubts what has been said or asserted, the question does not need to be answered. So, David Hume notwithstanding, it is by no means clear that the question cuts both ways rather than strongly against the traditional epistemologist.

B. Two Acceptable Responses

By way of confronting this pesky argument for the replacement thesis, another interesting response consists in asserting that we must begin by accepting the fact that we know something, and that just means that we must reject any and all core questions about human knowledge that can only be answered with a circular or question-begging response. So, the truth of the matter is that there is no non-question-begging way to answer questions such as "Are you justified in believing your definition of justification?" If we insist on answering such questions, however, we make global scepticism certain. Presumably, even naturalized epistemologists do not want to go that far. Consequently, such questions are not permissible. What this means is that generalizing from the facts of ordinary usage and scientific practice to determine what we mean by certain epistemic concepts is simply where we start and what we do to get clear about what human knowledge is. To ask that we be justified in the conclusions we draw here is to demand that we begin somewhere else when there is in fact nowhere else to go, and if we do not stop here or somewhere else (which will certainly happen if we allow the sceptic's eternal question "But are you justified in believing that?") there could be no knowledge about anything at all.

Is this a satisfactory response, or is it merely a wonderful way of begging the question against global scepticism which, if the original question is permissible, turns out to be forceful? Are we dismissing the question as meaningful merely because otherwise we would need to accept global scepticism? It is tempting to think not, but the sceptic will doubtless see things differently.

In the end what makes the sceptic's response here weak (and hence what counts in favor of this response to the naturalized epistemologist) is that the general sceptic on the question of justification is in the logically contradictory position of asserting as both logically privileged or justified the position that no beliefs are justified. For some peculiar reason, as yet unfathomed by the history of philosophy, general sceptics on the question of justification are not much moved by the observation that their position when honestly asserted is logically contradictory. Nevertheless, the traditional epistemologist will argue that any thesis leading to the acceptability of general scepticism on the question of justification is for that reason reduced to absurdity. Accordingly, because the alleged impossibility of offering a non-question-begging definition of justification leads to such an incoherent scepticism, the position stands refuted as does, by implication, the need to take seriously the question "Are you justified in accepting your definition of justification?" Indeed, if one's view is that what is wrong with generalized scepticism on the question of justification is that it is logically self-defeating because self-contradictory and incoherent, then that in itself would serve as a fine *reductio ad absurdum* of the need to justify one's definition of justification assuming that there is no non-question-begging definition to be offered.

If this last response is not enough, perhaps the more compelling response is that the question "Are you justified in accepting your definition of justification" is actually self-defeating in a way not at all obvious. Let me explain.

Whoever asks the question "Are you justified in accepting your definition of justification?" can be met with the response "What do you mean when you ask whether I am 'justified' in accepting this definition?" When anyone asks the question "Are you justified in accepting or believing your definition of justification?" he must have in mind just what it means to be justified, otherwise it is not a meaningful question because if he did not have in mind just what it meant, he would not know what would count for a good answer if an answer were possible. Thus, if the question makes any sense at all, the questioner must be prepared to say just what *he* means by justification when he asks the question "Are you justified in believing your definition of justification?" In fact, then, it is a necessary condition for this question being meaningful that the questioner be able to say what it would mean for someone to be justified in believing that a particular definition of justification is correct. If the questioner cannot answer the question "What do you mean?" then the question need not be taken seriously. If he can, then his question is easily answered. For example, if the questioner is asking for a good reason for accepting the definition, the response might well be that we have a good reason because the definition is a sound generalization of the facts of ordinary usage (and that's a good reason because evolution selects out this way of determining the meaning of expressions). In short, if the question is an honest one, then the questioner is asking for a justification, and if he cannot say what would count as an answer to his question (thereby saying what he means by "justification"), then we need not and will not take his question seriously. On the other hand, as soon as he tells us just what he means by "justification" his question seems meaningful and answerable.

However, now comes the rub. We can still refuse to take his question seriously because *we* can now raise the question of whether his understanding of "justification" is justified, because if it is not, we do not need to answer his question; and if he says our question is meaningless, then so too was his initial question. But now the shoe is on the other foot, as it were. The person who questions the original definition of justification can make sense of his question only if he is willing to say just what justification consists in; but if the original question makes sense then it will make equal sense when the question is asked of him—meaning that *he* has no non-question-begging way of answering a question necessary for his meaningfully asking "Are you justified in believing your definition of justification?" Thus it appears that we are justified in ignoring the question because the questioner cannot, *ex hypothesi*, satisfy a condition necessary for the meaningfulness of the proposed question. He cannot, *ex hypothesi*, answer in any non-question-begging way the question we can ask of him, namely, "Are you justified in accepting your definition of justification?"

More importantly, not only is the question meaningless because the questioner cannot answer in a non-question-begging way what he means by "justification," it is also semantically incoherent and self-defeating because a necessary condition for its being meaningfully asked, (namely, that one be able to defend one's definition of justification in a non-question-begging way), is precisely what the questioner denies that one can do.

Incidentally, it seems inescapable that this same conclusion applies with equal validity to all questions such as "Do you know that your definition of knowledge is correct?" or "Do you believe that your definition of correct belief is correct?"

Accordingly, we have two persuasive reasons why the above argument for naturalized epistemology and the death of traditional epistemology is not sound. This conclusion carries with it a strong reason why we should never accept as meaningful the question "Are you justified in accepting your definition of justification?" Of course, none of this implies that we have no way of assessing the relative merits of mutually exclusive definitions of justification. What it does mean, however, is that when we are involved in the practice of making such assessments we remind ourselves that we are not involved in the activity of justifying our definition of justification. Rather we are doing something else. We are determining which definition, if any, to accept as a more or less adequate generalization of our collective usage and practice in the relevant contexts. We do this because we believe that when it is done well it will produce a measure of understanding and enlightenment not otherwise available. Whether we are justified in this latter belief is an interesting question, but it is certainly not the question of justifying our definition of justification. For all the reasons mentioned above, we must not succumb to the temptation to characterize this activity as the activity of justifying our definition of justification.

VIII. CONCLUSION

Given the above considerations, it seems that, in spite of the popularity of the thesis, there is no sound argument presently available supporting the Quinean version of naturalized epistemology. Nor should we be tempted to suppose that because we have never achieved a consensus in traditional epistemology, it looks as though we have good inductive grounds that the program of traditional epistemology will never work. That sort of argument blatantly begs the question in favor of a concept of success that is appropriate to the methods of the natural sciences and so, by implication, begs the question in favor of the naturalized epistemology for which it is supposed to be an argument. The interesting question is whether there is something fundamentally incoherent about arguing philosophically for such a naturalized epistemology. As was suggested above in the discussion on Quine's argument, it certainly seems that offering a philosophical argument in favor of denying that philosophical arguments will count when it comes to answering questions about the nature of epistemology is incoherent when the point of it is to defend a particular view about the nature of human knowledge. But perhaps this is merely a philosophical point.

NOTES

* This paper is a revision of an earlier paper with the same title which appeared in the *American Philosophical Quarterly*, 27, no. 4 (Oct. 1990), pp. 263–79. The revisions consist in primarily reworking and expanding the arguments in section VII.

1. In *Ontological Relativity and Other Essays* (New York: Columbia University Press, 1969).
2. For a full discussion of Goldman's thesis as it occurs in *Epistemology and Cognition* (Cambridge: Harvard University Press, 1985), see R. Almeder and F. Hogg, "Reliabilism and Goldman's Theory of Justification," *Philosophia* 19 (1989) pp. 165–88.
3. In Hilary Kornblith, ed., *Naturalizing Epistemology* (Boston: MIT Press, 1985), pp. 71–85.
4. *Roots of Reference* (LaSalle, Il: Open Court, 1975).
5. In S. Guttenplan, ed., *Mind and Language* (Oxford: Clarendon Press, 1975).
6. See "Reply to Stroud," *Midwest Studies in Philosophy*, vol. 6, P. French, E. Uehling, and H. Wettstein, eds. (Minneapolis: University of Minnesota Press, 1981), p. 474.
7. See "Nature Unmirrored, Epistemology Naturalized," *Synthese* 55 (1983) p. 69.
8. See William Lycan, *Judgement and Justification* (Cambridge, England: Cambridge University Press, 1988).
9. This same point is made by P. Skagestadt in "Hypothetical Realism," in Brewer and Collins, eds., *Scientific Inquiry and the Social Sciences: A Volume in Honor of Donald T. Campbell* (San Francisco: Jossey-Bass, 1981), p. 92.
10. Ron Giere, *Explaining Science: A Cognitive Approach* (Chicago: University of Chicago Press, 1988).
11. See P. S. Churchland, *Neurophilosophy* (Cambridge: MIT Press, 1986); P. M. Churchland, "Eliminative Materialism and the Propositional Attitudes," *Journal of Philosophy* 78 (1981) pp. 67–90, and "Some Reductive Strategies in Cognitive Neurobiology," *MIND* 95 (1986), pp. 279–309. For a similar argument, see S. Stitch, *From Folk Psychology to Cognitive Science* (Cambridge: MIT Press, 1983).
12. For an interesting argument to the effect that folk psychology is not likely to be eliminated in the way the Churchland assert that it will, see Robert McCauley's "Epistemology in an Age of Cognitive Science," *Philosophical Psychology* 1, no. 2 (1988), pp. 147–49.
13. See, for example, P. S. Churchland, "Epistemology in an Age of Neuroscience" *Journal of Philosophy*,

32 (Dec. 1986) p. LXXXIV where she asserts, without benefit of proof, that the basic question in epistemology is indeed the question "How does the brain work?"

14. This same point is made by Ernest Sosa in "Nature Unmirrored: Epistemology Naturalised," *Synthese* 55 (1983), p. 70. Naturally, if one were able to defend a form of reliabilism similar to that offered by Alvin Goldman, the question "How does the brain work?" would turn out to be a most crucial question in epistemology; but at that point we would not be defending the sort of naturalized epistemology defended by Quine rather than the form offered and defended by Goldman.

15. See Harvey Siegel, *Philosophy of Science*, (1980), pp. 47, 297–321.

16. See P. S. Churchland, "Epistemology in the Age of Neuroscience," *Journal of Philosophy* (Oct. 1987).

17. See Michael Bradie, "Evolutionary Epistemology as Naturalised Epistemology," p. 3 (forthcoming).

18. See Peter Munz, *Our Knowledge of the Growth of Knowledge: Popper or Wittgenstein?* (London: Routledge and Kegan Paul, (1987), p. 371. For a defense of a similar argument, see also Michael Ruse's *Taking Darwin Seriously: A Naturalistic Approach to Philosophy* (Oxford: Basil Blackwell, 1986), and W. W. Bartley III, "Philosophy of Biology versus Philosophy of Physics," in G. Radnitzky and W. W. Bartley, III, eds., *Evolutionary Epistemology, Theory of Rationality and the Sociology of Knowledge* (LaSalle, IL: Open Court, 1987), p. 206.

19. See Hilary Kornblith, *Naturalizing Epistemology* (Cambridge: MIT Press, 1985), p. 4.

20. Nicholas Rescher, *Methodological Pragmatism* (Oxford: Basil Blackwell, 1977), chapter 6.

21. For further reasons why evolutionary epistemology has in fact failed to offer any compelling explanation of how what we take to be knowledge, especially scientific knowledge, has developed, see William Bechtel's "Toward Making Evolutionary Epistemology Into a Truly Naturalized Epistemology," in Nicholas Rescher, *Evolution, Cognition and Realism* (Washington, D.C.: University Press of America, 1990).

22. This is an informal reconstruction of the argument defended by Richard Ketchum in his paper "The Paradox of Epistemology: A Defense of Naturalism," *Philosophical Studies* (Oct. 1990).

23. In conversation, Marshall Swain offered this reply.

POSTSCRIPT

INTRODUCTION

    Peirce's "The Scientific Attitude and Fallibilism," at last, reasserts the robust realism that appears to typify scientists and their attitude toward theories. "The scientific imagination dreams of explanations and laws," he observes, where those who would become scientists should burn with the passion to learn merely to understand the natural world. Although scientists are among the best of society in their manners and their morals, too much morality can breed too much conservatism, because "morality is essentially conservative." Success in science requires the capacity for imagination and conjecture in contradicting and contravening accepted thought.

    Peirce suggests that scientific minds should not be supposed to be filled with propositions that are certain or even extremely probable, because "[an] hypothesis is something which looks as if it might be true. . . . The best hypothesis, in the sense of the one most recommending itself to the inquirer, is the one which can be the most readily refuted if it is false." Indeed, the most important maxim of science is: *Do not block the way of inquiry!* Do not make absolute assertions. Do not maintain that anything can never be known. Do not think we have discovered the ultimate and inexplicable. Do not imagine any theory has received its final and complete formulation.

    For Peirce, *the real* turns out to be "that whose characters are independent of what anybody may think them to be." The world is conceived as an objective, external reality that affects, or might affect, every inquirer. The process of experimental investigation by means of causal interactions with the world in subjecting our hypotheses and theories to empirical test thus affords a medium whereby different inquirers might be brought to a convergence of opinion. The pursuit of science may be said to be founded upon the conjecture of the existence of an external world that may or may not possess the properties that our hypotheses and theories assert about it.

    Peirce advances a pragmatic conception of truth according to which *the true* is the opinion that is destined to be agreed upon by the community of inquirers over the long run. But even if we could possess a complete description of the history of the world, we still might not know all the world's laws. Some laws, for example, might remain counterfactual and thus have no instances. Some regularities might be merely accidental, and therefore display no specific laws. Some frequencies might deviate from their generating probabilities "by chance." So if this is how things are, then the uncertainty of scientific knowledge would appear to be a direct effect of the nature of natural laws.

CHARLES S. PEIRCE

THE SCIENTIFIC ATTITUDE AND FALLIBILISM

I

f we endeavor to form our conceptions upon history and life, we remark three classes of men. The first consists of those for whom the chief thing is the qualities of feelings. These men create art. The second consists of the practical men, who carry on the business of the world. They respect nothing but power, and respect power only so far as it [is] exercised. The third class consists of men to whom nothing seems great but reason. If force interests them, it is not in its exertion, but in that it has a reason and a law. For men of the first class, nature is a picture; for men of the second class, it is an opportunity; for men of the third class, it is a cosmos, so admirable, that to penetrate to its ways seems to them the only thing that makes life worth living. These are the men whom we see possessed by a passion to learn, just as other men have a passion to teach and to disseminate their influence. If they do not give themselves over completely to their passion to learn, it is because they exercise self-control. Those are the natural scientific men; and they are the only men that have any real success in scientific research.

If we are to define science, not in the sense of stuffing it into an artificial pigeonhole where it may be found again by some insignificant mark, but in the sense of characterizing it as a living historic entity, we must conceive it as that about which such men as I have described busy themselves. As such, it does not consist so much in *knowing*, nor even in "organized knowledge," as it does in diligent inquiry into truth for truth's sake, without any sort of axe to grind, nor for the sake of the delight of contemplating it, but from an impulse to penetrate into the reason of things. This is the sense in which this book is entitled a History of *Science* [Editor's note—title of original volume where this essay first appeared]. Science and philosophy seem to have been changed in their cradles. For it is not knowing, but the love of learning, that characterizes the scientific man; while the "philosopher" is a man with a system which he thinks embodies all that is best worth knowing. If a man burns to learn and sets himself to comparing his ideas with experimental results in order that he may correct those ideas, every scientific man will recognize him as a brother, no matter how small his knowledge may be.

But if a man occupies himself with investigating the truth of some question for some ulterior purpose, such as to make money, or to amend his life, or to benefit his fellows, he may be ever so much better than a scientific man, if you will—to discuss that would be aside from the question—but he is not a scientific man. For example, there are numbers of chemists who occupy themselves exclusively with the study of dyestuffs. They discover facts that are useful to scientific chemistry; but they do not rank as genuine scientific men. The genuine scientific chemist cares just as much to learn about erbium—the extreme rarity of which renders it commercially unimportant—as he does about iron. He is more eager to learn about erbium if the knowledge of it would do more to complete his conception of the Periodic Law, which expresses the mutual relations of the elements.

When a man desires ardently to know the truth, his first effort will be to imagine what that truth can be. He cannot prosecute his pursuit long without finding that imagination unbridled is sure to carry him off the track. Yet nevertheless, it remains true that there is, after all, nothing but imagination that can ever supply him an inkling of the truth. He can stare stupidly at phenomena; but in the absence of imagination they will not connect themselves together in any rational way. Just as for Peter Bell a cowslip was nothing but a cowslip, so for thousands of men a falling apple was nothing but a falling apple; and to compare it to the moon would by them be deemed "fanciful."

It is not too much to say that next after the passion to learn there is no quality so indispensable to the successful prosecution of science as imagination. Find me a people whose early medicine is not mixed up with magic and incantations, and I will find you a people devoid of all scientific ability. There is no magic in the medical Papyrus Ebers. The stolid Egyptian saw nothing in disease but derangement of the affected organ. There never was any true Egyptian science.

There are, no doubt, kinds of imagination of no value in science, mere artistic imagination, mere dreaming of opportunities for gain. The scientific imagination dreams of explanations and laws.

A scientific man must be single-minded and sincere with himself. Otherwise, his love of truth will melt away, at once. He can, therefore, hardly be otherwise than an honest, fair-minded man. True, a few naturalists have been accused of purloining specimens; and some men have been far from judicial in advocating their theories. Both of these faults must be exceedingly deleterious to their scientific ability. But on the whole, scientific men have been the best of men. It is quite natural, therefore, that a young man who might develop into a scientific man should be a well-conducted person.

Yet in more ways than one an exaggerated regard for morality is unfavorable to scientific progress. I shall present only one of those ways. It will no doubt shock some persons that I should speak of morality as involving an element which can become bad. To them good conduct and moral conduct are one and the same—and they will accuse me of hostility to morality. I regard morality as highly necessary; but it is a means to good life, not necessarily coextensive with good conduct. Morality consists in the folklore of right conduct. A man is brought up to think he ought to behave in certain ways. If he behaves otherwise, he is uncomfortable. His conscience pricks him. That system of morals is the traditional wisdom of ages of experience. If a man cuts loose from it, he will become the victim of his passions. It is not safe for him even to reason about it, except in a purely speculative way. Hence, morality is essentially conservative. Good morals and good manners are identical, except that tradition attaches less importance to the latter. The gentleman is imbued with conservatism. This conservatism is a habit, and it is the law of habit that it tends to spread and extend itself over more and more of the life. In this way, conservatism about morals leads to conservatism about manners and finally conservatism about opinions of a speculative kind. Besides, to distinguish between speculative and practical opinions is the mark of the most cultivated intellects. Go down below this level and you come across reformers and rationalists at every turn—people who propose to remodel the ten commandments on modern science. Hence it is that morality leads to a conservatism which any new view, or even any free inquiry, no matter how purely speculative, shocks. The whole moral weight of such a community will be cast against science. To inquire into nature is for a Turk very unbecoming to a good Moslem; just as the family of Tycho Brahe regarded his pursuit of astronomy as unbecoming to a nobleman. (See Thomas Nash in *Pierce Pennilesse* for the character of a Danish nobleman.)

This tendency is necessarily greatly exaggerated in a country when the "gentleman," or recognized exponent of good manners, is appointed to that place as the most learned man. For then the inquiring spirit cannot say the gentlemen are a lot of ignorant fools. To the moral weight cast against progress in science is added the weight of superior learning. Wherever there is a large class of academic professors who are provided with good incomes and looked up to as gentlemen, scientific inquiry must languish. Wherever the bureaucrats are the more learned class, the case will be still worse.

The first questions which men ask about the universe are naturally the most general and abstract ones. Nor is it true, as has so often been asserted, that these are the most difficult questions to answer. Francis Bacon is largely responsible for this error, he having represented— having nothing but his imagination and no acquaintance with actual science to draw upon— that the most general inductions must be reached by successive steps. History does not at all bear out that theory. The errors about very general questions have been due to a circumstance which I proceed to set forth.

The most abstract of all the sciences is mathematics. That this is so, has been made manifest in our day; because all mathematicians now see clearly that mathematics is only busied about *purely hypothetical questions*. As for what the truth of existence may be the mathematician does not (*qua* mathematician) care a straw. It is true that early mathematicians could not clearly see that this was so. But for all their not seeing it, it was just as true of the mathematics of early days as of our own. The early mathematician might perhaps be more inclined to assert roundly that two straight lines in a plane cut by a third so as to make the sum of the internal angles on one side less than two right angles would meet at some finite distance on that side if sufficiently produced; although, as a matter of fact, we observe no such tendency in Euclid. But however that may have been, the early mathematician had certainly no more tendency than the modern to *inquire into the truth of that postulate*; but quite the reverse. What he really did, therefore, was merely to deduce consequences of unsupported assumptions, whether he recognized that this was the nature of his business or not. Mathematics, then, really was, for him as for us, the most abstract of the sciences, cut off from all inquiry into existential truth. Consequently, the tendency to attack the most abstract problems first, not because they were *recognized* as such, but because such they *were*, led to mathematics being the earliest field of inquiry.

We find some peoples drawn more toward arithmetic; others more toward geometry. But in either case, a correct method of reasoning was sure to be reached before many centuries of real inquiry had elapsed. The reasoning would be at first awkward, and one case would be needlessly split up into several. But still all influences were pressing the reasoner to make use of a diagram, and as soon as he did that he was pursuing the correct method. For mathematical reasoning consists in constructing a diagram according to a general precept, in observing certain relations between parts of that diagram not explicitly required by the precept, showing that these relations will hold for all such diagrams, and in formulating this conclusion in general terms. All valid necessary reasoning is in fact thus diagrammatic. This, however, is far from being obviously true. There was nothing to draw the attention of the early reasoners to the need of a diagram in such reasoning. Finding that by their inward meditations they could deduce the truth concerning, for example, the height of an inaccessible pillar, they naturally concluded the same method could be applied to positive inquiries.

In this way, early success in mathematics would naturally lead to bad methods in the positive sciences, and especially in metaphysics.

We have seen how success in mathematics would necessarily create a confidence altogether unfounded in man's power of eliciting truth by inward meditation without any aid from experience. Both its confidence in what is within and the absolute certainty of its conclusions lead to the confusion of *a priori* reason with conscience. For conscience, also, refuses to submit its dicta to experiment, and makes an absolute dual distinction between right and wrong. One result of this is that men begin to rationalize about questions of purity and integrity, which in the long run, through moral decay, is unfavorable to science. But what is worse, from our point of view, they begin to look upon science as a guide to conduct, that is, no longer as pure science but as an instrument for a practical end. One result of this is that all probable reasoning is despised. If a proposition is to be applied to action, it has to be embraced, or believed without reservation. There is no room for doubt, which can only paralyze action. But the scientific spirit requires a man to be at all times ready to dump his whole cartload of beliefs, the moment experience is against them. The desire to learn forbids him to be perfectly cocksure that he knows already. Besides positive science can only rest on experience; and experience can never result in absolute certainty, exactitude, necessity, or universality. But it is precisely with the universal and necessary, that is, with Law, that [con]science concerns itself. Thus the real character of science is destroyed as soon as it is made an adjunct to conduct; and especially all progress in the inductive sciences is brought to a standstill.

The effect of mixing speculative inquiry with questions of conduct results finally in a sort of half make-believe reasoning which deceives itself in regard to its real character. Conscience really belongs to the subconscious man, to that part of the soul which is hardly distinct in different individuals, a sort of community-consciousness, or public spirit, not absolutely one and the same in different citizens, and yet not by any means independent in them. Conscience has been created by experience just as any knowledge is; but it is modified by further experience only with secular slowness.

When men begin to rationalize about their conduct, the first effect is to deliver them over to their passions and produce the most frightful demoralization, especially in sexual matters. Thus, among the Greeks, it brought about paederasty and a precedence of public women over private wives. But ultimately the subconscious part of the soul, being stronger, regains its predominance and insists on setting matters right. Men, then, continue to tell themselves they regulate their conduct by reason; but they learn to look forward and see what conclusions a given method will lead to before they give their adhesion to it. In short, it is no longer the reasoning which determines what the conclusion shall be, but it is the conclusion which determines what the reasoning shall be. This is sham reasoning. In short, as morality supposes self-control, men learn that they must not surrender themselves unreservedly to any method, without considering to what conclusions it will lead them. But this is utterly contrary to the single-mindedness that is requisite in science. In order that science may be successful, its votaries must hasten to surrender themselves at discretion to experimental inquiry, in advance of knowing what its decisions may be. There must be no reservations.

The effect of this shamming is that men come to look upon reasoning as mainly decorative, or at most, as a secondary aid in minor matters—a view not altogether unjust, if questions of conduct are alone to interest us. They, therefore, demand that it shall be plain and facile. If, in special cases, complicated reasoning is indispensable, they hire a specialist to perform it. The result of this state of things is, of course, a rapid deterioration of intellectual vigor, very perceptible from one generation to the next. This is just what is taking place among us before our eyes; and to judge from the history of Constantinople, it is likely to go on until the race comes to a despicable end.

. . . The old-fashioned political economist adored, as alone capable of redeeming the human race, the glorious principle of individual greed, although, as this principle requires for its action hypocrisy and fraud, he generally threw in some dash of inconsistent concessions to virtue, as a sop to the vulgar Cerberus. But it is easy to see that the only kind of science this principle would favor would be such as is immediately remunerative with a great preference for such as can be kept secret, like the modern sciences of dyeing and perfumery. Kepler's discovery rendered Newton possible, and Newton rendered modern physics possible, with the steam engine, electricity, and all the other sources of the stupendous fortunes of our age. But Kepler's discovery would not have been possible without the doctrine of conics. Now contemporaries of Kepler—such penetrating minds as Descartes and Pascal—were abandoning the study of geometry (in which they included what we now call the differential calculus, so far as that had at that time any existence) because they said it was so UTTERLY USELESS. There was the future of the human race almost trembling in the balance; for had not the geometry of conic sections already been worked out in large measure, and had their opinion that only sciences apparently useful ought to be pursued [prevailed], the nineteenth century would have had none of those characters which distinguish it from the *ancien régime*.

True science is distinctively the study of useless things. For the useful things will get studied without the aid of scientific men. To employ these rare minds on such work is like running a steam engine by burning diamonds.

The evolutionary theory in general throws great light upon history and especially upon the history of science—both its public history and the account of its development in an individual intellect. As great a light is thrown upon the theory of evolution in general by the evolution of history, especially that of science—whether public or private.

The main theories of the evolution of organic species are three. First, the theory of Darwin, according to which the entire interval from Moner to Man has been traversed by successive purely fortuitous and insensible variations *in reproduction*. The changes on the whole follow a determinate course simply because a certain amount of change in certain directions destroys the species altogether, as the final result of successive weakenings of its reproductive power. Second, the theory of Lamarck, according to which the whole interval has been traversed by a succession of very minute changes. But these have not taken place in reproduction, which has absolutely nothing to do with the business, except to keep the average individuals plastic by their youth. The changes have not been fortuitous but wholly the result of strivings of the individuals. Third, the theory of cataclysmal evolution, according to which the changes have not been small and have not been fortuitous; but they have taken place chiefly in reproduction. According to this view, sudden changes of the environment have taken place from time to time. These changes have put certain organs at a disadvantage, and there has been an effort to use them in new ways. Such organs are particularly apt to sport in reproduction and to change in the way which adapts them better to their recent mode of exercise.

Notwithstanding the teachings of Weismann, it seems altogether probable that all three of these modes of evolution have acted. It is probable that the last has been the most efficient. These three modes of organic evolution have their parallels in other departments of evolution.

Let us consider, for example, the evolution of standards of weights and measures. In order to define the word "pound" in the *Century Dictionary*, I made a list of about four hundred pounds which had been in use in different parts of Europe—undoubtedly a very incomplete list, for it was confined in great measure to certain provinces concerning which I was able to obtain information. Each individual pound or measuring stick is from time to time copied; and at length the old one becomes destroyed. The measure of each copy is imperceptibly larger or smaller than its immediate prototype. If then these variations cannot, by gradual summation, produce a standard much smaller without that standard being destroyed as inconvenient while no such destruction would follow upon an increase of the standard, the average of the standards will slowly grow larger by Darwinian evolution. If there were a disposition on the part of owners of pounds to file them down, so as to make them lighter, though not enough to be noticed, then these filed pounds being copied, and the copies filed, there would be a gradual lightening of the pound by Lamarckian evolution. But it is very unlikely that either of these two modes has been a considerable factor in the actual evolution of weights and measures. As long as their circumstances are unchanged, human communities are exceedingly conservative. Nothing short of the despotism of a modern government with a modern police can cause a change in weights and measures. But from time to time changes occur which cause trade to take new routes. Business has to be adapted to new conditions; and under such influences we find all those habits of communities which are rendered unsuitable by the change become plastic enough. Then it is that a new pound or a new yard may be made which is a compromise between a desire to retain old ways and a desire to please new-comers.

In the evolution of science, a Darwinian mode of evolution might, for example, consist in this, that at every recall of a judgment to the mind—say, for example, a judgment in regard to some such delicate question as the marriage of the clergy—a slight fortuitous modification of the judgment might take place; the modified judgment would cause a corresponding modification of the belief-habit, so that the next recall would be influenced by this fortuitous modification, though it would depart more or less from it by a new fortuitous modification. If, however, by such summation of modifications an opinion quite untenable were reached, it would either be violently changed or would be associationally weak and not apt to be recalled. The effect of this would be in the long run that belief would move away from such untenable positions. It is possible that such a mode of influence may affect our instinctive feelings; but there can be nothing of this sort in science, which is controlled and exact. But another sort of Darwinian evolution undoubtedly does take place. We are studying over phenomena of which we have been unable to acquire any satisfactory account. Various tentative explanations recur to our minds from time to time, and at each occurrence are modified by omission, insertion, or change in the point of view, in an almost fortuitous way. Finally, one of these takes such an aspect that we are led to dismiss it as impossible. Then, all the energy of thought which had previously gone to the consideration of that becomes distributed among the other explanations, until finally one of them becomes greatly strengthened in our minds.

Lamarckian evolution might, for example, take the form of perpetually modifying our opinion in the effort to make that opinion represent the known facts as more and more observations came to be collected. This is all the time going on in regard, for example, to our estimate of the danger of infection of phthisis. Yet, after all, it does not play a prominent part in the evolution of science. The physical journals—say, for example, Poggendorff's [*Annalen der Physik*] and *Beiblätter*—publish each month a great number of new researches. Each of these is a distinct contribution to science. It represents some good, solid, well-trained labor of observation and inference. But as modifying what is already known, the average effect of the ordinary research may be said to be insignificant. Nevertheless, as these modifications are not fortuitous but are for the most part movements toward the truth—could they be rightly understood, all of them would be so—there is no doubt that from decade to decade, even without any splendid discoveries or great studies, science would advance very perceptibly. We see that it is so in branches of physics which remain for a long time without any decisive conquests. It was so, for example, in regard to the classification of the chemical elements in the lapse of time from Berzelius to Mendeléeff, as the valuable history of Venable shows. This is an evolution of the Lamarckian type.

But this is not the way in which science mainly progresses. It advances by leaps; and the impulse for each leap is either some new observational resource, or some novel way of reasoning about the observations. Such novel way of reasoning might, perhaps, be considered as a new observational means, since it draws attention to relations between facts which would previously have been passed by unperceived.

[I] illustrate by the discoveries of Pasteur, who began by applying the microscope to chemistry. He picked out the right- and left-handed crystals of tartaric acid. The two kinds have absolutely the same properties except in regard to direction of rotation of the plane of polarization and in their chemical relations to other "optically active" bodies. Since this method of picking out individual crystals was so slow, Pasteur looked for other means. Ferments of appropriate kinds were found to have the same effect. The microscope showed these were due to living organisms, which Pasteur began studying. At that time the medical world was dominated by Claude Bernard's dictum that a disease is not an entity but merely a sum of symptoms. This was pure metaphysics which only barricaded inquiry in that direction. But that was a generation which attached great value to nominalistic metaphysics. Pasteur began with the phylloxera. He found it influenced the "optical activity" of the sugar. This pointed to a ferment and therefore to an entity. He began to extend the doctrine to other diseases. The medical men, dominated by the metaphysics of Claude Bernard, raised all sorts of sophistical objections. But the method of cultures and inoculation proved the thing, and here we see new ideas connected with new observational methods and a fine example of the usual process of scientific evolution. It is not by insensible steps.

The last fifty years have taught the lesson of not trifling with facts and not trusting to principles and methods which are not logically founded upon facts and which serve only to exclude testimony from consideration.

Such, for example, was the dictum of Claude Bernard that a disease is not an entity—a purely metaphysical doctrine. But the observation of facts has taught us that a disease is in many, if not most, serious cases, just as much an entity as a human family consisting of father, mother, and children.

Such was the dictum of the old psychology which identified the soul with the ego, declared its absolute simplicity, and held that its faculties were mere names for logical divisions of human activity. This was all unadulterated fancy. The observation of facts has now taught us that the ego is a mere wave in the soul, a superficial and small feature, that the soul may contain several personalities and is as complex as the brain itself, and that the faculties, while not exactly definable and not absolutely fixed, are as real as are the different convolutions of the cortex.

Such were the dicta by means of which the internal criticism of historical documents was carried to such a height that it often amounted to the rejection of all the testimony that has come down to us, and the substitution for it of a dream spun out of the critic's brain. But archaeological researches have shown that ancient testimony ought to be trusted in the main, with a small allowance for the changes in the meanings of words. When we are told that Pythagoras had a golden thigh, we are to remember that to the ancients gold did not mean a chemical element of atomic weight 197.5 and specific gravity 19.3, melting at 1045°C. and forming saline compounds of the types AuX and AuX_3. It meant something of metallic lustre, warmer in color than electrum and cooler than copper. Dr. Schliemann's discoveries were the first socdolager that "higher criticism" received. It has since got many others. . . .

Such were the dicta by which everything of the nature of extraordinary powers connected with psychological states of which the hypnotic trance is an example were set down as tricks. At present, while the existence of telepathy cannot be said to be established, all scientific men are obliged by observed facts to admit that it presents at least a very serious problem requiring respectful treatment.

Persons who know science chiefly by its results—that is to say, have no acquaintance with it at all as a living inquiry—are apt to acquire the notion that the universe is now entirely explained in all its leading features; and that it is only here and there that the fabric of scientific knowledge betrays any rents.

But in point of fact, notwithstanding all that has been discovered since Newton's time, his saying that we are little children picking up pretty pebbles on the beach while the whole ocean lies before us unexplored remains substantially as true as ever, and will do so though we shovel up the pebbles by steam shovels and carry them off in carloads. An infinitesimal ratio may be multiplied indefinitely and remain infinitesimal still.

In the first place all that science has done is to study those relations between objects which were brought into prominence and conceiving which we had been endowed with some original knowledge in two instincts—the instinct of *feeding*, which brought with it elementary knowledge of mechanical forces, space, etc., and the instinct of *breeding*, which brought with it elementary knowledge of physical motives, of time, etc. All the other relations of things concerning which we must suppose there is vast store of truth are for us merely the object of such false sciences as judicial astrology, palmistry, the doctrine of signatures, the doctrine of correspondences, magic, and the like.

In the next place, even within the very bounds to which our science is confined, it is altogether superficial and fragmentary. Want of knowledge of the constitution of matter and of electricity. The conservation of forces, as Helmholtz first enunciated it, untenable; whether it can be universally true in any sense is a difficult problem. To strengthen it Helmholtz greatly insisted on discontinuities—a most objectionable theory from every point of view. Mind quite as little understood as matter, and the relations between the two an enigma. The forces we know can be but a small part of all those that are operative. Our ignorance of small things and great, of distant times and of very slow operations. We are equally ignorant of very rapid performances which nevertheless we know to take place. Our science is altogether middle-sized and mediocre. Its insignificance compared with the universe cannot be exaggerated.

It is a great mistake to suppose that the mind of the active scientist is filled with propositions which, if not proved beyond all reasonable cavil, are at least extremely probable. On the contrary, he entertains hypotheses which are almost wildly incredible, and treats them with respect for the time being. Why does he do this? Simply because any scientific proposition whatever is always liable to be refuted and dropped at short notice. A hypothesis is something which looks as if it might be true and were true, and which is capable of verification or refutation by comparison with facts. The best hypothesis, in the sense of the one most recommending itself to the inquirer, is the one which can be the most readily refuted if it is false. This far outweighs the trifling merit of being likely. For after all, what is a *likely* hypothesis? It is one which falls in with our preconceived ideas. But these may be wrong. Their errors are just what the scientific man is out gunning for more particularly. But if a hypothesis can quickly and easily be cleared away so as to go toward leaving the field free for the main struggle, this is an immense advantage.

II

Upon this first, and in one sense this sole, rule of reason, that in order to learn you must desire to learn, and in so desiring not be satisfied with what you already incline to think, there follows one corollary which itself deserves to be inscribed upon every wall of the city of philosophy:

> Do not block the way of inquiry.

Although it is better to be methodical in our investigations, and to consider the economics of research, yet there is no positive sin against logic in *trying* any theory which may come into our heads, so long as it is adopted in such a sense as to permit the investigation to go on unimpeded and undiscouraged. On the other hand, to set up a philosophy which barricades the road of further advance toward the truth is the one unpardonable offense in reasoning, as it is also the one to which metaphysicians have in all ages shown themselves the most addicted.

Let me call your attention to four familiar shapes in which this venomous error assails our knowledge.

The first is the shape of absolute assertion. That we can be sure of nothing in science is an ancient truth. The Academy taught it. Yet science has been infested with overconfident assertion, especially on the part of the third-rate and fourth-rate men, who have been more concerned with teaching than with learning, at all times. No doubt some of the geometries still teach as a self-evident truth the proposition that if two straight lines in one plane meet a third straight line so as to make the sum of the internal angles on one side less than two right angles those two lines will meet on that side if sufficiently prolonged. Euclid, whose logic was more careful, only reckoned this proposition as a *Postulate*, or arbitrary Hypothesis. Yet even he places among his axioms the proposition that a part is less than its whole, and falls into several conflicts with our most modern geometry in consequence. But why need we stop to consider cases where some subtilty of thought is required to see that the assertion is not warranted when every book which applies philosophy to the conduct of life lays down as positive certainty propositions which it is quite as easy to doubt as to believe?

The second bar which philosophers often set up across the roadway of inquiry lies in maintaining that this, that, and the other never can be known. When Auguste Comte was pressed to specify any matter of positive fact to the knowledge of which no man could by any possibility attain, he instanced the knowledge of the chemical composition of the fixed stars; and you may see his answer set down in the *Philosophie positive*. But the ink was scarcely dry upon the printed page before the spectroscope was discovered and that which he had deemed absolutely unknowable was well on the way of getting ascertained. It is easy enough to mention a question the answer to which is not known to me today. But to aver that that answer will not be known tomorrow is somewhat risky; for oftentimes it is precisely the least expected truth which is turned up under the ploughshare of research. And when it comes to positive assertion that the truth never will be found out, that, in the light of the history of our time, seems to me more hazardous than the venture of Andrée.

The third philosophical stratagem for cutting off inquiry consists in maintaining that this, that, or the other element of science is basic, ultimate, independent of aught else, and utterly inexplicable—not so much from any defect in our knowing as because there is nothing beneath it to know. The only type of reasoning by which such a conclusion could possibly be reached is *retroduction*. Now nothing justifies a retroductive inference except its affording an explanation of the facts. It is, however, no explanation at all of a fact to pronounce it *inexplicable*. That, therefore, is a conclusion which no reasoning can ever justify or excuse.

The last philosophical obstacle to the advance of knowledge which I intend to mention is the holding that this or that law or truth has found its last and perfect formulation—and especially that the ordinary and usual course of nature never can be broken through. "Stones do not fall from heaven," said Laplace, although they had been falling upon inhabited ground every day from the earliest times. But there is no kind of inference which can lend the slightest probability to any such absolute denial of an unusual phenomenon.

All positive reasoning is of the nature of judging the proportion of something in a whole collection by the proportion found in a sample. Accordingly, there are three things to which we can never hope to attain by reasoning, namely, absolute certainty, absolute exactitude, absolute universality. We cannot be absolutely certain that our conclusions are even approximately true; for the sample may be utterly unlike the unsampled part of the collection. We cannot pretend to be even probably exact; because the sample consists of but a finite number of instances and only admits special values of the proportion sought. Finally, even if we could ascertain with absolute certainty and exactness that the ratio of sinful men to all men was as 1:1; still among the infinite generations of men there would be room for any infinite number of sinless men without violating the proportion. The case is the same with a seven-legged calf.

Now if exactitude, certitude, and universality are not to be attained by reasoning, there is certainly no other means by which they can be reached.

Somebody will suggest *revelation*. There are scientists and people influenced by science who laugh at revelation; and certainly science has taught us to look at testimony in such a light that the whole theological doctrine of the "Evidences" seems pretty weak. However, I do not think it is philosophical to reject the possibility of a revelation. Still, granting that, I declare as a logician that revealed truths—that is, truths which have nothing in their favor but revelations made to a few individuals—constitute by far the most uncertain class of truths there are. There is here no question of universality; for revelation is itself sporadic and miraculous. There is no question of mathematical exactitude; for no revelation makes any pretension to that character. But it does pretend to be *certain*; and against that there are three conclusive objections. First, we never can be absolutely certain that any given deliverance really is inspired; for that can only be established by reasoning. We cannot even prove it with any very high degree of probability. Second, even if it is inspired, we cannot be sure, or nearly sure, that the statement is true. We know that one of the commandments was in one of the Bibles printed with[out] a *not* in it. All inspired matter has been subject to human distortion or coloring. Besides we cannot penetrate the counsels of the most High, or lay down anything as a principle that would govern his conduct. We do not know his inscrutable purposes, nor can we comprehend his plans. We cannot tell but he might see fit to inspire his servants with errors. In the third place, a truth which rests on the authority of inspiration only is of a somewhat incomprehensible nature; and we never can be sure that we rightly comprehend it. As there is no way of evading these difficulties, I say that revelation, far from affording us any certainty, gives results less certain than other sources of information. This would be so even if revelation were much plainer than it is.

But, it will be said, you forget the laws which are known to us *a priori*, the axioms of geometry, the principles of logic, the maxims of *causality*, and the like. Those are absolutely certain, without exception and exact. To this I reply that it seems to me there is the most positive historic proof that innate truths are particularly uncertain and mixed up with error, and therefore *a fortiori* not without exception. This historical proof is, of course, not infallible; but it is very strong. Therefore, I ask *how do you know* that *a priori* truth is certain, exceptionless, and exact? You cannot know it by *reasoning*. For that would be subject to uncertainty and inexactitude. Then, it must amount to this that you know it *a priori*; that is, you take *a priori* judgments at their own valuation, without criticism or credentials. That is barring the gate of inquiry.

Ah! but it will be said, you forget direct experience. Direct experience is neither certain nor uncertain, because it affirms nothing—it just *is*. There are delusions, hallucinations, dreams. But there is no mistake that such things really do appear, and direct experience means simply the appearance. It involves no error, because it testifies to nothing but its own appearance. For the same reason, it affords no certainty. It is not *exact*, because it leaves much vague; though it is not *inexact* either; that is, it has no false exactitude.

All this is true of direct experience at its first presentation. But when it comes up to be criticized it is past, itself, and is represented by *memory*. Now the deceptions and inexactitude of memory are proverbial.

. . . On the whole, then, we cannot in any way reach perfect certitude nor exactitude. We never can be absolutely sure of anything, nor can we with any probability ascertain the exact value of any measure or general ratio.

This is my conclusion, after many years study of the logic of science; and it is the conclusion which others, of very different cast of mind, have come to, likewise. I believe I may say there is no tenable opinion regarding human knowledge which does not legitimately lead to this corollary. Certainly there is nothing new in it; and many of the greatest minds of all time have held it for true.

Indeed, most everybody will admit it until he begins to see what is involved in the admission—and then most people will draw back. It will not be admitted by persons utterly incapable of philosophical reflection. It will not be fully admitted by masterful minds developed exclusively in the direction of action and accustomed to claim practical infallibility in matters of business. These men will admit the incurable fallibility of all opinions readily enough; only they will always make exception of their own. The doctrine of fallibilism will also be denied by those who fear its consequences for science, for religion, and for morality. But I will take leave to say to these highly conservative gentlemen that however competent they may be to direct the affairs of a church or other corporation, they had better not try to manage science in that way. Conservatism—in the sense of a dread of consequences—is altogether out of place in science—which has on the contrary always been forwarded by radicals and radicalism, in the sense of the eagerness to carry consequences to their extremes. Not the radicalism that is cocksure, however, but the *radicalism that tries experiments*. Indeed, it is precisely among men animated by the spirit of science that the doctrine of fallibilism will find supporters.

Still, even such a man as that may well ask whether I propose to say that it is not quite certain that twice two are four—and that it is even not probably quite exact! But it would be quite misunderstanding the doctrine of fallibilism to suppose that it means that twice two is probably not exactly four. As I have already remarked, it is not my purpose to doubt that people can usually *count* with accuracy. Nor does fallibilism say that men cannot attain a sure knowledge of the creations of their own minds. It neither affirms nor denies that. It only says that people cannot attain absolute certainty concerning questions of fact. Numbers are merely a system of names devised by men for the purpose of counting. It is a matter of real fact to say that in a certain room there are two persons. It is a matter of real fact to say that each person has two eyes. It is a matter of fact to say that there are four eyes in the room. But to say that *if* there are two persons and each person has two eyes there *will be* four eyes is not a statement of fact, but a statement about the system of numbers which is our own creation.

III

Let us now approach the subject of logic, and consider a conception which particularly concerns it, that of *reality*. Taking clearness in the sense of familiarity, no idea could be clearer than this. Every child uses it with perfect confidence, never dreaming that he does not understand it. As for clearness in its second grade, however, it would probably puzzle most men, even among those of a reflective turn of mind, to give an abstract definition of the real. Yet such a definition may perhaps be reached by considering the points of difference between reality and its opposite, fiction. A figment is a product of somebody's imagination; it has such characters as his thought impresses upon it. That those characters are independent of how you or I think is an external reality. There are, however, phenomena within our own minds, dependent upon our thought, which are at the same time real in the sense that we really think them. But though their characters depend on how we think, they do not depend on what we think those characters to be. Thus, a dream has a real existence as a mental phenomenon, if somebody has really dreamt it; that he dreamt so and so, does not depend on what anybody thinks was dreamt, but is completely independent of all opinion on the subject. On the other hand, considering, not the fact of dreaming, but the thing dreamt, it retains its peculiarities by virtue of no other fact that that it was dreamt to possess them. Thus we may define the real as that whose characters are independent of what anybody may think them to be.

But, however satisfactory such a definition may be found, it would be a great mistake to suppose that it makes the idea of reality perfectly clear. Here, then, let us apply our rules. According to them, reality, like every other quality, consists in the peculiar sensible effects which things partaking of it produce. The only effect which real things have is to cause belief, for all the sensations which they excite emerge into consciousness in the form of beliefs. The question therefore is, how is true belief (or belief in the real) distinguished from false belief (or belief in fiction). Now, as we have seen in the former paper, the ideas of truth and falsehood, in their full development, appertain exclusively to the experiential method of settling opinion. A person who arbitrarily chooses the propositions which he will adopt can use the word truth only to emphasize the expression of his determination to hold on to his choice. Of course, the method of tenacity never prevailed exclusively; reason is too natural to men for that. But in the literature of the dark ages we find some fine examples of it. When Scotus Erigena is commenting upon a poetical passage in which hellebore is spoken of as having caused the death of Socrates, he does not hesitate to inform the inquiring reader that Helleborus and Socrates were two eminent Greek philosophers, and that the latter, having been overcome in argument by the former, took the matter to heart and died of it! What sort of an idea of truth could a man have who could adopt and teach, without the qualification of a perhaps, an opinion taken so entirely at random? The real spirit of Socrates, who I hope would have been delighted to have been "overcome in argument," because he would have learned something by it, is in curious contrast with the naïve idea of the glossist, for whom (as for "the born missionary" of today) discussion would seem to have been simply a struggle. When philosophy began to awake from its long slumber, and before theology completely dominated it, the practice seems to have been for each professor to seize upon any philosophical position he found unoccupied and which seemed a strong one, to intrench himself in it, and to sally forth from time to time to give battle to the others. Thus, even the scanty records we possess of those disputes enable us to make out a dozen or more opinions held by different teachers at one time concerning the question of nominalism and realism. Read the opening part of the *Historia Calamitatum* of Abélard, who was certainly as philosophical as any of his contemporaries, and see the spirit of combat which it breathes. For him, the truth is simply his particular stronghold. When the method of authority prevailed, the truth meant little more than the Catholic faith. All the efforts of the scholastic doctors are directed toward harmonizing their faith in Aristotle and their faith in the Church, and one may search their ponderous folios through without finding an argument which goes any further. It is noticeable that where different faiths flourish side by side, renegades are looked upon with contempt even by the party whose belief they adopt; so completely has the idea of loyalty replaced that of truth-seeking. Since the time of Descartes, the defect in the conception of truth has been less apparent. Still, it will sometimes strike a scientific man that the philosophers have been less intent on finding out what the facts are, than on inquiring what belief is most in harmony with their system. It is hard to convince a follower of the *a priori* method by adducing facts; but show him that an opinion he is defending is inconsistent with what he has laid down elsewhere, and he will be very apt to retract it. These minds do not seem to believe that disputation is ever to cease; they seem to think that the opinion which is natural for one man is not so for another, and that belief will, consequently, never be settled. In contenting themselves with fixing their own opinions by a method which would lead another man to a different result, they betray their feeble hold of the conception of what truth is.

On the other hand, all the followers of science are animated by a cheerful hope that the processes of investigation, if only pushed far enough, will give one certain solution to each question to which they apply it. One man may investigate the velocity of light by studying the transits of Venus and the aberration of the stars; another by the oppositions of Mars and the eclipses of Jupiter's satellites; a third by the method of Fizeau; a fourth by that of Foucault; a fifth by the motions of the curves of Lissajoux; a sixth, a seventh, an eighth, and a ninth, may follow the different methods of comparing the measures of statical and dynamical electricity. They may at first obtain different results, but, as each perfects his method and his processes, the results are found to move steadily together toward a destined centre. So with all scientific research. Different minds may set out with the most antagonistic views, but the progress of investigation carries them by a force outside of themselves to one and the same conclusion. This activity of thought by which we are carried, not where we wish, but to a fore-ordained goal, is like the operation of destiny. No modification of the point of view taken, no selection of other facts for study, no natural bent of mind even, can enable a man to escape the predestinate opinion. This great hope is embodied in the conception of truth and reality. The opinion which is fated to be ultimately agreed to by all who investigate, is what we mean by the truth, and the object represented in this opinion is the real. That is the way I would explain reality.

. . . To satisfy our doubts, therefore, it is necessary that a method should be found by which our beliefs may be determined by nothing human, but by some external permanency—by something upon which our thinking has no effect. Some mystics imagine that they have such a method in a private inspiration from on high. But that is only a form of the method of tenacity, in which the conception of truth as something public is not yet developed. Our external permanency would not be external, in our sense, if it was restricted in its influence to one individual. It must be something which affects, or might affect, every man. And, though these affections are necessarily as various as are individual conditions, yet the method must be such that the ultimate conclusion of every man shall be the same. Such is the method of science. Its fundamental hypothesis, restated in more familiar language, is this: There are Real things, whose characters are entirely independent of our opinions about them; those Reals affect our senses according to regular laws, and, though our sensations are as different as are our relations to the objects, yet, by taking advantage of the laws of perception, we can ascertain by reasoning how things really and truly are; and any man, if he have sufficient experience and he reason enough about it, will be led to the one True conclusion. The new conception here involved is that of Reality. It may be asked how I know that there are any Reals. If this hypothesis is the sole support of my method of inquiry, my method of inquiry must not be used to support my hypothesis. The reply is this: I. If investigation cannot be regarded as proving that there are Real things, it at least does not lead to a contrary conclusion; but the method and the conception on which it is based remain ever in harmony. No doubts of the method, therefore, necessarily arise from its practice, as is the case with all the others. 2. The feeling which gives rise to any method of fixing belief is a dissatisfaction at two repugnant propositions. But here already is a vague concession that there is some *one* thing which a proposition should represent. Nobody, therefore, can really doubt that there are Reals, for, if he did, doubt would not be a source of dissatisfaction. The hypothesis, therefore, is one which every mind admits. So that the social impulse does not cause men to doubt it. 3. Everybody uses the scientific method about a great many things, and only ceases to use it when he does not know how to apply it. 4. Experience of the method has not led us to doubt it, but, on the contrary, scientific investigation has had the most wonderful triumphs in the way of settling opinion. These afford the explanation of my not doubting the method or the hypothesis which it supposes; and not having any doubt, nor believing that anybody else whom I could influence has, it would be the merest babble for me to say more about it. If there be anybody with a living doubt upon the subject, let him consider it.

FOR FURTHER READING

he following works are highly recommended as appropriate to study in the light of the present text. As a rule, they are listed in their order of relative difficulty, where the most accessible work is listed first, the next most accessible second, and the most difficult third. Every student of the philosophy of science, however, should acquire some background concerning logical positivism. The best place to begin, I believe, is with A. J. Ayer, *Language, Truth and Logic* (New York: Dover Publications, 1946).

I. THE LANGUAGE FRAMEWORK

Hempel, Carl G. *Fundamentals of Concept Formation in Empirical Science.* Chicago: University of Chicago Press, 1952.
There is a great deal more to learn from this work than is reprinted here.

Fetzer, James H., ed. *Definitions and Definability: Philosophical Perspectives.* Dordrecht: Kluwer Academic Publishers, 1991.
Studies in the theory of definition with Hempel as its point of departure.

Carnap, Rudolf. "Replies and Systematic Expositions." In *The Philosophy of Rudolf Carnap.* Edited by P. A. Schlipp. La Salle, IL: Open Court, 1963, pp. 859–1013.
Even Carnap acknowledged the potential of the intensional modalities.

II. LAWS AND LAWLIKENESS

Goodman, Nelson. *Fact, Fiction, and Forecast.* 4th ed. Cambridge: Harvard University Press, 1983.
This work has been among the most influential in philosophy of science.

Popper, Karl R. *The Logic of Scientific Discovery.* New York: Harper and Row, 1965.
A classic study with special emphasis on testing probability hypotheses.

Fetzer, James H. *Scientific Knowledge.* Dordrecht: D. Reidel, 1981.
Places ontology before epistemology in understanding science and laws.

III. THE STRUCTURE OF THEORIES

Suppe, Fred, ed. *The Structure of Scientific Theories.* 2nd ed. Urbana: University of Illinois Press, 1977.
Everything you could ever want to know about theories about theories.

Braithwaite, Richard B. *Scientific Explanation.* Cambridge, UK: Cambridge University Press, 1953.
A highly rigorous study of the standard conception of scientific theories.

Suppe, Fred. *The Semantic Conception of Theories and Scientific Realism.* Urbana: University of Illinois Press, 1989.
Explores relations between theories of theories and realism in science.

IV. EXPLANATION AND PREDICTION

Hempel, Carl G. *Aspects of Scientific Explanation.* New York: The Free Press, 1965.
The most influential work by the most influential student of explanation.

Kitcher, Philip and Wesley C. Salmon, eds. *Scientific Explanation.* Minneapolis: University of Minnesota Press, 1989.
Fascinating studies of past and present approaches toward explanation.

Salmon, Wesley C. *Scientific Explanation and the Causal Structure of the World.* Princeton, NJ: Princeton University Press, 1984.
The author of the S-R model shifts strongly in favor of the C-R model.

V. PROBABILITY AND INFERENCE

Skyrms, Brian. *Choice and Chance: An Introduction to Inductive Logic.* 3d ed. Belmont, CA: Wadsworth Publishing Company, 1986.
A very lucid introduction to basic concepts of probability and induction.

Fetzer, James H., ed. *Probability and Causality.* Dordrecht: Kluwer Academic Publishers, 1988.
A representative sampling of recent work on these difficult problems.

Kyburg, Henry E. and Howard Smokler, eds. *Studies in Subjective Probability.* Huntington, NY: Krieger, 1980.
A valuable collection of classic essays in subjective probability theory.

VI. THE PROBLEM OF INDUCTION

Salmon, Wesley C. *The Foundations of Scientific Inference.* Pittsburgh: University of Pittsburgh Press, 1965.
A fine introduction with special emphasis on the problem of induction.

Reichenbach, Hans. *Experience and Prediction.* Chicago: University of Chicago Press, 1938.
A brilliant presentation of the world view of a Humean frequentist.

Popper, Karl R. *Conjectures and Refutations.* New York: Harper and Row, 1968.
Classic essays by one of the most influential philosophers of science.

VII. THE GROWTH OF SCIENTIFIC KNOWLEDGE

Chalmers, Alan F. *What is this thing called Science?* Atlantic Highlands: The Humanities Press, 1976.
A lucid introduction to alternative theories about the nature of science.

Kuhn, Thomas S. *The Structure of Scientific Revolutions.* Chicago: University of Chicago Press, 1964.
This book created a revolution in the history and philosophy of science.

Lakatos, I. and A. Musgrave, eds. *Criticism and the Growth of Knowledge.* Cambridge: Cambridge University Press, 1971.
An invaluable collection of brilliant studies on scientific methodologies.

VIII. THE NATURE OF SCIENTIFIC KNOWLEDGE

Kornblith, Hilary, ed. *Naturalizing Epistemology.* Cambridge: MIT Press, 1985.
Diverse perspectives on the relations between science and philosophy.

Leplin, Jarrett, ed. *Scientific Realism.* Berkeley: University of California Press, 1984.
A representative sampling of current approaches to scientific realism.

Morick, Harold, ed. *Challenges to Empiricism.* Belmont, CA: Wadsworth Publishing Company, 1972.
A wide variety of fascinating alternatives to classic forms of empiricism.

INDEX OF NAMES

INDEX OF SUBJECTS